THE

WILLARD J. GRAHAM SERIES

IN ACCOUNTING

BOOKS IN

THE WILLARD J. GRAHAM SERIES IN ACCOUNTING

CONSULTING EDITOR   ROBERT N. ANTHONY   *Harvard University*

ANDERSON & SCHMIDT   *Practical Controllership*   rev. ed.
ANTHONY   *Management Accounting: Text and Cases*   4th ed.
ANTHONY   *Management Accounting Principles*   rev. ed.
BARR & GRINAKER   *Short Audit Case*
FREMGEN   *Managerial Cost Analysis*
GORDON & SHILLINGLAW   *Accounting: A Management Approach*   4th ed.
GRIFFIN, WILLIAMS, & LARSON   *Advanced Accounting*   rev. ed.
GRINAKER & BARR   *Audit Practice Case*
GRINAKER & BARR   *Auditing: The Examination of Financial Statements*
HAWKINS   *Corporate Financial Reporting: Text and Cases*
HENDRIKSEN   *Accounting Theory*   rev. ed.
HOLMES   *Basic Auditing Principles*   3d ed.
HOLMES, MAYNARD, EDWARDS, & MEIER   *Elementary Accounting*   3d ed.
HOLMES & OVERMYER   *Auditing: Principles and Procedure*   7th ed.
KENNEDY & MCMULLEN   *Financial Statements: Form, Analysis, and Interpretation*   5th ed.
LADD   *Contemporary Corporate Accounting and the Public*
MAURIELLO   *The Irwin Federal Income Tax Course: A Comprehensive Text*
MEIGS & LARSEN   *Principles of Auditing*   4th ed.
MIKESELL & HAY   *Governmental Accounting*   4th ed.
MOORE & STETTLER   *Accounting Systems for Management Control*
MURPHY   *Advanced Public Accounting Practice*
MURPHY   *Auditing and Theory: A CPA Review*
NEUNER & FRUMER   *Cost Accounting: Principles and Practice*   7th ed.
NIELSEN   *Cases in Auditing*
O'NEIL, FARWELL, & BOYD   *Quantitative Controls for Business: An Introduction*
PATON   *Corporate Profits*
PYLE & WHITE   *Fundamental Accounting Principles*   5th ed.
SCHAFER   *Elements of Income Tax—Individual*
SCHRADER, MALCOLM, & WILLINGHAM   *Financial Accounting: An Input/Output Approach*
SHILLINGLAW   *Cost Accounting: Analysis and Control*   rev. ed.
SPILLER   *Financial Accounting: Basic Concepts*   rev. ed.
STAUBUS   *Activity Costing and Input-Output Accounting*
VATTER   *Accounting Measurements for Financial Reports*
WELSCH, ZLATKOVICH, & WHITE   *Intermediate Accounting*   rev. ed.
WILLIAMS & GRIFFIN   *Management Information: A Quantitative Accent*

CORPORATE
FINANCIAL REPORTING
TEXT AND CASES

CORPORATE
FINANCIAL REPORTING
TEXT AND CASES

DAVID F. HAWKINS
Professor of Business Administration
Graduate School of Business Administration
Harvard University

1971

RICHARD D. IRWIN, INC.
HOMEWOOD, ILLINOIS 60430
IRWIN-DORSEY LIMITED, GEORGETOWN, ONTARIO

FIRST PRINTING, MAY, 1971

Library of Congress Catalog Card No. 78–149895

PRINTED IN THE UNITED STATES OF AMERICA

To Patricia

PREFACE

Published corporate profit figures can represent genuine managerial operating performance, or they can represent the illusion of performance. Investors who can tell the difference have a considerable advantage in making their investment decisions. Similarly, the corporate manager who knows how he or other managers can influence profits through the judicious use of alternative accounting practices is more likely to succeed than his less knowledgeable competitors. Ignorance of the options, uncertainties, and ambiguities of the practices underlying the construction of corporate financial statements can lead creditors to make poor credit decisions. On the other hand, unless those practicing public accountancy know how investors use financial data, how to identify and interpret the motives of managers issuing financial reports, and the relationship between business-operating and financial-reporting decisions, they can not satisfactorily fulfill their third-party responsibility to the issuers and users of corporate financial statements. In short, an intimate understanding of the practices and subtleties of financial accounting can be critical to the success of many of those who participate in our business system.

Today corporations have considerable leeway in the reporting of their financial condition and results of operations. Despite recent progress in eliminating undesirable reporting practices, there are many areas in which equally acceptable alternative practices exist for reporting essentially identical business situations. The profits of the reporting company will vary depending on which alternative is selected. Some of these alternatives are:

1. The investment in a capital asset can be written off against revenues by either a "fast" or "slow" depreciation method.
2. Expenditures for research and development can be charged to income

as incurred or carried as an asset and written off as expenses over several reporting periods.

3. Inventory can be valued at current costs or some other cost that may reflect 20-year-old price levels.

4. Investment tax-type credits can be recognized as income either in the year they are granted or over the life of the asset giving rise to the tax credit.

This book provides the reader with an understanding of the current state of these and many other financial reporting practices; the ways in which the corporate financial statements published in annual reports, prospectuses, and proxy statements influence our economic system; and the significant consequences of these data for the people who depend on its credibility. It is not a book on accounting methodology.

The subject matter is approached from a variety of points of view. First, and foremost, are the interests of those closest to the corporation, namely, the management publishing the financial statements; the existing and potential stockholders; financial analysts using the statements for investment recommendations; the grantors of trade and commercial credit; and the independent certified public accountant responsible for expressing an opinion on the fairness of the statements issued by the management. Also covered are the interests of others in a number of different business negotiations and transactions where the use and interpretation of financial statements has assumed major proportions, such as the determination of rates in regulated industries; the purchase and sale of businesses; government investigation of prices and other practices of particular industries and individual enterprises; and the determination by unions as to what to demand through collective bargaining.

Changing Accounting Principles

The accounting principles upon which corporate financial reports are based are continually being revised by the Accounting Principles Board of the American Institute of Certified Public Accountants. One way to keep abreast of these changes is to read either *The Wall Street Journal* or *New York Times*. Both of these newspapers cover proposed and actual changes in accounting principles. More complete, but less timely, coverage can be found in either *The Journal of Accountancy*, published by the American Institute of Certified Public Accountants, or the *Financial Executive*, published by the Financial Executives' Institute.

At the time this book went to press the Accounting Principles Board had either exposed releases for public comment or was considering drafts of future releases of accounting principles changes in these areas:

Long-term investments
Accounting changes

Long-term receivables and payables
Sources and application of funds statements
Accounting for income from films licensed to television
Long-term leases

Since each of these decisions will have important implications for the future, the reader is urged to follow the newspaper reports of the Board's deliberations on a current basis. To help the reader identify these proposed changes and put them in their proper perspective, each of the proposals is discussed briefly below. Later chapters cover them in greater detail.

Long-term Investments.   The Board had proposed that corporate holdings of common stock of less than 20 percent of the issuer's outstanding stock should be reported at their current market value rather than at their original cost or less. Furthermore, any changes in the market value of these marketable common stocks should be set forth as a separate item in the income statement during the period in which they occur. Since this proposal would recognize gains due to market price changes, rather than as the result of an actual sale, it represents a significant departure from two basic rules of accounting, namely, that income is not recognized until realized and that assets are not carried at their current market value if it is greater than their acquisition cost.

In addition, the Board has proposed that corporate investments in unconsolidated foreign subsidiaries, 50 percent owned companies, corporate joint ventures, and common stock holdings of 20 percent or more be shown at their original cost plus the parent company's proportionate share of the changes in the subsidiary's retained earnings since acquisition. The investing company's earnings would also include its proportionate share of the unconsolidated company's net income. The application of this method of asset valuation and income recognition to these investments is based on the assumption that the investment is substantial enough to give the investor an influence over the company's policy. At present most companies' investments of these kinds are carried at their cost or less, and income is recognized only to the extent dividends are received. A shift away from this current practice would represent in some people's opinion another significant step toward valuing assets at their current market value, rather than at their cost or less.

Accounting Changes.   The Board had proposed that changes in company accounting policies be restricted to those situations where it can be demonstrated that the new method will provide more useful information to investors than the former one. Any cumulative effect on past statements of the differences between the old and the new methods the Board proposed be included as a separate, clearly identified, extraordinary item in the determination of the current period's net income. Financial statements for prior years would not be restated, but the effect of the accounting change on those years would be disclosed as supplemental information.

If adopted, one of the results of this proposal would be to limit the use of accounting changes simply to improve reported earnings.

Long-term Receivables and Payables. The Board proposed that where a seller takes in return for the sale of an asset a long-term note bearing no interest or an interest rate much lower than the prevailing current rate for a comparable note, the sale price and the amount of the note should be reduced to the present value of the note using an imputed rate of interest. This imputed rate should approximate the prevailing market rate, at which the note could be sold or discounted. Similarly, the buyer would record the asset received and his note payable to the seller at this same present value amount. The effect for the seller would be to report a lower immediate profit on the sale. This reduction of profit would then be reported as interest income over the term of the note receivable. The effect on the buyer would be to report a lower cost of the asset, with correspondingly lower depreciation expense over the life of the asset. This reduction in his depreciation expense would be included as an addition to the interest expense over the terms of the note payable. Previously, accountants had not imputed interest on transactions since the appropriate interest rate could not be objectively verified. Now, the Board feels it is more important that the economic substance of business events be reflected in financial statements even though the resulting statements may be less objective.

Sources and Applications of Funds. The Board had proposed that the funds statement become part of the financial statements covered by the auditor's report.

Accounting for Income from Films Licensed to Television. The American Institute of Certified Public Accountants committee on accounting in the entertainment industries proposed that income realized by companies licensing films to television be recognized at the time each film is shown. This proposal is based on the traditional accounting concept that income is earned through performance. This is in contrast to the Board's proposals related to marketable securities that would recognize income as the result of market price changes.

Leasing. The Board had announced it planned to review the accounting for leases by lessees with the view to issuing a new opinion on this topic. The major proposed change being considered by the Board was to show certain types of leases on the lessee's balance sheet at the present value of the future lease rental payments. If this proposal is adopted it could lead to other changes in the current accounting for executory contracts and long-term commitments.

Textual Material

Each chapter consists of text and selected case studies. The split of pages between cases and text is about even. Thus, unlike a number of other casebooks, there should be sufficient textual material in this book to satisfy the noncollege user seeking to gain a better understanding of fundamentals and current practices in the area of corporate financial reporting. Such readers might include corporate executives, bankers, financial analysts, and individual investors.

A Clinical Approach

The case studies have been prepared as a basis for discussion of the topics covered in the related text. They have not been selected to present illustrations of either appropriate or inappropriate handling of financial reporting problems. To decide what is appropriate action is the purpose of the case discussion.

Most of the cases require a decision on the part of the student. Typically, he is asked to assume the role with a real sense of the professional and personal involvement of top management in a particular situation responsible for issuing financial data to the public. To make his decision realistically, the student must identify the administrative burdens of the decision maker; his opportunities for creative action; and his responsibilities. In particular, the student must be concerned with the relationship between financial reporting and the other areas of top management concern, such as stockholder relations, the market price of the company's stock, dividend policy, capital structure, union wage demands, product pricing, and antitrust actions. He must think through the implications for the company of the actions that investors, the company's independent auditor, the regulatory authorities, and others might take as a result of the company's decision. Seldom will there be a simple, easy answer to the problem posed.

Discussion of the case studies within a decision-making framework should give students an appreciation of:

a) The "real world" difficulties in resolving financial reporting issues.
b) The role of judgment in the selection of appropriate accounting practices.
c) The evolutionary state of accounting principles.
d) The significance and limitations of financial accounting data for decision-making purposes.
e) The need for managers to involve themselves in the financial reporting process.
f) The vital communication function financial reports play in our economic system.
g) The difficulties encountered in trying to develop an integrated statement of a basic theory of accounting that is acceptable to accounting theoreticians and at the same time is responsive to the subtleties of our complex economic system.

b) The relationship between the accounting systems and reports management uses for management control and financial reporting purposes.

i) The urgent need for the business and accounting professions to develop a set of accounting principles that eliminate the differences in accounting practices not justified by different circumstances.

Chapters 1, 2, and 3

The first three chapters do not include cases. They are presented as background material. The purpose of Chapter 1 is to familiarize the reader with (1) some of the fundamental issues in corporate reporting and (2) some of the key institutions that influence corporate reporting standards and practices. Chapter 2 provides a historical background for putting into perspective these issues and the roles of the key institutions. Chapter 3 briefly reviews the common tools of financial analysis used to interpret the data presented in financial statements. An understanding of the material in this chapter is important since many of the proposals for changing corporate reporting practices will influence the interpretation of the results obtained by financial ratio analysis.

Reading Plan

For a number of years the cases and chapters included in this book have been obtainable on an individual basis from a variety of different sources. As a result, a number of undergraduate and graduate courses have used these materials at both the introductory and advanced level. In each of these courses the order and manner in which the materials were used varied according to the student's prior background in the field and the instructor's course objectives. Consequently, it is unlikely that the materials included in this book could be put together in an order that would meet the needs of all readers and courses.

It is suggested that those readers with limited or no prior understanding of financial accounting start reading the book in the following chapter order: Chapters 1, 4, 5, 3, 2, 6, and then the rest of the chapters in order.

The reader with prior exposure at, say, the introductory level can follow the book's chapter sequence.

Acknowledgments

A number of people have helped in the preparation of this book and the financial accounting course at the Harvard Business School from which the book draws heavily. Professor Walter Frese provided the pedagogical and corporate-reporting-philosophy foundation for both the book and the financial accounting course. Two of my colleagues—Professor

Robert Madera and Mrs. Mary Wehle—were responsible for many of the original course materials that were subsequently incorporated into the book. The difficult and frustrating task of typing and controlling the manuscript in its many drafts was ably accomplished by Mrs. Gertrude Nierman. My wife, Patricia, provided both the inspiration needed and the continuing support that was required to squeeze out of a busy family and professional life the time needed to complete the manuscript. Professor Robert Anthony provided helpful editorial advice. I am grateful to all of these people and hope they will share with me a feeling of accomplishment and pride in this most recent outgrowth of the Harvard Business School's very successful financial accounting course. Finally, I wish to thank the President and Fellows of Harvard College for their permission to reproduce the case and textual materials copyrighted in their name, as well as Professors Robert Sprouse, Richard Vancil, Walter Frese, Robert Anthony, Brandt Allen, Russell Nelson, John Yeager, Andrew McCosh, Ross Walker, T. F. Bradshaw, C. A. Bliss, and Derek Newton for allowing me to use or adapt cases originally prepared by them. Others who have been associated with the development of the cases in the book include Len Savoie, Ed Jepson, David Macey, Arnie Ludwick, Don Bryant, David Koenig, Bob McInnis, and Jerry Brougher.

The cases in Chapter 11 are based on examples included in J. T. Ball's *Computing Earnings per Share*. The Holden case is based on an illustration presented in Accounting Research Study No. 6, *Reporting the Financial Effects of Price-Level Changes*. One case, John Sellers, is drawn directly from a release by the Securities and Exchange Commission.

April, 1971   David F. Hawkins

CONTENTS

PART IV. Income Determination

PART V. Asset Valuation and Expense Determination

and Events. *Opinion No. 11*. The Controversy, *Flow-Through Method. Comprehensive Allocation. Partial Allocation. Deferred Taxes: A Liability? Flow of Funds. Like Depreciation? Measurable Funds Effect. Extending the Argument. Income Measurement. Other Aspects of the Problem. Present Value Approach. Rate Changes. Liability Method: An Example. Deferral Method: An Example. Effective Tax Rate Reduction?* Public Utilities. *Tax Reform Act.* Loss Carry-Back—Carry-Forward Credits. Statement Presentation. *Income Statement.* Special Areas. *Continuing Controversy.*

Cases

Capitalization Criteria. Cost Basis. Expenditures Subsequent to Acquisition and Use. *Repairs and Maintenance. Betterments, Improvements, and Additions. Land. Wasting Assets.* Historical Costs and Accountability. *Donated Assets. Discovery Value. Appraisal Value of Plant Assets.* Alternative Proposals. Investment Tax Credit. *The Lessons.*

Cases

Computing Depreciation. *Estimating the Useful Life of Fixed Assets.* Depreciation Methods. *Straight-Line Depreciation. Accelerated Depreciation. Units-of-Production Depreciation.* Accounting for Depreciation. *Group and Composite Rate Depreciation. Depreciation and Federal Income Tax. Depreciation Schedule Revisions. Additions. Donated Assets. Written-Up Assets. Accounting for Retirements. Capital Investment Decisions. Depletion. Depreciation Decisions.*

Cases

Measures of Inflation. Business Considerations. Accounting Considerations. *Restatement Mechanism. Degree of Restatement. Other Issues.* An Example: The Cruzeiro Corporation.

Cases

Amortization Practices and Theory. Payments in Excess of Book Value. Income Tax Treatment. Specific Intangible Assets. *Research and Develop-*

ment Costs. *Advertising and Marketing Costs. Patents. Copyrights. Franchises. Trademarks and Trade Names. Leasehold Improvements. Organization Costs. Intangible Development Costs. Oil and Gas Exploration Costs.* Role of Judgment. *Profit Impact of Shift. Inappropriate Practices.*

Cases

17. INVENTORY PRICING   429

Periodic and Perpetual Inventory Systems. Pricing Bases. Cost Methods. Inventory Methods. *Specific Identification. Last Invoice Price. Simple Average. Weighted Average. Moving Average. First-In, First-Out. Last-In, First-Out. Lifo versus Fifo. Base Stock.* Cost or Market, Whichever Is Lower. *Retail Method.* Selling Price. Statement Presentation. Summary.

Cases

18. INTERCORPORATE INVESTMENTS AND BUSINESS
COMBINATIONS   454

Accounting Procedures. *Ownership Interests of Less than 50 Percent. Ownership Interests of More than 50 Percent. Ownership Interest of 50 Percent. Business Combinations: Two Approaches. Development of the* Business Combination Problem. Opinion No. 16, Business Combinations. *Conditions Requiring Pooling Treatment. The 90 Percent Test. Accounting Mechanics. Reporting Requirements. Disclosure of Poolings. Conditions Requiring Purchase Accounting.* Goodwill. *The Nature of Goodwill. "Negative Goodwill." Goodwill Tax Consideration.* Different Concepts. *Pooling of Interests. Purchase Method.* Research Efforts of the APB. *ARS No. 10. ARS No. 5. Criticisms.*

Cases

PART VI. Long-Term Commitments

19. ACCOUNTING FOR LEASES   493

Leasing Practices. Lessee's Statements. *Accounting Entries. Disclosure. Installment Purchases of Property. Sale and Lease-Back.* Lessor's Statements. *Operating Method. Financing Method. Accounting Entries.* Balance Sheet Presentation and Disclosure. *Initial Direct Cost.* Leasing by Manufacturers. *Accounting Entries. The Continuing Controversy.*

20. PENSION COSTS   525

Pension Plans. *Valuation. Assumptions. Funding Instruments and Agencies. Funding Methods. Income Tax Considerations in Plan Selection. Summary.* Accounting Considerations. *Cash versus Accrual. Opinion No. 8. An Overview. Pension Costs: Maximum and Minimum Limits. Income Taxes. Major Objective. After Opinion No. 8.*

21. LONG-TERM DEBT   551

Characteristics of Long-Term Debt. *Bond Prices. Registration. Financial Consideration.* Accounting Practices. *Issuance of Bonds. Amortization of Bond Premium and Discount. Retirement before Maturity. Refunding. Conversion. Debt Issued with Stock Warrants. Debt Issued with Conversion Privileges.* Accounting Practices: The Buyer. *Purchase of Bonds. Interest Payments Received.*

PART VII. Stockholders' Equity

22. EQUITY CAPITAL TRANSACTIONS   573

Owners' Equity. *Treasury Stock. Dividends. Stock Dividends and Splits. Stock Option and Purchase Plans. Convertible Securities.*

PART VIII. Special Accounting Problems

23. MEASURING OVERSEAS ACTIVITIES   593

Exchange Rates. *Devaluation.* Exchange Gains and Losses. Translation of Statements. *Stable Exchange Rate. Fluctuating Exchange Rate. Financial Method. Other Methods. Current Asset Method. Modified Financial Method. Net Asset Method. An Illustration.* Separating Price-Level and Translation Gains and Losses. Measurement and Motivation.

PART I

Corporate Reporting Environment

CHAPTER 1

INSTITUTIONS AND ISSUES

Accounting is the art of recording, classifying, and summarizing in a significant manner and in terms of money, transactions, and events which are, in part at least, of a financial character. Financial accounting is concerned with the process of using the content of these accounting records to measure, communicate, and interpret the financial condition and results of operations of business entities. The typical outputs of the process are the balance sheet, income statement, and funds flow statement. The financial data communicated through the financial statements are used both by management for decision-making purposes and a number of parties outside of the reporting entity who are interested in the results of the decisions made by management.

The management of the company publishing financial statements is responsible for their content. Many people mistakenly believe that the statements are the responsibility of the public accountant who audited them. A careful reading of the statement accompanying audited financial statements issued by the independent certified public accountant show he is only expressing his opinion as to (1) the fairness of statements, (2) their degree of conformity with the recognized generally accepted accounting principles, and (3) the consistency of the accounting practices used to prepare the statements with those followed in the previous accounting period.

The adequacy of financial statements is judged in terms of the fairness and usefulness of the data provided to all of the interested parties. These are difficult standards to define. There is considerable disagreement as to their definition. Nevertheless, a great number of generally accepted financial accounting conventions, concepts, principles, and standards of full and fair disclosure have evolved and been supported by recognized accounting authorities. These authorities include the Accounting Principles

Board (APB) of the American Institute of Certified Public Accountants (AICPA), and the Securities and Exchange Commission (SEC).

One of the early actions of the Securities and Exchange Commission was to rule that companies under its jurisdiction be audited by independent public accountants. Although the SEC was given the power to establish accounting rules by the Securities Exchange Act of 1933–34, very early in its existence the Commission made it known that it expected the accounting profession to assume the main part of this task. With few exceptions, the SEC has followed that policy to this day.

ACCOUNTING PRINCIPLES BOARD

The leading authority on accounting principles for business is the Accounting Principles Board of the AICPA. Periodically, it issues *Opinions* that are used as guidelines by businessmen and independent certified public accountants to determine the general acceptability of specific corporate financial reporting practices.

The Accounting Principles Board has 18 members elected by the Institute's Council for three-year terms. Typically, 15 of the members are certified public accountants in public practice, 1 is a financial executive from industry and 2 are from the academic field. Assisting the APB are a full-time administrative director and a research staff.

The AICPA's activities in the development of a formal statement of accounting principles began in 1938 when it formed a Committee on Accounting Procedure (CAP) to "narrow the areas of difference in corporate reporting" by gradually eliminating less desirable practices. Over a period of 20 years, 51 *Accounting Research Bulletins* (*ARB*'s) were issued, indicating preferred treatments of various items and transactions. Although these bulletins were advisory rather than binding, they became highly influential. They were supported by the SEC and the stock exchanges and were observed by the profession generally. (The SEC and the stock exchanges ordinarily will not accept a company's financial statements if the auditor's opinion contains an exception to the accounting principles used.)

Despite this progress, a feeling persisted, both within and without the profession, that there were still too many alternative accounting principles applicable in similar circumstances regarded as "generally accepted." It was also recognized that changed business conditions—new forms of financing, new tax laws, and the evolution of more complex corporate structures—required the development of some new accounting principles, and at a pace faster than had been previously considered necessary.

The AICPA in 1959 therefore created a new body, the APB, to succeed the Committee on Accounting Procedure and to carry on its work in a broader and more intensive way.

Later, the governing body of the AICPA adopted two important recommendations: (1) when a company audited by an Institute member uses
an accounting method other than that recommended by the APB, the
departure from the Board's position is to be disclosed in a footnote to
the financial statement or in the auditor's report; and (2) variations in the
treatment of accounting items generally should be confined to those justified by substantial differences in factual circumstances.

Formulation of an APB *Opinion* usually involves the following steps:

1. From a list of significant problems singled out by a planning subcom-
    mittee, the Board decides which projects should be undertaken in a
    given period.
2. In many cases the Board authorizes a formal research study under the
    direction of its Accounting Research Division.
3. When a study is completed it is published and widely circulated.
    Comments are invited, and APB members give careful consideration
    to all responses.
4. An APB subcommittee appointed by the chairman then reviews the
    study and recommends a course of action to the Board.
5. If the Board decides to issue an *Opinion*, the subcommittee prepares
    a first draft. Usually the subcommittee holds meetings with interested
    organizations representing industry and users of financial statements
    to discuss the basic points and to obtain informed views from them.
    Subsequent drafts are prepared until the Board reaches agreement that
    a draft is ready for "exposure."
6. The exposure draft of an *Opinion* is then mailed for comment to sev-
    eral thousand CPAs, business executives, security analysts, government
    officials, and others.
7. After a reasonable time (generally not less than 60 days), reactions to
    the exposure draft are summarized and studied. Following discussion
    of still further changes that may have been proposed, a final draft is
    prepared for balloting by the Board. Each member assents, dissents,
    or assents with qualification. In the latter two cases, a statement of the
    member's position is included with the *Opinion* as finally published.
    A two-thirds majority approval is required for issuance of a formal
    Opinion.

The time from start of a research study to issuance of an *Opinion* may
be several years.

THREE BASIC ISSUES

Underlying much of the contemporary controversy over corporate
financial reporting practices covered in this book are three basic issues:

1. Should corporate reports be reports *by* management or reports *on* management?
2. Should the accounting principles on which corporate reports are based be derived from business practice, their validity resting upon their general acceptance; or should they be developed conceptually, in a manner analogous to the principles of Euclidean geometry?
3. Should accounting principles be *uniform* in their application or should they permit *flexibility* on the part of the person responsible for the financial reports to choose from equally acceptable alternatives for reporting essentially identical transactions?

How each of these questions is ultimately decided will have an important impact on the means by which we measure and communicate managerial performance to investors.

Management's Statements

Today, management has the responsibility for measuring and reporting its own performance. A number of critics of the present corporate reporting system believe it is unreasonable to expect management to fulfill this public reporting responsibility objectively. In their opinion, the pressures upon management from stockholders to show a pattern of increasing annual earnings per share are so enormous that managers of companies in trouble find it hard to avoid puffing up their earnings through accounting policy decisions. Therefore, in order to ensure that stockholders obtain an objective measure of managerial performance, they believe it is necessary to shift the responsibility for the reports to a disinterested third party, such as the independent public accountant.

Others believe that the application of responsible management judgment is most likely to lead to the selection of the most meaningful accounting principles in particular situations. This point of view attaches importance to the need for each company to select accounting policies which best communicate its management's unique policies, objectives, and the factors which guided their decisions. Since few public accountants are trained to bring this perspective and understanding to the financial reporting process, it is argued that it can be accomplished best through the exercise of responsible management judgment.

Different Approaches

Most managers, public accountants and others involved in the corporate financial reporting process are uneasy about the present differences and inconsistencies in the preparation and presentation of financial information to stockholders. The AICPA, which represents the independent certified public accounting profession, and the American Accounting Association (AAA), which is comprised mostly of accounting professors, have programs which seek the improvement of financial accounting and reporting practices by reducing the number of acceptable alternative procedures. While the aims are common, their approaches are different. The AAA has adopted the conceptual approach to developing an overall framework for supporting accounting practice. The AICPA has followed a case-by-case approach to establishing accounting principles. This has been accomplished through the APB (and its predecessor, the CAP).

The advocates of the conceptual approach believe that if a consistent theory of financial accounting could be developed, many of the current controversies would be resolved. Those supporting this approach view conventional accounting practices as a collection of mutually inconsistent principles and practices which no systematic theory can describe. Therefore, they believe it is necessary to look elsewhere for a set of concepts which can be used to measure and communicate the results of business operations. There is little agreement on the methodology to be followed, however. The most popular approach has been to identify some accounting axioms and then use logic to construct a theory of accounting. Few of the recommendations resulting from this process have been adopted, principally because they have seemed impractical to most practicing accountants.

The AICPA's case-by-case approach, with its heavy reliance on acceptance, is more practical. Its efforts have been directed to identifying from the accounting practices that have evolved from actual business experience those principles that are generally accepted. It has exercised restraint in trying to impose unilaterally its own set of standards on the business community. Thus, the AICPA's role is more that of a catalyst than a prescriber of standards. This approach is based on the belief that fairness in financial reporting can not be fully realized unless it has a high degree of acceptance and is consistent with the modes of thought and customs of all segments of the business community.

Uniformity versus Flexibility

The broad accounting issue commonly known as "uniformity versus flexibility" arose during the 1950s, when an increasing number of thoughtful businessmen, accountants, and members of the financial community became concerned over the difficulties involved in making meaningful comparisons of the financial reports of different companies. These problems arose because businessmen could (and still can) choose between several equally authoritative accounting treatments to report to investors on such items as inventories, pensions, depreciation, and long-term contracts. The results? Profits vary greatly depending on the alternative chosen.

Some claimed that uniformity in the application of accounting princi-ples to similar transactions would be the solution to these inadequacies of accounting practice. Greater uniformity is needed to produce financial statements that are fair to all those who rely upon financial data. If such statements are not forthcoming, the supporters of uniformity predict a general lack of confidence in financial statements and an inevitable increase in governmental control over the accounting practices followed by in-dustry.

The supporters of a more flexible approach also recognized that gener-ally accepted accounting principles needed a thorough overhaul. How-ever, they cautioned against seeking uniformity solely for its own sake. Some flexibility must be retained, they argued, for management to choose between accounting principles, for only in this way can the variations in basic business policies and management attitudes toward risk which exist in actual business practice be reflected. The proponents of flexibility charge that to give these variations the appearance of comparability through uniform accounting, when in fact they are not uniform, would be misleading.

How this controversy will be resolved will depend in large part on how quickly and how far management will voluntarily improve the integrity of its financial representations to investors. For at the heart of this contro-versy is a strong desire by both camps to protect this integrity.

Furthermore, businessmen and others touched by this controversy must face up to the fact the answer to this issue is not a simple one. Specifically, if generally accepted accounting principles become too inflexible, it is possible that business practice may be unduly constricted. At the other extreme, if generally accepted accounting principles become too flexible, business practice may degenerate into confusion and mistrust. Both are undesirable situations. Where to draw the line is the critical issue.

In the future, as the APB's opinions on accounting matters are made known, the issue of uniformity versus flexibility will be faced again and again by businessmen. Management's decisions will have to be made on each opinion as it is offered, since there is no general, simple, ready-made solution to this broad issue. One fact is clear however. Some reform is needed if financial reports between different companies are to become more comparable. The character of these reforms will depend greatly on how the issue of uniformity versus flexibility in accounting principles is resolved.

MANAGER'S ROLE

The controversy over the three basic issues discussed above raises another basic question: What is management's role in the development and statement of generally accepted accounting principles?

Despite the obvious reasons why accounting principles are of vital interest to management, management has played only a small part in the development and statement of generally accepted accounting principles. In the absence of management participation the problems of financial reporting, which have a broad social impact, have had to be dealt with by the accounting profession. The unfortunate result is that the crucial need for management's recognition of its far-reaching public responsibilities in financial reporting, has been deemphasized among management people.

The outcome has been inevitable. A number of the less responsible individual managements, feeling no public responsibility, have been inclined to take advantage of the alternatives and gray areas of generally accepted accounting principles to report profits which best serve their individual purposes. Unhappily, these laggard managements all too often set the reporting standards of their industry. For, in the face of competitive pressures, it takes courage to report, say, lower profits just for the sake of supporting a more desirable accounting principle, when others regard it as only one of several equally authoritative alternatives.

This observation should not be interpreted as a general indictment of all business managers for lack of responsibility or for low morality. It is made solely to indicate that the unsatisfactory state of accounting principles and the acts of a few irresponsible businessmen have made it more difficult for business as a whole to fulfill its public responsibility in the area of corporate financial reporting.

If managements wish to lessen the probability of government control over financial reporting, they must support and participate in the accounting reform movement. Many are convinced that without responsible management participation, the accounting profession will be unsuccessful in its current efforts to narrow the areas of inconsistency in financial reporting practices. The accountants have recognized the necessity of joint effort with industry, appointing representatives from industry to the APB.

The controversy over accounting practices has alerted management to the fact that it shares a responsibility in setting realistic and workable ground rules for financial reporting. Whether or not uniformity or flexibility in accounting principles is fundamental to progress in formulating improved principles is yet to be decided. In deciding this and the other fundamental issues, however, the APB must have the assistance and support of the business community. For, in the end, the success or failure of the APB will rest largely with each businessman.

MANAGEMENT ACCOUNTING

This book focuses on *financial* accounting—accounting that has the goal of providing stockholders and other external parties to the company

useful financial information. Nearly all businesses have another closely related system of accounting which provides management with useful financial information for running the business. This internally oriented system is concerned with *management* accounting.

A company's management accounting need not conform to the generally accepted accounting principles that govern its financial accounting. However, in practice a close relationship between these two accounting systems usually exists. One of the principal functions of management accounting is to measure the performance of the various units of a company against a set of measurement standards. These measures of performance are selected on the basis that if the unit managers can be motivated to achieve these standards their actions will collectively move the company toward the realization of its overall corporate objectives. Since generally accepted accounting principles will be used to measure the total corporate progress, there must be a link between the two systems. It is not sensible to motivate unit managers to achieve results that look good according to internal accounting but poor when the same results are translated into external accounting terms. Also, if a company's rules for maintaining the internal and external systems are very different, the company must maintain two sets of books to record its business transactions. This can be very expensive. Therefore, to reduce their accounting costs, most companies collect and record their basic management accounting data according to financial accounting rules.

While most companies use essentially the same accounting principles for management and financial accounting purposes, a number of companies have explicitly decided not to adopt this practice. In their opinion some of the company's external reporting practices can not be used internally because they might introduce an undesirable behavioral bias in the decisions of unit managers. This practice raises a disturbing question: How can a company justify for external reporting the use of a generally accepted principle that does not lead to a useful measure of performance for internal purposes, because it either motivates managers to follow operating policies not desired by the company, provides top management with misleading measures of performance, or fails to reflect the company's real prospect?

BEHAVIORAL IMPLICATIONS

Research into the behavioral implications of management accounting and measurement systems has led some financial accounting authorities to conclude that generally accepted accounting principles can condition the decisions of managers as well as measure their performance for external reporting purposes. Unfortunately, in the opinion of these researchers, this has not always led to desirable results.

A number of these external reporting principles have a built-in bias which motivates managers under certain circumstances to adopt them in preference to alternative principles that may better reflect the operating results and financial condition of their company. In addition, other generally accepted accounting principles may induce managers to adopt specific operating policies to justify the use of these principles, even though these operating policies may not necessarily be the most appropriate.

The APB has reduced the number of behaviorally undesirable accounting principles, but some still persist. A number of people believe that the goal of the accounting and management professions should be to eliminate these remaining objectionable practices and to create a set of generally accepted principles that will motivate managers to make sound economic and factual reporting decisions. If this is not possible, our corporate reporting system should at least not encourage managers to act against what appear to be the best interests of their stockholders and society.

Those who hold this view believe the APB and others who influence the definition of what constitutes acceptable corporate financial accounting practices must ask themselves when considering the appropriateness of an accounting principle:

1. What might this accounting principle or practice motivate managers to do in their own selfish interest?
2. Could this possible action obscure actual managerial performance, give the illusion of performance where none exists, or lead to unsound economic actions?

If the answer to any part of the second question is yes, and the probability that it will occur is reasonably high in even a few cases, then the use of the accounting practice should not be encouraged, even though it may be sound from the technical viewpoint of accounting theory.

TAX ACCOUNTING

The objective of corporate tax planning is to minimize the current tax liability and then to defer the payment of this liability to the government as long as possible. A firm's taxable income is established by two sets of accounting rules and conventions that impinge upon each other. One set is established by the Internal Revenue Service. The other set is generally accepted accounting principles.

In general, a firm's taxable income is determined by the accounting system based on generally accepted accounting principles that it uses in the normal course of its business. However, with one major exception involving inventory accounting, the tax code allows companies to deviate from this practice in specific areas when calculating taxable income without having to change the corporate financial reports issued to stockholders.

As a result, in such areas as fixed asset accounting, a company can maintain two sets of accounting data: one for determining the current tax payments to the government, another for preparing the statements for public reporting purposes. This is legal. However, it does create financial accounting problems related to how to account for the current corporate income tax expenses in financial reports to stockholders. These will be discussed at considerable length in Chapter 12.

From time to time somebody advocates that greater harmony, if not complete agreement, should exist between the income figures determined for income tax and financial reporting purposes. This position fails to recognize that the objectives of financial and tax accounting are different. The objective of financial accounting is to present fairly the results of operations and the financial condition of a company to its stockholders and other interested parties external to the firm, such as employees and creditors. Tax accounting's objective is to raise tax revenues and to help carry out the government's economic, political, and social policies. For example, tax surcharges and investment credits are adopted to manipulate the growth of the economy. The provision in the 1969 Tax Reform Act permitting 60-month amortization of certain pollution control facilities is an example of congressional concern over the ecological problem of pollution. In addition, some tax accounting practices are based on administrative practicalities. For example, a basic tax concept is that the timing of a tax liability should be influenced by when the taxpayer can most readily pay and the government can most readily collect. Clearly, this concept is at odds with the accrual concept of financial accounting, which says income should be recognized when it is earned.

In general, business has been unwilling to accept an accounting principle for financial reporting purposes that reduces financial income unless it produces a tax reduction. For example, many businessmen oppose the amortization of goodwill (i.e., excess cost of assets acquired in acquisitions over their fair market value) for financial reporting purposes because it is not a deductible expense for determining income tax payments. Similarly, many believe it is the inability to claim a tax deduction for employee stock options that justifies the similar treatment for financial accounting purposes, despite the fact that many accounting authorities believe that stock options represent a form of compensation that should be charged to earnings. Thus, while we often argue that because of their different objectives, tax and financial accounting should be kept separate, in practice tax accounting does influence financial accounting.

AN APPROACH TO FINANCIAL REPORTING DECISIONS

The process of analyzing and resolving financial reporting problems is similar to that followed in other business decision-making situations, except

that the decision maker must usually work with the constraints of generally accepted accounting principles. Typically, the businessman is faced with a problem to which there is more than one possible solution. His task is to choose what he believes to be the best possible course of action. He can do this intuitively or through careful, systematic consideration and weighting of the anticipated consequences; or some combination of these two approaches. Whatever the approach used, he must eventually make a decision.

The evaluation of the alternative courses of action can be facilitated if "yardsticks" or criteria, weighted by their relative importance, are first developed. Then, for any particular problem these criteria can be used as guides to distinguish between acceptable and unacceptable solutions. The criteria can also be used to rank the acceptable solutions in their relative order of attractiveness.

In the case of financial reporting problems, the decision criteria are usually developed from an analysis of the company's overall objectives and the operating strategy to achieve those objectives. This is done by answering these questions: Given the company's objectives and operating plan, what characteristics must the financial reporting policy satisfy if it is to significantly contribute to the realization of these plans? What are the implications for the company's financial reporting policies of the characteristics of the company's particular operations, relations with external groups, competitors' policies and plans, industry, financial structure, and management? Answers to these questions require a detailed analysis of such areas as the company's operations and plans, the stock market's evaluation of such companies, the company's business environment, and the public interest and regulatory requirements that may be present.

The identification and correct definition of the problem to be solved is a critical stage in the decision-making process. Unless this is done well, the decision maker may solve the wrong issue or only part of the problem, which may leave him with a more unsatisfactory situation than before he took action. In most of the cases presented, at least part of the problem is fairly evident. How well one is able to clearly and fully state the problem will depend in large part on the quality of the operating and environmental analysis described above.

Financial reporting problems usually involve the selection of the appropriate generally accepted accounting principles to handle a specific item. These problems involve at least five interrelated considerations:

1. Which principles are the most appropriate?
2. How should the decision on this accounting policy application be communicated to the public?
3. As a result of this decision what other adjustments, if any, must be made in the particular mix of generally accepted accounting princi-

ples that collectively constitute the company's financial reporting policy?

4. What operating or financial bias will this decision have on management's future business decisions or policies?

5. How will this decision contribute to the real or apparent achievement of management's objectives?

The third question recognizes that a company's earnings per share and financial image is the net result of applying accounting policy decisions to a variety of individual transactions. Therefore, a change in one part of this mix may necessitate changes in other parts to achieve the overall effect management is seeking.

The alternative solutions to financial reporting problems usually involve a choice between different generally accepted accounting principles. Therefore, in order for the decision maker in any particular situation to fully appraise and consider the full range of solutions open to him, he must be familiar with generally accepted accounting principles, the conditions justifying the usage of particular principles, and the principal theoretical arguments for and against each principle.

Once the criteria, the problem, and the possible solutions are identified the decision maker must sift through the facts available to him to extract those that are relevant to the problem.

These facts, of which some are measurable and others are not, must be related to the solutions so that the advantages and disadvantages of each solution can be identified. The decision maker must then use judgment to decide which solution has the greatest net advantage.

There is seldom a right answer to financial reporting problems, or even an answer to which everyone will agree. The decision maker must make the best decision he can with the facts available to him, knowing that two people may interpret or weigh the same facts differently and reach quite different conclusions. Decision making under these circumstances is a complicated and difficult task, fraught with uncertainty.

THE CHALLENGE

The challenge to those who define generally accepted accounting principles is to develop a set of principles that are both behaviorally and technically sound. They should be behaviorally sound in that they:

1. Inhibit managers from taking undesirable operating actions to justify the adoption of an accounting alternative.

2. Inhibit the adoption of accounting practices by corporations which create the illusion of performance.

The traditional approach to defining generally accepted accounting principles has focused principally on technical considerations. Typically,

this has been done well The time has come, however, to pay greater attention to the possible impact of accounting practices on people's actions. If this is also done well, financial accounting will do a better job of communicating the financial facts of a business situation, rather than being a convenient vehicle for unscrupulous managers to mislead unwitting investors.

SUGGESTED FURTHER READINGS

LADD, DWIGHT D. *Contemporary Corporate Accounting and the Public.* Homewood, Ill.: Richard D. Irwin, 1963.

ZEFF, STEPHEN, and KELLER, THOMAS. *Financial Accounting Theory.* New York: McGraw-Hill, 1964.

CHAPTER 2

THE DEVELOPMENT OF CORPORATE REPORTING PRACTICES

From 19th-century traditions of corporate secrecy, American manufacturers have moved slowly toward more public and credible financial disclosure practices. This chapter examines the variety of political, technical, social, and economic pressures from the business community, the accounting profession, the government, and the public which have impelled this movement and governed its direction and tempo. An appreciation of this process is necessary to put our contemporary practices and problems into proper perspective. People with such a sense of history seem to be more closely in touch with reality and able to deal with change more creatively. The study of corporate reporting history also sharpens one's sense of when to introduce change and how long it may take.

As late as 1900, the amount of financial information presented to stockholders by the managers of most publicly owned American manufacturing corporations was meager. After 1900, the level and frequency of corporate financial disclosure by industrial management began to rise slowly and the credibility of its representations began to improve. These changes in the quality of the financial reporting practices of American manufacturing concerns have four principal causes: (1) gradual recognition by some managers of their public responsibility; (2) increasing criticism of management accounting and reporting practices by a number of influential groups and individuals outside of the management class; (3) direct federal government regulation, such as the Securities Acts of 1933 and 1934; (4) the recognition by the American accounting profession, and acceptance by the business community, of some common accounting and reporting standards. Underlying and contributing to these forces for change

16

have been a number of social, political, and economic factors such as the emergence of a large number of small investors, the evolution of big business, and the increasing willingness of the public to seek government action to reform undesirable commercial practices.

NINETEENTH CENTURY

The modern reviewer of management financial reporting practices during the 19th century is immediately struck by the limited amount of information made public by manufacturing firms—even the larger ones with widespread public ownership. Not only was there inadequate financial disclosure, but some companies were irregular in the frequency with which they issued reports. For example, between 1897 and 1905, the Westinghouse Electric and Manufacturing Company neither published an annual financial report to its stockholders nor held an annual meeting.

This lack of financial information pertaining to manufacturing concerns was in contrast to the reporting practices of public utilities, insurance companies, banks, and railroads, whose activities (being more in the public service) were more closely regulated and more fully reported. Even here, however, practice varied in accordance with state requirements, and there were some notable nonreporters. For instance, in 1866, the treasurer of the Delaware, Lackawanna, and Western Rail Road Company, in response to a request for information from the New York Stock Exchange replied simply: "The Delaware Lackawanna R.R. Co. make no reports and publish no statements and have done nothing of the sort for the last five years."

Before 1900, for the few publicly held manufacturing corporations in existence, it was possible for investors to obtain some information pertaining to the companies' capitalization, if not from management, from the standard financial sources such as *Hunt's Merchant's Magazine*, and later, the *Commercial and Financial Chronicle*. Less frequently was a simple balance sheet available and seldom were sales and profit figures released— an income statement showing sales less the major expense items was rare. In addition, few of these published financial facts were accompanied by either a company or independent auditors' certificate, since neither the theory nor practice of these procedures was common in America. The public had to rely upon management's integrity in determining if published financial information was reliable.

After 1890, a few of the newly created industrial combinations sometimes published more detailed financial statements. By modern standards, even in these cases, the amount of data released was sketchy. Companies, such as American Tobacco, which issued the more detailed financial reports usually did so because of enlightened managers or because of their heavy dependence on outside sources for capital.

Generally, as might be expected, the small and the closely held manufacturing corporations were the more secretive. Yet as late as 1900 there were some notoriously secretive managements among the large publicly traded corporations. This group included such companies as the American Tin Plate Company, a large publicly owned company, which controlled 95 percent of the tin-plate production in the United States and whose stock was traded on the New York and Chicago stock exchanges. It published in 1900 a balance sheet containing only four asset and five liability accounts.

FACTORS CONTRIBUTING TO FINANCIAL SECRECY

The principal reasons why corporate managers were so secretive with regard to their companies' financial affairs during most of the 19th century were four in number: (1) there was no tradition of publicity, for no one would have thought of asking individual proprietors, partners, or early family owners to divulge such information; (2) management believed the public had no right to information on these matters; (3) managers feared that by revealing financial information they would unwittingly assist their competitors; (4) to many, the doctrine of *caveat emptor* seemed as applicable to buyers of securities as to purchasers of horses. For instance, during the testimony heard before the Industrial Commission in 1899, Henry O. Havemeyer, the president of American Sugar Refining Company, and commission member Thomas Phillips had the following exchange:

PHILLIPS: You think, then, that when a corporation is chartered by the State, offers stock to the public, and is one in which the public is interested, that the public has no right to know what its earning power is or to subject them to any inspection whatever, that the people may not buy stock blindly?

HAVEMEYER: Yes; that is my theory. Let the buyer beware; that covers the whole business. You cannot wet-nurse people from the time they are born until the day they die. They have got to wade in and get stuck and that is the way men are educated and cultivated.

The testimony of another witness before the commission, Charles W. King, secretary and general manager of the New Jersey Corporation Agency,[1] illustrates another of the reasons for secrecy:

LIVINGSTON (commission member):   Now, then, when the people ask for information, why not just give it? You say because it would be giving away

---

[1] The New Jersey Corporations Agency was formed in 1895 for the purpose of furnishing corporations chartered in New Jersey but operating out of state with the necessary facilities for complying with the state's liberal incorporation laws. Mr. King's office represented several hundred such corporations, including the Amalgamated Copper Company, the American Car and Foundry Company, the American Thread Company, the Pressed Steel Car Company and the American Soda Fountain Company.

your private business. Well, you did not think of that when you went to the public for your franchise, did you?

KING: The public may not be your competitors, but you may have competitors, and in giving it to the public you would have to give it to your competitors.

These comments of Havemeyer and King represented in part an inheritance by late 19th-century management of a number of the attitudes of the owner-managers of the century's earlier industrial ventures. Ownership and management, if not the same persons, were closely related, and the owners were in continual personal touch with the affairs of the enterprise. Because there were few or no outside investors, there was little need for management to think about the problems of financial disclosure. Under these conditions a company's financial statements were considered private, just as were the financial affairs of any private citizen.

State corporation laws reflected this antipublicity sentiment of managers and their agents. By 1900, reports of some kind were required in 27 states. The remainder of the states required no report whatsoever.

About half the states provided for reports to stockholders. In general, these statutes merely specified that an "annual report" be provided the stockholders. Seldom were the contents of the report specified or a provision included to require the mailing of annual reports to those stockholders who were unable to attend the stockholders' meeting. To have imposed the burden of detailed public reports upon management would not have improved a state's chances of attracting incorporations—a lucrative business few states wished to discourage.

The accepted method of marketing new industrial securities also placed little pressure upon management for greater financial disclosure. During the 19th century, investors bought securities primarily on the basis of their confidence in the promoter or the investment banker offering the issue. In particular, investment bankers, it was widely believed, undertook searching investigations of all securities before they were offered to the public, only offered securities of investment quality, and practically guaranteed the security. Consequently, prospectuses offering new industrial securities seldom ran more than two pages and contained sketchy financial data. The first test of a security was the reliability of the investment bankers involved, not the financial conditions of the issuing company. Under these conditions, as long as companies paid their dividends, investors rarely needed, or demanded, financial statements.

Finally, the absence of a strong accounting profession and an established body of accounting theory in America contributed to the inadequacy of management's financial reports. Not only was there nondisclosure, but when information was released it was of dubious value, since different companies used different accounting concepts to measure and report similar transactions. For instance, the concept of depreciation was little

understood. A number of firms made no provisions for depreciation. Some related depreciation expense to changes in appraised asset values. There were also several other areas where accounting practice was far from standardized and the use of different accounting practices created confusion—including the treatment of unusual charges and credits, the valuation of assets, and the consolidation of subsidiaries.

These accounting vagaries existed partly because little attention had been given in the United States to the logic of accounting. Prior to 1900, nearly all of the American textbooks pertaining to the subject were concerned principally with the rules of bookkeeping.

In addition, the function of public accountants and their reports was misunderstood. For a company to call in independent auditors to examine its books was often taken by the public as an indication of suspected fraud, irregularity, losses, and doubt regarding the reporting company's financial strength. Some managers regarded such action as a reflection on their integrity. Even as late as 1900, many businessmen were still reluctant to call in an accountant, and many investigations by public accountants were made secretly, often at night and on Sundays. Consequently, it is not surprising that an English chartered accountant wrote of American practice before 1905: "the profession of accounting has hitherto been little understood in America. The accountant in the United States was little known, little recognized, little wanted, most accountants neither could nor desired to modify management's desire for corporate secrecy.

TOWARD THE SECURITIES ACTS
AND IMPROVED DISCLOSURE, 1900–33

Almost as soon as business became big, a number of people became disturbed by its growth in power and critical of its practices. It was argued by many, for instance, that the large combinations should be dissolved, since the very existence of these new and powerful industrial groups threatened the fundamental civil liberties and morality of American society.

One of the most popular remedies suggested to rectify this imbalance of power and to end the predatory methods of large corporations was improved corporate financial publicity. For example, in 1900, the Industrial Commission recommended to Congress:

> The larger corporations—the so-called trusts—should be required to publish annually a properly audited report, showing in reasonable detail their assets and liabilities, with profit or loss; such report and audit under oath to be subject to Government inspection. The purpose of such publicity is to encourage competition when profits become excessive, thus protecting consumers against too high prices and to guard the interests of employees by a knowledge of the financial condition of the business in which they are employed.

The increasing number of investors, it was thought, would also be protected by improved corporate publicity. While little correlation between the issuance of informative reports and willingness on the part of investors to buy stock was noted, public opinion nevertheless was appalled by the stock market manipulations of many managements and promoters who sought to enrich themselves at the expense of their stockholders. According to one contemporary observer:

The suppression and misstatement of facts by corporations have in recent years misled investors as well as speculators to buy shares in concerns financially unsound and on the verge of bankruptcy. To prevent the "watering" of stock or to find some method of furnishing investors a basis of judging the condition of companies has absorbed the attention of the "public mind" for some time. "Secrecy" was said to be the evil; nor is it to be wondered at that "publicity" was the remedy suggested. No one word has been more frequently upon the lips of the American public in the last three years [1900–1903] than "publicity."

These pre–World War I demands for fuller financial disclosure, both by the critics of big business and the public, were generally ignored by management. Few companies, for instance, followed United States Steel Corporation's declared policy of presenting full and definite financial information, which first found expression in the 35 pages of financial data contained in the company's annual report of 1902. In contrast, most managements did not seem to care about public opinion. They disregarded it. In fact, some companies which had previously published financial statements quit issuing financial reports altogether. For instance, in 1901, George Westinghouse, president of Westinghouse Electric and Manufacturing, said:

. . . if some should be surprised that more complete statements have not been previously submitted to them, it can only be said that the Directors as well as the stockholders who own the largest amounts of stock, have believed that in view of the existing keen competition and the general attitude toward industrial enterprises, the interests of all would be served by avoiding, to as great an extent as possible, giving undue publicity to the affairs of the Company.

While the pioneer critics of big business had little direct impact on management, they greatly influenced, nevertheless, those who later played important roles in increasing the federal government's control over business affairs. For instance, before World War I, among early advocates of greater publicity of corporate affairs, few became more widely read and respected than the future associate justice of the Supreme Court, Louis D. Brandeis. In 1913, Brandeis said: "Publicity is justly commended as a remedy for social and industrial diseases. Sunlight is said to be the best of disinfectants; electric light the most efficient policemen." Later in 1933, it was Mr. Frankfurter—surrogate for Justice Brandeis—in his visits with President Roosevelt who argued for this approach to business regulation.

Following World War I, and until the economic and stock market disasters of 1929, there was a shift in the American political, social, economic, and ethical climate. The nation became more prosperous and the public grew weary and disillusioned with the crusades of the preceding progressive era. Businessmen were regarded with a new respect. The public, instead of disapproving, now looked upon the large-scale efforts to rig the securities market by such market operators as Harry F. Sinclair, Percy A. Rockefeller, and Bernard E. Smith with breathless admiration.

Consequently, during the period 1918–29, the public appeal of the critics of business waned but did not disappear. In 1926, for instance, Professor William Z. Ripley of Harvard University created "quite a flutter in financial centers" when he proclaimed: "let the word go forth that the Federal Trade Commission is henceforth to address itself vigorously to the matter of adequate and intelligent corporate publicity, and taken in conjunction with the helpful agencies at work the thing is as good as done." Ripley was particularly disturbed by the "enigmatic" accounting practices which made possible financial "obfuscation" and "malfeasance." Another who spoke in the same vein was the young Adolph Berle, Jr., who, as part of his notion of "social corporation," demanded as an expression of the public responsibility of management fuller disclosure of corporate affairs, particularly to investors.

As with that of their predecessors, the immediate impact of such critics as Ripley was almost nil; but after 1930, when the nation lay in economic disorder, businessmen were more easily discredited. The public once again became sympathetic to the opinions of those critical of business and finance, and it was the critics' standards—not those of management—by which managers were finally judged.

Between 1900 and 1933, others more closely allied with management sought to raise the level of financial reporting, including the New York Stock Exchange, the Investment Bankers Association of America, and the public accounting profession. Of these private groups, the New York Stock Exchange was perhaps the leading influence in the promotion of adequate corporate disclosure the world over. The exchange's direct influence, however, was limited to companies listed on the exchange. The influence of the Investment Bankers Association and the public accounting profession was severely curtailed by the unwillingness of much of their membership to act independently of management.

The New York Stock Exchange

As early as 1869, the New York Stock Exchange's Committee on Stock List adopted a policy that companies should agree that once listed on the exchange they would publish some form of an annual financial report. Few companies, however, agreed to observe this stipulation. In fact, it

was not until the Kansas City (Missouri) Gas Company listing agreement of 1897 that the exchange extracted from a listed company a substantive promise to observe some minimum reporting requirements. Nevertheless, from 1910 onward, the exchange influenced improvements in financial reporting practices of listed companies.

Before 1900, so reluctant was the exchange to enforce its reporting requirements upon industrial management that in 1885 it created the so-called Unlisted Department. This department sought to grasp business then going to outside street markets where fewer restrictions were placed upon issuers. The companies whose stocks were noted by the Unlisted Department (mainly industrials) were not required to furnish the exchange with financial information relevant to the issue. Nevertheless, these shares were traded with regularly listed securities, unlisted stocks being distinguished on quotation sheets only by an asterisk. In this manner, such active stocks as those of Amalgamated Copper and the American Sugar Refining Companies were dealt in on the exchange for many years without the public having any information regarding their affairs. They were in effect conducted and maintained as "blind pools." Those in control were then enabled to use their information for speculative purposes.

In 1910, under growing threats of government regulation, the New York Stock Exchange abolished its Unlisted Department. Thereafter, over the next 20 years, the exchange's Committee on Stock List actively sought to improve the reporting practices of listed companies, particularly with respect to the frequency with which they published financial statements. For example, in 1916, General Motors Company agreed to publish semi-annually a consolidated income statement and balance sheet. In 1924, Inland Steel Company modified its original listing agreement and agreed to issue a public statement of quarterly earnings.

In 1926, the NYSE officially recommended the publication of quarterly reports by all listed companies. Also, by this time, nearly all listed manufacturing companies had adopted the practice of issuing annual reports covered by an independent auditor's opinion certificate, a practice made mandatory by the exchange in 1933. Such progress was not easy, however, since as late as 1931 many an executive of a listed company held the exchange's suggested publicity requirements to be arbitrary and unreasonable.

The exchange's control, of course, was restricted only to those corporations which sought to list securities. The securities handled on the over-the-counter markets and the securities listed on the regional exchanges—Chicago, Boston, Pittsburgh—were not only beyond the New York Stock Exchange's control, but were also subject to less rigorous requirements so as to attract local lesser corporations, more closely controlled and less susceptible to educational appeal. Yet, these were the very corporations where the most need for improved financial reporting existed.

The Investment Bankers Association of America

Between 1920 and 1927, the Investment Bankers Association of America on several occasions sought, through voluntary action of its membership, to standardize the information regarding industrial securities presented to the public, particularly that in prospectuses. The initial impetus for these reform efforts grew out of a desire on the part of some association members to protect investors, to protect legitimate investment bankers from the growing public resentment against the sellers of fraudulent securities, and to forestall federal and state governmental regulation of securities. Already, by 1920, some 20 states, alarmed by the prevalence of fraudulent stock promotions, had passed so-called blue-sky laws, and on the federal level, security bills had been placed before Congress in 1918, 1919, and 1921, respectively.

On at least six occasions between 1920 and 1928 the Investment Bankers Association issued reports setting forth recommended minimum standards for financial disclosure in prospectuses. In general, these reports, three of which were related to industrial companies, called for an "adequate" and "understandable" balance sheet with some comments on such items as inventory, working capital and depreciation policy, as well as a presentation of earnings by years. In the case of holding companies, it was suggested that investors be provided with a consolidated balance sheet, a consolidated statement of earnings, and an income statement for the holding company.

Few of these recommendations were ever followed in practice by investment bankers or their corporate clients. The reasons for the failure of the association's voluntary reform program were many. A number of members of the association were indifferent with respect to these recommendations. Also, among those companies that issued securities, some of the bigger and better known companies objected to allowing financial information to go beyond the eyes of their investment bankers.

In addition, a number of investment bankers still preferred to follow the 19th-century practice of selling securities on the basis of the investment banker's reputation alone, rather than on the merits of the issue and issuer. As late as 1923, "confidence," one investment banker said, "was the bulwark in the relationship between the dealer and the client." Earlier, in 1918, another investment banker had stated, "The questions of brick and mortar and turnover and rate of profit and all the other fine points are secondary considerations." Other investment bankers relied upon the 19th-century custom of nondisclosure to justify the hiding of weakness in the dubious securities they offered.

Clearly, such attitudes as these were hardly likely to lead to universal voluntary acceptance among investment bankers of the association's sug-

gestions regarding financial disclosure. Some investment bankers, it would seem, were just as desirous as their corporate clients of fostering financial secrecy.

The Accounting Profession

During the years 1900 to 1933, with the growing dependence of business on outside sources of capital, with the introduction of the income tax law in 1913, and with the passage of the excess profits tax in 1917, the accounting profession became an essential part of American business life. Credit granters came to depend upon financial statements as the basis for credit decisions, and complete and accurate accounting records became necessary for income tax purposes.

As a result, the public accounting profession expanded and accounting instruction was increasingly included in college curricula. In 1917 and 1930, the profession, through its principal society—the American Institute of Accountants (later renamed the American Institute of Certified Public Accountants)—undertook two important programs to improve corporate disclosure practices. The first was in conjunction with the Federal Trade Commission and the Federal Reserve Board; the second with the New York Stock Exchange.

Throughout most of this 33-year period the primary force among accountants for improved corporate financial disclosure came from three sources: educators, individual practitioners, and the American Institute of Accountants. Around 1900, because of a growing recognition of the importance of business in American life, universities added to their curricula business courses which included accounting as a primary subject. University professors began to probe behind accounting practice and explore its logic, and the first university department of accounting, as such, was established by New York University in 1900. For the first time in the United States, accounting education was rising above the level of bookkeeping, and an ideology for accounting technology was slowly developed.

Among businessmen, perhaps a more influential group were the leading practitioners of the accounting profession. Such men as George O. May and A. Lowes Dickinson of Price Waterhouse & Company, and Robert H. Montgomery of Lybrand, Ross Brothers & Montgomery, through their day-to-day contacts—literary and personal—with other accountants and businessmen, sought to raise the level of industrial financial disclosure and hasten the adoption of sounder accounting practices. In general, these men, whose early training had been in England, believed that the disclosure standards included in the English Companies Acts should be adopted by American businessmen. Later, the framers of the securities acts exhibited a similar belief when they based the disclosure philosophy underlying the Securities Act of 1933 on the existing English Company Law.

The genesis of the modern American Institute of Certified Public Accountants (American Institute of Accountants) and its work to raise the standards of the American accounting profession can be traced back to similar earlier attempts in Great Britain before 1880. In Great Britain, a vital and influential accounting profession had existed since about 1850. Beginning in the 1880s, a number of these British chartered accountants came to the United States, principally to audit the various British investments there. To these transplanted Britishers the first steps necessary to improve the stature of accounting in the United States appeared to be the establishment of a nationwide society of accountants, along the lines of the Institute of Chartered Accountants in England and Wales.

The first organized body of professional accountants in the United States was formed in New York in 1886. Soon after, other state and national accounting bodies were founded. In 1905, the contending national organizations were united to form one principal organization: the American Association of Public Accountants. In 1916, the association was reorganized as the American Institute of Accountants.

The first attempt of the Institute to set some auditing and reporting standards came in 1917 when it joined with the Federal Trade Commission and the Federal Reserve Board in publishing *Uniform Accounting*, the most comprehensive and authoritative document related to corporate financial disclosure and balance sheet audits yet published in the United States. Over the years, the Federal Trade Commission, in the course of its investigation of business conditions, had become disturbed over the lack of uniformity in balance sheet audits and financial reports. As the very first step toward standardization of practices relating to the compiling and verifying of corporate reports, the Commission requested the Institute to prepare a memorandum on balance sheet audits.

The Institute's memorandum was eventually prepared by a committee under George O. May's direction, approved by the Federal Trade Commission, and given tentative endorsement by the Federal Reserve Board. This tentative document was then submitted to bankers throughout the country for their consideration and criticism. Later in 1917, the final draft of *Uniform Accounting* was published by the Federal Reserve Board. In 1918, it was reissued under the name, *Approved Methods for the Preparation of Balance Sheet Statements*. Subsequently, in 1929, it was revised by the Institute for the Federal Reserve Board, republished, and renamed *Verification of Financial Statements*.

Uniform Accounting and its later versions were widely distributed. The bulk of this document related to balance sheet audits. Its last three pages, however, presented suggested forms for comparative income statements and balance sheets. The model income statement provided for some 29 revenue and expense items. The asset side of the proposed balance sheet called for details under the following headings: cash, notes and accounts

receivable (less provision for bad debts), inventories, other quick assets, securities, fixed assets (less reserves for depreciation), deferred charges, and other assets. The liability side of the balance sheet indicated detailed information should be presented under these headings: unsecured bills and notes, unsecured accounts, secured liabilities, other current liabilities, fixed liabilities, and net worth.

Despite their prestigious backers, the recommendations outlined in *Uniform Accounting* were not quickly adopted by corporations, bankers, or the accounting profession—chiefly because bankers, out of fear of driving away customers, refrained from insisting upon audited statements from their clients. Nevertheless some progress was made.

Except for the recommendations pertaining to inventories and disclosure of asset values, few of the improvements ever found their way into public reports. Businessmen in general believed that the standard form of financial statements outlined in the Federal Reserve Board's publication called for too much information and would be used to their detriment by competitors.

Encouraged by the publication of *Uniform Accounting*, the Institute directed its main educational efforts for the next nine years toward encouraging businessmen to use balance sheet audits for credit purposes. By 1926, George O. May declared to the accounting profession that, among prominent industrial companies, the practice of having audits "had become almost universal." Now, he said, the time had come for the Institute to assume a larger responsibility and "render a higher service to the community." The new goal he proposed for the profession was the adoption by industrial corporations of the financial disclosure standards embodied in the English Companies Act. To achieve this end, he suggested that the Institute cooperate with "such bodies as the leading stock exchange, the investment bankers and the commercial banks which grant credit." It was impractical, May believed, to consider bringing about improved corporate disclosure in the United States through direct legislation, as had happened in England.

During the next four years, the Institute undertook two cooperative efforts along the lines suggested by May. The first undertaking with the Investment Bankers Association of America in 1928 produced little. The second was much more fruitful. In 1930, with the long-standing urging of J. M. B. Hoxsey, the executive assistant on stock list of the New York Stock Exchange, and May, reinforced by the effects of the market crash of 1929, the Institute appointed a committee to cooperate with the exchange "in consideration of all problems which are of common interest to investors, exchanges, and accountants."

Hoxsey's concern was principally for the protection of investors, of whom there were some 10 million in 1930. "Accounting," Hoxsey told the Institute, "is a matter of convention but it is questionable whether these

conventions have kept pace with the changes in modern business conditions."

At Hoxsey's suggestion, the American Institute appointed a Special Committee on Cooperation with Stock Exchanges, with George O. May as chairman, to work with the New York Stock Exchange to explore the issues raised by Hoxsey. This undertaking was a significant development as it represented a change in outlook by the accounting profession. *Uniform Accounting* had been prepared with an institution concerned with the quality of credit and the recommendations contained therein made with the credit granter in mind; the new undertaking was with the New York Stock Exchange and the accounting problems were to be considered from the standpoint of those who traded in securities—that is, investors.

On September 22, 1932, the Institute's special committee submitted its report to the exchange's Committee on Stock List. The report, which was published in 1933 under the title *Audits of Corporate Accounts*, listed four principal objectives the committee thought the exchange should "keep constantly in mind and do its best to gradually achieve." These goals were: to bring about a better recognition by the public that balance sheets did not show present values of the assets and liabilities of corporations, to encourage the adoption of balance sheets which more clearly showed on what basis assets were valued, to emphasize the cardinal importance of the income account, and to make universal the usage by listed corporations of certain broad principles of accounting which had won fairly general acceptance. On this last point the report warned the exchange against attempting "to restrict the right of corporations to select detailed methods of accounting deemed by them to be best adapted to the requirements of their business." In addition, the report suggested each listed corporation should submit to the exchange a clear and detailed statement of the accounting principles it observed when compiling financial statements.

This document, which was the most specific statement yet formulated on just how financial reports could be made more informative and reliable, was given warm approval by the Controllers Institute and the Investment Bankers Association. Taking a lead from the report's recommendations, on January 6, 1933, the exchange announced that henceforth corporations seeking listing must submit financial statements audited by independent public accountants and agree to have all future reports to stockholders similarly inspected. In addition, the scope of the audit was to be no less than that indicated in *Verification of Financial Statements*.

The accountants read Whitney's announcement with "a feeling of hearty gratification" according to Richardson, the editor of the *Journal of Accountancy*. Richardson had campaigned long and hard for such a listing requirement and hailed the announcement as probably the "most important forward step in the history of accounting within recent years."

Such joy was short-lived. Within six months the envisioned role of the

Committee on Stock List and that of the Institute's special committee in effect passed to a federal agency—first to the Federal Trade Commission and then to the Securities and Exchange Commission. In 1934, many accountants, including George O. May, believed that the profession might in the future "all too easily, find itself merely the ciphering agency for vitally unreviewable bureaucrats." To date, such has not been the case.

Management and Financial Disclosure

Between 1900 and 1933, the financial disclosure practices of industrial corporations improved somewhat. Nevertheless, despite such exceptions as United States Steel Corporation, Bethlehem Steel Corporation, and General Motors Company, the financial reporting practices lagged far behind the recommendations for greater and more useful corporate financial disclosure made by the New York Stock Exchange. Also, the numerous alternative accounting principles which had caused so much confusion during the late 19th century were still observed in practice.

As time passed, however, the statements of industrial corporations became more uniform as to the degree and form of disclosure. By 1933, most publicly owned manufacturing corporations were publishing annual reports containing fairly detailed balance sheets. Furthermore, in line with the shift of emphasis in common stock evaluation techniques from the balance sheet to the income statement, a sketchy income statement showing sales, several major expense items, and current profits was now usually included. Auditing by outside accountants was also becoming more common.

Yet some of the larger companies still refused to provide stockholders with written financial statements. For instance, the Singer Sewing Machine Company did not issue annual reports, information regarding the company's affairs being given orally at the annual stockholders' meetings. As late as 1927 the Royal Baking Powder Company had issued no financial statement whatsoever. In addition to the nonreporting companies, a number of large companies rendered their reports to the public well after the close of their fiscal year.

There were two basic reasons for management's slow progress in improving corporate financial reporting. First, managers did not consider public reports a matter of prime importance. Second, and more important, businessmen were still inclined toward financial secrecy, principally because of their fear of assisting competitors.

Financial chicanery and business custom were also responsible for corporate secrecy. Unfortunately, there were still a few industrial directors and officers who practiced financial secrecy so as to profit in their stock market activities through the use of corporate information not available to others. While the motivation of management in such cases was clearly to deceive or mislead, in most instances of nondisclosure, it should be

noted, corporate financial secrecy resulted primarily because it was simply a custom that had been handed down from generation to generation to tell as little as possible.

In addition, there were still few external restraints upon management's financial reporting practices. State corporation laws relating to corporate financial reports had not advanced much beyond the 19th-century stage. Federal law was still silent on industrial financial publicity, as it was assumed this was a state matter. Also, after 1914, public opinion was indifferent to the attempts to improve the financial reports of industrial companies. In particular, investors, the very group the reformers sought to protect, were usually satisfied with generalities and did not request detailed financial statistics.

Similarly, accounting practice placed few restrictions on industrial management. There was an inviting variety of alternatives approved by accountants and employed by businessmen. For example, there still were many different theories of depreciation. No consensus yet existed as to the degree of ownership which warranted consolidation. Frequently, no distinction was made between operating income and other income. And a variety of methods pertaining to the recording of asset values persisted. Such accounting freedom unfortunately tempted a number of managements to inflate reported profits through questionable adjustments to surplus and profits. These adjustments were seldom revealed to the public.

Finally, the reformers were powerless to force their proposed financial reporting standards upon industrial management. Businessmen, in the absence of regulatory restraints, held the balance of power vis-à-vis the would-be reformers. The efforts of the Investment Bankers Association were thwarted by its own membership and the accounting profession was not yet willing to be truly independent. Even the New York Stock Exchange was unable to enforce its authority upon the recalcitrant listed companies.

Thus, as late as the 1920s, industrial management could ignore with impunity the demands for improved financial disclosure. The economic depression of 1930, the subsequent shift in the public's attitude toward business, the election of Franklin D. Roosevelt as President in 1932, and the passage of the Securities Acts of 1933 and 1934 brought this situation to an end. Henceforth, for most publicly owned industrial companies, the Securities and Exchange Commission became the final arbiter in matters of financial disclosure, not management.

THE SECURITIES ACT AND ITS AFTERMATH

On May 29, 1933, President Roosevelt requested Congress to enact a federal securities bill which would add "to the ancient rule of *caveat emptor*, the further doctrine, 'let the seller also beware.' " The President's

bill proposed to put the burden of telling the whole truth on those connected with the sale of securities—corporate officers, investment bankers, and accountants. Congress responded to the President's request and on May 27, 1933, Roosevelt signed into law the Securities Act—"an act to provide full and fair disclosure of the character of the securities sold in interstate and foreign commerce. . . ."

The Securities Act was originally administered by the Federal Trade Commission, but in 1934, the act was amended to provide for the creation of a special body—the Securities and Exchange Commission—to assume its administration. Specifically, the Securities and Exchange Commission's task was to regulate the degree of disclosure, financial and non-financial, associated with new public security offerings as well as to require reports from those companies whose securities were already traded on the public security markets. Furthermore, the Commission was given broad statutory authority to state accounting rules for registered companies and to enforce them.

In line with its power to prescribe accounting practices, the SEC quickly standardized the format of required financial statements it received. More important, the Commission issued, from time to time, a number of opinions on accounting principles to encourage the development of uniform standards and practices in major accounting questions.

These opinions, however, cover but a small number of accounting practices. In those cases where no opinion has been expressed by the Commission, its policy is to accept a registrant's accounting practice "if the points involved are such that there is a substantial authoritative support," which in most instances has meant acceptance by the accounting profession. So far, these opinions of the SEC, it should be noted, apply only to those publicly available, prescribed statements which registrants are required to file with the Commission. The management representations contained in periodic reports to stockholders have not yet been placed under the direct control of the Commission. However, the Commission will not permit registered companies to disclose information in their reports to stockholders which is different from that filed with the SEC.

Next, beginning in 1939 and continuing through 1958, the Committee on Accounting Procedure of the American Institute issued a series of 51 *Accounting Research Bulletins*, touching upon a number of accounting problems and procedures. The principal objective of the bulletins was "to narrow areas of difference and inconsistency in accounting practices, and to further the development and recognition of generally accepted accounting principles." Each bulletin's opinions and recommendations "would serve as criteria for determining the suitability of accounting practices reflected in financial statements and representations of commercial and industrial companies." The authority of the opinions set forth in these

bulletins rested "upon their general acceptability" among accountants and businessmen. In practice, however, the bulletins' authority has been greatly strengthened by the reliance placed upon them by the New York Stock Exchange and the Securities and Exchange Commission in determining the acceptability of any questionable accounting practice.

Today, the reports filed by corporations with the Securities and Exchange Commission and the national stock exchanges are perhaps the most comprehensive, reliable, and detailed financial statements available publicly anywhere in the world. The financial statements published in periodic reports to stockholders, while less detailed, are nevertheless a great improvement over pre-1933 reports.

In recent years, a number of prominent, influential, and responsible public accountants, security analysts, social critics, and accounting educators have become increasingly disturbed by what they perceive to be inadequacies in management's financial disclosure practices. The motives of these modern-day critics are similar to those of the earlier critics of management already discussed. Some want to protect investors from fraud and blind speculation. Others desire to make management more accountable to stockholders for its actions. A few wish to contain, or even destroy, big business. Several hope to increase the independence of the accounting profession.

In 1959, faced with the growing discontent over current financial reporting practices and the increasing demand for more uniformity in accounting principles, the American Institute of Certified Public Accountants [2] dissolved its Committee on Accounting Procedure, the group that had issued the *Accounting Research Bulletins*, and created the Accounting Principles Board. This substitution was intended to intensify efforts toward defining accounting "principles." The Board was provided with both an administrative director and the services of a research staff (the Accounting Research Division).

Eleven research studies have been prepared for publication under the sponsorship of the Accounting Principles Board. All but one of the studies were prepared by a leading scholar or practitioner. Two of the studies represent attempts to provide a theoretical basis for accounting: *The Basic Postulates of Accounting*, by Maurice Moonitz (study #1); and *A Tentative Set of Broad Accounting Principles for Business Enterprises*, by Robert T. Sprouse and Maurice Moonitz (#3). Paul Grady's *Inventory of Generally Accepted Accounting Principles* (#7) approaches the definition of principles through codification of current practice. Research has also concentrated on specific areas of concern, such as *Reporting of Leases in Financial Statements* (#4), by John H. Myers; *Accounting*

---

[2] The American Institute of Accountants was renamed the American Institute of Certified Public Accountants in 1957.

for the Cost of Pension Plans (#8), by Ernest L. Hicks; *Interperiod Allocation of Corporate Income Taxes (#9)*, by Homer A. Black; and *Financial Reporting in the Extractive Industries (#11)*, by Robert M. Field. Concern with the problems of corporate mergers and combinations is reflected in two studies, *A Critical Study of Accounting for Business Combinations (#5)*, by Arthur R. Wyett; and *Accounting for Goodwill (#10)*, by George R. Catlett and Norman O. Olson. Finally, two aspects of financial statement presentation were studied in *Cash-Flow Analysis and the Funds Statement (#2)*, by Perry Mason; and *Reporting the Financial Effects of Price Level Changes (#6)*, by the staff of the Accounting Research Division.

Each of the research projects was developed in response to contemporary accounting problems and areas of disagreement. None of the studies were "accepted" by the Accounting Principles Board; rather, these studies were published to provide impetus toward general discussion by both accountants and managers. Although a subcommittee acted as liaison between researchers and the full Board, many of the studies which were published included strong dissents by individual Board members.

There has not always been a direct relationship between Board-sponsored research and the *Opinions* of the Accounting Principles Board. Seventeen *Opinions* had been issued by late 1970:

1. New Depreciation Guidelines and Rules.
2. Accounting for the "Investment Credit."
3. The Statement of Source and Application of Funds.
4. Accounting for the "Investment Credit." (Amending No. 2)
5. Reporting of Leases in Financial Statements of Lessee.
6. Status of Accounting Research Bulletins.
7. Accounting for Leases in Financial Statements of Lessors.
8. Accounting for the Cost of Pension Plans.
9. Reporting the Results of Operations:
     I.   Net Income and the Treatment of Extraordinary Items and Prior Period Adjustments.
     II. Computation and Reporting of Earnings per Share.
10. Omnibus Opinion—1966.
     Consolidated Financial Statements.
     Poolings of Interest—Restatement of Financial Statements.
     Tax Allocation Accounts—Discounting.
     Offsetting Securities against Taxes Payable.
     Convertible Debt and Debt Issued with Stock Warrants.
     Liquidation Preference of Preferred Stock.
     Installment Method of Accounting.
11. Accounting for Income Taxes.

12. Omnibus Opinion—1967.
    Classification and Disclosure of Allowances.
    Disclosure of Depreciable Assets and Depreciation.
    Deferred Compensation Contracts.
    Capital Changes.
    Convertible Debt and Debt Issued with Stock Warrants.
    Amortization of Debt Discount and Expense or Premium.
13. Amending Paragraph 6 of APB Opinion No. 9, Application to Commercial Banks.
14. Accounting for Convertible Debt and Debt Issued with Stock Purchase Warrants.
15. Earnings per Share.
16. Business Combinations.
17. Intangible Assets.

The diversity of these opinions and of the Accounting Research Studies indicates the breadth of the accounting problems which the accounting profession must face. Controversy continues as to the treatment of leases and many other areas, despite the Accounting Principles Board's continued efforts.

Some predict that if the APB cannot succeed in its task, it is quite possible that the government will promulgate accounting principles, as has been done in several European countries.

SUMMARY: EVOLVING STANDARDS AND LAGGING PRACTICE

The financial disclosure practices of modern American industrial management have nearly all developed since 1933. Yet modern standards have sprung from an earlier reaction to the secrecy which surrounded the financial affairs of most 19th-century manufacturing firms. This reaction, which began around 1900, is the historical base upon which recent developments rest. Improvements in reporting practices came principally as the result of continuing pressure from individuals outside the managerial group for improved corporate publicity. This nonmanagement group included such diverse characters as the so-called critics of big business and leaders of the public accounting profession, and set the evolving standards by which the public evaluated corporate financial disclosures. The tempo of these critics' activities varied directly with the public attitude toward business, increasing markedly during those periods when management had fallen from popular favor.

Persistently, management's financial reporting practices lagged far behind the externally set standards, since management favored corporate secrecy and the would-be reformers were powerless to force their recommendations upon managers. Eventually, because management generally

had not voluntarily adjusted its financial reporting practices to society's evolving financial informational needs (as perceived by management's critics), amid the business disorder following the 1929 stock market collapse the federal government intervened in the field of corporate financial disclosure, in 1933.

Thereafter, some authoritative, but nevertheless permissive, accounting standards were developed by the Securities and Exchange Commission and the Committee on Accounting Procedure of the American Institute of Certified Public Accountants. To comply with these new standards industrial management rapidly improved its financial reporting practices in a number of areas. Yet, in the meantime, the demand for fuller, more reliable, and more comparable financial data again outstripped management practice and the expressed standards of the accounting profession.

Once more, the possibility of further government intervention in industrial reporting matters is imminent, principally because of the difficulty the accounting profession has had in its efforts to narrow the areas of difference in accounting principles and the resistance of some managements to the critics' demands for improved corporate financial disclosure. Whether or not it will be necessary to expand government authority in the area of industrial accounting practice will probably depend upon the acceptance by both management and its critics of the authority and contents of the pronouncements of the Accounting Principles Board, as well as the Board's willingness and ability to resolve quickly the issues confronting it. In any case, the historical evaluation of acceptable standards of financial disclosure among American industrial firms is far from complete.

SUGGESTED FURTHER READINGS

CHATFIELD, MICHAEL. *Contemporary Studies in the Evolution of Accounting Thought.* Belmont, Calif.: Dickenson Publishing Co., 1968.

LITTLETON, A. C., and YAMEY, B. S. (eds.). *Studies in the History of Accounting.* London: Sweet & Maxwell; and Homewood, Ill.: Richard D. Irwin, 1956.

LITTLETON, A. C., and ZIMMERMAN, V. K. *Accounting Theory: Continuity and Change.* Englewood Cliffs, N.J.: Prentice-Hall, 1962.

CHAPTER 3

USES OF FINANCIAL DATA

The analysis of financial statements provides an important basis for valuing securities and appraising managerial performance. Consequently, one measure of the usefulness of financial statements is how well they help investors to appraise the financial condition of the issuing company and the effectiveness of its management in earning a return on its invested capital. This chapter introduces some of the basic concepts of financial ratio analysis and common stock valuation. The valuation of debt securities is discussed in Chapter 21. A knowledge of these techniques is essential to appreciate fully the communications aspect of financial reports. It is not sufficient just to be familiar with generally accepted accounting principles.

FINANCIAL ANALYSIS

Financial analysis is a tool for interpreting financial statements. It can provide insight into two important areas of management: the return on investment earned and the soundness of the company's financial position. This technique compares certain related items in the statements to each other in a meaningful manner. The analyst evaluates these results against the particular characteristics of the company and its industry. The astute analyst seldom expects answers from this process. Rather, he hopes it will provide him with clues as to where he should focus his subsequent analysis.

Financial ratios fall into four classes: ratios appraising liquidity, ratios measuring solvency, ratios evaluating funds management, and ratios measuring profitability. The categories indicate that different ratios may be more helpful than others for particular purposes. Therefore, rather than calculating ratios indiscriminately, the experienced analyst precedes his ratio computation with some consideration of the kinds of insights he be-

lieves will be helpful in understanding the problem he faces. He then calculates those ratios that best serve his purpose. To get the most meaningful results, the analysis compares these ratios over a period of several years against some standard; examines in depth major variations from this standard; and cross-checks the various ratios against each other.

The 1968 balance sheet and income statement of the Ampex Corporation, a retailing business, will be used to illustrate some of the more common ratios (see Illustrations 3–1 and 3–2).

Liquidity Ratios

Liquidity ratios appraise a company's ability to meet its current obligations. These ratios compare current liabilities, which are the obligations

ILLUSTRATION 3–1

AMPEX CORPORATION

Comparative Balance Sheets, December 31, 1967 and 1968
(in thousands of dollars)

ASSETS	1967	1968
Current Assets:		
Cash	$ 30	$ 20
Accounts receivable (net)	95	95
Inventory	110	130
Total Current Assets	$235	$245
Fixed Assets:		
Land	$ 10	$ 10
Building and equipment (net)	100	120
Total Fixed Assets	$110	$130
Other Assets:		
Goodwill and organization costs	$ 10	$ 10
Total Assets	$355	$385

LIABILITIES AND STOCKHOLDERS' EQUITY		
Current Liabilities:		
Accounts payable	$ 40	$ 50
Estimated income taxes payable	10	10
Total Current Liabilities	$ 50	$ 60
Fixed Liabilities:		
Mortgage bonds, 4 percent	$ 50	$ 50
Total Liabilities	$100	$110
Stockholders' Equity:		
Preferred stock, 5 percent	$ 20	$ 20
Common stock (10,000 shares outstanding)	50	50
Retained earnings	185	205
Total Stockholders' Equity	$255	$275
Total Liabilities and Stockholders' Equity	$355	$385

ILLUSTRATION 3–2

AMPEX CORPORATION

Condensed Income Statement, 1968
(in thousands of dollars)

Gross sales	$1,516	100.66%
Less: Returns and allowances	10	0.66
Net sales	$1,506	100.00%
Less: Cost of goods sold	1,004	66.67
Gross profit	$ 502	33.33%
Operating expenses *	400	26.56
Operating profit	$ 102	6.77%
Interest	2	0.13
Profit before taxes	$ 100	6.64%
Income tax expense	50	3.32
Net income	$ 50	3.32%
Less: Preferred dividends	1	0.07
Common dividends	29	1.93
Change in Retained Earnings	$ 20	1.32%

* Includes lease rental costs of $30,000 and depreciation of $10,000.

falling due in the next 12 months, and current assets, which typically provide the funds to extinguish these obligations. The difference between current assets and current liabilities is called "net working capital."

Current Ratio

$$\frac{\text{Current assets}}{\text{Current liabilities}} = \frac{\$245,000}{\$ 60,000} = 4.1 \text{ times, or 4.1 to 1}$$

The meaningfulness of the current ratio as a measure of liquidity varies from company to company. Typically, it is assumed that the higher the ratio, the more protection the company has against liquidity problems. However, the ratio may be distorted by seasonal influences, slow-moving inventories built up out of proportion to market opportunities, or abnormal payment of accounts payable just prior to the balance sheet date. Also, the nature of some businesses is such that they have a steady, predictable cash inflow and outflow, and a low current ratio is appropriate for such a business.

Acid-Test or Quick Ratio

$$\frac{\text{Quick assets}}{\text{Current liabilities}} = \frac{\$115,000}{\$ 60,000} = 1.9 \text{ times, or 1.9 to 1}$$

The acid-test or quick ratio measures the ability of a company to use its current assets to immediately extinguish its current liabilities. Quick assets include those working capital items that presumably can be quickly

converted to cash at close to their book value. Such items are cash, stock investments, and accounts receivable. Like the working capital ratio, this ratio implicitly implies a liquidation approach and does not recognize the revolving nature of current assets and liabilities.

Solvency Ratios

Solvency ratios describe a company's ability to meet long-term debt payment schedules. There are a number of ratios which compare stockholders' equity to funds provided by creditors. All of these ratios are designed to give some measure of the extent to which ownership funds provide protection to creditors should a company incur losses.

Times Interest Earned

$$\frac{\text{Operating profit}}{\text{Long-term debt interest}} = \frac{\$102,000}{\$\ \ 2,000} = 51 \text{ times}$$

This coverage ratio is calculated on a pretax basis, since bond interest is a tax deductible expense. The ratio in the example implies that operating profits cover interest payments 51 times. This indicates the extent to which income can decline without impairing the company's ability to pay the interest on its long-term debt.

Some analysts prefer to use operating profit plus noncash charges as the numerator of this ratio. This modification indicates the ability to the company to cover its cash outflow for interest from its cash inflow from operations. For example, the only so-called noncash charge in the Ampex income statement is depreciation; i.e., no cash outflow results from incurring this expense. Adding the company's $10,000 depreciation expense to operating profit changes the numerator to $112,000 and increases the coverage to 56 times.

Coverage ratios can be computed for preferred stock dividends and other fixed charges, such as lease rentals. The preferred-stock-dividend-coverage ratio is calculated on an aftertax basis, since preferred stock dividends are not considered a tax deductible expense. For example, the Ampex *preferred-stock-dividend-coverage* ratio is:

$$\frac{\text{Profits after taxes}}{\text{Preferred stock dividends}} = \frac{\$50,000}{\$\ 1,000} = 50 \text{ times}$$

A coverage ratio for all of a company's fixed charges is called the times-fixed-charges-earned ratio. The denominator of this ratio includes such items as lease rentals, interest, and preferred dividends converted to a pretax basis. The numerator is operating profit before these charges. The *times-fixed-charges-earned* ratio for Ampex is:

$$\frac{\text{Operating profit before fixed charges}}{\text{Lease rentals, interest, preferred dividends}} = \frac{\$136,000}{\$\ 34,000} = 4.0 \text{ times}$$

Debt-to-Equity Ratios.   The relationship of borrowed funds to owner-ship funds is an important solvency ratio. Capital from debt and other creditor sources is more risky for a company than equity capital. Debt capital requires fixed interest payments on specific dates and eventual repayment. If payments to a company's creditors become overdue, the creditors can take legal action which may lead to the company being de-clared bankrupt. Ownership capital is less risky. Dividends are paid at the discretion of the directors, and there is no provision for repayment of capital to stockholders. It is generally assumed that the more ownership capital relative to debt a company has in its capital structure, the more likely it is that the company will be able to meet its fixed obligations. An excessive amount of ownership capital relative to debt capital may not necessarily indicate sound management practices, however. Equity capital is typically more costly than debt capital. Also, the company may be forgoing opportunities "to trade on its equity," that is, borrow debt at relatively low interest rates and hope to earn greater rates of returns on these funds. The difference between these two rates on a large invest-ment base can increase earnings per share without having to increase the number of common shares outstanding.

There are a number of debt-to-equity ratios. Three of the most com-mon are:

$$\frac{\text{Total debt}}{\text{Total assets}} = \frac{\$110,000}{\$385,000} = 28.6\%, \text{ or } 0.286 \text{ to } 1$$

This ratio indicates the proportion of a company's total assets financed by short-term and long-term credit sources.

$$\frac{\text{Long-term debt}}{\text{Capitalization}} = \frac{\$50,000}{\$275,000} = 18.2\%, \text{ or } 0.182 \text{ to } 1$$

This measure, which excludes current liabilities, reflects management's policy on the mix of long-term funds obtained from ownership and non-ownership sources.

$$\frac{\text{Total debt}}{\text{Stockholders' equity}} = \frac{\$110,000}{\$275,000} = 40\%, \text{ or } 0.4 \text{ to } 1$$

This ratio is another way of measuring the relative mix of funds provided by owners and creditors. Ampex appears to have an adequate cushion of ownership funds against losses from operations, decreases in the book value of assets, and poor estimates of future cash flows.

Funds Management Ratios

The financial situation of a company turns in large measure on how its investment in accounts receivable, inventories, and fixed assets is man-

aged. As a business expands its sales, it is not uncommon to find that the associated expansion of these three items is so great that despite profitable operations the company is short of cash. In such situations the management of trade credit becomes critical. It is a source of capital which should expand along with the increased sales.

Receivables to Sales

$$\frac{\text{Receivables (net)}}{\text{Net sales}} = \frac{\$\ \ 95,000}{\$1,506,000} = 6.3\%$$

In the absence of an aging of accounts receivable (classification of receivables by days since billing) or other detailed credit information, the receivables-to-sales ratio, computed over a number of years, can give a crude indication of the trend in a company's credit policy. In those cases where a company sells for cash and credit, only net credit sales should be used in the denominator. Receivables include accounts receivables, trade receivables, and trade notes receivable. The rather low receivables-to-sales percentage for Ampex is indicative that this retailer's sales most probably include a high proportion of cash sales.

Average Collection Period

$$\left(\frac{\text{Receivables}}{\text{Sales}}\right) \times \text{days in the period} = \text{Collection period}$$

$$6.3\% \qquad \times \qquad 365 \qquad = 23 \text{ days}$$

A two-step method to get the same result is:

a)   Calculate the average daily sales:

$$\frac{\text{Sales}}{\text{Days}} = \frac{\$1,506,000}{365} = \$4,126 \text{ per day}$$

b)   Calculate the days' sales represented by receivables:

$$\frac{\text{Receivables}}{\text{Sales per day}} = \frac{\$95,000}{\$\ 4,126} = 23 \text{ days}$$

To appraise the quality of accounts receivable, the average collection period can be related to the typical credit terms of the company. A collection period substantially longer than this standard might indicate poor credit management, resulting in an increasing amount of funds being tied up in this asset. On the other hand, a significantly shorter collection period than is typical in the industry might mean profitable sales to slower paying customers were being missed. This may well be the case at Ampex, since 23 days seem very short for a retail business.

Average Accounts Payable Period.   Similar tests can be made of accounts payable to see how well they are managed. In this case the accounts

payable are compared to the purchases for the period (costs of goods sold plus inventory changes). The calculation of the average day's payables is made as follows:

a) Calculate the average daily purchases:

$$\frac{\text{Purchases}}{\text{Days}} = \frac{\$1,024,000}{365} = \$2,805 \text{ per day}$$

b) Calculate the day's purchases represented by payables:

$$\frac{\text{Accounts payable}}{\text{Purchase per day}} = \frac{\$50,000}{\$\ 2,805} = 18 \text{ days}$$

The day's-payables ratio becomes meaningful when compared to the credit terms given by the suppliers of the industry. If a company's average day's payables is growing larger, it may mean trade credit is being used increasingly as a source of funds. If the period is less than the average for the industry, it may indicate that management has not used this source of funds as much as is possible. If it is longer, it may mean the company is overdue on its payables and is using this source of funds beyond the normal trade limits.

Rarely is the purchase figure available to people outside of the company. Consequently, the analyst has to approximate this figure. One way is to take the cost-of-goods-sold figure, adjust it for inventory changes, and then try to estimate how much of the resulting figure represents outside purchases. In merchandising situations, like the Ampex illustration, this is less difficult. The merchandiser's cost of goods sold is the price he paid his suppliers for the goods sold. In manufacturing situations, this is not such an easy task. The cost-of-goods-sold expense includes direct labor, raw materials, and some manufacturing overheads. If the raw materials portion of the cost-of-goods-sold and inventories figures are available, they can be used to calculate an approximation of the raw materials purchases, which in most cases represents the minimum level of purchases.

Another difficulty is that the accounts payable figure may include payables incurred for other than items included in cost of goods sold. As a result of this problem and the other measurement problems, this ratio is usually not regarded as being a particularly reliable indication of the quality of the accounts payable.

Inventory Turnover

$$\frac{\text{Cost of sales}}{\text{Average inventory}} = \frac{\$1,004,000}{\$\ 120,000} = 8.4 \text{ times}$$

The inventory turnover ratio shows how fast the inventory items move through the business. It is an indication of how well the funds invested in inventory are being managed. The analyst is interested in two items: the absolute size of the inventory in relationship to the other fund needs of

the company, and the relationship of the inventory to the sales volume it supports. A decrease in the turnover rate indicates that the absolute size of the inventory relative to sales is increasing. This can be a warning signal, since funds may be tied up in this inventory beyond the level required by the sales volume, which may be rising or falling.

Average inventory is used in the denominator because the sales volume is generated over a 12-month period. The average inventory is obtained by adding the opening inventory and closing inventory balances and dividing the sum by two.

If the cost-of-goods-sold figure is not available, an approximation of the inventory turnover rate can be obtained by using the sales figure in the numerator. If profit margins have remained fairly steady, then this sales-to-average-inventory ratio can provide, over a period of years, an indication of inventory management trends.

By dividing the turnover rate into 365 days, the analyst can estimate the average length of time items spent in inventory:

$$\frac{365 \text{ days}}{\text{Inventory turnover}} = \frac{365}{8.4} = 43 \text{ days}$$

Fixed Asset Turnover.   A similar turnover ratio can also be calculated for fixed assets. It provides a crude measure of how well the investment in plant and equipment is being managed relative to the sales volume it supports. The usefulness of this measure is reduced considerably because book values seldom approximate market values or are comparable from company to company due to different depreciation policies.

$$\frac{\text{Net sales}}{\text{Average fixed assets}} = \frac{\$1,506,000}{\$ 120,000} = 12.6 \text{ times}$$

Profitability Ratios

The analysts look at profits in two ways: first, as a percentage of sales; second, as a return on the funds invested in the business.

Profit Margin.   Profit margins relative to sales can be evaluated in a number of different ways.

a) Net profit after taxes as a percentage of sales measures the total operating and financial quality of management, since net profit after taxes includes all of the costs of doing business:

$$\frac{\text{Net profit}}{\text{Sales}} = \frac{\$ 50,000}{\$1,506,000} = 3.32\%$$

b) Net profit before taxes and interest is indicative of management's operating ability. Interest is excluded because it relates to financing policy rather than operating efficiency:

$$\frac{\text{Earnings before interest and taxes}}{\text{Sales}} = \frac{\$ 102,000}{\$1,506,000} = 6.77\%$$

c) Gross margin (sales minus cost of sales) as a percentage of sales is an indication of the ability of the management to mark up its products over their costs:

$$\frac{\text{Gross margin}}{\text{Sales}} = \frac{\$ \ 502,000}{\$1,506,000} = 33.3\%$$

In addition to these ratios, it is often informative to express as a percentage of net sales all of those expense items relevant to the area being explored (see Illustration 3–2).

Return on Investment. The relationship between profitability and investment is considered the key ratio by many analysts. It provides a broad measure of management's operating and financial success. Several different return-on-investment ratios are commonly used.

a) *Return on Total Assets*

$$\frac{\text{Net profit before taxes and interest}}{\text{Average total assets}} = \frac{\$102,000}{\$370,000} = 27.6\%$$

This ratio gauges how well management has managed the total resources at its command, before consideration of taxes and credit costs. It focuses on the earning power of the assets and is not influenced by how they are financed. Average total assets is used as the denominator since profit is earned over a 12-month period.

b) *Return on Total Assets*

$$\frac{\text{Net profit after taxes and interest}}{\text{Average total assets}} = \frac{\$ \ 50,000}{\$370,000} = 13.5\%$$

This variation of (*a*) measures the return on total assets from the point of view of the profits accruing to the stockholders.

c) *Return on Total Capital*

$$\frac{\text{Net profit after taxes}}{\text{Average total capital}} = \frac{\$ \ 50,000}{\$315,000} = 15.9\%$$

Another ratio measuring return on investment equates investment with total long-term capital (equity capital plus long-term liabilities). This ratio indicates how well management has invested the permanent funds at its disposal. The ratio can be computed on a before- or aftertax basis. If interest is paid on short-term liabilities, then this amount is sometimes deducted from the net profit figure, since it relates to the financial management of those items.

d) *Return on Net Worth*

$$\frac{\text{Net profit after taxes}}{\text{Average stockholders' equity (net assets)}} = \frac{\$ \ 50,000}{\$265,000} = 18.9\%$$

This method measures the return on ownership capital after all taxes and interest payments. It is perhaps the most common return-on-investment figure published by financial services.

e) *Return on Tangible Net Worth*

$$\frac{\text{Net profit after taxes}}{(\text{Average net worth} - \text{average intangible assets})} = \frac{\$50,000}{(\$265,000 - 10,000)}$$
$$= 19.6\%$$

This modification of (d) measures the return on net worth less the intangible assets, such as goodwill and capitalized organization costs. The principal use of this ratio is to present a more conservative measure of the investment base than (d).

Investment Turnover. A ratio similar to the inventory and asset turnover ratios can also be calculated for investment:

$$\frac{\text{Sales}}{\text{Average total capital}} = \frac{\$1,506,000}{\$\ 315,000} = 4.78 \text{ times}$$

This ratio, when combined with the net-profit-to-sales ratio, produces the return-on-investment total capital rate:

Investment turnover × net profit ratio = Return on investment
4.78 times × 3.32%   = 15.9%

This formula indicates that a business return on investment can be improved by increasing the sales volume per dollar of investment; by generating more profit per dollar of sales; or some mix of these two factors. Thus, a store earning 2 percent on sales with an inventory turnover of 10 can be doing just as good a job as another company with a profit margin of 10 percent and an inventory turnover of 2 times. Both have the same return on investment, 20 percent.

A number of other ratios are closely related. The analyst often uses these relationships to learn more about a particular area of interest. For example, a greater appreciation of the relationship between asset turnover and profit rates can be obtained as follows:

$$\frac{\text{Net profit}}{\text{Sales}} = 3.32\%$$

$$\text{Asset turnover} = \frac{\text{Net sales}}{\text{Average total assets}} = 4.07 \text{ times}$$

$$\frac{\text{Net profit}}{\text{Net sales}} \times \frac{\text{net sales}}{\text{average total assets}} = \frac{\text{Net profit}}{\text{Average total assets}}$$
$$3.32\% \qquad \times \ 4.07 \text{ times} \qquad = \ 13.5\%$$

A similar set of ratios which have more meaning when examined together are the components of the current ratio. For example, an examination of the relationship between inventory turnover and the receivables and payables periods demonstrates how changes in these working capital items influence funds flow.

Common Stock Ratios. Buyers and sellers of common stocks use a number of ratios relating market values to earnings and dividends. The significance of these ratios is discussed in the "Security Valuation" section of this chapter.

Earnings per Share. The most straightforward computation of earnings per share is for companies with simple capital structures. In these situations the calculation is:

$$\frac{\text{Net profit after taxes}}{\text{Common shares outstanding}} = \frac{\$49,000}{10,000} = \$4.90 \text{ per share}$$

Preferred stock dividends, if any, are deducted from net profit before calculating earnings per share. The divisor is the weighted average number of shares determined by relating (*a*) the portion of time within a reporting period that a number of shares of a certain security has been outstanding, to (*b*) the total time in that period.

The number of earnings-per-share figures a company may report will vary with the complexity of its capital structures and whether or not its net income calculations involve extraordinary items.

Since the adoption of *Opinion No. 9, Results of Operations* [1] by the Accounting Principles Board, the net profit figure used by some analysts is the net profit either after or before extraordinary items, or both.

The term net income per share should be used only in those cases where the capital structure of the company is such that there are no potentially dilutive convertible securities, options, warrants, or other agreements providing for contingency issuances of common stock outstanding. *Opinion No. 15, Earnings per Share* [2] recommends that companies with complex capital structures present with equal prominence two types of earnings-per-share amounts on the face of the income statement: one, primary earnings per share; the other, fully diluted earnings per share. Primary earnings per share is the amount of earnings attributable to each share of common stock outstanding, including securities that are equivalent to common stock, i.e., convertible preferred stock with a relatively low dividend rate at issue. Fully diluted earnings per share is the amount of current earnings per share reflecting the maximum dilution that would have resulted from conversions, exercises, and other contingent issues that individually in the future may decrease earnings per share and in the

---

[1] *Opinion No. 9* is discussed in detail in Chapter 10.
[2] *Opinion No. 15* is discussed in detail in Chapter 11.

aggregate might have a dilutive effect. Because of the variety of earnings-per-share data which is possible in some situations, it is always dangerous to use these figures without insisting first on knowing which definition is being used.

It is not uncommon to see different earnings-per-share figures for the same company reported in the financial press and services. Frequently, the financial press simply reproduces the earnings per share highlighted by the company in its press releases. All too often, these releases do not clearly indicate whether or not the earnings per share are before or after adjustments for extraordinary items. The better financial services frequently look beyond the press releases to the annual report and try to distinguish between earnings per share before and after extraordinary items. In addition, these services check whether or not the appropriate number of shares has been used in the computation of primary and fully diluted earnings-per-share data.

Typically, financial analysts eliminate nonrecurrent items from a single-year analysis of companies but include them in long-term analysis. In single-year analysis, financial analysts tend to want to know whether or not the current earnings are in line with the "normal" earnings of the company. Consequently, unusual items such as material refunds of over-paid taxes are excluded from these analyses.

In long-run analyses of historical data, financial analysts tend to include in income every profit and loss item, unless it is quite unrelated to normal operations. This practice recognizes that many of these so-called unusual items are elements of profit and loss that would have been included in income if the accounting period had been longer than, say, one year. In this latter case, the tax refund excluded from the single-year analysis would be included. Examples of items typically excluded from long-term analyses are gains and losses from property sales and voluntary markup or markdown of capital items, such as plant.

Price-Earnings Ratio. Assuming the average price for the Ampex stock is $40, the price-earnings ratio is:

$$\frac{\text{Market price per share}}{\text{Earnings per share}} = \frac{\$40.00}{\$\ 4.90} = 8.2 \text{ to } 1$$

Typically, the earnings-per-share figure in this ratio is based upon the net profit after extraordinary gains or losses.

The reciprocal of the price-earnings ratio gives the *capitalization rate:*

$$\frac{\text{Earnings per share}}{\text{Market price per share}} = \frac{\$\ 4.90}{\$40.00} = 12.2\%$$

In some cases this percentage may reflect the rate of return the marketplace expects from this type of investment.

Dividend Yield. In situations where cash dividends have been increased at the last payment date, the current dividend rate converted to a yearly basis is often used for the numerator:

$$\frac{\text{Cash dividends per share}}{\text{Price per share}} = \frac{\$\ 2.90}{\$40.00} = 7.3\%$$

Stock dividends are not included in this calculation. The *payout ratio* is the percentage cash dividends paid on common stock are of earnings per share:

$$\frac{\text{Cash dividends per share}}{\text{Earnings per share}} = \frac{\$2.90}{\$4.90} = 59\%$$

Basis of Comparison

The results of financial ratio analysis take on real meaning when compared to a standard appropriate to the company's stage of development, seasonal pattern, and industry and management plans. The selection of a relevant standard is always difficult.

The management of a company can use its budgets as a basis of comparison. These are rarely available to the outside analyst. Therefore, he must seek other sources. By comparing a company's current results as showing in its financial reports to similar data in past reports the analyst can get some indication of how much "better" or "worse" things are compared to the past.

Important sources of average ratios for a particular industry are Dun & Bradstreet's *Modern Industry*, Moody's *Manual of Investment*, and Standard and Poor's *Corporation Records*. Another source of comparison bases are the publications of the various trade associations. Often, these publications report selected financial ratios for industries broken down by sales volume categories. These ratios can be used to highlight variations from the average company situation.

Another source of standards can be ratios computed from the data in the annual reports of individual companies in the same industry. This type of external comparison when used with good judgment can indicate the relative quality of the company's operating performance and funds management compared to its competitors.

The experienced analyst rarely relies on any one standard. He uses several standards. He also looks at a variety of related ratios and knows from experience that he must have a good appreciation of the particular company's business before he should take action based upon his analysis.

A Warning

Financial ratio analysis can be a useful analytical tool if used wisely. It has many limitations which the unsophisticated analyst must remember.

First, it deals only with numerical items. It does not look at nonmeasurable factors such as management's ethical values or the quality of the middle management. These are important considerations which should be taken into account when evaluating a company.

Second, management can take certain short-run actions prior to the statement dates to influence the ratios. For example, a company with a better than 1:1 current ratio can improve this ratio by paying off as many of its current liabilities as possible just prior to the balance sheet date.

Third, comparison of ratios between companies can be misleading due to differences in accounting practices in such areas as depreciation, income recognition, and intangible assets.

Fourth, different definitions of common ratios are used by different analysts. Often, two analysts' reports may include the same ratios for a particular company but give very different results.

Fifth, because accounting records are maintained in historical dollars, a change in the value of the dollar can distort the comparability of ratios computed for different time periods.

Finally, ratios show relationships as they existed in the past. The analyst interested in the future should not be misled into believing that the past data necessarily reflect the current or future situation.

SECURITY VALUATION

Valuation of securities problems arise in such situations as the pricing of new issues, the purchase or sale of securities, and the exchange of stock in mergers or reorganizations. There are a variety of ways to determine value. The approach to valuation used in any particular situation depends on the particular circumstances of the buyer and seller.

Asset Valuation

There are three basic asset valuation approaches: book value, reproduction value and liquidation value.

The *book value* of a company's common stock is the difference between the accounting value assigned to its assets and the sum of the liabilities and preferred stock, if any. This amount divided by the number of shares outstanding gives the book value per share. A more conservative approach also eliminates the intangible assets, such as organization expense and bond discounts, from the total asset values shown on the books. The resulting amount is labeled "tangible book value."

The principal weakness of the book value approach is its dependence on the accounting policies of the company. Comparing the book value of different companies is therefore difficult. Some analysts try to overcome this problem by readjusting the accounting statements to some comparable basis. This is a difficult and potentially dangerous task, since putting all

companies on the same accounting basis may obscure important differences between the companies.

Book value rarely approximates the market value of the owner's equity in a company or its assets, principally due to the accountant's use of the historical cost convention. Consequently, book values are usually appropriate only in appraising companies, such as mutual funds, whose assets are mostly liquid and reflect current market values.

Reproduction value is the cost of reproducing at current prices the physical assets of a going concern. The principal deficiency of this approach is that the value of a going business is typically more than the sum of its individual physical asset values, which individually can be appraised reasonably accurately. What value to assign to the company's reputation and other intangible assets is much more difficult. This approach is sometimes used by governmental agencies as a basis for setting public utility rates and in valuation situations where physical assets are the principal asset of the company, such as in real estate businesses, where reproduction of the buildings would be the principal cost of going into business.

Liquidation value focuses on the resale value of assets, principally their scrap value. It usually sets the lower valuation limit.

Sometimes the liquidation value approach is used in conjunction with the earnings approach. In cases where a company is bought for its income potential, but has excess assets, the excess assets can be valued without reference to the company's value based on earning power and then properly added to the earning power value of the company. This approach is called the "redundant asset method." Similarly, if the potential purchaser must acquire additional assets to maintain a company's earning power, the value of these additional assets can be subtracted from the value derived from the earnings approach.

Capitalized Earnings

The current value of a business is determined in many cases by the estimated future earnings it can produce, adjusted for the degree of risk the investor associates with realizing his earnings projections. In these situations the stockholder values the income flow rather than the physical and intangible assets themselves which give rise to this income. This concept is widely accepted, but it is not easy to apply.

There are two steps in the capitalization of earnings valuation method: first, future earnings available to stockholders must be estimated; and second, a capitalization rate must be selected to apply to this estimate.

Typically the analyst bases his estimate of a company's future earnings on its average earnings for the last few years plus or minus some adjustment to reflect his feelings about the company's prospects over the next five or so years. Rather than trying to predict earnings for each of these

future years, he simply settles on an average earnings figure for this period or projects a smooth trend line. His adjustments to the historical pattern of earnings may reflect anticipated changes in the national economy, new product introductions, potential mergers, conversion to common stock of convertible senior securities, and other similar factors which influence earnings per share.

The *capitalization rate* is the price-earnings ratio upside down. It reflects the rate at which the market is capitalizing the value of current earnings. For example, multiplying an average earnings figure by a capitalization rate of 10 percent (or 10 times) is equivalent to calculating the present value of a stream of equal annual earnings over a long period of time discounted at 10 percent. Similarly, a capitalization rate of 20 percent is equivalent to a price-earnings ratio of five times, which when multiplied by the average projected earnings gives a value which is the present value of an equal earnings stream discounted at 20 percent. Clearly, earnings streams are not constant over time. However, because of the high degree of uncertainty as to what the actual earnings will be in any particular year, the analyst feels more comfortable simplifying the problem by using an average projected earnings estimate.

In most situations, the more certain the analyst is that his projected earnings will be realized, the higher the capitalization rate he is willing to apply to those earnings. For example, in the case of a business with very stable earnings historically and the prospect of continued stable earnings, the analyst might use a capitalization rate of 7 percent. Assuming projected earnings were $5 per share, this rate would imply a market value of about $70 ($5/.07 = $71.43). Similarly, the analyst valuing high-risk businesses can use either a conservative earnings forecast or a low capitalization rate. In the case of companies with outstanding growth potential, a very low capitalization rate is sometimes applied to the current earnings. In these cases the rate can approach 1 percent.

The selection of the appropriate capitalization rate is very subjective. It is a function of the estimated risk associated with realizing the projected earnings stream and the willingness of the investor to bear this risk given his financial condition and attitude toward risk bearing. For example, based upon earnings estimates, an analyst may decide a 15 percent capitalization rate is appropriate. However, an investor may decide this is too low, given the fact that if the company fails to reach its projected earnings his stock losses will eliminate most of his life savings. Consequently, the investor may demand a capitalization rate of 30 percent before undertaking this type of investment. One guide to appropriate capitalization rates is the price-earnings ratios range assigned by the market to the current earnings of particular industries.

Considerable controversy surrounds the role of cash dividends in security valuation. The capitalization of earnings approach assumes that a dollar

of earnings is equally valuable to an investor whether it is paid out in dividends or retained for reinvestment in the company. Eventually, how the individual investor incorporates the dividend factor in his formula for stock valuation will depend on his financial needs and resources and the company's earnings prospects relative to the investor's potential rate of return on dividends.

Fair Market Value

If a stock is publicly traded, its current market price may not necessarily reflect a reasonable valuation. There are a number of reasons for this conclusion.

First, the markets for many listed and unlisted stocks is "thin." That is, there are few prospective buyers or sellers. In these cases, the price of the stock can fluctuate significantly with the addition of a small number of buy or sell orders.

Second, some stock prices are maintained at an artificial level by deliberate attempts to manipulate the price. A legal illustration of this practice is the price stabilization support often given initially to new issues by their underwriters.

Third, the marketplace tends to exaggerate upward and downward stock price movements. Consequently, at the peaks and troughs of price swings the market may not reflect necessarily reasonable values.

Finally, the market price of most stocks reflects transactions involving relatively small numbers of shares. Often it is not appropriate to use these prices as a basis for valuing large blocks of shares. The price of a large block of shares may be at a discount from the current market, since if they were dumped on the open market they might depress the price of the stock. However, if the sale gives the purchaser control of the company, the buyer may have to pay a premium for the stock.

These objections to current stock prices as a measure of value have led to the development of the "fair market value" or "intrinsic value" method. This method tries to establish the price at which a security would trade in a free market between fully informed, rational buyers and sellers. As a result, the intrinsic value method looks at the valuation problem from the point of view of the buyer and seller, using some of the asset and capitalized earnings valuation techniques described earlier.

Range of Values

The three principal security valuation methods help set the range of possible values for a company's common stock. In the case of the capitalization of earnings and intrinsic value methods, ratio analysis techniques can be helpful in getting a feel for a company's risk characteristics and

the appropriateness of different capitalization rates. In any particular situation, the actual stock value settled upon will probably be based on an approach involving several of these methods, modified by the negotiating skills of the buyer and seller.

SUGGESTED FURTHER READINGS

FOULKE, ROY A. *Practical Financial Statement Analysis.* 5th ed. New York: McGraw-Hill, 1961.

GRAHAM, BENJAMIN; DODD, DAVID L.; and COTTLE, SIDNEY. *Security Analysis: Principles and Technique.* 4th ed. New York: McGraw-Hill, 1963.

HELFERT, ERICH A. *Techniques of Financial Analysis.* Homewood, Ill.: Richard D. Irwin, 1967.

KENNEDY, RALPH DALE, and McMULLEN, STEWART YARWOOD. *Financial Statements: Form, Analysis, and Interpretation.* 4th ed. Homewood, Ill.: Richard D. Irwin, 1962.

MYER, JOHN N. *Financial Statement Analysis: Principles and Techniques.* 3d ed. Englewood Cliffs, N.J.: Prentice-Hall, 1961.

PART II

Corporate Reporting Fundamentals

CHAPTER **4**

BASIC CONVENTIONS

Financial accounting decisions reflect a number of basic conventions which are commonly accepted as useful guides to selecting appropriate accounting policies. These conventions have grown out of the experiences of accountants and businessmen in trying to measure and communicate the results of operations and the financial condition of corporations. Accounting conventions are utilitarian. Their degree of acceptance stems from their usefulness to those making decisions involving accounting data. This usefulness is determined in turn by the convention's congruence with the social and economic conditions, needs, and concepts of the time. Clearly, as these factors change over time, so must accounting conventions.

This chapter briefly describes 14 basic conventions. Not everyone will agree with this list. Some may argue certain conventions should be combined or dropped. Others might try to break the list into categories which distinguish between postulates and principles. Many of these proposals have merit. The purpose of our list, however, is simply to cover the basic conventions included in a number of the outstanding books on this subject. Some of these include: The APB's Statement No. 4, "Basic Concepts and Accounting Principles Underlying Financial Statements of Business Enterprises," Grady's *Inventory of Generally Accepted Accounting Principles for Business Enterprises*, Moonitz's *The Basic Postulates of Accounting*, and Sprouse and Moonitz's *A Tentative Set of Broad Accounting Principles for Business Enterprises*. All of these works, excluding Statement No. 4, are accounting research studies of the AICPA.

Enforceable Private Property Rights

In the United States, nearly every accounting entry assumes that the property rights of those involved are legally enforceable. Also, account-

ing assumes that society and government will continue to recognize that individuals have the right to invest and enjoy their property rights, as long as they do not interfere with the rights of others or the public interest. These conditions do not prevail in all nations and, in those countries it is doubtful if statements prepared according to American practice would be very meaningful.

Business Entity

The business entity convention assumes that the financial statements are for the business entity, as distinct from its owners. Consequently, the analysis of business transactions involving costs and revenues is expressed in terms of the changes in the firm's financial condition. Similarly, the assets and liabilities devoted to business activities are entity assets and liabilities. Also, since business activity is carried on between particular firms, financial statements must clearly identify the specific companies involved. This separation of ownership and management also recognizes the fiduciary responsibility to the stockholders of those who manage the business.

The boundaries of the business entity are sometimes difficult to establish. Typically the accountant defines these boundaries in terms of the firm's economic activities and administrative control, rather than legal relationships. For example, consolidated financial statements often present the financial condition and results of operations of different entities with common ownership in a single set of statements, thus treating the various entities as a single economic unit, even though they consist of several legal entities. Here the accountant is trying to present useful statements which look beyond the legal relationships to the underlying economic and managerial relationships. The legal considerations are relevant only insofar as they define or influence economic activities and managerial control.

The entity concept applies equally to incorporated, unincorporated, small, and big businesses. In the case of incorporated, widely held, publicly owned companies, such as General Motors, it is not difficult to keep separate the affairs of the business and its owners. However, in the case of small unincorporated businesses where the owners exert day-to-day control over the affairs of the business and personal and business assets are intermingled, the definition of the business entity is more difficult for financial—as well as managerial—accounting purposes.

The entity concept recognizes the long-standing belief that management has a stewardship responsibility to owners. Owners entrust funds to management and management is expected to use these funds wisely. Periodically, management must report to the owners the results of management's actions. Financial statements are one of the principal means whereby management fulfills this reporting responsibility. In the case of owner-

manager businesses, the stewardship responsibility is assumed to exist principally because of the analytical value of separating how well the owner-managers did as investors in contrast to managers.

Going Concern

Unless evidence suggests otherwise, those preparing accounting statements for a business entity assume it will continue operations into the foreseeable future. This convention reflects the normal expectation of management and investors. So that readers of financial statements will not be misled, the statements of business entities with limited lives must clearly indicate the terminal data and type of liquidation involved (i.e., receiver's statements, etc.). Otherwise, the reader will assume that the accounts are based on the presumption that the enterprise has an indefinitely long life.

Accounting emphasizes and reflects the continuing nature of business activity. Consequently, in the normal situation the accountant is not concerned with the current or liquidation values of assets. For example, the accountant expects that the company in the normal course of business will receive the full value of accounts receivable. Accordingly, he records these items at their face value, less some deductions for anticipated bad debts, rather than at current liquidation value. Similarly, the expenditures made to create finished goods inventories are recorded as assets, since the accountant assumes the inventories will be disposed of later in the normal course of operations. Fixed assets are reported at cost. Their current resale value is irrelevant for the accountant's task. His statements assume the fixed assets will not be sold as such, but will be a cost input to future production output.

The going-concern convention leads to the corollary that individual financial statements are part of a continuous, interrelated series of statements. This further implies that data communicated are tentative and that current statements should disclose adjustments to past-year statements revealed by more recent developments.

Monetary

Accounting is a measurement process dealing only with those events which can be measured in monetary terms. This convention reflects the fact that money is the common denominator used in business to measure the exchangeability of goods, services, and capital. Obviously, financial statements should indicate the money unit used.

The monetary convention leads to one of the limitations of accounting. Accounting, for example, does not record or communicate the state of the president's health, the attitude of the labor force, or the relative advan-

tage of competitive products. Consequently, the most important aspects of a business may not be reflected in the financial statements.

Accounting Period

For decision-making purposes, management and investors need periodic "test readings" of the progress of their business. Accounting recognizes this need and breaks the flow of business activity into a series of reporting or fiscal periods. These periods are usually 12 months in length. Most companies also issue quarterly or semiannual statements to stockholders. These are considered to be *interim*, and essentially different from annual statements. For management use, statements covering shorter periods such as a month or week may be prepared. Irrespective of the length of the period, the statements must indicate the period covered.

The success of a business can only be determined accurately upon liquidation. Consequently, the periodic financial statements are at best estimates which are subject to change as future events develop.

Breaking business activity into a series of discrete segments creates a number of accounting problems. For example, given the uncertainties surrounding the life of an asset and its scrap value, how should the cost of the asset be allocated to specific periods? How should the income and costs associated with long-term contracts covering several accounting periods be treated? Should research and development costs be expensed as incurred or carried as assets to be expensed in later periods when revenues may be derived from these outlays? Such questions must be resolved in the light of the particular circumstances. There is no easy, general solution. The accountant and businessman must rely upon their experience, knowledge, and judgment to come to the appropriate answer.

The timing of the accounting period will depend upon the nature of the business. For most companies the accounting period runs from January 1 to December 31. Some companies use a different period, principally because their yearly business cycle does not conform to the calendar year. For example, typically the annual statements of department stores are more meaningful if their fiscal period ends January 31. This is a time when inventories are low and the Christmas selling peak is over.

Consistency

The consistency convention requires that similar transactions be reported in a consistent fashion from period to period. Clearly, for example, comparison of interperiod results would be difficult if a company changed its depreciation policy each year. The consistency concept is not inflexible, however. Changes in accounting policies are appropriate when justified by changing circumstances.

Accountants place considerable emphasis on consistency. When expressing an audit opinion the accountant notes whether or not the statements were prepared "on a basis consistent with that of the preceding year." If changes were made, he notes these in his opinion and insists that the nature and impact of these changes be fully disclosed.

The consistency concept does not necessarily mean uniformity exists among the accounting practices of affiliated business units or even within a single company. For example, one unit may value inventory on the so-called Lifo basis whereas another may use the Fifo basis. Similarly, a single unit might use both methods to value different parts of its inventory. In either case the policy should be disclosed and consistently followed.

The consistency concept does not imply uniformity in the treatment of particular items among different independent companies. One of the characteristics of American accounting practice is the accounting diversity among different companies, almost all of which meets the criterion of "generally accepted accounting principles."

Historical Cost

For accounting purposes, business transactions are normally measured in terms of the actual prices or costs at the time the transaction was consummated. This convention applies to both the initial recording and subsequent reporting of transactions. While agreeing with the need to record historical costs initially, some influential accountants argue accounting would be "more useful" if estimates of current and future values were substituted for historical costs under certain conditions. The extent to which cost and value should be reflected in the accounts is central to much of the current accounting controversy.

The market value of assets may change with time. Typically, accounting does not recognize these changes in value. Thus, the cost of assets shown on financial statements seldom reflects their current market value. This accounting practice flows from the going-concern concept, which implies that since the business is not going to sell its assets as such there is little point in revaluing assets to reflect current values. In addition, for practical reasons, the accountant prefers the reporting of actual costs to less certain estimates which are difficult to verify. By using historical costs, the accountant's already difficult task is not further complicated by the need to keep additional records of changing market values.

In practice, there are a number of modifications to the historical cost concept. For example, under special conditions inventory may be reported at market values if this value is less than the historical cost. Assets acquired for stock are recorded at the estimated market value of the stock exchanged. Mutual funds and some pension funds whose assets consist

almost entirely of securities report the market value of their investments, taking the gain or loss into income at the end of each reporting period. Similarly, donated assets may be carried at their appraised value at the time of acquisition.

Realization

For accounting purposes, revenue is realized during the period either when services or goods are exchanged for a valuable consideration or when the amount of the revenue can be verified with a reasonable degree of objectivity. In practice, no one test, such as sale or delivery, has proven satisfactory, given the diversity of industry's production, sale, and credit practices. Consequently, the timing of revenue realization ranges from the act of production, in the case of gold mining operations, to the receipt of cash, in the case of some installment sales contracts. Clearly, the application of the realization concept depends upon the circumstances of each case.

Some authorities claim revenue is earned during the process of operations, rather than, say, entirely at the time of sale. All activities related to production and sales contribute to the final product and, hence, to revenue, they argue. Accordingly, they state that accounting should recognize revenue in proportion to the costs accumulated to date of such activities. In practice, one method of accounting for long-term construction contracts covering several accounting periods does recognize revenue as it is earned by permitting revenues to be recognized in the proportion the estimated progress bears to the total job, provided it is anticipated that the contract can be completed and the originally estimated profit obtained. In the absence of firm contracts or reasonable certainty as to the course of future events, accounting practice does not normally recognize revenue during production.

Matching of Costs and Revenues

Accounting income or profit is the net result of the accountant's trying to match the related costs and revenues of the period. This process can be described as matching "effort and accomplishments," where costs measure effort and revenue the related accomplishments. Often this ideal cannot be achieved, since costs cannot be easily identified with specific current or anticipated revenues. In these cases the accountant normally relates the costs to the time period during which they were incurred.

The matching of costs and revenues may require deferring recognition of expenses and revenues to future periods. For example, cash may be spent today for product development which is expected to generate revenues two years hence. In this case, the accountant may defer recognizing the product development outlay as a cost until the expected revenues

materialize. At this time the costs and the revenues would be matched. In the meantime, however, the product development cost would be reported as an asset (i.e., capitalized). Whether or not costs should be deferred is a difficult question to resolve in practice.

The matching process is usually achieved through application of the accrual method of accounting rather than the cash method. The cash method of accounting records cash receipts and disbursements and focuses on the changes in the cash account. The accrual method seeks to measure changes in the owner's equity during the accounting period. Events which decrease the owner's equity are usually called expenses. Events which increase the owner's equity are typically called revenues. The net difference between these movements is net income for the period. These changes in owner's equity may not necessarily result in changes in the cash account. For example, a $100 sale on credit will increase accounts receivable and owner's equity. The accrual method recognizes the fact that the service has been performed and a valuable asset received. If a cash method was being used, no record of the event would be made until the customer's $100 cash was received.

Dual Aspect

The dual aspect convention recognizes that someone has a claim on all the resources owned by the business. These resources are called "assets." The creditor's claims against these assets are usually referred to as "liabilities." The owners' claims are called either "stockholders' equity," "owners' equity," or "proprietorship." Consequently, since the total assets of the business are claimed by somebody, it follows that:

$$Assets = Liabilities + Stockholders' Equity$$

Assets are things of value owned by the reporting entity which have been acquired through a current or past transaction and are expected to have some future economic benefits. Assets are recorded at no more than their original cost to the entity, less any reduction of this value due to use or decline in potential usefulness. An asset can have value for several reasons:

1. The asset may be used to acquire other assets. Cash is the principal example of an asset that derives its value from its purchasing power.
2. The asset represents a claim upon another entity for money—for example, accounts receivable, which are amounts owed to the company for credit sales.
3. The asset can be converted to cash or a money claim. Finished goods inventories that will be sold in the normal course of business are an example.

4. The asset has potential benefits, rights, or services which will result in the entity earning something from its use in some future accounting period. Such assets include items like buildings, patents, and raw materials.

The term liabilities may be defined as the entity's obligations to convey assets or perform services resulting from past or current transactions involving creditor relationships. These obligations require future settlement and represent claims on the entity's assets by nonownership interests. Accounts payable to trade creditors, bonds payable, and taxes payable are examples of liabilities.

Stockholders' equity is the claim upon the company's assets of the ownership interest. This is a residual claim. It is the excess of the entity's total assets over its liabilities. This amount is also equal to the owners' capital invested in the business plus profits retained by the business.

Accounting systems are designed so that events are recorded in terms of their influence on assets, liabilities, or owners' equity. Every event has a dual aspect. For example, assume John Smith invested $5,000 in a new business; the accounting entry would recognize the $5,000 asset of the business and John Smith's claim upon this asset:

$$\text{Assets, } \$5,000 = \text{Stockholders' Equity, } \$5,000$$

Now, if the company borrowed $1,000 from the bank, the firm's accounting statement would be:

ASSETS		LIABILITIES AND STOCKHOLDERS' EQUITY	
Cash	$6,000	Bank loan payable	$1,000
		Stockholders' equity	5,000
Total	$6,000	Total	$6,000

Next assume the business used $2,000 of its cash to acquire some inventory, the new statement would be:

ASSETS		LIABILITIES AND STOCKHOLDERS' EQUITY	
Cash	$4,000	Bank loan payable	$1,000
Inventory	2,000	Stockholders' equity	5,000
Total	$6,000	Total	$6,000

Thus, the *double-entry* system requires two entries for each event. Other systems are possible, such as a single-entry system, but the double-entry system is the most widely used.

All creditors and owners with claims against the assets of a company

can be considered as having an equity in those assets. Therefore, some accounting authorities prefer to state the basic equation as follows:

$$\text{Assets} = \text{Equities}$$

Those holding this point of view believe that the dual aspect of accounting transactions results in accounting entries which record changes in assets and equities.

A few accounting authors argue that the traditional accounting equation with its definition of assets, liabilities, and net worth is an outmoded concept and, therefore, the notion of the basic equation should be changed to reflect current thinking in finance and business.

One such approach suggests that contemporary financial accounting practice is becoming increasingly concerned with maintaining a continuing record of capital invested in an enterprise from a two-sided point of view: the *sources* and *uses* of funds, with funds broadly defined as all financial resources. This concern, it is argued, is in line with modern financial theory and practice, which tends to view assets as funds invested within the business, and liabilities and net worth as financial resources obtained from sources external to the firm. As a result, the balance sheet can be regarded as a report, at an instant of time, of the status of funds obtained from sources external to the business and the items in which these funds (and those generated by drawing down other assets) are invested.

The growing use of a "no-man's land" category between the customary liabilities and stockholders' equity section of the balance sheet, for items (such as tax deferrals) created by using different accounting methods for book and tax purposes, serves as evidence that it is no longer practical to present fairly all external sources of funds as flowing through either the liabilities or stockholders' equity sections. Such items as deferred profit on sale and leaseback transactions and pension accruals in excess of legal requirements seem to fall into this new account section. They are somehow thought to belong on the right-hand side of the balance sheet, but don't neatly fit the definition of the traditional categories. Also, these transactions are not regarded as contributing directly to income at the time the transaction occurs.

Those who take this position maintain that in our current economic environment, accounting needs to remove the shackles of trying to classify all sources of capital reflected in the balance sheet as either pure "liabilities" or pure "ownership equity." What is needed now is to give explicit recognition to the fact that current business conditions require a more flexible approach to classifying "external sources of capital" on the right side of the balance sheet and then proceed from there.

Those who support this point of view express the dual aspect of transactions in terms of sources and uses of funds. Since for each use of funds

there must be a matching source and for each source a use, the basic accounting equation suggested is:

$$\text{Items in which capital is invested (assets)} = \\ \text{External sources of capital (equities)}$$

Reliability of Evidence

Accountants recording events rely heavily upon objective, verifiable documentary evidence, in contrast to the subjective judgments of a person who may be biased. Acceptable evidence includes such items as approved sales or purchase invoices. This desire to base decisions on objective evidence is one of the principal supports of the historical cost convention.

In practice, accountants find it difficult to apply the absolute standard of objective, verifiable evidence. Many major decisions, such as the allocation of costs between periods, must be based on reasonable estimates after considering all of the relevant facts. In many instances it is not feasible for an auditor to verify the recording of every event. As a result, he bases his opinion in large part upon his assessment of management's internal controls, which are the measures adopted by management to safeguard assets, check the reliability and accuracy of data, and encourage adherence to operating policies and programs.

Disclosure

The disclosure convention requires that accounting reports disclose enough information so that they are not misleading to those investors who are careful and reasonably well informed in financial matters. Special disclosure is made of unusual items, changes in expectations, significant contractual relations, and new activities. The disclosure can be in the body of the financial statements, the auditor's opinion, or the footnotes to the statements.

The disclosure convention has received increasing attention in recent years. For example, financial analysts have been pressing for fuller disclosure of sales and profits by divisions and major product lines. It is anticipated that the pressure for fuller disclosure will continue. In general, while management has cooperated with these demands, it has refused to disclose information of a "competitive" nature. The question of what constitutes "competitive" information has yet to be settled, however.

Conservatism

The conservatism convention prescribes that when choosing between two permissible accounting alternatives, some added weight be given to

the alternative that understates current income and assets. If not carefully applied, this convention can lead to abuses which result in unnecessary or dishonest understatement. Also, by understating income in one period, income in another period will be overstated. Thus, the application of this convention requires considerable judgment, especially since an accountant may be sued if he condones grossly misleading statements.

Materiality

Accounting conventions apply only to material and significant items. Inconsequential items can be dealt with expediently. However, in applying this convention, care must be taken to see that the cumulative effect of treating a series of immaterial items does not materially alter the total statements. Whether or not an item is immaterial depends on judgment and the particular circumstances. One common test of materiality is: Would the investment decision of a reasonably well informed user of the statements be altered if the item was treated differently? If the decision would change, the item is material.

Application

The application of these conventions in specific instances is left to the judgment of management and the accountants. The relative importance of these conventions changes from decision to decision. Also, in any one instance, two or more conventions may be in conflict. The problem facing the accountant or businessman is to select those conventions most relevant to the facts of his situation and the particular needs of the dominant user of the statements. Whether or not a convention leads to a feasible solution will also determine its relevance.

SUGGESTED FURTHER READINGS

ACCOUNTING PRINCIPLES BOARD. "Basic Concepts and Accounting Principles Underlying Financial Statements of Business Enterprises," Statement No. 4. New York: AICPA, 1970.

AMERICAN ACCOUNTING ASSOCIATION. *A Statement of Basic Accounting Theory*. Evanston, Ill.: AAA, 1966.

CHAMBERS, R. J. *Accounting, Evaluation and Economic Behavior*. Englewood Cliffs, N.J.: Prentice-Hall, 1966.

EDWARDS, E. O., and BELL, P. W. *The Theory and Measurement of Business Income*. Berkeley and Los Angeles: University of California Press, 1961.

GRADY, PAUL. *Inventory of Generally Accepted Accounting Principles for Business Enterprises*, Accounting Research Study No. 7. New York: American Institute of Certified Public Accountants, 1965.

MATTESSICH, RICHARD. *Accounting and Analytical Methods*. Homewood, Ill.: Richard D. Irwin, 1964.

MOONITZ, MAURICE. *The Basic Postulates of Accounting*, Accounting Research Study No. 1. New York: AICPA, 1961.

PATON, W. A., and LITTLETON, A. C. *An Introduction to Corporate Accounting Standards*. Evanston, Ill.: AAA, 1962.

SPROUSE, ROBERT T., and MOONITZ, MAURICE. *A Tentative Set of Broad Accounting Principles for Business Enterprises*, Accounting Research Study No. 3. New York: AICPA, 1962.

CASES

Case 4–1. **OMEGA NOVELTY SHOP**
Economic versus Accounting Concepts

Early in 1968, Paul Stone submitted to the Research Division of an eastern business school the profit and loss statement for his retail novelty shop shown in Exhibit 1.

EXHIBIT 1

OMEGA NOVELTY SHOP

Profit and Loss Statement
For Year Ending December 31, 1967

Gross sales	$104,850.48	
Returns and allowances to customers	4,500.00	
Net sales		$100,350.48
Net inventory of merchandise at beginning of year	$ 50,258.79	
Purchases of merchandise at billed cost	74,762.67	
Inward freight, express, and parcel postage	428.61	
Gross cost of merchandise handled	$125,450.07	
Cash discounts taken	1,276.95	
Net cost of merchandise handled	$124,173.12	
Net inventory of merchandise at end of year	55,245.84	
Net cost of merchandise sold		68,927.28
Gross margin		$ 31,423.20
Total salaries and wages	$ 9,480.39	
Advertising	1,702.56	
Boxes and wrappings	556.41	
Office supplies and postage	1,220.73	
Taxes, insurance, repairs, and depreciation of real estate	2,616.30	
Heat, light, and power	515.79	
Taxes	342.00	
Insurance	863.31	
Depreciation of store equipment	660.00	
Interest on borrowed capital	178.80	
Miscellaneous expense	1,533.63	
Income taxes	1,125.30	
Total expense		20,795.22
Net Profit		$ 10,627.98

On writing to Mr. Stone for supplementary information, the division learned that of the net profit of $10,627.98 shown on his statement, Mr. Stone had withdrawn $4,500. He did not make a charge for his own services as manager, but up to 1966 he had been employed in a similar capacity in another store at a salary of $5,400 a year. Mr. Stone stated that he owned his store building, which had a rental value of $3,900 a year. From the balance sheets submitted for this firm, the division computed the net worth of the business exclusive of real estate to be $98,677.98. Interest on this sum at 6 percent, which Mr. Stone stated to be the local rate on reasonably secure long-time investments, amounted to $5,920.68.

On the basis of these additional data, the division adjusted the profit and loss statement for the Stone store and sent it back as shown in Exhibit 2.

EXHIBIT 2

OMEGA NOVELTY SHOP

Profit and Loss Statement
For Year Ending December 31, 1967

Merchandise Statement

Gross sales		$104,850.48	
Less: Returns and allowances to customers		4,500.00	
Net sales		$100,350.48	100.00%
Net inventory of merchandise at beginning of year	$ 50,258.79		
Plus: Purchases of merchandise at billed cost	74,762.67		
Inward freight, express, and parcel postage	428.61		
Gross cost of merchandise handled	$125,450.07		
Less: Cash discounts taken	1,276.95		
Net cost of merchandise handled	$124,173.12		
Less: Net inventory of merchandise at end of year	55,245.84		
Net cost of merchandise sold		68,927.28	68.69
Gross margin		$ 31,423.20	31.31%

Expense Statement

Proprietor's salary	$ 5,400.00		5.38%
All other salaries and wages	9,480.39		9.45
Total salaries and wages	$ 14,880.39		14.83%
Advertising	1,702.56		1.70
Boxes and wrappings	556.41		0.55
Office supplies and postage	1,220.73		1.21
Rent	3,900.00		3.89
Heat, light, and power	515.79		0.51
Taxes	342.00		0.34
Insurance	863.31		0.86
Depreciation of store equipment	660.00		0.66
Interest on borrowed capital	$ 178.80		
Interest on owned capital invested in the business	5,920.68		
Total interest		6,099.48	6.08
Miscellaneous expense		1,533.63	1.53
Total expense		$ 32,274.30	32.16%

EXHIBIT 2 *(Continued)*

Net Gain Statement

Net loss			$ 851.10	0.85%
Interest and rentals earned.				
Interest on owned capital invested in the business		$ 5,920.68		
Rent of owned store building $3,900.00				
Less: Expense on owned store building (taxes, insurance, repairs, depreciation, interest on mortgages).............. 2,616.30		1,283.70		
Total interest and rentals			7,204.38	
Net Gain			$ 6,353.28	
Provision for federal and state income taxes ...... $ 1,125.30				
Withdrawals		4,500.00	5,625.30	
Surplus for the Year			$ 827.98	

After receiving this adjusted profit and loss statement, Mr. Stone wrote the following letter to the division on July 13, 1968:

Dear sirs:

I have received a copy of my 1967 profit and loss statement as adjusted by you, and I am at a loss to understand some of the changes you have made.

For instance, the statement which I sent you showed a net profit of $10,627.98 but the copy which you have returned to me shows a net loss of $851.10. I notice that you have charged $5,400 as my salary. I do not draw any regular salary from the business, and since I am in business for myself I consider that I am not working for a salary but for profits. Also you have shown a rental expense of $3,900. Since I own the building, I consider that the item of rent is adequately taken care of by the expenses incurred in connection with the building, such as taxes, insurance, and so on. Furthermore, you have shown an expense of $5,920.68 for interest on owned capital. I have worked hard to put this business in a position where I would not have to borrow money, but if I have to charge interest on my own capital, I do not see where I am any better off, according to your version of affairs, than if I were continually in debt to banks and wholesalers.

In short, it seems to me that your adjustment of my statement amounts merely to shifting money from one pocket to another and calling it salary, rent, or interest, as the case may be; whereas what I am really interested in is the profit that I make by being in business for myself rather than working for somebody else.

An explanation from you will be appreciated.

Yours very truly,
PAUL STONE

Questions

1. Did Mr. Stone make a profit from his novelty business in 1967? How much, if any? How may the difference between Mr. Stone's computation of profits and that of the Research Division be explained?

2. Was Mr. Stone a successful businessman?
3. Should Mr. Stone have sold his novelty business?
4. What were the incentives which motivated Mr. Stone?

Case 4–2. **THE GETTY FORMULA**
Different Concepts of Value

On June 16, 1960, George F. Getty II, president of Tidewater Oil Company, addressed a regular luncheon meeting of the New York Society of Security Analysts. According to Mr. Getty, the appraised value of Tidewater Oil Company can be estimated by using the following generally accepted method:

1. Proven and developed crude oil and liquids reserves are valued at $1 per barrel.
2. Proven and developed natural gas reserves are valued at $0.05 per MCF (thousand cubic feet).
3. Probable reserves of liquids and natural gas are appraised at one fourth of the unit values above.
4. Refining, marketing, transportation, and other miscellaneous assets, including investments and advances, are assessed at net book value.
5. Add net working capital.
6. Deduct long-term debt and preferred stock.

The appraised value of Tidewater's common stock at December 31, 1959 determined by this method is about $80.00 per share. This appraised value of $80.00 per share is four times the current market value.[1]

This case uses Mr. Getty's formula (1) to explore the meaning and significance of "value" to majority and minority owners, potential owners, managers, security analysts, and accountants; and (2) to establish the usefulness of accounting information in measuring "value." To emphasize the importance of "value," information about a proposed merger between Tidewater and the Skelly Oil Company is included.

Tidewater Oil Company

Tidewater Oil Company, a medium-sized, domestic, integrated firm operated in all phases of the oil business. The company was engaged in

---

[1] The price of Tidewater common was $24 on December 31, 1959; on June 16, 1960, it was $17.50.

exploration, development, and production of crude oil and natural gas. It operated an extensive transportation system consisting of pipelines and a fleet of tankers. Tidewater's refinery capacity placed it 11th in a list of top United States refiners. The eastern refinery, located in Delaware, was generally regarded as the most advanced in the world. Tidewater also engaged in retail distribution, selling its products through retail outlets principally on the east and west coasts of the United States.

Instead of cash dividends Tidewater had followed the practice, since 1955, of declaring a 5 percent stock dividend each year.

After 1952, Tidewater was especially active in finding new oil and gas reserves. From 1953 to 1959 its proven reserves of petroleum liquids (crude oil and natural gas liquids) increased 30 percent, to 693.3 million barrels, from 533.3 million barrels, or more than twice the rate of increase for the industry. Proven natural gas reserves increased even more dramatically, to 3,510 billion cubic feet from 1,674 billion cubic feet, nearly four times the rate of increase in the industry. In addition, the company owned probable reserves of 134 million barrels of crude and 424 billion cubic feet of natural gas.

During 1959, Tidewater earned $34 million from sales of $600 million. Tidewater's 1959 balance sheet is shown in Exhibit 1. Information concerning the earnings, dividends, and market price of Tidewater and other selected oil companies during several recent years is presented in Exhibit 2.

Proposed Merger with Skelly Oil Company

The merger negotiations between Tidewater and Skelly Oil Company which began during April 1959 gave rise to considerable discussion regarding the value of Tidewater stock. Skelly, one of the smaller integrated domestic companies, was engaged in the production, refining, pipeline transportation, and marketing of petroleum products. With crude production about 50 percent greater than its refinery capacity, it seemed a natural complement to Tidewater, which had excess refinery capacity and whose operations were hampered by import quotas on foreign oil. The Tidewater and Skelly marketing organizations were also complementary, since Skelly's outlets were concentrated in the middle, southwest, and southern states. Combining the two firms would help to balance their refining operations and lead to national distribution.

In contrast to Tidewater, Skelly had paid a cash dividend of $1.80 in each of the last five years.

As the merger talks progressed, joint committees representing the two companies were established. These committees, together with technical experts and appraisers, examined all phases of the two firms' operations. Earnings were recalculated on comparable bases for several past years and forecasts of operations and earnings were prepared. Reserves were valued

EXHIBIT 1

TIDEWATER OIL COMPANY

Consolidated Balance Sheet as of December 31, 1959
(in thousands)

ASSETS

Cash	$ 36,183	
U.S. government securities	390	
Accounts receivable	74,560	
Inventories *	61,618	
Deferred charges	9,955	
Total Current Assets		$182,706
Investments and advances		15,476
Plant, property, and equipment, net **		658,231
Total Assets		$856,413

LIABILITIES

Accounts payable	$ 50,553	
Accrued taxes payable	15,734	
Dividends payable	739	
Current portion of long-term debt	25,973	
Total Current Liabilities		$ 92,999
Long-term debt		284,751
Preferred stock	$ 62,393	
Less preferred stock in treasury	697	61,696
Common stock	$139,594	
Less common stock in treasury	2,901	$136,693
Paid-in capital		69,298
Retained earnings		210,976	416,967
Total Liabilities		$856,413

° Crude oil and products, $42,409; materials and supplies, $19,209.
°° These items include:

	Gross	Depreciation	Net
Production	$ 545,878	$324,542	$221,336
Transportation	141,943	42,654	99,289
Manufacturing	331,250	101,347	229,903
Marketing	142,930	46,831	96,099
Miscellaneous	12,648	1,044	11,604
Totals	$1,174,649	$516,418	$658,231

SOURCE: Adapted from Tidewater *Annual Report,* 1959.

EXHIBIT 2

TIDEWATER AND OTHER SELECTED OIL COMPANIES

Earnings, Dividends, and Market Price, 1955–59

	1959	1958	1957	1956	1955
Tidewater:					
Earnings per share	$2.23	−$0.03	$2.31	$2.58	$2.53
Cash flow per share	6.67	3.94	7.08	5.89	6.19
Dividends per share	5% stock	5% stock	5% stock	5% stock	5% stock
Price range:					
High	28⅛	27⅛	38⅜	41⅜	38¾
Low	20	18⅛	17⅞	28⅝	20
Continental:					
Earnings per share	$2.85	$2.40	$2.38	$2.65	$2.38
Cash flow per share	4.34	3.99	3.82	3.97	3.71
Dividends per share	1.70	1.60	1.60	1.52½	1.42½
Price range:					
High	69¾	64	70¼	69	52½
Low	45⅛	38⅝	41½	27	35
Phillips:					
Earnings per share	$3.05	$2.45	$2.80	$2.77	$2.78
Cash flow per share	6.61	6.14	6.40	6.03	5.47
Dividends per share	1.70	1.70	1.70	1.60	1.50
Price range:					
High	52¾	49¼	53¼	56¾	41⅞
Low	41	36⅜	35⅜	39⅜	34¾
Pure:					
Earnings per share	$3.32	$3.35	$4.13	$4.26	$4.05
Cash flow per share	6.56	6.40	7.14	7.14	6.93
Dividends per share	1.60	1.60	1.60	1.60	1.51¼
Price range:					
High	48⅛	45	48⅞	51¾	41½
Low	34⅛	29	29¾	37¾	32
Skelly:					
Earnings per share	$4.87	$4.82	$6.40	$5.93	$5.61
Cash flow per share	9.74	10.35	11.87	11.29	10.63
Dividends per share	1.80	1.80	1.80	1.80	1.80
Price range:					
High	74¼	72⅜	80¾	73	57½
Low	50¼	48	49	52⅞	46¼
Sun:					
Earnings per share	$3.48	$2.60	$3.86	$4.56	$3.89
Cash flow per share	7.76	7.54	8.88	9.16	8.90
Dividends per share	0.95	0.92½	0.87½	0.82½	0.76
Price range:					
High	62⅝	63⅞	71½	71½	62½
Low	52⅞	54½	61⅛	57¾	52¼
Mean P/E ratio for					
the industry	11.16	17.1	11.8	14.0	13.7

SOURCES: *Moody's Industrial Manual*; Standard & Poor's *Industry Surveys*.

and stock prices were compared. Nevertheless, D. H. Miller, the president of Skelly, stated that:

> After several months of studying and comparing asset values of the companies . . . it became apparent that there was a wide difference between the companies in their estimates of the relative value of the common stocks.[2]

During October, negotiations were terminated. In commenting on the failure of the companies to agree on merger terms, George Getty noted that the indicated exchange ratio of Tidewater to Skelly stock, when based on appraised value, was three for two, while market prices suggested a ratio closer to three for one. According to Getty, this "created a gulf between us that appraisals and so forth could not bridge."[3]

Excerpts from George Getty's Speech to the Security Analysts

During the postwar years prior to 1953, the principal objective of Tidewater's management was the retirement of the large debt accumulated by the company during the late 1920s and early 1930s. This philosophy was reflected in the company's aging plant and equipment, in its static organization, and in its timid attitude toward postwar expansion opportunities. When new management entered Tidewater Oil Company in May 1953, it was faced immediately with the necessity of rebuilding and revitalizing the company. Promptly, plans were laid for strengthening the company's organization, for rebuilding its physical facilities and for expanding the scope and magnitude of its operations.

This program got under way in 1954 and required a vast amount of money, demanding a reversal of the company's long-standing, ultraconservative financial policy. Long-term financing was arranged at attractive rates; cash dividends on the common stock were eliminated to conserve internally generated funds. Since 1954, the company has paid no cash dividend on its common stock, but has, instead, paid an annual 5 percent stock dividend. I do not anticipate a resumption of cash dividends in the near future.

During the years 1954 through 1959, Tidewater's capital expenditures for rebuilding, modernization, and expansion amounted to $775 million, of which 60 percent was internally generated. Sources of funds for this capital program were:

Long-term borrowing	$310 million
Depreciation, depletion, and amortization	300
Retained earnings	165

These expenditures again placed Tidewater in a leading competitive position in the oil industry.

Our shareholders are benefiting from this more aggressive financial policy and from the fact Tidewater has avoided the pitfall of borrowing money to pay dividends. Since 1953, the common shareholder's equity has increased by

---

[2] "President's Letter," *Annual Report*, Skelly Oil Company, 1959.
[3] "J. Paul Getty's Well-Heeled Woe," *Forbes*, October 15, 1959, p. 43.

more than 50 percent—from $19.32 a share to $30.49 per share at March 31, 1960. This, of course, does not reflect the real value of oil and gas reserves, which are carried on our books at cost. . . .

Tidewater's common stock is traded on the New York and Pacific Coast Stock Exchanges. Also, Tidewater can be purchased at a discount through Mission Development Company which owns 1.41 shares of Tidewater per each Mission Development share, yet currently sells around 17 compared to around 19 for Tidewater. Mission Development Company's sole holding is 6,942,955 shares or 47.48 percent of the outstanding common shares of Tidewater. . . .

Turning now to Tidewater's operations, in 1953 we recognized that while markets for our products would continue to grow, competition for those markets would increase in intensity. We felt the only way we would be able to compete successfully for future markets would be on the basis of efficiency and quality. The four refineries we had in 1953 met neither of these requirements. Therefore, we have since closed down three of our refineries, built the new Delaware refinery from the ground up and modernized our large refinery in California. Thus, we have two, large, modern, manufacturing centers, with capacity of 275,000 barrels per calendar day, capable of supplying us with the quantity and quality of products demanded by our customers.

For many years Tidewater has been a large purchaser of raw materials. On a net basis, we purchase half the raw materials processed in our refineries. One of our objectives in 1953—as it is today—was to increase our self-sufficiency in crude oil production. . . . Our efforts to become increasingly self-sufficient have been enhanced by the excellent results of our exploratory drilling. More than one third of Tidewater's exploratory wells drilled in the United States in the past five years have produced oil or gas, compared with only one sixth for the domestic industry as a whole.

As a result of this success, Tidewater's proved reserves reached new highs in 1959—693 million barrels of petroleum liquids and 3.5 trillion cubic feet of natural gas. As a measure for your consideration, this represents the equivalent per common share of stock of 50 barrels of petroleum liquids and 250,000 cubic feet of natural gas. At current valuations, these oil and gas reserves are worth $62.50 per share. . . .

Tidewater's picture will not be complete for you as analysts, I know, unless we take a look at the immediate future.

Our forecast is for a modest percentage rise in domestic oil consumption in 1960. Actually, this small percentage gain tends to obscure the fact that domestic oil consumption has been growing at an average rate of a thousand barrels every day for the last 15 years. This means that some 365,000 barrels of new oil a day are required each year to satisfy the constantly growing demand for petroleum products in the United States. I expect oil demand in the United States to grow at the rate of a thousand barrels or more a day for the foreseeable future.

We expect that Tidewater will share in the increase in business in 1960 as it did in 1959. While we cannot safely predict our 1960 earnings at this time, because so much depends upon the level of product prices, I anticipate they will be about the same as those of 1959. Our capital expenditures for the year are budgeted at $100 million, about the same as last year.

In summary, then, since 1953 Tidewater has changed its financial policies, built up the quality and effectiveness of its organization, modernized or rebuilt its principal operating plants, added significant new facilities, and expanded the scope and magnitude of its operations.

We stand now on the threshold of the sixties with an aggressive management, a strong and efficient organization, and the finest facilities in our entire history. Our achievements during this decade should be outstanding.

Reactions to the Getty Speech

According to *Forbes* magazine: "There is just one big drawback to Getty's formula: oilmen use it, but very few security analysts do." [4] Another view was expressed by Professor Donald A. Corbin of the University of California, Riverside:

It appears that oil company balance sheet figures for assets deviate materially from their current values. . . . Income was earned (but not reported because it was not "realized") when oil and gas reserves were discovered. . . . If the assets in the company's balance sheets are undervalued, then income statement figures are understated also.[5]

Questions

1. Identify the different concepts of value in this case. How do they differ from each other? Why?
2. How should the management of Tidewater Oil Company reflect in the company's financial statements the "value" of the oil and gas reserves discovered as a result of the exploration program?
3. Why do Tidewater and Skelly Oil value the Tidewater stock differently?

---

[4] "The Getty Formula," *Forbes*, July 1, 1960, p. 22.
[5] Donald A. Corbin, "Current Reading," *Journal of Accountancy*, October 1960, pp. 91–92.

CHAPTER 5

BASIC FINANCIAL STATEMENTS

The typical corporate annual report to stockholders contains four basic statements: a balance sheet, a statement of net income, a reconciliation of retained earnings, and a funds flow statement. In practice there are many variations in the titles, form, content, and coverage of these statements. For example, they may be for a parent company alone or for a consolidated entity representing the parent and its subsidiaries. Annual statements, in contrast to interim statements, are nearly always covered by a certified public accountant's opinion and are presented on a comparative basis with the previous year. Irrespective of their title or whether they are annual or interim statements, the function of these four basic statements is to communicate useful quantitative information of a financial nature about a business to stockholders, creditors, and others interested in the reporting company's financial condition, results of operations, and uses and sources of funds.

This chapter describes the purpose and contents of the typical balance sheet and income statement and the basic accounting mechanics used to record the transactions summarized by these statements. The statement of changes in retained earnings is discussed also. Chapter 5 also expands upon some of the definitions and concepts discussed in the previous chapter. The funds flow statement is covered in Chapter 7.

Objectives

According to the Accounting Principles Board *Statement No. 4*, "Basic Concepts and Accounting Principles Underlying Financial Statements of Business Enterprises," the general objectives of financial statements are:

1. To provide reliable financial information about the economic resources and obligations of a business enterprise and the changes in these items.

2. To provide reliable information about changes in the net resources of an enterprise that result from its profit-directed activities.
3. To provide financial information that assists in estimating the earnings potential of the enterprise.
4. To disclose to the extent possible other information related to the financial statements, such as the company's accounting policies, that is relevant to the statement user's needs.

General Requirements

All financial statements must carry the name of the reporting company, the dates of the period covered, and an indication of whether or not the statements and accompanying footnotes are audited. Unless otherwise indicated, it is presumed that the statements are for a going concern. However, in practice this assumption should not be accepted literally in all cases, since the future prospects of reporting companies for survival over the long run varies greatly. In addition, companies under the jurisdiction of the Securities and Exchange Commission should not publish statements that differ materially from those required to be filed with the Commission on an annual and interim basis.

Financial statements should present data that can be understood by users of the statements and in a form and with terminology compatible with the user's range of understanding. In practice, this requirement assumes the users have some basic familiarity with the business activities of the reporting entity, the financial accounting process, and the technical language used in financial statements.

Another basic requirement is that the comparative statements issued by a company be comparable. This requires that (1) the format of the statements be identical, (2) the same items from the underlying accounting records are classified under the same captions, (3) the accounting principles followed in preparing the statements are not changed (or if they are changed the changes and their effects are disclosed), (4) changes in the circumstances of the enterprise are disclosed, and (5) the comparative reporting periods are of equal length.

Other requirements include: the statements must be complete for the periods covered; the data must be communicated soon enough after the close of the accounting period to be useful to the statement users; and the disclosure of all data relevant to the users' needs must be adequate.

BALANCE SHEET

The balance sheet presents data related to a company's financial condition as of a specific time, based on the conventions and generally accepted principles of accounting. The amounts shown on this statement are the balances at the date of the statement in the various accounts listed in the company's accounting records. Thus, since any transactions will change these account balances in the company's books, all transactions can be described in terms of their effects on the balance sheet. It is for this reason that the balance sheet is often considered to be the fundamental accounting statement.

All balance sheets do not follow the same precise format or use the same account titles. However, within reasonable limits of flexibility the items on a balance sheet are typically grouped in the following general categories:

ASSETS	LIABILITIES AND OWNERS' EQUITY
Current assets xxx	Liabilities:
Long-term investment xxx	Current liabilities xxx
Fixed assets xxx	Long-term liabilities xxx
Other assets (sometimes divided into noncurrent, prepaid and deferred charges, and intangible assets) xxx	Other liabilities (sometimes divided into deferred credits and accumulated provisions).. xxx
	Total Liabilities xxx
	Owners' Equity:
	Capital stock xxx
	Other paid-in capital xxx
	Retained earnings xxx
	Total Owners' Equity xxx
Total Assets xxx	Total Liabilities and Owners' Equity xxx

The totals of the amounts listed in each of three major categories of the balance sheet conform to the basic accounting equation:

$$\text{Assets} = \text{Liabilities} + \text{owners' equity}$$

ASSETS

Assets represent valuable economic resources that are recognized and measured in conformity with generally accepted accounting principles and are acquired through the investment of the funds available to the business. These resources may be considered valuable for a variety of different reasons. For example, some expenditures, such as capitalized [1] research and development expenditures, are called assets because it is thought that they will contribute to the generation of income in future accounting periods. Some assets represent resources that can readily be converted into cash, such as accounts receivable. Other resources are called assets because they represent valuable property rights, such as the land owned by the business. Irrespective of the principal criterion used to determine if an item is

---

[1] An expenditure is said to be capitalized when it is recorded as an asset rather than an expense.

an asset or not, assets should not be carried at a value more than the lower of either their original cost or net realizable value through direct sale or use in future operations.[2]

Illustration 5–1 presents the asset section of a major corporation's consolidated balance sheet. The assets are divided into four categories that are common to many other statements—current assets, investment, property at cost, and other assets. The asset items are clearly described and the format is easy to follow. Although they are not shown, the footnotes to the statements provided additional information relevant to understanding the data in the asset section of the statement. For example, the method used to determine inventory values and the company's depreciation accounting policy were disclosed. This illustration will be used to explain briefly the nature of the asset accounts found on most balance sheets. A fuller explanation of these items is presented in subsequent chapters.

ILLUSTRATION 5–1

Asset Section of a Major Corporation's Consolidated Balance Sheet,
December 31, 1970
(in thousands)

Current Assets:

Cash	$ 39,274
United States government and other marketable securities, at lower of cost or market (quoted market value: 1970, $3,726,000)	3,722
Notes and accounts receivable (less estimated losses, 1970, $4,251,000)	165,288
Inventories	193,795
Prepayments and other current assets	9,979
Total Current Assets	$ 412,058

Investments:

Investments in jointly owned companies, at equity	$ 36,068
Investments in subsidiaries not consolidated, at cost or less	9,690
Other, at cost or less	9,739
Total Investments	$ 55,497

Property (at cost):

Land, buildings, machinery and equipment, etc.	$1,199,489
Less: Accumulated depreciation and depletion	594,085
Net Property	$ 605,404

Other Assets:

Excess of cost of investments in consolidated subsidiaries over equities in net assets, unamortized balance	$ 11,165
Deferred charges	10,629
Total Other Assets	$ 21,794
Total Assets	$1,094,753

---

[2] In early 1971 the Accounting Principles Board proposed that marketable securities be carried at their market value. Furthermore, it was proposed that any unrealized change in this value, irrespective of whether or not it represented appreciation or depreciation, was to be included in current income. If this practice were adopted it would be an important exception to the lower of cost or net realizable value rule.

Current Assets

According to APB Statement No. 4, "current assets include cash and other assets that are reasonably expected to be realized in cash or sold or consumed during the normal operating cycle of the business or within one year if the operating cycle is shorter than one year." The operating cycle can be represented as that period during which the series of events described in Illustration 5–2 occur in sequence.

ILLUSTRATION 5–2

Normal Operating Cycle Illustrated

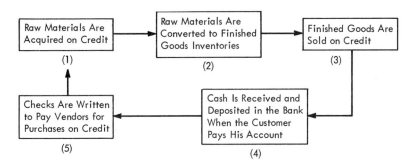

For most companies the operating cycle is less than 12 months. However, there are some notable exceptions. For example, one large bowling equipment manufacturer sold bowling alley equipment in return for long-term notes with payment schedules ranging up to seven years. These notes receivable from customers were classified as a current asset on the grounds that the company's "normal operating cycle" was seven years, since it took that long to complete all of the events related to each sale. Other more common examples of industries with operating cycles longer than one year are the distilling and tobacco industries. Their inventories must age for a long period of time before being offered for sale. In other cases, such as land development companies, no distinction is made between current and noncurrent assets, since the period during which land must be held for sale can be very long and the period over which the purchase price is paid by the buyer of the land even longer.

Current assets include cash, accounts receivable, marketable securities, and inventories. Cash is shown at its face value and includes cash on hand, undeposited checks at the date of the balance sheet, cash in banks and checks in transit to banks. Checks written by the company but not yet deposited and charged to the company's bank account are treated as if they had been deposited.

Sometimes corporations invest surplus cash on a temporary basis in securities that can be readily sold under normal conditions. These marketable securities are held for investment purposes rather than to control the operations of the entity issuing the securities. Typically these securities, as in Illustration 5–1, are short-term obligations of the United States government. Marketable securities are presented at the lower of their cost or current market. In addition, their current market value is shown parenthetically (i.e., in brackets next to the account).

Notes and accounts receivable represent the claims against customers generated by credit sales for amounts still due to the company. The balance of such an account only includes billings for services performed on or before the balance sheet date. The amount presented in the balance sheet is net of the company's estimated losses from uncollectible accounts. The procedures used to estimate these amounts is described in Chapter 9.

Inventories include tangible items that will be either sold directly or included in the production of items that will be sold in the normal course of operations. The inventory account shown in Illustration 5–1 probably includes three types of inventory: a finished goods inventory, consisting of products ready for sale; a work in process inventory, consisting of products in various stages of production; and a raw materials and supplies inventory, consisting of items that will enter directly or indirectly into the production of finished goods.

Inventories are carried at cost, unless their utility is no longer as great as their cost. The so-called "lower of cost or market" rule to determine if the carrying value of inventories should be written down below cost is covered in Chapter 17. This same chapter discusses also the alternative methods for determining the cost value of inventories shown on the balance sheet. These methods include the first-in, first-out method, which values the inventory on the balance sheet date at the most recent cost; and the last-in, first-out method, which uses the oldest cost of goods in inventory to value the asset inventory.

The current assets category may include other accounts which will be realized during the normal operating cycle. Examples are unbilled costs on construction contracts performed by contractors for customers, prepaid insurance and expenses where the benefits to be derived from the prepayment extend beyond the current accounting period, and tax refunds receivable. Even though they do not result in a conversion into cash, prepaid expenses are listed among current assets. This practice is followed because the use of cash during the operating cycle would be required if there were no prepayment.

It is customary to list current assets in their descending order of liquidity. For example, in Illustration 5–1 cash is listed first, marketable securities next, and then accounts receivable. Marketable securities precede accounts receivable because, of the two items, marketable securities can more easily be turned into cash by management. For a similar reason, inventories are listed after accounts receivable but before prepayments.

Long-Term Investments

Investments made in other companies are carried on the balance sheet as noncurrent items when the investing company's objective is one of control, affiliation, or some continuing business relationship with the company and the circumstances of the investment do not require the subsidiary to be consolidated. These investments may be common stock, debt securities, or long-term advances. It is not customary to state the market value of such noncurrent investments, since it is assumed that there is no present intention to sell the securities. These securities may be carried at their original cost or at an amount equal to the investing company's original cost plus its proportional share of the subsidiary's retained earnings. This latter approach is called the equity method. Chapter 6, "Consolidated Statements," explains the cost and equity methods in greater detail.

Illustration 5–1 shows three types of long-term investments and their valuation basis: investments in joint ventures, valued according to the equity method; investments in unconsolidated subsidiaries, valued by the cost method at their original cost or less (these subsidiaries could be overseas subsidiaries in countries with unusual economic or political problems that limit the parent company's *control* over their operations); and other miscellaneous long-term investments, shown at cost or less. Investments are shown at less than their original cost when there has been a permanent loss in their value.

Fixed Assets

Long-lived tangible assets, such as equipment acquired to produce goods for sale, are referred to as "fixed assets." Assets in this category are land, buildings, machinery, equipment and any other long-lived tangible items used in the company's operations. These assets are stated at their original cost less depreciation, rather than at their replacement value or current market value. The one exception is land, which is always stated at its original cost.

Depreciation represents the decline in the useful economic value of an asset due to use and obsolescence. An annual charge for depreciation is included in the expenses of current operations. The amount of this depreciation expense is related to the anticipated useful life of the asset, which may be computed on the basis of either expected years of service or actual use (i.e., hours of operation, units produced, etc.). The accumulated amount of depreciation expense related to the fixed assets still carried on the books of the company is presented on the balance sheet in an account called "accumulated depreciation." Sometimes the term "reserve for depreciation" is used. However, it is gradually being abandoned in favor of "allowance for depreciation" or "accumulated depreciation."

Chapter 14, "Depreciation Accounting," discusses the various depreciation methods. The two principal approaches to depreciation are the straight-line and accelerated methods. Straight-line depreciation allocates the cost of a fixed asset, less any estimated salvage value, equally to operations over the life of the asset. Accelerated depreciation methods charge a greater proportion of an asset's total depreciation to operations during the early years of its life than during the latter years.

It is customary, as presented in Illustration 5–1 under the caption "property (at cost)," to show both the original cost and the depreciated book value of the fixed assets available for use in operations. The difference between these two amounts, accumulated depreciation, is shown as a deduction from the total original cost of the fixed assets to arrive at the net book value of the assets. This net book value, called "net property" in Illustration 5–1, seldom reflects the current market value of the asset. It is simply the balance left in the property accounts of the company's accounting books or records after deducting the related accumulated depreciation charges.

Illustration 5–1 refers to "accumulated depreciation and depletion." The term *depletion* relates to investments in natural resources, whereas the term *depreciation* is associated with plant and equipment investments. Depletion is the amount of a company's investment in natural resources that is charged to operations over the period during which these resources are extracted or exhausted. Accumulated depletion is the cumulative total of these charges related to the natural resource investments still available to the company for the generation of future revenues. Depletion is often charged on a units-of-production basis.

Other Assets

Items included in the "other assets" category include tangible assets and deferred charges. Intangible assets are long-term assets that are not of a tangible nature. Assets that fall into this category are patents, trademarks, copyrights, and franchises. To be recorded, these assets must be created or acquired through a business transaction. Intangible assets are carried at cost initially and then charged to operations in a systematic manner over their useful life. Chapter 16 covers the topic of intangible assets in greater detail.

Illustration 5–1 lists an intangible asset labeled "excess of cost of investments in consolidated subsidiaries over equities in net assets, unamortized balance." The popular name for this item is "goodwill." It arises when a company purchases another company for a price in excess of the net book or fair market value of its assets. Goodwill, which is the difference between the purchase price and the net asset values acquired, must be charged to operations over a period of not more than 40 years. However, the actual period used varies greatly from company to company. The accounting for business acquisitions and goodwill is covered in Chapter 18, "Intercorporate Investments and Business Combinations."

Deferred charges are very similar in nature to prepaid expenses, since both are payments or accruals recognized before the balance sheet date that properly should be charged to operations subsequent to that date. However, it is important to distinguish between them, since prepaid expenses are a current asset and deferred charges are assigned to the other-asset category. Prepaid expenses relate to amounts paid for services yet to be received from the seller. In contrast, deferred charges represent amounts paid for services already received by the business. For example, the prepayment of the premiums on a three-year insurance policy is a prepaid expense, since the insurance protection has yet to be received. In contrast, expenditures for product research and development that are expected to produce benefits beyond the current period are considered a deferred charge, since the company has already received the service.

LIABILITIES

The APB's Statement No. 4 defines liabilities as:

Economic obligations of an enterprise that are recognized and measured in conformity with generally accepted accounting principles. Liabilities also include certain deferred credits that are not obligations but that are recognized and measured in conformity with generally accepted accounting principles.

Liabilities include all of those claims of a nonownership type against the business by outsiders. Stated another way, they represent the amounts owed to creditors. These obligations include such items as amounts due to vendors, bank loans payable, and debentures outstanding.

Liabilities are claims against all assets. In those cases where liabilities relate to specific assets, it is not acceptable to show the liability as a deduction from the asset. For example, the mortgage on a building is shown on the right-hand or liability side of the balance sheet and the asset "building" is listed on the left-hand side.

The accounting concept of liabilities is broader than liabilities in the popular sense of legal debts and obligations. The accounting concept includes certain deferred credits that do not involve a debtor-creditor relationship. For example, for accounting purposes, the seller's profit on a sale and lease-back transaction is not recognized in the income statement as a gain at the time of the sale. The preferred treatment is to list the profit as a deferred credit on the right-hand side of the balance sheet and allocate this amount to the income statement as a reduction to lease rentals over the life of the lease. This practice leads to a better matching of costs and revenues.

Illustration 5–3 presents an example of the right-hand side of a major corporation's consolidated balance sheet, the liabilities and owners' equity section. Taken together, Illustrations 5–1 and 5–3 comprise this company's entire balance sheet with the exception of the related footnotes.

Current Liabilities

Current liabilities are defined as: (1) those liabilities that the company expects to satisfy with either assets classified as current in the same balance sheet or the creation of other current liabilities; (2) all obligations arising from operations directly related to the company's operating cycle; or (3) those liabilities expected to be satisfied during the following year. The one-year rule is widely considered to be the cutoff between current and noncurrent liabilities. However, if the enterprise's operating cycle is longer than 12 months, an exception is made to this rule.

Current liabilities include the current portion (i.e., due within 12 months) of notes payable to banks, amounts owed to trade creditors, wages earned by employees but not paid to them, and funds received in advance for services not yet rendered. The order of presentation followed in the current liability section of Illustration 5–3 is typical of most balance sheets.

The captions of the various current liabilities listed in Illustration 5–3 are almost self-explanatory. Notes payable to banks represent the company's obligations to banks arising from short-term borrowing arrangements. The amount shown as the current maturities on long-term debt is a portion of the long-term debt's principal that must be repaid during the next 12 months. Accounts payable represent the claims of trade creditors for goods and services provided on an open account basis. If these trade obligations were evidenced by a note or similar written promise to pay, they would be included with notes payable. The sundry accruals combined with the accounts payable in Illustration 5–3 are most probably items such as wages owed to employees or deposits owed to customers on returnable containers not yet returned. The taxes owed as of the balance sheet date to various taxing authorities that will be paid during the next 12 months are included in the obligation listed as "domestic and foreign taxes on income."

Long-Term Liabilities

Long-term liabilities are all of an enterprise's noncurrent liabilities. They are often subdivided on the balance sheet into several different categories.

ILLUSTRATION 5–3

Liability and Owners' Equity Section of a Major Corporation's
Consolidated Balance Sheet, December 31, 1970
(in thousands)

LIABILITIES

Current Liabilities:
Notes payable—banks	$ 59,504
Current maturities of long-term debt	7,953
Accounts payable and sundry accruals	113,953
Domestic and foreign taxes on income	19,700
Total Current Liabilities	$ 201,110

Long-Term Debt:
5⅝% Sinking fund debentures	$ 125,000
4½% Term loan	42,088
Other	26,666
Total Long-Term Debt	$ 193,754

Deferred credits:
Deferred income tax	$ 36,186
Investment credit—unamortized balance	17,959
Other	1,793
Total Deferred Credits	$ 55,938

Accumulated Provisions:
Maintenance and repairs	$ 6,623
Insurance and unfunded and uninsured pensions	3,733
Foreign operations	543
Total Accumulated Provisions	$ 10,899

Capital and Retained Earnings:
Cumulative preferred stock—authorized 5,000,000 shares, without par value; no shares issued	....
Common stock—authorized, 50,000,000 shares, par value $2.50 each; issued, 1970, 21,721,988 shares	$ 212,850
Earnings retained for use in the business	462,972
Less common stock in treasury, 1970, 1,245,420 shares at cost	(42,770)
Total Capital and Retained Earnings	$ 633,052
Total Liabilities	$1,094,753

For example, the long-term liabilities shown in Illustration 5–3 are presented in three groups: long-term debt, deferred credits, and accumulated provisions.

Long-term debt represents those debt obligations of a company that will mature beyond one year's time. These obligations are recorded at their principal value. In the case of bank loans, this is the amount borrowed. Similarly, bonds, debentures and other long-term debt instruments are recorded at the amount of principal stated on the face of the instrument. The current interest on these obligations is charged to operating income as the interest obligation is incurred. Chapter 21 discusses the accounting for long-term debt in greater detail.

Deferred credits are the opposite of deferred charges. They are unearned revenues, such as subscriptions collected in advance of providing the service; or deferred profits, such as the deferral of profit on a sale and lease-back transaction. Another important class of deferred credits results from charges required by generally accepted accounting principles to current or past income in advance of the actual expenditure or obligation being incurred, such as the deferred credit resulting from income tax allocation requirements (see below). Some deferred credits, such as subscriptions received in advance, are obligations, whereas others, such as deferred sale and lease-back profits, are not.

Illustration 5–3 shows two significant deferred credits: namely, the deferred income tax and the unamortized investment credit items. Both of these accounts and the controversy surrounding them are covered in Chapter 12.

Deferred income tax represents the amount of the company's potential income tax obligation that the company has deferred from past periods to future periods by following different accounting practices for book and tax purposes. For example, deferred income tax arises in situations where a company uses straight-line depreciation for book purposes and accelerated depreciation for its tax returns. If the company's depreciable assets are new, this can result in a lower income for tax purposes than that reported to stockholders, since the depreciation charge for tax reporting purposes is bigger than the book depreciation expense. In such situations, the Accounting Principles Board decided that the tax expense calculation for book purposes should be based on the profits before tax reported to stockholders, rather than the taxable income actually used to determine the company's current income tax payments. Thus, in the example, the company's current book tax expense will be greater than actual payments due to the government. The difference between the tax actually due and the book tax expense recognized is the addition to the deferred tax account. This amount is not a legal obligation like long-term debt. It simply results from the accounting requirement to reconcile book tax expenses recognized and actual taxes paid. Double-entry bookkeeping forces the recognition of this deferred tax item on the liability side of the balance sheet when the cumulative tax payments actually made or due to the government lag behind the cumulative tax expenses recognized for book purposes.

During the 1960s the federal government granted an investment tax credit for certain qualified investments in tangible property. In the case of qualified property with a life of eight or more years, an investment credit was granted equal to 7 percent of the property's cost. This amount was deducted from the company's current tax bill. Some companies, for book purposes, recognized the full benefit of this reduction of taxes during the period in which the credit was granted. Other companies spread the tax expense reduction benefit over the life of the asset giving rise to the credit. This is the method adopted by the company in Illustration 5–3.

Accumulated provisions are estimates of (*a*) an admitted liability of an uncertain amount, as in the case of reserves for possible storm damages; (*b*) the probable amount of disputed claims, such as reserves for additional taxes; or (*c*) a liability or loss which is not certain to occur but is so likely to do so as to require current recognition, as in the case of a reserve for self-insurance. Illustration 5–3 presents three examples of accumulated provisions. Each of these represents an item that the company concedes may involve future obligations that are not precisely determinable in amount, but nevertheless can be estimated currently with a reasonable degree of reliability. Each of these accounts is discussed below.

In some companies, the need for maintenance and repairs is level and the annual charges are constant. In other companies, the need fluctuates from year to year. Many companies in these industries charge to operations a fixed amount each year for maintenance and repairs. These charges to income are accumulated in the liability account "accumulated provision for maintenance and repairs." Actual expenditures for maintenance and repairs are then charged directly to this liability account.

The account "insurance and unfunded and uninsured pensions" listed in Illustration 5–3 results from charges to income to establish a reserve for self-insurance against certain future losses. In particular, the company appears to be making some provision for future pension obligations that might arise because the company's pension fund is not fully funded or insured. This can occur when the company knows it has a liability under the pension plan but the ultimate amount of the liability is not determinable with confidence because of the uncertainty inherent in the actuarial estimates used to determine the potential liability.

The provision for foreign operations represents the recognition by management that they have sustained some losses overseas, but the amount of the losses is uncertain. The provision was set up by a charge to income. When the extent of the losses is known, they will be charged to the liability account. Any actual losses in excess of the amount set aside in the liability account will be charged to income directly.

OWNERS' EQUITY

Owners' equity represents the interest of the owners in an enterprise. It is the balance that remains after deducting the total liabilities of the enterprise from its total assets. For most companies the residual owners' interest determined in this fashion bears little relationship to the actual market value of that interest. Two companies identical in all respects except their accounting policy could show in the balance sheets very different values for their owners' equity. The company with the more conservative accounting practices would report the lower book value for owners' equity. Yet the market value of the two companies should be the same.

Illustration 5–3 presents the owners' equity for our example company under the caption "capital and retained earnings." Other terms used to describe the owners' equity are "net worth," "net assets," and "stockholders' equity." Chapter 22 covers equity capital transactions.

The *capital* section of the balance sheet lists (1) the amount and type of capital stock authorized, (2) the number of shares issued, (3) the net amount received by the company for the issued stock, and (4) the number of shares and acquisition costs of the company's own stock held by the company. Illustration 5–3 shows that the company's stockholders have authorized five million shares of no-par value preferred stock, but none have been issued. The authorized number of shares represents the maximum number of shares the company may sell under the terms of its charter. Thus, the principal source of the company's capital from stock issues was the 21.7 million shares of $2.50 par value common stock sold at various times to the public for a total consideration of $212 million.

Rather than showing, as in Illustration 5–3, the value of the total consideration received from the issuance of common stock, a preferred approach is to value the common stock account at the par value of the securities issued. Then, if the company sells any of this stock for more than its par value, this excess is shown in an account labeled "capital received in excess of par value of stock issued." This account appears immediately below the common stock account.

The *earnings retained in the business* (or simply, retained earnings) account represents the balance of net profits, income, and gains and losses of the enterprise from the date of incorporation, after deducting distributions of dividends to shareholders. In addition, under some circumstances transfers may be made from retained earnings to the capital stock accounts. As indicated in Illustration 5–3, this account presents the value of the resources, earned by the business through profit-directed activities, that are retained for use in the business. Another common but less acceptable term used to describe this item is "earned surplus."

Data related to issued stock reacquired by the issuing company are presented in the *treasury stock* account. This stock is carried at its acquisition cost and is always presented as a deduction from the owners' equity. Accounting regards only the stock actually in the hands of the stockholders as outstanding stock for computing earnings per share. This is different from the legal position that considers all stock not formally retired to be outstanding.

INCOME STATEMENT

The results of operations of a business for a period of time are presented in the income statement.[3] From the accounting systems point of view, the

---

[3] Common alternative titles are: statement of profit and loss, statement of earnings, and statement of operations.

income statement is subordinate to the balance sheet, since the income statement simply presents the details of the changes in the retained earnings balance sheet account. In contrast to this limited perspective, however, for most users of financial statements the income statement is a more important source of information than the balance sheet.

Statement No. 4

The elements of a business's profit-directed operations and their net results can be represented by the equation:

$$\text{Revenues} - \text{expenses} = \text{Net income (net loss)}$$

The income statement presents the details of this expression in a commonly agreed upon format according to generally accepted accounting principles.

Revenue is defined in Statement No. 4 as

Gross increases in assets or gross decreases in liabilities recognized and measured in conformity with generally accepted accounting principles that result from those types of profit-directed activities of an enterprise that can change owners' equity.

Not all increases in assets or decreases in liabilities are included in revenue. For example, the receipt of cash from a bank loan is not revenue. This transaction does not change owners' equity. It increases an asset (cash) and a liability (bank loans payable). In contrast, a cash sale of inventory in the normal course of business is revenue. It increases the asset cash and changes the owners' equity account retained earnings. If the goods are sold at a profit, retained earnings will increase by the amount of the profit.

Statement No. 4 defines *expenses* as:

Gross decreases in assets or gross increases in liabilities recognized and measured in conformity with generally accepted accounting principles that result from those types of profit-directed activities of an enterprise that can change owners' equity.

Like revenues, expenses can only result from profit-directed activities that change owners' equity. The reduction of inventory as the result of a sale is an expense, since the net result of this transaction is a change in the owners' equity account retained earnings. The purchase of an inventory on credit is not an expense, since this does not change owners' equity. The purchase increases the asset inventory and the liability trade payables.

Although the payment of dividends reduces owners' equity, it is not an expense. This transaction reduces cash and the owners' equity account returned earnings, but it is not a profit-directed activity. It is a distribution of capital.

Given these definitions of revenues and expenses, Statement No. 4 concludes that net income (net loss) is.

The excess (deficit) of revenue over expenses for an accounting period, which is the net increase (net decrease) in owners' equity (assets minus liabilities) of an enterprise for an accounting period from profit-directed activities that is recognized and measured in conformity with generally accepted accounting principles.

Chapter 9 discusses the many problems associated with income recognition. Particular aspects of expense measurement are discussed in a number of different chapters.

Basic Conventions

Four basic conventions discussed in the last chapter influence the preparation of the income statement. These are the accrual concept, the accounting period concept, the realization concept, and the matching concept. Each will be reviewed here briefly.

The *accrual concept* relates revenues and expenses to changes in owners' equity, not cash. Statements prepared on this basis recognize and report the effects of transactions and other events on the assets and liabilities of a business in the time period to which they relate, rather than only when cash is received or paid. Accordingly, for example, wage expense is recognized when labor services are performed, not when the workers are paid.

The *accounting period* is the segment of time covered by the income statement. All events affecting income determination occurring during this period should be measured and recorded in the company's accounting records and assigned to this period for income determination purposes. The accounting period is bounded by a beginning and ending balance sheet. The income statement relates to the changes in owners' equity from one balance sheet date to another due to profit-directed activities.

The *realization concept*, according to Statement No. 4, holds that "revenue is generally recognized when both of the following conditions are met: (1) the earnings process is complete or virtually complete and (2) an exchange has taken place." For example, interest revenue from loans to others is recognized as time passes, since that, assuming the borrower is solvent, is the critical event dictating the timing and amount of interest receivable.

The *matching concept* recognizes that some costs have a presumed direct association with specific revenues or time periods. This is a process of associating cause and effect. It is through this matching process that income is determined.

Expenditures and Expenses

A troublesome accounting problem is the determination whether a purchase results in an asset or an expense. An expenditure occurs whenever an asset or service is purchased. At the moment of the transaction, all expenditures for purchases can be thought to result in assets. These assets will then become expenses if they (*a*) are directly or indirectly related or associated with the revenue of the period, or (*b*) suffer a loss during the period in their future revenue-generating capacity, such as in the case of assets destroyed by fire or patents carried as assets in prior periods that now become worthless due to the development of a new technology.

Statement Format

A common order of items in the income statement is:

1. Revenues (the sales for the period).
2. Cost of sales (the manufacturing or acquisition costs of the goods sold during the period).
3. Gross profit or margin (the difference between revenues and cost of sales; item 1 less item 2).
4. Operating expenses (the selling, administration, and general expenses associated with operating the company's principal business activity during the period).
5. Operating income (item 3 less item 4).
6. Nonoperating revenues (revenues derived from sources other than operations during the period, such as interest on the temporary investment of excess cash).
7. Nonoperating expenses (expenses not directly related to the principal business activity and the financial costs of borrowed money).
8. Provision for taxes (the income tax expense, based on item 5 plus item 6 less item 7).
9. Income before extraordinary items (item 5 plus item 6 less item 7 plus item 8).
10. Extraordinary items.[4] (These are nonrecurring, unusual gains or losses not related to the company's normal operations or business activities. These items are all shown net of their tax effect.)
11. Net income (item 9 less item 10).

An alternative form of income statement is shown in Illustration 5–4. This statement omits the gross and operating profit calculations. It is

---

[4] Chapter 10, "Results of Operations," discusses extraordinary items.

ILLUSTRATION 5-4

EXAMPLE: A MAJOR CORPORATION'S SINGLE-STEP
INCOME STATEMENT

Statement of Earnings for the Year Ended December 31, 1970

Net sales	$1,962,487,755
Costs and expenses:	
Cost of products sold	$1,445,785,281
Selling, advertising, general, and administrative expenses	182,507,421
Interest and debt expense	7,581,223
	$1,635,873,925
Earnings before provision for taxes	$ 326,613,830
Provision for federal and state taxes on income	176,569,000
Net Earnings	$ 150,044,830

known as single-step statement. Each of the items on this statement will be discussed briefly.

The *net sales* figure represents the company's net sales during the calendar year 1970. It is derived by deducting from gross sales any sales returns, allowances, and discounts. The gross sales amount is the invoice price of the goods and services sold. Sales returns and allowances result from the credit given to customers for sales returns or defective goods. Sales discounts are discounts granted to customers for prompt payment of amounts owed to the seller. Sometimes this item is shown as a sales expense rather than as a reduction of gross sales. Discounts from list price granted to members of the seller's trade do not enter into the accounting records. These sales are recorded at the actual invoice price.

Cost of products sold is the manufactured cost or, in the case of merchandising companies, the purchase price of the goods sold during the period. The manufactured cost includes the cost of direct labor, raw materials, and some manufacturing overhead. The amount of cost of goods sold expense matched with current revenues will depend in large part on the company's inventory valuation practices, since any current expenditures for products not included in cost of products sold must be assigned to the inventory account.

Selling, advertising, general, and administrative expenses are all of the expenses incurred for these activities during the accounting period. Generally these expenditures are not assumed to have a lasting value beyond the current period. Therefore they are related directly to the current accounting period for income determination purposes.

Interest and debt expenses are financial charges. It is customary to segregate these items from operating expenses. This approach assumes that users of the statements wish (1) to identify and evaluate the cost of financing operations, and (3) to determine whether or not management's return from operations is adequate, given the financing costs.

Earnings before provision for taxes are the basis for determining the company's tax expense. It should be remembered that this amount most likely will be different from the taxable income shown on the company's tax returns. Two common reasons for this difference are that some cost items included in the income statement are not recognized for tax purposes, and that some revenue items recognized currently to determine book income are deferred to future periods for tax purposes.

Provisions for federal and state taxes on income will, for most companies, consist of two parts: the taxes actually payable based on the income shown in the current tax return, and the taxes recognized for book purposes for which there is no current tax liability. This latter type of account expense is the source of the changes in deferred tax liability discussed earlier.

Net earnings, or net income, is the final figure on the statement. It represents the net impact of profit-directed activities on owners' equity after considering all items of profit and loss recognized during the period.

Interrelationship

The items on the income statement and the balance sheet are interrelated. For example, when a credit sale is made revenues and accounts receivable both increase. In addition, the sale causes finished goods inventory to decline and cost of goods sold to increase, and the increased tax expense related to the profit on the sale causes taxes payable to increase. Therefore, in order to gain a full appreciation of any item on one statement, it is necessary to examine also the related items on the other.

Changes in Owners' Equity

The income statement alone can not be relied upon to present all of the changes in owners' equity during an accounting period. It relates only to profit-directed activities. Therefore, to describe the changes due to capital additions and disbursements an additional statement or disclosure is required.

Typically, the changes in retained earnings are presented in a statement of changes in retained earnings and any changes in the capital stock accounts are described in the notes to the financial statements. The statement of retained earnings is the link between the net income figure and changes in the retained earnings during the period. Usually, it follows this format:

1. Beginning retained earnings (the balance at the beginning of the accounting period).
2. Net income (shown in the income statement for the period).
3. Dividends paid to common stockholders.

4. Ending retained earnings (the amount appearing in the balance sheet at the end of the period—equal to item 1 plus item 2 less item 3).

OTHER CONSIDERATIONS

Footnotes

Financial statements are inevitably accompanied by footnotes. These are an integral part of the statements. The functions of footnotes are:

1. To amplify the numerical data and descriptive captions presented on the face of the statements by giving such details as the requirements of bond indentures and the terms of lease agreements.
2. To present additional information on events that may subsequently affect the data reported, such as contingencies that may arise from outstanding legal suits or the future audit of current tax returns by the tax authorities.
3. To disclose events that have occurred subsequent to the balance sheet date that may materially affect the statement users' evaluation of the data presented but not require adjustment to the statements, such as an issue of debentures after the balance sheet date.
4. To identify the particular accounting methods used to prepare the statements and the impact on key financial statistics of any changes in these methods.
5. To disclose commitments of an unusual nature, such as a major plant expansion program.

Auditor's Report

The auditor's report accompanying financial statements should always be read in conjunction with the statements. It is important for anyone using the statements to know the auditor's appraisal of the statements.

Financial statements are the direct responsibility of the management and directors of the reporting company. Although the company's public auditor may assist and advise management in its preparation of the statements, management alone is responsible for their contents. Management is not compelled to follow the auditor's advice. However, the auditor does have a responsibility in his report accompanying the statements to state whether or not he agrees with the fairness of the financial presentation. In practice, it is this duty of the auditor to state exceptions in his report that brings reluctant managements to accept the auditor's recommendation in those cases where differences of opinion exist between management and auditors. Chapter 8 discusses in greater detail the nature of the auditor's opinion and his basis for reaching this opinion.

Interim Statements

Most corporations publish at least quarterly condensed income statements for the quarter and the year to date on a comparative basis with the same periods during the previous year. A few companies also present in their quarterly reports a condensed balance sheet as of the end of the quarter.

Considerable caution should be exercised when using quarterly statements, since:

1. There is no common agreement as to whether or not the statements should be reports on (*a*) the actual events that occurred during the period, or (*b*) the actual events modified in some way to make the report more useful as a prediction of year-end results.
2. Quarterly statements are usually unaudited. Some managements in trouble take advantage of this to hide their problems from stockholders during the year in the hope that all can be made right by year-end.
3. Adjustments to data reported in earlier interim statements and decisions to change accounting methods are made usually during the fourth quarter. This results from the fact more data are available as year-end approaches; management has a better feel of whether or not it can reach its earnings goals as a result of operations; and lax accounting practices are revealed by the auditor, who during this period is spending an increasing amount of time with the company conducting his audit related to the annual statements.
4. Comparisons of the current interim results with those of the same period during the prior year may not be entirely valid, because the structure of the business may be constantly expanding and changing.
5. Annual predictions based on interim results may be misleading due to the seasonality of the business.

Despite these limitations, a number of authorities on stock price determinants believe interim results influence stock market price movements more than the information in annual statements.

Many hope that the impetus for improving the reporting standards governing quarterly financial statements will be the new SEC regulation requiring that quarterly statements be filed with the Commission.

Pro Forma Statements

Few companies include pro forma statements for future periods or dates in their public reports. Pro forma statements sometimes appear in a prospectus to show the expected results of combining or modifying historical statements of companies being acquired or combined. Some accounting authorities advocate that annual reports should disclose in summary form the reporting companies' budgeted results for the next annual period. It is argued that these data would provide stockholders with a better basis for evaluating management's planning capabilities and how well management achieved its objectives for the reporting period. In addition, it would put the current results into better perspective.

The accounting profession has not encouraged pro forma reporting because of the problems associated with objectively auditing these reports. Managements have been reluctant to publish these data, since they often consider budget data to be competitive data that should not be revealed publicly.

Summary of Financial Results

In addition to the financial statements covered by the auditor's opinion, annual reports typically include two sets of summary financial statistics. First, inside the front cover, and opposite the chief executive officer's letter to the stockholders that inevitably begins the text of the report, selected statistical data on a two-year comparative basis are shown related to such items as current earnings per share, sales volume, dividends per share, return on investment, net income as a percentage of sales, and the ratio of current assets to current liabilities. Second, usually following the footnotes to the financial statements, a 10-year statistical summary is presented. The basic data included in this summary are similar to that covered in the two-year statistical presentation at the beginning of the report. Additional statistics presented may include such data as the number of employees, the number of common shares outstanding, and the preferred dividends paid per share.

These statistical summaries are not covered by the auditor's opinion. However, for companies under the jurisdiction of the SEC these disclosures should not be materially different from the data presented in the audited statements.

Text

Most annual reports include textual material describing, primarily in qualitative terms, the companies' activities, plans, and problems. A thorough reading of this material is essential for anyone trying to determine the significance of the communication contained in the financial statements.

BASIC ACCOUNTING MECHANICS

So far, we have discussed the effect of individual transactions in terms of their impact on the balance sheet, with little concern for accounting mechanics. This section of Chapter 5 will present a systematic procedure to record and summarize transactions. It might be called simple book-keeping, but it is not our objective to train bookkeepers. The objective is to help the reader learn how to reduce, in an efficient manner, a complex set of business facts to the comprehensible set of relationships expressed in financial statements.

Accounts

Accountants use a series of accounts to record transactions. These accounts correspond to the items shown on the financial statements. The simplest form of account, and the one we will use, is a T account. The cash account of a company might look like this:

Cash

	(Increases)	(Decreases)
Beginning balance	100,000	3,000
	5,000	8,000
	20,000	40,000
	10,000	
	135,000	51,000
New beginning balance	84,000	

All of the increases in cash are shown on one side. All of the decreases are recorded on the other. The new balance is determined by (1) adding all of the amounts listed on the increases and decreases side, and (2) subtracting these totals from each other.

Debit-Credit Mechanism

Each accounting transaction has two parts. This is the dual aspect convention discussed in Chapter 4. It is reflected in the statement "the payment of an accounts receivable increases cash and reduces accounts receivable." This statement uses laymen's language to describe what occurred. The accountant would describe this transaction in terms of the debit-credit mechanism.

The accountant uses the term *debit* (dr.) to describe that part of a transaction that:

1. Increases an asset account.
2. Decreases a liability account.
3. Decreases an owners' equity account.
4. Decreases a revenue account.
5. Increases an expense account.

The term *credit* (cr.) is used to describe that part of the transaction that:

1. Decreases an asset account.
2. Increases a liability account.
3. Increases an owners' equity account.
4. Increases a revenue account.
5. Decreases an expense account.

The reader is encouraged to memorize these debit-credit rules rather than to try and determine their algebraic relationship to the basic accounting equation: Assets = Liabilities + owners' equity.

Here are some examples of the debit-credit terminology used to describe transactions:

1. A company borrows $10,000 cash from the bank. The accounting effect of the transaction is:

    Dr. Cash 10,000
    Cr.   Bank Notes Payable 10,000

2. The company repays the loan. The accountant would describe the transaction as:

    Dr. Bank Notes Payable 10,000
    Cr.   Cash 10,000

The words debit and credit have no meaning in accounting other than the following: debit means the amount is entered on the left-hand side of the T account; credit means the amount is entered on the right-hand side of the T account. The words carry no moral judgment. Depending on the account involved, they can be "desirable" or "undesirable" from the company's point of view. These are neutral terms.

Illustration 5–5 shows the relationship between T accounts and the debit-credit mechanism. The reader should note that because debit and credit are used to signify the left and right sides of the T account, the side used to record an increase or a decrease depends on the account. For example, increases in assets are recorded on the left or debit side, whereas increases in liabilities are listed on the right or credit side.

An Example

The following problem will be used to illustrate the steps in the process that you can use to prepare the financial statements required in your case problems.

Climax Industries, Inc., a new company started on January 1, 1970, sold at the beginning of the year 10,000 shares of $5 par value common stock for $50,000. The company bought for cash $20,000 worth of raw materials and processing equipment worth $10,000. During the year the company had sales of $45,000, of which $5,000 was still owed by customers at year-end; consumed $15,000 worth of raw materials; spent

ILLUSTRATION 5-5

Debit-Credit Rules

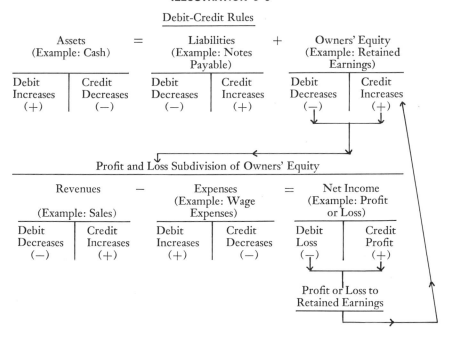

$10,000 cash on wages; and paid $5,000 cash for administration, rent, and selling activities. During the year the company also bought $15,000 of raw materials for which it still owed $5,000 at the end of the year. Dividends of $2,000 were declared and paid at year-end. The company anticipates it will have no bad debts. Your assignment is to prepare an income statement for the period and a balance sheet as of the end of the year. (Disregard taxes.)

The first step is to *analyze* the transactions and record them in the debit-credit form. This is called *journalizing original entries.* It is purely mechanical. Here are the journal entries. To help you understand the debit-credit decisions better, each account will be labeled *A* if it is an asset account, *L* if it is a liability account, and *OE* if it is an owners' equity account.

1. To record the sale of capital stock for cash:

    Dr. Cash (*A*) 50,000
    Cr.   Capital Stock (*OE*)   50,000

2. To record the initial purchase of raw materials for cash:

    Dr. Raw Materials Inventory (*A*) 20,000
    Cr.   Cash (*A*)   20,000

3. To record the purchase of processing equipment for cash:

    Dr. Processing Equipment (*A*) 10,000
    Cr.   Cash (*A*)   10,000

4. To record the sales during the period:

    Dr. Cash (A) ....,,,,,,,   ,,,,,,,,........ 40,000
        Accounts Receivable (A) 5,000
    Cr.   Sales (OE) 45,000

5. To record the period's wage expense:

    Dr. Wage Expense (OE) 10,000
    Cr.   Cash (A) 10,000

6. To record the period's administration, rent and selling expense:

    Dr. Administration, Rent and Selling Expense (OE) 5,000
    Cr.   Cash (A) 5,000

7. To record the purchase of raw materials during the year:

    Dr. Raw Materials Inventory (A) 15,000
    Cr.   Cash (A) 10,000
        Accounts Payable (L) 5,000

8. To record dividend declaration and payment:

    Dr. Retained Earnings (OE) 2,000
    Cr.   Cash (A) 2,000

9. To record the raw materials inventory withdrawals during the year: [5]

    Dr. Raw Materials Expenses (OE) 15,000
    Cr.   Raw Materials Inventory (A) 15,000

10. To record the processing equipment's depreciation expense (see below for the debit-credit treatment of this "contra asset" account):

    Dr. Depreciation Expense (OE) 1,000
    Cr.   Accumulated Depreciation (L) 1,000

This last journal entry is called an adjusting entry. There is no transaction with parties outside the entity to prompt the recording of the event or to determine the amounts. These entries are made at the end of the period. They are the adjustments to assets or liabilities previously recorded that are required to achieve a proper periodic matching of costs and revenues. These entries require considerable judgment to determine the amounts involved.

Using the scheme of T accounts similar to those in Illustration 5–5, the next step is to post the journal entries to the appropriate T accounts. The results of this process are shown in Illustration 5–6. The numbers beside each amount refer to the journal entries describing the transaction.

Illustration 5–6 shows the accumulated depreciation account under the "liabilities" caption. The debit-credit mechanism treats this account as a

---

[5] Beginning inventory ... $20,000
    Plus: Purchases   15,000
    Less: Withdrawals ...   15,000
    Ending inventory $20,000

ILLUSTRATION 5-6

T Accounts for Climax Industries, Inc. Example

ASSETS = **LIABILITIES** + **OWNERS' EQUITY**

LIABILITIES

Accounts Payable

−	+
0	5,000 (7)
	5,000

Accumulated Depreciation*

−	+
0	1,000 (10)
	1,000

OWNERS' EQUITY

Capital Stock

−	+
0	50,000 (1)
	50,000

Retained Earnings

−	+
2,000 (8)	14,000 (13)
2,000	14,000
	12,000

ASSETS

Cash

+	−
50,000 (1)	20,000 (2)
40,000 (4)	10,000 (3)
	10,000 (5)
	5,000 (6)
	10,000 (7)
	2,000 (8)
	57,000
90,000	
33,000	

Raw Materials

+	−
20,000 (2)	15,000 (9)
15,000 (7)	15,000
35,000	
20,000	

Processing Equipment

+	−
10,000 (3)	0
10,000	

Accounts Receivable

+	−
5,000 (4)	0
5,000	

* Contra asset account.

Retained Earnings Subdivisions

REVENUES − **EXPENSES** = **NET INCOME**

REVENUES

−	+
45,000 (11)	45,000 (4)
45,000	45,000

EXPENSES

+	−
10,000 (5)	31,000 (12)
5,000 (6)	
15,000 (9)	
1,000 (10)	
31,000	31,000

NET INCOME

−	+
31,000 (12)	45,000 (11)
14,000 (13)	
45,000	45,000

liability. However, for statement purposes it is shown as a deduction, or a contra account, to the asset "processing equipment."

The next step is to calculate the *ending balances* in the asset and liability accounts, *close out* the expense and revenue accounts to the net income account, and then close the balance in this account to retained earnings. Here are the required journal entries to reduce the revenue, expense and net income accounts to zero:

11.   To close the revenue account:

Dr.	Revenues	45,000	
Cr.	Net Income		45,000

12.   To close the expense account:

Dr.	Net Income	31,000	
Cr.	Expenses		31,000

13.   To close the net income account:

Dr.	Net Income	14,000	
Cr.	Retained Earnings		14,000

Now the statements can be prepared. Illustration 5–7 presents the company's income statement combined with a statement of changes in retained earnings. Illustration 5–8 presents the balance sheet of Climax Industries, Inc.

ILLUSTRATION 5–7

CLIMAX INDUSTRIES, INC.

Statement of Earnings and Changes in Retained Earnings
for the Year Ended December 31, 1970

Sales		$45,000
Cost of goods sold:		
Raw materials	$15,000	
Direct labor	10,000	
Manufacturing depreciation	1,000	26,000
Gross profit		$19,000
Selling, rent, and administration		5,000
Net Income		$14,000
Less: Common stock dividends declared		2,000
Additions to Income Retained in the Business ...		$12,000

ILLUSTRATION 5–8

CLIMAX INDUSTRIES, INC.

Statement of Financial Condition, December 31, 1970

ASSETS			LIABILITIES AND OWNERS' EQUITY		
Current Assets:			Current Liabilities:		
Cash		$33,000	Accounts payable		$ 5,000
Accounts receivable (net)		5,000	Long-Term Liabilities		....
Raw materials inventory		20,000	Total Liabilities		$ 5,000
Total Current Assets		$58,000			
Property (at cost):			Owners' Equity:		
Processing equipment	$10,000		Capital stock		$50,000
Less: Accumulated			Retained earnings		12,000
depreciation	1,000		Total Owners' Equity		$62,000
Net Property		$ 9,000	Total Liabilities and		
Total Assets		$67,000	Owners' Equity		$67,000

SUGGESTED FURTHER READINGS

FINNEY, H. A., and MILLER, HERBERT E.   *Principles of Accounting.* Englewood Cliffs, N.J.: Prentice-Hall, 1957.

MEIGS, WALTER B., and JOHNSON, CHARLES E.   *Accounting.* New York: McGraw-Hill, 1962.

SEILER, ROBERT E.   *Elementary Accounting.* Columbus, Ohio: Charles E. Merrill Books, 1963.

CASES

Case 5-1. **OTTOMAN CAR COMPANY**

Preparation of Journal Entries,
Balance Sheet, and Income
Statement

Fred Ottoman was a fire truck salesman for many years, while Bill, his brother, worked as a book salesman for a major publishing house. Although they had done fairly well financially they wanted to "be their own bosses," so they decided to go into business together.

They agreed that selling cars would be a good line for them to go into as both had been interested in sports cars for many years. Also the small town in Ohio where they lived did not have any automobile dealerships. The nearest dealer, a Ford dealer, was some 30 miles away.

After some searching, they chose a suitable site for their proposed operation. It was situated on a popular shopping street. A dilapidated apartment building which had been condemned by the local authorities stood on the site.

At this point in time, the brothers decided to incorporate the business. The services of a lawyer were obtained to draw up the legal papers and to handle all aspects of the execution of the incorporation. The fee for this service was $200, and each of the brothers paid half of it.

Fred purchased 1,800 shares of the company's stock for $18,000 and Bill purchased 500 shares for $5,000. The above-mentioned payments for legal services were considered part of these investments. Further purchases of the company's shares could be made only at the prevailing book value per share at the time of the purchase and only if both parties agreed to the transaction. If either brother wished at any time to sell his shares back to the company, this transaction would also be conducted at the prevailing book value of the shares. The brothers also agreed that they should each receive salaries of $6,000 per year at all times during which they were engaged on the company's business on a full-time basis.

108

On November 1, 1969, with the aid of a $10,000 bank loan and $8,000 of the company's money, Fred purchased the property which had been selected. The same day, he left his job to devote his full attention to the new enterprise.

First, Fred arranged to have the old building demolished. A cursory examination revealed there was nothing of any significance that could be salvaged, except for some building stone. Mr. Mahoney, the wrecker, agreed to clear the site for $3,500, provided he could have the stone. Otherwise, he would want $4,500. Fred was convinced he could get a better price for the stone, so he instructed Mr. Mahoney to clear the site and store the stone in a corner of it. This work was started immediately, and completed before Christmas. Mr. Mahoney agreed to defer collection of payment until May 31, 1970.

In the meantime, Fred got in touch with a large automobile manufacturer, National Cars, Inc., who had previously indicated interest in the projected dealership. Fred asked National for financial help to construct the buildings needed to carry on business. National agreed to provide all the finances needed for the building through a loan repayable in 10 equal annual installments, provided Ottoman Cars sold only National models. The loan earned an interest rate of 4 percent per year, payable from April 1, 1970. The first repayment, including interest, would fall due on March 31, 1971.

On December 31, National Cars sent a check for $10,000 to get Ottoman Cars started. Fred deposited the check in the business's bank account. The remainder of the loan would be forthcoming when the building was completed.

Next Fred arranged through a consulting architect for several construction companies to bid for the job. The lowest bidder was the Birkett and Snell Company. They agreed to construct the specified building for $31,500. On the advice of his architect, however, Fred Ottoman decided to accept the Holmes Bros. Construction Company bid of $35,000; the architect knew Birkett and Snell Company was less reliable than Holmes in meeting promised completion dates.

The construction was started immediately, Holmes promising completion by the end of March 1970. Progress payments on certificates from the architects were to be made at the end of January, the end of February, and the date of completion in amounts of $10,000, $10,000, and $15,000.

During the winter period, Fred tried to obtain some orders for the 1970 model cars, which he planned to deliver directly to customers from National's warehouse in Cleveland. Fred had some success with the model he had recently bought for himself. Between January 1 and March 30, Fred sold 17 of this model at an average cash cost to Ottoman Cars of $2,250. Nothing was paid to National for these cars during the period. These 17 sales realized $45,900, whereof $14,500 represented trade-in allowances, $28,000 was in cash, and the rest was outstanding at March 30. Fred sold all the trade-in cars for $13,700 cash before March 30. Bill and Fred agreed that the latter should receive $10 for every new car sale as compensation for using his private car as a display model.

At the end of March, the building was completed. However, there was an additional charge of $600 for materials, which Ottoman had to pay according to the provisions of the building contract. At the same time, the architect's bill for $650 arrived.

Fred sent the progress payments to the builder as previously arranged, making the January payment with $10,000 of the company's money and the February payment with the National loan. On March 31 the last $15,000 progress payment and the $600 materials surcharge were paid. The $10,000 bank loan plus interest of $300 was repaid by check on March 30.

On March 30, Bill quit his job with the publishing house and joined Ottoman Cars on a full-time basis. At Bill's request, it was agreed that financial statements would be prepared, to allow the two brothers to see where they stood as at the end of March. National Cars, Inc. asked that a portion of the amount the dealership owed the manufacturers for cars be regarded as the payment due to the dealership under the building contract, and Fred accepted this arrangement on behalf of Ottoman Cars. The two brothers agreed that they would invite Mr. William Hurley, an accountant who was a mutual friend of theirs to prepare the accounts.

Questions

1. As Mr. Hurley, prepare journal entries to record the events that have taken place in the business up to March 31, 1970.
2. From these journal entries, prepare a balance sheet as of March 31, 1970, and an income statement for the period to that date.
3. Based on your financial statements, what is the value of each brother's equity in the company?
4. Prepare a statement showing the sources and uses of cash from the formation of the business until March 31, 1970.

Case 5–2. **PETER FULLER**

Determining Financial Reporting Policy and Preparation of Projected Financial Statements

Peter Fuller was the inventor of a metal hoseclamp for automobile hose connections. Having confidence in its commercial value, but owning no surplus funds of his own, he sought among his friends and acquaintances for the necessary capital to put it on the market. The proposition which he placed before possible associates was that a corporation should be formed with capital stock of $30,000, that he be given $16,000 par value of stock for his patent, and that the remaining $14,000 be sold for a sum as near par as possible.

The project looked attractive to a number of the individuals to whom the inventor presented it, but the most promising among them—a retired manufacturer—said he would be unwilling to invest his capital without knowing what uses were intended for the cash to be received from the proposed sale of stock. He suggested that the inventor determine the probable costs of experimentation and of special machinery, and prepare for him a statement of the estimated assets and liabilities of the proposed company when ready to begin actual operations. He also asked for a statement of the estimated transactions for the first year of production and sales operations, together with an analysis of the operating results indicated by those expectations. This information would be based on the studies the inventor had made of probable markets and costs of labor and materials. It would include a listing of resulting assets and liabilities; an analysis of expected sales, expenses, and profits; and an explanation of expected flow of cash over the course of the year.

After consulting the engineer who had aided him in constructing his patent models, Fuller drew up the following list of data relating to the transactions of the proposed corporation during its period of organization and development.

1. Probable selling price of $14,000 par value of stock, $18,000.
2. Probable cost of incorporation and organization, $825, which includes estimated officers' salaries during developmental period.
3. Probable cost of developing special machinery, $13,000. This sum includes the cost of expert services, materials, rent of a small shop, and the cost of power, light, and miscellaneous expenditures.
4. Probable cost of raw material, $500, of which $300 is to be used in experimental production.

Fuller drew up the first of the statements desired by his prospective associate in the following manner:

Probable Assets and Liabilities of the Proposed Company
when Ready to Begin Actual Operations

ASSETS		LIABILITIES AND PROPRIETORSHIP	
Patent	$16,000	Capital stock at par	$30,000
Machinery	13,000	Plus premium on stock	4,000
Organization costs	825	Capital paid in	$34,000
Experimental costs	300		
Raw materials and supplies	200		
Cash	3,675		
Total Assets	$34,000	Total Liabilities	$34,000

With this initial part of his assignment completed, the inventor set down the following estimates as a beginning step in furnishing the rest of the information desired.

1. Expected sales, $28,000, all to be received in cash by the end of the first year following completion of organization and initial experimentation.
2. Expected additional purchases of raw materials and supplies during the course of this operating year, all for cash, paid by end of year, $9,000.
3. Expected help from the banks during year—but loans, including $50 interest, to be repaid before close of year—$2,000.
4. Expected payroll and other cash expenses and manufacturing costs for the operating year, $14,000 (of which $3,000 is to be for selling and administrative expenses).
5. Expected inventory of raw materials and supplies at close of period, at cost, $1,800.
6. No inventory of unsold process or finished stock expected as of the end of the period. All goods to be sold "on special order"; none to be produced "for stock."
7. All experimental and organization costs, previously capitalized as essentially going-concern assets or "valuations," to be charged against income of the operating year.
8. Estimated depreciation of machinery, $1,300, based on a 10-year life. (However, Fuller was aware of a plastic hoseclamp being developed by a major corporation that might make his product and the equipment used to produce it obsolete in about four years' time. If this occurred, Fuller thought that it might be possible to convert special machinery into general purpose equipment at a cost of several thousand dollars.)
9. Machinery maintenance, cash, $75.
10. New machinery and equipment to be purchased for cash, $1,000.
11. Profit distributions of net cash proceeds of sales, $3,000.

The above transaction data were for the most part cumulative totals, and should not be interpreted to mean that the events described were to take place in the precise order or sequence indicated.

Questions

1. Prepare the information wanted by the retired manufacturer.
2. What kind of a financial image do you think Fuller should present to the retired manufacturer? Do your statements communicate this image?

CHAPTER 6

CONSOLIDATED FINANCIAL STATEMENTS

Consolidated financial statements present the financial position and the results of operation for a parent company and its subsidiaries as if the group were a single company. The corporation owning a major portion (more than 50 percent) of the outstanding capital stock of another corporation is the parent, while the controlled corporation is the subsidiary. The parent and its subsidiaries are sometimes called affiliated companies.

Businessmen and accountants generally recognize: "Where there is a parent company and one or more subsidiaries, there is a presumption that consolidated statements are more meaningful than separate statements." [1] Although it is customary for parent corporations controlling subsidiaries to publish statements consolidating domestic subsidiaries, the practice regarding foreign subsidiaries is less standardized.

Consolidated statements treat affiliated corporations as though they were a single economic unit, even though the affiliated companies are legally separate entities. Financial information is combined as if the corporations involved were merely departments or divisions of a larger corporation. The consolidating procedure cancels out on work sheets all offsetting reciprocal pairs of assets and liabilities, revenues and costs, and investment and equity accounts which appear on the statements of affiliated corporations. For example, a parent may lend its subsidiary $100,000. This will appear as a loan receivable on the parent's statements. It will be carried as a loan payable on the subsidiary's books. When the statements of the two companies are consolidated, these items will be eliminated.

---

[1] Principle E–2 in Paul Grady, *Inventory of Generally Accepted Accounting Principles for Business Enterprises*, Accounting Research Study No. 7 (New York: American Institute of Certified Public Accountants, 1965), p. 67.

Similarly all such transactions involving intercompany investments and gains and losses on intercompany transactions are reversed on the work sheets so that only events involving the economic unit and outside parties will show on the consolidated statements.

Consolidation Policy

At least two conditions should be present to justify consolidation: control and homogeneity of operations.

Control.   In general, the parent must have presently, and expect to continue, ownership and management control over the subsidiary. Not everyone agrees on the degree of control, however. Some consider the minimum ownership of "more than 50 percent" is too low. They insist that 60 percent, 75 percent, or some higher ownership percentage is necessary.

Irrespective of the degree of ownership control, however, managerial control is a prerequisite for consolidation. Adequate control is not considered to be present if the parent-subsidiary relationship is hampered or threatened by currency, dividend, legal, or political restrictions. Principally for these reasons, foreign subsidiaries are excluded from consolidation when there are significant limitations or threats to the economic flexibility or the continuity of these operations. Also, these conditions justify the nonconsolidation of bankrupt or insolvent subsidiaries.

Homogeneity.   In earlier periods, it was believed that statements for a parent and its consolidated subsidiaries should represent a homogeneous economic unit. However, increasing corporate diversification and the increase in "conglomerates" has resulted in substantial relaxation of this requirement. So long as the parent retains control, nonhomogeneous subsidiaries may be and often are consolidated.

Disclosure.   The parent company policy regarding consolidation policy is frequently disclosed in footnotes to the financial statements, as in the following example:

Youngstown Sheet and Tube

. . . .
Note 1: *Principles of Consolidation.* The consolidated financial statements include all wholly owned subsidiary companies. Dividends received from a 53% owned subsidiary company not consolidated exceeded the equity in its 1967 income by $403,000.

Accounting Concepts Peculiar to Consolidated Statements

Most items appearing on consolidated financial statements are comparable to those found on statements of the individual corporations. There are four items which are peculiar to consolidated statements: minority interest, goodwill, consolidated net income, and consolidated retained earnings.

Minority Interest. Financial statements prepared for single corporations do not distinguish between the individuals or groups owning a single
class of capital stock. In the case of consolidated statements, if the parent
does not own 100 percent of the capital stock of a subsidiary, that part
of ownership equity not owned by the parent is presented separately on
the consolidated balance sheet and identified as minority interest. This
practice conforms to the concept of preparing consolidated financial statements from the point of view of the parent company which exercises
controlling ownership over its subsidiaries.

After total net income for the affiliated group is determined, a deduction is made for that part of the subsidiary's earnings applicable to the
minority ownership. Thus, the minority interest shown on the consolidated balance sheet consists of a pro rata share of net worth based on
capital contribution plus accumulated earnings less any dividends paid.

From the parent's point of view, some accountants argue that the
minority interest has characteristics of a liability. Others claim it represents a separate class of equity. As a result, in practice "minority interest"
is usually recorded between liabilities and ownership rather than being
included in either category.

Goodwill. Ordinarily, the intangible asset goodwill is recognized only
when a going business is acquired at a price greater than the value of the
net assets.[2] When a parent acquires an interest in a subsidiary under these
circumstances, this excess of investment is not separated on the parent's
unconsolidated statements. It remains as an unidentified part of parent's
total investment in the subsidiary, which is listed as an asset.

When the subsidiary giving rise to the goodwill is consolidated, along
with all the other intercompany investments this investment account on
the parent's balance sheet must be offset against the subsidiary's equity
accounts. If there is an excess of investment over the subsidiary's net assets,
goodwill results, and it must be descriptively recognized on the consolidated balance sheet.

Consolidated Net Income. Consolidated income statements present the
total net income during the period for the affiliated group as if it were
operating as a single corporation. To achieve this, all intercompany transactions giving rise to gains or losses are eliminated. Also, those earnings
applicable to minority ownership are deducted from consolidated net
income and included as part of minority interest. The resulting consolidated net income consists of parent company earnings plus the parent's
share of subsidiary earnings for the period arising from external transactions.

Consolidated Retained Earnings. Consolidated retained earnings include all of the retained earnings of the parent plus the parent's share of

---

[2] The nature and handling of goodwill will be treated in greater detail in Chapter
18.

the subsidiary's retained earnings from the date of acquisition. Of course, earnings applicable to the minority interest have been removed. Also, dividends paid by subsidiary companies to the parent have been eliminated, since they are merely transfers of cash within the consolidated entity.

Investment in Subsidiary

The parent company can adopt one of two alternative methods for *recording in its accounts* its ownership interest in a subsidiary corporation. These are the cost or equity methods. Typically, the cost method is used where appropriate for investments ranging anywhere from 0–100 percent interest in an unconsolidated subsidiary. The equity method is generally limited to investments of more than 50 percent.[3] In early 1971, the APB was considering a proposal to extend the application of the equity method, when appropriate, to investments of more than 20 percent.

Cost Method.   Under the cost method, the original price paid for the subsidiary is recorded on the parent's records as the "investment in subsidiary." This original investment figure remains unchanged by the subsequent activities of the subsidiary. Neither subsequent profits nor losses of the subsidiary are given any recognition in the parent's accounts. However, any cash dividends received from the subsidiary are recorded as income at the time of receipt.

Equity Method.   Under the equity method, initially the acquisition price is recorded on the parent's books as "investment in subsidiary," as under the cost method. Subsequently, this investment account is increased by the parent's pro rata share of the subsidiary's additions to stockholders' equity (or decreased by reduction in stockholders' equity). The parent's share of the subsidiary's profits (or losses) are recognized on the parent's books as "other income" (or "other expense") at the close of each accounting period. Cash dividends received by the parent from the subsidiary are recorded as reductions to the investment account. Thus, the account labeled "investment in subsidiary" reflects the original cost plus (or minus) the parent's share of changes in the subsidiary's net worth from the date of acquisition.

Opinion No. 10.   In *Opinion No. 10, Omnibus Opinion—1966*, the Accounting Principles Board expressed the opinion that if a domestic subsidiary controlled by the parent is not consolidated, the equity method should be used to report investment in the subsidiary. The Board deferred consideration of the appropriate treatment of investments in unconsolidated foreign subsidiaries until its accounting research study on accounting for foreign investments and operations was published.

---

[3] Accounting for intercorporate investments is discussed in greater detail in Chapter 18. The focus of Chapter 6 is on consolidated statements.

In *Opinion No. 10*, the Accounting Principles Board also declared that for periods subsequent to December 31, 1966 the accounts of subsidiaries whose principal business activity is leasing property or facilities to their parent should be consolidated. Previously most companies had used the equity method of recording their investment in such subsidiaries. The Board believed this practice obscured the significance of the leasing subsidiary's assets and liabilities to the consolidated financial position of the enterprise.

Consolidation Procedures

A number of alternative methods involving work sheets are used to accomplish consolidation. The act of consolidation occurs only on the work sheet used for assembling the consolidated data, not in the accounts or records of the affiliated corporations. Each affiliate's accounting records and its financial statements are based upon the principle that each affiliate is a separate legal entity.

None of the alternative work sheet procedures, or methods of recording ownership of subsidiaries prior to consolidation, have any distinguishing effect upon the final consolidated financial statements. The reader of the consolidated statements can not determine which alternative was used.

Confusion in consolidating procedures is minimized if one is mindful constantly that (1) consolidating adjusting and eliminating entries are never recorded in the accounts of the affiliated group, and (2) each periodic or annual consolidation is made as if it were the initial consolidation.

A common procedure for preparing consolidated financial statements involves the following steps:

1. Arrange vertically in parallel columns on a work sheet the unconsolidated statements of the parent and of the subsidiaries to be consolidated, as shown in Illustration 6–1.

2. Make any preconsolidating adjustments necessary to bring consistency into the statements. For example, a work sheet adjustment would be required if an affiliate had forwarded cash to another affiliate in payment of a debt but the other affiliate had not yet received the cash as of the closing date. In this case the statement of the affiliate to whom the cash was sent would be adjusted as if the cash had been actually received. All intercompany relationships such as these must be reconciled and brought into agreement before eliminations can be made. (The receipt of cash such as $10,000 for payment of accounts receivable by the parent from the subsidiary is shown as adjustment (1) in the illustration.)

3. Eliminate intercompany assets and liabilities. All debtor-creditor relationships between affiliates to be consolidated are offset on the work sheet. This is achieved by making work sheet entries which cancel the

asset of one affiliate against the liability of another affiliate. The effect of these eliminations is reversal of transactions which created the intercompany assets and liabilities in the accounts of affiliates. For example, if a subsidiary borrowed $175,000 from its parent, the subsidiary would enter the transaction on its books by debiting Cash $175,000 and crediting Loans Payable $175,000. The parent's records will reflect an entry debiting Loans Receivable and crediting Cash $175,000. On the consolidating work sheet the eliminating entry will debit Loans Payable and credit Loans Receivable for $175,000. (See adjustment number (2).) This entry involves accounts which are in the statements of different corporations. The effect of this entry is to reverse the entries made on the books of the affiliates, but no entries to Cash are necessary because assets and liabilities of all affiliates will be combined. As noted earlier, all eliminating entries are made only on the consolidating work sheets and are not entered in the accounts of the individual corporations.

4. Eliminate (or cancel out) any intercompany revenue against the appropriate costs or expenses. Adjustment number (3) shows the entries reversing $150,000 of intercompany sales. This entry assumes none of the goods sold to the subsidiary are still in its inventory account.

5. Eliminate the effect of dividends declared by a corporation to another member of the affiliated group. (None shown in the example.)

6. Eliminate from the accounts all intercompany profits or losses which may be cumulatively included in asset accounts of the purchaser and in equity accounts of the seller. The gains or losses of prior periods of affiliation as well as those of the current period must be canceled.

Illustration 6–1 does not include an example of this kind of adjustment. If such an adjustment were required, however, it might be handled as follows: Assume the parent had sold 3 years earlier to its subsidiary a machine for $20,000, including the parent's $2,000 profit, and the subsidiary was depreciating this machine over 10 years, the adjustments would be

a) to eliminate the profit on the intercompany sale from the gross carrying value of the assets of the subsidiary and the retained earnings of the parent

Retained Earnings (Parent) 2,000
    Plant and Equipment (Sub) 2,000

b) to eliminate the depreciation expense based on the intercompany profit of $2,000 included in the subsidiary's fixed asset account. This requires $200 (or $2,000/10 years) to be deducted from this year's depreciation expense and an elimination from the subsidiary's retained earnings of $400 representing the last two year's depreciation charged by the subsidiary on the intercompany profits included in its asset base.

Accumulated Depreciation (Sub) 600
    Depreciation Expense (Sub) 200
    Retained Earnings (Sub) 400

7. Eliminate the investment account of the parent in those subsidiaries being consolidated and adjust those subsidiaries' equity accounts for any minority interests that may be present. The minority interest is equal to the minority stockholders proportional share of the subsidiaries *current* net worth.

The computation of the minority interest is:

> Minority Interest (in Subsidiary)
> Capital Stock .... 20% × $200 = $40
> Retained Earnings .... 20% × $100 = 20
> $60

The adjusting entries in Illustration 6–1 (number 4) are

> Capital Stock (Sub) 40
> Retained Earnings (Sub) 20
>   Minority Interest 60

If the parent's investment in the subsidiary exceeded its proportional share of the subsidiary's equity capital and retained earnings accounts at the *acquisition date* an adjustment will also be required to determine the goodwill amount on the consolidated statements. To illustrate, assume the $400 "Investment in subsidiary" balance shown in Illustration 6–1 represents an 80 percent interest in the subsidiary's equity and the subsidiary's retained earnings were zero at the time the investment was made. (The retained earnings is now $100.)

The goodwill calculation is:

> Goodwill
> Investment (Parent) $400
> Common Stock (Sub), 80% × 200 .... $160
> Retained Earnings (Sub), 80% × $0   0   160
> $240

The adjusting entries in Illustration 6–1 (number 5) are

> Common Stock (Sub) 160
> Retained Earnings (Sub)   0
> Goodwill 240
>   Investment in Subsidiary (Parent) 400

The goodwill amount, if positive, is usually labeled descriptively as "excess of cost over book value" and presented as an asset on the consolidated balance sheet. A negative balance is identified as "excess of book value over cost" and is handled in one of a number of different ways, depending upon the underlying circumstances which gave rise to the amount. (See Chapter 18.)

8. Combine all remaining statement amounts for all affiliates being considered. The balances can then be arranged in the traditional financial statement form, modified for the four concepts peculiar to consolidation described previously.

Consolidated Federal Income Tax Returns. The choice of filing consolidated federal income tax returns by an affiliated group is completely independent of financial reporting practices. In general, domestic industrial corporations which are related by a minimum of 80 percent control (or have this degree of common ownership) may elect to report on a consolidated basis. The complex regulations governing the filing of consolidated returns provide for elimination of intercompany gains and losses and for offsetting profits of one affiliate against losses of another member of the group.

Limitations of Consolidated Financial Statements. The underlying assumption that consolidated financial statements are more meaningful than separate statements for affiliated companies needs to be qualified.

ILLUSTRATION 6–1

Consolidation Working Papers

			Adjustments		Consolidated
	Parent	Subsidiary	Debits	Credits	Statement
ASSETS					
Cash	$ 400	$ 20	(1) 10		$ 430
Accounts receivable	700	125		(1) 10	815
Inventory	1,200	275			1,475
Investment in subsidiary	400			(5) 400	—
Note due from subsidiary ...	175	—		(2) 175	—
Plant and equipment (net) ..	300	200			500
Goodwill			(5) 240		240
Other assets	25	10			35
Total Assets	$3,200	$630			$3,495
LIABILITIES					
Accounts payable	$ 200	$100			$ 300
Notes payable	400	30			430
Loans payable—bank	1,000	25			1,025
Loans payable—parent		175	(2) 175		—
Common stock	1,000	200	⎰(4) 40 ⎱(5) 160		1,000
Retained income	600	100	⎰(4) 20 ⎱(5) 0		680
Minority interest				(4) 60	60
Total Liabilities	$3,200	$630			$3,495
INCOME STATEMENT					
Sales	$1,200	$475	(3) 150		$1,525
Cost of goods sold	800	125		(3) 150	775
Gross margin	$ 400	$350			$ 750
Selling expense	$ 50	$ 75			$ 125
Operating expense	75	125			200
Total expense	$ 125	$200			$ 325
Operating profit	$ 275	$150			$ 425

Since consolidated financial statements ignore the separate legal character of affiliated corporations, information concerning any of the individual companies included in the consolidated statements cannot be obtained from the statements. For example, creditors and investors can not evaluate the profitability or financial condition of any single corporation within the group on the basis of the consolidated statements. The analyst is unable to identify the assets and liabilities of the consolidated group with any of the individual corporations. Similarly, the statements are of limited value to the minority stockholder interested in a subsidiary company.

SUGGESTED FURTHER READINGS

FINNEY, H. A., and MILLER, HERBERT E. *Principles of Accounting, Advanced.* Englewood Cliffs, N.J.: Prentice-Hall, 1960.

KARRENBROCK, WILBERT E., and SIMMONS, HARRY. *Advanced Accounting.* Cincinnati: South-Western Publishing Co., 1961.

MOONITZ, MAURICE. *The Entity Theory of Consolidated Statements.* Bloomington, Ind.: American Accounting Association, 1944.

CASES

Case 6–1. **COMPANY P AND SUBSIDIARY COMPANY S**

Preparation of Consolidated Statements

Company P purchased 80 percent of the outstanding capital stock of Company S from individual stockholders for $290,000 cash on January 1, 1966. On this date the retained earnings of Company S were $30,000.

Company S was primarily, but not exclusively, engaged in marketing goods purchased from Company P. Though purchases from Company P during the year 1970 were $1,200,000, the inventory held by Company S at the beginning or the close of the year did not include any merchandise acquired from Company P. On December 31, 1970, the balance due to Company P for these intercompany purchases was $280,000.

All plant and equipment owned by Company S was acquired for cash from Company P on January 1, 1968, and has been depreciated on the basis of its estimated life of 10 years, using the straight-line method without salvage value. In 1968, Company P recorded a $50,000 profit on the sale of these fixed assets to its subsidiary.

A 10 percent cash dividend was declared and paid by Company S on its outstanding capital stock on July 1, 1970.

Financial statements of Company P and of Company S are presented in vertical form on the accompanying work sheet (Exhibit 1) to facilitate assembly of information for consolidated statements.

Questions

1. Complete the work sheet provided (or use any method you prefer) to assemble the information necessary for:
   a) A consolidated income statement,
   b) A consolidated retained earnings statement, and
   c) A consolidated balance sheet.

EXHIBIT 1

COMPANY P AND SUBSIDIARY COMPANY S

Working Papers for Consolidated Statements for the Year Ended December 31, 1970
(in thousands; parentheses indicate deductions)

	Company P	Company S	Adjustments and Eliminations Dr.	Cr.	Consolidated Statements
Income Statement					
Sales	$1,500	$1,800			
Cost of sales	(900)	(1,400)			
	$ 600	$ 400			
Depreciation	(40)	(20)			
Operating expenses	(440)	(290)			
Net income from operations	$ 120	$ 90			
Dividend income	24				
Minority net income					
Net Income	$ 144	$ 90			
Retained Earnings Statement					
Retained earnings, Jan. 1, 1970:					
Company P	$ 248				
Company S		$ 70			
Net income (as above).....	144	90			
Dividends:					
Company P	(72)				
Company S		(30)			
Retained earnings,					
Dec. 31, 1970	$ 320	$ 130			
Balance Sheet					
Cash	$ 110	$ 150			
Accounts receivable (net)..	375	410			
Inventories	310	75			
Plant and equipment	885	200			
Accumulated depreciation.	(265)	(60)			
Investment in Co. S (at cost)	290				
Goodwill					
Total Assets	$1,705	$ 775			
Accounts payable	$ 385	$ 345			
Minority interest					
Capital stock:					
Company P	1,000				
Company S		300			
Retained earnings (as above)	320	130			
Total Liabilities	$1,705	$ 775			

2. Compare the financial condition of Company P on an unconsolidated basis with that presented by the consolidated statements. Your comparison should include computations of:
   a) Working capital.
   b) Total assets.
   c) Long-term capital.
   d) Any other ratios or relationships you think significant.
3. Compare the profitability of Company P on an unconsolidated basis with that shown by the consolidated statements.
4. How meaningful are consolidated statements to you as:
   a) A stockholder of Company P?
   b) A minority stockholder of Company S?

Case 6–2. MOHAWK PRODUCTS, INCORPORATED

Determination of the Consolidated Entity

In 1933, Edwin Franklin, following the inheritance of a large fortune, established Mohawk Products, Inc. in Greensville, Quebec, Canada, to manufacture textile products. Between 1933 and 1970 the company prospered and expanded to the point where it was one of the largest privately held companies in the nation. In 1970 its operations included two foreign and one domestic textile subsidiaries, a real estate subsidiary, a finance subsidiary, an electronics subsidiary, a bank, and a farm equipment company. Mohawk Products or one of its subsidiaries established each of these companies and owned 100 percent of their outstanding common stock.

In early 1970, James Franklin, president and principal stockholder of Mohawk Products, was considering the possibility of making a small private offering to a limited number of investors of some of his Mohawk Products common stock. Several members of the Franklin family thought a wider market holding of their stock would simplify the valuation of their holdings in the company for estate tax purposes. In 1970 Mohawk had outstanding, and in the hands of the Franklin family, one million shares of common stock.

To date, Mohawk had carried its subsidiaries on Mohawk's financial statement as an "investment in unconsolidated subsidiaries." This investment was valued according to the cost method.

Mr. Franklin was considering whether it would be better for the purposes of the stock offering to present the company's financial statements on a consolidated basis. In addition, if he decided to change the parent company's consolidation policy, he was not sure which subsidiaries he should consolidate. He was determined, however, to continue using the cost method to value all unconsolidated subsidiaries.

Mr. Edwin Franklin, Mohawk's founder, believed "every tub should stand on its own bottom." In line with this policy, it had been Mohawk's practice to reinvest the earnings of its subsidiaries in the subsidiary creating the earnings; to minimize intercompany investment and operating transactions; and to satisfy the needs of the Mohawk stockholders for dividends from the current earnings of the parent. To date, the parent had never received dividends from its subsidiaries. For income tax purposes, the company submitted unconsolidated returns.

Textile Companies. Mohawk Products owned three subsidiaries in the textile area: Iroquois Woolens, Inc.; Bull Dog Linens Proprietary, Ltd.; and Mohawk Products (Australia) Ltd. Iroquois Woolens was formed in 1939 to manufacture blankets in Madison, Quebec. Bull Dog Linens, the company's British subsidiary, was created in 1953 to produce fine linen goods for the British and European markets. Bull Dog's two plants were located in Manchester and Liverpool. During recent years, repeated labor troubles had plagued Bull Dog Linens. The Australian subsidiary, Mohawk Products (Australia) was formed in 1963 to operate a small textile mill near Sydney, Australia.

Banking Company. In 1939, following the collapse of Greensville's two banks, Mr. Edwin Franklin created the Franklin Trust Company in Greensville. Since the Mohawk mill was the major company in Greensville, Mr. Franklin saw an opportunity for Mohawk Products to make a profit by becoming its own banker and the banker for its employees, their relatives, and the many local tradesmen who relied upon the mill and its employees for their livelihood. Over the years new companies moved into the town and its population increased considerably. Throughout this period, the Franklin Trust was the town's only bank and its business expanded.

Since it had been founded, the Franklin Trust had held all of Mohawk's cash balances. However, it had never loaned money to its parent or its subsidiaries. This "no loan" practice followed Mr. Edwin Franklin's promise to the townspeople and the province's banking commission that the bank would avoid conflict-of-interest situations, such as lending money to its parent or any of its parent's subsidiaries. As a result, whenever Mohawk or its subsidiaries needed financing they obtained it from Franklin's correspondent bank in Montreal.

Farm Equipment Company. In 1937, Mr. Edwin Franklin's youngest daughter married John Atkins, the sales vice president for one of the largest farm equipment manufacturers in the country. As a wedding present, Mr. Franklin used Mohawk Products' cash to buy at a distress price the Eastern Canadian franchise to distribute and sell the well-known Walpole farm equipment line and made Mr. Atkins the president of the new company, Consolidated Farm Equipment, Inc. Mr. Atkins quickly developed an effective system of subdistributors and the company made progress, despite the unfavorable state of the farm economy.

In early 1939, the franchise became worthless when the Walpole Farm Equipment Company of Canada went bankrupt. Mr. Atkins, aware of the growing threat of war in Europe, bought the assets of Walpole at book value, with the expectation that in the event of war Consolidated Farm Equipment could use the Walpole plants to profitably manufacture tanks and small arms. Mohawk guaranteed the loans Consolidated Farm Equipment used to finance this acquisition. Accordingly, during World War II, Consolidated Farm Equipment manufactured farm equipment, tanks, and small arms. The company's wartime profits were used to extinguish the loans obtained to buy Walpole.

With the advent of peace, the company turned its attention to developing the Walpole farm equipment line on a national basis. Since World War II, Consolidated Farm Equipment had been profitable, except during 1964 and 1965, when the company introduced a new line of farm equipment at the same time as the level of farm equipment purchases fell drastically.

Finance Company. In early 1966, for tax, financial, and administrative reasons, Consolidated Farm Equipment created a wholly owned finance subsidiary, Consolidated Finance Corporation, to finance the company's credit sales to dealers. Beginning in 1966, Consolidated Farm Equipment began a major program to increase both the number of its dealers and the levels of their inventories. As part of this program, Consolidated Farm Equipment sold equipment to its dealers on extremely favorable credit terms. In turn, Consolidated Farm Equipment sold at a discount its dealers' accounts receivable to Consolidated Finance. As part of this arrangement, the banks lending to Consolidated Finance forced Consolidated Farm Equipment to agree to take back any dealer receivables falling in default.

Electronics Company. In 1968, Mohawk bought a patent covering a new technique for manufacturing transistors. In order to exploit this patent, Mohawk established a new company called Transiton, Inc. Within six months, the company was in business and rapidly developed a market for its transistors. Unlike the other Mohawk subsidiaries, Transiton had yet to earn a profit.

Real Estate Company. For tax reasons, Transiton leased its buildings from Equity Real Estate Company, a wholly owned subsidiary of Mohawk. In 1970, the Equity Real Estate Company did not have any other business. Sometime in the future, however, Mr. James Franklin planned to extend Equity's activities in the real estate area to include some form of non-Mohawk business.

Exhibit 1 presents the profits after taxes of Mohawk Products and its subsidiaries for the period 1960–69, inclusive. Exhibit 2 shows condensed balance sheets for Mohawk Products and its subsidiaries as of December 31, 1968 and 1969, respectively.

Questions

1. What subsidiaries should be included in the consolidated statements for prospectus purposes?
2. Given your answer to question 1, what will Mohawk's annual earning per share be for the last seven years (assume one million shares outstanding in each of the seven years)?
3. Should Mr. Franklin change Mohawk's consolidation policy for annual reporting purposes to stockholders? Why?

EXHIBIT 1

MOHAWK PRODUCTS, INC.

Mohawk Products and Subsidiaries, Profits After Taxes, 1960–69
(millions of dollars; 0 = less than $100,000)

	1969	1968	1967	1966	1965	1964	1963	1962	1961	1960
Mohawk Products	4.2	4.5	4.1	4.5	3.2	3.1	5.1	4.7	4.8	4.2
Iroquois Woolens	2.9	3.2	3.1	2.9	1.9	1.4	2.9	2.8	2.7	2.6
Franklin Trust	0.5	0.4	0.3	0.2	0.1	0.1	0.2	0.1	0.2	0.1
Consolidated Farm	2.8	2.9	3.9	1.9	(0.4)	(1.0)	3.4	3.7	3.6	2.4
Bull Dog Linens	(0.4)	(0.6)	0.4	0.7	0.6	0.4	0.5	0.4	0.1	0.1
Mohawk (Australia)...	2.5	1.9	1.3	(0.6)	0.8	0.9	(0.4)			
Consolidated Finance ..	0.2	0.2	0.2	0.1						
Transiton	(0.6)	(1.5)								
Equity Real Estate	0.0	0.0								

EXHIBIT 2. MOHAWK PRODUCTS AND SUBSIDIARIES

Condensed Balance Sheets

(millions of dollars; 0 = less than $100,000)

December 31, 1968

	Mohawk Products	Iroquois Woolens	Franklin Trust	Consolidated Farm	Bull Dog Linens	Mohawk (Australia)	Consolidated Finance	Transition	Equity Real Estate
ASSETS									
Cash	3.8	2.3	4.9	1.7	0.9	1.2	0.7	0.8	0.
Accounts (loans) receivable	8.7	5.4	77.0	-0-	1.4	4.0	30.7	2.3	-0-
Investment in subsidiaries (at cost)	36.5	-0-	-0-	2.5	-0-	-0-	-0-	-0-	-0-
Other assets	81.3	69.2	10.2	48.4	7.1	12.5	2.3	6.8	3.2
Total Assets	130.3	76.9	92.1	52.6	9.4	17.7	33.7	9.9	3.2
EQUITIES									
Accounts payable (deposits)	5.7	5.8	81.2	3.1	1.3	2.0	-0-	2.1	-0-
Other current liabilities	8.7	2.7	2.3	3.6	0.7	1.8	0.7	4.3	0.5
Long-term debt	-0-	-0-	-0-	-0-	-0-	5.0	30.0	-0-	2.5
Capital stock*	50.0	10.0	3.5	8.5	4.0	5.0	2.5	5.0	0.2
Retained earnings	65.9	58.4	5.1	37.4	3.4	3.9	0.5	(1.5)	0.●
Total Equities	130.3	76.9	92.1	52.6	9.4	17.7	33.7	9.9	3.2

December 31, 1969

	Mohawk Products	Iroquois Woolens	Franklin Trust	Consolidated Farm	Bull Dog Linens	Mohawk (Australia)	Consolidated Finance	Transition	Equity Real Estate
ASSETS									
Cash	4.2	2.1	5.2	1.4	0.7	1.3	0.6	0.7	0.
Accounts (loans) receivable	9.2	5.2	76.9	-0-	1.5	4.3	32.3	2.4	-0-
Investment in subsidiaries (at cost)	36.5	-0-	-0-	2.5	-0-	-0-	-0-	-0-	-0-
Other assets	80.7	72.7	12.7	51.3	6.7	15.0	2.2	6.5	3.
Total Assets	130.6	80.0	94.8	55.2	8.9	20.6	35.1	9.6	3.2
EQUITIES									
Accounts payable (deposits)	4.9	6.2	83.3	2.7	1.4	2.3	-0-	3.7	-0-
Other current liabilities	7.7	2.5	2.4	3.8	0.5	1.9	0.7	3.0	0.2
Long-term debt	-0-	-0-	-0-	-0-	-0-	5.0	31.2	-0-	2.
Capital stock*	50.0	10.0	3.5	8.5	4.0	5.0	2.5	5.0	0.2
Retained earnings	68.0	61.3	5.6	40.2	3.0	6.4	0.7	(2.1)	0.2
Total Equities	130.6	80.0	94.8	55.2	8.9	20.6	35.1	9.6	3.2

* Original investment.

CHAPTER 7

FUNDS FLOW STATEMENTS

Funds flow statements present a company's sources and uses of funds during an accounting period. There are a number of possible different definitions of funds, of which "all financial resources" is the most common (see below). Growing interest in cash flow and funds flow analytical techniques by investors and security analysts has led an increasing number of companies to include a funds flow statement as a supplement to the more traditional balance sheet and income statement. This trend has been encouraged by the Accounting Principles Board, and funds flow statements are frequently covered by the auditors' opinion.

Current Practice

Opinion No. 3 of the Accounting Principles Board, issued in October 1963, encouraged companies to present statements of sources and application of funds:

The Board believes that a statement of source and application of funds should be presented as supplementary information in financial reports. The inclusion of such information is not mandatory, and it is optional as to whether it should be covered in the report of the independent accountant.

The concept of "funds" underlying the preparation of a statement of source and application of funds should be consistent with the purpose of the statement. In the case of statements prepared for presentation in annual reports, a concept broader than that of working capital should be used which can be characterized or defined as "all financial resources," so that the statement will include the financial aspects of all significant transactions, e.g., "non-fund" transactions such as the acquisition of property through the issue of securities. . . .

The presentation of comparative and consolidated statements of source and application of funds should conform to the policies adopted for the basic

129

financial statements. A statement of source and application of funds which is cumulative for a period of years is sometimes prepared in addition to the statement for the current year, and is often helpful in furnishing a broad review of the financial activities over a period of time.

Using the APB's definition of funds, sources and uses of funds may be defined as:

Sources of Funds	Uses of Funds
Increases in Liabilities	Decreases in Liabilities
Increases in Net Worth	Decreases in Net Worth
Decreases in Assets	Increases in Assets

Nature of the Funds Flow Statement

Funds flow reporting can be distinguished from the other concepts of financial reporting. The funds flow statement shows changes in the firm's assets, liabilities, and equity accounts during a specified period of time. In contrast, the balance sheet presents the company's financial position at an instant of time. The income statement shows revenues, expenses, and profit for a period of time.

Causes for changes in the firm's financial position can be readily observed in a well-prepared funds flow statement. Funds flowing from operations, borrowing, sale of properties, and equity contributions are related to outflows for property acquisitions, dividends, and debt retirement. Answers are provided to such questions as: What happened to profits generated by operations? How was it possible for the firm to distribute dividends? What happened to money borrowed during the period? What caused the change in the working capital position?

Funds flow statements are most commonly entitled "The Source and Application of Funds," although other titles may be used.

Definition of "Funds"

The term "funds" as used in funds flow analysis can be defined in at least five different ways. These definitions, beginning with the narrowest and moving to the broadest, define funds flows as *changes* in (1) cash, (2) the sum of cash and marketable securities, (3) net monetary assets, (4) working capital, and (5) all financial resources. Each of these definitions leads to emphasis being placed on a different aspect of funds flow. The appropriateness of any definition will depend upon the particular circumstances of the firm and the purpose of the user of the statement.

Whether or not a particular accounting transaction is defined as a funds flow will depend on the definition of funds used. For example, the *declaration* of dividends changes a company's net monetary assets, net working capital, and "all financial resources." Thus, in a company that used a funds definition based on changes in any one of these items this transaction would be regarded as a funds flow for accounting purposes. If the company used a funds definition related to changes in cash or cash and marketable securities, this transaction would not be recorded as a funds flow, since it does not change either of these two asset accounts (only the liability and net worth accounts are changed). On the other hand, the *payment* of the dividends previously declared (and recorded on the company's books as "dividends payable") would be regarded as a funds flow in companies defining funds as changes in either cash, cash and marketable securities, or all financial resources. This transaction changes these items. However, since the transaction did not change the company's monetary assets or working capital, it would not be regarded as a funds flow if these balance sheet categories were the basis for the funds definition.

These five definitions of funds are demonstrated below. The funds flow statements resulting from each definition will be based upon the simplified balance sheets and statement of retained earnings for the Carter Company shown in Illustration 7–1. As the various funds flow statements are devel-

ILLUSTRATION 7–1

CARTER COMPANY

Balance Sheets at December 31, 1967 and 1968

	1967	1968	Difference
ASSETS			
Cash	$ 28	$ 30	$ 2
Marketable securities	10	15	5
Receivables	32	40	8
Inventories	40	35	(5)
Fixed assets (net)	130	140	10
Total Assets	$240	$260	$20
LIABILITIES			
Current payables	$ 54	$ 47	$(7)
Long-term debt	46	53	7
Capital stock	100	105	5
Retained earnings	40	55	15
Total Liabilities	$240	$260	$20

Statement of Retained Earnings
For the Year Ended December 31, 1968

Balance, December 31, 1967	$40
Net income for the year	20
	$60
Less: Dividends	5
Balance, December 31, 1968	$55

Additional data: Depreciation of $8 was charged against operations in 1968. Long-term debt of $10 was issued for fixed assets in the same amount.

oped, it must be remembered that each is entirely based upon the balance sheet and statement of retained earnings. That is, each statement must be considered independently, rather than as part of a continuing illustration.

1. Funds Defined as Cash. When funds are defined as cash, the increase in the cash account of $2 in Illustration 7–1 can be explained by a rearrangement of differences in the balance sheet accounts other than cash. (Some accounting authorities distinguish between cash flow and funds flow statements. For our purposes this distinction is not important.)

ILLUSTRATION 7–2

CARTER COMPANY

Cash Flow Statement
For the Year Ended December 31, 1968

Funds provided:			
From operations:			
Net income	$20		
Depreciation	8	$28	
From decrease in inventories		5	
From increase in capital stock		5	
Total		$38	
Funds applied:			
To increase in marketable securities	$ 5		
To increase in receivables	8		
To increase in fixed assets	8		
To decrease in current payables	7		
To decrease in long-term debt	3		
To payment of dividends	5		
Total		36	
Net Increase in Funds (Cash)....................		$ 2	

The handling of the investment in fixed assets is tricky in this case. The amount shown in the cash flow statement (Illustration 7–2) for "increase in fixed assets" is $8, not the $10 indicated in Illustration 7–1. The issuance of $10 of long-term debt for fixed assets is ignored in the cash statement, since it did not result in a change in cash. (See "additional data" note to Illustration 7–1.) If the $10 is deducted from both fixed assets and long-term debt in the 1968 balance sheet, fixed assets for 1967 and 1968 are $130. Since depreciation of $8 was charged in 1968, fixed assets must have been increased by $8 in 1968 (i.e., 1967 balance − 1968 depreciation + 1968 additions = 1968 ending balance).

Depreciation is added to net income to determine total funds provided from operations as depreciation charges requiring no expenditure of funds were subtracted in the determination of net income.

2. Funds Defined as Cash and Marketable Securities. Under this definition of funds, arrangement of balance sheet accounts other than cash and marketable securities will result in the funds flow statement shown in

ILLUSTRATION 7–3

CARTER COMPANY

Changes in Cash and Marketable Securities
For the Year Ended December 31, 1968

Funds provided:
  From operations:
    Net income $20
    Depreciation 8 $28
  From decrease in inventories 5
  From increase in capital stock 5
      Total $38
Funds applied:
  To increase in receivables .... $ 8
  To increase in fixed assets 8
  To decrease in current payables 7
  To decrease in long-term debt 3
  To payment of dividends 5
      Total 31
Net Increase in Funds
  (Cash and Marketable Securities) .... $ 7

Illustration 7–3. This statement differs from the preceding illustration only in that marketable securities are considered as funds in addition to cash.

3. Funds Defined as Net Monetary Assets. Under this alternative, funds are identified as net quick assets. For the Carter Company the total of cash, marketable securities, and receivables reduced by current payables is $16 and $38 at the close of 1967 and 1968 respectively. This net increase in funds of $22 can be explained by are funds flow statement shown in Illustration 7–4.

ILLUSTRATION 7–4

CARTER COMPANY

Changes in Net Monetary Assets
For the Year Ended December 31, 1968

Funds provided:
  From operations:
    Net income $20
    Depreciation 8 $28
  From decrease in inventories 5
  From increase in capital stock 5
      Total $38
Funds applied:
  To increase in fixed assets .... $ 8
  To decrease in long-term debt 3
  To payment of dividends 5
      Total 16
Net Increase in Funds (Quick Assets) $22

4. Funds Defined as Working Capital. This definition of funds treats current assets less current liabilities as a single body of funds. The working capital of the Carter Company can be summarized as shown in Illustration 7–5.

ILLUSTRATION 7–5

| | December 31 | | |
	1967	1968	Difference
Current Assets:			
Cash	$ 28	$ 30	$ 2
Marketable Securities	10	15	5
Receivables	32	40	8
Inventories	40	35	(5)
	$110	$120	$10
Less: Current Liabilities:			
Current payables	$ 54	$ 47	$ 7
Working Capital	$ 56	$ 73	$17

The funds flow statement is prepared by analyzing all noncurrent balance sheet accounts to explain the increase in working capital of $17, as shown in Illustration 7–6.

ILLUSTRATION 7–6

CARTER COMPANY

Changes in Working Capital
For the Year Ended December 31, 1968

Funds provided:		
From operations:		
Net income	$20	
Depreciation	8	$28
From increase in capital stock		5
Total		$33
Funds applied:		
To increase fixed assets	$ 8	
To decrease long-term debt	3	
To payment of dividends	5	
Total		16
Net Increase in Funds (Working Capital)........		$17

5. Funds Defined as All Financial Resources. This concept of funds is recommended by the APB for general usage. When funds are defined in this broad manner, the preceding working capital concept of funds flow is extended to include all transactions involving resources available to the firm, even though working capital is not directly affected. For example, the Carter Company issued $10 long-term debt directly for fixed assets; current asset and liability accounts were not changed in any way. Funds flow statements prepared under previous narrower definitions of funds deliberately excluded the effect of this transaction. It might be argued that such omission obscures an important event in Carter's financial affairs. Therefore the transaction is now recognized in the funds flow statement *as if* the issuance of debt resulted in a receipt of cash which was immediately paid for fixed assets. The funds flow statement resulting from application of this broadest concept of funds is shown in Illustration 7–7.

ILLUSTRATION 7–7

CARTER COMPANY

Source and Application of Funds
For the Year Ended December 31, 1968

Funds provided:		
From operations:		
Net income	$20	
Depreciation	8	$28
From increase in capital stock		5
From increase in long-term debt		10
Total		$43
Funds applied:		
To increase in fixed assets		$18
To decrease long-term debt		3
To payment of dividends		5
To increase working capital		17
Total		$43

The $10 increase in long-term debt is listed as a source of funds and the $3 retirement of long-term debt is included as an application of funds. As an alternative, these items might be netted and the resulting $7 increase would be included as a source of funds. Since the underlying objective of the funds flow statement is to provide useful information to the reader, it seems appropriate to present all material information in gross terms.

Funds flow statements are provided in many forms. Often the details of the changes in working capital are not summarized, but shown in detail, as in Illustration 7–8.

Statement of Balance Sheet Changes

For a number of analytical purposes, a rough approach to funds flow analysis can be accomplished by summarizing increases and decreases in comparative balance sheet accounts without adjustments. Such a statement for the Carter Company might appear as shown in Illustration 7–9.

ILLUSTRATION 7 0

CARTER COMPANY

Funds Flow Statement
For the Year Ended December 31, 1968

Funds provided:
From operations:

Net income	$20	
Depreciation	8	$28
From increase in capital stock		5
From increase in long-term debt		10
From decrease in inventories		5
Total		$48

Funds applied:

To increase in fixed assets	$18
To decrease in long-term debt	3
To payment of dividends	5
To increase in receivables	8
To decrease in current payables	7
To increase in cash and marketable securities ...	7
Total	$48

ILLUSTRATION 7–9

CARTER COMPANY

Changes in Balance Sheet Items
For the Year Ended December 31, 1968

Sources:
Decreases in assets:

Inventories	$ 5

Increases in liabilities and net worth:

Long-term debt	7
Capital stock	5
Retained earnings	15
Total	$32

Applied:
Increases in assets:

Cash	$ 2
Marketable securities	5
Receivables	8
Fixed assets	10

Decreases in liabilities and net worth:

Current payables	7
Total	$32

Working Papers for Funds Flow Statements

It was noted earlier that the funds flow statements would be prepared directly from an analysis of the differences between balance sheet accounts at the beginning and close of the accounting period. Minimum analysis of account balances is ordinarily required to obtain the needed information. When the number of accounts is unusually great or when transactions are complex, it may be desirable to prepare working papers to assemble the information for the funds flow statement in an orderly manner.

The working paper for the funds flow statement of the Dexter Company is presented in Illustration 7–10 as an example of the procedure which might be used to eliminate inaccuracy and confusion. A typical broad definition of funds as all financial resources is used. The following additional information is offered to make the illustration more comprehensive. During the year Dexter issued $12,000 in long-term notes payable for fixed assets, charged goodwill to earnings, and received $10,000 for its capital stock with a par value of $8,000. Operations resulted in net income after taxes of $20,000 and dividends of $5,000 were declared during 1968.

The working paper consists of five pairs of columns in which net changes in the balance sheet accounts are computed, adjusted if necessary, and classified to assemble information needed for preparation of the funds flow statement. In the first pair of columns, the balance sheet accounts at the beginning and close of the period are listed and net changes during the year are extended into the second pair of columns. In the Adjustments columns, certain of the net changes are eliminated, combined, or separated into component items after considering the effect upon funds flow. New accounts are created in the lower part of the work sheet to handle reclassification or labeling of items for the funds flow statement. The noncurrent items explaining funds flow are extended into the Funds Applied and Funds Provided columns, while current assets and liabilities are extended into the final pair of Working Capital columns. The computation of the balance "increase in working capital" in the fourth and fifth pairs of columns aids in proving mathematical accuracy of the work sheet.

The eight keyed adjustments of the working paper are explained briefly:

(1) Net income of $20,000 for the year is entered as the explanation for increased retained earnings.
(2) Dividends of $5,000 required the expenditure of funds and caused a corresponding decrease in retained earnings.
(3) Amortization of goodwill is recorded as an addition to income, as the charge did not result in a funds outflow.
(4) Depreciation charged for the year of $35,000 (the amount of the increase in accumulated depreciation) is recorded as an addition to net income to compute total funds derived from operations.
(5) The $12,000 issue of long-term notes payable for fixed assets is recognized. In the strictest sense, working capital was not affected by this transaction. However, in order to present funds flow in a broader manner, the event is treated as though notes payable had been issued for cash which was immediately paid for fixed assets.

ILLUSTRATION 7-10

Brown Company
Working Paper: Source and Application of Funds
For the year ended December 31, 1968 (in thousands of dollars)

Accounts	Balances 1967	Dec. 31 1968	Net Change Dr	Net Change Cr	Adj. ref	Adj. Dr	Adj. Cr	Funds Applied Dr	Funds Provided Cr	Working Capital Increase Dr	Working Capital Decrease Cr
Debits											
Cash	50	60	10							10	
Marketable securities	20	25	5							5	
Receivables	71	65		6							6
Inventories	74	82	8							8	
Fixed assets	320	373	53		(3)		53				
Goodwill	5	–		5		5					
	540	605									
Credits											
Accumulated depreciation	65	100		35	(4)	35					
Current payables	105	100	5							5	
Long-term notes payable	80	90		10	(5)	12	2				
Capital stock – at par	180	188		8	(6)	8					
Other paid-in capital	20	22		2	(8)	2					
Retained earnings	90	105		15	(1)	20	5				
	540	605	81	81							
Funds provided by operations:											
Net income per income statement					(1)		20		60		
Add: depreciation					(4)		35				
Add: amortization of goodwill					(3)		5				
Funds applied to dividends					(2)	5		5			
Funds provided by long-term notes					(5)		12		12		
Funds applied to purchase fixed assets						53		53			
Funds applied to retirement of long-term notes					(7)	2		2			
Funds provided by sale of capital stock							10		10		
						142	142	60	82	28	6
Increase in working capital								22			22
								82	82	28	28

(6) The acquisition of fixed assets for $53,000 is entered. (This amount includes $12,000 acquired by issuing long-term notes payable. See (5) above.)

(7) Payment of long-term notes payable of $2,000 can be inferred from the net increase of $10,000 during the year and the effect of adjustment (5) above. The notes payable account increased by $10,000. However, we know that $12,000 of notes payable were issued. Therefore, $2,000 of notes payable were retired.

(8) Proceeds from the sale of capital stock is identified on the working paper as a single item by bringing together the net increases in the capital stock and other paid-in capital accounts.

The working paper should not be considered a substitute for the funds flow statement. It merely provides means for assembly of the information for the statement. The formal funds flow statement can be easily prepared from the amounts extended into the Funds Applied and Provided columns, as shown in Illustration 7–11.

ILLUSTRATION 7–11

DEXTER COMPANY

Sources and Application of Funds
For the Year Ended December 31, 1968

Funds sources:
    From operations:
        Net income for the year $20
        Depreciation and amortization of goodwill 40 $60
    Increase in long-term debt 12
    Sales of capital stock 10
        Total $82

Funds applications:
    Dividends paid .... $ 5
    Purchase of capital equipment 53
    Repayment of long-term debt 2
    Increase in working capital 22
        Total $82

A number of alternative forms of the funds flow working paper might be used instead of the particular columnar headings and procedures illustrated. For example, the entire working paper could be simplified significantly by omitting the first and last pairs of columns and using only net changes in the noncurrent accounts along with the single balancing amount of the net increase (or decrease) in working capital. Simplifications of this type emphasize that funds flow statements may ordinarily be prepared directly from comparative balance sheets with a minimum analysis of accounts.

Cash Flow Per Share

In recent years, as part of the growing use of funds flow analysis, security analysts and financial reporting services have given greater weight to cash flow per share, which is usually defined as net profit after taxes plus noncash expenses such as depreciation. Often, the impression is given that cash flow per share is a superior measurement to net income as a measure of management performance. In response to this development, the Accounting Principles Board in *Opinion No. 3* stated:

The amount of funds derived from operations cannot be considered as a substitute for or an improvement upon properly determined net income as a measure of results of operations and the consequent effect on financial position. Misleading implications can result from isolated statistics in annual reports of "cash flow" which are not placed in proper perspective to net income figures and to a complete analysis of source and application of funds. "Cash flow" and related terms should not be used in annual reports in such a way that the significance of net income is impaired, and "cash earnings" or other terms with a similar connotation should be avoided. The Board regards computations of "cash flow per share" as misleading since they ignore the impact of cash expenditures for renewal and replacement of facilities and tend to downgrade the significant economic statistic of "earnings per share."

SUGGESTED FURTHER READINGS

FINNEY, HARRY A., and MILLER, HERBERT E. *Principles of Accounting: Introduction*, chaps. 22, 23. 6th ed. Englewood Cliffs, N.J.: Prentice-Hall, 1963.

KARRENBROCK, WILBERT, and SIMONS, HARRY. *Intermediate Accounting*, chap. 28. Cincinnati: South-Western Publishing Co., 1958.

MASON, PERRY. *"Cash Flow" Analysis and the Funds Statement*, Accounting Research Study No. 2. New York: American Institute of Certified Public Accountants, 1961.

CASES

Case 7–1. **WALTHAM COMPANY, INCORPORATED**

Funds Flow Analysis

Mr. Joseph Johnson, in line with his objective of assisting small companies through their early periods of growth and development, was beginning to take a closer look at the Waltham Company, Inc. Mr. Johnson had recently purchased a major block of stock from one of the original stockholders and had accepted a position on the company's board of directors. The company had a good profit record and Mr. Johnson felt that the general nature and reputation of its product lines gave it some real potential for future growth.

In anticipation of taking over his duties as a director, Mr. Johnson began looking at the unaudited financial statements prepared by the company bookkeeper for the year 1969. These consisted of comparative balance sheets for December 31, 1968 and 1969; and year-end statement of retained earnings and capital surplus for 1969; and a 1969 condensed income statement. These statements are reproduced in Exhibits 1 and 2.

Upon reviewing these statements Mr. Johnson was alarmed, and somewhat puzzled, to note that the working capital of the company had declined nearly $100,000. He thought this was particularly serious since the cash position had declined substantially in the face of a before-tax profit of $335,000 and an aftertax profit of $233,000. He planned to discuss this situation with management, but first he wanted to obtain as complete an analysis of the causes of the decrease in working capital as he could from the financial statements and supplementary data presently available to him.

In an attempt to better acquaint himself with accounting principles and practices, Mr. Johnson often discussed the financial statements he received with Franklin Addison, a partner in a local accounting firm. Mr. Addison had been a close friend and advisor to Mr. Johnson for a number of years.

EXHIBIT 1

WALTHAM COMPANY, INC.

Comparative Balance Sheets at December 31
(in thousands)
(unaudited)

	1968		1969	
ASSETS				
Current Assets:				
Cash	$129		$ 42	
Marketable securities	55		25	
Accounts receivable (net)	110		160	
Inventory	152	$ 446	222	$ 449
Long-Term Assets:				
Plant and equipment	$370		$460	
Less: Accumulated depreciation	108	262	90	370
Goodwill		90		
Patents		50		110
Other intangibles		20		40
Investment in subsidiary companies		500		580
Other assets		14		96
Total Assets		$1,382		$1,645
LIABILITIES AND STOCKHOLDERS' EQUITY				
Current Liabilities:				
Accounts payable	$210		$250	
Accrued charges	60		80	
Accrued taxes	62	$ 332	97	$ 427
Mortgages payable		125		100
Reserve for deferred taxes		30		50
Capital stock ($100 par)	$500		$540	
Capital surplus	200		190	
Retained earnings	195	895	338	1,068
Total Liabilities and Stockholders'				
Equity		$1,382		$1,645

Mr. Johnson remembered a discussion several months back concerning a statement called the Statement of Sources and Applications of Funds. Although he did not fully understand this statement, he understood that this type of analysis would help him to gain the insight he wanted into the financial operations of the Waltham Company and would help to explain why working capital had decreased.

Questions

1. Prepare a brief memorandum which will provide Mr. Johnson with a greater understanding of the financial condition and operations of this company. Include a statement of sources and applications of funds in your memorandum. What accounting and reporting practices appear to be questionable? In what respects do these obscure significant information?

2. Point out to Mr. Johnson specific lines of inquiry which you think he should undertake with the management of the company (with reasons therefor) on the basis of the information revealed by your analysis of the financial statements.

EXHIBIT 2

WALTHAM COMPANY, INC.

Income Statement and Changes in Surplus for Year Ended
December 31, 1969
(in thousands)
(unaudited)

Sales		$3,500
Less: Cost of sales		2,600
Gross profit		$ 900
Less: Selling expenses	$400	
Administrative expenses	135	535
Net profit from operations		$ 365
Other income and expenses:		
Deduct: Other expenses	$ 40	
Add: Equity in 1969 earnings of subsidiary	10	30
Profit before taxes		$ 335
Income taxes		102
Profit after taxes		$ 233

Analysis of Changes in Surplus

Capital surplus:		
Balance, December 31, 1968		$ 200
Add: Premium on sale of capital stock		80
		$ 280
Deduct: Write-off of goodwill		90
Balance, December 31, 1969		$ 190
Retained earnings		
Balance, December 31, 1968		$ 195
Add: Profit after taxes		233
		$ 428
Deduct: Amortization of patents	$ 45	
Loss on sale of buildings and equipment *	30	
Cash dividend	15	90
Balance, December 31, 1969		$ 338

* Because of a modernization program undertaken by the company, some excess facilities were disposed of by sale. Book value at time of sale was $110,000; originally the facilities cost $200,000.

Case 7–2. **LAKELAND AIRLINES, INCORPORATED**

Determination of Funds Flow Disclosure Policy

On January 15, 1970, the board of directors of Lakeland Airlines, Inc. was considering a recommendation by Mr. Peter Prentiss, the company's controller, that Lakeland include a funds flow statement in its 1969 annual report to stockholders. Mr. Prentiss believed the addition of a funds flow statement would greatly enhance the ability of stockholders to analyze the company's activities as well as provide management with a useful means of communication with stockholders. Also, Mr. Prentiss indicated that the American Institute of Certified Public Accountants and the New York Stock Exchange had recommended that companies include a funds statement in their annual reports.

In general, the board members were sympathetic toward Mr. Prentiss's proposal, but before approving his suggestion they wanted to resolve a number of issues concerning the format of the statement, its location in the annual report, and whether or not their public accountant should include the funds flow statement in the materials covered by his opinion report.

The Company

Lakeland Airlines, Inc. was founded in 1952 by Mr. John Drew, a former military air transport pilot. Originally the airline's only aircraft, a Korean war surplus Douglas DC–3, operated between Philadelphia and a number of small towns in upper Pennsylvania. During the following years, as more and more cities built airports and existing feeder lines went out of business, the company acquired CAB approval to fly additional routes throughout the mid-Atlantic states, Ohio, West Virginia, Kentucky, and upper New York state.

Initially, Mr. Drew financed this expansion through the sale of common stock and convertible debentures to a number of the major industrial companies within the area serviced by his company. These companies bought Lakeland stock so that the cities where their plants were located would have reliable air service. In 1960, in order to finance the acquisition of a number of turbo-prop Viscount aircraft, Lakeland offered some common shares to the public. This offering was well received and the securities were traded actively on the New York over-the-counter market. Subsequently, in 1965, a larger common stock offering was made in order to finance the purchase of several Caravelle jet aircraft. As of December 31, 1969, Lakeland had over 2,500 stockholders, of which 25 were corporations in towns serviced by Lakeland.

EXHIBIT 1

LAKELAND AIRLINES, INC.

Income Statement for the Year Ended December 31, 1969
(millions of dollars)

Operating revenue:

Commercial revenue	25.6
Federal subsidy	4.2
Total operating revenue	29.8

Operating expense:

Flying operations	7.3
Direct maintenance, flight equipment	4.5
Depreciation, flight equipment *	1.0
Total direct expense	12.8
Direct maintenance, ground equipment	0.3
Maintenance burden	1.9
Passenger servicing	1.1
Aircraft servicing	2.9
Traffic servicing	3.4
Reservation and sales	2.9
General and administrative	1.5
Depreciation, ground equipment *	0.3
Development and preoperating costs	0.1
Total indirect expense	14.4
Total operating expense	27.2

Operating profit	2.6

Nonoperating expense:

Interest and amortization of debt expense	0.3
All other expense (income)	(0.1)
Total nonoperating expense	0.2
Net income before taxes and special item	2.4

Provision for federal income taxes *

Current	1.0
Deferred	0.1
Total income taxes	1.1
Net earnings before special item	1.3

Special item:

Amortization of goodwill	0.1
Net Earnings Retained for the Year	1.2

* See Note D to Exhibit 2.

EXHIBIT 2

LAKELAND AIRLINES, INC.

Balance Sheets at December 31, 1969 and 1968
(millions of dollars)

RESOURCES	1969	1968
Current Assets:		
Cash	2.1	0.8
Accounts receivable:		
U.S. government agencies	0.7	0.9
Airline traffic, less reserve	2.2	2.0
Other, less reserve	0.3	0.3
Inventories (Note A)	1.9	1.7
Prepaid expenses	0.3	0.2
Total Current Assets	7.5	5.9
Assets Applied to Aircraft Order (Note B):		
Cash deposits, restricted	0.0	3.6
Deposits on aircraft and engines	4.3	0.5
Aircraft acquisition costs	0.4	0.3
Total	4.7	4.4
Operating Property and Equipment (at cost):		
Flight equipment (Notes B, C)	13.5	12.4
Ground property and equipment	2.0	1.7
Construction in progress	0.0	0.1
Total	15.5	14.2
Less: Amortization and depreciation provisions (Note D)	6.9	6.0
Net Operating Property and Equipment	8.6	8.2

LIABILITIES AND SHAREHOLDERS' EQUITY	1969	1968
Current Liabilities:		
Equipment obligations (Note B)	0.5	0.3
Accounts payable and accrued expenses	3.6	4.0
Accrued taxes on income (Note D)	1.0	0.2
Unearned transportation revenue	0.2	0.1
Total Current Liabilities	5.3	4.6
Long-Term Debt (Note C):		
Equipment obligations	0.7	0.4
Subordinated notes and debentures	6.4	9.2
Total Long-Term Debt	7.1	9.6
Future Liabilities:		
Deferred income taxes (Note D)	0.4	0.3
Lease and purchase commitments (Notes B, E)	0.0	0.0
Total Future Liabilities	0.4	0.3
Shareholders' Equity:		
Capital stock, common, $1 par, authorized shares, 3,000,000; outstanding shares:		
1,770,142, less 57,220 in treasury	1.7	
1,143,906, less 57,220 in treasury		1.1
Additional paid-in capital	5.8	3.2
Retained earnings	1.6	0.4
Total Shareholders' Equity	9.1	4.7

Deferred Charges:		
Development and preoperating costs	0.3	0.2
Discount and expense on debt	0.1	0.2
Total Deferred Charges	0.4	0.4
Other Assets:		
Investments and advances	0.1	0.1
Notes receivable:		
Officers, secured by capital stock	0.0	0.1
Goodwill	0.4	0.0
Capital stock expense	0.2	0.1
Total Other Assets	0.7	0.3
Total Resources	21.9	19.2
Total Liabilities and Shareholders' Equity	21.9	19.2

A. *Inventories.* The company's inventories consist of operating supplies and aircraft expendable parts. These inventories are carried at cost less valuation reserves established to provide for estimated losses from obsolescence and deterioration.

B. *Replacement of Flight Equipment.* The company has signed contracts and letters of intent under which it will during 1970–73 sell or trade most of its present aircraft and will purchase BAC 1–11 fan-jet and FH 227 turbo prop aircraft. Net cost of the 25 new aircraft is estimated at $49 million. Under contractual agreements the company has made payments aggregating $4.3 million in advance of delivery on its purchase of BAC 1–11 aircraft and Rolls-Royce fan-jet engines. Preacquisition costs, including financing expense, incurred for purpose of acquiring these aircraft have been capitalized.

C. *Notes Payable and Long-Term Debt.* Equipment obligations and subordinated notes and debentures mature in various amounts over a 14-year period ending 1983. Six of the company's aircraft are pledged to secure equipment notes. The company has a bank loan commitment for $6 million and an informal agreement to obtain loans aggregating as much as $34 million in connection with its acquisition of new aircraft.

D. *Income Taxes.* Current income taxes are shown net after deducting allowable investment credits. Adjustments of relatively immaterial amounts have been made in deferred income taxes to reflect changes caused by the Revenue Act of 1964. Deferred income tax liability results primarily from use of straight-line depreciation and amortization rates suggested by the Civil Aeronautics Board for statement purposes, while accelerated methods are used in computing deductions for current income taxes.

E. *Lease Commitments.* The company's headquarters and primary maintenance plant, as well as facilities in communities served by Lakeland, are entirely leased. Terms of these leases and contracts vary from 30 days to 25 years. It is estimated that present commitments will require annual net payments of approximately $1.3 million.

Through its 17-year history, Lakeland had almost constantly been short of cash, principally because of its policy of using the most modern aircraft available for its type of business and the increasing investments required to service its expanding route system. Consequently, small dividends had been declared only twice, and the company had entered into a number of bank loans. While no stockholder had ever questioned the "no dividend–heavy bank loan" policy, Mr. Drew believed many of the stockholders did not really understand the company's financial policy.

In early 1969, Lakeland acquired the Pioneer Airlines, a major feeder line servicing parts of West Virginia, Ohio, and Kentucky. Lakeland exchanged shares with a market value of $2.5 million for the Pioneer plant, equipment, and routes. These assets were carried on Pioneer's books at $2 million. The excess of investment over these values was added to the Lakeland goodwill account. The board intended to write this goodwill off as a special charge against income over a five-year period, beginning in 1969.

To bring the Pioneer service up to Lakeland's high standards of quality, two second-hand Convair 440's were added to the Pioneer fleet at a cost of $1.7 million. In order to finance this purchase, $1 million was borrowed from the Marine Merchants Bank, New York, and $0.7 million of stock was sold to several insurance companies. In the near future, Mr. Drew planned to replace these aircraft with British Aircraft Corporation 1–11 fan-jets.

John Drew's ambition was to build Lakeland into a major airline before he retired in 1980. Therefore, he anticipated there would be more stock issues, more route acquisitions, more bank loans and more equipment investments during the remaining 10 years of his presidency.

Exhibits 1 and 2 present the financial statements management planned to include in the 1969 annual report to stockholders.

Questions

1. Should Lakeland include a funds flow statement in its 1969 annual report to stockholders?

2. Which definition of "funds" do you think Lakeland should adopt?

3. Construct the funds flow statement you believe Lakeland should present to its stockholders. Where in the annual report would you include your statement? Would you ask Lakeland's public accountant to include your statement in materials covered by his report?

4. Prepare a one-paragraph interpretive comment explaining the significant flows indicated by your statement.

PART III

Role of Certified Public Accountants

CHAPTER **8**

THE AUDITOR'S OPINION

Published financial statements are usually accompanied by a signed auditor's report. This report means that a member of a licensed profession, who is morally bound to exercise his competent independent judgment, has examined management's financial statements to the extent he thinks necessary and stakes his professional reputation upon his opinion that the financial statements present fairly the financial position and results of operations of the company. The criteria upon which he bases this opinion are "generally accepted auditing standards" and "generally accepted accounting principles."

It is important to note that the auditor in his report expresses his professional *opinion* as to the *fairness* of financial statements prepared and presented by management. For many years, until the early 1930s, it was customary for auditors to use the phrase "we hereby certify" in their reports on financial statements. Even today the term "auditor's certificate" is used interchangeably with "auditor's report." This unfortunate terminology may be partly responsible for the confusion as to the nature of the auditor's work. The professional auditor may well be certified by a state licensing board, but he does not certify financial statements.

Almost all publicly owned businesses offer audited statements, because they are required by stock exchange regulations or federal or state laws or because management recognizes a responsibility to include auditor's opinions in its report to stockholders.

THE AUDITOR'S PROFESSION

The professional auditor has two characteristics which make his opinion on published financial statements useful: namely, independence and competence. The role of the auditor will continue to be significant only to the extent that the public generally continues to attribute these two qualities to the profession of public accountancy.

From the public's point of view, independence is perhaps the more important of the auditor's characteristics; certainly it is the more difficult for the auditor to achieve. A basic conflict arises because the client whose financial statements are examined pays for the services of the auditor. To be independent, the professional auditor must be prepared to place his responsibilities to third-party readers of financial reports higher than a desire to continue offering his services to a particular client. This attitude of public responsibility and service is an essential element which characterizes a profession and distinguishes it from commercial enterprise. Because public accountants have been able to achieve this sense of public responsibility, they have earned the right to call auditing a "profession."

Competence is the second characteristic which the auditor must achieve and maintain. The professional accountant offering his services to the public must comply with the licensing restrictions of the states in which he practices. Public accountancy boards are appointed by the state governors to administer each state's public accounting regulations. All those wishing to become certified public accountants must pass a two-and-one-half day examination prepared and graded by the American Institute of Certified Public Accountants. This exam is given simultaneously by each state board in May and November. Typically, candidates must meet qualifying requirements of citizenship, education, experience, and personal character. These licensing requirements have developed over a period of some 70 years to protect the public interest by restricting the practice of public accountancy to those who have a demonstrated proficiency in accounting and its applications.

The American Institute of Certified Public Accountants is a national organization with more than 60,000 members, all of whom are certified public accountants and have met certain experience requirements. All of the Institute's extensive programs are directed toward enhancing the level of the profession. Its members are subject to a code of professional ethics adopted voluntarily and enforced by the group. Training and professional development programs are sponsored continuously. The Institute has, as the voice of the accounting profession, assumed the position of leadership in the development of auditing standards and accounting principles. Its publications include the monthly *Journal of Accountancy*, Accounting Research Studies, Statements on Auditing Procedures, and many technical and professional books and pamphlets.

The auditor, as a member of a profession, has a legal responsibility to his client and to third parties who might be injured by shortcomings in his audit opinions. As a general rule, the client may recover damages from an auditor who has been negligent in the performance of his examination, and third parties may claim damages in case of the auditor's fraud or gross negligence.

The professional accountant offers his services to the public in a number of areas related to financial reporting and management. Traditionally he is best known as an auditor reviewing the accounting statements and records of business firms so that his opinion can be given. The work of the professional accountant includes preparation of tax returns and counseling in related matters, installation of accounting systems, and the newer and expanding field of management services. The following comments are concerned only with auditing.

THE AUDITOR'S REPORT

The auditor's report is addressed to the directors and stockholders of the client corporation. It usually follows closely a standard form and language. The short-form report recommended by the Committee on Auditing Procedure of the American Institute of Certified Public Accountants is:

Date

To the XYZ Corporation, its Directors, and its Stockholders:

We have examined the balance sheet of the XYZ Company as of December 31, 19___ and the related statement(s) of income and retained earnings for the year then ended. Our examination was made in accordance with generally accepted auditing standards, and accordingly included such tests of the accounting records and such other auditing procedures as we considered necessary in the circumstances.

In our opinion, the accompanying balance sheet and statement(s) of income and retained earnings present fairly the financial position of XYZ Company at December 31, 19___, and the results of its operations for the year then ended, in conformity with generally accepted accounting principles applied on a basis consistent with that of the preceding year.

ABC
Certified Public Accountants

Each word and phrase in this report has been carefully chosen to describe concisely the examination and to state the opinion to which the examination has led.

The first paragraph of the standard short-form report is called the "scope paragraph" and emphasizes that the auditor's examination has conformed to "generally accepted auditing standards." Auditing standards are the criteria for measuring the quality of the auditor's performance in his engagements. The auditing standards generally accepted by the profession have been described by the American Institute of Certified Public Accountants Committee on Auditing Procedure and approved by the membership of the Institute. They are: [1]

---

[1] These standards are explained in greater detail in *Statements on Auditing Procedure, No. 33* published by the American Institute of Certified Public Accountants in 1963.

General Standards

1. The examination is to be performed by a person or persons having adequate technical training and proficiency as an auditor.
2. In all matters relating to the assignment an independence in mental attitude is to be maintained by the auditor or auditors.
3. Due professional care is to be exercised in the performance of the examination and the preparation of the report.

Standards of Field Work

1. The work is to be adequately planned and assistants, if any, are to be properly supervised.
2. There is to be a proper study and evaluation of the existing internal control as a basis for reliance thereon and for the determination of the resultant extent of the tests to which auditing procedures are to be restricted.
3. Sufficient competent evidential matter is to be obtained through inspection, observation, inquiries, and confirmations to afford a reasonable basis for an opinion regarding the financial statements under examination.

Standards of Reporting

1. The report shall state whether the financial statements are presented in accordance with generally accepted principles of accounting.
2. The report shall state whether such principles have been consistently observed in the current period in relation to the preceding period.
3. Informative disclosures in the financial statements are to be regarded as reasonably adequate unless otherwise stated in the report.
4. The report shall either contain an expression of opinion regarding the financial statements, taken as a whole, or an assertion to the effect that an opinion cannot be expressed. When an over-all opinion cannot be expressed, the reasons therefor should be stated. In all cases where an auditor's name is associated with financial statements the report should contain a clear-cut indication of the character of the auditor's examination, if any, and the degree of responsibility he is taking.

The second paragraph of the standard short-form report is called the "opinion paragraph." In a single sentence the auditor attests that the financial statements:

1. Present fairly the financial position and the results of operations.
2. Are in conformity with generally accepted accounting principles.
3. Are on a basis consistent with that of the prior year.

The phrase "present fairly" means that the opinion applies to the statements taken as a whole. The auditor does not imply that any single item on the statements is exact or precisely correct. Instead he professes that the statements as a whole are a complete disclosure and free from any material bias or misstatement.

"Generally accepted accounting principles" is perhaps the most debated phrase in the area of financial accounting. Though the term has been commonly used for at least a quarter of a century, there has been no single definition or listing of principles which has been universally accepted by accounting theorists and practitioners. Accounting principles have been compared to English spelling and pronunciation in that usage by those considered competent becomes the generally accepted standard. Probably the most authoritative enumeration of accounting principles has been published by the AICPA in its *Accounting Research Bulletins* and *Opinions* of the Accounting Principles Board. Members of the AICPA are required to disclose departures from these principles in financial statements for fiscal years beginning after December 31, 1965. Other sources of information about accounting principles include publications of the American Accounting Association and the U.S. Securities and Exchange Commission. The Accounting Principles Board in 1970 published Statement No. 4, "Basic Concepts and Accounting Principles Underlying Financial Statements of Business Enterprises," to encourage discussion of accounting principles and practices. Statement No. 4 is not an official pronouncement of the APB, but it does appear to be the most complete codification of accounting principles and practices available currently.

The auditor's reference to "consistency" assures the reader that alternative accounting procedures and statement presentation methods used for the current period do not vary from those of the previous year. This uniformity allows useful comparisons of financial position and operating results for successive periods.

Forms of the Audit Report

There are four different forms in which the auditor's opinion might be expressed. They are (1) an unqualified opinion, (2) a qualified opinion, (3) an adverse opinion, and (4) a disclaimer of opinion. The choice of the form of opinion and the language used in departures from the recommended short-form opinion are a part of the auditor's responsibility for the application of informed judgment in all matters concerning the audit.

The auditor's standard short-form report presented earlier illustrated an unqualified opinion. The auditor made no reservations and stated no conditions precedent to his opinion about the fairness of management's financial statements. Typically, in most audit engagements, conditions which might lead to a restricted opinion can be eliminated by agreement between the auditor and the client to extend the auditing procedure or revise the financial statements.

The qualified opinion includes a statement indicating that the auditor is unable to express a full unqualified opinion. There are a number of reasons why this style of opinion might be appropriate. The client's unwillingness to permit some essential auditing procedure, such as confirming accounts receivable or observation of the taking of inventories, would require qualification of the auditor's opinion. Failure of the auditor to agree with the propriety of an accounting method or a presentation on the financial statements would also result in a qualification. Phrases including "except" or "exception" are usually inserted in either or both paragraphs of the short-form opinion together with necessary explanation why the auditor used a qualified opinion. Occasionally an opinion notes another type of qualification; the phrase "subject to" followed by an explanation of uncertainties about valuation or realization of assets or prediction of contingent liabilities is used when the auditor has reservation regarding these items as represented by management.

An adverse opinion is a completely negative expression by the auditor about the fairness of the financial statements. If exceptions concerning fairness of presentation are so material that a qualified opinion would not be justified, the auditor must state that in his opinion the statements "do *not* present fairly" the financial position and results of operations. A separate paragraph inserted between the scope and opinion paragraphs of the short-form report presents the reasons for the adverse opinion. This type of report is rarely published. Indeed, the engagement leading to an adverse opinion would probably be terminated prior to its completion.

The disclaimer of opinion is a pronouncement by the auditor that he is unable to express any of the preceding three types of opinion on the financial statements. A disclaimer is used when the auditor has not obtained "sufficient competent evidential matter" to form an opinion on the fairness of the financial statements. The reasons for the use of the disclaimer, which must be fully disclosed, might include a serious limitation on the scope of the examination or the existence of unusual uncertainties concerning the amounts reported in the statements.

Frequently the auditor's examination results in a so-called long-form report. This report contains all of the essential elements of the more familiar short-form but includes supplementary information about the business entity and its financial position and operations. Comments about the history of the business, comparative analyses, ratios, and a statement of application of funds might be presented. Management and creditors may find this type of report more useful for their purposes. The examining procedures used and the responsibility of the auditor are the same for both the short-form and long-form reports.

Typically, the auditor's short-form report presented in annual reports to stockholders covers the comparative balance sheet, income statement, statement of retained earnings, and funds flow statement. Other financial and nonfinancial information included elsewhere in the annual report is not usually covered by the auditor's opinion.

THE AUDITOR'S WORK

Auditors use a variety of techniques to examine the financial statements of a company. The techniques applied in carrying out an "audit program" can be grouped into four categories: internal analysis, inspection, external communication, and analytical review. The specific auditing procedures used in any engagement will be determined by relevance of the "Standards of Field Work" to the particular situation. As noted earlier, these standards relate to planning and supervision, evaluation of the internal control system, and evidential matter.

The Audit Program

The auditor prepares his audit program early in his examination after appraisal of the company's situation. The audit program is a schedule of audit procedures and the extent to which they will be applied during the course of the audit. This formalized plan of audit procedures prepared by the auditor in charge of the engagement serves several vital needs. First, it enables him to anticipate time and manpower requirements. Second, it permits effective assignments to assistants and aids coordination of their efforts. Third, the audit program serves as a master list of the audit procedures facilitating indexing of working papers prepared during the examination. Some audit forms have developed standard "check-list" programs which are used on all engagements to insure that no essential procedure is omitted. Other firms insist that the auditor-in-charge prepare a program specifically for each engagement. In any event, each audit will require program modifications to fit the requirements of the investigation. The audit program is subject to constant revision as the aduit progresses and new circumstances are revealed by the examination. In this sense, the audit program is not in final form until the entire audit is completed and the auditor's report has been drafted.

Since the audit is essentially an examination of the financial statements, it is logical that investigations of the financial accounts are, in general, accomplished in the order of their appearance on the balance sheet and on the income statement. The interrelationship of the accounts makes it impractical to audit any single segment of the client's operations without recognizing the effect upon other accounts. For example, the examination of accounts receivable will directly relate to cash receipts, income recognition, and finished goods shipments. Therefore, the audit proceeds by investigation of various areas of functional activity rather than of individual account balances.

Evaluation of Internal Controls

Early in the examination, the auditor must make a study of the internal controls existing in the organization. The system of internal controls includes all measures instituted by management: (1) to insure accuracy and dependability of financial data, (2) to protect assets from improper or inefficient use, and (3) to control and evaluate operations. The present-day concept of internal control is much broader than that of a generation ago, when internal controls were almost limited to prevention of fraud and clerical inaccuracy. The modern auditor is concerned with all administrative aspects of the business entity he examines, as well as its financial records and properties.

The extent of the auditing procedures to be required by the auditor will depend almost entirely upon the adequacy of the system of internal controls he observes. The evaluation of internal controls continues throughout the entire course of the audit. Financial and administrative procedures are investigated by inquiry and observation. Usually the results of this essential part of the examination are summarized in a separate report to management, together with recommendations for improved internal controls. The auditor's evaluation of internal controls is the basis for determining the degree of reliability of the resulting financial statements. Obviously, there is an inverse relationship between reliability of financial data and the amount of evidential matter the auditor requires to reach his opinion on the financial statements.

Auditing Procedures

A comprehensive view of auditing procedures would require detailed consideration of the many groups of accounts which make up the financial statements. Auditing procedures might be classified by the types of investigative activities employed by the auditor: (1) internal analysis, (2) inspection, (3) external communication, and (4) analytical review. Each of these groups is considered briefly to describe the varied techniques used by the auditor to help form his opinion of management's financial statements.

The principles of testing and sampling must be extensively employed throughout the audit procedure. It would be impractical (and probably impossible) for the auditor to examine and review all records and activities of a business entity. The auditor's judgment, supplemented to an increasing extent by scientific sampling methods, is the basis for determining testing procedures.

1. Internal Analysis. A major part of the auditor's time is devoted to an analysis of the company's internal financial records. The extent of his internal analysis to verify mathematical accuracy is minimized by the presence of internal controls. Many of the accounts are analyzed so that the auditor may independently verify changes and balances. For example, receivable and payable accounts may be analyzed and listed for subsequent investigation. Plant asset and security investment accounts are analyzed to show necessary details of balances. Supporting business documents such as purchase invoices, checks issued, and cash remittance receipts are traced and compared to the accounting entries. The client's employees may assist with clerical work, but the auditor's independence must be maintained by close supervision and verification.

2. Inspection. Auditors make extensive visual inspections of their client's properties in order to independently satisfy themselves that assets are properly presented. Cash on hand is counted and securities are inspected for reconciliation with records. Physical inventories taken by the client's employees are observed by the auditor. Plant assets may be inspected in at least a limited manner. These inspections and observations must of necessity be coordinated with the client's business operations and with preparation of appropriate analyses of the financial accounts.

3. External Communication. The auditor frequently communicates directly with individuals, businesses, and institutions having dealings with his audit client. These external communications or confirmations aid the auditor in verifying relationships independently of the client's records. In all instances, information is requested from outsiders only with the client's approval and cooperation. Confirmations might be obtained (1) from banks, to verify balances of cash on deposit and amounts of indebtedness; (2) from trade creditors; (3) from customers; (4) from corporate transfer agents and registrars; (5) from sinking fund trustees; (6) from public warehouses; and (7) from others, such as appraisers and attorneys. Typically, these direct communications with third parties produce evidence that is considered highly credible by the auditor in forming his independent opinion.

4. Analytical Review. An analytical review of the relationships between data shown by the financial records and revealed during the audit examination add significantly to the auditor's satisfaction with resulting financial statements. It is in this general area that the ingenuity and imagination of the auditor become especially important. For example, comparisons of the client's current bad debt losses with those of prior periods and with those for other businesses in the industry provide insights into the adequacy of the client's bad debt provisions. Analysis of changes in departmental gross profit rates and inventory turnover may help substantiate the recorded income and inventory levels. Comparison of income from securities with records of security ownership adds assurance that financial statements present consistent data. Property tax payments will corroborate property ownership.

SUMMARY

Auditing procedures include an almost unlimited variety of investigations designed by the auditor so that he can form his independent professional opinion of management's financial statements. This opinion is expressed in his audit report. In an unqualified report the auditor states to management and owners that: (1) he has completed his examination of the business in a manner required by the application of generally accepted auditing standards, and (2) he offers his opinion, backed by his competence and independence, that management's financial statements present fairly the entity's financial position and the results of its operation in accordance with "generally accepted accounting practices."

SUGGESTED FURTHER READING

AMERICAN INSTITUTE OF CERTIFIED PUBLIC ACCOUNTANTS. *Audit Guides* (various dates and subjects). New York: AICPA.

DAVIS, GORDON B. *Auditing and EDP.* New York: AICPA, 1968.

HOLMES, ARTHUR W. *Basic Auditing Principles.* Homewood, Ill.: Richard D. Irwin, 1966.

MONTGOMERY, ROBERT H. *Montgomery's Auditing.* New York: Ronald Press Co., 1957.

CASES

Case 8–1. **COMET SERVICE, INCORPORATED**

Testing Internal Controls for Cash Receipts and Disbursements

Comet Service, Inc. was engaged in servicing and repairing elevator equipment. Maintenance service contracts were the major source of revenue. Substantial repair jobs furnished the remainder of the company's revenue. Annual sales were approximately $10 million and there were about 150 men engaged in service and repair work.

The company had not been previously audited. Your public accounting firm has been engaged to make annual examinations. You have been assigned to review and test the cash receipts and disbursements procedures and to make suggestions for improvements where the internal accounting controls appear to be deficient.

The company's accounting staff consists of:

1. Cashier.
2. Assistant cashier, who also posted the detail accounts receivable ledger.
3. Bookkeeper.
4. Assistant bookkeeper.
5. Billing and job cost clerk.
6. Two general clerks—filing, general office work, incoming and outgoing mail.
7. Secretary.
8. Messenger.

The vice president, who is engaged mostly in the technical end of the business, is also the treasurer. You are favorably impressed with the caliber of the staff, who appear to carry out their duties efficiently. The accounting records are kept on a manual basis.

The following is a brief summary of the procedures as you have recorded them in your notes:

Cash Receipts

a) All incoming remittances were received by check.

b) Incoming mail was opened by one of the general clerks.

c) Clerk prepared two adding machine tapes of checks as a means of control, one tape of checks accompanied by remittance advices and another of checks for which remittance advices were not received. On the latter tape, the clerk noted against each item the name of the customer for the information of the accounts receivable ledger clerk in posting collections. Tapes were delivered to the ledger clerk, who was also the assistant cashier.

d) Clerk delivered checks to the cashier, who endorsed them, prepared bank deposit, agreed amount with tapes, and wrote up cash receipts entry, which was supported by the adding machine tapes and remittance advices received from customers.

e) Bank deposit was taken to the bank by the assistant cashier.

Cash Disbursements

a) Invoices were processed for payment by assistant bookkeeper; invoices were matched up with receiving reports (received directly from receiving department) and with copies of purchase orders as to quantity, description, and price; invoices were matched with freight and trucking charges (if any); mathematical accuracy of invoices was checked; work done was not initialed for by the assistant bookkeeper.

b) On the 10th and 25th of the month (or on discount date), invoices were assembled by vendor and vouchered for payment by the assistant bookkeeper, who also kept the accounts payable ledger. Amounts vouchered were entered in the accounts payable ledger.

c) The vouchers with documents attached were sent to the cashier, who prepared the checks and entered them in the cash disbursements book.

d) Checks and vouchers with attached documents were sent by the cashier to the vice president–treasurer; he reviewed the vouchers and supports, initialed the vouchers, signed the checks (one signature only on checks), and sent them back to the cashier. The vouchers and supporting documents were not canceled with a dated paid stamp or by machine.

e) As the recording of checks was time-consuming, the cashier abbreviated somewhat by using initials only instead of full names for some companies (e.g., TCSI for Technical Control Systems, Inc.).

Apparently, some of the larger suppliers emphasized initials on their invoices and letterheads and they had no difficulty cashing checks prepared in this manner.

f) Upon occasion, a representative of the company was required to visit certain suppliers to expedite shipments of sorely needed material for jobs. For psychological reasons, it was decided that the request for early shipments would be aided by the presentation of a check in payment of past orders, and therefore certain checks were secured from the mail clerk before mailing.

g) No examination of endorsements on paid checks was made at any time by the cashier in making the monthly bank reconciliation.

Questions

1. On the basis of the foregoing information, what recommendations would you make for improvement in internal accounting controls over cash receipts and disbursements?

2. Based on your appraisal of the company's internal controls, what audit steps would you undertake to examine cash receipts and disbursements and related areas?

Case 8–2. **EAGLE BRANDS, INCORPORATED**

Audit Tests of Year-End Inventories when Physical Inventory Is Taken at an Interim Date

Eagle Brands, Inc. manufactured a line of small hand tools and machines. Your public accounting firm audited the company's books and you have been assigned responsibility for the inventory items.

Eagle's perpetual inventory records were maintained for raw materials and finished goods, showing quantities and dollar amounts; general ledger control accounts were maintained for raw materials and finished goods. No work in process records were maintained, since the production time of each of the company's lines was generally one day. The cost of raw materials put into process and productive labor was charged directly to the finished goods account.

Charges to the raw material perpetual records were made from vendors' invoices and receiving reports. Credits for materials put into production were based on material requisitions, priced at weighted average cost.

A lot (or production) order was issued for the manufacture of quantities to be produced of each type of tool or machine, and a requisition was prepared for the required amount of raw materials to produce the quantity of finished product ordered. Labor tickets prepared by shop workers showed lot order number, hours worked, and units processed. These time tickets were extended for labor charges by the cost clerk; the hours were agreed with time-clock cards. Daily production line inspection counts were made by the timekeeper of finished products, and the quantities were agreed by the cost clerk with the production reported by the shop workers. A summary by lot orders was made by the cost clerk of materials, labor charges, and quantities produced, and the totals were charged to the perpetual records of finished products. A new weighted average was computed each time a production order was completed, and this new average was used by the cost clerk to calculate the cost of the sales made under shipping reports.

Requisitions for additional raw materials to replace items spoiled in manufacture, and an estimate of labor spent on the spoiled materials, were charged to shop overhead (spoilage account), with an offsetting credit to finished goods.

Monthly trial balances of the perpetual stock records of raw materials and finished products were reconciled monthly by the bookkeeper with the general ledger control accounts. Overhead was apportioned to inventory at year-end only (December 31), based on the relation of overhead for the year to direct labor costs for the year.

Because Eagle experienced heavy production demands during the month of December and business was relatively slow in late summer, a complete physical inventory was taken at September 30, after shutting down production and clearing all in-process work. Your accounting firm had generally found the inventory to be carefully taken and the perpetual records to be reasonably accurate. Shipping and receiving cutoffs were properly recorded. The physical inventory at the interim date was priced as follows:

1. Raw materials at the latest weighted average cost of purchases.
2. Finished goods at the latest weighted average cost per unit (material and labor only).

Question

1. Your audit tests have satisfactorily established the reasonableness of the company's inventory as at the interim date. What audit tests do you suggest to determine that the inventories in the company's financial statements at the year-end are reasonably stated?

Case 8–3. **WILEY INTERNATIONAL OIL**

Confirmation of Accounts Receivable

Wiley International Oil Company, a medium-sized integrated oil company, maintained three large sales divisions in the United States and three small sales divisions outside the United States. In addition, a separate sales division in the head office handled all large special sales and direct refinery shipments.

Divisions in the United States sold both at retail and wholesale. Retail accounts receivable arose through sales on credit cards. There were some 115,000 active credit card accounts. There were about 30,000 wholesale accounts and 200 general sales (special and refinery shipment) accounts. The accounts receivable and annual sales by divisions are summarized below (all *dollar* amounts are in thousands):

| | Accounts Receivable | | | | Annual Sales | |
| | Retail | | Wholesale | | | |
	No. of Accounts	Amount	No. of Accounts	Amount	Retail	Wholesale
Divisions in U.S.:						
No. 1	50,000	$ 700	10,000	$2,500	$10,000	$20,000
No. 2	35,000	500	10,000	2,000	7,000	18,000
No. 3	30,000	450	8,000	1,500	5,000	15,000
Divisions outside U.S.:						
No. 4			800	250		3,000
No. 5			1,000	400		4,000
No. 6			200	100		1,000
Special Division			200	3,000		35,000
Total	115,000	$1,650	30,200	$9,750	$22,000	$96,000

The company's system of internal accounting control at the three United States divisions was satisfactory, the accounting staff at each of the sales divisions being sufficiently large to permit adequate segregation of duties. The company maintained a staff of internal auditors at each of the U.S. divisions.

The number of employees at each of the sales divisions outside the United States was small and a certain amount of overlapping of duties existed. The company auditors did not regularly visit these divisions, their last visit having been about five years ago.

The company used the cycle method of billing retail accounts; that is, the accounts were divided into five groups or cycles, the billings of which were staggered throughout the month, one cycle being billed every five days. Trial balances of past due accounts only were run for each cycle immediately before the cycle billing, and current billings were entered on these trial balances in one amount to balance to the controls maintained for each cycle. The cycle controls were balanced monthly with the divisional ledger.

Wholesale accounts were kept on bookkeeping machines, from four to six machines being used at each United States division. The accounts were segregated by area, and separate controls were maintained for each marketing area, of which there were between 60 and 100 in each division.

The number of transactions in the special sales division was relatively small and the internal accounting control was considered adequate. The company auditors did not examine the records of this division.

The company maintained a credit section at each of the sales divisions, and the head office credit department controlled and supervised the divisional credit sections and received for review copies of all divisional trial balances.

Early in the year the chief internal auditor submitted his proposed program of circularization (confirmation) of accounts receivable as of an interim date and told you that it was similar to those of the past five years:

1. No work would be undertaken at any of the divisions outside the United States or at the special sales division.
2. Retail accounts: 100 accounts at each United States division would be circularized by use of the positive form of confirmation (i.e., the customer would be requested to confirm his balance shown in the confirmation letter, regardless of whether or not the balance was correct). The chief auditor explained that only a token number of retail accounts would be circularized because (1) the credit risk was well spread, (2) it was his experience that most replies were unsatisfactory because of cycle billing, and (3) he considered a test of a significant portion of the accounts to be impracticable.
3. Wholesale accounts: 5 percent of the wholesale accounts at each United States division would be circularized by use of the positive form. The chief auditor maintained records of the ledgers circularized each year, so that over a period of years all ledgers would be circularized. The ledgers which he selected each year included some from each of the bookkeepers.
4. Accounts written off: twenty-five percent of the accounts written off in the preceding two years would be circularized. This work would include examination of the credit files on accounts circularized.

5. Second requests would be mailed to all regular wholesale accounts failing to reply at the end of one month if such accounts had not then been paid in full. Second requests would not be mailed on accounts written off. Confirmation requests returned unclaimed would be remailed if another address could be determined.
6. All incoming mail for a period of 10 days would be opened and remittances received noted for subsequent tracing to individual accounts.
7. All postings to wholesale accounts for a two-day period would be checked.
8. A report summarizing the results of the circularization would be prepared and furnished to you for review. The internal auditors' working papers would also be made available to you.

Questions

1. The work of the internal auditors is considered satisfactory by the external auditor. On that basis, to what extent should the independent certified public accountant circularize accounts receivable in his examination for the year ending December 31?
2. In reviewing the work of the internal auditors, what points would you keep in mind?
3. Do you recognize any situations in the facts stated that might call for recommendations to Wiley? What might customers' replies disclose that could prove helpful to management?

Case 8–4. ENGINEERING SYSTEMS, INCORPORATED
The Audit Opinion

Engineering Systems, Inc. manufactured complete custom hydraulic shafting machines on a contract basis. The selling prices of these machines ranged from $100,000 for the smaller models to $300,000 for larger ones.

While the company had attained a reputation for quality custom workmanship, it lost money in 1968 and 1969 because of the high proportion of engineering costs involved in designing and customizing each machine to specific customer requirements. To put the company on a profitable basis, its officers planned to make a basic change in manufacturing policy.

Instead of building custom engineered machines, as was the general custom in the industry, the management felt that three or four "lines" of machines could be designed which would be largely standard models. Customizing would be done through minor design changes and the use of accessories.

During the year ended December 31, 1970, the corporation completed and shipped one of each of three newly standardized models for contract amounts of $120,000, $210,000, and $290,000. These three machines were actually custom engineered per customer request, but the engineering department spent $750,000 in excess of the normal engineering costs for these three machines in research and development to standardize the design of the lines, which would be offered to customers over the next five years. Customers ordering the standardized models would be permitted to request only minor changes in individual end products. No strictly custom orders would be accepted after June 30, 1971.

The company had taken the position that the $750,000 represented non-recurring research and development costs pertaining to the design of the three standard machine models, which should be deferred as applicable to future orders of similar machines.

The engineering department and the accounting department worked out the following cost allocation:

Model	R. & D. Cost
A	$100,000
B	250,000
C	400,000

In addition, the accounting department and the sales department developed the following forecast of sales for each model over the next five years:

Model	Sales per Year	Average Price
A	5	$150,000
B	4	225,000
C	3	285,000

Based on the foregoing information, a unit of production method of amortization was chosen and the following amortization schedule resulted:

Model	Total to Be Produced	R. & D. Cost	R. & D. Cost per Machine
A	25	$100,000	$ 4,000
B	20	250,000	12,500
C	15	400,000	26,667

Assuming that the estimated number of units for each model were produced and sold in 1971, the total amortization charge for the year would be $150,000.

As the independent public accountant for Engineering Systems, Inc., you believed that the custom nature of their prior machines was an important element in the company's ability to sell and you questioned whether the company could sell these "standard" machines at a price high enough to absorb the present deferred engineering development costs and still show a profit on the contract. You also had reservations as to the amount of engineering costs which could be saved on each future contract based on the standard engineering work performed on the three contracts. You thought that customers will still insist upon a certain amount of customizing in their machines.

As of the completion of the December 31, 1970 audit, orders for two machines had been received and were in the early stages of production. However, it was not possible to determine the amount of savings that could be obtained.

At the close of the 1970 audit, you noted that the company's total assets amount to $6,500,000. With the deferral of $750,000 of research and development costs recorded, the company's income statement showed a $50,000 profit before federal income taxes. For tax purposes, the company had elected to expense the $750,000 in the current year.

Questions

1. Would you express an unqualified, qualified, or adverse opinion, or a disclaimer of opinion, on Engineering System's financial statements?
2. Briefly outline the information you would provide in a note to the financial statements pertaining to this deferred development cost. Write the note.
3. Write the opinion paragraph which you would provide in your report.
4. Discuss the company's decision to expense the entire $750,000 for tax purposes in 1970.

PART IV

Income Determination

CHAPTER 9

INCOME RECOGNITION

The matching of costs and revenues to determine periodic net income is a principal purpose of accounting practice. This is a difficult task, since it requires allocating the various activities of a continuing business into arbitrary time periods which rarely coincide with the periods during which each of the various activities comprising the total business is started and completed. Nevertheless, managers try to accomplish this matching by associating as best they can their companies' accomplishments of the period (revenues) with the efforts expended to achieve these accomplishments (expenses). The result of this matching process is net income or profit.

The Critical Event

The recognition of income is generally considered to be determined in large part by the timing of revenue recognition, since the sale of goods and services is generally considered a necessary prerequisite to earning income. Starting from this position, management must still determine what the critical event is in the typical chain of business events from production through receiving an order to actual payment of an account receivable. In many cases, this requires the application of considerable management judgment in the light of a thorough and objective analysis of the particular circumstances.

No one accounting rule or practice covers all revenue recognition situations. Nevertheless, an analysis of revenue recognition practices seems to indicate that revenue is typically recognized when the event which reduces the risk of ultimately receiving the revenue is reduced to a minimum level which is considered to be prudent by those issuing and using financial statements. However, in a number of cases, there can be disagreement as to the nature of the critical event and what is prudent.

While income recognition seems to turn on the timing of revenue recognition, the final measurement of income must also include a consideration of the costs related to the revenue recognized. In practice, management appears to tolerate slightly more uncertainty in the recognition of costs than it does in the case of revenues. However, if the total amount of revenue from a transaction is certain and the eventual costs of obtaining the revenue are fairly uncertain, the revenue should be capitalized and held back from the income statement until the costs are more certain. To do otherwise might be misleading and imprudent. Again, the decision is a management one, involving a responsible and careful consideration of the particular facts.

Revenue Recognition Methods

The recognition of income varies from the time of production, in the case of certain mining operations, to the actual receipt of cash, in some installment sale situations. These variations fall into four revenue recognition categories:

a) Recognition at the time of sale (i.e., sales method).
b) Recognition at the time the sale price is collected (i.e., installment sales method).
c) Recognition at the time the product is completed (i.e., production method).
d) Recognition proportionally over the performance of a contract (i.e., percentage-of-completion method).

Sales.   The time of sale is the most common revenue recognition method. Chapter 1A, paragraph 1, of *ARB No. 43* states:

> Profit is deemed to be realized when a sale in the ordinary course of business is effected, unless the circumstances are such that the collection of the sale price is not reasonably assured.

Typically, the act of invoicing, accompanied by delivery or consignment to a common carrier, is considered to constitute a sale for accounting purposes, rather than the legal criterion of title passing. In recognition of the fact that the cash eventually received from sales will fall short of the invoiced sales, a number of estimated deductions are made directly from the sales. These include: cash discounts taken and allowances for returns, warranty or service guarantees, and cash discounts. Allowances for bad debts are usually reported as an expense rather than a revenue deduction. Also, sometimes cash discounts are deducted from a customer's account at the time of sale and then any discounts not taken are reported as a separate revenue item.

Installment Sales.   An installment sale involves a down payment and a specified series of payments over time. The gross profit from such sales can be recognized in one of two ways: at the time of sale, or proportionally as the cash payments are received. This latter approach is known as the installment method. Many retailers use the installment method for calculating tax payments while recognizing the income at the time of sale for accounting purposes. In the absence of circumstances that indicate the collection of the sales price is not reasonably assured, *Opinion No. 10* concluded that the installment method of recognizing revenue is not acceptable. However, if the collection of revenues is not reasonably assured, then the installment method is appropriate.

A third approach—the cost-recovery method—is seldom used. This method does not recognize any gross profit from the sale until the cumulative total of the payments received equals the cost of the item sold.

Production. There are some industries where the sale or the collection of cash is not the critical event in the recognition of income. For example, in the case of a number of extractive industries, there is a market that stands ready to take their product at the going price. The company has merely to make the decision as to when and where it will convert its inventory of products into a sale. For such companies, production is the critical event in the recognition of income. Chapter 4 of *ARB No. 43* discussed the recognition of income at the time the product is completed as follows:

It is generally recognized that income accrues only at the time of sale, and that gains may not be anticipated by reflecting assets at their current sales prices. For certain articles, however, exceptions are permissible. Inventories of gold and silver, when there is an effective government-controlled market at a fixed monetary value, are ordinarily reflected at selling prices. A similar treatment is not uncommon for inventories representing agricultural, mineral, and other products, units of which are interchangeable and have an immediate marketability at quoted prices and for which appropriate costs may be difficult to obtain. Where such inventories are stated at sales prices, they should of course be reduced by expenditures to be incurred in disposal, and the use of such basis should be fully disclosed in the financial statements.

Long-Term Contracts. There are two methods for recognizing income from contracts covering a long period of time: the completed contract method, and the percentage-of-completion method. Both of these methods are acceptable for federal income tax purposes, and it is possible to use one method for calculating income tax payments and the other for measuring accounting profit.

The percentage-of-completion method recognizes income as the work on the contract progresses. *ARB No. 45, Long-Term Construction-Type Contracts,* issued in October 1955, discussed this method and its application:

The percentage-of-completion method recognizes income as work on a contract progresses. The committee recommends that the recognized income be that percentage of estimated total income either:

(*a*) that incurred costs to date bear to estimated total costs after giving effect to costs to complete based upon most recent information, or

(*b*) that may be indicated by such other measures of progress toward completion as may be appropriate having due regard to work performed.

Under this method current assets may include costs and recognized income not yet billed, with respect to certain contracts; and liabilities, in most cases current liabilities, may include billings in excess of costs and recognized income with respect to other contracts.

When the current estimate of total contract costs indicates a loss, in most circumstances provision should be made for the loss on the entire contract. If there is a close relationship between profitable and unprofitable contracts, such as in the case of contracts which are parts of the same project, the group may be treated as a unit in determining the necessity for a provision for loss.

There are two principal advantages of the percentage-of-completion method. First, periodic income is recognized currently rather than irregularly as contracts are completed. Second, the status of the uncompleted contracts is provided through the current estimates of costs to complete or of progress toward completion.

The principal disadvantage of the percentage-of-completion method is that it is necessarily dependent upon estimates of ultimate costs and consequently of currently accruing income. Typically, these are subject to the uncertainties frequently inherent in long-term contracts.

In discussing the completed-contract method, *ARB No. 45* stated:

The completed-contract method recognizes income only when the contract is completed or substantially so. Accordingly, costs of contracts in process and current billings are accumulated but there are no interim charges or credits to income other than provisions for losses. A contract may be regarded as substantially completed, if remaining costs are not significant in amount.

When the completed-contract method is used, it may be appropriate to allocate general and administrative expenses to contract costs rather than to periodic income. This may result in a better matching of costs and revenues than would result from treating such expenses as period costs, particularly in years when no contracts were completed. It is not so important, however, when the contractor is engaged in numerous projects and in such circumstances it may be preferable to charge those expenses as incurred to periodic income. In any case there should be no excessive deferring of overhead costs, such as might occur if total overhead were assigned to abnormally few or abnormally small contracts in process.

Although the completed-contract method does not permit the recording of any income prior to completion, provision should be made for expected losses in accordance with the well-established practice of making provision for foreseeable losses. If there is a close relationship between profitable and unprofitable contracts, such as in the case of contracts which are parts of the same project, the group may be treated as a unit in determining the necessity for a provision for losses.

When the completed-contract method is used, an excess of accumulated costs over related billings should be shown in the balance sheet as a current asset, and an excess of accumulated billings over related costs should be shown among the liabilities, in most cases as a current liability. If costs exceed billings on some contracts, and billings exceed costs on others, the contracts should ordinarily be segregated so that the figures on the asset side include only those contracts on which costs exceed billings, and those on the liability side include only those on which billings exceed costs. It is suggested that the asset item be described as "costs of uncompleted contracts in excess of related billings" rather than as "inventory" or "work in process," and that the item on the liability side be described as "billings on uncompleted contracts in excess of related costs."

The principal advantage of the completed-contract method is that it is based on final results, rather than on estimates for unperformed work which may involve unforeseen costs and possible losses.

The principal disadvantage of this method is that it does not reflect current performance when the period of any contract extends into more than one accounting period. Under these circumstances, it may result in irregular recognition of income.

The Committee on Accounting Procedure believed the use of the percentage-of-completion method was preferable in those situations where the estimates of costs to complete and the extent of progress toward completion are reasonably dependable. The committee also indicated interim billings should not be used as a basis for recognizing income, since considerations other than those acceptable as a basis for the recognition of income frequently enter into the determination of the timing and the amounts of interim billings.

Magazine publishers recognize profit on subscription sales proportionally as the magazines are delivered. This accounting practice is analogous to the completed-contract method. When the subscription is sold the full subscription price is usually received in cash. The accounting entries increase cash and an accompanying liability account, such as deferred subscription liability. As the magazine subscription is fulfilled, the liability account is reduced and income recognized.

Services

Income from services is recognized during the period in which the service is rendered. For example, in the case of services such as the use of money or facilities, the interest or rent income is accrued and included in income as the services are used over time.

Because services can not be stored, they must be marketed before they are provided. If these activities involve substantial outlays, some portion of the revenue from the sale of services may be attributed to the marketing costs. For instance, leasing companies spend a considerable sum on selling and negotiating leasing contracts before any receipts are received from lease agreements. For a number of years prior to *Opinion No. 7*, in order to cover these costs, many leasing companies at the time the lease agreement was signed recognized for income determination purposes some portion of the lease rental receipts before they were received. *Opinion No. 7* rejected this practice. It expressed a preference for spreading these costs over the life of the lease.

ACCOUNTING FOR BAD DEBTS

Revenues are ordinarily accounted for at the time a transaction is completed, with appropriate provision for uncollectible amounts. This section presents alternative procedures used by businesses in recognizing and reporting losses from uncollectible receivables.

Every enterprise extending credit to customers sustains some losses from bad debts. An account receivable becomes a bad debt when all reasonable expectation of collection is exhausted. The amounts of bad debt loss to the business firm will depend upon such factors as the type of customer served, policies regarding investigative procedures prior to granting credit, and policies employed in the collection of receivables. In spite of efforts to minimize these losses, uncollectible accounts will result from the inability to predict the certainty of payments by customers. Bad debt losses can be avoided only if a firm receives payment in cash at the time of sale.

There are two basic reasons for recognizing bad debt losses in the financial records. First, the determination of net income based upon the proper matching of revenue and expense must include these unavoidable losses. Second, the valuation of receivables in the balance sheet requires consideration of these losses to present a realistic estimate of the anticipated funds that will flow from the collection of receivables.

Accounting for bad debt losses can be accomplished by either of two methods: (1) the direct write-off method, or (2) the bad debt estimation method. For federal income tax purposes, the deduction for bad debt expense can be determined by either of these two methods. In fact, one method can be used for financial reporting purposes while the other method is used for income tax purposes. However, for practical reasons, the method adopted by a business for tax or book purposes is usually used for both purposes.

Direct Write-Off Method

The direct write-off method of accounting for bad debt expense ignores the possibility of any bad debt loss until individual accounts receivable prove to be uncollectible. No advance provision is made for doubtful accounts. Under this method, the bad debt expense represents the amount of receivables which have actually become uncollectible during the operating period.

When an account receivable is considered uncollectible, the following entry is made:

```
Bad Debt Expense ..............................................  000
    Accounts Receivable (Customer A)...........................       000
```

This entry has the effect of charging an asset account (Accounts Receivable) directly to an expense account (Bad Debt Expense) and gives this method its descriptive name.

If subsequent events prove that an account previously written off can be collected, the entry required to reinstate the receivable is:

```
Accounts Receivable (Customer A)...............................  000
    Bad Debts Recovered (or Bad Debt Expense).................       000
```

At the close of the accounting period, Bad Debts Recovered must be recognized as revenue while Bad Debts Expense is deducted in the determination of net income. Alternatively, recoveries and expenses might be netted to show only the excess or deferment of write-offs over recoveries.

The direct write-off method has two severe limitations. First, the bad debt expense may be deducted from the revenue of an accounting period subsequent to the original sale. Hence, it fails to properly match income and expense of a particular operating period. Second, current assets in the balance sheet may be overstated, since no recognition is given to the probable uncollectibility of some part of the receivables. For these reasons, the direct write-off method is not widely used by businesses of significant size. However, its simplicity makes it a popular method among very small businesses.

Bad Debt Estimation Method

Matching of revenue and expense and a realistic valuation of accounts receivables is achieved by including an estimate of bad debt expense in the financial statements.[1] The estimated amount of bad debt losses which will eventually result from sales of an accounting period is treated as an expense of the period. That part of the estimated loss which cannot be identified with particular receivables is deducted from total receivables on the balance sheet to show the expected amount to be collected eventually.

The unique feature of the bad debt estimation method is the creation of the asset valuation account deducted from receivables. This contra-

---

[1] This method is sometimes called the "reserve" method. However, preferred modern terminology disapproves of the reserve label previously given to the accumulated estimate of uncollectibility.

asset account, called Allowance for Doubtful (or Uncollectible) Accounts, is increased as estimated bad debt expense is recorded and decreased by recognition of actual bad debt losses.

There are several different approaches to the estimation of bad debt expense. The estimated bad debt losses for a business enterprise can usually be estimated with a high degree of accuracy based upon its own experience of actual bad debt losses over a period of time or upon the experience of similar businesses. For estimating purposes, this experience can be related on a percentage basis to: (1) sales for a period of operations, or (2) to the amount of receivables at the close of the operating period. Either of these approaches will, over a period of time, theoretically result in proper charges to income and proper valuation of receivables.

Percentage of Sales.   The estimate for bad debt losses may be expressed as a percentage of sales. For example, historical experience might indicate that actual bad debt losses averaged 2 percent of sales. This rate for estimating bad debt losses might be applied in successive operating periods until actual experience suggests that the rate be adjusted upward or downward to achieve greater accuracy. Frequently the rate is determined on the basis of a sales figure adjusted by eliminating cash sales and sales returns, in recognition that bad debts result only from net credit sales to customers.

Percentage of Receivables.   The estimate for bad debt losses may be expressed as a percentage of receivables at the close of an accounting period. For example, prior experience might indicate that on the average 5 percent of the balance of receivables subsequently proves uncollectible. In each operating period sufficient bad debt expense might be charged to maintain the Allowance for Doubtful Accounts at 5 percent of receivables until actual experience requires revision of this rate.

To obtain greater accuracy in estimating uncollectibility, an analysis grouping accounts receivable by "age" from date of sale may be prepared. Since older accounts are more likely to be uncollectible, separate consideration of each group of accounts might suggest that the provision for uncollectibility should be equal, for example, to 1 percent of receivables 0 to 30 days old, 3 percent of receivables 31 to 60 days old, and 25 percent of receivables over 60 days old.

Accounting Entries for Bad Debt Estimation Method

The following accounting entries are typically required to handle estimated and actual bad debt losses under the estimation method.

1.   To record estimated bad debt expense:

Bad Debt Expense 000
    Allowance for Doubtful Accounts   000

This entry is usually made only at the close of the accounting period immediately before financial statements are prepared. The amount of the entry will be either (1) the amount of bad debt expense computed as a percentage of sales, or (2) the amount necessary to bring the Allowance for Doubtful Accounts to a computed percentage of receivables.

2.   To write off an account determined to be uncollectible:

```
Allowance for Doubtful Accounts ...............................  000
    Accounts Receivable (Customer A)...........................       000
```

In this entry, specific collectible receivables are identified with the bad debt expense previously recognized on an estimated basis.

3.   To recognize collectibility of a receivable previously written off:

```
Accounts Receivable (Customer A)...............................  000
    Allowance for Doubtful Accounts ...........................       000
```

This entry will reflect the amount expected to be collected from the customer. Reinstatement of the receivable previously written off is accomplished so that a complete history of dealings with customers is maintained in the accounts receivable records. The actual collections on the reinstated account will then be recorded as though the account had never been written off.

Financial Statement Presentation

Bad debt expense recorded on the basis of an estimate is reported as an expense on the income statement. Usually this expense is classified as selling expense or as administrative expense, depending upon responsibility within the firm for the granting of credit.

The allowance for doubtful accounts is subtracted from the total of the related receivables in the current asset section of the balance sheet. This net amount presents the expected cash proceeds from subsequent collection of the receivables.

WARRANTIES AND SERVICE GUARANTEES

Some merchandise is sold with a warranty against defects or a service guarantee, which when fulfilled is usually paid in labor and materials rather than cash. These items are similar to bad debts in that the future expense and accompanying liability are unknown at the time of sale. Therefore, initially, they must be estimated.

The accounting for warranty or service guarantees is analogous to bad debt accounting. The estimated expense is recognized at the time of the sale and an offsetting liability is established. This liability is then reduced when the guarantee or warranty is paid. Sometimes the estimated costs are shown as a revenue offset instead of an expense.

REALIZATION CONTROVERSY

Accounting practice has relied heavily on the realization principle as a guide to recognizing income. With the exceptions discussed earlier, this principle states that income arises at the point of sale. A number of accounting authors do not accept this concept and its related practices as an essential feature of accounting. They claim it lacks analytical precision. Also, it is in more or less continual conflict with the going-concern convention, which places emphasis on the continuity and whole process of business activity. In contrast, the realization principle places undue emphasis on the act of selling, which is only one point in a company's total economic activity.

The critics of the realization concept believe the proper function of accounting is the measurement of the resources of specific entities and of changes in these resources. These changes are attributable to the whole process of business activity. Accordingly, the principles of accounting should be directed at the fulfillment of this function. In their opinion changes in resources (income) should be classified among the amounts attributable to:

a) Price level changes which lead to restatement of capital, but not to revenues and expenses.

b) Changes in the replacement costs of assets beyond the effect of price level changes.

c) The recognition through sales and other operating related transfers of net realizable value which leads to revenue or gain.

d) Other causes, such as the accretion or discovery of previously unknown natural resources.

This approach requires the use of price level accounting and current values (i.e., replacement costs) of assets rather than the presently more accepted historical cost principle.

The supporters of the realization principle argue that it is difficult to determine the fairness and reasonableness of appraisals which seek to restate plant and equipment in terms of current replacement costs. They cite as evidence the disillusionment of investors from the experiences of the 1920s, when companies wrote up asset values only to have to write them down again during the 1930s. Those who argue for the realization concept do so principally on its demonstrated practical utility. In addition, they believe it is not prudent to recognize gains before they are realized.

Relaxation of the realization principle to reflect price level changes has been approved in countries with severe inflation. In the United States, Accounting Principles Board *Statement No. 3* in June 1969 approved the issuance of supplemental statements showing gains or losses due to inflation.

To date, despite the advocacy of many academic accountants, the Accounting Principles Board has not approved the inclusion in income of unrealized gains and losses due to changes in replacement costs. Despite some relaxation of the realization principle, there still exist many different theories to explain the current practices of when to match costs and revenues. Many hope the accounting profession will give special attention to the development of a single theory for the timing of income recognition.

SUGGESTED FURTHER READING

BEDFORD, NORTON M. *Income Determination Theory: An Accounting Framework*. Reading, Mass.: Addison-Wesley, 1965.

HANSEN, PALLE. *The Accounting Concept of Profit: An Analysis and Evaluation in the Light of the Economic Theory of Income and Capital*. Amsterdam: North-Holland Publishing Co., 1962.

THOMAS, ARTHUR L. *Revenue Recognition*, Michigan Business Report No. 49. Ann Arbor: Bureau of Business Research, Graduate School of Business Administration, University of Michigan, 1966.

WINDAL, FLOYD. *The Accounting Concept of Realization*, Occasional Paper No. 5. East Lansing: Bureau of Business and Economic Research, Michigan State University, 1961.

CASES

Case 9–1. **GOLDFINGER INCORPORATED**

Alternative Realization Criteria

Early in 1970, Goldfinger Incorporated was formed to acquire and operate a Nevada mining property using newly developed extraction methods capable of processing profitably low grade ores containing small quantities of gold.

Operations began promptly in 1970. Engineers' reports based upon extensive geological surveys indicated that 1.6 million ounces of gold would be recovered over the life of the mining properties. The mining properties were located in an arid mountainous area and would have no residual value after the gold deposits were exhausted. The existing equip-

EXHIBIT 1

GOLDFINGER INCORPORATED

Schedule of Cash Receipts and Disbursements for the Year 1970
(in thousands)

Cash receipts:		
Sales of capital stock at par value		$10,000
Collections from sales (30,000 ounces		
at $35 per ounce)		1,050
Total receipts		$11,050
Cash disbursements:		
Cost of mining properties *	$8,000	
Production costs	2,250	
Delivery expenses	25	
Administrative expenses	150	
Total disbursements		10,425
Cash on Hand, Balance at December 31, 1970		$ 625

° Including all mineral rights, engineers' surveys, roads, mine shafts, and equipment.

184

ment and property improvements were expected to be used during the period of production and abandoned thereafter. All production and operating expenses were paid during the year. Goldfinger's cash receipts and disbursements for the year are summarized in Exhibit 1.

The Gold Reserve Act of January 1934 defined the United States dollar as 15 and 5/21 grains of gold 9/10 fine. Since there are 480 grains of pure gold to the ounce, the mint price for 9/10 fine gold became $35. Since the adoption of the gold bullion standard, it is illegal for the ordinary citizen to have in his possession more than a nominal amount of gold. The United States Treasury stands ready to buy gold from miners or importers at the $35 mint price, and to sell to industrial users, dentists, foreign governments, or central banks at the same price. Thus, gold is readily marketable at the fixed price of $35 and this price is subject to change only by the federal government.

Goldfinger's production records for 1970 show the following information (amounts are ounces of 9/10 fine):

Sold, delivered, and proceeds collected	30,000
Sold and delivered, but proceeds not collected	20,000
Produced but not sold or delivered	40,000
Total production	90,000

Questions

1. Prepare a balance sheet at December 31, 1970, and an income statement for the year based on each of the following:
   a) Revenues are recognized upon the receipt of cash.
   b) Revenues are recognized at time of sale and delivery.
   c) Revenues are recognized upon the basis of production.
   (Ignore any income tax considerations.)
2. Evaluate the three sets of statements which you prepared in terms of the criteria of:
   a) Usefulness.
   b) Feasibility.
   c) Conformity to accepted definitions of income.

Case 9–2. **RAVENWOOD OIL CORPORATION**
Carved-Out Oil and Gas Production Contracts

The Ravenwood Oil Corporation was formed in 1961 by a group of Denver businessmen to engage in oil exploration in the western part of the

United States. Its operations included exploration, development, and production activities in scattered areas from Texas to Canada and west to California. More than one half of the four million shares of common stock authorized by its Delaware charter were issued to the incorporators and about 750 investors through public offerings.

This case deals with the accounting methods used by the corporation to report *profits* from the sales of carved-out oil and gas production payments in 1968, 1969, and 1970.

To obtain funds for exploration or other purposes, the owner of a producing oil property may sell carved-out oil production payments. In exchange for an immediate payment in cash, the purchaser of the carved-out oil production payment receives the right to a certain amount of money to be paid from a specified percentage of the oil produced from an existing producing property. For example, Ravenwood, as an owner of oil properties, might sell to an investor for $100,000 cash the right to receive up to $125,000 from the proceeds of 20 percent of the oil produced from one of its producing properties. Ravenwood would continue to operate the property and bear all costs of producing the oil. The trans-

EXHIBIT 1

RAVENWOOD OIL CORPORATION

Balance Sheets at December 31
(in thousands)

ASSETS	1969	1968
Cash	$ 262	$ 178
Receivables (net)	1,852	1,838
Materials and supplies (at cost)	158	162
Other current assets	98	44
Total Current Assets	$ 2,370	$ 2,222
Net property	6,846	6,640
Undeveloped leases	1,644	1,214
Other assets	137	114
Total Assets	$10,997	$10,190
LIABILITIES AND STOCKHOLDERS' EQUITY		
Accounts payable	$ 306	$ 496
Notes payable	520	2,468
Accrued expenses	430	88
Total Current Liabilities	$ 1,256	$ 3,052
Long-term notes payable	2,980	1,886
Total Liabilities	$ 4,236	$ 4,938
Stockholders' equity:		
Common stock (par value $1)	$ 2,428	$ 2,396
Paid-in surplus	2,748	2,274
Retained earnings	1,585	582
Total Stockholders' Equity	$ 6,761	$ 5,252
Total Liabilities and Stockholders' Equity	$10,997	$10,190

action is considered a sale of the oil under the ground; no liability for repayment is created by such sale. As the owner of the oil, the purchaser of the oil payment will receive the proceeds from the sale of the oil directly from the buyer of the crude oil. The excess of the oil payment over the cash paid by the investor indicates the risk assumed by the investor regarding the certainty that production will be sufficient to satisfy the payment. Typically, the level of risk assumed by the buyer of this carved-out oil payment is low.

Initially, Ravenwood's operations had been a disappointment to the incorporators. Between 1961 and 1967 irregular profits and losses had been reported, and at the close of 1967 retained earnings were $90,000.

EXHIBIT 2

RAVENWOOD OIL CORPORATION

Income Statements for the Year Ended December 31
(in thousands)

	1969	1968
Income:		
Sales of oil and gas	$4,775	$4,228
Operating costs and expenses:		
Lease operations	$ 752	$ 864
Production and ad valorem taxes	234	216
Administrative and general	470	464
Interest on long-term debt	126	144
Other interest	26	14
Miscellaneous	4	2
	$1,612	$1,704
Other costs:		
Intangible development costs	$ 728	$ 716
Dry holes and abandonments	102	166
Depreciation and depletion	1,012	1,034
Released or expired interests	318	116
	$2,160	$2,032
Total costs and expenses	$3,772	$3,736
Net Income	$1,003	$ 492

Operations in 1968 and 1969 resulted in profits of $492,000 and $1,003,000, respectively, however (see Exhibits 1 and 2). Profits from carved out oil payments sold but not satisfied by production before year-end were $116,000 in 1968 and $1,360,000 in 1969. These amounts had been recognized as income at the time of sale and were included in the sales of oil and gas reported in those years, after making adequate provision for estimated future production costs. All oil payments were satisfied by production within 12 months following the sale of the oil payment.

On April 10, 1970, after the 1969 annual statements were issued to stockholders but before interim statements for the first quarter of 1970 weie prepared, the company changed its method of accounting for the profits from the sale of carved-out oil production payments. Effective January 1, 1970, all such profits were to be deferred until the oil and gas was produced. So that the 1969 statements would be comparable to the 1970 statements prepared using the newly adopted accounting method, it was necessary to recast the 1969 financial statements applying this new policy.

Operations for the year 1970 resulted in a net loss of $275,000 exclusive of any consideration of profits from sales of oil production payments. By December 31, 1970, all oil payments sold in previous years had been satisfied by oil production. The single carved-out oil production payment sold in 1970 resulted in a profit of $255,000 but no oil was produced from this property in 1970.

To date, the company had not declared any dividends.

Questions

(NOTE: Ignore income tax considerations in your answers.)

1. What net income would Ravenwood report in 1970 if the accounting method used previously had been continued?
2. What is the net income for each of the years 1968, 1969, and 1970 under the newly adopted method of deferring profits from sales of carved-out oil production payments until production takes place?
3. What are the earnings per share in each of the three years under:
   a) The accounting method originally used?
   b) The newly adopted accounting method?
4. What reasons can you suggest for adoption of the new accounting method?
5. How do you think Ravenwood should report its profits from sales of carved-out oil production payments? Why?

Case 9–3. **UNIVERSAL FILMS**

Sale of Television
Screening Rights

Universal Pictures Company, Inc., was one of the oldest and most active companies in the motion picture industry. In 1957 Universal granted the television rights to a number of its films to Screen Gems, a subsidiary of Columbia Pictures. In 1963, the company entered a similar agreement with the Seven Arts Distributing Corporation. This case deals with the accounting for the revenues from these transactions. Exhibit 1 presents some financial highlights for the years 1963 and 1962.

EXHIBIT 1

UNIVERSAL PICTURES COMPANY, INC.

Financial Highlights, 1962–63 *

	1963	1962
Film rentals and sales	$77,488,000	$72,839,000
Net earnings before federal and foreign income taxes	10,241,000	8,914,000
Federal and foreign taxes on income	4,890,000	4,492,000
Net earnings after taxes	5,351,000	4,422,000
Net earnings per share of common stock, based on shares outstanding excluding shares in the treasury, at year-end	6.22	4.96
Cash dividends on preferred stock	48,000	93,000
Cash dividends on common stock:		
Per share	1.25	1.25
Total	1,074,000	1,101,000
Current assets	49,146,000	49,269,000
Current liabilities	15,796,000	16,379,000
Net working capital	$33,350,000	$32,890,000
Shares of common stock outstanding, excluding shares in the treasury, at year-end	853,236	874,408
Book value per share of common stock, based on shares outstanding excluding shares in the treasury, at year-end	$ 46.84	$ 42.44
Shares of preferred stock outstanding in hands of the public at year-end	—	15,420

° 1963 includes $5 million down payment from Seven Arts Distributing contract.

Impact of Television on Film Industry 1950–63

The advent of television presented both opportunities and threats to the film industry. The programming needs of television opened up a new market for the industry's large inventory of old films with limited theatrical reissue possibilities, as well as creating a new demand for the utilization of the industry's film-making capacity. Offsetting these opportunities, television sharply reduced box-office receipts and domestic film rental income. In response to this trend, the film industry shifted its theatrical releases to the so-called "block-buster" type of film.

By 1958 it became clear that "people just don't go to the movies any more; they go to see a particular movie." The public's taste had veered sharply from the moderately budgeted pictures which had been the backbone of the releasing programs of companies like Universal. Also, while box-office receipts in the domestic market from pictures of this kind were declining, the costs of production were steadily rising. Clearly, the trend in public taste was toward the so-called "block-buster," which is a picture based upon a well-known literary or dramatic property, with star-studded cast—often a picture of epic proportion, but in each instance a most expensive as well as lavishly produced picture. Along with the higher costs associated with the block-buster film, the probability of a loss increased significantly.

The introduction and increasing popularity of color television during the early 1960s created a great demand for color programs which exceeded the television industry's ability to supply such programs. An obvious answer to this problem was the movie industry's inventory of color films, most of which had been produced during the 1950s. Thus, a technicolor film withdrawn from theatrical distribution in, say, 1958 could have a residual value of up to $500,000 if leased to television distributors, whereas several years earlier its residual value for television purposes had been about $150,000.

Television Rights

In July 1957, Universal Films granted the United States and Canadian television distribution rights to its pre-1948 pictures to Screen Gems for seven years. Under the terms of the agreements, Universal was guaranteed annual minimum income of $2 million for the first year and $3 million for each of the ensuing six years, ending June 30, 1964, for a total of $20 million. Columbia Pictures Corporation, Screen Gems' parent company, furnished a guarantee of performance of the obligations of its subsidiary.

As a result of this agreement, the United States Government instituted an antitrust suit against the company, Columbia Pictures, and Screen Gems. The government sought to invalidate the agreement and also requested an injunction restraining the companies from acting thereunder. The companies contested the government's actions and the suit was dismissed by a federal court during 1960.

In 1957, Universal adopted the policy of taking "a pro rata share of the annual minimum guarantee . . . into operations each monthly accounting period." Between 1957 and 1963, Universal included in income, under this agreement, the amounts shown in Exhibit 2.

EXHIBIT 2

(in thousands)

Fiscal Year	Amount	Cumulative Amount
1957	$ 692	$ 692
1958	2,346	3,038
1959	3,000	6,038
1960	3,000	9,038
1961	3,000	12,038
1962	3,000 *	15,557 †
1963	3,000	18,557

* During 1962, the company changed its year-end from the last Sunday of October to the last Sunday of December. The $3 million is the amount recognized during fiscal year 1962.

† The difference between the 1962 and 1961 cumulative amounts represents the income recognized over a 14-month period.

In July 1963, Universal licensed the distribution over a period of 10 years by Seven Arts Distributing Corporation, for free television in the United States and Canada, of 215 of the company's post-1948 pictures released originally between 1948 and 1956. Under the terms of the agreement, the company was guaranteed a minimum net rental of $21.5 million, of which $5 million was to be received on execution of the agreement. The contract also provided that a minimum of $3.6 million was to be received by July 10, 1965, and a minimum of $4.3 million was to be received in each of the ensuing three years, ending July 10, 1968. On the basis of contracts for showing the films written to date by Seven Arts Distributing Corporation, Universal expected that at least the minimum guarantee due in 1965 would be received in 1964.

Questions

1. How should Universal Pictures account for the revenues from the Seven Arts distributing agreement?
2. Do you agree with the company's accounting for the revenues from the Screen Gems agreement?

Case 9–4. **LECTRO-MAGIC COMPANY**

Accounting for Bad Debt and Warranty Service Costs

The Lectro-Magic Company was incorporated in Ohio, in April 1969, to produce and sell a new line of small electrical appliances. Organizational leadership for Lectro-Magic was provided by Roger Wiswell, who left his position as district sales manager for a national electrical appliance firm. Reluctant to accept a promotion requiring transfer to the West Coast, Wiswell had for more than a year been alert to an opportunity to use his abilities in a smaller firm in the Cleveland area.

In mid-1968, Wiswell was introduced to a young electrical engineer who had developed a miniature power unit around which he designed a number of unusual and effective small appliances. After a six-month investigation of product marketability and anticipated costs, the two decided to pool their resources to produce and market the line.

The limited financial resources of the promoters were supplemented by investments of four mutual friends. These investors were not interested in direct participation in the management of the enterprise. However, all six planned to serve as the firm's board of directors. After the corporate charter was granted by the State of Ohio, 100,000 of the 500,000 authorized $1 par value shares of capital stock were issued to the six incorporators at $3 per share. Roger Wiswell was elected president of the new corporation.

Several tentative agreements made prior to incorporation were now formalized by contracts. The corporation agreed to pay a 5 percent royalty, based on the selling price of appliances, to the engineer-inventor in return for exclusive rights to the use of his patents. Two small electrical and metal stamping firms agreed to manufacture and assemble the appliances at prices subject to periodic revision based upon negotiation.

Early in the planning stages of the venture, the principal promoters agreed that the mechanical nature of the products would require extensive servicing after sale in order to gain customer acceptability. Therefore, from the outset, all appliances were sold with a two-year warranty. Lectro-Magic was to provide unlimited service and repairs for this period without charge to the ultimate purchaser. Only transportation costs were paid by appliance owners under this liberal service policy. The manufacturer who contracted to produce the electrical components agreed to provide the required service and repairs for Lectro-Magic under a cost-plus arrangement.

By October 1969, Lectro-Magic's operations were well under way. Sizable expenditures for promotion and introduction of the product line resulted in almost immediate customer acceptance. During the balance of the year, efforts were concentrated upon marketing activities in a selected six-state area.

From the beginning, the firm's accounting and related clerical activities were supervised by a competent but inexperienced young accountant. His attention had been entirely directed toward establishing procedures and records for control of cash, inventories, accounts receivable, and accounts payable. Since Wiswell's time was taken by more pressing matters, accounting and reporting practices were given little consideration by him beyond the selection of a calendar-year closing date.

Early in January 1970, the company accountant prepared a balance sheet at December 31, 1969 and an income statement covering 1969 operations. These statements are shown in the first columns of Exhibits 1 and 2. All accounts payable and accruals of monetary liabilities had been recorded. Cash, receivables, and inventories had been carefully reconciled. A net loss from operations had been expected during this initial period, and no income tax liability was anticipated.

Several events in January 1970 brought President Wiswell's attention directly to accounting matters. These related to bad debts and warranty service costs.

During the year 1969, bad debt losses had not been anticipated. Shipments had been made to retailer customers after cursory reference to a publication of a credit reporting service. In January, however, Lectro-Magic was notified that a customer owing $4,000 had been declared bankrupt. There was little prospect of even a partial recovery of the unpaid balance.

In a review of the warranty service contract, Wiswell noted that costs to the end of 1969 had exceeded earlier projections. The costs taken into account in pricing the company's line were estimated to be 12 percent of the total sales price. These service costs were expected to be incurred as follows: 2 percent in the year of sale, 6 percent in the succeeding year, and 4 percent in the second year following sale. Wiswell noted, however, that a number of minor changes made in product design late in 1969 were expected to reduce the need for repairs and service from these projected levels.

While conferring with the company's legal counsel late in January, Wiswell was reminded that Lectro-Magic's federal income tax return would be due on March 15, 1970. The attorney suggested that it might be wise

EXHIBIT 1

LECTRO-MAGIC COMPANY

Balance Sheets at December 31
(in thousands)

ASSETS	1969 (Actual)	1970 (Estimated)
Current Assets:		
Cash	$125	$201
Accounts receivable	70	125
Inventories	30	151
Total Current Assets	$225	$477
Plant and equipment	$213	$213
Less: Accumulated depreciation	4	12
Net book value	$209	$201
Total Assets	$434	$678
LIABILITIES AND EQUITY		
Current Liabilities:		
Accounts payable	$137	$235
Taxes payable	—	45
Other accruals	13	35
Total Current Liabilities	$150	$315
Stockholders' Equity:		
Capital stock	$100	$100
Other paid-in capital	200	200
Retained earnings	(16)	63
Total Stockholders' Equity	$284	$363
Total Liabilities and Equity	$434	$678

to retain a certified public accountant to make an audit of the firm's operations and prepare the income tax returns. He noted that accounting methods used by taxpayers in initial periods must generally be continued in subsequent periods unless prior permission for change is obtained within 90 days after the beginning of the taxable year.[1] In addition, borrowing or security offerings to finance possible expansion would probably require financial statements with an independent accountant's opinion.

Immediately after returning to his office, Wiswell asked the company's accountant to prepare estimated statements for the year 1970 based upon projections of sales, costs, and expenses. These estimated statements appear in the second columns of Exhibits 1 and 2.

EXHIBIT 2

LECTRO-MAGIC COMPANY

Income Statements for the Years 1969 and 1970
(in thousands)

	1969 (Actual)	1970 (Estimated)
Sales	$200	$600
Cost of sales:		
Production costs	$100	$300
Royalties	10	30
Total	$110	$330
Gross profit	$ 90	$270
Expenses:		
Warranty service costs	$ 6	$ 24
Selling expenses	16	48
General and administration	24	50
Bad debts	—	4
Promotional expenses	60	20
Total	$106	$146
Net income before taxes	$(16)	$124
Provision for income taxes *	—	52
Net Income after Taxes	$(16)	$ 72

* Federal income tax rates on corporations for 1969 and 1970 were: the normal tax rate of 22 percent on all taxable income, plus a surtax of 26 percent on taxable income over $25,000. (This does not include a special surtax imposed in 1969–70, which should not be considered in computation.)

Mr. Wiswell planned to spend the evening studying the financial statements for 1969 and 1970.

---

[1] As a general rule, estimated expenses cannot be deducted for federal income tax purposes. Expenses may be deducted only in the period in which they actually accrue. Special statutory provisions do, however, permit deduction of reasonable additions to a "reserve" for bad debts instead of a deduction for specific bad debt items.

Questions

1. How, if at all, should the company's financial statements reflect:
   a) Warranty service costs?
   b) Bad debt expense?
2. What other areas of financial reporting should be considered by management?
3. Using available information and any assumptions you choose to make, recast 1969 statements and 1970 estimates to reflect fairly the financial position and the results of operations.

Case 9–5. GUIDO ANTONINI (A)
Accounting For Franchises

In May 1968, Guido (Guy) Antonini surveyed with pride his new business: the "Easy Day Car Wash of Providence, Inc.," completed, ready to operate, and only slightly months behind schedule.

Mr. Antonini had been a very successful produce dealer in Philadelphia, finally employing six men and five trucks. He was then in his early fifties, and with two children educated and married, he decided that he and his wife Anna could retire and enjoy life. Anna had long wished to move back to Providence, where her family lived, and Guy had agreed. The decision was made in early 1966; by March the business and their home had been sold.

Guy found life moving very slowly once he and Anna had settled in Providence. After a month of retirement, he started looking for something to do. The produce market in Providence was too small, and tightly controlled. After 30 years of being his own boss, Guy had no desire to look for a regular job—even if he could find one where they would consider working experience more important than the fact that he had quit high school in the 10th grade.

Guy seriously considered opening a pizza parlor—his brother-in-law Rocco was doing very well with his—but Rocco was willing to work every night until midnight, and Guy was not interested in those hours. He searched for a location for a fruit and flower shop, but found none to his satisfaction.

In mid-July, another brother-in-law, Tony Cabrese, the service manager for a large Providence auto dealer, told him that the ARS Automotive Company was looking for a man to run a pilot car wash for them in the Providence area. Guy had been suggested by Tony as a "savvy businessman"; several days later, the local ARS representative called him and Guy indicated interest in the enterprise.

ARS was a leading manufacturer of automotive finishes, making paints, polishing compounds, and a line of liquid and solid automotive waxes. ARS had spent about $100,000 on consulting contracts, looking for diversification opportunities, and had determined that a car-wash operation presented potential for both sales of company products and for financial growth.

ARS had formed a subsidiary corporation, the Easy Day Car Wash Franchises, Inc. It assigned its $100,000 investment in research and development to EDCWF, Inc. and paid $40,000 cash in exchange for 140,000 shares of no-par common stock out of the total of 500,000 shares authorized. Mr. Stanley White was appointed president of EDCWF, Inc.; he had previously been vice-president, sales, for ARS. Although Mr. White had no experience with franchising, he had extensive experience in the sale of ARS products, especially waxes and polishes.

Under Mr. White's leadership, the Easy Day Car Wash Franchises, Inc. set as its goal the installation of 200 car-washing facilities in the northeastern and central Atlantic areas within the next five years. To be able to finance the predicted expansion, the board of directors of EDCWF planned to offer 40 percent of its authorized common stock to the public as soon as possible. Based on the experience of other franchisors, the board felt that a public offering price of $15 to $20 a share would be possible.

EDCWF entered into a development agreement with the Drexsler Machine Company. Drexsler would design and build a self-contained unit for the proposed car wash at its own expense, if EDCWF would agree to use Drexsler equipment exclusively and would contract to purchase 30 machines, including the prototype, for $55,000 each over a period of two years. A penalty of $5,000 would be assessed for each of the 30 machines not ordered at the end of the two-year period. Drexsler developed the specialized equipment suitable for handling ARS detergents and waxes by early 1966. In addition, an architectural firm was retained to design a distinctive shell for a fee of $10,000.

Easy Day Car Wash Franchises, Inc. agreed to purchase all its washing and wax compounds from ARS for a per-drum price equivalent to $0.05 a car for each wash and $0.05 for each wax. This pricing agreement would be reviewed annually.

Guy Antonini was selected as the first franchisee; the Providence location was sufficiently close to company headquarters to permit close supervision of the pilot operation. The terms of EDCWF's agreement with Guy were relatively straightforward. The fee for the perpetual franchise was to be $15,000, payable $5,000 immediately and $1,000 a year for the next 10 years. Four percent interest was to be charged on any unpaid balance. In addition, Antonini would pay the franchiser $200 a month, or 2 percent of gross receipts, whichever was the greater in any month. EDCWF would supply bookkeeping supervision and technical consultation.

Guy purchased the equipment from EDCWF for $60,000; $10,000 at once and the remainder payable over the next five years, at $10,000 each year, plus 5 percent interest on the unpaid balance. The equipment had an expected life of 10 years.

The franchise agreement was signed December 10, 1967, and the initial fee paid. Construction and installation of equipment was scheduled to begin January 30, 1968.

EDCWF purchased the property on which the car wash was to be located from a local trust for $20,000 on January 1, 1968, and arranged for the construction of a shell building for $25,000 to house the equipment. The construction was to be supervised by EDCWF, Inc.; a rental of $3,000 a year and locally assessed taxes were to be paid by the franchisee. The initial lease period was five years, with provision for renewal for five years. The agreement was between Easy Day Car Wash Franchises, Inc. and Easy Day Car Wash of Providence, a Rhode Island corporation in which Guido and Anna were the sole stockholders. The Antoninis had paid $16,000 cash for 1,000 shares of common stock.

EDCWF supervised the construction of the shell and Drexsler the machinery installation, which allowed a double line of traffic to move through. The opening was delayed for two months by the unanticipated demand of the Providence Public Works Department that the Easy Day Car Wash of Providence install special sewage lines connecting with a main city line one-half mile distant. The cost of the sewer connection was $7,000, paid by the franchiser.

Easy Day of Providence opened June 1, 1968, with Guido as manager and Anna as bookkeeper-cashier. For the month of June, the special car wash and wax price was $2.50 instead of the regular price of $3 for washing and $1.50 additional for the wax. The Easy Day of Providence had a $15,000 line of credit at a local bank, guaranteed by EDCWF, Inc.

Questions

1. As the treasurer of EDCWF, Inc., how would you prepare a:
   a) Balance sheet on December 31, 1967?
   b) Balance sheet and income statement June 30, 1968?

2. Prepare a financial statement for Easy Day of Providence, Inc., on June 30, 1968. Sales were $3,600; cash wages, $925; electricity and water, $275; supplies, $72; annual salaries, Guido, $10,000, and Anna, $5,000. Ignore supplies inventory.

Case 9–6. **GUIDO ANTONINI (B)**
Accounting For Franchises

In early December 1969, Stanley White, president of the Easy Day Car Wash Franchises, Inc. received the following letter forwarded from his sales manager, Frederic Behr:

Dear Mr. Behr:

I've decided to get out of the car-wash business. I've been shorthanded since last August when those college kids left. Anna and I have decided to go back to Philadelphia for Christmas, and we want to be out of this mess by then.

Guido Antonini

Since 1966, Easy Day Car Wash Franchises, Inc. had opened eight car-wash franchises in the New England and middle-Atlantic areas. Guido Antonini's franchise had been the first to be granted. The next six wash operations would be opened July 1, 1970.

After two days of discussion with Guido, Mr. Behr determined that he was serious. It was decided that EDCWF, Inc. would buy Guido's stock of Easy Day of Providence, Inc., after distribution of the cash, for $45,000, and would pay $5,000 for an agreement that Guido would stay out of the car-wash business within 50 miles of Providence for two years. Guido would pay the debts of Easy Day of Providence before making the stock transfer. EDCWF, Inc. was uncertain as to whether or not they would operate the franchise or would attempt to sell it to another franchise.

Questions

1. If you were EDCWF, Inc., with a fiscal year ending December 31, how would you account for the stock purchase? (Include the A case facts where relevant.) Do you think this is "fair"?
2. What are the alternative methods? Under what criteria would they be more appropriate?

Case 9–7. **JOHN SELLERS**
Real Estate Sales

John Sellers, a staff member of the research department of a major accounting firm, was reviewing six cases involving real estate transactions where profits had been taken into account at the time the transactions were recorded. Sellers' task was to determine if a "clean opinion" should be issued by the firm.

Case 1

On the last day of its fiscal year, a client of the accounting firm engaged principally in the development of real estate sold a block of 1,000 lots to a nonaffiliated construction company for $1.1 million, receiving a cash payment of $100,000 and a nonrecourse note of $1 million due in one year, secured only by the lots transferred. Interest was limited to 6 percent for one year or $120 per house. A profit of $500,000 before taxes was recorded on the transaction.

The transaction was subject to, among others, the following conditions and arrangements:

a) Each lot was to be released upon payment of $1,000 plus interest at the time of closing the sale of a house and lot.

b) The client company was to make the determination of when the houses were to be constructed and to arrange the construction loans.

c) The client company was to be exclusive sales agent for the construction company, and to arrange financing and conduct closings with the home buyers.

d) The construction company was to be paid a maximum of $500 profit and an additional $100 to cover overhead expenses on each house sold. Profits to be received by the construction company were to be applied against the note owed to the client company.

Case 2

In September 1970, a client sold a block of improved properties to another corporation for a consideration of $3.5 million in cash, a $3.5 million noninterest-bearing note, and 50,000 shares of the Class A stock of the purchaser, which had a current market price of $15 per share. This sale was recorded at these amounts and showed a gain of $2 million after provision of $500,000 for possible loss and $1 million for federal income taxes. The noninterest-bearing note was payable during the period from 1979 to 1989. Until 1979, the purchaser has the option of liquidating the note by the issuance of capital stock, the number of shares to be determined by dividing the face amount of the note, $3.5 million, by the lesser of $15 per share or 125 percent of the then current market price. After 1979, the client may call for payment of the note in stock at $17 per share, and if such call is made, the purchaser may elect to pay the note in full in cash.

Case 3

In September 1970, a client acquired approximately 500 acres of undeveloped land for $300,000 in cash and a mortgage of $900,000 and immediately sold the property to an affiliate of the original seller for $2.2 million. The purchaser paid $300,000 in cash, issued a $1 million noninterest-bearing deed of trust note maturing in 18 months, and assumed the $900,000 mortgage. Simultaneously, the client company loaned $1 million to the purchaser on a 6 percent note maturing in 18 months and made a commitment to loan an additional $1 million. The client recorded a gross profit of $1 million against which a reserve for possible loss in the amount of $260,000 was provided.

Case 4

In June 1970, a client company purchased 20,000 acres of undeveloped land for $1 million cash and a 5 percent note for $3 million. Simultaneously, the client sold the property to another company, for a $3 million noninterest-bearing deed of trust note payable in installments of $1 million in June 1971, $500,00 in June 1972, and $500,000 in June 1973, and for the assumption by the purchaser of the $3 million first lien note. A gross profit on the sale of $1 million was recorded, and a reserve of $400,000 was provided for a possible loss.

Case 5

A client company purchased a tract of land for a cash payment of $100,000 and a 10-year nonrecourse noninterest-bearing note in the amount of $800,000, with annual maturities of $80,000. On the same date, the land was sold to a nonaffiliated group for a cash payment of $15,000 and a nonrecourse noninterest-bearing purchase money note for $1,785,000. The latter obligation required annual payments of approximately $100,000 for seven years and a payment of approximately $1.1 million at the end of the eighth year. At the time of the sale, the client company also advanced to the purchaser $350,000 for use in advertising. The proceeds from the sales of land by the purchaser were assigned to the client company until the $350,000 advance was paid. The client recorded a profit of $900,000 at the date of sale.

Case 6

Shortly before the close of its fiscal year, the company recorded the sale of a block of 150 lots for a total consideration of $375,000. Cash of $75,000 was paid on the settlement date and the purchaser then took title to 30 lots. The balance of the consideration consisted of four notes of $75,000 each bearing interest at 5 percent per year, due 6, 12, 18, and 24 months after settlement. The purchaser was to take title to 30 lots at the time of settlement of each note. The notes were secured only by a mortgage on the property, and there was no personal liability on the purchaser to complete the payments. In the unaudited statements completed shortly after the close of the fiscal year, this transaction was recorded as a sale in the total amount of $375,000, with an indicated gross profit of $44,000 on the uncollected portion after provision for deferred taxes of $47,000.

Question

1. What advice should John Sellers give to the partners in charge of these six accounts?

CHAPTER 10

RESULTS OF OPERATIONS

One of the oldest and most controversial areas of accounting is the treatment of nonrecurring unusual gains and losses of a noncapital nature in the measurement of periodic net income. This controversy has acquired added significance in recent years as (*a*) the income statement emerged as the investor's most popular financial statement, and (*b*) greater emphasis was placed by investors on earnings per share as the most important statistic in the income statement.

Companies will occasionally have to report unusual gains and losses, no matter how carefully judgment is applied and estimates are made in determining periodic net income. Unusual gains and losses are of two main types: (1) those that relate to past years' transactions, such as the receipt of a tax refund not previously anticipated or the results of litigation claims relating to prior periods; and (2) those that occur in the current period, but are not related to the company's normal operations. Examples of such events are the profit or loss on the sale of a fixed asset, the write-down of inventories, the loss of foreign assets, and uninsured losses due, say, to a hurricane.

Many profit and loss items are unusual and material simply because of the shortness of the accounting period, which is typically one year. If the accounting period were 5, 10, or 20 years, a number of these items would be considered a part of "normal" operating results. Also, over the longer period, a number of these so-called unusual items would be considered less material and, hence, not subject to special treatment.

AUTHORITATIVE PRONOUNCEMENTS

In 1953, the AICPA's Committee on Auditing Procedures, in Chapter 8 of *Accounting Research Bulletin No. 43*, recommended that nonrecurring and extraordinary gains and losses should be recognized during the period in which they occur, but shown separately. In addition, the committee argued there should be a general presumption that all gains and losses should be included in the periodic income statement, unless they were material in relation to the company's net income and clearly not related to the usual business operations of the firm.

In this latter case, the committee suggested that the extraordinary gains or losses should be written off directly to retained earnings when their inclusion in the calculation of net income would lead to misleading inferences as to the significance of reported income. According to the CAP, extraordinary nonrecurring gains or losses which might be excluded from the determination of current income included material charges or credits related to (*a*) prior years' operations, (*b*) sale of assets not acquired for resale, (*c*) unusual losses not usually insured against, (*d*) write-off intangible assets, or (*e*) unamortized bond discount or premium expense.

Irrespective of how the unusual item was handled in the accounts, the committee was very explicit that the amounts involved and the method used should be fully disclosed.

Because of the committee's failure to take a strong stand, practices among companies continued to vary widely. In addition, studies of reports to stockholders showed that some companies had a tendency to report favorable items as part of income and unfavorable items as direct charges to retained earnings. This tendency was particularly disturbing to the Securities and Exchange Commission. Since 1950, it had required all unusual items to be reported in a "Special Items" category directly after the caption "Net Income or Loss" in reports filed with the Commission.

In 1966, the Accounting Principles Board, concerned with the increasing emphasis placed on earnings-per-share figures and the diversity of practices followed for reporting nonrecurring and extraordinary items, issued *Opinion No. 9*, dealing with *Reporting the Results of Operations*. This opinion, which superseded Chapter 8 of *ARB No. 43*, distinguished between extraordinary items which should be shown as an element of current income and those which should be considered prior-year adjustments, and consequently excluded from income. It was the Board's belief that prior period adjustments were rare. Consequently, most extraordinary items would be included in the determination of income. This opinion also reaffirmed the long-standing practice of excluding items of a capital nature from the determination of periodic operating income under all circumstances.

The Board's opinion introduced a new format for the "net income" section of the income statement. It also distinguished between unusual items which occurred during the current period. The new format was:

Income before extraordinary items 000
Extraordinary items (less applicable income tax) 000
Net income 000

Unusual items, such as inventory write-downs, which relate to a company's customary business activity are included as a regular item in the calculation of "income before extraordinary items." In other words, no matter how material the item is, it is not considered to be an extraordinary item. Other unusual items, such as a gain on sale of fixed assets, which are not expected to occur frequently and are not typically considered in any evaluation of the ordinary operating process of the business, are included in the extraordinary item category.

All-Inclusive versus Current Operating Performance

For a number of years, the controversy over what constituted net income revolved around two dominant concepts of income—the so-called "all-inclusive" and "current operating performance" concepts. Despite the issuance of *Opinion No. 9*, this controversy persists. The all-inclusive supporters claim that the most useful concept of income includes all items affecting the net increase in net worth, except dividend distribution and capital transactions. The current operating performance advocates place considerable emphasis on the usefulness of an income figure that reflects the earnings from normal operations under the operating conditions of the period. Consequently, this concept excludes from the measurement of current income all material extraordinary items which are not clearly related to operations. Those items excluded from income are treated as direct adjustments to retained earnings. *ARB No. 43* considered both of these theories acceptable.

Chapter 8 of *ARB No. 43* summarized the major arguments for and against the all-inclusive and current operating performance concepts thus:

Proponents of the *all-inclusive* type of income statement insist that annual income statements taken for the life of an enterprise should, when added together, represent total net income. They emphasize the dangers of possible manipulation of the annual earnings figure if material extraordinary items may be omitted in the determination of income. They also assert that, over a period of years, charges resulting from extraordinary events tend to exceed the credits, and the omission of such items has the effect of indicating a greater earnings performance than the corporation actually has exhibited. They insist that an income statement which includes all income charges or credits arising during the year is simple to prepare, is easy to understand, and is not subject to variations resulting from the different judgments that may be applied in the treatment of individual items. They argue that when judgment is allowed to enter the picture with respect to the inclusion or exclusion of special items, material differences in the treatment of borderline cases develop and that there is a danger that the use of *distortion* as a criterion may be a means of accomplishing the equalization of income. With full disclosure of the nature of any special or extraordinary items, this group believes the user of the financial statements can make his own additions or deductions more effectively than can the management or the independent accountant.

Those who favor the *all-inclusive* income statement largely assume that those supporting the *current operating performance* concept are mainly concerned with establishing a figure of net income for the year which will carry an implication as to future earning capacity. Having made this assumption, they contend that income statements should not be prepared on the *current operating performance* basis because income statements of the past are of only limited help in the forecasting of the earning power of an enterprise. This group also argues that items reflecting the results of unusual or extraordinary events are part of the earnings history of the company, and accordingly should be given weight in any effort to make financial judgments with respect to the company. Since a judgment as to the financial affairs of an enterprise should involve a study of the results of a period of prior years, rather than of a single year, this group believes that the omission of material extraordinary items from annual income statements is undesirable since there would be a greater tendency for those items to be overlooked in such a study.

On the other hand, those who advocate the *current operating performance* type of income statement generally do so because they are mindful of the particular business significance which a substantial number of the users of financial reports attach to the income statement. They point out that, while some users of financial reports are able to analyze a statement and eliminate from it those unusual and extraordinary items that tend to distort it for their purposes, many users are not trained to do so. Furthermore, they contend, it is difficult at best to report in any financial statement sufficient data to afford a sound basis upon which the reader who does not have an intimate knowledge of the facts can make a well-considered classification. They consider it self-evident that management and the independent auditors are in a better position than outsiders to determine whether there are unsual and extrordinary items which, if included in the determination of net income, may give rise to misleading inferences as to current operating performance. Relying on the proper exercise of professional judgment, they discount the contention that neither managements nor the independent auditors, because of the absence of objective standards to guide them, have been able to decide consistently which extraordinary charges and credits should be excluded in determining earning performance. They agree it is hazardous to place too great a reliance on the net income as shown in a single annual statement and insist that a realistic presentation of current performance must be taken for what it is and should not be construed as conveying an implication as to future accomplishments. The net income of a single year is only one of scores of factors involved in analyzing the future earnings prospects or potentialities of a business. It is well recognized that future earnings are dependent to a large extent upon such factors as market trends, product developments, political events, labor relationships, and numerous other factors not ascertainable from the financial statements. However, this group insists that the net income for the year should show as clearly as possible what happened in that year under that year's conditions, in order that sound comparisons may be made with prior years and with the performance of other companies.

The advocates of this *current operating performance* type of statement join fully with the so-called *all-inclusive* group in asserting that there should be full disclosure of all material charges or credits of an unusual character, including those attributable to a prior year, but they insist that disclosure should be made in such manner as not to distort the figure which represents what the company was able to earn from its usual or typical business operations under the conditions existing during the year. They point out that many companies, in order to give more useful information concerning their earning performance, make a practice of restating the earnings of a number of prior years after adjusting them to reflect the proper allocation of items not related to the years in which they were first reported. They believe that material extraordinary charges or credits may often best be disclosed as direct adjustments of surplus. They point out that a charge or credit in a material amount representing an unusual item not likely to recur, if included in the computation of annual net income, may be so distorting in its results as to lead to unsound judgments with respect to the current earning performance of the company.

APB *Opinion No. 9*

The APB's *Opinion No. 9* did not adopt either of the "current operating performance" or "all-inclusive" points of view in their entirety, although it did move current practice close to the all-inclusive concept. The Board concluded that all items of profit and loss should be included in the deter-

ILLUSTRATION 10–1

Illustrative Comparative Statement Presentation
(amounts, except per-share figures, in thousands)

	1970	1969
Income before extraordinary items	$10,130	$ 7,990
Extraordinary items, net of applicable income tax of $1,880,000, in 1970 (Note 1)	(2,040)	(1,280)
Net income	$ 8,090	$ 6,710
Retained earnings at beginning of year:		
As previously reported	$28,840	$25,110
Adjustments (Note 2)	(3,160)	(1,760)
As restated	$25,680	$23,350
	$33,770	$30,060
Cash dividends on common stock, $0.75 per share ..	4,380	4,380
Retained Earnings at End of Year	$29,390	$25,680
Per share of common stock:		
Income from ordinary operations	$1.73	$1.37
Extraordinary items, net of tax	(0.34)	(0.22)
Net Income	$1.39	$1.15

Note 1. During 1970, the Company sold one of its plants at a net loss of $2,040,000 ($0.35 per share), after applicable income tax reduction of $1,880,000 ($0.32 per share). During 1969, the Company sold an investment in marketable securities at a loss of $1,280,000 ($0.22 per share), with no income tax effect.

Note 2. The balance of retained earnings at December 31, 1969 has been restated from amounts previously reported to reflect a retroactive charge of $3,160,000 for additional income taxes settled in 1970. Of this amount, $1,400,000 ($0.24 per share) is applicable to 1969 and has been reflected as an increase in tax expense for that year, the balance (applicable to years prior to 1969) being charged to retained earnings at January 1, 1969.

mination of net income, with the exception of items which were essentially adjustments to the results reported in prior periods. These prior-period adjustments were to be treated as adjustments to the period's beginning retained earnings. In addition, the Board recommended extraordinary items, net of their related tax effect, should be segregated in the income statement from the results of normal operations.

Under the proposed approach, extraordinary items and prior-year adjustments might be reported in comparative statements, as shown in Illustration 10–1. It is important to note in Illustration 10–1 that (a) the earnings-per-share calculation is made for both the "income before extraordinary items" and "net income" amounts; (b) the earnings-per-share data are shown on the face of the income statement; and (c) the earnings-per-share amount for the extraordinary items and prior-period adjustments are disclosed. These practices were not always followed prior to *Opinion No. 9.*

In the case of, say, five-year summaries, the comparative income statements might disclose the data shown in Illustration 10–2.

The APB believed its approach to reporting net income had the following advantages and disadvantages:

The principal advantages are: (a) inclusion of all operating items related to the current period, with segregation and disclosure of the extraordinary items;

ILLUSTRATION 10–2

Illustrative Five-Year Historical Summary

	1966	1967	1968	1969	1970
Income before extraordinary items..	$7,340	$7,400	$7,480	$7,990	$10,130.
Extraordinary items, net of applicable income tax (Note A)	—	380	—	(1,280)	(2,040)
Net Income (Note B).............	$7,340	$7,780	$7,480	$6,710	$ 8,090
Per share of common stock: Income before extraordinary items	$1.26	$1.27	$1.28	$ 1.37	$ 1.73
Extraordinary items, net of income tax	—	$0.06	—	$(0.22)	$(0.34)
Net Income	$1.26	$1.33	$1.28	$ 1.15	$ 1.39

Note A. The extraordinary items consist of the following: 1967, gain as a result of condemnation of idle land, less applicable income tax of $127; 1969, loss on sale of investment in marketable securities, with no income tax effect; 1970, loss on sale of plant, less applicable income tax reduction of $1,880.

Note B. The amounts of net income for 1966, 1967, and 1969 have been restated from amounts previously reported to reflect additional income taxes for such years settled in 1970. These retroactive adjustments reduced net income for such years by $860 ($0.15 per share), $900 ($0.15 per share) and $1,400 ($0.24 per share), respectively, as follows:

	1966	1967	1969
Previously reported	$8,200	$8,680	$8,110
Adjustments	860	900	1,400
As adjusted	$7,340	$7,780	$6,710

(*b*) a reporting of current income from operations free from distortions resulting from material items directly related to prior periods; and (*c*) proper retroactive reflection in comparative financial statements of material adjustments relating directly to prior periods. . . . [The principal disadvantages are] (*a*) occasional revision of previously reported net income for prior periods to reflect subsequently recorded material items directly related thereto, (*b*) difficulty in segregating extraordinary items and items related to prior periods and (*c*) the possibility that disclosures regarding adjustments of opening balances in retained earnings or of net income of prior periods will be overlooked by the reader.

Opinion No. 9 set forth a number of criteria to assist in determining what constitute extraordinary items related to the current period. In general, extraordinary items are those material gains and losses whose character in the judgment of the businessman and his accountant is significantly different from the "typical or customary" business of the firm. According to the opinion, the criteria for extraordinary items related to the current period are as follows.

The segregation in the income statement of the effects of events and transactions which have occurred during the current period, which are of an extraordinary nature and whose effects are material, requires the exercise of judgment. (In determining materiality, items of a similar nature should be considered in the aggregate. Dissimilar items should be considered individually; however, if they are few in number, they should be considered in the aggregate.) Such events and transactions are identified primarily by the nature of the underlying occurrence. They will be of a character significantly different from the typical or customary business activities of the entity. Accordingly, they will be events and transactions of material effect which would not be expected to recur frequently and which would not be considered as recurring factors in any evaluation of the ordinary operating processes of the business.

Examples of extraordinary items, assuming that each case qualifies under the criteria outlined above, include material gains or losses (or provisions for losses) from (*a*) the sale or abandonment of a plant or a significant segment of the business,[1] (*b*) the sale of an investment not acquired for resale, (*c*) the write-off of goodwill due to unusual events or developments within the period, (*d*) the condemnation or expropriation of properties, and (*e*) a major devaluation of a foreign currency. As indicated above, such material items, less applicable income tax effect, should be segregated, but reflected in the determination of net income.

Certain gains or losses (or provisions for losses), regardless of size, do not constitute extraordinary items (or prior period adjustments) because they are of a character typical of the customary business activities of the entity. Examples include (*a*) write-downs of receivables, inventories, and research and development costs; (*b*) adjustments of accrued contract prices; and (*c*) gains

---

[1] Operating results prior to the decision as to sale or abandonment should not be considered an element of the extraordinary gain or loss.

or losses from fluctuations of foreign exchange. The effects of items of this nature should be reflected in the determination of income before extraordinary items. If such effects are material, disclosure is recommended.

The Board believed prior-period adjustments were rare in modern business. The opinion defined prior-period adjustments as those material adjustments related to transactions or events which occurred in a prior period, the accounting effect of which could not be determined with reasonable assurance at the time, usually because of some major uncertainty then existing. More specifically, the Board proposed the following criteria for identifying prior-period adjustments:

Adjustments related to prior periods—and thus excluded in the determination of net income for the current period—are limited to those material adjustments which (a) can be specifically identified with and directly related to the business activities of particular prior periods, and (b) are not attributable to economic events occurring subsequent to the date of the financial statements for the prior period, and (c) depend primarily on determinations by persons other than management, and (d) were not susceptible of reasonable estimation prior to such determination. . . . Evidence of such an uncertainty would be disclosure thereof in the financial statements of the applicable period, or of an intervening period in those cases in which the uncertainty became apparent during a subsequent period. Further, it would be expected that, in most cases, the opinion of the reporting independent auditor on such prior period would have contained a qualification because of the uncertainty. Examples are material, non-recurring adjustments or settlements of income taxes, of renegotiation proceedings, or of utility revenue under rate processes. Settlements of significant amounts resulting from litigation or similar claims may also constitute prior period adjustments.

Treatment as prior period adjustments should not be applied to the normal, recurring corrections and adjustments which are the natural result of the use of estimates inherent in the accounting process. For example, changes in the estimated remaining lives of fixed assets affect the computed amounts of depreciation, but these changes should be considered prospective in nature and not prior period adjustments. Similarly, relatively immaterial adjustments of provisions for liabilities (including income taxes) made in prior periods should be considered recurring items to be reflected in operations of the current period. Some uncertainties, for example those relating to the realization of assets (collectibility of accounts receivable, ultimate recovery of deferred costs or realizability of inventories or other assets), would not qualify for prior period adjustment treatment, since economic events subsequent to the date of the financial statements must of necessity enter into the elimination of any previously existing uncertainty. Therefore, the effects of such matters are considered to be elements in the determination of net income for the period in which the uncertainty is eliminated. Thus, the Board believes that prior period adjustments will be rare.

A change in the application of accounting principles may create a situation in which retroactive application is appropriate. In such situations, these changes should receive the same treatment as that for prior period adjustments. Examples are changes in the basis of preparing consolidated financial statements or in the basis of carrying investments in subsidiaries (e.g., from cost to the equity method).

In the case of extraordinary items, the Board believed the effects of restatement should be fully disclosed in the basic statements included in the first annual report issued subsequent to such restatement. This restatement should disclose the amounts involved, both gross and net of taxes, and the effect of the adjustments on the beginning retained earnings. If comparative statements are presented, the prior years' income should also be adjusted to reflect the restatement. Ordinarily, the opinion stated, disclosure of such restatements is not required in subsequent reports. The Board also believed these disclosure standards should be observed in any published historical summaries of financial data.

SUMMARY

The Board's recommended procedures for handling extraordinary items follow very closely the preferred financial analysis practices described in the principal security analysis texts. The recommendations also reflect a strong desire on the part of the Board to make corporate financial statements more useful to stockholders and those who analyze and compile business earnings statistics from annual reports.

The determinations of periodic income will always be an imprecise measure of performance involving human judgment. Those who seek to refine its computations, as well as those who rely on net income figures, would be well advised to reflect upon the words of the late Robert Frost: "No figure has ever caught the whole thing."

SUGGESTED FURTHER READING

BERNSTEIN, LEOPOLD. *Accounting for Extraordinary Gains and Losses.* New York: Ronald Press Co., 1967.

CASES

Case 10–1. COMPTON MILLING, INCORPORATED

Accounting for
Discontinued Operations

In April 1970, David Strange, president, Compton Milling, Inc. (CMI) said: "We believe it is clearly in the best interests of stockholders to discontinue CMI's feed business, to sell the assets of the Feed Division, and release capital funds for operations that offer greater opportunities for profit and growth." This case deals with the accounting issues facing the CMI top management as a result of their decision to discontinue the Feed Division.

The Company

In 1970, CMI was a large convenience foods manufacturer with diversified interests in specialty chemicals, electronics, materials testing equipment, and related fields. Sales for the fiscal year ended May 31, 1969 exceeded $575 million and net earnings after taxes were almost $13 million for the same period. (See Exhibits 1 and 2 for financial statements.) The company's operations included more than 50 flour mills, terminal elevators, flour and food packaging plants, and chemical and electronic installations throughout the United States and in a number of foreign countries.

CMI was incorporated in 1936 to acquire several grain-handling and milling firms in the midwest. Numerous acquisitions in related areas were made in the years following. During its early years, the company was essentially a holding company; but in 1945, most of the subsidiary corporations were dissolved and the firm became an operating company. Rapid expansion followed as the company integrated vertically and developed brand-name consumer goods including breakfast cereals, cake mixes,

EXHIBIT 1

COMPTON MILLING, INC.

Consolidated Balance Sheet at May 31
(in thousands)

ASSETS	1969	1968
Cash	$ 12,541	$ 15,211
Accounts receivable (net)	44,825	42,515
Inventories	69,513	55,879
Total Current Assets	$126,879	$113,605
Sundry costs chargeable to future periods	8,767	7,268
Land, buildings, and equipment (net)	124,780	121,048
Miscellaneous assets	2,816	2,790
Goodwill, patents, trade names, and other intangibles	4,646	3,970
Total Assets	$267,888	$248,681

LIABILITIES AND EQUITY		
Notes payable	$ 7,250	—
Accounts payable and accrued expenses	29,611	$ 22,597
Accrued taxes	12,833	12,513
Thrift accounts of officers and employees	3,665	3,539
Dividends payable	277	277
Total Current Liabilities	$ 53,636	$ 38,926
Long-term debt	45,444	45,200
Reserves for self-insurance, price declines, and other purposes	4,837	4,959
Total Liabilities	$103,917	$ 89,085
Stockholders' Equity:		
Preferred stock, 5% cumulative	$ 22,147	$ 22,147
Common stock	46,276	45,123
Retained earnings	95,787	92,658
Treasury stock (deduct)	(239)	(332)
Total Stockholders' Equity	$163,971	$159,596
Total Liabilities and Equity	$267,888	$248,681

and similar products based upon its basic milling activities. Livestock feed products were an integral part of operations throughout most of the company's history.

One of the factors contributing to the company's rapid growth was the development of supermarket chains which emphasized preselling, self-service, and rapid turnover. The development of nationally branded food products by CMI complemented these innovations in food marketing. In the 1950s, however, supermarket chains introduced private brands, and profit margins dropped substantially for all food manufacturers.

Increased competition and declining profit margins caused CMI to seek more rapid growth by diversification into chemicals, electronics, oil-seed processing, and for a short time into small household appliances. Sales

EXHIBIT 2

COMPTON MILLING, INC.

Consolidated Income Statement for the Fiscal Year Ended May 31
(in thousands)

	1969	1968
Sales of products and services	$575,512	$537,818
Costs:		
Costs of products and services sold, exclusive of items shown below	$431,060	$405,256
Depreciation	8,427	7,681
Interest	2,989	2,502
Contribution to employees' retirement plans	2,779	2,435
Selling, general, and administrative expenses	105,966	97,582
Federal taxes on income	11,459	10,847
Total costs	$562,680	$526,303
Earnings for the Year	$ 12,832	$ 11,515

increased only modestly in the 1950s and early 1960s and profits moved erratically. CMI found itself competing for sales in industries that were dominated by large companies and where, again, margins were very low or even nonexistent. This was the case for a number of years in the company's Feed Division.

The company also sought to reach wider markets on an international scale. In 1962, productive and marketing facilities were constructed in Canada for several food products. In the early 1960s, acquisitions were made in Central and South America, in Pakistan, and in Europe. Most of these international ventures were wholly owned subsidiaries, but a few were joint enterprises with firms in foreign nations. The nature of these foreign operations varied from food product marketing and raw material processing to electronic activities.

The company's 1969 sales volume was distributed among the major segments of the company as follows: consumer foods, $260 million; flour, $161 million; feed, $78 million; specialty products, $28 million; chemicals, $15 million; and electronics, $33 million.

Change in Management and Company Policy

In December 1969, several important changes were made in the CMI top management. David Strange, who had come to the company from a top management position in the food industry, was named president. Several new vice presidents and divisional managers were also announced about this time.

The change in management was followed by a change in corporate policy directed toward improved profitability and growth through concentration in the areas of convenience foods and specialty chemicals. Early in 1970, in response to a stockholder's question, "Where is the company's profit potential?" management published its succinct answer in *CMI News*, a quarterly publication directed to stockholders: "Our combined chemical and electronics business was still less than 10 percent of total sales in the last fiscal year. We expect growth in these areas, but our greatest profit potential is in packaged convenience food products." A large consumer foods research facility was completed, and expenditures for research and development and for advertising were increased markedly. Management believed that development and marketing of new convenience food products would bring the desired higher sales and wider profit margins.

All areas of the company's activities were reorganized to conform to this new policy. For example, several further changes were made in the organization and personnel of the company's Electronic Group, which had been created a year earlier to combine all electronic, mechanical, aerospace and related operations into a single unit. In line with these changes, management was considering the discontinuance of several of its electronic operations at a later date.

Decision to Liquidate the Feed Division

For several years the entire operation of the Feed Division of CMI had been under study. Management could not see any means of changing operations to make a satisfactory return on investment in the future, despite efforts to build needed volume in the highly competitive, low-margin feed industry through extensive expansion into poultry, broiler, and turkey growing operations. Prices of broilers and turkeys during most of the 1970 fiscal year were below the costs of production. In addition, many direct feed customers, suffering from the same depressed prices, were unable to buy in normal volumes and some could not meet their financial obligations. Increasing bad debt losses from uncollectible receivables added to the company's operating losses in this area.

Feed Division operating losses had been substantial for several prior years, and losses for the fiscal year to end May 31, 1970, were expected to exceed $5 million before tax credits. Total company sales and profits were expected to be significantly lower than those reported in the 1969 fiscal year.

The decision to begin liquidation of the Feed Division was announced in April 1970. An orderly withdrawal extending over a two- or three-year period was planned. During this period, all plant facilities of the division were to be sold. Operations were to be continued into the 1971 fiscal accounting period, but only to honor existing firm contracts which were to require several months for completion. The 900 or more employees were to be transferred and absorbed into other CMI operations or to be terminated with benefits in line with existing company policies.

Reporting the Feed Division Liquidation to Stockholders

The decision to liquidate the unprofitable division had been announced less than two months before the approaching close of the 1970 fiscal year on May 31. Management faced a reporting problem with two dimensions. First, it was necessary to choose the *time* at which anticipated losses from liquidation would be reported; and second, a decision was required for the *method* of presenting these losses in the financial statements.

The controller's office was asked to prepare a projection of the amounts involved in the Feed Division liquidation so that consideration could be given to the alternatives in proper perspective. His report was submitted to the CMI executive committee early in May. The controller's projections were made to May 31, 1970 and gave recognition to the operations and partial liquidation transactions that were expected to occur prior to that date. A summary of his detailed report is shown as Exhibit 3.

The analysis pointed out that neither the timing nor the method of reporting the liquidation in the annual report to stockholders would have any effect upon income tax reporting. The estimated total book loss of

EXHIBIT 3

COMPTON MILLING, INC.

Projection of Estimated Costs and Losses Arising from
Feed Division Liquidation as of May 31, 1970

Accounts receivable charged off	$5,110,461	
Less bad debt allowance provided from operations to date	3,644,536	
	$1,465,925	
Estimated future additional uncollectible receivables ...	570,000	$ 2,035,925
Losses and write-down of land, building, and equipment:		
Recorded to date	$1,465,425	
Estimated additional losses in future dispositions	6,867,608	8,333,033
Costs and expenses related to discontinuance of operations:		
Incurred to date	$2,294,559	
Estimated future liquidation costs	2,803,073	5,097,632
Total		$15,466,590
Less income tax credits *		11,027,752
Total after Income Tax Credits		$ 4,438,838

* Income tax credits will be claimed against actual tax liability when expenses are incurred or when properties are sold. Loss carry-over provisions in the tax law will provide full benefit of losses not used currently. Tax credits include benefit of write-off of feed division goodwill not carried on books as an asset. This goodwill resulting from acquisitions of feed companies in earlier years was written off the books, but a deduction for income taxes was not allowable until liquidation of feed operations.

more than $15 million was significantly reduced by computed tax benefits, to a projected net loss of $4,438,838.

1.   *Timing of Reporting Losses.* Two basic points of view were taken by the executive committee in trying to decide the time at which liquidation losses would be reported to stockholders in annual reports.

Since operations were planned for a least several months extending into the next fiscal year, one possibility was to give recognition to liquidation transactions only as they were completed. Following this procedure, operating losses on disposal of properties would be reported within the period of disposition. Under this line of reasoning, losses would be recognized and reported historically as they materialized.

The other viewpoint in choosing the time for reporting liquidation losses held that the decision to discontinue feed operations represented a significant change in activities and that all losses should be anticipated and reported completely, insofar as possible, in the 1970 fiscal year within which the decision was made.

2.   *Method of Reporting Losses.* Regardless of the choice in timing of the loss recognition, another basic question was posed. Where in the financial statements should the losses be presented?

Considerations Affecting the Reporting Decision

The executive committee believed the decisions for selecting the timing and the method of reporting losses on liquidation of the Feed Division were dependent upon a number of factors which were to be considered and weighed.

For many years, the annual financial reports to stockholders consisted of a consolidated balance sheet, an abbreviated single-step consolidated income statement, and a separate consolidated statement of retained earnings. Management preferred to continue the use of this format unless there was an important need for change.

Although CMI had basically used the all-inclusive or clean-surplus concept in annual reports to stockholders, there were no company precedents applicable to the present decision. In the preceding 10 years, only two charges had been made to retained earnings aside from the regular quarterly dividends on preferred and common stock. Both of these events had occurred before the issuance of APB *Opinion No. 9*. In 1963, the intangible assets acquired several years earlier in connection with the purchase of a subsidiary were written down to $1 when the product line failed to meet expectations. The unamortized balance of these intangibles of $1,761,-846 was charged to retained earnings. In the following year, an insignificant premium on the retirement of preferred stock of $741 was charged against the same account. All other gains or losses of any character had been brought into retained earnings through the traditional income statement. There had not been in the company's history any dispositions or liquidations comparable to the announced Feed Division liquidation. No particular reporting practices had developed in the industry; variations in accordance with current concepts of generally accepted accounting principles had been used for presenting similar matters over the last 10 years.

CMI's financial statements had been examined for many years by a national firm of certified public accountants; unqualified opinions had been issued on annual statements to stockholders, the New York Stock Exchange, and the Securities and Exchange Commission. To date, the public accounting firm had not expressed its preference for any reporting procedures for the Feed Division liquidation.

The loss on liquidation was significant in amount in comparison to both net income and financial size. The character of the loss was viewed from two different points of view by members of top management. One view held that the decision to liquidate the unprofitable division was a drastic departure from activities constituting the firm's ordinary business operations and should therefore be considered as an unusual and nonrecurring item in financial reports. The opposite opinion expressed was that disposition of the properties of the Feed Division simply represented the final phase in an ordinary part of the animal and poultry feed business which had extended over some 30 years. Proponents of this attitude suggested that losses incurred in liquidation were essentially adjustments of depreciation charges and cost allocations made during the lengthy period of feed operations.

Over a period of several years, CMI had accumulated "reserves for self-insurance, price declines, and other purposes" by charges against net income. These reserves totaled $4,836,654 on the consolidated balance sheet at May 31, 1969, of which $2,855,786 applied to the Feed Division. This amount would no longer be required after liquidation of the division. The controller's analysis of estimated losses in Exhibit 4 was before possible credits from these reserves.

The terms of the sizable long-term promissory note indebtedness of CMI placed a restriction upon the payment of dividends to common stockholders. In general the dividends paid or declared after May 31, 1959 could not exceed 85 percent of consolidated net earnings since that date. At May 31, 1969, $30,411,380 of retained earnings was free of this restriction.

Management was very much aware of its position in the competitive environment in which it operated. Selected information for several firms in the milling and consumer foods industries is shown in Exhibit 4.

In mid-April 1970, the market price of CMI's common stock had dropped to $28 after being in the middle thirties in the last few months of 1969. Although sales for the six months ended November 30, 1969 had exceeded those of the corresponding period for the previous year, earnings

EXHIBIT 4

COMPTON MILLING, INC.

Selected Industry Data †

	Sales *	Net Income after Taxes *	Earn-ings per Sales Dollar	Earn-ings per Share	Divi-dends per Share	Price Range High—Low	
Compton Milling:							
1965	$ 527,701	$12,235	2.3%	$1.63	$1.00	$ 23	$19
1966	529,820	14,694	2.8	1.98	1.00	30	20
1967	545,998	16,817	3.1	2.26	1.00	38	30
1968	537,818	11,515	2.1	1.46	1.15	34	24
1969	575,512	12,832	2.2	1.63	1.20	39	31
Processers United:							
1965	$ 331,362	$ 4,006	1.2%	$2.02	$1.25	$ 22	$20
1966	350,610	5,641	1.6	2.90	1.25	37	21
1967	359,657	7,913	2.2	3.70	1.25	50	37
1968	373,818	6,541	1.8	3.03	1.40	47	32
1969	384,962	7,911	2.1	3.62	1.40	77	44
Parker Foods:							
1965	$ 438,261	$14,569	3.3%	$2.28	$0.80	$ 31	$23
1966	493,527	17,468	3.5	2.71	1.00	52	25
1967	530,571	17,784	3.4	2.74	1.20	52	42
1968	527,816	18,915	3.6	2.76	1.20	45	39
1969	581,042	19,908	3.4	3.03	1.35	45	39
National Foods:							
1965	$ 971,334	$42,399	4.4%	$1.81	$1.95	$ 25	$20
1966	1,008,897	48,397	4.8	1.99	2.00	40	24
1967	1,052,964	54,145	5.1	2.21	2.30	54	37
1968	1,087,076	61,071	5.6	2.48	2.60	75	62
1969	1,160,177	66,821	5.8	2.69	2.10	108	69
Consumer Products:							
1965	$1,432,319	$44,058	3.1%	$3.18	$1.80	$ 39	$33
1966	1,451,245	45,544	3.1	3.27	1.80	50	38
1967	1,605,725	49,362	3.1	3.51	1.95	54	46
1968	1,667,176	50,667	3.0	3.59	2.00	66	45
1969	1,790,834	50,211	2.8	3.51	2.00	79	59

† Fiscal year endings for the companies are: Compton Milling and Processors United Co., May 31; Parker Foods Co., Sept. 30; National Foods, Inc., March 31; and Consumer Products Corporation, Dec. 31.

° In thousands. All data adjusted for stock splits and dividends.

per share had declined to $0.55 from $0.75 for the same period. Market analysts were anticipating that earnings for the year ending May 31, 1970 would cover the $1.20 annual dividend and that in the longer run the stock price would recover to the 1969 levels.

Perhaps the most important single factor considered by management in choosing the method of reporting Feed Division liquidation losses was the anticipated effect upon stockholder and prospective investor attitudes toward the company. Throughout its entire history, CMI had maintained an ideal relationship with its stockholders, and the new management would not consider any reporting alternative which stockholders would be likely to interpret as improper or uninformative. Management was aware that the amount of net income reported for the fiscal year ending May 31, 1970 might have an effect upon the market price of the company's common stock. Not only was there a concern to preserve the position of present stockholders, but there was a strong possibility that in the near future additional issues of common might be offered to facilitate further acquisitions for expansion in the area of convenience foods. Management was therefore anxious to avoid any reporting alternative which might have a significant, continuing adverse effect upon its relations in the stockholder and financial communities.

Question

1. How should the liquidation of the Feed Division be reflected in the company's financial statements?

Case 10–2. DOW CHEMICAL COMPANY

Accounting for Extraordinary Items

Dow Chemical Company's earnings per share advanced by an average of about 10 percent per year for the five-year period 1964–69. The breakdown of the company's 1969 sales of $1.8 billion was:

Chemicals and metals	49%
Plastics and packaging	34
By-products and consumer products	17

Dow's earnings in 1969 prompted Alan Abelson to write the following in his "Up and Down Wall Street" column in the March 30, 1970 issue of *Barron's:*

While we're at it, we might raise a figurative eyebrow at Dow Chemical's earnings. Virtually alone among the big chemical producers, Dow has enjoyed an uninterrupted rise in profits over the past decade, from $2.03 a share in '61 to last year's $4.91. That the company has been able to do so well, despite the miserable price pattern in its industry through much of this period, speaks well of its competitive fiber. Last year, however, to keep its enviable skein unbroken, the company seemingly relied at least as heavily on the uses of bookkeeping as on the tools of enterprise.

Thus, for 1969, Dow reported profits of $148.7 million, or $4.91 a share, compared with $135.96 million, or $4.51 a share, in 1968. On the face of it, therefore, earnings last year ran about 10 percent higher than the year before. The gain, sad to say, doesn't withstand a close look at Dow's income statement. To begin with, a footnote discloses that the total includes $6.3 million after taxes, "from discontinuance of several small product lines." That sounds rather nonrecurring to us; it adds up to 20 cents a share. Half the '69 gain, then, came from the sale of some small operations.

Another 12–13 cents a share stemmed from a tax break, created by Dow's practice of recording "the income tax effect of significant timing differences between accounting and taxable income." Further, investment tax credits amounted to $18.1 million last year vs. $8.9 million in 1968; the difference

EXHIBIT 1

DOW CHEMICAL COMPANY AND SUBSIDIARY COMPANIES

Consolidated Statement of Income

	Year Ended December 31	
	1969	1968
Products and services:		
Net sales	$1,797,057,283	$1,652,492,908
Operating costs and expenses:		
Cost of sales	$1,155,954,658	$1,053,295,887
Depreciation	177,882,468	157,227,205
Selling and administrative	223,532,962	213,474,777
	$1,557,370,088	$1,423,997,869
Products and services operating income	$ 239,687,195	$ 228,495,039
Nonproducts and services:		
Investment and financial:		
Profit on investment turnover	$ 11,117,707	$ 9,273,142
Income from sundry investments	2,572,591	2,922,409
Equity in earnings of Swiss banking subsidiary	2,112,725	1,648,018
Administrative expenses	(1,286,113)	(833,112)
Investment and financial income	$ 14,516,910	$ 13,010,457
Other:		
Dividends from associated companies	9,278,203	8,562,401
Sundry income—net	26,213,026	15,789,540
Interest expense—net	(54,315,243)	(33,915,575)
Nonproducts and services income (loss)	$ (4,307,104)	$ 3,446,823
Income before provision for taxes on income and minority interests	$ 235,380,091	$ 231,941,862
Provision for taxes on income	81,500,000	92,000,000
Income before minority interests	$ 153,880,091	$ 139,941,862
Minority interests' share in income	5,157,778	3,982,023
Net Income (Note H)	$ 148,722,313	$ 135,959,839
Earnings per Share	$ 4.91	$ 4.51

amounts to 30 cents a share. Ex the added benefits and nonrecurring profits. Dow's earnings last year approximated $4.30 a share. That, of course, is lower than the previous year's $4.51 a share. Come to think of it, it also is below '67 earnings of $4.41.

Exhibit 1 shows Dow's Consolidated Statement of Income as it appeared in the 1969 annual report. Note H to this statement read as follows:

> H. *Profit on Discontinuance of Product Lines.* Net income for 1969 includes $6,305,000 after providing for income taxes of $1,623,000, representing net profit on discontinuance of several small product lines.

Abelson's contention that the $6.3 million was nonrecurring implied that Dow should have used the income statement format prescribed in paragraph 20 of *Opinion No. 9* of the Accounting Principles Board. If the $6.3 million had been treated as an extraordinary item, *Opinion No. 9* would have led Dow to show:

	Opinion 9 Format	As Reported
Income before extraordinary items	$4.71	
Extraordinary items (less applicable income tax)	0.20	
Net Income	$4.91	$4.91

Dow reports for previous years contained the items shown in Exhibit 2 under the "Sources" portion of the "Sources and Applications of Funds" statements.

The 1968 report contained the following statement in the president's letter:

> Our earnings also benefited from the inclusion of profit, amounting to 23 cents per share, on the sale of temporary investments. Income from temporary investments has become a normal recurring part of our increasingly diversified business.

Note C to the 1968 financial statements added:

> Net income for 1968 includes a credit of $6,976,847, after providing for income taxes of $2,296,295, representing the profit on sale of sundry investments.

EXHIBIT 2

(in millions)

End of Year	Items	Amounts	Total Sources for the Year
1964	Sale of fixed assets and other receipts	$ 2.0	$291.4
1965	Sale of fixed assets and other receipts	8.3	459.2
1966	Sales of fixed assets, investments, and other receipts	14.2	365.9
1967	Disposal of fixed assets and other receipts	10.0	366.9
1968	Disposal of sundry assets and other receipts	24.7	494.3
1969	Disposal of sundry assets and other receipts	21.2	525.6

In the 1969 annual report, Dow commented on its newly formed Ventures Division as follows:

Our activities in the investment and financial services area were consolidated in the new Ventures, Investment and Finance Company Division, which has a character to broaden Dow's participation in new enterprises. This division will be instrumental in the acquisition activities of the Company and also will handle the disposition of those Dow operations which no longer fit the Company's long-term pattern of development.

Writing in the July 1970 issue of *Journal of Accountancy*,[1] Professor Bernstein made the following observations regarding actual financial accounting and reporting practice since the advent of *Opinion No. 9*, i.e., fiscal periods beginning after December 31, 1966:

1. Some major corporations elected to report as extraordinary items events and transactions which amounted to less than 1 percent of normal operating income, e.g., Delta Air Lines with 0.5 percent and North American Phillips with 0.4 percent (extraordinary item as a percentage of income before extraordinary item).

2. Major food processing and bottling companies opted to show their inventory losses, which resulted from the government's ban on cyclamates, as extraordinary items, when it could have been argued that these write-downs were quite simply part of the normal incidence of business risk and thus should have been treated just like any normal inventory write-down.

3. Some firms stated "moving, start-up, rearrangement, relocation, and consolidation expenses" as extraordinary items. Again, it could have been argued that these activities are quite typical and customary for nearly any business to experience.

Following Abelson's article, the Dow stock dropped 1⅛, to 70⅝ on Monday, March 30, 1970. It then recovered 1¼ points the following day.

Questions

1. To be "extraordinary," must an item be both "nontypical, noncustomary, *and* nonrecurring"?
2. Where should the line be drawn on the definition of "material"?
3. How should "extraordinary" be defined for the conglomerates and multi-companies who, some believe, have little, if any, limit on their range of activities?
4. Do Dow's funds flow statements from 1964 to the present substantiate Dow's 1968 assertion that "income from temporary investments has become a *normal, recurring* part of our increasingly *diversified* business"? (Italics added.)

---

[1] Leopold A. Bernstein, "Reporting the Results Of Operations—A Reassessment of APB Opinion No. 9," *Journal of Accountancy*, July 1970.

5. What kind of an income figure is the most meaningful and useful to:
   a) A stockholder?
   b) A security analyst?
   c) A banker?
   d) The capital markets in general?

CHAPTER 11

EARNINGS PER SHARE

Earnings-per-share data are the key financial statistics for most investors. These ratios represent, on a per-share basis, the common stockholder's equity in a company's current profits after considering potential dilution by senior convertible securities, warrants, and options. Typically, this calculation involves some adjustments to the net income figure shown on the income statement. However, it is important to note that these adjustments are made only for the purpose of calculating earnings per share. The net income figure shown on the statements is not affected by these adjustments.

Depending on its capital structure, a company may present two earnings-per-share figures: "primary" and "fully diluted" earnings per share. Furthermore, if the company's earnings computation involve extraordinary items, each of the two earnings-per-share figures will also be presented for both the "income before extraordinary items" and "net income" amounts. Thus, depending on the circumstances, as many as four different earnings-per-share figures may be shown on the face of an income statement.

Earnings-per-share data can be very useful, together with other data, in evaluating management's past performance and predicting future earnings potential. However, overreliance on published earnings-per-share figures has several pitfalls. First, the earnings-per-share data tend to be accepted without examining the details of the income statement. This can lead to misleading inferences. Second, the emphasis on a single share earnings figure tends to shift the investor's attention away from the enterprise's total operations.

Two APB opinions relate to earnings-per-share computations. Part I of *Opinion No. 9* covers the proper handling of extraordinary items in the calculation of earnings per share. It was discussed in a previous chapter. *Opinion No. 15* deals exclusively with the computation of earnings per share and is covered in this chapter. This *Opinion* superseded Part II of *Opinion No. 9,* in which the APB first recommended that dual earnings-per-share figures be presented.

DUAL PRESENTATION: SUMMARY

In addition to the problems related to the handling of extraordinary items in earnings-per-share data, another class of problems relates to the question of what should properly be included in the earnings per share divisor. For a number of years some financial analysts believed that the earnings-per-share figures of companies with complex capital structures involving convertible securities, warrants, or stock options were misleading unless they reflected the potential dilutive effect of all of these securities. Others believed that the divisor should at least include all securities that were in substance equivalent to common stock, because of their terms, the circumstances under which they had been issued, or the way the market valued the securities.

The APB initially, in Part II of *Opinion No. 9,* and subsequently, in *Opinion No. 15,* accepted both of these points of view. In addition, after trying unsuccessfully for many years to deemphasize the significance of earnings per share in accounting reports, the Board switched its position in Part II of *Opinion No. 9* and required these data to be displayed on the earnings statement.

The factors contributing to this decision were: (*a*) the widespread use of these data; (*b*) the importance people attached to them; (*c*) the apparent misleading use of this figure by certain companies to boost their stock prices through the issuance of securities with common stock characteristics which did not enter into the earnings-per-share calculation; (*d*) the increasing use of warrants and convertible securities which had the potential effect of diluting earnings per share; and (*e*) the apparent unwillingness of other accounting authorities to deal forcefully with the inconsistencies, confusion, and abuses in this area.

In contrast to the then current practice, Part II of *Opinion No. 9* stated that the primary earnings-per-share computation must give consideration to the existence of all of a company's common stock and common stock equivalents.[1] It also stated that when this primary earnings-per-share calculation was subject to future dilution from the conversion of senior securities, a second earnings-per-share figure should be published showing the full effect of this dilution. Prior to *Opinion No. 9* these computations

---

[1] *Opinion No. 9* used the term "residual securities" to describe the same security issues referred to as "common stock equivalents" in *Opinion No. 15.* As will be explained later, the test for a common stock equivalent was different, in *Opinion No. 9,* from that eventually adopted in *Opinion No. 15.*

of earnings-per-share data were seldom presented, except in prospectuses and proxy statements.[2]

Henceforth, companies with complex capital structures had to present with equal prominence on the face of the income statement the company's primary earnings-per-share and fully diluted earnings-per-share amounts.[3] Both of these statistics represented new interpretations of the earnings-per-share concept.[4]

Primary earnings per share was defined by *Opinion No. 15* as the amount of earnings attributable to each share of issued common stock and common stock equivalent. A common stock equivalent was defined as any security which, because of its terms or the circumstances under which it was *issued*, was in substance equivalent to common stock.[5]

Fully diluted earnings per share was defined in *Opinion No. 15* as the amount of current earnings per share reflecting the maximum dilution that would result from the conversion of convertible securities and exercise of warrants and options that individually would decrease earnings per share and in the aggregate would have had a dilutive effect. All such issuances are assumed to have taken place at the beginning of the period (or at the time the contingency arose, if later).[6]

Opinion No. 15 specified that the term "earnings per common share" should be used without qualifying language *only* when *no* potentially dilutive convertible securities, options, warrants or other agreements providing for contingent issuances of common stock were outstanding. In all other cases, qualifying language (such as the word "primary") must be used with the term "earnings per share."

Finally, even if some securities are regarded as common stock equivalents, they should not be included in the computation of primary or fully diluted earnings per share if their inclusion will have the effect of increasing the earnings per share or decreasing the loss per share otherwise computed. This effect is referred to as being "antidilutive."

Opinion No. 15 is a very controversial opinion. Several prominent accounting authors have described it as reading like an episode from "Alice

---

[2] *ARB No. 43* had earlier suggested that the divisor include common stock and other residual securities. A residual security was defined as a security other than common stock which could be considered the substantial equivalent of common stock. This residual security concept was seldom followed in practice, however.

[3] *Opinion No. 9* referred to this earnings data as "pro forma earnings per share." The term "fully diluted" was first used in *Opinion No. 15.*

[4] Previously, the single earnings-per-share figure presented in annual reports was a company's net profits after taxes less preferred dividends, if any, divided by the number of common shares held by stockholders. This figure represents the legal claim of common stockholders on current earnings. Until such time as the holders of convertible securities convert their securities and the holders of warrants and options exercise their rights, they have no legal claim on these earnings.

[5] See later discussion entitled "At Issue" for further clarification.

[6] See later discussion entitled "Fully Diluted Earnings per Share" for further clarification.

in Wonderland." Some of its critics believe the Board should never have issued the *Opinion*, since the subject matter is one of financial analysis, not accounting principles. Others disagree with the novel concepts and methods introduced in this *Opinion* and the prominence it gives to the earnings-per-share figure in income statements. In addition, others believe that the *Opinion*'s recommendations are inconsistent and do not reflect the ways investors calculate and use earnings-per-share data.

Because the fully diluted earnings-per-share calculation reduces the earnings per share of a company to the lowest figure possible, a number of analysts tend to use this figure in preference to primary earnings per share. In addition, some analysts claim that the fully diluted data is more indicative of a company's future earnings-per-share potential. However, a number of other analysts believe the Board's definition of common stock equivalents is arbitrary and has little practical justification. Hence, they consider the resulting earnings-per-share data meaningless for the purpose of predicting long-term market values. However, until analysts and investors acquire more experience with the new concepts of earnings per share introduced by *Opinion No. 15*, it is likely that no one concept will be universally preferred over all others.

Legal Considerations

The new requirements for calculating earnings per share presented in *Opinion No. 15* did not change in any way the legal rights of the various security holders. Thus, the long-term capital section of the balance sheet still reflects the legal relationships between the various classes of securities. Also, the interest expense related to convertible debt shown as an expense in the computation of net income remains unchanged regardless of how the related debt securities are treated for earnings-per-share calculation purposes.

OPINION NO. 15

Opinion No. 15 was issued in May 1969. It sets forth some general standards and specific methods for (1) computing earnings per share in a consistent manner and (2) presenting this data in a meaningful manner in reports to stockholders.

Opinion No. 15 concluded that the extent of the earnings-per-share data shown on the face of the income statement and the captions used should vary with the complexity of the company's capital structure. Accordingly, the *Opinion* distinguished between companies with simple and complex capital structures. The primary and fully diluted earnings-per-share concepts introduced by the *Opinion* apply only to companies with complex capital structures.

Simple Capital Structures

In the case of companies with relatively simple capital structures, a single presentation of earnings per share is appropriate. Such cases include companies whose capital stock consists only of common stock and includes no other securities, options, or warrants that upon conversion could materially dilute earnings per share. (Any reduction through conversion of less than 3 percent of the aggregate earnings-per-share figure was defined by *Opinion No. 15* as immaterial, and hence need not be included in the computation of earnings per share.)

Illustration 11–1 presents the disclosure of earnings-per-share data for a company with a simple capital structure. (This and all subsequent exhibits in Chapter 11 assume that *Opinion No. 15* was effective for all periods covered.) The numbers of shares assumed for Illustration 11–1 are as follows:

	1968	1967
Common stock outstanding:		
Beginning of year	3,300,000	3,300,000
End of year	3,300,000	3,300,000
Issued or acquired during year	None	None
Common stock reserved under employee stock options granted	7,200	7,200
Weighted average number of shares	3,300,000	3,300,000

The shares issuable under employee stock options are excluded from the weighted average number of shares on the assumption that their effect is not dilutive (i.e., that it is less than 3 percent).

ILLUSTRATION 11–1

Example of Disclosure of Earnings per Share; Simple Capital Structure
Conclusion of Income Statement
(in thousands, except per-share data)

	1968	1967
Income before extraordinary item *	$ 9,150	$7,650
Extraordinary item—gain on sale of property, less applicable income taxes	900	....
Net Income	$10,050	$7,650
Earnings per common share:		
Income before extraordinary item	$2.77	$2.32
Extraordinary item	0.28	...
Net Income	$3.05	$2.32

* The claims of senior securities, such as nonconvertible preferred stock or other securities that have preferential rights and are not a common stock or common stock equivalent, should be deducted from net income and income before extraordinary items before computing earnings per share. Dividends on cumulative preferred stock should be deducted from net income or loss irrespective of whether or not they are earned. If the claims of senior securities are payable only if earned, then the amount deducted should be limited to the extent income is available therefor.

Complex Capital Structures

Corporations with complex capital structures are required by *Opinion No. 15* to present on the face of the income statement two types of earnings-per-share data with equal prominence. If a company had no common stock equivalents, the *Opinion* suggested that it use the titles:

"Earnings per common share, assuming no dilution."
"Earnings per common share, assuming full dilution."

If common stock equivalents are present, the titles are to read approximately as follows (exact titles were not prescribed in the *Opinion*):

"Earnings per common and common equivalent share."
"Earnings per common and common equivalent share, assuming full dilution."

The *Opinion* described these data as follows:

The first presentation is based on the outstanding common shares and those securities that are in substance equivalent to common shares and have a dilutive effect. The second is a pro-forma presentation which reflects the dilution of earnings per share that would have occurred if all contingent issuances of common stock that would individually reduce earnings per share had taken place at the beginning of the period (or time of issuance of the convertible security, etc., if later). For convenience in this Opinion, these two presentations are referred to as "primary earnings per share" and "fully diluted earnings per share," respectively, and would in certain circumstances be supplemented by other disclosures and other earnings-per-share data.

In practice, the terms "primary earnings per share" and "fully diluted earnings per share" have been adopted extensively.

At Issue

The Board concluded that the determination of whether or not a convertible security is a common stock equivalent should be made at the time of issuance and that as long as the security is outstanding it retains this status. The tests for determining a convertible stock's status are:

Convertible securities should be considered common stock equivalents if the cash yield to the holder at time of issuance [7] is significantly below what would be a comparable rate for a similar security of the issuer without the conversion option. Recognizing that it may frequently be difficult or impossible to ascertain such comparable rates, and in the interest of simplicity and objectivity, the

---

[7] This is generally the data when agreement as to terms has been reached and announced, even though such agreement is subject to certain further actions, such as directors' or stockholders' approval.

Board has concluded that a convertible security should be considered as a common stock equivalent at the time of issuance if, based on its market price, it has a cash yield [8] of less than 66⅔% of the then current bank prime interest rate.[9] For any convertible security which has a change in its cash interest rate or cash dividend rate scheduled within the first five years after issuance, the lowest scheduled rate during such five years should be used in determining the cash yield of the security at issuance.

The Board believes that the current bank prime interest rate in general use for short-term loans represents a practical, simple and readily available basis on which to establish the criteria for determining a common stock equivalent, as set forth in the preceding paragraph.

The Board recognizes that there are other rates and averages of interest rates relating to various grades of long-term debt securities and preferred stocks which might be appropriate or that a more complex approach could be adopted. However, after giving consideration to various approaches and interest rates in this regard, the Board has concluded that since there is a high degree of correlation between such indices and the bank prime interest rate, the latter is the most practical rate available for this particular purpose.

Investment Value Test Rejected

The adoption of this "at issue" test marked a significant departure from the test for common stock equivalents recommended in Part II of *Opinion No. 9*, which was based on a comparison of the current market price and the investment value of the security throughout its existence whenever earnings-per-share data were presented. According to *Opinion No. 9:*

When more than one class of common stock is outstanding or when an outstanding security has participating dividend rights with the common stock, or when an outstanding security clearly derives a major portion of its value from its conversion rights or its common stock characteristics, such securities should be considered (common stock equivalents) and not "senior securities" for purposes of computing earnings per share.

According to the typical interpretations of the "major-portion-of-value" test of *Opinion No. 9*, a security was a common stock equivalent if it "derived more than half its value from its common stock characteristics." Thus, a $1,000 convertible bond that was selling in the market for $2,000 was clearly a common stock equivalent. However, in practice this

---

[8] Cash yield is the cash received by the holder of a security as a distribution of accumulated or current earnings or as a contractual payment for return on the amount invested, without regard to the par or face amount of the security. As used in this *Opinion*, the term "cash yield" refers to the relationship or ratio of such cash, to be received annually, to the market value of the related security at the specified date. For example, a security with a coupon rate of 4 percent (on par of $100) and a market value of $80 would have a cash yield of 5 percent.

[9] If convertible securities are sold or issued outside the United States, the most comparable interest rate in the foreign country should be used for this test.

test was interpreted differently if the bond was selling between $1,500 and $1,999. Also, changes in the equity and debt market conditions could affect the security's price, and hence its common stock equivalent status, at any particular time. For example, if a $1,000 convertible bond price fell from $2,500 to $1,200, it would shift from the common stock equivalent category to the senior security class. Subsequently, if its price again rose to $2,100, it would once more be classified as a common stock equivalent.

These difficulties led the Board to replace the *Opinion No. 9* test of common stock equivalents with the at issue test presented in *Opinion No. 15*. Henceforth, irrespective of what happened to the market price of a convertible security after issue, if its effective yield at issue was, say, 3 percent and the prime rate 7 percent, it would always be classified as a common stock equivalent, since its yield at issue was less than 66⅔% of the prime bank rate.

Fully Diluted Earnings per Share

The purpose of the fully diluted earnings-per-share presentation is to indicate on a prospective basis the maximum potential dilution of current earnings per share. Securities whose conversion, exercise, or other contingent issuance would have an antidilutive effect are excluded from this computation.

Fully diluted earnings-per-share data are required to be shown on the face of the income statement for each period presented:

. . . if shares of common stock (*a*) were issued during the period on conversions, exercises, etc., or (*b*) were contingently issuable at the close of any period presented and if primary earnings per share for such period would have been affected (either dilutively or incrementally) had such actual issuances taken place at the beginning of the period or would have been reduced had such contingent issuances taken place at the beginning of the period. The above contingencies may result from the existence of (*a*) senior stock or debt which is convertible into common shares but is not a common stock equivalent, (*b*) options or warrants, or (*c*) agreements for the issuance of common shares upon the satisfaction of certain conditions (for example, the attainment of specified higher levels of earnings following a business combination). The computation should be based on the assumption that all such issued and issuable shares were outstanding from the beginning of the period (or from the time the contingency arose, if after the beginning of the period). Previously reported fully diluted earnings-per-share amounts should not be retroactively adjusted for subsequent conversions or subsequent changes in the market prices of the common stock.

Earnings Data Adjustments: Convertible Securities

The new concepts of earnings per share introduced by *Opinions No. 15* and *No. 9* require adjustments, for the earnings-per-share calculation *only*, of a company's profit after taxes, preferred dividends, and interest expense. This is necessary to reflect the fact that the reporting company's net income before and after preferred dividends includes payments that are deducted in arriving at these figures but which would be avoided if these securities were converted as is assumed in the earnings-per-share calculations.

Two possible approaches were considered by the Board to handle interest charges and preferred dividends applicable to the common stock: namely, the "if-converted" and the "two-class" methods of computation. The if-converted method is a method of computing earnings-per-share data that assumes conversion of convertible securities as of the beginning of the earliest period reported (or at time of issuance, if later). The two-class method is a method of computing primary earnings per share that treats common stock equivalents as though they were common stocks with different dividend rates from that of common stock.

Opinion No. 15 expressed a preference for the if-converted method in the case of most convertible securities. The *Opinion* described these two methods and their application:

The "if converted" method recognizes the fact that the holders of convertible securities cannot share in distributions of earnings applicable to the common stock unless they relinquish their right to senior distributions. Conversion is assumed and earnings applicable to common stock and common stock equivalents are determined before distributions to holders of these securities.

The "if converted" method also recognizes the fact that a convertible issue can participate in earnings, through dividends or interest, either as a senior security or as a common stock, but not both. The two-class method (see below) does not recognize this limitation and may attribute to common stock an amount of earnings per share less than if the convertible security had actually been converted. The amount of earnings per share on common stock as computed under the two-class method is affected by the amount of dividends declared on the common stock. . . .

Although the two-class method is considered inappropriate with respect to [most convertible securities] . . . its use may be necessary in the case of participating securities and two-class common stock. This is the case, for example, when these securities are not convertible into common stock.

Under the two-class method, common stock equivalents are treated as common stock with a dividend rate different from the dividend rate on the common stock and, therefore, conversion of convertible securities is not assumed. No use of proceeds is assumed. Distributions to holders of senior securities, common stock equivalents and common stock are first deducted from net income. The remaining amount (the undistributed earnings) is divided by the total of common shares and common share equivalents. Per share distributions to the common stockholders are added to this per share amount to arrive at primary earnings per share.

Computation Examples

To illustrate the recalculations of earnings per share as required by *Opinion No. 15*, assume the ABC Company has a net income of $60,000 after interest and taxes, but before preferred dividends of $10,000; paid a dividend of $0.30 per common share; and had the following long-term capital structure:

Convertible 4% bonds (convertible into 100,000 common shares).... $ 500,000
Convertible 2½% preferred stock (convertible into 50,000
   common shares) 400,000
Common stock (250,000 shares authorized, 50,000 outstanding)...... 2,000,000

The if-converted method recommended by *Opinion No. 15* is initially used in these examples. Later, the same example is used to illustrate the two-class method.

First, assume that the ABC Company has a simple capital structure. That is, the yield at issue of *neither* the convertible bonds *nor* the convertible preferred was such as to require these securities to be classified as common stock equivalents. The computation of the ABC Company's "earnings per share, assuming no dilution," according to *Opinion No. 15*, is:

$$\text{Earnings per share, assuming no dilution} = \frac{\text{Net profit after taxes} - \text{preferred dividends}}{\text{Weighted average number of common stock outstanding}}$$

$$= \frac{\$60,000 - \$10,000}{50,000 \text{ shares}}$$

$$= \$1 \text{ per share}$$

Now, assume that the convertible preferred stock, but *not* the convertible debt, had been classified at issue as a common stock equivalent. This would give the ABC Company a complex capital structure. As a result, the computation of the company's primary earnings per share (or earnings per common and common equivalent shares) is:

$$\text{Primary earnings per share} = \frac{\text{Profit after taxes before preferred dividends}}{\text{Common stock outstanding} + \text{common stock equivalent of preferred stock}}$$

$$= \frac{\$60,000}{(50,000 + 50,000) \text{ shares}}$$

$$= \$0.60 \text{ per share}$$

This calculation reflects the fact that if the convertible preferred stock were converted, the need to pay preferred dividends would be eliminated.

Continuing with the same ABC Company complex capital example, the company's fully diluted earnings per share (or earnings per common and common equivalent share, assuming full dilution) is calculated as follows:

$$\text{Fully diluted earnings per share} = \frac{\begin{array}{c}\text{Profits after taxes} \\ \text{before} \\ \text{preferred dividends}\end{array} + \begin{array}{c}\text{aftertax equivalent} \\ \text{of convertible} \\ \text{debt interest}\end{array}}{\begin{array}{c}\text{Common shares} \\ \text{outstanding}\end{array} + \begin{array}{c}\text{common stock equivalent} \\ \text{of convertible preferred} \\ \text{stock plus common stock} \\ \text{potentially issuable to} \\ \text{convertible debt holders}\end{array}}$$

$$= \frac{\$60,000 + \$10,000}{(50,000 + 50,000 + 100,000) \text{ shares}}$$

$$= \frac{\$70,000}{200,000 \text{ shares}}$$

$$= \$0.35 \text{ per share}$$

This last calculation reflects the elimination of the preferred dividends and the interest cost after the assumed conversion of the convertible preferred and debt issues.

Two-Class Method

The two-class method seeks to determine an earnings base that reflects (1) the fact that the common stock equivalent (convertible preferred in the ABC Company complex capital example) has a disportionate preference to earnings relative to the common stock, and (2) that actual amounts were paid to the holders of these common stock equivalents based on the stock's actual relationship, preference, and privileges. Accordingly, the following calculation is based on the assumption that amounts already paid to the common stock equivalent holders cannot logically be attributed to any other security during the current period. Continuing to use the same ABC Company complex capital example, the ABC Company's primary earnings per share calculated by the two-class method would be:

$$\text{Primary earnings per share} = \frac{\begin{array}{c}\text{Earnings after distribu-} \\ \text{tion to senior securities,} \\ \text{common stock equivalents} \\ \text{and common stock}\end{array}}{\begin{array}{c}\text{Common stock and} \\ \text{equivalents}\end{array}} + \begin{array}{c}\text{per-share common} \\ \text{stock cash} \\ \text{distributions}\end{array}$$

$$= \frac{\$(60,000 - 10,000 - 15,000)}{(50,000 + 50,000) \text{ shares}} + \$0.30 \text{ per share}$$

$$= \$0.65 \text{ per share}$$

As noted earlier, the two-class method may be required to compute earnings per share in the case of companies whose capital structure includes:

a) Securities which may participate in dividends with common stocks according to a predetermined formula with, at times, an upper limit on the extent of participation.

b) A class of common stock with different dividend rates or voting rights from those of another class of common stock, but without prior or senior rights.

In addition, some of these securities may be convertible into common stock. In the case of convertible securities the two-class method may be used only if it results in greater dilution than the if-converted method.

To illustrate the application of the two-class method for nonconvertible securities, assume that a corporation had 5,000 shares of $100 par value nonconvertible preferred stock and 10,000 shares of $50 par value common stock outstanding during 1969 and had a net income of $65,000. The preferred stock is entitled to a noncumulative annual dividend of $5 per share before any dividend is paid on common. After common has been paid a dividend of $2 per share, the preferred stock then participates in any additional dividends on a 40:60 per-share ratio with common. That is, after preferred and common have been paid dividends of $5 and $2 per share respectively, preferred participates in any additional dividends at a rate of two thirds of the additional amount paid to common on a per-share basis. Also assume that for 1969, preferred shareholders have been paid $27,000 (or $5.40 per share) and common shareholders have been paid $26,000 (or $2.60 per share).

Under the two-class method for nonconvertible securities, earnings per share for 1969 would be computed as follows:

Net income		$65,000
Less dividends paid:		
Preferred	$27,000	
Common	26,000	53,000
Undistributed 1969 earnings		$12,000

Allocation of undistributed earnings:

5,000 Shares Preferred

$$\frac{0.4}{2,000}$$

$$\frac{2,000}{8,000} \times \$12,000 = \$3,000$$

$$\frac{\$3,000}{5,000} = \$0.60/\text{share}$$

$+$

10,000 Shares Common

$$\frac{0.6}{6,000}$$

$$\frac{6,000}{8,000} \times \$12,000 = \$9,000$$

$$\frac{\$9,000}{10,000} = \$0.90/\text{share}$$

$= 8,000$ "equivalent shares"

Earnings per share:

	Preferred	Common
Distributed earnings	$5.40	$2.60
Undistributed earnings	0.60	0.90
	$6.00	$3.50

Because of the great variety of features which these participating and two-class common stock securities have in practice, the *Opinion* did not set detailed specific guidelines for determining when they should be considered common stock equivalents. Rather, it stated simply:

Dividend participation does not per se make a security a common stock equivalent. A determination of the status of one of these securities should be based on an analysis of all the characteristics of the security including the ability to share in the earnings potential of the issuing corporation on substantially the same basis as the common stock.

Earnings Data Adjustments: Options and Warrants

Options, warrants, and similar arrangements, such as securities with a low cash yield that require payment of cash upon conversion, are regarded by *Opinion No. 15* as common stock equivalents at all times. Typically, these securities have no cash yield and whatever value they have is derived from their right to obtain common stock at a specific price during a specified time period. Accordingly, the *Opinion* maintains that primary earnings per share should reflect the assumption that these securities have been exercised.

The earnings-per-share effect of such securities is computed by the "treasury stock" method. This approach assumes (1) that the warrants and options are exercised at the beginning of the period (or at time of issuance, if later); and (2) that any proceeds received by the issuing company are used to purchase its common stock, up to 20 percent of the outstanding stock, at the average market price during the period.[10] If funds from assumed exercises of options and warrants are still available after this 20 percent limit is reached, their assumed application must follow specific rules outlined in paragraph 38 of the *Opinion* (see below). These computations should not, however, reflect the exercise or conversion of any security if its effects on earnings per share is antidilutive, except as indicated in paragraph 38 of the *Opinion*.

---

[10] For example, if a corporation has 10,000 warrants outstanding exercisable at $54 and the average market price of the common stock during the reporting period is $60, the $540,000 which would be realized from exercise of the warrants and issuance of 10,000 shares would be an amount sufficient to acquire 9,000 shares; thus, 1,000 shares would be added to the outstanding common shares in computing primary earnings per share for the period.

As a practice, the Board recommended that the assumed exercise not be reflected in primary earnings-per-share data until the market price of the common stock obtainable had been in excess of the exercise price for substantially all of three consecutive months, ending with the last month of the period to which earnings-per-share data relate. Therefore, under the treasury stock method, options and warrants have a dilutive effect (and are, therefore, reflected in earnings-per-share computations) only when the average market price of the common stock obtainable upon exercise during the period exceeds the exercise price of the options or warrants. Previously reported earnings-per-share amounts should not be retroactively adjusted, in the case of options and warrants, as a result of changes in market prices of common stock.

The Board recognized that the funds obtained by issuers from the exercise of options and warrants are used in many ways, with a wide variety of results that cannot be anticipated. Application of the treasury stock method in earnings-per-share computations is "not based on an assumption that the funds will or could actually be used in that manner" required by this method. Nevertheless, the Board believed it represented a practical approach to reflecting the dilutive effect that would result from the issuance of common stock under option and warrant agreements at an effective price below the current market price.

The Board concluded, however, that the treasury stock method can be inappropriate, or should be modified, in certain cases. For example, some warrants contain provisions that permit, or require, the tendering of debt (usually at face amount) or other securities of the issuer in payment for all or a portion of the exercise price. The terms of some debt securities issued with warrants require that the proceeds of the exercise of the related warrants be applied toward retirement of the debt. Also, some convertible securities require cash payments upon conversion and are, therefore, considered to be the equivalent of warrants. In all of these cases, the if-converted methods should be applied as if retirement or conversion of the securities had occurred and as if the excess proceeds, if any, had been applied to the purchase of common stock under the treasury stock method. However, exercise of the options and warrants should not be reflected in the primary earnings-per-share computation unless (*a*) the market price of the related common stock exceeds exercise price, or (*b*) the security which may be (or must be) tendered is selling at a price below that at which it may be tendered under the option or warrant agreement and the resulting discount is sufficient to establish an effective exercise price below the market price of the common stock that can be obtained upon exercise. Similar treatment should be followed for preferred stock bearing similar provisions or other securities having conversion options permitting payment of cash for a more favorable conversion rate from the standpoint of the investor.

The methods described above should be used to compute fully diluted earnings per share also if dilution results from outstanding options and warrants. However, in order to reflect maximum potential dilution, the market price at the close of the period reported upon should be used to determine the number of shares which would be assumed to be repurchased if this market price is higher than the average price used in computing primary earnings per share. Common shares issued on exercise of options or warrants during each period should also be included in fully diluted earnings per share from the beginning of the period, or from date of issuance of the options or warrants if later. In addition, the computation for the portion of the period prior to the date of exercise should be based on market prices of the common stock when exercised.

Computation Example

For example, assume the following data:

Net income for year	$2,000,000
Shares outstanding	1,000,000
Warrants and options to purchase equivalent shares (outstanding for full yrs.)	100,000
Exercise price per share	$15
Average price	$20
Year-end market price	$25

Then primary earnings per share would be computed as:

$$\left(\frac{20-15}{20}\right) \times 100,000 = 25,000 \text{ shares}$$

$$\frac{\$2,000,000}{100,000 + 25,000} = \$1.95$$

Fully diluted earnings per share would be:

$$\left(\frac{25-15}{25}\right) \times 100,000 = 40,000 \text{ shares issued}$$

$$\frac{\$2,000,000}{1,000,000 + 40,000} = \$1.92$$

Paragraph 38: Twenty Percent Test

The treasury stock method of reflecting use of proceeds from options and warrants may not adequately reflect potential dilution when options or warrants to acquire a substantial number of common shares are outstanding. Accordingly, the Board concluded in paragraph 38 of *Opinion No. 15:*

... if the number of shares of common stock obtainable upon exercise of outstanding options and warrants in the aggregate exceeds 20% of the number of common shares outstanding at the end of the period for which the computation is being made, the treasury stock method should be modified in determining the dilutive effect of the options and warrants upon earnings-per-share data. In these circumstances all the options and warrants should be assumed to have been exercised and the aggregate proceeds therefrom to have been applied in two steps:

(*a*) As if the funds obtained were first applied to the repurchase of outstanding common shares at the average market price during the period but not to exceed 20% of the outstanding shares: and then

(*b*) As if the balance of the funds were applied first to reduce any short-term or long-term borrowings and any remaining funds were invested in U.S. government securities or commercial paper, with appropriate recognition of any income tax effect.

The results of steps (*a*) and (*b*) of the computation (whether dilutive or anti-dilutive) should be aggregated and, if the net effect is dilutive, should enter into the earnings-per-share computation.

Illustration 11–2 demonstrates the application of paragraph 38. Case 2 in the illustration shows a dilutive effect despite a market price below exercise price.

ILLUSTRATION 11–2

Application of Paragraph 38

	Case 1	Case 2
Assumptions:		
Net income for year	$ 4,000,000	$ 2,000,000
Common shares outstanding	3,000,000	3,000,000
Options and warrants outstanding to purchase equivalent shares	1,000,000	1,000,000
20% limitation on assumed repurchase	600,000	600,000
Exercise price per share	$ 15	$ 15
Average and year-end market value per common share to be used	$ 20	$ 12
Computations:		
Application of assumed proceeds ($15,000,000):		
Toward repurchase of outstanding common shares at applicable market value	$12,000,000	$ 7,200,000
Reduction of debt	3,000,000	7,800,000
	$15,000,000	$15,000,000
Adjustment of net income:		
Actual net income	$ 4,000,000	$ 2,000,000
Interest reduction (6%) less 50% tax effect	90,000	234,000
Adjusted net income (A)	$ 4,090,000	$ 2.234,000
Adjustment of shares outstanding:		
Actual outstanding	3,000,000	3,000,000
Net additional shares issuable (1,000,000—600,000)	400,000	400,000
Adjusted shares outstanding (B)	3,400,000	3,400,000
Earnings per share:		
Before adjustment	$ 1.33	$ 0.67
After adjustment (A ÷ B)	$ 1.20	$ 0.66

Contingent Issues

Some agreements call for the further issuance by companies of shares either directly or from escrow accounts contingent on such conditions as the attainment of specific earnings levels. Such contingent issuable shares should be considered as outstanding in both the primary and fully diluted earnings computations if the conditions for their issuance are currently being attained. If these conditions are not being met, they should be included only in the fully diluted earnings calculation.

The number of shares contingently issuable may depend on some future market price of the stock. In such cases the current earnings-per-share computations should use the number of shares that would be issuable based on the market price of the stock at the close of the period. If the number of shares issued or contingently issuable subsequently changes because of market price changes, the earnings per share reported for prior periods should be restated. A similar approach should be used if the number of shares contingently issuable is dependent on both future earnings and future stock prices.

Securities of Subsidiaries

In some cases warrants, options, or securities issued by subsidiaries must be considered as common stock equivalents when computing consolidated and parent company earnings per share which reflect the subsidiary's results of operations through consolidation or the use of the equity method. Circumstances requiring this approach and the appropriate rule to follow in reporting consolidated or parent company earnings include:

a) Certain of the subsidiary's securities are common stock equivalents in relation to its own common stock.

In this case, the earnings per share should include the portion of the subsidiary's income that would be applicable to the consolidated group based on its holdings and the subsidiary's primary earnings per share.

b) Other of the subsidiary's convertible securities, although not common stock equivalents in relation to its own common stock, would enter into the computation of its fully diluted earnings per share.

Under these conditions, only the portion of the subsidiary's income that would be applicable to the consolidated group based on its holdings and the fully diluted earnings per share of the subsidiary should be included in consolidated and parent company fully diluted earnings per share.

c) The subsidiary's securities are convertible into the parent company's common stock.

Such securities should be considered as issued and treated the same way as the related parent stock in the computation of primary and fully diluted earnings per share.

d) The subsidiary issues options and warrants to purchase the parent company's common stock.

These rights should be considered as common stock equivalents by the parent company.

Further Requirements

The complexity of the earnings-per-share calculation requires additional disclosures to explain (*a*) the pertinent rights and privileges of the various securities outstanding, and (*b*) the assumptions and adjustments made to calculate primary and fully diluted earnings per share. The disclosure of rights and privileges should include: dividends and liquidation preferences, participation rights, call prices and dates, conversion or exercise prices or rates and pertinent dates, sinking fund requirements, and unusual voting rights.

The disclosure of how the earnings-per-share amounts were obtained should not be shown in such a manner as to imply that an earnings-per-share amount which ignores the effect of common stock equivalents constitutes an acceptable presentation of primary earnings per share. In addition, earnings-per-share data are required to be presented for all periods covered by the statement of income or summary of earnings. If it is necessary to previous periods' income, the prior periods' earnings-per-share data must also be restated.

Dividends-per-share presentations in comparative statements should reflect the actual dividends declared during the appropriate period adjusted for any subsequent stock splits or dividends. Following a pooling of interest, the dividends-per-share presentation for periods prior to the pooling creates a problem. In these cases, the typical practice is to disclose the dividends declared per share by the principal constituent.

Weighted Average Computations

The divisor for the earnings-per-share calculation should be the weighted average of the number of common shares and, if any, common share equivalents outstanding during each period presented.

This number is determined by relating (*a*) the portion of time within a reporting period that a particular number of shares of a certain security has been outstanding to (*b*) the total time in that period. Thus, for example, if 100 shares of a certain security were outstanding during the first quarter of a fiscal year and 300 shares were outstanding during the balance of the year, the weighted average number of outstanding shares would be 250. The use of a weighted average is necessary so that the effect of changes in the number of shares outstanding is related to the operations during the portion of the accounting period affected.

If the company reacquires its shares, these shares should be excluded from the weighted average calculation from the date of their acquisition.

Computations of earnings-per-share data should give retroactive recognition in all periods presented to changes in the capital structure due to stock splits, stock dividends, or reverse stock splits. If the capital structure is changed by such events after the close of the period but before the completion of the financial report, the per-share calculations for the period should be based on the current capitalization. This presumes that the reader's primary interest is related to the current capitalization.

When a business is acquired for stock, the transaction can be accounted for as either a purchase or a pooling of interest depending on the particular circumstances. When a business combination is accounted for as a purchase, the new shares should be included in the computation of earnings per share only from the acquisition date. In the case of a pooling of interest, the computation should be based on the aggregate of the weighted average outstanding shares of the merged business, adjusted to the equivalent shares of the surviving business for all periods presented. These computations reflect the difference in accounting for income under the two methods of accounting for business combinations. (In a purchase, the income of the purchaser includes the income of the purchased company only from the date of acquisition. In a pooling of interest, the net incomes of the two companies are combined for all periods presented.)

Effective Date

The effective date of *Opinion No. 15* was for fiscal periods beginning after December 31, 1968. It applied to all primary, fully diluted, and supplementary earnings-per-share data regardless of when the securities involved in the computations were issued, except for securities issued prior to June 1, 1969 entering into the computation of primary per-share data.

In the case of securities issued prior to June 1, 1969, the following election could be made with respect to these securities in computing earnings per share: they could either be classified according to the common stock equivalent tests established in *Opinion No. 15*, or they could be classified according to the tests included in *Opinion No. 9* regardless of how they would be classified in *Opinion No. 15*. If the *Opinion No. 15* tests were elected, the provisions of *Opinion No. 15* should be used in the computation of both primary and fully diluted earnings-per-share data for all periods presented.

The Board also recommended that in comparative statements in which the information for some periods is subject to *Opinion No. 15* and for others is not, the *Opinion* be applied to all periods covered, based on the conditions existing in the prior periods.

CONFLICTING VIEWPOINTS

Opinion No. 15 has been criticized widely. In fact, the *Opinion* was not wholeheartedly endorsed by 8 of the 18 members of the Board (three "dissented" and five "assented with qualification"). The principal reservations of these eight Board members, as well as the viewpoints of others not endorsing *Opinion No. 15*, are:

1. The required dual presentation of earnings per share dignifies one figure above all others. This practice runs counter to the profession's position that fair presentation of financial condition and results of operations is achieved by the whole presentation, not by the specific location of any item. Accordingly, the *Opinion* should not be so specific on the location of the dual presentation of earnings per share.

2. The determination of common stock equivalence is a subjective one which cannot be accommodated within prescribed formulas or mathematical rules. This determination, however, does begin with the one factually determinable figure of earnings per actual outstanding common share. Therefore, it does not serve the interests of meaningful disclosure to deny corporations the right to report on the face of the income statement as a basis for investor pro forma per-share calculations this one factually determined figure. Given this figure as a base, plus adequate disclosure of information related to capital structure that falls within the present bounds of fair disclosure, the calculation of pro forma common stock equivalence should be left to the investor to do in a way that he believes best serves his purpose. Accounting should not preempt the investor's judgment.

3. Investors have a right to view the primary earnings-per-share data as a realistic attribution of the earnings of the issuer to the various complex elements of its capital structure based on the current economic realities—not those existing years earlier when securities were issued. Investment value tests such as proposed by *Opinion No. 9* are a more realistic test of common stock equivalence, since they reflect current conditions. In addition, the at-issue test disregards the fact that both the issuers and holders of newly issued convertible securities that are not classified as common stock equivalents at issue recognize the possibility that as the value of the underlying common stock increases, the convertible features become increasingly significant. Therefore, the common stock equivalent concept should have validity at issuance and subsequently.

4. The use of the bank prime rate for the cash-yield test does not differentiate among types of security issued and the credit standing of the issuers.

5. It is erroneous to attribute earnings to securities that do not currently, and may never, share in those earnings, particularly when part or all of those earnings may have already been distributed to others as dividends. Furthermore, until convertible securities are converted, the common stockholders are in control of earnings distributions. Therefore, to show an amount per share which assumes conversion is improper.

6. It is potentially baffling to investors that convertible debt is debt in the statement of earnings but is common stock equivalent in the statement of earnings per share, and that dividends per share are based on the actual numbers of shares outstanding while earnings per share are based on a different and larger number of shares. Others go further and claim that the source of potential confusion is the fact that there is no such category as "common stock equivalent" in reality and the concept involves assumptions and intricate determinations which result in figures of questionable meaning which are more confusing than enlightening.

7. The argument that the investment value test and its application subsequent to issue has a "circular" effect [11] does not recognize the fact that analysts give appropriate recognition to the increasing importance of the common stock characteristics of convertible securities as the market rises or falls. Therefore, it is the argument against the investment value test that is illogical, not the test.

8. A third approach—the market parity method—to determining the common stock equivalence of securities has been proposed by some. This approach compares a convertible security's market value with its conversion value. If the two values are substantially equivalent and in excess of redemption price, the convertible security is considered to be a common stock equivalent. The advantage of this method as compared to the investment value test, which requires an estimate of investment value, is that it uses amounts that are readily available and ascertainable.

9. The financial statements should be consistent with the method used to determine earnings per share. Accordingly, the convertible debt considered to be the equivalent of common stock should be classified in the balance sheet in a combined section with common stock under a caption such as "equity of common stockholders and holders of common stock equivalents." In addition, in the income statement the interest paid on common stock equivalents should be shown as a distribution of income with a caption such as "distributions to holders of common stock equivalents."

---

[11] The reported earnings per share influence the market price, which, in turn, influences the classification of the security's status, which, in turn, influences the computation of earnings per share, which, in turn, influences the market.

10. Similarly, it is considered inconsistent and misleading by some that the income of subsidiaries reflected in consolidaetd and parent company statements disregards the existence of the subsidiary's common stock equivalents, whereas the earnings-per-share calculation reflects these securities.

11. The requirement that options and warrants whose exercise price is at or above the market price of related common stock be taken into account in the computation of primary earnings per share destroys the usefulness of the dual presentation of primary and fully diluted earnings per share. It fails to disclose the magnitude of the contingency arising from the outstanding warrants and options. Also, it is inconsistent with the determination of the status of convertible securities at time of issuance only, since it is an apparent recognition of the fact that market conditions subsequent to issuance can determine the status of a security.

12. The 20 percent limitation on the use of the treasury stock method of applying proceeds from the assumed exercise of options and warrants is arbitrary and unsupported.

13. It is inconsistent, in computing fully diluted earnings per share, to measure potential dilution by the treasury stock method in the case of most warrants and to assume conversion in the case of convertible securities. This inconsistency results in required recognition of potential dilution attributable to all convertible securities and at the same time, through the use of the treasury stock method, understatement or no recognition of potential dilution attributable to warrants.

14. The treasury stock method is unsatisfactory and other methods are preferable. One alternative proposed is that the number of equivalent shares be computed by reference to the relationship between the market value of the option or warrant and the market value of the related common stock. This method results in options and warrants having an impact on earnings per share whenever they have a market value, and not only when the market price of the related common stock exceeds the exercise price, as in the treasury stock method.

15. Some argue that the treasury stock method is improper since it (a) fails to recognize dilution unless the market price of the common stock exceeds the exercise price, and (b) assumes substantial blocks of treasury stock can be acquired without influencing the current market price, which is based on current actual trades.

16. There are more preferable approaches to the uses of funds assumed to be received from the exercise of outstanding warrants and options. Other uses proposed include the application of these funds to (a) reduce short- or long-term borrowings, (b) invest in government obligations or commercial paper, (c) invest in operations of the issues, or (d) fulfill other corporate purposes.

17. The inclusion of stock issuable in connection with a business combination on a purely contingent basis should not be included in the com-

putation of primary earnings per share if its issuance is wholly dependent upon the future movement of market prices. As a general practice, it is unsound for the determination of earnings to depend on the fluctuations of security prices, since it makes earnings per share a function of market price movements. The earnings per share should affect market price, and not vice versa.

18. Finally, there are some who claim that no matter how long the Board labors to solve the problems associated with computing earnings per share, no real progress will be made until the Board develops a sounder definition of net income.

SUGGESTED FURTHER READING

BALL, J. T. *Computing Earnings-Per-Share.* New York: American Institute of Certified Public Accountants, 1970.

CASES

Case 11-1. GENERAL POWER CORPORATION
Weighted Average Number of Shares

The General Power Corporation had 25,000 shares of common stock outstanding during a year and also had granted options which resulted in the following incremental shares, computed using the treasury stock method: 500 in the first quarter; none in the second quarter, because they would have been antidilutive; 1,400 in the third quarter; and 1,000 in the fourth quarter.

Question

1. Compute the weighted average of shares for computing the company's annual primary earnings per share.

Case 11-2. WILEY COMPANY
Calculating Incremental Stock Issues

The Wiley Company has 100,000 common shares outstanding, and 10,000 warrants outstanding which are exercisable at $20 per share to obtain 10,000 common shares. Assume also the following market prices per share of common stock during a three-year period:

	Year 1		Year 2		Year 3	
Quarter	Average	Ending	Average	Ending	Average	Ending
1	$18*	$22	$24	$25	$20	$18
2	20*	21	22	21	18	22
3	22	19	20	19	24	21
4	24	23	18	17	22	25

* Assume market prices had been more than $20 for substantially all of a previous quarter.

Questions

1. Compute the number of incremental shares related to the warrants to be included in each quarter's calculation of (*a*) primary earnings per share, and (*b*) diluted earnings per share.
2. Compute the number of incremental shares included in the year-to-date weighted average for calculating (*a*) primary earnings per share, and (*b*) fully diluted earnings per share.

Case 11–3. THE THOMAS COMPANY
Calculation of Earnings per Share

The Thomas Company was located in Boston, Massachusetts. Its stock was traded in the local over-the-counter market. Trading seldom reached a thousand shares a day. Certain data related to the company's earnings, capital structure and security prices are presented below:

Market Price of Common Stock. The market price of the common stock was as follows:

	1970	1969	1968
Average price:			
First quarter	$50	$45	$40
Second quarter	60	52	41
Third quarter	70	50	40
Fourth quarter	70	50	45
December 31 closing price ...	72	51	44

Cash Dividends. Cash dividends of $0.125 per common share were declared and paid for each quarter of 1968 and 1969. Cash dividends of $0.25 per common share were declared and paid for each quarter of 1970.

Convertible Debentures. Four percent convertible debentures with a principal amount of $16 million due in 1988 were sold for cash at a price of $100 in the last quarter of 1968. Each $100 debenture was convertible into two shares of common stock. No debentures were converted during 1968 or 1969. The entire issue was converted at the beginning of the third quarter of 1970 because the issue was called by the company.

Convertible Preferred Stock. At the beginning of the second quarter of 1969, 600,000 shares of convertible preferred stock were issued for assets in a purchase transaction. The annual dividend on each share of this convertible preferred stock was $0.20. Each share was convertible into one share of common stock. This convertible stock has a market value of $53 at the time of issuance and the bank prime rate was 5.5 percent.

Holders of 500,000 shares of this convertible preferred stock converted their preferred stock into common stock during 1970. (Assume even conversion throughout the year.)

Warrants. Warrants to buy 500,000 shares of common stock at $60 per share for a period of five years were issued along with the convertible preferred stock mentioned above. No warrants have been exercised.

Common Stock. The number of shares of common stock outstanding was as follows (in thousands):

	1970	1969
Beginning of year	3,300	3,300
Conversion of preferred stock	500	-
Conversion of debentures	200	—
End of year	4,000	3,300

Net Income. The 1969 and 1970 net income before dividends on preferred stock was (in thousands):

1969:	Net income	$10,300
1970:	Income before extraordinary item	12,900
	Net income	13,800

Taxes in 1969 were 48 percent; in 1970 they were 52.8 percent.

Questions

1. Compute the company's primary and fully diluted earnings per share for 1970 and 1969. The prime rate was 6 percent in 1968.
2. Starting with the "income before extraordinary item" line of the comparative 1970 and 1969 statements, complete the remaining portion of the bottom of the income statement for presentation in the company's annual

report. (The last line should disclose the company's net income per share, assuming full dilution.)

3. Prepare the footnote to accompany the per-share data presented in the 1970 income statement.

4. Does paragraph 38 of *Opinion No. 15* apply in this case?

Case 11–4. MOREHEAD CORPORATION

Two-Class Method

The Morehead Corporation had 10,000 shares of Class A common stock (the "ordinary" common) and 5,000 shares of Class B common stock outstanding during 1969 and had a net income of $65,000. Each share of Class B is convertible into two shares of Class A. The Class B is entitled to a noncumulative annual dividend of $5 per share. After Class A has been paid a dividend of $2 per share, Class B then participates in any additional dividends on a 40 to 60 per-share ratio with Class A. For 1969, the Class A shareholders have been paid $26,000 (or $2.60 per share) and the Class B shareholders have been paid $277,000 (or $5.40 per share).

Questions

1. Compile the earnings per share for 1969 (*a*) under the "if converted" method; (*b*) under the two-class method.

2. Could the two-class method be used in this case to report earnings per share?

3. Which method do you think results in the better measure of earnings per share?

PART V
Asset Valuation and Expense Determination

CHAPTER 12

ACCOUNTING FOR INCOME TAXES

Income taxes are an expense of doing business, and should be allocated to income and other accounts in the same fashion as other expenses. However, a number of companies report items of income and expense for income tax purposes on a basis different from that followed for financial reporting to stockholders and creditors. This raises a fundamental accounting question: Should the annual income tax expense reported in the published income statement be based on the taxable income reported to the Internal Revenue Service on the company's tax return for that year, an amount computed on the basis of the pretax income reported on the financial statements, or some other amount? *Opinion No. 11* of the Accounting Principles Board discusses this issue.

ORIGINS OF THE PROBLEM

The income tax allocation controversy is a direct outgrowth of the federal government's increasing use of income taxes as a positive or negative stimulus in the economy. The use of taxes as a stimulus takes a variety of forms:

1. "Across the board" stimulus, in the form of general changes in the tax rate.
2. Specific modifications to the continuing rules of determining taxable income, such as exemptions of certain revenues from taxable income.
3. Changes in the pattern of payment of the tax liability.
4. Changes in the timing of recognizing taxable revenues or tax deductible expenses.

There is general agreement that it is appropriate to reflect the effects of the changes specified above in the first two categories directly in the income statement during the period in which they occur. Such changes are, by law and regulation, directly relatable to items entering currently into the determination of income subject to tax.

The third type of stimulus—changes in the pattern of tax payments—affects a company's funds flow rather than income pattern. The delay in the payment of the tax increases the taxes payable liability account, and as such represents a source of funds. The eventual payment, which draws down the cash account, is a use of funds. The size of the tax expense is unaffected. To the extent that corporate tax payments are moving closer to a pay-as-you-go basis, an important source of funds from delayed tax payments is being taken away from businessmen.

The tax allocation accounting issue arises when the government employs the fourth category of stimuli; i.e., it allows a different timing pattern for revenues and expenses on tax returns from that employed in the financial accounting reports.

Permanent and Timing Differences

Differences between the income reported in the financial statement and that reported on the tax return may be either (1) permanent, or (2) related to timing differences. *Permanent* differences arise due to specific statutory concessions or exclusions of the tax code. For example, items of reported income such as domestic dividends may be omitted, in part, from a corporation's income on its tax return. Similarly, expenses allowable for financial reporting, such as premiums on officers' life insurance or amortization of goodwill, may not be deducted in the computation of taxable income.

Timing differences arise from the recognition in the financial reports and tax returns of income and expense in different periods. For example, a retailer may be required under *Opinion No. 10* to use in his published financial reports the accrual method, which recognizes income from installment sales at the time of sale. However, for tax purposes the retailer may elect to use the installment method, which recognizes the profit from the sale proportionately as the installment debt is paid. Other common examples of timing differences include: the use of straight-line depreciation in financial reports but accelerated depreciation in tax returns; the capitalization of research and development costs for stockholder reporting which are expensed as incurred for tax purposes.

There are four general types of timing differences. The individual transactions giving rise to these timing differences originate in one period and reverse themselves in subsequent periods:

1. Revenues are included in taxable income later than they are included in pretax accounting income, as in the installment sales example.
2. Expenses are deducted later in determining taxable income than in determining financial statement income, as in the case of warranty costs, which are deductible from taxable income only when incurred.
3. Revenues are included earlier in taxable income than in pretax accounting income. For example, rent payments received in advance may be reported when received for tax determination, but as earned for financial reporting purposes.
4. Expenses or losses are deducted in determining taxable income earlier than in determining pretax book income, such as in the case of research and development expenses that may be deducted immediately on a tax return but amortized in the financial statements over several years.

The major accounting problem arising from the timing differences is the method of recognizing the tax effects of timing differences. Permanent differences between pretax accounting income and taxable income present no problem, since, under applicable tax laws and regulations, current differences are not offset by corresponding differences in later periods.

Timing differences which reverse or turn around in later periods result in an equivalent reversal of the tax effects. Often the impact of the reversal of these differences is indefinitely postponed as similar new transactions balance out the reversal. A basic question develops as to whether the tax effect of timing differences should be recognized in view of the possibility of indefinitely postponing the actual payment of the tax.

THREE APPROACHES

Three methods of recognition of the tax effects arose in response to this problem. One widely held concept is that the income tax expense of a period should equal the tax payable for the period. Advocates of this "flow-through" method argue that there is no tax liability created until a later period; thus, there is no need to create an additional tax expense applicable to the current book pretax income.

Others argue for the "comprehensive allocation" method of reporting the income tax expense. This point of view holds that the tax expense reported in the financial statements should be the same as if the book profit were the profit actually reported for tax purposes. Any difference between this tax calculation and the tax currently due to the Internal Revenue Service is recorded as a potential tax liability labeled "deferred tax liability." *Opinion No. 11* recommends this approach.

A third view is expressed by proponents of "partial allocation." They would recognize in the determination of current income only those taxes deferred that are reasonably certain to be paid during, say, the next three to five years.

EXAMPLE

The problem of recognizing timing differences is illustrated in the following example. In early January 1968, retailer Smith sold a TV set for $360 on an installment sale basis. The installment sales contract called for no down payment and 36 payments of $10 per month plus interest on the unpaid balance. The retailer's gross margin was 20 percent of the sales price. (The interest and any carrying charges related to the installment payments can be ignored in this discussion.)

According to Accounting Principles Board *Opinion No. 10* (December 1966), the retailer must use the so-called accrual method of handling the transaction *on his books*, rather than the installment method, since the circumstances of the sale were such that the collection of the sales price was reasonably assured. Therefore, Smith must recognize the full pretax profit of $72 at the time of the sale. If he had been able to use the installment approach, he would have shown a $2 before-tax profit at the time each $10 installment payment was received. The accounting entries for recognizing the income under the two methods are:

Accrual Method

Accounts Receivable	360	
Cost of Goods Sold		288
Profit		72
To record sale.		

Cash	120	
Accounts Receivable		120
To record collections *each* year.		

Installment Method

Cash	120	
Cost of Goods Sold		96
Profit		24
To record installments received *each* year.		

The timing of the pretax profit recognition under the two methods is compared in Illustration 12–1.

ILLUSTRATION 12–1

Accrual versus Installment Treatment of Pretax Profit

	Accrual	*Installment*
1968	$72	$24
1969	—	24
1970	—	24
Total	$72	$72

First-Year Taxes

For calculating his tax payments, however, the retailer still has the option of using either the accrual or the installment method. If, in order to conserve his cash, Smith decides to use the installment method for tax purposes, he creates a tax deferral situation: he has recorded on his books the full $72 profit at the time of the sale, but for tax purposes he defers the actual payment of taxes on this profit until the time of the collection.

The aftertax profit consequences of using the accrual method for book purposes and the installment basis for tax purposes depend on whether Smith uses the flow-through treatment for handling the tax deferral or the comprehensive allocation method.

The flow-through approach records for book purposes the current year's tax payment actually shown on the retailer's tax return. If we assume a 50 percent tax rate, its application in this case would lead to the incremental effect on profits shown in Illustration 12–2.

ILLUSTRATION 12–2

Flow-Through Tax Accounting Illustrated

	Pretax Profit	Tax *	Net Profit
1968	$72	$12	$60
1969	—	12	(12)
1970	—	12	(12)
Total	$72	$36	$36

* 50 percent of the 20 percent profit included in the installments collected.

Given the pretax profit of $72 on the company's books in the year of sale, the comprehensive allocation approach leads to a profit of $36 after taxes. This treatment puts the profit effect of the installment rate on the same basis as an equivalent cash sale. The difference between the $36 tax expense shown on the books and the actual tax of $12 paid to the Internal Revenue Service in 1968 is set up as a deferred tax account of $24 on the liability side of the balance sheet. This account is reduced incrementally each subsequent year by the amount of taxes paid on the profit from the installment payments received during that year. So, in this example, the deferred tax account would be reduced by $12 each year over the remaining two-year installment payment period. The income statement is not affected by these subsequent tax payments or installment collections.

The accounting entries for the tax effect would be:

Comprehensive Allocation

Year 1:

Tax Expense		36
Taxes Payable	12	
Deferred Tax Liability	24	

Years 2 and 3:

Deferred Tax Liability	12	
Taxes Payable	12	

Flow-Through

Year 1:

Tax Expense	12	
Taxes Payable	12	

Years 2 and 3:

Tax Expense	12	
Taxes Payable	12	

A comparison of the results obtained from applying the flow-through and the comprehensive allocation methods, when Smith uses different book and tax income recognition timing, is shown in Illustration 12–3. (The cash flow effect of this sale depends on whether the retailer sells for cash or on an installment basis and on the method he chooses to use on his tax return to recognize the profit from the sale. The financial accounting handling of the deferred taxes, if any, does not change his cash flow.)

ILLUSTRATION 12–3

Flow-Through versus Comprehensive Tax Accounting:
Aftertax Book Profits

	Flow-Through	Comprehensive	Differential
1968	$60	$36	$24
1969	(12)	—	(12)
1970	(12)	—	(12)
Total	$36	$36	$ 0

Second-Year Taxes

In addition to realizing a first-year profit differential of $24, the flow-through approach provides an opportunity to offset the $12 reduction in second-year profits (see Illustration 12–3.) Smith can accomplish this by making a similar $360 TV set installment sale in 1969. Again, the aftertax profit differential between the flow-through and comprehensive allocation treatment would be $24. But he would offset this amount with the second-year $12 profit reduction associated with the 1968 sale. So the net profit in the second year would be $12. This effect is shown in Illustration 12–4.

ILLUSTRATION 12–4

Flow-Through versus Comprehensive Tax Accounting:
Aftertax Book Profits

	Flow-Through	*Comprehensive*	*Differential*
1968	$60	$36	$24
1969	48	36	12
1970	(24)	—	(24)
1971	(12)	—	(12)
Total	$72	$72	$ 0

If the retailer in the second example is using the comprehensive allocation approach, the deferred tax item appearing on the balance sheet at the end of the first year would be $24. This deferral would rise to $36 at the end of the second year (the $24 difference between the tax payment recognized by the second-year sale handled on an accrual versus an installment basis, less the $12 reduction for taxes related to the first-year sale's actual tax payments made during the second year). If Smith sells one $360 TV set each year on a three-year installment sale basis, his deferred tax will remain at $36. If he increases his installment sales volume, the deferred tax item will increase. It is this so-called "permanent" deferral that the partial allocation advocates claim should be included in earnings.

Thus, if flow-through accounting is used, the retailer could establish on a long-term basis a profit differential between himself and other retailers making similar installment sales who are using the accrual method for book purposes and the installment method for tax purposes, but are handling their tax accounting on a comprehensive allocation basis. This differential would be proportionately greater if the retailers installment sales volume were growing.

So far we have looked only at recognizing the full book profits at the time of sale. Let us go back to the original one TV set sale example and lay aside for a moment the Board's earlier 1966 accrual basis decision. If the retailer, Smith, had handled his installment sale in exactly the opposite way to the previously assumed method—that is, if he reported the sale on an accrual basis for tax purposes and on an installment basis for book purposes—the sale would have the aftertax effect on book profits shown in Illustration 12–5. The first-year pretax profits on the installment method are $24 and the taxable income on the accrual method reported to the

ILLUSTRATION 12–5

Flow-Through versus Comprehensive Tax Accounting:
Aftertax Book Profits

	Flow-Through	Comprehensive	Differential
1968	$(12)	$12	$(24)
1969	24	12	12
1970	24	12	12
Total	$ 36	$36	$ 0

government is $72. In years 2 and 3 the book pretax profit is $24 each year. There is no profit reported on the tax return since it was all recognized in year 1. In Illustration 12–5, if comprehensive allocation were applied, the deferred tax item would show up on the asset side of the balance sheet, since the first-year profit recorded for taxes would be greater than the profit recorded for financial accounting purposes. In a sense, the company has overpaid, or prepaid, some taxes.[1]

EARLY PROPOSALS AND EVENTS

The present controversy about how to handle differences between the income reported for financial and for tax purposes originated in the early 1950s. To promote the development of productive facilities needed for support of the Korean War, the federal government granted certificates of necessity which permitted amortization for tax purposes of new "emergency facilities" over a period of 60 months. *Accounting Research Bulletin 43*, Chapter 9, Section C, discussed the accounting problems raised by this provision of the tax code. The committee stated that from an accounting standpoint, there is nothing inherent in the nature of emergency facilities which required the depreciation or amortization of their cost for financial accounting purposes over either a shorter or longer period than would be proper if no certificate of necessity had been issued.[2] Accordingly, the committee believed that during the tax amortization period, if there was a material difference between book and tax depreciation, a charge should be made in the income statement to recognize the income

---

[1] Situations giving rise to deferred tax assets include those where rents or royalties are taxed as collected but deferred in the accounts to later periods; and the sale of carved-out production payments, where the tax is due when the sale is made but for book purposes the income from the sale is reported as the underlying minerals are produced.

[2] The Tax Reform Act of 1969 created an analogous situation by giving taxpayers, under certain conditions, the choice of amortizing the cost of qualifying air and water pollution facilities over a 60-month period in lieu of depreciating the assets over their useful life.

tax to be paid in the future on the amount by which amortization for income tax purposes exceeded the depreciation that would be allowable if certificates of necessity had not been issued. This estimated amount should be based on normal and surtax rates in effect during the period covered by the income statement.

In accounting for this deferment of income taxes, the committee believed it desirable to treat the charge as additional income tax expense. The related credit in such cases would properly be made to an account for deferred income taxes. Under this method, in the later period after the emergency amortization period, the annual charges for income taxes would be reduced by charging to the account for deferred income taxes that part of the income tax in excess of what would have been payable had the amortization deduction not been claimed for income tax purposes in the amortization period. The committee concluded that by this procedure the net income would more nearly reflect the results of a proper matching of costs and revenues.

Under the proposed method, the purchase of a $50,000 machine with a 10-year life under a certificate of necessity would permit write-off of the full cost (assuming no salvage value) of the equipment over a period of five years or less for tax purposes. Illustration 12–6 shows the effect of the committee's recommendation if income is assumed to be $10,000, and the tax rate 50 percent.

ILLUSTRATION 12-6

Preferred Method of Handling Differences in Depreciation for Book Tax Purposes

| | Tax Return | | | Financial Statements | | | |
Year	Income	Deprecia-tion	Tax Paid	Income	Deprecia-tion	Tax Expense	Cumulative Tax Deferred
1	$ 10,000	$10,000	–0–	$ 10,000	$ 5,000	$ 2,500	$ 2,500
2	10,000	10,000	–0–	10,000	5,000	2,500	5,000
3	10,000	10,000	–0–	10,000	5,000	2,500	7,500
4	10,000	10,000	–0–	10,000	5,000	2,500	10,000
5	10,000	10,000	–0–	10,000	5,000	2,500	12,500
6	10,000	–0–	$ 5,000	10,000	5,000	2,500	10,000
7	10,000	–0–	5,000	10,000	5,000	2,500	7,500
8	10,000	–0–	5,000	10,000	5,000	2,500	5,000
9	10,000	–0–	5,000	10,000	5,000	2,500	2,500
10	10,000	–0–	5,000	10,000	5,000	2,500	–0–
	$100,000	$50,000	$25,000	$100,000	$50,000	$25,000	–0–

In *Accounting Research Bulletin No. 44* (revised), issued in 1958, the committee recommended the same deferral procedures for concerns using declining-balance depreciation for income tax returns and straight-line for financial reporting.

These statements of the committee supporting tax deferral tax accounting were opposed by the SEC's 1945 *Accounting Series Release No. 53.* In this release, the Securities and Exchange Commission took the position that income tax allocation was not appropriate. The release concluded that "the amount shown as provision for taxes should reflect only actual taxes believed payable under the applicable tax laws." However, the commission never insisted that this provision be followed.

OPINION NO. 11

In December 1967, after many years of debate, the Accounting Principles Board issued *Opinion No. 11*, requiring comprehensive tax allocation for income taxes. The Board concluded:

. . . that comprehensive interperiod tax allocation is an integral part of the determination of income tax expense. Therefore, income tax expense should include the tax effects of revenue and expense transactions included in the determination of pretax accounting income. The tax effects of those transactions which enter into the determination of pretax accounting income either earlier or later than they become determinants of taxable income should be recognized in the periods in which the differences between pretax accounting income and taxable income arise and in the periods in which the differences reverse. Since permanent differences do not affect other periods, interperiod tax allocation is not appropriate to account for such differences.

The Board has concluded that the deferred method of tax allocation should be followed since it provides the most useful and practical approach to interperiod tax allocation and the presentation of income taxes in financial statements.

The tax effect of a timing difference should be measured by the differential between income taxes computed with and without inclusion of the transaction creating the difference between taxable income and pretax accounting income. The resulting income tax expense for the period includes the tax effects of the transaction entering into the determination of results of operations for the period. The resulting deferred tax amounts reflect the tax effects which will reverse in future periods. The measurement of income tax expense becomes thereby a consistent and integral part of the process of matching revenues and expenses in the determination of results of operation.

THE CONTROVERSY

Flow-Through Method

Advocates of the flow-through method recognize as taxes only those amounts immediately payable based upon the current tax returns. They believe that only the current taxes are a legal liability and that to recognize future taxes results in undesirable income normalization. Further, since, in the case of many companies, tax deferrals are unlikely to be paid in the foreseeable future, continuation of the policy of deferring taxes may result in an ever-increasing amount on the liabilities side of the balance sheet which does not represent a legally enforceable claim against the corporation.

Comprehensive Allocation

Comprehensive allocation proponents base their arguments on the accounting convention that profits result from matching revenues and related costs. They argue that tax expenses should be recorded in the same accounting period as that in which the related revenue and expense items are recognized for book purposes.

Given this approach, when there is a timing difference between the recognition and payment of taxes, the logic of the debit-credit mechanism requires a deferred balance to be placed on the appropriate side of the balance sheet. This, a credit entry to offset the debit to tax expense is made to the liability account, deferred taxes. This liability item, they argue, is only a "residual" entry, and as such does not have all the usual characteristics of a liability or an asset.

Advocates of comprehensive allocation argue that the fact that reversal of timing differences may be more than offset by new timing differences does not alter the fact that the reversals do occur, and may be readily identified as to their tax effect. Accounting principles, they state, cannot be predicated on a reliance that these offsets will continue. They therefore conclude that the fact that the tax effects of two transactions happen to go in opposite directions does not invalidate the necessity of recognizing separately the tax effects of the transactions as they occur.

Partial Allocation

The partial allocation concept is often considered a modification of the flow-through method. The flow-through approach recognizes only those taxes which are payable in the current period. Partial allocation proponents would modify this approach to include those deferred taxes which are reasonably certain to become payable in the immediate future, as, say, within three to five years. Holders of this view believe that when recurring differences between taxable income and pretax accounting income give rise to an indefinite postponement of an amount of tax payments or to continuing tax reductions, tax allocation is not required, since taxes not reasonably expected to be payable should not affect net income. Furthermore, partial allocation advocates believe that indefinite postponement of taxes involves contingencies which are at best remote, and the inclusion of such taxes in the determination of the current book tax expenses results in a misstatement of that expense and of net income. For example, it is argued, comprehensive tax allocation will result in an understatement of net income in the case of a company with a relatively stable or growing investment in depreciable assets which uses straight-line depreciation in determining pretax accounting income but an accelerated method in determining taxable income as it will continue to defer taxes so long as it continues to invest in capital equipment.

Those who favor partial allocation also argue that it is misleading to show the full tax allocation, since it does not represent a legally enforceable claim by outsiders on the company's assets. Therefore, since it is not a liability, it should not be included in the balance sheet. This position should be modified only in those instances in which specific nonrecurring differences between taxable income and pretax accounting income would lead to a material misstatement of income tax expense and net income. If such nonrecurring differences occur, income tax expense of a period for financial accounting purposes should be adjusted to include those amounts expected to be paid within the immediate four- to five-year period.

Opponents of partial allocation believe that partial allocation artificially inflates income; that it does not follow the matching concept; and that it leaves to management judgment the computation of income tax expense, which can, in fact, be directly determined in an objective manner.

Deferred Taxes: A Liability?

Whether or not deferred taxes are a liability has been the focus of much of the controversy over deferred tax accounting. This argument has created problems for the proponents of both partial and comprehensive allocation, since neither has been able to satisfactorily explain the nature of the deferred tax item.

Advocates of partial allocation and flow-through methods correctly claim that the deferred tax item does not satisfy the traditional asset or liability conventions. Some believe the weakness of this argument is exposed by the partial allocation advocates' admission that they would set up a deferred tax item on the balance sheet in certain cases. Also, it is pointed out, partial allocation proponents offer no explanation of what their limited deferral item is, beyond saying that it is that portion of postponed taxes which might have to be paid in the near future. Some comprehensive allocation advocates argue that the "no liability" argument is not relevant, since the conventional definition of a liability is outmoded by current financial reporting practices. In addition to deferred taxes, for example, such items as deferred profits on sale and leaseback transactions and pension accruals appear as liabilities, although they do not fit the conventional definition of a liability.

In the past, supporters of comprehensive allocation also have failed to develop an adequate explanation of the deferred tax item on the balance sheet. This has subjected this method to continuing criticism. Businessmen have been concerned that users of financial statements might include deferred tax credits as debt in the debt-equity or the working capital ratios, despite the fact that these deferrals do not have the characteristics of debt. This apprehension has made it difficult for many to see how comprehensive allocation produces fairer, more useful results than partial allocation.

Flow of Funds

It has been advocated that the adoption of the source of funds approach suggested earlier in the "Basic Conventions" chapter may help to resolve many of these theoretical difficulties.

Contemporary financial accounting is increasingly concerned with maintaining a continuing record of capital invested in an enterprise from a two-sided point of view: that of the sources and uses of funds, with funds broadly defined as all financial resources. This concern is in line with modern financial theory and practice, which tends to view assets as funds invested within the business, and liabilities and net worth as financial resources obtained from sources external to the firm. As a result, the balance sheet is regarded by many as an instant report of the status of funds obtained from sources external to the business and the items in which these funds are invested. Closely related to this trend is the growing importance of the funds flow statement to the users of financial statements. These funds flow statements are typically derived from the balance sheets for the related period.

In addition, increasingly, businessmen and accountants are challenging the customary two-part division of the balance sheet. The growing use of a "no-man's land" category for items between the customary liabilities and equity section of the balance sheet serves as evidence that it is no longer practical to present fairly all external sources of funds as flowing through either the traditional "liabilities" or "net worth" sections of the balance sheet. Items such as deferred taxes or deferred pension costs fall into this new category. They are thought to belong on the right-hand side of the balance sheet, but don't neatly fit traditional categories. On the other hand, these transactions are not regarded as contributing directly to income at the time the transaction occurs.

Proponents of this funds flow view of the balance sheet believe that this gives explicit recognition to the fact that current business conditions require a more flexible approach to classifying "external sources of capital" on the right side of the balance sheet. In the case of tax allocation, this approach avoids the seemingly endless and frustrating arguments that revolve around the nature of the deferral items. The deferral item is a special source of funds from the postponement of taxes due to timing differences and is clearly labeled as such on the balance sheet, along with the sources of funds from creditors and owner equity sources.

Like Depreciation?

Some accountants argue that deferred taxes are not technically a funds source. Rather they are similar to depreciation; that is, simply a nonfund bookkeeping adjustment.

The funds flow advocates agree that depreciation is not a source of funds. They acknowledge that the real funds flow associated with depreciation occurs when an asset giving rise to depreciation is acquired. In their view, the depreciation adjustment to reported profits is simply a device to obtain a better measure of the funds from operations which represent both a return on and a return of capital.

Deferred taxes, the funds approach suggests, are different in character from depreciation, and it is these differences that make them a genuine source of funds. Deferred taxes relate to the accounting period in which they occur rather than to some past period, as does depreciation. The funds are obtained in the current period through a postponement of the timing of cash outflows to the taxing authorities *and* a decision by management that the pattern of expenses recognized for tax purposes is not appropriate for book purposes. Both conditions must be present.

If one starts with the assumption that management uses for book purposes the most appropriate depreciation policy for its particular business and assets, then its use of another method for tax purposes must be motivated and justifiable only as a tax strategy maneuver to change the flow of cash related to income tax obligations. A company using accelerated depreciation for *both* tax and book purposes can delay the payment of taxes. However, in this case the delayed taxes don't represent a special source of funds, because the company is using for tax purposes the same depreciation method it believes is the most appropriate for measuring the results of its operations for financial reporting purposes. The federal government has not made any special concessions in such a situation, beyond letting the company use the same method for book and tax purposes.

The source of funds is created by a difference between the company's "real" depreciation policy and its tax depreciation policy. The company using straight-line for book purposes and accelerated depreciation for tax purposes has been able to take advantage of a special concession from the government: namely, to use for tax purposes a depreciation method that does not, in the opinion of management, reflect fairly the results of operations.

Some critics of the funds flow justification for comprehensive allocations maintain that this approach assumes that the funds source results from a comparison between, say, the accelerated depreciation actually used for tax purposes and a hypothetical tax use of straight-line depreciation. Implicit comparisons of this kind, they then claim, are not consistent with the traditional accounting model, and hence the funds approach is invalid.

The funds advocates believe the error of this criticism lies in a mistaken assumption as to what creates the funds. The funds result from a timing difference between book and tax items, not between the actual tax timing used and some alternative approach to tax recognition of revenues and costs.

Other critics claim corporations deferring taxes do not receive a check from the government for the amount deferred. Consequently, they conclude, there is no source of funds.

The supporters of the funds approach claim this point of view represents a narrow bookkeeping approach to accounting. In their opinion, it completely disregards the effect of tax deferrals on the corporation's total funds flow. It also fails to reflect the view of most businessmen that tax deferrals are a source of funds. Furthermore, the funds advocates point out that businessmen know that to avoid paying out funds is as valuable as receiving the same amount from somebody outside the corporation. They do not appear to be troubled by the absence of a check from the government.

Measurable Funds Effect

The partial allocators maintain that under certain circumstances income tax payments postponed can be permanently deferred, and that these deferred taxes cannot be construed to be liabilities. They argue that the government does not tax individual items of revenue or give offsetting refunds for the tax impact of individual expense items. The tax is levied on the results of bringing individual revenues and expense items together. Given this fact, they claim it is possible to offset the eventual tax impact of particular tax deferral transactions by recurring transactions of a similar nature. Thus, the accumulated tax effect of revenues not yet included in tax returns and expenses taken into tax returns at a faster rate than on the financial statements are theorized out of existence.

Legally, the income tax liability is a function of the net profit item shown on the tax return. However, this figure is a *net* result of a multitude of taxable revenue and tax deductible expense items, each of which has a calculable impact on the ultimate tax assessment. The individual elements which created the tax and the actual tax payment are inextricably tied together. It would be misleading to consider each element of the tax calculation without regard to its ultimate tax effect either in (1) making decisions which give rise to revenues and expenses, or (2) evaluating the financial results of these decisions. The fact that the individual revenue and expense items shown on the tax return might be brought together at a different time than on the accounting reports does not—assuming the typical case of a profitable entity—remove the calculable tax effect which they create individually.

Another line of reasoning followed by critics of comprehensive allocation also fails to reflect the way businessmen look at the tax impact of individual decisions. Their permanent deferral claim glosses over the fact, well recognized among businessmen, that revenues recognized now, but not included in current tax returns, will create an upward push on the amount of future income taxes. Also, businessmen typically assume that exercising the privilege of taking some deductions for certain expenses on the current year's income tax returns will most likely cause an upward push on future income taxes. Fewer future effects are more predictable than these events in the company with reasonable prospects for future profits. It is a natural result and in line with the common business practice which relates, for decision-making purposes, the tax effects with the individual transactions which collectively determine taxable income, such as in capital investment appraisals.

Extending the Argument

Extending the "permanent deferral" argument to other items on the balance sheet leads to clearly unacceptable results. For example, the accounts receivable and accounts payable balances of most companies have some part which is permanent in amount and is "rolling over" constantly. Applying the permanent deferral approach to these items would mean sales would have to be reduced by the amount of funds related to the "permanently" deferred accounts receivable, which, of course, would not be shown on the balance sheet. Similarly, the "permanent" portion of the funds derived from accounts payable would be left off the balance sheet and expenses reduced to the extent these payables were related to expense items.

Of course, supporters of the flow-through type of approach argue against these "roll-over" objections by claiming that items like accounts payables involve real invoices and real creditors. This is true. However, are they that different a source of funds from deferred taxes? In fact, from a businessman's point of view, deferred taxes are an even more valuable source of funds, since no direct, immediate creditor claim exists. Some claim this is an important reason for showing this special source of funds on the balance sheet.

Income Measurement

Some critics of the funds flow justification for comprehensive allocation claim that funds flow arguments support their opposing position equally as well. Deferred tax, they claim, is a meaningful source of capital obtained through operations and should be included in income for the period giving rise to the deferral. The turning point in deciding whether funds obtained through tax deferral should be included in the income statement is the definition of income one adopts.

Proponents of comprehensive allocation believe that net income measures principally how effectively management has added to the capital of the business through operations utilizing the capital already invested in the enterprise. Exercise by management of the privilege afforded by the income tax code to postpone taxes does not, in their opinion, constitute improved operating performance, no matter how long may be the prospect of continuing the tax postponement. They view tax postponement as providing an opportunity to perform better in the future as a result of being able to conserve funds currently for use in the business.

Consequently, they state that this funds retention benefit should be reflected in terms of a favorable capital "funds flow," rather than in terms of an immediate increase in funds from operations, as proposed by the partial allocators. Furthermore, the income benefits flowing from the deferral of tax payments should be reflected in income only as management earns profits through reducing financial charges or improving operations as a result of using effectively the funds retained.

Funds flow advocates feel that a standard recognizing income as earned only through "honest-to-goodness" operating efficiency is vital to maintaining some semblance of integrity in the earnings figures as a measure of performance. The partial allocation method fails to meet this objective. For example, the partial allocation approach would permit a company in expanding investment situations, simply by using straight-line depreciation on its books and accelerated depreciation on its tax returns, to get credit for an additional profit improvement equal to 48 percent of the difference in expense charges between these two methods when the rate is 52%.

Similarly, a retailer with increasing sales who sells on the installment basis would show higher profits than another retailer with identical sales who sells for cash. To achieve this result, the credit sales would be recorded on the accrual basis for book purposes and the installment basis for tax purposes. Obviously, any accounting procedure that permits higher aftertax gross margin profits from credit sales than from cash sales is undesirable since it substitutes the illusion of performance for the realities.

Those favoring comprehensive allocation believe that postponement of tax payments is equivalent in practice to an interest-free loan from the government which should be disclosed in the balance sheet. In contrast, the partial allocation approach does not show this source as an identifiable item on the balance sheet. Rather, it is included as an unidentified part of the source of funds from profitable operations, since income will be higher in most cases using the partial allocation, due to the lower tax expense shown. Thus, an important source of funds is not fully disclosed.

Other Aspects of the Problem

Advocates of the funds flow approach believe it also solves certain other specific problems inherent in accounting for deferred taxes.

In the rare cases where management decisions lead to timing differences resulting in higher income for tax purposes than recorded in the books, the funds approach argues that the resulting increase in deferred tax debit balances is a use of funds, and as such, belongs on the left-hand or asset side of the balance sheet, since, in a sense, the debit represents an overpayment or prepayment of taxes. Also, placing emphasis on the amount of resources obtained currently from tax deferrals rather than the amount owed removes the need to determine and report the deferrals on a discounted basis.

Present Value Approach

Accounting Research Study No. 9, *Interperiod Allocation of Corporate Income Taxes*, proposed that certain long-term tax allocation accounts be presented on a present value basis. Laying aside the practical difficulties of determining the discount rate and period, the funds advocates claim that this proposal misinterpreted the real nature of the deferred tax item. It reflected the typical accounting theory approach to liabilities. As a result, it focused heavily on their payment characteristics. This concern, in turn, led to a proposal that was consistent with conventional accounting theory related to long-term debts.

The advocates of the funds approach to liabilities believe their point of view reflects the emphasis businessmen place on the amount of funds obtained currently from tax deferrals rather than on the amount owed. Using this approach, they argue, there is no need to determine and report the deferrals on a discounted basis. It is of little interest and relevance. Consequently, in their opinion, the current practice, which does not report discounted deferred taxes, is correct.

Rate Changes

The appropriate handling of changes in the corporate income tax rate which occur after the establishment of the original tax deferrals on the balance sheet presents a thorny problem. There are two principal points of view, both of which are consistent with the comprehensive allocation approach to tax deferral accounting. The supporters of the liability method argue that rate changes should be reflected in current income. The advocates of the deferral method maintain that the rate change only affects balance sheet items. *Opinion No. 11* and the funds view of financial accounting support the deferral method.

The liability method supporters argue that the deferred tax portion of the current tax expense should be computed at the rate expected to be paid in the future, when the taxes deferred become payable. The typical assumption is that tax rates will, in the absence of definite evidence to the contrary, be no less than the current rate. However, if it is known that the tax rate will rise in a subsequent year, that tax rate must be applied in the current year.

Under the liability method, given an increase in the tax rate, the tax expense in the rate change year (or the year when the future rate change is known) would reflect both (1) the difference in the previous years' deferrals still on the balance sheet, restated as if the new rate had been in effect in previous years, and the original balance before adjustment; and (2) the deferred tax expense provision for the current period at the new rate. The first step of this procedure can result in adding to the tax expense for the rate change year an element of tax expense for which there is no related income.

The rate change problem affects all companies with tax deferrals, particularly those companies where the items creating the deferral roll over during relatively short periods of time. Consequently, there is widespread objection to this method among businessmen who might agree with comprehensive allocation, but who would oppose it because of potential income distortion due to income tax rate changes if the liability method approach to comprehensive allocation had been adopted. For example, many in the retail trade felt this approach was not consistent with the matching convention. They believed that it was not appropriate to make this additional charge to tax expense in a single year in those cases where the deferred tax account related to installment sales is growing and will most likely not be drawn down in the foreseeable future.

Liability Method: An Example

Under the liability method Company ABC would start with the following balance sheet:

Assets xxx	Liabilities xxx
	Deferred tax (@ 50%)...$20,000
	Net worth xxx
Total xxx	Total xxx

If the pretax accounting income for the year were $40,000, the pretax income for tax return purposes was $10,000, the rate had changed from 50 to 55 percent, and all of the previous year's deferral was to be paid this year, the following computation would be made:

Profit before tax $40,000
Income tax:
  Current .... $ 7,500

> Tax on $10,000 of the current
> profit recognized for tax
> purposes @ 55% $5,500
> Adjustment of prior deferral for
> 5% rate increase on $40,000
> income previously deferred $2,000

  Deferred portion   16,500

> Tax on $30,000 of current profit
> deferred for tax purposes at 55%

Total tax   24,000
Profit after tax $16,000

The impact on the deferred tax account would be (assuming that the prior year's deferral was payable this year):

Beginning balance (prior deferred portion)..... $20,000
Increase: Current portion   7,500
         Deferred portion   16,500
                               $44,000
Decrease: Payment of tax   27,500
Ending balance $16,500

Deferral Method: An Example

The deferred method restricts the accounting impact of the rate change to the balance sheet. Stated simply, a tax rate increase reduces the source of funds shown on the balance sheet due to past postponement accruals. A tax rate decrease increases this source. No income adjustments are needed.

To illustrate the deferred method, assume Company ABC has the same balance sheet income and tax assumptions as in the example above, i.e.:

Assets xxx	Liabilities xxx
	Deferred tax (@ 50%)...$20,000
	Net worth xxx
Total xxx	Total xxx

The required tax computation on the current pretax profit of $40,000 would be:

Profit before tax		$40,000
Tax:		
Current	$ 5,500	
Deferred	16,500	22,000
Profit after tax		$18,000

The impact on the deferred tax account would be:

Beginning balance (deferred portion)..........	$20,000
Increase: Current portion (on current income)	5,500
Deferred portion	16,500
	$42,000
Decrease: Payment of tax	27,500
Ending balance	$14,500

Effective Tax Rate Reduction?

Some authorities believe that the change in the timing for recognition of taxable revenues and deductions is essentially similar to a change in the pattern of payment of the tax liability. Both change the timing of tax payments. Both are changes in the sources of funds created by the government's decision to allow corporations to delay payments. Neither reduces the ultimate tax expense.

Those who hold this view believe comprehensive allocation to be consistent with the facts of the situation. Representatives of the Treasury during the late 1960s disagreed with this view of the nature of the timing differences. They argued that this kind of tax stimulus, which permits timing differences, represents a reduction in the effective tax rate to the corporation taking advantage of the timing difference provisions of the code. Comprehensive allocation, they claim, masks the effect of rate reduction due to timing differences and as such, gives a misleading picture of the administration's tax policy. Also, by reducing the profits of corporations (compared to the flow-through and partial allocation methods), comprehensive allocation leads to an unnecessary understatement of corporate profits, and a consequent understatement of the economy's health.

Those who disagreed with the Treasury's point of view believed that, first, if deferral of tax payments constitutes a rate reduction in taxes, speeding up the payment schedule must be the equivalent of a rate increase. They felt it was doubtful that the Treasury would agree to this extension of their position. Second, the Treasury argument was based upon a cash-flow approach to financial accounting. Corporate reporting had long abandoned cash basis reporting systems for the more useful and fair accrual method. Third, it was suspected that the Treasury Department might have been seeking to fashion corporate reporting principles for political ends. Adoption of noncomprehensive methods would tend to soften the impact of increased corporate tax rates and give the impression of greater growth in the economy than had actually occurred.

PUBLIC UTILITIES

A number of public utilities subject to rate-making processes have elected to use accelerated depreciation on their income tax returns and straight-line depreciation on their reports to stockholders. In these circumstances, some regulatory commissions have permitted the public utility neither to record deferred taxes in their accounts nor include deferred taxes as an allowable cost for rate-making purposes.[3] In these cases, most of the affected public utilities follow flow-through accounting for reporting their current tax expense to stockholders. This creates several problems for public accountants: Should an unqualified opinion be given on financial statements that do not provide for deferred taxes? What constitutes full and fair disclosure when flow-through accounting is used?

Paragraph 8 of *Accounting Research Bulletin No. 44* (revised) provides that comprehensive tax allocation need not be followed by public utilities with transactions involving timing differences "if it may be reasonably expected that the increased future income taxes resulting from the earlier deduction of declining-balance depreciation, for tax purposes only, will be allowed in future rate determinations." Consequently, the public accountant does not qualify his opinion on the statement of "flow-through" public utilities if there is basis for a reasonable expectation that taxes deferred will be allowed in the future as a recoverable cost in rate determinations.

There is no common understanding or objective standard for determining what constitutes the basis for a "reasonable expectation" in this public utility exception to comprehensive tax allocation accounting. Many accountants assume that if current regulatory commissions do not allow deferred taxes for rate-making determination, future commissions will continue to support this practice and will allow increased taxes in the future when the annual tax return accelerated depreciation charges are lower than the straight-line charges used in the accounts. Some accountants believe this is a dangerous assumption, since future commissions may not necessarily be bound by the decisions of prior commissions. Also, in the opinion of some accountants, the public utility expectation of *ARB No.*

---

[3] In a regulated industry, the price of the product is determined by a formula which permits the utility to recover from its operating revenues its operating costs plus a fair return on the cost or fair market value of property used in the public service.

44 (revised) is based on an untenable concept that accounting resulting from rules prescribed by rate-making bodies may be unconditionally approved by public accountants notwithstanding the fact that the accounting result of applying the rule is not in accordance with generally accepted accounting practices.

Those public utilities regulated by "flow-through" commissions claim that in their circumstances either to force them to use deferred tax accounting in their accounts or to require the public accountant to issue a qualified opinion would be misleading to users of their reports and unfair to the issuer. For example, assume that, according to the applicable rate formula, a utility is allowed a return of $2 million on its net worth ($1,750,000 for common dividends plus $250,000 for retained earnings), in addition to its allowable operating costs and interest expense. If such a company is forced by its public accountants to include in its accounts a deferred tax cost of $400,000 which is not allowed for rate determination purposes, its common dividends will not be covered out of current profits. This is an intolerable position for such companies. On the other hand, those opposed to paragraph 8 of *ARB No. 44* claim that if deferred taxes are not provided for in the accounts, retained earnings will be overstated to the extent of this cost.

Flow-through accounting for regulated utilities covered by paragraph 8 is opposed by some accountants on the ground that it encourages regulatory commissions to adopt rate determination formulas that transfer costs to future customers that are properly applicable to current customers. Costs currently deducted for tax purposes exert an upward pressure on taxes in future years, since these deductions are unavailable in future years. Therefore, it is argued, the decision allows the tax deferment benefit arising from the use of accelerated depreciation for tax purposes to flow to the current customers. This also increases the risk to security holders, since it is possible that these deferred tax costs may not be allowed in future rate determinations, or that if they are allowed the revenues realized may not be sufficient to cover them and interest costs.

Paragraph 20 of APB *Opinion No. 6*, issued in October 1965, sets the standards for disclosure for "flow-through" utilities:

> When a company subject to rate-making processes adopts the declining-balance method of depreciation for income tax purposes but adopts other appropriate methods for financial accounting purposes in the circumstances described in Paragraph 8 [*ARB No. 44* (revised)] and does not give accounting recognition to deferred income taxes, disclosure should be made of this fact.

This disclosure requirement differed from an earlier one set forth in paragraph 9 of *ARB No. 44*. It required that "full disclosure should be made of the *amount* of deferred income taxes." Several members of the Board objected to the removal of this requirement by the APB in *Opinion*

No. 6, on the grounds that "the Accounting Principles Board is inappropriately sponsoring the viewpoint that investors and other users of financial statements should be told of the practice but need not be furnished the information to judge its significance." The "flow-through" segment of the public utility industry agreed with the Board's decision. In their opinion, to disclose the current amount of taxes deferred may cause some investors to erroneously discount current earnings in the belief that the tax deferment is a current cost. Such investor action could adversely affect the utilities' ability to raise common equity.

Tax Reform Act

The Tax Reform Act of 1969 contained a major innovation in tax policy for utilities, in that henceforth the availability of an accelerated tax depreciation method is dependent on the rate practice of the regulatory commission and the utility's accounting policy. This policy was adopted to avoid a federal revenue loss projected to be between $1.5 and $2 billion annually, as additional utilities were being forced by rate-making bodies to shift to flow-through accounting for book and rate determination purposes.

This provision of the act established "normalization" as the preferred standard for public utilities in this country. (A utility is using the normalization method of accounting if it includes any deferred taxes in current expenses for accounting *and* rate purposes, *and* records any accumulated deferred taxes in a balance sheet reserve account.) Henceforth, public utilities, as defined in the act, would be limited to the use of straight-line tax depreciation unless they normalize or unless they had already established conditions specified in the act by August 1969 which would classify them as being flow-through companies.

LOSS CARRY-BACK—CARRY-FORWARD CREDITS

Where an operating loss for income tax calculation purposes occurs, a corporation may offset the loss against the taxable income of the preceding three years to the extent that the entire loss is offset. This is accomplished by filing amended tax returns for the prior years. The difference between tax liability on the amended and original returns can be claimed by the corporation as a tax refund.

If taxable income during the previous three years is less than the current year's loss, the unabsorbed portion of the current year's loss may be carried forward five years to reduce taxable income. Where two loss years occur, the amount of the first loss is offset in full before the second loss is matched retroactively or prospectively against taxable income.

The carry-back and carry-forward provisions of the tax code create an accounting problem, since the realization of the benefits of the loss carried forward generally is not assured in the loss periods. The issue is: Should the tax reductions resulting from the carry-forwards be included in net income for the year in which the tax benefit is realized, or should they be applied to the prior year in which the losses occurred, as a partial recovery of such losses?

The Accounting Principle Board's conclusions on this topic (including its views on the proper accounting for loss carry-backs) is contained in paragraphs 44–47 of *Opinion No. 11*. The Board concluded that:

1. The tax effects of any realizable loss carry-backs should be recognized in the determination of net income of the loss periods. The tax loss carry-back and the related tax refund claim are measurable and realizable in the current period.

2. The tax effects of loss carry-forwards should not be recognized until they are realized, since realization of the tax benefits of the loss periods is dependent on future income.

3. In certain unusual circumstances, the loss carry-forward tax benefit may be recognized in the loss period when future realization of these benefits is assured beyond any reasonable doubt at the time the loss carry-forwards arise.

4. When tax benefits of loss carry-forwards are not recognized until realized in full or in part in subsequent periods, the tax benefits should be reported as extraordinary income items.

5. In contrast, in those rare cases where the tax benefit of the carry-forward is recognized in the loss period, the tax benefit should be included in the determination of the results of operations. The offsetting asset (and the tax benefit) should be computed at the corporate tax rates expected to be in effect at the time of realization. If the applicable tax rates should change from those used to compute the amount of the asset, the effect of the rate change should be accounted for in the period of the change as an adjustment to the asset account and the current income tax expense.

6. Disclosure should be made of the amounts of any loss carry-forwards not recognized in the loss period and the expiration date of such carry-forwards.

Prior to the issuance of *Opinion No. 11*, the accounting for tax carry-backs and carry-forwards varied considerably among companies. While recognizing that the opinion filled a need for greater uniformity in this area, some of its critics claim that the handling of realized tax loss carry-forwards as extraordinary items does not result in the most meaningful financial statement presentation. In their opinion, proper matching of costs and revenues requires that the tax benefits of carry-forwards of operating losses be related to the years in which the losses occurred. Also, since the loss carry-forward represents a potentially valuable asset, it should be recorded on the face of the balance sheet in preference to being disclosed only in a footnote. This could be achieved by adding the benefits when realized directly to retained earnings for retroactive application to the years that gave rise to the loss, less a reserve for any amount of the carry-forward not reasonably expected to be realized on the basis of the existing circumstances or the company's future plans. This point of view places greater emphasis on the "matching" concept than the "realization" concept supported by the Board in *Opinion No. 11*.

STATEMENT PRESENTATION

Deferred taxes are part of the tax expense recognized in the determination of current income. Therefore, the portion of taxes deferred should not be included in the balance of the stockholders' equity. This practice is supported by the Accounting Principles Board and the Securities and Exchange Commission, even though some accounting authors and many businessmen argue that the portion of income taxes deferred indefinitely should be considered as part of the stockholders' equity.

Despite the fact that deferred taxes do not represent receivables or payables in the traditional sense, they should nevertheless be presented in a manner that is consistent with the customary distinction between current and noncurrent items. The general rule is that deferred taxes should be classified in the balance sheet in the same manner as that related to assets and liabilities giving rise to the deferred taxes. For example, that portion of deferred taxes arising from the use of different plant depreciation methods should be classified as a long-term liability. This corresponds to the plant's classification as a long-term asset.

The authority for this practice is *Accounting Series Release No. 102*, issued in December 1965 by the Securities and Exchange Commission, and *Opinion No. 11*, issued by the Accounting Principles Board in December 1967.[4] *Release No. 102*, which dealt specifically with the classification of deferred income taxes related to installment receivables, stated:

> The classification of deferred income taxes related to installment receivables as noncurrent is significant when considered in light of the practice of classifying assets and liabilities as current or noncurrent in accordance with the normal operating cycle of the business. In Regulation S–X the Commission recognized the operating cycle treatment in the determination of working capital.
>
> The installment receivables and related deferred income taxes pertaining to the same operating cycle clearly are both either current or noncurrent. There is no justification from the standpoint of either proper accounting or fair financial reporting for the use of the operating cycle approach for installment receivables and not for the related deferred income taxes. Obligations for items which have entered into the operating cycle and which mature within the

---

[4] A similar conclusion was included in the exposure draft of *Opinion No. 6* of the Accounting Principles Board. This portion of the draft was deleted from the final opinion issued in October 1965. Subsequently, Arthur Andersen & Co. filed a petition with the Securities and Exchange Commission requesting the Commission to issue an accounting release supporting this deleted portion of the exposure draft of *Opinion No. 6*. The Commission responded favorably to this request and issued *Accounting Series Release No. 102*.

operating cycle should be included in current liabilities when the related receivables are included in current assets, in order to present fairly the working capital position.

In *Release No. 102* the SEC did not accept the theory advanced by some that the deferred taxes related to installment sales should be offset against the installment receivables as a contra item. In the Commission's opinion, the current value of the receivable is not affected by the amount of the tax deferral. The deferral is not a valuation reserve (such as reserves for anticipated bad debts). Rather, it is a credit or liability item, representing cash retained in the business by the deferral of tax payments.

The opposed point of view argued that it was preferable to deduct the deferred tax from the installment receivable. According to Arthur Andersen & Co.:

> Such a practice would recognize that the particular asset arises from the same transactions as does the income being deferred for tax purposes and that the asset includes the uncollected amount which is not yet taxable. Therefore, the real asset is the receivable less the future tax to be paid. Likewise, if the income on installment sales were deferred for both book and tax purposes, there would be no deferred tax, and the preferable practice in such a case would be to deduct the deferred income from the related receivables.
>
> Deferred taxes become a definite tax liability when and as the receivables are collected, since prior to that time there is only a provision for payment of future taxes. Therefore, if such deferred taxes are deducted from the related asset, the deferred taxes should be transferred to current liabilities as the receivables are collected.

Income Statement

The components of the tax expense shown on the current income statement should be disclosed by the following categories:

1. Taxes estimated to be payable currently.
2. Tax effects of timing differences.
3. Tax effects of operating losses.

These amounts should be allocated to (*a*) income before extraordinary items, and (*b*) extraordinary items.

In addition, the Board recommends that significant variations in the normal ratio of income tax expense and pretax accounting income that are not otherwise apparent from the company's financial statements or business activities should be explained.

SPECIAL AREAS

Opinion No. 11 does not apply to certain specific industries where the tax consequences of some transactions are similar to those discussed for timing differences. The Board decided to defer any conclusion as to whether interperiod tax allocation should be required in these special areas, pending further study and consideration. It was anticipated that opinions on these areas would be issued at a later date.

Commenting on these special areas, *Opinion No. 11* said:

> These transactions result in differences between taxable income and pretax accounting income in a period and, therefore, create a situation in which tax allocation procedures may be applicable in the determination of results of operations. These transactions are also characterized by the fact that the tax consequences of the initial differences between taxable income and pretax accounting income may not reverse until an indefinite future period, or conceivably some may never reverse. In addition, each of these transactions has certain unique aspects which create problems in the measurement and recognition of their tax consequences. These special areas are:
>
> *a*) Undistributed earnings of subsidiaries.
> *b*) Intangible development costs in the oil and gas industry.
> *c*) "General reserves" of stock savings and loan associations.
> *d*) Amounts designated as "policyholders' surplus" by stock life insurance companies.
> *e*) Deposits in statutory reserve funds by United States steamship companies.

Paragraph 16 of *ARB No. 51, Consolidated Financial Statements*, states that:

> When separate income tax returns are filed, income taxes usually are incurred when earnings of subsidiaries are transferred to the parent. Where it is reasonable to assume that a part or all of the undistributed earnings of a subsidiary will be transferred to the parent in a taxable distribution, provision for related income taxes should be made on an estimated basis at the time the earnings are included in consolidated income, unless these taxes are immaterial in amount when effect is given, for example, to dividend-received deductions or foreign tax credits. There is no need to provide for income tax to the parent company in cases where the income has been, or there is evidence that it will be, permanently invested by the subsidiaries, or where the only likely distribution would be in the form of a tax-free liquidation.

The Board has decided to defer any modification of the above position until the accounting research study on accounting for intercorporate investments is completed and an Opinion is issued on that subject.

Intangible development costs in the oil and gas industry are commonly deducted in the determination of taxable income in the period in which the costs are incurred. Usually the costs are capitalized for financial accounting purposes and are amortized over the productive periods of the related wells. A question exists as to whether the tax effects of the current deduction of these costs for tax purposes should be deferred and amortized over the productive periods of the wells to which the costs relate. Other items have a similar, or opposite, effect because of the interaction with "percentage" depletion for income tax purposes. The Board decided to defer any conclusion on these questions until the accounting research study on extractive industries was completed and an Opinion was issued on that subject.

The "general reserves" of stock savings and loan associations, amounts designated as "policyholders' surplus" by stock life insurance companies, and deposits in statutory reserve funds by United States steamship companies each have certain unique aspects concerning the events or conditions which may lead to reversal of the initial tax consequences.

Continuing Controversy

Following the issuance of *Opinion No. 11*, most of the topics discussed in this chapter no longer represent a problem in practice. However, the subject of deferred income tax accounting continues to be controversial and is of deep interest to those interested in the development of generally accepted accounting principles. A full appreciation of this area is essential to those who seek to appraise investment opportunities through the analysis of the funds flow of corporations and the relationship of the pretax and aftertax operating results.

SUGGESTED FURTHER READING

ARTHUR ANDERSEN & COMPANY. *Accounting for Income Taxes.* Chicago, 1962.

BEVIS, DONALD, and PERRY, RAYMOND E. *Accounting for Income Taxes: An Interpretation of APB Opinion No. 11.* New York: American Institute of Certified Public Accountants, 1969.

BLACK, HOMER, A. *Interperiod Allocation of Corporate Income Taxes,* Accounting Research Study No. 9. New York: AICPA, 1966.

COMMERCE CLEARING HOUSE. *Master Tax Guide, 1970.* New York: Commerce Clearing House, 1970.

PRICE WATERHOUSE & COMPANY. *Are Deferred Taxes Misleading?* New York, 1967.

CASES

Case 12–1. **FRANKLIN STORES, INCORPORATED**
Accounting for Income Tax Expense

In June 1970, the board of directors of Franklin Stores, Inc., a large chain of discount stores, approved a recommendation from the company's president, Joe Franklin, that Franklin Stores offer its customers the opportunity to purchase goods on an installment sales basis. Prior to this time, all of Franklin Stores' sales had been on a cash basis.

As part of this decision, the board had to consider a recommendation concerning the accounting treatment of the installment sales made by Peter Lewis, the company's financial vice president. Lewis recommended that Franklin account for its installment sales by the installment sales method for tax purposes. That is, the profit from the sale would be recognized as collections were made from the customer, or when the installment sales contract was sold to a finance company. He claimed that this method would defer the payment of income taxes arising from the sales and, thus, help the company's cash position. He likened the deferred taxes to an "interest-free loan from the government."

Lewis recommended that Franklin adopt the accrual method for public reporting purposes, however. The accrual method, he said, recognized the profit on the transaction at the time the goods giving use to the installment sales contract were sold. In his opinion, this method gave a better matching of costs and revenues.

Following Lewis' recommendation, the board approved the use of the installment method for tax purposes, principally because their public accountant had recommended it. However, before approving the recommendation to use the accrual method in public reports, several directors asked Lewis to explain the nature of the deferred tax account created by

282

the use of the installment method for the calculation of income taxes and the accrual method for determining profit in the financial reporting to stockholders. Excerpts from this conversation are presented later in the case.

Franklin Stores, Inc.

Franklin Stores, Inc. was founded in 1957 by Joe Franklin, his brother William, and Peter Lewis to sell television sets at a discounted price. The company's merchandising policy was an instant success—so much so that customers began to ask the store to obtain other appliances for them at a discount. As a result of these requests, the founders decided to expand their business to include a full line of household appliances. Initially, this move met with opposition from some manufacturers and local department stores. However, this was eventually overcome and, by 1960, the company was the largest retailer of appliances in its market area.

In 1962, the founders decided to expand their operations to include other cities. Accordingly, during the next five years they established new Franklin Stores in three cities. Also during this same period, Franklin stores expanded its operations to include records, home furnishings, musical instruments, toys, and a variety of other goods. This expansion was financed by a large public stock offering. Eventually, Mr. Franklin hoped to have Franklin Stores in every major city of the nation.

Beginning in the late 1960s the company began to experience greater competition from other discount stores and department stores. The competing discount stores cut heavily into Franklin's sales by improving their store layouts, installing more attractive displays, and granting liberal credit terms. The department stores became more competitive by lowering their prices to meet the discounted items, offering better service on the goods sold, and granting more liberal and varied credit terms.

These industry trends forced Franklin to adopt an installment sales plan. The plan was a fairly simple one: Customers could purchase merchandise by paying as little as 10 percent of the purchase price at the time of purchase and then paying the outstanding balance over the next 12, 24, or 36 months in equal installments. A service charge of 2 percent of the outstanding balance was charged each month. Under this plan, Franklin continued to hold title (reduced by the buyer's equity as established by payments) to the merchandise until the final payment. Before a customer could use the installment plan, he was checked out by the company's credit bureau to see if he was able to comply with the terms of the installment sales contract.

June Board Meeting

After the decisions concerning installment sales were made, the following discussion related to deferred taxes occurred at the June board of directors meeting.

LEWIS: Let me begin by saying that whenever you report items of income and expense for income tax purposes on a basis different from that followed for financial accounting purposes, the provision for the income tax expense does not represent the taxes actually paid, but the taxes properly allocated to the profit shown in the income statement.

Let me illustrate this problem with an example: Suppose we sold a freezer unit for $800 on August 1, 1970. The customer paid $80 down and agreed to pay $720 in equal installments over the next 36 months. Furthermore, let us assume the freezer cost us $600. So, we made $200 on the sale. As a percentage of the sales price, this represents a 25 percent gross margin.

Now here's how we'd account for the sale using the installment method.

On August 1 we'd record the sale, the creation of an installment receivable, and the initial down payment thus:

Installment Receivable	800	
Inventory [1]		600
Deferred Gross Profit on Installment Sales		200
Cash	80	
Installment Receivable		80

Now, on September 1, and monthly thereafter for 36 months as the payments are received, the following entries will be made:

Cash	20	
Installment Receivables		20

Of course, there'd be an entry recognizing the service charge, but for the purposes of this example let's not worry about it.

Next, at the close of the fiscal year during which the sale was made we'd recognize the profit on the collections. Here's the journal entry:

Deferred Gross Profit on Installment Sales	40	
Recognized Gross Profit on Installment Sales		40

The $40 is the sum of the payments received times the percentage gross margin on the sale: that is, $160 × 25 percent.

Now the entries for the same transaction are . . . [Lewis went on to explain the accounting for the accrual method and to demonstrate how the deferral and actual taxes were calculated].

SMALL (director, retired businessman): That was an excellent explanation. However, I still don't understand why we have to provide for deferred taxes.

LEWIS: Well, it is the generally accepted way to handle such situations by businessmen and the public accounting profession. In fact, the general principle of income tax allocation is supported by *Opinion No. 11* of the Accounting Principles Board.

SMALL: Oh, yes. I recall you mentioned that at our last meeting. Nevertheless, I think we ought to have some good business reasons for following this deferred tax method. Irrespective of how much authority such statements may have among accountants, I don't see why we should blindly follow them.

---

[1] Franklin Stores, Inc. maintained perpetual inventory records.

FRANKLIN: You may have a good point there, but I have another question for Peter: Where is this deferred tax item carried on the balance sheet?

LEWIS: That's a tough question to answer. Personally, I think it ought to be reported as a current liability, since the installment receivables giving rise to the deferred taxes are covered as current assets. The SEC insists upon this approach for registered companies.

SMALL: What are some of the alternative ways?

LEWIS: While these would not be necessarily regarded as being generally acceptable methods, here are some alternatives: first, as a deduction from the related asset; second, as a current liability; third, below current liabilities, but above long-term debt; and finally, below long-term debt, but above stockholders' equity.

MURPHY (director, president of utility company): At one time didn't American Electric Power Company try to show as part of net worth the deferred taxes arising from using different depreciation policies for tax and book purposes?

LEWIS: Yes. They claimed it was part of the stockholders' equity. However, the Securities and Exchange Commission issued a "Statement of Administrative Policy" stating they considered classifying the deferred tax liability as part of common stock equity was misleading for financial statement purposes. The AICPA also issued a similar pronouncement. After discussions with the SEC and the AICPA, a compromise was reached. The item was placed between net worth and long-term debt. In addition, all parties agreed the amount was to be considered as neither long-term debt nor common stock equity.

FRANKLIN: Clearly, this question of the location of deferred taxes on the balance sheet is of some importance, since it will have a direct impact on our financial ratios. I think we ought to direct the executive committee to look further into this deferred tax business and make a recommendation as to how we should explain it to our stockholders and where it should be reported on the balance sheet. Are there any other questions related to this topic you want the executive committee to consider?

PETERSON (vice president, public relations): Yes, as I said earlier when the recommendation was first made, I'm not at all convinced we ought to use the accrual method in published statements for installment sales. Now, after listening to this discussion of deferred taxes, I'm even less convinced. It seems to me that we can avoid this whole deferred tax business by using the installment method in our published statements. And, unlike Peter, I happen to think the installment method does match costs and revenues. In my opinion, when we make an installment sale, we don't make a profit until at least about 80 percent of the monthly collections are made. In previous discussions with Peter, he tells me that some opinions of the Accounting Principles Board suggest strongly that we should use the accrual sales method. However, we are new at the installment sales business, and without any track record to guide us in estimating the probability of collections, I think we ought to be very conservative in recognizing income.

FRANKLIN: Any other items for the executive committee?

SMALL: Yes, Peter's example was very helpful, but it dealt with only one sale. As I see it, our installment sales volume is going to continue growing over the years and I'm curious just how big this deferred tax account is going to be in, say, 1973. Are we talking of $1 million or $10 million?

LEWIS: I'll get that figure to you by the next board meeting.

LORENZ: I'd like to know what our auditors will say if we include the deferred tax item in current liabilities this year and then in several years' time we classify it somewhere between long-term debt and net worth. Would they note a consistency exception in their opinion?

FRANKLIN: Of course, we have been discussing this matter with our auditors. In fact, it's clear to me now that I made a mistake by not asking Frank Towle [the audit partner in charge of the Franklin Stores account] to come to this meeting. I'll make sure he comes to the next executive committee meeting, however. . . .

Questions

1. Complete the freezer example Peter Lewis presented to the board. What are the accounting entries for the installment sale, using the accrual and the installment methods? Assuming a 50 percent income tax rate, what will be the actual tax payments for 1970, 1971, 1972, and 1973? What will be the deferred tax accounting entries during these years?
2. The following projections of Franklin Stores' operations are available (all amounts are millions of dollars):

	Sales			Cash Collected on Installment Receivables	Selling and General Expense
	Install-ment	Cash	Total		
1970	$ 8	$20	$28	$ 2.8	$4.2
1971	18	22	40	9.5	6.0
1972	24	26	50	18.2	7.5
1973	30	30	60	24.1	9.0

Assuming a constant 25 percent gross margin and a 50 percent income tax rate, and ignoring service charges, compute the amounts of net income after taxes, income taxes payable, deferred gross profit on installment sales, and deferred income taxes at the close of each year, 1970 through 1973, under each of these alternatives:

a) The accrual method is used for financial reporting and for income tax purposes.

b) The installment method is used for financial reporting and for income tax purposes.

c) The accrual method is used for financial reporting, and the installment method is used for income tax purposes.

3. Where on the balance sheet should Franklin present its deferred tax liability? Why?
4. Should Franklin use the installment or accrual method in its public financial statements? Why?

Case 12–2. ALLIS-CHALMERS MANUFACTURING COMPANY

Accounting for Losses Carried Forward

In the first few paragraphs of his letter to stockholders in the 1968 annual report, the new president of Allis-Chalmers Manufacturing Company, David C. Scott, outlined the company's situation:

We began in September 1968 to take decisive action that will place this company in the forefront of American industry. Included in these actions are steps to face financial reality, build a new management team, reorganize along decentralized lines, market new products and negotiate new ventures. . . .

EXHIBIT 1

ALLIS-CHALMERS MANUFACTURING COMPANY

Statement of Income (Loss)
Allis-Chalmers Manufacturing Company and Consolidated Subsidiaries

	Year Ended December 31	
	1968	1967*
Sales and other income:		
Sales	$767,313,100	$821,764,535
Discounts, interest earned, and other income	11,152,147	6,428,597
Income of finance subsidiaries	9,901,233	6,893,641
	$788,366,480	$835,086,773
Costs and expenses:		
Materials, plant payrolls, and services (Note 3)......	$703,041,018	$689,225,155
Depreciation (Note 6)	16,024,167	18,713,666
Selling, general, and administrative expense (Note 3) .	131,352,862	100,216,572
Discount and interest on receivables sold to finance subsidiaries	21,662,133	11,158,812
Other interest expense	9,380,927	9,590,531
	$881,461,107	$828,904,736
Income (loss) before income taxes and extraordinary charges	$(93,094,627)	$ 6,182,037
Federal, state and Canadian income taxes (Notes 3 and 6)	51,942,000	(1,180,200)
Income (loss) before extraordinary charges	$(41,152,627)	$ 5,001,837
Extraordinary charges, net of income taxes of $15,057,211 (Note 3)...........................	(13,437,093)	....
Net Income (Loss) for the Year	$(54,589,720)	$ 5,001,837

* 1967 has been restated to conform with the current year's classifications.

Sales totaled $761 million in 1968, compared with the company's sales volume of $821 million in 1967. The net loss reported for 1968 is $54 million, divided into (1) $22 million from regular operations, (2) $19 million identified as new charges and reserves, and (3) $13 million from extraordinary and non-recurring charges. As explained in Note 6 to the financial statements, in 1968 the company changed its method of computing depreciation and extended the application of tax allocation accounting procedures. These changes had the effect of reducing the net loss for the year by $8.9 million. In 1967, net income totaled $5 million. . . .

Our 1968 operating results were adversely affected by reduced sales and extraordinary expenses involving costs and reserves related to closing down unprofitable plants for optimum utilization of manufacturing space and cutting out slow moving inventory not associated with profitable product lines. . . .

The 1968 income statement presented in the 1968 annual report is shown in Exhibit 1. Notes 3 and 6 read as follows:

NOTE 3: *Special Reserves and Income Taxes.* During the last quarter of 1968 a major change took place in the company's management. The new management made an extensive study of the company's operations, products, and markets. This study resulted in changes in company philosophy and policies relating to organization, products and production facilities, marketing, and relations with dealers and customers. The company has estimated that implementation of these policy changes will result in substantial costs and losses for (a) parts replacement, warranty costs, repossession losses, and price allowances, and (b) relocation and discontinuance of facilities and products. Provisions were recorded in the last quarter of 1968 to establish special reserves totaling $68,754,410 for these anticipated costs and losses. Of this amount, $28,494,304 ($13,437,093 net of taxes), associated with relocation and discontinuance of products and facilities, is shown as an extraordinary charge in the consolidated statement of income (loss). The remaining provisions, totaling $40,260,106, were charged to sales ($5,627,178); materials, plant payroll, and services ($28,190,928); and selling, general, and administrative expenses ($6,442,000).

Although the costs and losses to be charged to the special reserves cannot be finally determined at the present time, management believes, based on the company's extensive studies and evaluations which were reviewed in depth by the independent auditors, that the provisions recorded in 1968 represent a fair and reasonable determination of the amounts required.

The net loss for the year has been determined after giving recognition to income taxes recoverable ($14,345,721) from carry-back to prior years of operating losses and to estimated future tax benefits ($50,900,000) of unused losses, including $6,836,276 relating to an accounting change described in Note 6 to the financial statements. The amounts recoverable from carry-back to prior years are included in current assets in the consolidated balance sheet, together with 1968 tax refunds receivable of $3,970,000 and estimated future income tax benefits of $17,303,304 relating primarily to normal book-tax timing differences applicable to amounts included in current assets and liabilities. The realization of estimated future income tax benefits which total $60,275,704 is dependent upon the company's ability to generate future taxable income. This amount is included in the financial statements because, in the opinion of management, the realization of such tax benefits is assured beyond any reasonable doubt.

The company has unrecorded investment tax credit carry-forwards of $6,098,722, applicable to the years 1962 through 1968, which may be used to reduce income taxes payable in future years.

NOTE 6: *Accounting Changes.* The company has adopted, for financial reporting purposes, the straight-line method of computing depreciation for substantially all plants and equipment. These fixed assets were previously depreciated on an accelerated basis. This change, effective January 1, 1968, reduced depreciation expense by $4,505,109 and decreased the net loss by $2,126,411, equal to $0.21 per common share.

In 1968, the company extended the application of tax allocation accounting procedures to certain reserve accounts to comply fully with new tax accounting requirements effective this year. The extension of these procedures decreased the net loss by $6,836,276, equal to $0.66 per common share.

An article entitled "A Bit of Rouge for Allis-Chalmers" appeared in the May 1969 issue of *Fortune*. It stated:

The accounting that appears in annual reports sometimes serves a cosmetic purpose—it is not there so much to inform stockholders as to help management keep them happy, or at least quiet, by touching up blemishes and brightening beauty spots. When a company is not doing well, and at the same time is trying to fend off unwanted merger, the cosmeticians of accountancy can sometimes perform wonders—even when they are limited to shades of red. Quite a number of companies in this year's directory used bookkeeping devices of various kinds to brighten their results. But Allis-Chalmers Manufacturing outdid them all at the rouge pot.

As 1968 ended, long-suffering Allis-Chalmers, No. 130 among the 500, found itself with some conflicting needs and desires. It presumably wanted to put the best possible face on 1968 results in order to maintain stockholder support in a bitter battle against a takeover by White Consolidated Industries, No. 143. But the new president of Allis-Chalmers, David C. Scott, who took office September 1, wanted to write off at once the tremendous charges associated with past mistakes and thereby turn the company around. To do that, he had to slap stockholders with some very bad news just when White Consolidated's onslaught was hotting up.

Allis-Chalmers resolved this conflict with some intricate accounting that let it accept Scott's write-off while minimizing the bad news that had to be reported to stockholders. The published results were still pretty dismal: on sales of $767,313,100, the company reported a loss of $54,589,720. That was, however, a whole lot better than the $121,588,931 that the company *actually* lost last year.

To understand how an actual loss of $122 million can become a reported loss of $55 million requires some comprehension of tax accounting. It is well known, of course, that a corporate dollar earned is roughly 50 cents lost to the tax collector. The converse is also true, i.e., *a dollar lost is 50 cents earned*. Allis-Chalmers simply claimed a credit on its profit-and-loss statement for the taxes that it saved by achieving a loss. The company said, in effect: "If Uncle Sam deserves his slice of profits, he also deserves his slice of the losses. We cannot be said to have lost $122 million when we thereby hung on to something over $60 million in taxes that we otherwise would have had to pay."

Allis-Chalmers had deducted from its operating loss of $93,094,627 "federal, state and Canadian income taxes" of $51,942,000. Part of this was provided by a loss carry-back of $14,345,721, effectively refunding taxes paid in 1965, 1966, and 1967. The remainder was supplied by potential carry-forward benefits. It would be necessary for Allis-Chalmers to earn a total of $86 million over the next five years to obtain the full benefit of the tax carry-forward. The company listed as a current asset "income tax refunds and future income tax benefits" of $35,619,025, and an additional asset, between current and long-term assets "estimated future income tax benefits" of $42,972,400 (see Exhibit 2).

APB *Opinion No. 11* (effective for periods beginning after December 31, 1967) had stated:

> If operating losses are carried backwards to earlier periods under provisions of the tax law, the tax effects of the loss carry-*backs* are included in the results of operations of the loss period, since realization is assured. If operating losses are carried forward under provisions of the tax law, the tax effects usually are not recognized in the accounts until the periods of realization, since realization of the benefits of the loss carry-*forwards* generally is not assured in the loss periods. The only exception to that practice occurs in unusual circumstances

EXHIBIT 2

ALLIS-CHALMERS MANUFACTURING COMPANY

ASSETS	December 31 1968	1967*
Current Assets:		
Cash	$ 23,483,905	$ 32,778,384
Receivables, less reserves of $16,171,800 and $12,990,000, respectively	126,836,883	125,835,967
Inventories, at lower of approximate cost (10% valued at Lifo) or market, less progress payments of $14,286,644 and $13,816,887, respectively	234,115,066	231,107,182
Income tax refunds and future income tax benefits (Note 3)	35,619,025	21,590,000
Other current assets	3,997,779	4,496,240
Total Current Assets	$424,052,658	$415,807,773
Estimated future income tax benefits (Note 3)	42,972,400	....
Investments and Other Assets:		
Investment in finance subsidiaries, at equity in net assets	$ 53,498,936	$ 46,594,803
Investment in other subsidiaries, at cost, less reserves (Note 1)	18,524,117	23,748,137
Intangible assets arising from acquisition (Note 2)	7,389,935	7,389,935
Other investments, assets, and deferred charges (Note 5)	6,366,775	5,244,786
	$ 85,779,763	$ 82,977,661
Plants and equipment at cost:		
Land and buildings	$110,168,287	$103,163,467
Machinery and equipment	190,005,484	180,635,390
Tools and fixtures	32,212,797	29,925,202
Furniture and fixtures	7,136,070	6,391,647
	$339,522,638	$320,115,706
Accumulated depreciation and amortization (Note 6)	186,714,838	178,989,166
	$152,807,800	$141,126,540
	$705,612,621	$639,911,974

EXHIBIT 2 *(Continued)*

	1968	*1967**
LIABILITIES AND EQUITY		
Current Liabilities:		
Notes payable and current maturities of long-term debt	$106,382,295	$ 50,797,500
Accounts payable and payrolls	68,970,051	69,978,681
Federal, state, and Canadian income taxes	883,458	4,072,998
Reserves for completion of contracts and product corrections and current portion of special reserves	69,486,985	12,611,115
Other current liabilities	20,606,507	19,237,153
Total Current Liabilities	$266,329,296	$156,697,447
Special Reserves (Note 3):		
Estimated costs of parts replacement, warranty costs, repossession losses, and price allowances	$ 40,260,106	....
Estimated costs and losses associated with relocation and discontinuance of facilities and products	28,494,304	....
	$ 68,754,410	....
Less amount included in current liabilities	48,000,000	....
	$ 20,754,410	....
Long-Term Debt (Note 4):		
Notes payable	$ 66,000,000	$ 69,000,000
Sinking fund debentures	45,000,000	45,000,000
Other long-term debt	3,361,924	4,228,487
	$114,361,924	$118,228,487
Deferred income taxes	....	$ 1,449,260
Share Owners' Equity (Notes 5 and 9):		
Preferred stock, $100 par value, 500,000 shares authorized, 134,594 shares, 4.20% cumulative convertible series outstanding in 1967	....	13,459,400
Common stock, $10 par value, 12,500,000 shares authorized, 10,410,292 and 9,881,481 shares outstanding after deducting 42,869 and 82,869 shares held in treasury, respectively	$104,102,920	98,814,810
Capital in excess of par value of capital stock	122,548,752	113,198,182
Earnings retained	77,515,319	138,064,388
Total Share Owners' Equity	$304,166,991	$363,536,780
	$705,612,621	$639,911,974

* 1967 has been restated to conform with the current year's account classifications.

when realization is assured beyond any reasonable doubt in the loss periods. Under an alternative view, however, the tax effects of loss carry-*forwards* would be recognized in the loss periods unless specific reasons exist to question their realization.

The auditor's opinion on the 1968 financial statements read:

. . . As explained in Note 3 to the financial statements, in the last quarter of 1968 the Company recorded substantial amounts associated with (*a*) reserves for anticipated costs and losses, and (*b*) estimated income tax benefits expected to be realized in the future. Although these reserves and anticipated tax benefits reflect the best current judgment of the Company's management, we cannot determine at this time the amounts of costs and losses which ultimately will be charged against the reserves, and the amounts of future tax benefits which ultimately will be realized.

In our opinion, subject to the effect of any adjustments which may result from ultimate determination of the matters referred to in the preceding paragraph, the accompanying consolidated financial statements examined by us present fairly the financial position of Allis-Chalmers Manufacturing Company and its subsidiaries at December 31, 1968 and the results of their operations for the year, in conformity with generally accepted accounting principles applied on a basis consistent with that of the preceding year, except for the changes in accounting for depreciation and income taxes as explained in Note 6 to the financial statements.

The 1969 first quarter earnings were $11.7 million, less a provision for taxes, for a net profit of $5.1 million. The tax carry-forward benefit had been taken completely in 1968 for book purposes. Hence, it was not available for 1969. In contrast, the actual tax payment benefits could only be realized as future profits were reported for tax purposes.

Questions

1. Appraise the current and prospective corporate implications of the corporate reporting decisions discussed in the Allis-Chalmers case.
2. Comment on the appropriateness of these decisions from the point of view of "fairness" and "generally accepted accounting principles."
3. What is your appraisal of the comments included in the *Fortune* article?
4. What is your evaluation of the auditor's opinion?

CHAPTER 13

FIXED ASSET ACCOUNTING

Tangible fixed assets include all of those assets of a physical substance with a life of more than one year that are used in operations but are not intended for sale as such in the ordinary course of business. Tangible fixed assets can be classified in three different categories: (*a*) those subject to depreciation, such as plant and equipment; (*b*) those subject to depletion, such as natural resources; and (*c*) those not subject to depreciation or depletion, such as land used for plant sites. Fixed assets are normally carried at their original cost, less any accumulated depreciation. Depreciation, the process of allocating the cost of fixed assets over the useful life of the asset so as to match the cost of an asset with the benefits it creates, is covered in Chapter 14. This chapter focuses on the measurement of investments in fixed assets.

Fixed assets are shown on the balance sheet as follows:

```
Fixed Assets:
    Plant and equipment (original cost).... xxxx
    Less: Allowance for depreciation .... xxxx
        Net Plant and Equipment ......... xxxx
```

Ordinarily no mention is made of a fixed asset's market value or replacement cost in the balance sheet.

CAPITALIZATION CRITERIA

Considerable judgment is sometimes required to determine whether or not an expenditure related to fixed assets should be capitalized or expensed as incurred. Generally, those expenditures whose usefulness is expected to extend over several accounting periods or that extend the useful life of a fixed asset are capitalized. Conversely, expenditures should be expensed when they neither extend the useful life of a fixed asset beyond the original estimates nor generate benefits beyond the current accounting period. Such expenditures are known as "revenue expenditures." Companies usually establish minimum cost limits below which all amounts are expensed, even if they might otherwise be properly capitalized. The minimum amount selected should be set at that point which still results in fair financial reporting but which does not place an unreasonable burden on the accounting system.

COST BASIS

Unless otherwise indicated, the cost of a purchased fixed asset is the price paid for the asset plus all of the costs incidental to acquisition, installation, and preparation for use. Judgment must be applied to assure the inclusion of all material identifiable elements of cost, such as purchasing, testing, and similar items. All available cash discounts irrespective of whether or not they are taken should be excluded from the amount capitalized. Discounts not taken should be charged as a current financial expense.

Fixed assets may be acquired by manufacture or by exchange. The cost of assets manufactured for use in the business generally includes the materials, labor, and manufacturing overhead directly related to the construction. How much, if any, of the general factory overhead is included in the construction cost depends on whether or not the plant constructing the asset is operating at or below capacity.

When the plant is operating at or near capacity, the use of the scarce productive facilities to construct an asset for internal use reduces the opportunity to produce regular items for sale. Because of this lost profit opportunity, a fair share of general manufacturing overhead is typically charged to an asset construction project, thereby relieving the income statement of costs that, in the absence of the construction, would have generated some offsetting revenue.

Under below-capacity conditions, it is debatable whether or not a fair portion of general manufacturing overhead should be charged to the cost of assets constructed for a company's own use. The arguments for charging a portion of general manufacturing overhead include: (a) the current loss from idle capacity will be overstated unless a cost for the idle capacity used for construction is capitalized; (b) the construction will have future benefits, so all costs related to acquiring these benefits should be deferred; and (c) the construction project should be treated the same as regular products, which are charged with general overhead.

The principal arguments opposing this point of view are: (a) the cost of the asset should not include general overhead costs that would still have been incurred in the absence of the construction; (*b*) the general overhead was probably not considered as a relevant cost in making the decision to construct the asset for the company's own use, since the costs would be incurred irrespective of whether or not the asset was constructed; (*c*) by capitalizing part of the general overhead, current income will increase due to construction rather than the production of salable goods; and (*d*) it is more conservative not to capitalize general overhead.

Increasingly, the practice of charging fixed assets constructed for a company's own use with general overhead on the same basis and at the same rate as regular goods produced for sale is being adopted, irrespective of the prevailing capacity conditions. This trend reflects a movement away from conservatism for its own sake and a growing concern for the proper allocation of costs to reduce distortions of periodic income due to undervaluation of assets or overcosting of inventory.

Assets manufactured for a company's own use may cost less than their purchase price. This saving should not be recorded as profit at the time the asset is completed, since profits result from the use of assets, not their acquisition. The advantage of the saving will accrue to the company over the life of the asset through lower depreciation charges than would have been incurred if the asset had been purchased.

Assets costing more to construct than their purchase price are sometimes recorded at their purchase price in the interests of conservatism. The difference between construction cost and purchase price is charged to income upon completion of the asset.

Assets acquired in trade or exchange transactions are valued at their fair market value at the time of acquisition. The difference between this market value and the book value of the exchanged asset is treated as a gain or loss. If an asset is acquired for a cash payment plus property, the cost of the acquired asset is its market value plus the cash payment. Any difference between this sum and the exchanged asset's book value is recognized as a gain or loss on exchange.

Trade-in allowances on exchanged assets are often greater than their market value. Consequently, the use of trade-in allowances to value a newly acquired asset may lead to misleading results through an overstatement of its cost and subsequent depreciation charges. Caution must be exercised in trade-in situations, since assets acquired through exchanges should not be recorded at a price greater than would have been paid in the absence of a trade-in.

For income tax purposes, "no gain or loss is recognized if the taxpayer exchanges property held for productive use in his trade or business, together with cash, for other property of like kind for the same use." The depreciation base of the newly acquired property is the book value shown for tax purposes of the exchanged property plus the cash payment. Accountants reject this approach for financial reporting purposes, since it blurs the distinction between old and new asset costs by carrying over in the fixed asset account the allowances for depreciation related to retired assets.

The interest cost on funds borrowed for construction purposes may also be capitalized, although this practice is rare today except in the case of public utility rate determinations.

EXPENDITURES SUBSEQUENT TO ACQUISITION AND USE

After a fixed asset is acquired and put into use, a number of expenditures related to its subsequent utilization may be incurred. The manager must decide whether or not these expenditures should be capitalized as part of the asset cost or expensed as incurred. The general practice is to capitalize those expenditures that will generate future benefits beyond those originally estimated at the time the asset was acquired. However, if there is substantial uncertainty as to whether the benefits will ever be realized, such expenditures are charged to current income. Also, all expenditures related to fixed assets that are necessary to realize the benefits originally projected are expensed.

Repairs and Maintenance

Maintenance and repair costs are incurred to maintain assets in a satisfactory operating condition. When these expenditures are ordinary and recurring, they are expensed. Significant expenditures made for repairs which lead to an increase in the asset's economic life or its efficiency beyond the original estimates should be charged to the allowance for depreciation. This effectively raises the asset's book value. In addition, the asset's depreciable rate should also be changed to reflect the new use, life, and residual value expectations. Extraordinary expenditures for repairs that do not prolong an asset's economic life or improve its efficiency probably represent the cost of neglected upkeep of the asset, and as such should be charged to income as incurred.

Repairs made to restore assets damaged by fire, flood, or similar events should be charged to loss from casualty up to the amount needed to restore the asset to its condition before the damage. Expenditures beyond this amount should be treated like any other expenditure that prolongs the economic life of an asset.

When some assets are acquired, it is anticipated that unusually heavy maintenance costs, such as repainting, may be incurred at different points during their lives. In these situations, some managers establish an "allowance for repairs and maintenance" account to avoid unusually large charges against income. This practice, which is permissible, charges income with a predetermined periodic maintenance expense based upon management's estimate of the total ordinary and unusual maintenance costs over the asset's life. The credit entry is to the liability account, repairs and maintenance allowance. When the actual expenditures for the anticipated maintenance are incurred, the allowance account is charged with this amount. Since the allowance represents a future charge to current assets, it is sometimes treated as a current liability. In other cases, it is reported as a contra account to fixed assets, along with the allowance for depreciation account. Credit balances are deducted from original cost in determining book value. Debit balances are regarded as temporary additions, and as such increase book value. For income tax purposes, only the actual expenditures for maintenance are deductible. Therefore, the establishment of an allowance usually has deferred tax accounting implications also.

Betterments, Improvements, and Additions

Expenditures for betterments and improvements, such as replacing wooden beams in a building with steel girders, usually result in an increase in an asset's economic life or usefulness. As such, these expenditures are properly capitalized and subsequently charged to the related asset's allowance for depreciation. Also, the asset's depreciation rate should be redetermined to reflect the economic consequences of the expenditure. Minor expenditures for betterments and improvements are typically expensed as incurred.

Additions to existing assets, such as a new wing to a plant, represent capital expenditures, and as such should be recorded at their full acquisition cost just like the original investment in fixed assets.

Land

Land is a nondepreciable asset, since its life is assumed to be indefinitely long. Land should be shown separately on the balance sheet.

The cost of land includes the purchase price, all costs incidental to the purchase, and the costs of permanent improvements, such as clearing and draining. Expenditures made for improvements with a limited life, such as sidewalks and fencing, should be recorded in a separate account, Land Improvements, and written off over their useful lives.

If land is held for speculative purposes, it should be captioned appropriately and reported separately from the land used for productive facilities. The carrying costs of such land can be capitalized, since the land is producing no income and the eventual gain or loss on the sale of the land is the difference between the selling price and the purchase price plus carrying charges. For income tax purposes, the carrying charges can be either capitalized or deducted as incurred.

Wasting Assets

Mineral deposits and other natural resources that are physically exhausted through extraction and are irreplaceable are called "wasting assets." Until extracted, such assets are classified as fixed assets. The cost of land containing wasting assets should be allocated between the residual value of the land and the depletable natural resource. If the natural resource is discovered after the purchase of the land, it is acceptable to reallocate the original cost in a similar way.

Companies in the business of exploiting wasting assets on a continuing basis incur exploration costs to replace their exhausted assets. As indicated in Chapter 16, these exploration costs can be either expensed or capitalized. Because of the great uncertainty associated with the extractive industry, the typical practice is to capitalize only those costs identifiable with the discovery and development of productive properties and expense the rest as incurred.

HISTORICAL COSTS AND ACCOUNTABILITY

The general practice of recording fixed assets at cost can lead to situations where there is a conflict between adherence to the cost principle and management accountability for the use of the assets at their disposal. In some of the cases where this conflict arises, it is permissible to depart from the cost principle. They include: recording of donated assets at market value; write-up of unexpectedly discovered valuable natural resources to appraised value; write-down of book value due to a significant and permanent decline in an asset's economic utility; and, under very unusual circumstances, the write-up of the cost of such assets as plant and equipment to a higher appraised value. Each of these situations is discussed below.

Donated Assets

Valuable property may be acquired at no cost or at a cost which inadequately measures its economic worth. For accounting purposes, a fair market value is assigned to such assets, rather than the purchase price, if any. The difference between the cost and the fair market value is credited to a paid-in capital account appropriately titled to identify its source. Some argue that this practice departs from the cost principle, and as such should not be permitted. However, since financial accounting is concerned with management accountability and the measurement of management performance, it seems appropriate to hold management responsible for the fair market value at the time of acquisition of donated and similar assets.

If use of the donated asset is contingent upon certain conditions being met, the contingent nature of the asset should be fully disclosed and the account balance shown "short" (i.e., listed on the balance sheet, but not included in the total amounts). When clear title is obtained, the asset should be transferred to the appropriate regular asset account.

Discovery Value

When valuable material resources are discovered on land after its acquisition, it is acceptable to record the wasting asset at its fair market value determined by appraisal after providing for the residual value of the land. The offsetting credit to the increased appraisal should be to the capital account "appraisal capital."

Appraisal Value of Plant Assets

Another departure from the application of the cost principle to fixed asset accounting is the practice of substituting the appraisal value for the book value of plant assets whose replacement value has increased significantly since acquisition, due, say, to increased price levels. This practice is acceptable only under exceptional circumstances and can only be justified on the ground that the use of appraisal values will significantly improve the usefulness of the financial statements. Accountants and managers are wary of writing up fixed assets to appraisal value, since some questionable accounting practices in this area during the late 19th and early 20th centuries were used to justify fictitious stock values. The resulting scandals brought the accounting profession and management into disrepute.

To record asset appreciation a debit entry to the asset account is made for the value increase. The offsetting credit entry is to Appraisal Capital. The balance sheet should clearly indicate that the asset is carried at an appraised amount. The source, date, and basis of the appraisal should also be disclosed in the accompanying footnotes.

When assets recorded at appraised values are sold, all evidence of the appraisal is eliminated. The net effect of the sale on retained earnings is the same as if the asset had been recorded at cost rather than an appraised amount.

To illustrate, assume land is purchased for $10,000. Subsequently, its carrying value is changed to its appraised value of $100,000. Later, the land is sold for $150,000.

The entries to record the change in carrying value are:

Land 90,000
    Appraisal Capital—Land 90,000

The sale is accounted for as follows:

Cash 150,000
Appraisal Capital—Land 90,000
    Land 100,000
    Gain on Sale 140,000

ALTERNATIVE PROPOSALS

Historical cost and, under certain rare circumstances, appraisal value are the only two accepted bases for measuring plant and equipment and related depreciation charges in published financial statements. A number of other approaches have been proposed by accounting authors. These include: making the carrying value of assets more responsive to their current market values, adjusting the historical cost base to reflect price level changes, and the use of replacement costs as the basis for calculating annual depreciation charges.

Those who oppose the use of historical costs to value fixed assets do so principally on the ground that it does not, in their opinion, lead to useful financial statements. The desirability of historical costs in terms of objectivity and feasibility over other alternative methods for measurement of fixed assets is not challenged.

The supporters of historical cost argue that this basis is useful and part of the discipline of management: it holds management responsible for the funds invested in fixed assets. Also, the users of financial reports are fully aware that historical costs do not represent value, but merely unexpired costs. The weight of convention, experience, and acceptance is clearly on the side of historical costs; therefore, it is argued, the burden of proving some alternative basis more useful rests with those who oppose the use of historical costs to measure assets.

The *essence of the price-level and market value approaches* can be illustrated as follows: A farmer's sole business asset is land purchased 15 years ago for $8,000. The current appraisal of the land's market value is $300,000. Based upon this appraisal, the farmer obtained a mortgage loan of $350,000 for the construction of a new shopping center on the land, the total value of which will be $650,000. During the 15 years the farmer held the land, the price levels doubled.

An historical cost statement for this farmer just prior to the bank loan would show assets of $8,000 and net worth of $8,000 (other items excluded). If price-level adjustments were made, the statement would show assets of $16,000 and a similar amount for net worth. If market values were used, the statements would show assets at $300,000 and net worth at $300,000, which would consist of $8,000 original investment plus $292,000 appreciation by reason of holding the land in a rising market. If the price-level and market value approaches were combined, the assets would remain the same, but net worth would now consist of the $8,000 original investment, the $8,000 price-level gain, and the $284,000 appreciation in the market value of the land after adjusting for price-level changes.

Price-level adjustment attempts to state historical costs incurred in different years in terms of a current and common monetary unit. It is not a valuation method. In countries with rapidly rising price levels, it is common practice to adjust the historical acquisition costs of fixed assets for general price-level changes. This results in a measurement of fixed assets and their related depreciation charges in terms of the general purchasing power invested and expiring. Under conditions of rapid inflation, few question the wisdom of this practice. However, many, including the Accounting Principles Board, argue that the annual rate of inflation in the United States is not high enough to justify converting the historical costs invested in assets during prior years to current dollars having the same purchasing power. Nevertheless, in those cases where management believes price-level-adjusted statements are more meaningful than historical-cost-based statements, the Accounting Principles Board has encouraged the use of supplemental disclosure of the price-level-adjusted data. Price-level accounting is covered in greater detail in Chapter 15.

The case for the *market value method* of asset valuation is expressed as follows: Assets are recorded at cost initially, because this is the economic measure of their potential service value. After acquisition, the accounting goal should continue to be the expression of the economic value of this service potential. This is difficult to measure directly. However, the current market price others are willing to pay for similar assets approximates in most cases this value. Therefore, to the extent that market values are available they should be used to measure fixed asset carrying values and their subsequent consumption in the production of goods and services. Property values are more useful to managers and stockholders than historical costs because market values determine the collateral value of property for borrowing purposes, fix liability for property taxes, establish the basis for insurance, and reflect the amount an owner might expect to realize, upon sale of the property.

The principal objection to market value is that it is often difficult to determine objectively. The proponents of market value answer this argument by indicating that the notion of market value has some important qualifications. For example: recognition should only be given to fairly determined market values when the disparity between market value and cost is likely to prevail for a fairly long period of time. Furthermore, recognition of market value should occur only when there is reliable evidence as to the market value of the asset involved. Also, the notion of market value probably has little relevance to nonstandardized equipment, or special fixed assets for which no readily available market exists, Historical costs must suffice in these cases.

The market value approach has significant implications for the income statement. The market value advocates claim that management continually faces the alternative of using or disposing of assets. Income statements based on historical cost do not show how well management has appraised this alternative, since in no way is the "cost" of the alternative foregone included in the statements. In a case where the market value of an asset is greater than its historical cost, historical-cost-based depreciation leads to an overstatement of the incremental benefit gained by using rather than selling, since the book depreciation basis is understated. The reverse is true when the market value is less than the book value. It is claimed that market-value-based depreciation would overcome this weakness. The incremental benefit of continuing to use the asset would be determined after a depreciaiton charge based on the "cost" of the income foregone by not disposing of the asset.

There is a difference in opinion among market value supporters as to how changes in the carrying value of the assets should be recorded. Some would treat the increases or decreases in stockholder's equity in much the same way as appraisal adjustments are recorded. Others propose including the changes as part of the income determination, in a fashion similar to the adjustments to income for gains or losses on foreign exchange.

The *replacement cost approach* advocates carrying assets at the cost of reproducing equivalent property, not identical property, as some critics of replacement cost assume. This approach is based on a concept of income which maintains that no profit is made until adequate provision through depreciation charges is made for the eventual cost of replacing the capacity represented in the existing assets with an asset of more modern design. Based on this theory, in periods of rising replacement costs, traditional depreciation, which recovers original cost from revenues, does not adequately provide for future replacement and so leads to an overstatement of profits. As a result, excessive dividends, wages, and income taxes may be paid, to the detriment of the company's ability to maintain its current level of capacity.

The replacement cost approach involves the application of specific price indexes to an asset's original cost. The result approximates the replacement cost of an asset derived through an appraisal. Such price indexes are available and widely accepted for specific categories of assets. The replacement cost proponents argue that their method has the advantage of the objectivity associated with recording the original cost of the asset at acquisition, plus minimizing the role of judgment in subsequent revaluations. Thus, the net result of their approach, they argue, is a more useful income figure without any sacrifice in objectivity.

Accounting Research Bulletin No. 43 recognizes the potential erosion of capital inherent in applying cost-based depreciation in periods of rising replacement costs, but concludes that increasing depreciation charges against income is not an appropriate solution. It recommends "annual appropriations of net income or surplus in contemplation of replacement of such facilities at higher price levels" as a more satisfactory solution.

INVESTMENT TAX CREDIT

To encourage investment in productive assets, the Revenue Act of 1962 allowed taxpayers a credit against income taxes of up to 7 percent of the acquisition cost of certain tangible personal property used in business operations. Originally, taxpayers qualifying for the investment credit were required for income tax purposes to reduce the depreciation basis of the property to which the credit related by the amount of the credit. This requirement was eliminated in the Revenue Act of 1964. In October 1966, the credit was suspended by Congress. It was restored again in May 1967. The 1969 Tax Reform Act abolished the investment tax credit.

To illustrate the calculation of the investment tax credit, assume a qualified piece of machinery with a 10-year life and zero salvage is purchased for $200,000 during 1969. The company's profits before taxes, but after depreciation, on all other items except the new machinery is $1,320,000. Therefore, the company's taxable income is:

Profit after all depreciation, but before taxes and depreciation on new equipment	$1,320,000
Less: Depreciation on new machinery ($200,000 × 0.10)	20,000
Taxable income	$1,300,000

The effect of the purchase on the company's 1969 payment is:

Income taxes before investment credit (50% of taxable income)	$ 650,000
Less: Investment Credit ($200,000 × 0.07)	14,000
1969 tax payment due	$ 636,000

It is important to note that the investment tax credit is a direct reduction of the tax otherwise payable.

The granting of the investment tax credit created a serious accounting problem. Although most people [1] agreed that the credit was a factor which

---

[1] It was argued by some that the credit was in effect a subsidy by way of a contribution to capital and, hence, should be so recorded directly as an increase in owners' equity. This position was not considered by the Accounting Principles Board, since it ran counter to widespread belief that the credit increased income.

influenced the determination of net income, they could not agree on how the credit increased income.

A number of businessmen and accountants supported the flow-through method for handling the credit. Under this method, the investment tax credit was considered as being in substance a selective reduction in taxes which otherwise would have been payable and which were related to the taxable income of the year in which the credit was granted. This approach considered the credit as being related to taxable income rather than to the cost of using assets. Also, since the credit was not relatable to, or dependent on, future revenues, the flow-through advocates maintained that the credit was earned during the period in which it was obtained.

The supporters of the deferral approach believed that the investment tax credit should be put on the balance sheet as deferred income and reflected in earnings as a separately identifiable item as the related asset was used and depreciated. They rejected the flow-through approach, principally on the ground that the credit did not enhance the integrity of the earnings figure if earnings could be increased simply by buying an asset.

To illustrate the effect of these different approaches to handling the investment credit, assume that the Hampton Company bought a new piece of equipment costing $100,000. The expected life of the equipment was 10 years. Consequently, the company qualified to receive an investment tax credit of $7,000. Handling the credit on a flow-through basis would improve 1968 aftertax profits by the full $7,000, but on a deferral basis by only $700. In both cases, the cash flow would be the same. However, the use of the flow-through method would boost the Hampton Company 1968 aftertax profits by $6,300 over using the deferral method. Alternatively, the adoption of the deferral method would result in future profits for each of the next nine years being $700 higher than they would have been if the flow-through method had been adopted.

In December 1962 the Accounting Principles Board issued *Opinion No. 2, Accounting for the "Investment Credit,"* which supported the deferral method and explicitly rejected the flow-through approach. Later, in January 1963, the Securities and Exchange Commission, in *Accounting Series Release No. 96,* indicated that the Commission would accept statements using either the deferral or the flow-through approach, principally because of the substantial diversity of opinion among responsible people as to the appropriate accounting for the credit. As a result of the Commission's decision and the significant number of companies adopting the flow-through method, the Accounting Principles Board issued *Opinion No. 4,* which amended *Opinion No. 2* to approve both the flow-through and deferral methods. However, the Board still expressed a preference for the deferral approach.

Subsequently, in 1967, the Board issued an exposure draft of *Opinion No. 11,* which again proposed that the deferral method be adopted as the only acceptable way to account for the investment credit. This proposal aroused the ire of many corporate executives, accountants, and government officials and was withdrawn from the final draft of the opinion for further study.

The exposure draft of *Opinion No. 11* would also have permitted companies to apply its pronouncements "retroactively to periods prior to the effective date in order to obtain comparability in financial presentations for the current and future periods." This would have enabled some companies, by retroactively applying the decision, to take part of their past investment tax credits into aftertax profits a second time. To illustrate this proviso:

Assume that the Hampton Company had bought the machine in 1964, rather than 1968, and had accounted for the full $7,000 investment tax credit on a flow-through basis then. To apply the exposure draft's decision retroactively, the company would have had to reconstruct its past financial statements as if it had adopted the deferral approach in 1964. To do this, the company would in essence take the following steps:

1. Reduce the 1968 beginning retained earnings balance by the credit of $7,000 previously included in 1964 aftertax earnings.
2. Increase the 1968 beginning retained earnings balance by the $2,800 aftertax profit which would have been included in aftertax profits for the years 1964 through 1967 if the item had originally been accounted for on a deferral basis.
3. Include in 1968 income a $700 credit related to the 1964 purchase.
4. Show the remaining $3,500 credit as a deferred item on the balance sheet, to be taken into income during the 1969–73 period.

Thus, the Hampton Company would be able to run $4,200 of its original credit through the income account twice. At the end of 1968, however, the company's retained earnings would be $3,500 less than they would have been if the retroactive accounting change had not been made.

The Board's decision on the investment tax credit was important to many industries and the users of their products. For example, one letter to the Board from an investment banking firm claimed that adoption of the deferral approach would reduce the airline industry's profits and retained earnings by about $1.5 billion over the next decade. The reduction in retained earnings, the letter claimed, would impair the industry's ability to borrow capital to finance expansion; and as a result, more expensive equity capital would have to be used, and the carriers would have to raise fares to cover this extra cost.

The Lessons

The 1969 Tax Reform Act made the investment tax credit a dead issue for the time being. However, in future cases of investment tax credits that are available to all companies on the same basis, there will be considerable pressure on the APB not to condone two very different methods for handling it. Also, the SEC's action in overruling the Board's original *Opinion No. 2* and the subsequent defiance of this opinion by businessmen indicated that (1) the Board must work closely with the SEC in drafting future opinions, and (2) the Board's opinions are unenforceable without the SEC's approval. The Board seems to have learned its lesson. Hopefully, it will not forget it in the future, since the investment tax credit episode did much to undermine public confidence in the Board. On the other hand, if the SEC fails to support the Board, the SEC may find itself having to take over the Board's task. To date, the SEC had indicated a distinct preference for leaving this work to the Board. Thus, while the investment tax credit issue is dead, its history contains many valuable lessons for those charged with the future development of what constitutes acceptable corporate financial reporting standards.

SUGGESTED FURTHER READING

SPROUSE, ROBERT T. (ed.). *The Measurement of Property, Plant and Equipment in Financial Statements.* Boston: Harvard University, 1964.

CASES

Case 13–1. BRAZOS PRINTING COMPANY

Problems in Fixed Asset Transactions

The Brazos Printing Company was founded as a one-man job printing firm in a small southwestern town. Shortly after its founding, the owner decided to concentrate on one specialty line of printing. Because of a high degree of technical proficiency, the company experienced a rapid growth.

However, the company suffered from a competitive disadvantage in that the major market for this specialized output was in a metropolitan area over 300 miles away from the company's plant. For this reason, the owner 12 years later decided to move nearer his primary market. He also decided to expand and modernize his facilities at the time of the move. After some investigation, an attractive site was found in a suburb of his primary market, and the move was made.

A balance sheet prepared prior to the move is shown in Exhibit 1. The transactions that arose from this move are described in the following paragraphs.

1. The land at the old site together with the building thereon was sold for $35,000. The land had originally cost $5,000. The building appeared on the company's books at a cost of $76,000 and a depreciation allowance of $45,000 had been accumulated on it.

2. Certain equipment was sold for $4,500 cash. This equipment appeared on the books at a cost of $16,700 less accumulated depreciation of $9,700.

3. New bindery equipment was purchased. The invoice cost of this equipment was $20,000. A 2 percent cash discount was taken by the Brazos Company, so that only $19,600 was actually paid to the seller. The Brazos Company also paid $80 to a trucker to have this equipment deliv-

ered. Installation of this equipment was made by Brazos workmen, who worked a total of 40 hours. These men received $1.50 per hour in wages, but their time was ordinarily charged to printing jobs at $4 per hour, the difference representing an allowance for overhead ($2.10) and profit ($0.40).

4. The city to which the company moved furnished the land on which the new plant was built as a gift. The land had an appraised value of $20,000; the appraisal had been made recently by a qualified appraiser. The company would pay property taxes on its assessed value, which was $15,000.

5. The Brazos Company paid $4,000 to have an old building on the gift plot of land torn down. (The value of this building was not included in the appraised or assessed values named above.) In addition, the company paid $2,000 to have permanent drainage facilities installed on the new land.

EXHIBIT 1

BRAZOS PRINTING COMPANY

Condensed Balance Sheet

ASSETS

Current Assets:		
Cash		$ 91,242
Other current assets		69,720
Total Current Assets		$160,962
Fixed Assets:		
Land		5,000
Buildings	$76,000	
Less: Accumulated depreciation	45,000	31,000
Equipment	$65,822	
Less: Accumulated depreciation	42,340	23,482
Total Assets		$220,444

LIABILITIES

Current Liabilities	$ 41,346
Common stock	100,000
Retained earnings	79,098
Total Equities	$220,444

6. A new strip caster with an invoice cost of $4,500 was purchased. The company paid $3,000 cash and received a trade-in allowance of $1,500 on a used strip caster. The used strip caster could have been sold outright for not more than $1,200. It had cost $3,000 new, and accumulated depreciation on it was $1,200.

7. The company erected a building at the new site for $90,000. Of this amount $70,000 was borrowed on a mortgage.

8. After the equipment had been moved to the new plant, but before operations began there, extensive repairs and replacement of parts were

made on a large paper cutter. The cost of this work was $1,100. Prior to this time, no more than $100 had been spent in any one year on the maintenance of this paper cutter.

9. Trucking and other costs associated with moving equipment to the new location and installing it there were $1,400. In addition, Brazos Company employees worked an estimated 120 hours on that part of the move that related to equipment.

10. During the moving operation, a piece of equipment costing $3,000 was dropped and damaged; $400 was spent to repair it. Mr. Timken believed, however, that the salvage value of this equipment had been reduced to $200. Up until that time, the equipment was being depreciated at $240 per year, representing a 10 percent rate after deduction of estimated salvage of $600. Accumulated depreciation was $960.

Questions

1. Analyze the effect of these transactions on the items in the balance sheet.
2. In your opinion, should the transactions which affect net worth in the case be accounted for in the profit and loss account or carried directly to retained earnings? If in the profit and loss account, where should these items appear in the profit and loss statement?

Case 13–2. MILLER SALT COMPANY

In February 1961, Mr. Morgan Nicholas, president of Miller Salt Company, was confronted with the problem of deciding how the newly acquired assets of Caribou Valley Salt Company should be shown on Miller's balance sheet. He had held several conferences with his own executives, agents from the Internal Revenue Service, and representatives of the American Appraisal Company; but in the final analysis, he was the only one who could make this important decision relative to asset valuation on the company's balance sheet. Since Miller's fiscal year had ended on December 31, 1960, Mr. Nicholas knew he must come to his final decision very soon. Because of this deadline, he decided to devote the rest of the day to reviewing, analyzing, and pondering the results of his decision to acquire Caribou Valley Salt Company.

Miller Salt Company

The Miller Salt Company of Detroit, Michigan, was one of the oldest producers of salt in the country. It was founded late in the 19th century and had grown from a small one-man operation to a large multiplant company that accounted for 5 to 10 percent of the total salt production of the United States. Selected income data for the Miller Salt Company are given in Exhibit 1.

EXHIBIT 1

MILLER SALT COMPANY

Comparative Income Statistics
(in thousands)

	Net Sales	Net Income	Dividends Paid *
Miller Salt:			
1950	$ 7,271	$ 913	$ 448
1951	8,840	1,058	498
1952	9,109	979	498
1953	8,898	872	498
1954	10,275	2,208	797
1955	10,956	1,992	996
1956	12,035	2,108	1,096
1957	11,703	1,743	1,096
1958	12,450	1,735	946
1959	12,915	1,660	946
Caribou Valley:			
1950	$ 1,743	$ 220	
1951	2,075	232	
1952	2,457	221	
1953	2,158	206	
1954	2,615	249	
1955	1,834	156	
1956	2,125	191	
1957	2,507	237	
1958	2,817	277	
1959	3,514	520	

* This information not available for Caribou Valley.

The common stock of Miller had been closely held for many years, but because of the company's rapid growth, financing had been solicited from outside sources, and by 1960 the capital stock of Miller was widely distributed. Mr. Nicholas had been appointed president in late 1958 during an executive reorganization motivated by shareholder dissatisfaction with the company's recent growth relative to the growth of the total salt market. The shareholders had also expressed dissatisfaction with the company's recent earnings record.

Miller Salt Company had had salt-producing and refining plants in Michigan, New York, Pennsylvania, and Ohio, prior to its acquisition of Caribou Valley. The company's primary market embraced heavy chemical industries in the north central, northeastern, and middle Atlantic states. These chemical industries used salt in the manufacture of most sodium and chlorine compounds and in the production of petroleum products and plastics. Since most of these industrial consumers had branch plants in various parts of the country, and because of the high cost of transporting salt for any great distance, Miller Salt Company might supply the northern branch of a company but be unable to supply its western branch because of the high cost of transporting salt from a northern mining and refining center to a western market.

Because of Millers' weak market position in the West, and because many branch plants of companies with which Miller had established lines of supply in the North and East were located in the West, Mr. Nicholas as one of his first acts of office began negotiations to acquire an established market outlet in the West. He felt that such action would boost Miller's sales and improve its profit picture. After negotiating with Caribou Valley Salt Company on the basis of the value of its assets, the extent, strength, and brand loyalty of the Caribou Valley market, and the remaining recoverable deposits in the mine, Miller had acquired all of the outstanding Caribou capital stock (held by the Chadwick and Northland families) for a cash payment of $4.5 million in January of 1960. Miller also assured Caribou's top executives a berth in its executive cadres if they so desired.

Caribou Valley Salt Company

In 1917, John Chadwick and Walter Northland, two chemical wholesalers from Los Angeles, California, purchased Caribou Valley, a wooded peninsula jutting into the Pacific Ocean near San Juan Capistrano, with the intention of creating a private hunting and fishing preserve for Los Angeles businessmen. The peninsula, 125 acres in size, was tucked deep in a bay and thus had access not only to the sea but also to adjacent swampland. While drilling for water to supply their lodge, Chadwick and Northland hit rock salt at 100 feet. Subsequent exploration disclosed that the peninsula was the cap of a massive rock salt deposit 6,300 feet in diameter and several thousand feet deep.

Roughly 15 percent of the deposit was beneath the peninsula, but an additional 420 acres of developable deposit extended into the adjacent bay, which was owned by the State of California. A 50-year lease of the state's mineral rights was secured in 1920, under which the state was to be paid six cents per ton of salt mined.

Since the salt deposit came to a peak under the peninsula, Chadwick and Northland had to sink a shaft to an 800-foot depth before the lateral area of the deposit was extensive enough to permit economical mining. Because of this, open-pit mining (mining from the land surface) had not been feasible. At the same time, mill buildings had been constructed, and primary and secondary crushers, classifiers, evaporators, recrystallization equipment, and other machinery had been put into place. The mine began operation in 1922 at the 800-foot level and produced 2,620,932 tons of salt at this level prior to 1940, when the impurity of the salt at this level made it desirable to extend the mining operations to the 1,000-foot level; and subsequently work at the 800-foot level was abandoned. After the installation of certain new equipment, mining commenced at the 1,000-foot level, and 4,757,086 tons of salt had been removed from that level by the end of 1959. (See Exhibit 2 for tonnage summary.)

EXHIBIT 2

MILLER SALT COMPANY

Salt Production of the Caribou Valley Salt Company
(in tons)

| | Source | | Total |
	Caribou Land	State Land	Production
1959	15,874	432,723	448,597
1958	13,018	311,403	324,421
1957	6,402	283,079	289,481
1956	34,375	205,207	239,582
1955	80,097	132,675	212,772
1954	168,682	130,343	299,025
1953	165,734	82,652	248,386
1952	146,346	98,836	245,182
1951	156,953	79,033	235,986
1950	170,963	66,749	237,712
1922–40, 800-foot level	N.A.	N.A.	2,620,932
1941–59, 1,000-foot level	N.A.	N.A.	4,757,086
Total production, 1922–59	N.A.	N.A.	7,378,018

But at this point, Caribou Valley Salt Company faced a dilemma. They had retained Wambly & Raymond, consulting geologists and mining engineers of Chicago, to determine (1) the remaining tonnage at the 1,000-foot level, (2) the feasibility of reworking the 800-foot level, and (3) the possibility of operating a third level at 1,200 feet. The engineers' report estimated that only 2.2 million tons of rock remained at the 1,000-foot level (five sixths of which was on state land); that the 800-foot level had been "worked out" on the basis of the quality of rock salt necessary to make the present shaft-mining operation feasible; and that if the shaft were extended to the 1,200-foot level, new hoists, drive motors, and ventilating equipment would have to be installed to support the increased mine depths. The salt deposit extended down several thousand feet, so the mineral was there, but the problem existed in getting it out. The report also indicated that a large amount of salt would have to be left intact at the 1,200-foot level in order to support the weight of the salt and earth above the tunnels, since the salt at this level had a relatively low compressive strength. At best, the report indicated that only marginal safety could be maintained at the 1,200-foot level.

Mr. Chalwick and Mr. Northland, both in their late sixties, were quite upset over the geologists' report; and because of this report and the fact that neither of them had heirs who were interested in running the company, they decided to sell the company. It was at this point that Mr. Nicholas of Miller Salt Company negotiated the purchase of Caribou Valley Salt Company.

Miller's Acquisition of Caribou Valley

Mr. Nicholas became interested in Caribou Valley because of its strong penetration of the western salt market. Caribou Valley Salt Company had built a solid market position for its product and had been able to acquire many major industrial salt users in the West as its customers. It had been able to do this by insuring exceptional quality, by guaranteeing prompt delivery on short notice, and by selling for less than national competition because of lower freight costs relative to its closeness to the market. The product was considered by many industrial concerns as the finest that could be obtained (see Exhibit 3).

Also, Mr. Nicholas felt that a new mining technique that was in the final stages of development in Miller's research laboratory could be profitably employed both in mining salt from depths greater than 1,000 feet and in recovering salt from the 800-foot and 1,000-foot levels which had previously been considered of a quality too poor to mine. However, controversy existed among various mining experts as to whether or not this new technique would be applicable at the Caribou Valley mining property. Miller had no previous experience in shaft mining, as all of its mines were of the open-pit or forced well variety. A forced well mine was operated by forcing water under pressure down a pipe into the layer of salt. The water dissolved the salt and was then forced out another pipe as additional fresh water was forced into the cavity. The salt water was then evaporated, leaving salt behind as a residue. Mr. Nicholas was confident that even if the new mining technique did not prove operational at the Caribou Valley mine, Miller would still be able to purchase salt from other local salt mines, process it on Caribou Valley's recrystallization equipment, and sell it through Caribou's sales organization under the well-established Caribou Valley brand name.

Aside from the operational aspects of the Caribou Valley property, Miller faced the problem of establishing a valuation on the assets acquired from Caribou Valley. This was a particularly difficult task, since Miller had paid $4.5 million for Caribou's total net worth of only $2,717,110 (Exhibit 4). The difference of $1,782,890 must then have been paid for

EXHIBIT 3

MILLER SALT COMPANY

Comparative Statement of Income of Caribou Valley Salt Company
For the Periods Ended December 31, 1959 and 1958

	1959	%	1958	%	Increase–Decrease
Tons sold	442,075		323,693		118,382
Gross sales	$3,530,763		$2,825,306		$705,457
Less: Adjustments	16,532		8,382		8,150
Net sales	$3,514,231	100.0	$2,816,924	100.0	$697,307
Cost of sales	1,797,896	51.2	1,607,156	57.1	190,740
Gross profit	$1,716,335	48.8	$1,209,768	42.9	$506,567
Operating expenses:					
Selling	$ 499,250	14.2	$ 500,595	17.8	$−1,345
Administrative	399,989	11.4	322,548	11.4	77,441
Total operating expenses	$ 899,239	25.6	$ 823,143	29.2	$ 76,096
Gross profit from operations	$ 817,096	23.2	$ 386,625	13.7	$430,471
Other income credits:					
Total income credits	55,801	1.6	18,761	0.7	37,040
Gross income	$ 872,897	24.8	$ 405,386	14.4	$467,511
Other income charges:					
Total income charges	57,769	1.6	7,016	0.3	50,753
Net income before provision for income taxes	$ 815,128	23.2	$ 398,370	14.1	$416,758
Provision for income taxes	294,567	8.4	120,975	4.3	173,592
Net Income	$ 520,561	14.8	$ 277,395	9.8	$243,166

goodwill, for assets not shown on Caribou's balance sheet, or because Miller considered that Caribou's assets were worth more than the amount at which they were shown on the balance sheet. Mr. Nicholas, Mr. Jamieson (Miller's controller), and other members of the board of directors felt that an appraisal by an outside consultant was necessary in order to determine properly the value at which the new assets should be carried. They also specified that only the fixed assets (property) should be appraised, since it was their opinion that the current assets could be brought onto Miller's books at Caribou's book value. The notes and accounts receivable had been guaranteed collectible by Northland and Chadwick, and the inventory of $323,780 was composed of $199,200 of boxed salt against which purchase orders had already been received; $49,800 in bags, bales, and labels which Miller expected to use immediately in its packaging operations; and $74,780 of salt in the process of being recrystallized, for which a ready market existed.

Mr. Nicholas felt that a correct or reasonable property valuation was extremely important for three reasons:

1. The asset valuation established would be used in determining the amount of depreciation allowed by the Internal Revenue Service and would therefore have a direct effect on the amount of profit remaining for Miller's shareholders after taxes. The importance of this item was further stressed by Mr. Schwingle of American Appraisal in his initial conference with Mr. Nicholas. (See section on property appraisal.)
2. Second, the asset valuations would be used for casualty insurance assessments. This involved maintaining appropriate amounts of insurance as well as affecting co-insurance requirements.
3. Finally, the appraisal was needed for internal and external accounting purposes, i.e., relation of costs to pricing, return on investment, extent of dividend payout or retention to provide for future equipment replacement, booking depreciation, and others. Further, Mr. Nicholas felt that since he had only recently been appointed president, the shareholders would be carefully scrutinizing any figures reported in the 1960 annual report.

Because of the importance of setting "correct" values on the assets, Mr. Nicholas retained the American Appraisal Company of Milwaukee, Wisconsin, to carry out this appraisal work.

Exhibit 4 gives Caribou's balance sheet as compiled by Caribou's controller as of the date of acquisition.

Organizing For The Property Appraisal

During the initial conference which was held between Mr. Nicholas and Mr. Schwingle, American Appraisal's representative from the Milwaukee office, Mr. Schwingle stated that he felt the paramount problem faced in the appraisal was that of allocating the $4.5 million purchase to the tangible and intangible, depreciable and nondepreciable assets of Caribou in such a way that full benefit could be taken of the 1954 Revenue Code.

As permitted by the code, Miller could bring the acquired assets onto their tax books at cost, which was the price which had been paid for the Caribou stock. However, the code stipulated that the price paid (cost to Miller) must be allocated "equitably" to all tangible and intangible assets acquired. The code did not allow any depreciation deduction for goodwill and certain other types of intangible assets. It would therefore be to Miller's advantage to set as high a value as possible on depreciable assets, such as machinery, buildings, and office equipment, thus minimizing the allocation to nondepreciable assets such as goodwill.

Moreover, it would be to Miller's advantage to minimize the value placed on the salt deposits and the mine shaft, since the code permitted a percentage depletion deduction on these assets regardless of the original cost assigned to them. Thus, the smaller the value assigned to depletable assets, the higher the value that could be assigned to depreciable assets, with no effect on the depletion deduction allowed under the code.

EXHIBIT 4

MILLER SALT COMPANY

Comparative Balance Sheet of Caribou Valley Salt Company

| | December 31 | | Increase– |
ASSETS	1959	1958	Decrease
Current Assets:			
Cash	$1,051,701	$ 825,340	$ 226,361
Notes and accounts receivable:			
Customers	$ 800,559	$ 458,042	$ 342,517
Sundry	24,291	18,118	6,173
Total notes and accounts receivable	$ 824,850	$ 476,160	$ 348,690
Less reserve for doubtful accounts	4,150	4,150	0
Net notes and accounts receivable	$ 820,700	$ 472,010	$ 348,690
Inventories	323,780	298,647	25,133
Total Current Assets	$2,196,181	$1,595,997	$ 600,184
Property:			
Land	$ 70,665	$ 7,055	$ 63,610
Salt deposits—arbitrary constant	$ 100,000	$ 83,000	$ 17,000
Shaft construction and developments	309,971	309,971	0
Total depletable property	$ 409,971	$ 392,971	$ 17,000
Less reserve for depletion	282,641	277,375	5,266
Net depletable property	$ 127,330	$ 115,596	$—11,734
Buildings, machinery, and equipment	$2,351,791	$2,278,636	$ 73,155
Automobiles and trucks	62,302	73,310	—11,008
Furniture and fixtures	51,780	54,299	— 2,519
Canal development	47,717	47,717	0
Total depreciable property	$2,513,590	$2,453,962	$ 59,628
Less reserve for depreciation	1,520,341	1,502,181	18,160
Net depreciable property	$ 993,249	$ 951,781	$ 41,468
Construction in progress	$ 30,102	$ 21,703	$ 8,399
Net Property	$1,221,346	$1,096,135	$ 125,211
Intangible Assets:			
Rights of way	$ 747	......	$ 747
Deferred Charges:			
Prepaid insurance	$ 59,002	$ 66,279	$ —7,277
Dissolver expense	4,262	6,611	—2,349
Other	4,826	6,407	—1,581
Total Deferred Charges	$ 68,090	$ 79,297	$—11,207
Total Assets	$3,486,364	$2,771,429	$ 714,935

EXHIBIT 4 (continued)

LIABILITIES AND NET WORTH	December 31 1959	December 31 1958	Increase– Decrease
Current Liabilities:			
Vouchers payable	$ 267,746	$ 111,032	$ 156,714
Dividends payable	......	70,787	−70,787
Accrued taxes	314,016	139,284	174,732
Other accrued accounts:			
Salaries and wages	$ 10,762	$ 12,960	$ −2,198
Bonuses and commissions	146,882	97,392	49,490
Miscellaneous accrued accounts	29,848	28,623	1,225
Total other accrued accounts	$ 187,492	$ 138,975	$ 48,157
Total Current Liabilities	$ 769,254	$ 460,078	$ 309,176
Net Worth:			
Capital stock:			
Common: authorized, 50,000 shares without par value; issued and outstanding, 50,000 shares	$1,018,485	$1,018,485	......
Total capital stock	$1,018,485	$1,018,485	......
Surplus:			
Capital	$ 62,393	$ 62,393	
Earned	1,636,232	1,230,473	$ 405,759
Total surplus	$1,698,625	$1,292,866	$ 405,759
Total Net Worth	$2,717,110	$2,311,351	$ 405,759
Total Liabilities and Net Worth	$3,486,364	$2,771,429	$ 714,935

Depletion was defined in the code as "the gradual diminution of the original amount of a mineral deposit because of any operation which removed the mineral from its natural state. In such a case, the owner or lessor of the deposit is entitled to a depletion allowance of 10 percent (on salt deposits) of gross sales from the property. However, this allowance must not exceed 50 percent of the property's taxable income, but may not be less than the deduction computed under the cost of units method."

The two methods which Miller might use—the percentage depletion method or the cost of units method—are illustrated in Exhibit 5. Once a company had adopted either of these methods, it was committed to this method and could not elect to change from one to the other. Under the cost of units method, the cumulative total of the annual cost recoveries ($50,000 in the example) was not allowed to exceed the original purchase price ($500,000 in the example); while under the percentage depletion method, the original purchase price had no bearing on the amount allowed as a depletion deduction.

Mr. Schwingle further pointed out, "The task cannot involve setting unrealistically high valuations on property units with the sole purpose being to allocate the entire purchase price to depreciable assets, but it must involve identifying *all* depreciable assets and establishing a supportable

FXHIBIT 5

(in thousands)

Example (1) Percentage Depletion Method:

Gross salt sales	$4,000
Cost of sales	2,000
Gross profit	$2,000
Less other operating and nonoperating expenses	$1,000
Net income before tax	$1,000
Less depletion deduction of 10% of gross sales (but not to exceed 50% of 1,000,000 or be less than $50,000 computed as the deduction under the cost of units method, example 2).................	400
Taxable Income	$ 600

Example (2) Cost of Units Method: *

Gross salt sales (500,000 tons)........................	$4,000
Cost of sales (other than cost of raw salt).............	2,000
Gross profit	$2,000
Less other operating and nonoperating expenses	1,000
Net income before tax	$1,000
Less cost of salt computed under the cost of units method (500,000 tons × 10¢ per ton).............	50
Taxable Income	$ 950

° In which the original cost of salt deposit and mine shaft is $500,000, and the estimated tons of salt in deposit are five million. Therefore the cost imputed to each ton mined is $500,000 ÷ 5,000,000 = 10¢ unit cost per ton mined.

value thereon. The appraisal must exhibit high-level professional integrity in order to make the allocation acceptable to the Internal Revenue Service."

After an estimated appraisal fee of $25,000 had been agreed upon, American's field dispatch unit assigned three men from its structural department to appraise the buildings, four men from the mechanical department to evaluate machinery and equipment, and two men to study the land. Several additional men were assigned to do research on special projects such as leasehold improvements, lease and royalty contracts, and costs and operation methods at other competitive salt mines in various geographical areas. The final results of the appraisal have been reproduced as Exhibit 6. This exhibit indicates for each major asset item its: (1) original cost, (2) accumulated depreciation to December 31, 1959, on Caribou's books, (3) net book value on Caribou's books, (4) "cost of reproduction new," (5) fair market value, and (6) the asset's estimated remaining life.

Performance of the Property Appraisal

In general, the American Appraisal Company structured its appraisal operation as diagrammed in Exhibit 7. Specifically, in appraising the assets

EXHIBIT 6

MILLER SALT COMPANY

Book Value, Reproduction Value New, and Fair Market Value
of Caribou Valley's Property Assets

	Asset Value on Caribou Valley Books			American Appraisal Valuation		
	Original Cost	Accumulated Depreciation*	Net Book Value	Cost of Reproduction New	Fair Market Value	Estimated Remaining Life (Years)
Land	$ 70,665	$	$ 70,665	$ 29,880.00	$ 29,880.00	:...
Mine shaft	309,971	$ 282,641	27,330	1,141,250.00	456,500.00	15
Canal	47,717	6,410	41,307	55,361.00	44,288.80	35
Buildings	954,509	732,653	221,856	1,694,766.58	1,010,538.03	18
Machinery and equipment	1,397,282	744,872	652,410	2,517,775.42	1,477,817.75	10
Office furniture and fixtures ...	51,780	28,106	23,674	73,460.40	49,232.81	8
Automobiles and trucks	62,302	8,300	54,002	70,006.03	65,448.17	4
Salt deposits, owned	......	......	......	24,900.00	24,900.00	10
Salt deposits, state leased	100,000	......	100,000	249,000.00	249,000.00	10
Totals	$2,994,226	$1,802,982	$1,191,244	$5,856,399.43	$3,407,605.56	

* To Dec. 31, 1959.

EXHIBIT 7

MILLER SALT COMPANY

American Appraisal Company's Operations Flow Chart

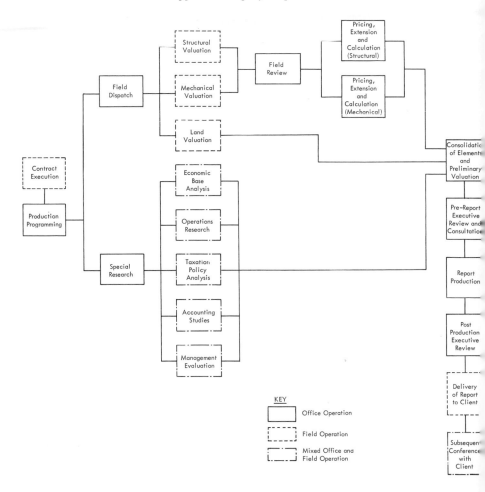

KEY

Office Operation

Field Operation

Mixed Office and
Field Operation

of Caribou Valley Salt Company, American's engineers were confronted
with four major tasks.

1. _Identify Assets._ It was necessary to identify all tangible and intangible, depreciable and nondepreciable assets of Caribou Valley.

2. _Establish the "Cost of Reproduction New" of Each of These Assets._
Cost of reproduction new was the amount that would be required to recreate an asset fully in its original condition at today's costs. This figure became a partial bench mark for calculating present values after physical depreciation and functional obsolescence were considered.

In setting a value for Caribou's land, American's field appraisers checked sales of similar salt properties within California and in other parts of the nation. In the selection of these comparable land sales, several conditions had to be present if they were to have validity. The sales had to occur, for example, in a reasonably free market with willing sellers and willing buyers. There must have been equity to both parties to the sale and both parties must have had equal access to the facts about the property. Once the comparable sales data were collected, the appraisers made adjustments to eliminate circumstances peculiar to each sale so that they would become truly comparable to the Caribou case.

In establishing the cost of reproduction new of the mine shaft, the canal, and the buildings, American's appraisers determined what materials in what quantities, what input of labor, what overhead expenses, and what other elements of cost would be required to rebuild each of these facilities new at the date of the appraisal. Information to support these cost findings was obtained partially from American's architectural and structural pricing library at Milwaukee and partially from checks with contractors, labor unions, and materials suppliers in the Caribou Valley area.

The mechanical valuation engineers who worked on cost of reproduction of machinery and equipment relied heavily on American's mechanical pricing library at Milwaukee, but checks were also made with equipment manufacturers. Perhaps most important, the mechanical men were specialists in mining equipment familiar with the machinery and its characteristics.

The cost of reproduction new for office furniture and fixtures, automobiles, and trucks was determined in a manner similar to that for machinery and equipment.

The salt deposits were valued with the aid of consulting geologists who calculated the remaining mineable tonnage at the 800- and 1,000-foot levels. American's appraisers then figured the cost of recovery, royalty payments for salt in the state lands, royalty savings on the owned lands, processing, and other costs in setting value. No value was assigned salt below the 1,000-foot level because its recovery was speculative and because its development would not occur for at least 10 years. Precisely what cost and mining conditions would be realized in several years could not be known at the time of the appraisal, and consequently, no supportable value could be given the lower deposits.

Preliminary field values were sent to American's Milwaukee office where they were checked, calculated, and extended.

3. *Establish the Fair Market Value of the Assets.*   Fair market value—the figure that would be equivalent to current book value—was not necessarily cost of reproduction less accrued depreciation with provision for functional obsolescence, nor was it the amount that would be obtained in the used machinery and equipment market. Fair market value in this case, Schwingle reasoned, would be the value of the assets as part of a going concern.

The hoist and cage equipment in the mine shaft, for example, were old, and no mining company would install such equipment today. If offered in the used equipment market, the hoist and cage would probably have little more than scrap value. Yet they had been well maintained and were functional.

To Caribou Valley, therefore, the equipment had value as part of the enterprise substantially above scrap and used equipment value. The fair market value as determined by American was cost of reproduction less accrued depreciation from all causes, less a penalty for the slight inefficiency and added operating cost induced through use of this equipment as opposed to more modern machinery.

On the other hand, the current used automobile market was used as a base in determining fair market value for automobiles, since used autos were exchanged freely between sellers and buyers without consideration of their value as part of the enterprise.

4. Establish Remaining Useful Lives of the Assets. In determining the remaining useful lives of the buildings, machinery and equipment, mine shaft, canal, office furniture and fixtures, and automobiles and trucks, American's valuation engineers relied heavily on their judgment about the assets and sought to determine the amount of time remaining before each asset would either exhaust its useful life because of wear and tear or become functionally obsolete. In the case of power shovels and mucking machines used in the mine, the appraisers knew that their physical lives would extend several years beyond the time at which new equipment would make them functionally obsolete, and the estimated date of functional obsolescence was therefore used to set the remaining lives on these pieces of machinery.

In setting a 35-year life on the canal, American's engineers estimated the time that would elapse before silting and slippage would require re-dredging equivalent to a complete rebuilding of the canal.

The remaining useful lives established varied from asset to asset, and in American's Milwaukee office, as the final report was given executive review, argument developed because the lives of several assets were longer than the estimated life of the salt deposits. "If the salt gives out in 10 years," Mr. Gaus, a field review man, argued, "what earthly value have the buildings, the machinery, and the mine shaft?" Schwingle replied that although the salt below 1,000 feet had not been valued and had been given no life, a new process which was in the final stages of development at Miller might permit its exploitation. Besides, he continued, the surface works could be used to process salt from other nearby sources.

In final executive review at Milwaukee, a determination had to be reached as to whether the total appraised value could be supported by the anticipated profits that the business would earn. Based on experience of the five prior years, and without attempting an income forecast, the valuation study indicated that a profit of approximately 10 percent on the investment (after taxes and depreciation) could conservatively be anticipated annually over the next 10 years. The annual aggregate weighted depreciation, if figured on a straight-line basis, was given at 8.37 percent. When combined, the profit on the investment and the recovery of the investment yielded an annual cash flow of 18.37 percent. This figure was high enough to justify the purchase price and the fair market value established by the appraisal, and it compared well with comparable rates gathered in analysis from 10 other similar mining companies.

Internal Revenue Service Reaction to Property Appraisal

Miller Salt Company submitted American's appraisal of its acquired assets to the IRS for a ruling as to reasonability. In a subsequent conference which was held with two IRS agents, the IRS contested the valuation placed on the following items:

1. Valuation of Salt Deposits. The IRS agents contended that the 10-year estimated life was unrealistic, and in their opinion the life should be some indefinite period. They also contended that the value of the deposits should be $850,000 rather than the $273,900 proposed by the American Appraisal Company.

2. Value of Mine Shaft. It was Mr. Howe's (IRS agent) opinion that the "hole in the ground" had not decreased in value since its inception, and since American's appraisal set the cost of reproduction for the entire shaft including shorings at $1,141,250, Mr. Howe believed the value of the hole should be related to that amount. The IRS did not consider the mine shaft as a depreciable asset, but ruled that it was depletable property, and therefore no depreciation could be allowed on the shaft itself. From this, he contended that the 15-year life set on the shaft was completely erroneous.

3. Canal. Why should a canal be considered as a depreciable asset? Mr. Howe contended that a canal was similar to land, and therefore no depreciation could be claimed.

4. Inconsistency of Estimated Lives. Why weren't the various valuations based on a single consistent term, say 10 years, the date when the state lease was to expire? Mr. Howe stated that it was inconsistent to assign salt deposits a 10-year life, the mine shaft a 15-year life, buildings an 18-year life, etc. Mr. Howe further commented that in light of the inconsistencies, the 18-year life of the building was far too short a time. At this point, Mr. Nicholas charged Mr. Howe with being inconsistent in his criticism of inconsistency. Mr. Howe replied that he did not intend to imply that he or the IRS would have accepted American's estimated lives even if a consistent 10-year term had been used.

No final agreement was reached with the IRS agents on any of the above items, but a second meeting was scheduled. Legal counsel for Miller Salt Company said that negotiations with the IRS might continue for several months and perhaps longer if the company decided to challenge the final IRS decision in the tax courts. In the lawyer's opinion, Miller's tax position would not be unduly prejudiced if the company handled the transaction differently for book (stockholder reporting) purposes, since differences between tax and book treatments were common, particularly for companies permitted to deduct depletion allowance for tax purposes.

Reaction of Miller Salt Company Executives to American's Property Appraisal

As Mr. Nicholas contemplated what decision he should make relative to the valuation of the acquired property assets on Miller's books, he mulled over the points of view expressed by various members of Miller's board of directors at a meeting where the acquisition of Caribou Valley had been the topic of discussion.

Mr. Jamieson, Miller's controller, advocated the use of Caribou's book values as of the date of acquisition as the basis at which the acquired property should be carried. He agreed that for tax purposes the appraised values should be used, but he contended that the assets weren't worth any more to Miller than they had been to Caribou, and thus the book value ($1,221,346) of the property assets should be shown on Miller's books. He admitted that his method might be on the conservative side, but that this was far superior to using appraisal values which had obviously been stated at a maximum for income tax purposes. He commented, "American's appraisal is absolutely silly. They say that the assets we purchased are worth more than we paid for them ($3,407,605.56 appraised property + $2,196,181 current assets − $769,254 current liabilities = $4,834,-532.56 net worth purchased for $4,500,000), and this indicates to me that American arrived at inflated asset values. This is fine for our tax books, but isn't it misleading to management and to our stockholders?" He thought that the difference between the purchase price and the total asset book values should be written off as an extraordinary loss of the period, but justified in the annual report on the basis that such a loss was necessary to the establishment of a foothold in the western market. This idea had not appealed to Mr. Nicholas because he was afraid that the shareholders would become quite perturbed if a large acquisition loss appeared on the first income statement after he had become president, regardless of what justification he gave.

Mr. Crowder, a director of Miller and partner in a local stock brokerage house, stated that he saw no reason why the assets should not be shown at their appraised values. After all, he pointed out, "We hired the American Appraisal Company to evaluate our assets, and if we can't rely on their judgment and values which have been meticulously determined, we had better give up. There is absolutely no justification for tinkering around with the values they arrived at." He further pointed out that the shareholders were interested in the *actual* realistic values of the assets which had been purchased, and not in some meaningless book value as determined by Caribou's bookkeeper. "The book value shown on Caribou's balance sheet has absolutely no relevance in determining the asset values which we should show on our books," was his concluding remark.

Finally, Mr. Jevelekian, vice president of marketing, had disagreed violently with this approach and told Mr. Crowder that he had evidently forgotten the prime reason for purchasing Caribou in the first place. He reminded the board that the prime reason for purchasing Caribou had been to acquire its western market and brand image and not the value of the mining assets themselves. He agreed with Jamieson that the assets acquired should be shown at book value, not at appraised value, but that the difference between the purchase price and book value should not be shown as the value of the markets and customer lists which had been built up under the Caribou Valley brand name and for which the company had been acquired. He even went one step further than Jamieson when he said, "For that matter, we could disregard the value of the assets *completely* and could allocate the entire purchase price to 'value of markets acquired,' which would then be shown as a permanent asset on our balance sheet. Isn't this the most accurate presentation of the facts, since we don't know that further mining of salt is possible even with our new method?"

After mulling over each of these points of view, after considering the comments made by the IRS agents after their examination of American's appraisal, and with American's appraisal before him, Mr. Nicholas thought he could now decide on a course of action relative to valuation of Caribou's property assets which he felt would be reasonable.

Questions

1. What value should be assigned to the fixed assets? What life?
2. How should the difference between the purchase price and the book value of the acquired assets be treated?

CHAPTER **14**

DEPRECIATION ACCOUNTING

The term depreciation, as used in accounting, refers to the process of allocating the cost of a tangible fixed asset to the accounting periods covered during its expected useful life to a business. Some of the difficulties encountered in connection with depreciation result from failure to recognize the meaning of the term in this accounting sense. Outside the area of accounting, depreciation is generally used to denote a reduction in the value of property; misunderstandings are caused by attempts to substitute this concept for the more specialized accounting definition.

Depreciation was defined by the American Institute of Certified Public Accountants in its *Accounting Terminology Bulletin No. 1:*

Depreciation accounting is a system of accounting which aims to distribute the cost or other basic value of tangible capital assets, less salvage (if any), over the estimated useful life of the unit (which may be a group of assets) in a systematic and rational manner. It is a process of allocation, not of valuation.

Depreciation for the year is the portion of the total charge under such a system that is allocated to the year. Depreciation can be distinguished from other terms with specialized meanings used by accountants to describe asset cost allocation procedures. Depreciation is concerned with charging the cost of man-made fixed assets to operations (and not with determination of asset values for the balance sheet). Depletion refers to cost allocations for natural resources such as oil and mineral deposits. Amortization relates to cost allocations for intangible assets such as patents and leaseholds. The use of the term depreciation should also be avoided in connection with valuation procedures for securities and inventories.

COMPUTING DEPRECIATION

Depreciation expense for a period of operations can be determined by a variety of means, all of which satisfy the general requirements of consistency and reasonableness. Depreciation accounting requires the application of judgment in four areas: (1) determination of the cost of the asset depreciated (covered in Chapter 13), (2) estimation of the useful life of the asset, (3) estimation of the salvage value at the end of expected useful life, and (4) selection of a method of computing periodic depreciation charges.

Estimating the Useful Life of Fixed Assets

The estimated useful life of most fixed assets is expressed in terms of a period of calendar time. For example, a time basis for determining depreciation charges is suitable for general purpose assets like buildings. The useful life of an asset might be expressed in units other than time, however. For instance, the life of a motor vehicle could be estimated as 100,000 miles, while the life of a unit of specialized machinery could be estimated as 200,000 units of output or as 5,000 operating hours.

The estimated life of an asset should be the period during which it is of use to the business. Thus, the estimate should take into account such factors as the use of the asset, anticipated obsolescence, planned maintenance, and replacement policy. The period of useful life may be less than the entire physical life of the asset. For example, machinery with an expected physical life of 10 years under normal conditions will have a useful life for depreciation purposes of six years if company policy is to trade or dispose of such assets after six years or if technological improvements are expected to make the machine obsolete in six years.

Salvage value of fixed assets represents estimated realizable value at the end of the expected life. This may be the scrap or junk proceeds, cash sale proceeds, or trade-in value, depending upon the company's disposition and replacement policies.

Depreciable cost is determined by subtracting salvage value from the cost of the fixed asset. This depreciable cost is the amount allocated to the operating periods comprising the asset's useful life.

DEPRECIATION METHODS

Any depreciation method which results in a logical, systematic, and consistent allocation of depreciable cost is acceptable for financial accounting purposes. The procedures most commonly used are based upon straight-line, declining-balance, sum-of-the-years'-digits, and units-of-production (or service-life) depreciation methods. The commonly used depreciation methods are illustrated and discussed separately below. Several rarely used and comparatively complex depreciation methods which take into account the imputed earning power of investments in fixed assets will not be discussed. This group includes the annuity and sinking fund methods.

Straight-Line Depreciation

The most simple method of computing depreciation is the straight-line method. For purposes of illustration, a machine with a cost of $6,000 and estimated salvage value of $1,000 at the end of its expected five-year useful life is assumed. Depreciation expense for one year is computed thus:

$$
\begin{array}{lr}
\text{Cost of machinery} & \$6,000 \\
\text{Less: Estimated salvage value} & 1,000 \\
\text{Depreciable cost} & \$5,000 \\
\end{array}
$$

$$
\frac{\text{Depreciable cost}}{\text{Estimated life}} = \text{Depreciation expense}
$$

$$
\frac{\$5,000}{5 \text{ years}} = \$1,000 \text{ per year}
$$

The straight-line method's strongest appeal is its simplicity. Until accelerated depreciation methods were permitted for income tax purposes, this method was used almost universally. Objections to the straight-line method center on the allocation of equal amounts of depreciation to each period of useful life. Identical amounts are charged in the first year for use of a new and efficient machine and in the later years as the worn machine nears the salvage market.

Accelerated Depreciation

Accelerated depreciation methods provide relatively larger depreciation charges in the early years of an asset's estimated life and diminishing charges in later years. The double-declining-balance method and the sum-of-the-years'-digits method are the two best known methods.

Double-declining-balance depreciation for each year is computed by multiplying the asset cost less accumulated depreciation by twice the straight-line rate expressed as a decimal fraction. Using the earlier example—machinery with a cost of $6,000 and a five-year estimated useful life, which is equal to 20 percent per year—depreciation is computed as follows:

$$
\begin{array}{lll}
\text{First year:} & \$6,000 \times 0.40 & \$2,400 \\
\text{Second year:} & (\$6,000 - \$2,400) \times 0.40 & 1,440 \\
\text{Third year:} & (\$6,000 - \$3,840) \times 0.40 & 864 \\
\text{Fourth year:} & (\$6,000 - \$4,704) \times 0.40 & 518 \\
\text{Fifth year:} & (\$6,000 - \$5,222) \times 0.40 & 311 \\
\text{Total} & & \$5,533 \\
\end{array}
$$

Note that estimated salvage value is not used directly in these computations, even though the asset has salvage value. Since the double-declining-balance procedure will not depreciate the asset to zero cost at the end of the estimated useful life, the residual balance provides an amount in lieu of scrap or salvage value. Ordinarily, however, depreciation is not continued beyond the point where net depreciated cost equals a reasonable salvage value. Also, it is common practice to switch from double-declining-balance depreciation to straight-line depreciation over the remaining life of an asset when the annual depreciation charge falls below what the charge would have been if straight-line depreciation had been used originally.

Sum-of-the-years'-digits depreciation for the year is computed by multiplying depreciable cost of the asset by a fraction based upon the years' digits. The years' digits are added to obtain the denominator $(1+2+3+4+5 = 15)$, and the numerator for each successive year is the number of the year in reverse order.

The formula for determining the sum of the years' digits is:

$$SYD = n \left(\frac{n+1}{2} \right)$$

Again using the facts for the illustration of straight-line depreciation, annual depreciation computed by the sum-of-the-years'-digits method would be:

First year:	$5,000 × 5/15	$1,667
Second year:	$5,000 × 4/15	1,333
Third year:	$5,000 × 3/15	1,000
Fourth year:	$5,000 × 2/15	667
Fifth year:	$5,000 × 1/15	333
Total		$5,000

Accelerated depreciation methods provide larger depreciation charges against operations during the early years of asset life, when the asset's new efficient condition contributes to greater earnings capacity. Further, the increasing maintenance and repair costs in the later years of asset use tend to complement the reducing depreciation charges, thereby equalizing the total cost of machine usage. Therefore, it is claimed that accelerated depreciation methods more properly match income and expense than does the straight-line method.

Units-of-Production Depreciation

The units-of-production depreciation method is based upon an estimated useful life in terms of units of output, instead of a calendar time period. Units-of-production (or service-life) methods are appropriate in those cases where the useful life of the depreciable asset can be directly related to its productive activity.

Under the units-of-production method, depreciation is determined by multiplying the actual units of output of the fixed asset for the operating period by a computed unit depreciation rate. This rate is calculated by dividing the depreciable cost by the total estimated life of the asset expressed in units of output. A $6,000 machine is estimated to have a $1,000 salvage value after producing 100,000 units of output. The depreciation rate for the machine is:

$$\frac{\$5,000}{100,000 \text{ units}} = \$0.05 \text{ per unit}$$

And, the depreciation charge for a year in which 25,000 units are produced upon this machine is $1,250 (25,000 units × $0.05 per unit).

The units-of-production depreciation method relates fixed asset cost directly to usage. It is argued this method best matches depreciation costs and revenues. However, the life of an asset is not necessarily more accurately estimated in units of output than in terms of time. Further, this depreciation method requires a record of the output of individual assets, which may not be readily available without significant additional effort and cost.

A hybrid straight-line and production method is sometimes used by companies in cyclical businesses. The straight-line portion is treated as a period cost and is the minimum depreciation charge. In addition, when production increases beyond a "normal" operating level, an additional depreciation charge is made to reflect the use of assets which are idle at normal production levels.

ACCOUNTING FOR DEPRECIATION

Regardless of the method chosen for computing depreciation, the accounting entry required to record depreciation applicable to a period of operations is:

Depreciation Expense xxx
    Accumulated Depreciation xxx

In addition, both account titles should indicate the type of fixed assets involved, i.e., buildings, machinery, office equipment, etc. This aids in proper handling of the accounts in the financial statements.

Depreciation expense is listed in the income statement according to the nature of the fixed asset giving rise to the depreciation. Depreciation expense on factory machinery is included in factory overhead, while depreciation on office equipment is included among the administrative expenses.

Accumulated Depreciation (sometimes called Allowance for Depreciation or labeled with the outdated title of Reserve for Depreciation) is deducted from the related fixed asset account on the balance sheet. This account's credit balance is increased as assets are depreciated in successive accounting periods. Of course, the allocation of fixed asset cost could be accomplished by crediting the amount of depreciation directly to the fixed asset accounts. This procedure is not recommended because the cost of the fixed asset is merged with estimated depreciation charges, and the users of financial statements would be denied information about fixed asset investment and depreciation policies.

Depreciation charges are continued systematically until the asset is disposed of or until the asset is depreciated to salvage values. Fully depreciated assets remaining in service are carried in the accounts until disposition. From time to time, significant changes in a company's circumstances may require a switch from one depreciation method to another. The APB has proposed any required adjustments to the depreciation allowance be handled as extraordinary charges.

Group and Composite Rate Depreciation

Depreciation is frequently computed for a group of assets owned by a business. In preceding illustrations, it was assumed that depreciation was calculated separately for each fixed asset; such procedures are called unit methods. If the asset units can be grouped together in some general category, such as machinery, delivery equipment, or office equipment, it may be desirable to compute depreciation for the total of each group. This practice minimizes detailed analyses and computations. Also, errors in estimates of useful life and salvage value tend to balance out for the group. Estimated useful life is established for the entire group of assets and depreciation is computed on the basis of weighted-average or composite rates. These group depreciation procedures necessitate arbitrary assumptions in handling dispositions and replacements in the accounting records. However, both unit and group methods will theoretically achieve the same results of charging fixed asset costs to operations during the period of expected useful life.

Depreciation and Federal Income Tax

Federal income tax laws recognize depreciation as an expense in the computation of taxable income. The law permits a deduction of a reasonable allowance for the "exhaustion," "wear and tear," and "obsolescence" of property used in a business. As a general rule, the taxpayer bears the burden of proof to justify depreciation charges claimed.

There is no requirement that the same depreciation methods be used for both tax and financial reporting purposes. It is not uncommon for a business to adopt an accelerated depreciation method to maximize income tax deductions while using the straight-line depreciation method for financial reporting. Material differences in depreciation charges under this procedure will require appropriate deferred tax accounting in the financial statements.

In recent years, the tax laws related to depreciation have been modified so as to stimulate the economy by encouraging investment in fixed assets. For example, in 1954, the law for the first time specifically described and permitted the use of accelerated depreciation under either the declining-balance or sum-of-the-years'-digits methods for subsequent tax years. Since 1958, a special additional 20 percent bonus depreciation has been permitted in the year of acquisition on certain fixed asset purchases, up to a total of $10,000 fixed asset cost for each taxpayer.

In mid-1962, the Treasury Department issued new depreciation guidelines and rules which generally permitted more generous depreciation deductions by reducing prescribed estimated lives for groups of assets with similar physical characteristics.

Depreciation Schedule Revisions

Depreciation schedules are based upon management's best estimate of the future utilization of an asset at the time it is acquired. During the life of the asset, these estimates may prove to be improper due to circumstances that indicate that either the asset's useful life or the disposal value, or both, should be revised. Under these conditions, management might wait until the asset is retired to recognize any over- or underdepreciation as a gain or loss on sale of the asset. However, the preferred approach is to either:

a) Leave the book value as it is and alter the rate of future depreciation charges.

b) Revise the book value through an immediate charge to income and base the modified future depreciation charges on the revised book value.

The first method is found more often in practice than the second. It is argued that costs charged to revenue in prior periods are permanent assignments and the only costs subject to modification are future costs. Also, the depreciation charged to income through the depreciation expense account over the life of the asset is the same as the original depreciable cost, which is not the case if the second method is used, since the book value adjustment is a special charge to income.

Those supporting the second method argue that the depreciation recognized each period should be the best possible estimate given the evidence available. The first method does not meet this goal, since it compensates for past errors by including them in subsequent depreciation charges. Thus, both the past and future periodic income measurements are distorted.

The accounting profession generally prefers the first method over the second. However, if the first method results in significant distortion in the measurement of future periodic income, then the second method is preferred.

Additions

For depreciation purposes, an addition to fixed assets should be depreciated over its own economic life or that of the original asset, whichever is shorter.

Donated Assets

Fixed assets donated on a conditional basis to a company raise a difficult issue: Should income be charged with depreciation on such assets before full title is obtained? Since the company does not own the asset, it can be argued that depreciation should not be charged. On the other hand, the economic life of an asset is not dependent on who owns it. Therefore, if depreciation is not charged until title is obtained, the full depreciation charge must be applied to the economic life of the asset remaining after this event. This practice, which relates depreciation to ownership rather than the period of use, results in a misleading variation of income charges during two similar operating periods. Therefore, it is argued the depreciation for such assets should be charged to operations during the full period of use.

Written-Up Assets

The write-up of depreciable assets requires, in addition to the recognition of appraisal capital, an adjustment to the depreciation accounts. The related allowance for depreciation must be increased to reflect the fact that inadequate depreciation has been taken in the past. The amount added to the Appraised Capital account is the net difference between the appraised value and the original cost minus the adjustment to the Allowance for Depreciation account. In addition, if the asset's appraised life remaining is different from the remaining life implicit in book value of the asset, the past depreciation allowance based on cost should also be adjusted to reflect the new estimated life.

To illustrate, assume the following information related to a manufacturing plant: cost, $100,000; estimated life, 50 years; period used, 20 years; allowance for depreciation, $40,000. An appraisal of the plant indicates that it would cost $200,000 to replace the plant with an identical new plant. (This amount is the so-called reproduction cost.) The estimated actual depreciation to date is $100,000 based upon the reproduction cost. Hence, the sound value or reproduction cost less estimated actual depreciation to date based on this value is $100,000. Therefore, the estimated actual depreciation is 50 percent, rather than the 40 percent assumed in the company's books.

The appraisal indicates that the accounts should be adjusted as follows:

a) The depreciation allowance based on cost must be increased by $10,000 to reflect the fact that 50 percent of the asset's life has been consumed in operations. The new allowance for depreciation is $50,000. The accounting entries are:

> Depreciation Expense—Adjustment for Understatement
> of Prior Period Depreciation Charges 10,000
> Allowance for Depreciation 10,000

b) The $100,000 original cost of the asset must be increased to its $200,-000 reproduction cost. In addition, the allowance for depreciation must be increased to 50 percent of the reproduction cost. Therefore, since the allowance for depreciation account is now $50,000, after adjusting it for accumulated depreciation charges based on original cost, an additional $50,000 must be added. The net result is the new book value, equal to the asset's sound value. The entries are:

> Building—Appraisal Increase 100,000
> Allowance for Depreciation of
> Building—Appraisal Increase 50,000
> Appraisal Capital—Building 50,000

Whether periodic depreciation should be based on the original cost or the appraisal value is an unsettled issue. Both approaches have been followed in practice.

ARB No. 43, Chapter 9, Section B indicates that when appreciation is entered on the books, the company is obliged to make periodic depreciation charges that are consistent with the increased valuation rather than the historical cost basis. This position can be supported on the ground that current revenues ought to be matched with the current costs of replacing assets. This position reflects a conviction that a company does not earn any distributable profits until enough is recovered through depreciation charges to provide for the eventual replacement of assets consumed during the period.

Those advocating retaining the original cost basis for depreciation maintain that costs can only be incurred through actual expenditures. Income, they state, is obtained through the matching of actual dollar costs and revenues. Providing for replacement is a financial—rather than accounting—problem. Therefore, it should not be allowed to interfere with the measurement of income.

Depreciation of appraised asset values on the basis of costs is recorded in the usual way. This results in a cost-based income statement and an appraisal-based balance sheet. The entry reconciling these two statements is a debit to appraisal capital and a credit to appraisal allowance for depreciation. This has the effect of: (*a*) reducing the net appraisal value of the asset; and (*b*) transferring an amount equal to the reduction in appraisal value from appraisal capital to retained earnings. Appraisal capital is reduced, and the profits added to retained earnings are greater than they would otherwise have been if depreciation had been charged on the full appraised value.

To illustrate, assume assets with an original cost of $100,000 and accumulated depreciation of $60,000 are revalued upward to $300,000. The appraiser believes the existing depreciation schedule, which assumes a 10-year life and straight-line depreciation is still valid. After appraisal, the assets are shown as follows on the balance sheet:

Fixed assets (original cost)	$100,000	
Less allowance for depreciation	60,000	$ 40,000
Fixed assets—appraisal increase	$200,000	
Less allowance for depreciation—appraisal increase	120,000	80,000
Total Fixed Assets		$120,000

The entries to record the annual depreciation charge are:

Depreciation Expense	10,000	
Allowance for Depreciation		10,000
Appraisal Capital	20,000	
Allowance for Depreciation—Appraisal Increase		20,000

If depreciation is based on appraised values that are higher than original cost, income will be understated relative to cost-based accounting income. To correct the resulting understatement of retained earnings, Appraised Capital is debited and Retained Earnings credited for the amount of the understatement.

To illustrate, using the same example used above, the entries to record periodic depreciation are:

Depreciation Expense	30,000	
Appraisal Capital	20,000	
Allowance for Depreciation		10,000
Allowance for Depreciation—Appraisal Increase		20,000
Retained Earnings		20,000

Some people object to the transfer of appraisal capital to retained earnings. In their opinion, appraisal capital should be viewed as permanent capital and, hence, not transferable to retained earnings through operating charges or sale. Others believe that the transfer of appraised capital to retained earnings should be achieved through a net income adjustment account, so as to show net income on both an appraisal and a historical cost basis.

Accounting for Retirements

The accounting for asset retirement is fairly straightforward. At the time an asset is retired, its original cost is credited to the appropriate asset account and the related accumulated depreciation is charged to the accumulated depreciation account. Any gain or loss on the retirement after adjusting for the cost of removal and disposition should be recognized as an extraordinary gain or loss.

To illustrate, assume the Cleveland Company purchased a piece of equipment for $100,000. After two years, the company sold the equipment for $50,000. At the time of the sale the asset's book value was $60,000 and the related accumulated depreciation was $40,000.

The entries to record the purchase are:

Machinery	100,000	
Cash		100,000

The entries to record the subsequent sale are:

Cash	50,000	
Accumulated Depreciation	40,000	
Loss on Sale of Machinery	10,000	
Machinery		100,000

Capital Investment Decisions

Some fault current depreciation accounting on the ground that it does not lead to a measurement of return on investment which matches the

ILLUSTRATION 14–1

Year	Total Earnings (a)	Return at 8% on Investment Outstanding (b)	Balance Capital Recovery (c)=(a−b)	Investment Outstanding End of Year (d)
0	—	—	—	$1,000
1	$250	$80	$170	830
2	250	66	184	646
3	250	52	198	448
4	250	36	214	234
5	250	19	231	3*

° Due to rounding.

economic concept of return on investment used by many companies in making asset investment decisions.

To illustrate, assume a company approves a proposed investment of $1,000, which is estimated to earn $250 *cash* per year after taxes for five years and expected to earn 8 percent on the amount, at risk, as indicated by Illustration 14–1. The economic return on this investment is 8 percent, since the investor's principal is recovered over the life of the investment and each year he receives an 8 percent return on the principal balance outstanding.

ILLUSTRATION 14–2

Year	Gross Assets	Average Net Assets*	Net** Income	Computed Return On Gross	On Net
1	$1,000	$900	$50	5%	5.5%
2	1,000	700	50	5	7.1
3	1,000	500	50	5	10.0
4	1,000	300	50	5	16.7
5	1,000	100	50	5	50.0

° Beginning and ending book values divided by two.
°° Cash earnings, $250, minus depreciation, $200. Income taxes are included in the calculation of net earnings.

Assuming a straight-line depreciation method, this investment will be reported for financial accounting purposes as shown in Illustration 14–2. From this illustration it is clear that the financial reports in no year show a return of 8 percent. This problem is eliminated if the periodic cost-based depreciation of an asset is shown as the difference between the present value of the related future service benefits at the beginning and end of the accounting period discounted by the internal rate of return [1] calculated in the purchase decision analysis. In practice, it is difficult to measure the future service benefits accurately enough to apply this approach with confidence, so managers resort to using the various depreciation methods discussed above.

Depletion

Depletion is the process of allocating the cost of an investment in natural resources through systematic charges to income as the supply of the physical asset is reduced through operations, after making provision for

---

[1] The internal rate of return is the discount rate which reduces the present value of the future benefits to the present value of the investment.

the residual value of the land remaining after the valuable resource is exhausted.

There are two depletion methods: the production method and percentage method. The production method is acceptable for accounting purposes, whereas the percentage method is not. It is commonly used for computing income tax payments, however.

The production method establishes the depletion rate by dividing the cost of the depletable asset by the best available estimate of the number of recoverable units. The unit costs are then charged to income as the units are extracted and sold. The unit can be the marketing unit (ounces of silver) or the extractive unit (tons of ore), although the marketing unit is preferred. It is permissible to adjust the depletion rate when it becomes apparent that the estimate of recoverable units used to compute the unit cost is no longer the best available estimate.

To illustrate the cost-based depletion method, assume a coal mine containing an estimated profitable output of 10 million tons of coal is developed to the point of exploitation at a cost of $1 million. Furthermore, during the first year of operations, 500,000 tons of coal are mined and 450,000 tons are sold. The depletion unit charge is the total development cost divided by the estimated profitable output, or 10 cents per ton, i.e., $1 million/10 million tons. The total depletion charged to the inventory in the first operating year is $50,000, i.e., total production (500,000 tons) times the depletion unit cost ($0.10). The depletion charged to income as cost of goods sold during this period is $45,000, i.e., total production sold (450,000 tons) times the depletion unit cost of ($0.10). Consequently, $5,000 of the year's depletion charge is still lodged in the inventory account.

Depletion differs from depreciation in several respects: depletion charges relate to the actual physical exhaustion of an asset, and as such are directly included in inventory costs as production occurs. In contrast, depreciation recognizes the service exhaustion of an asset and is allocated to periodic income, except for depreciation related to manufacturing facilities, which is included in inventory costs on an allocated basis.

The percentage or statutory method, which is permissible for tax purposes only, computes depletion as a fixed percentage of the gross income from the property. The percentage varies from 5 to 22 percent according to the type of product extracted and is specified in the Internal Revenue Code and Regulations. The depletion deduction is limited to 50 percent of the net income from the property before consideration of depletion, however. This method, which can result in depletion deductions greater than the original cost of the property, is applicable to all mineral investments for tax purposes. The cost method is also permissible for determining income tax payments. Companies are not obliged to use the same depletion method for book and tax purposes.

Depreciation Decisions

The accounting criteria for choosing one depreciation method rather than another in any particular situation are fuzzy.

The decision to use one of the depreciation methods over another should be made on the basis of a close examination of the asset's characteristics and the way management viewed these characteristics in their investment decision. Empirical and theoretical evidence suggests that most productive assets tend to become less and less valuable over time. Maintenance costs rise and the quality of the asset's service declines as time goes on. Also, as technological advances are made, the quality of the existing equipment declines relative to alternative more modern equipment, even though quality does not deteriorate absolutely. Based on this evidence, it is believed by some that productive equipment in most cases depreciates on an accelerated basis rather than, as thought for a long time, on a straight-line basis. Similar studies indicate straight-line depreciation is a reasonable approximation of the depreciation rate of buildings and plant structures.

When an asset is utilized in a project whose future success is more uncertain than the typical situation, some managements believe it is prudent to use accelerated depreciation. Others object to this practice on the ground that the high depreciation charges in the early years will increase the likelihood that the project will be viewed as unsuccessful due to the lower profits. Thus, the action taken to reflect the excessive risk involved contributes to the worst fears of management being realized.

More often than not, depreciation accounting is used as an instrument of management's financial policy. Management selects the depreciation method or mix of methods that contributes to the desired financial results they hope to achieve over time. For example, in some cases accelerated depreciation methods have been used to hold earnings down and conserve funds by reducing stockholder pressure to increase dividend distributions. It also provides an argument against pay increases. In other situations, straight-line depreciation has been utilized to smooth earnings. And, in times of depressed profits, some companies have switched from accelerated to straight-line depreciation to boost earnings with the hope that this will maintain the market price of the company's stock. The choice of service life can also be used in a similar way to further the achievement of management's financial objectives.

The different nature of assets argues for retaining the present wide range of permissible depreciation methods. However, the apparent use of depreciation as a tool of financial policy, due to the difficulty in practice of determining which method is the most appropriate for any given asset, has led some to conclude that depreciation methods should be standardized for similar categories of assets. To date, nobody has seriously pursued this proposal. However, unless some managements adopt a more responsible attitude towards depreciation accounting, some action limiting management's flexibility in this area may be necessary.

SUGGESTED FURTHER READING

GRANT, EUGENE L., and NORTON, PAUL T., JR. *Depreciation.* New York: Ronald Press Co., 1955.

TERBORGH, GEORGE. *Realistic Depreciation Policy.* Chicago: Machinery and Allied Products Institute, 1954.

CASES

Case 14-1. UNITED STATES STEEL CORPORATION

Selection of Appropriate Depreciation Methods

United States Steel Corporation is the nation's largest steel producer, with approximately 25 percent of United States producers' shipments. The corporation's operations are highly integrated; it produces a substantial portion of its required stock of coal, iron ore, limestone, and electric power. Additionally, it operates steamships, barges, and stock facilities for the transportation of raw materials and steel products.

The following discussion pertains only to U.S. Steel's depreciation accounting policies and its treatment of the investment credit between 1946 and 1968.

The Environment (1947)

For a number of years prior to 1947, the management of U.S. Steel had been concerned with the effects of the steady rise in the general price level on the company's capital replacement program. This concern arose from the realization that the amounts being deducted from earnings as depreciation and amortization of plant and equipment were insufficient to provide for the replacement of worn-out or obsolete physical facilities. Depreciation was based on the original cost of plant and equipment, despite the fact that general price levels and replacement costs had risen markedly. U.S. Steel executives believed that failure to take action on this well-recognized problem would be failure to discharge a major management responsibility to corporate stockholders: the preservation of the company's capital.

The management of U.S. Steel believed that unless price, wage, and dividend policies were predicated upon a full recognition of the need to replace worn-out plant and equipment, the company would dissipate capital in the course of normal operations. First, selling prices, based on cost, would be insufficient to recover the real costs of wear and exhaustion of facilities (i.e., replacement costs). Second, the misleading net profit figure might be used as the argument for higher wage or dividend payments than were actually justified.

The relaxation of governmental price controls in late 1946 and early 1947 resulted in an immediate surge in prices, further aggravating the problem of providing for plant and equipment replacement. The effect of these price increases is indicated in Exhibit 1, which shows the increase in price for typical equipment and services purchased by U.S. Steel during the period. In the same period, the wholesale price of iron and steel rose 50 percent and that of finished steel 39 percent.

EXHIBIT 1

	Increase, 1947 over 1940
Wire drawing machine	91%
Standard electric crane	105
Reheating furnace	108
Blast furnace	105
By-product coke ovens	150
Mine locomotive	44
Large electric motor	50
Continuous rolling mill	84
Concrete construction	124
Brick construction	250

As a step toward stating depreciation in an amount which would recover in current dollars of diminished buying power the same purchasing power represented by the original plant expenditure, the company deducted, in arriving at net income for 1947, an amount of $26.3 million over and above its regular depreciation charge (based on the straight-line method). Although the federal tax authorities would not allow the extra depreciation as a deduction in arriving at taxable income for that year, the company's executives considered it essential to recognize this element of cost in arriving at a measure of income to be used in other matters of company management.

In its 1947 annual report, the management stated that while awaiting accounting and tax acceptance, U.S. Steel believed that it was prudent for it to give some recognition to increased replacement costs rather than to sit idly by and witness the unwitting liquidation of its business should inadequate recording of costs result in insufficient resources to supply the tools required for sustained production.

The additional depreciation charge was shown in the company's income statement as a separate item in the section under "Wear and Exhaustion of

Facilities" and labeled, "Added to Cover Replacement Cost"; it was shown in the balance sheet, on the liability side, as "Reserve for Replacement of Properties." The sum of $26.3 million, which amounted to approximately 30 percent of the regular depreciation based on original cost, was arrived at partly on the basis of cost increases actually experienced by the company and partly through study of construction cost index numbers (notably the *Engineering News-Record Index*). The management pointed out that, although the amount was actually much less than that which could be substantiated by actual cost increases, it was all that was deemed appropriate in view of the newness of the application of such a method of computing depreciation.

The company's independent auditors noted that the 1947 financial statement lacked consistency, since the corporation had included in costs additional depreciation of $26.3 million "in excess of the amount determined in accordance with the generally accepted accounting principle heretofore followed of making provision for depreciation on the original cost of facilities."

U.S. Steel was not alone in its concern over the effect of rising prices. In the late 1940s, several other large corporations, among them Crane Company, E. I. du Pont de Nemours & Company, and Libbey-Owens-Ford Glass Company, also made accounting provisions for replacement costs.

Carman G. Blough, director of research of the American Institute of Certified Public Accountants (at that time the American Institute of Accountants), commented on this practice as follows:

> There can be no argument but that a going concern must be able to replace its productive assets as they are used up if it is to continue to do business. It is also important for management to understand that the difference between cost and estimated replacement value may be significant in determining production and pricing policies. It does not follow, however, that the excess of the cost of replacement over the cost of existing assets should be accounted for as current charges to income. All who have dealt with appraisal values know how very difficult it is just to determine current replacement costs, but the most striking difficulty in this respect is the impossibility of predicting what will be the eventual cost of replacing a productive asset. How many men are prepared to state what the price level will be two years from today, to say nothing of trying to guess what it will be five or ten years hence when many of these assets are to be replaced? [1]

The AICPA Committee on Accounting Procedure issued in late 1947, *Accounting Research Bulletin No. 33* (later restated as *APB No. 43*, Chapter 9, Section A, paragraphs 4–9), in which it stated that it disapproved

---

[1] "Replacement and Excess Construction Costs," *Journal of Accountancy*, Vol. 84 (October 1947), p. 335.

immediate write-downs of plant cost by charges against current income in amounts believed to represent excessive or abnormal costs occasioned by current price levels. However, the committee calls attention to the fact that plants expected to have less than normal useful life can properly be depreciated on a systematic basis related to economic usefulness.

1948

United States Steel Corporation continued through the first three quarters of 1948 its practice of charging additional depreciation to cover higher costs of replacing worn-out facilities, and in view of the continued increase in the cost of facilities during 1948, advanced the additional charge from 30 to 60 percent of the depreciation based on original cost.

In the release of its quarterly statements for the third quarter of 1948, however, the company stated that in view of the position taken by the AICPA and the discussions between the corporation and the Securities and Exchange Commission, further study was being made in an effort to agree upon principles satisfactory to the commission for "determining and reflecting additional wear and exhaustion cost."

In its annual report for 1948, U.S. Steel announced that it was abandoning the policy adopted in 1947 of charging to costs an amount over and above the regular depreciation on original cost and was substituting in its place a method of charging "accelerated depreciation on cost." The following quotation from the notes to the financial statements in the 1948 annual report provides a brief description of the formula to be used in determining the amount of annual charge for accelerated depreciation:

The accelerated depreciation is applicable to the cost of postwar facilities in the first few years of their lives when economic usefulness is greatest. The amount thereof is related to the excess of current operating rates over U.S. Steel's long-term peacetime average rate of 70 percent of capacity. The annual accelerated amount is 10 percent of the cost of facilities in the year in which the expenditures are made and 10 percent in the succeeding year, except that this amount is reduced ratably as the operating rate may drop, no acceleration being made at 70 percent or lower operations. The accelerated depreciation is an addition to the normal depreciation on such facilities, but the total depreciation over their expected lives will not exceed the cost of the facilities.

This method was made retroactive to January 1, 1947, and there was included in the $55,335,444 deducted for accelerated wear and exhaustion of facilities for 1948 an amount of $2,675,094 to cover a deficiency in the $26,300,000 sum reported in 1947 as "depreciation added to cover replacement cost." In other words, the new method when applied to the 1947 situation resulted in a deduction that exceeded the figure actually reported in 1947. It was again pointed out at this time that the accelerated depreciation was not "presently deductible for federal income tax purposes."

The company's independent auditors apparently interpreted the concept of accelerated depreciation as being within AICPA standards as a "systematic basis related to economic usefulness"; for they stated in their report to the stockholders for 1948 that they "approved" the new policy.

The management's convictions on the change in policy were, however, clearly set forth by the chairman of the board of directors in the following quotation from the company's annual report for 1948:

U.S. Steel believes that the principle which it adopted in 1947 and continued in 1948 is a proper recording of the wear and exhaustion of its facilities in terms of current dollars as distinguished from the dollars which it originally expended for those facilities. However, in view of the disagreement existing among accountants, both public and private, and the stated position of the American Institute of Certified Public Accountants, which is supported by the Securities and Exchange Commission, that the only accepted accounting principle for determining depreciation is that which is related to the actual number of dollars spent for facilities, regardless of where or what buying power, U.S. Steel has adopted a method of acceleration based on cost instead of one based on purchasing power recovery.

1949 to 1952

U.S. Steel continued its policy of charging accelerated depreciation through 1952; more than $201 million was deducted from income on the 1946–52 financial statements. Deduction of the "excess portion" (above straight-line) was not permitted in computing taxable income.

In its annual report for 1949, U.S. Steel restated its belief that:

. . . a manufacturer should be able to recover out of receipts from customers through depreciation and through income remaining for reinvestment after equitable dividends, an amount sufficient to replace and keep modern his plant and equipment so as continuously to retain his productive capacity on a competitive basis.

In its annual report for 1952, management commented:

. . . so long as depreciation that is deducted for tax purposes is measured by the relatively smaller number of dollars of greater buying power expended in an earlier period, it will be inadequate to recover the original purchasing power invested in the facilities consumed in production. Real wear and exhaustion costs are thus understated, real profits are overstated, and there results an erosion of capital through taxation.

Although the continuing concern for capital replacement provision was expressed in 1952, U.S. Steel was deducting from both taxable and reported income substantial additional amounts of depreciation under "certificates of necessity."

To increase productive capacity necessary for the support of the Korean War, the Internal Revenue Code of 1950 provided for a 60-

month amortization of "emergency facilities" constructed under (and evidenced by) "certificates of necessity," regardless of the facility's probable economic life.

The AICPA through an accounting research bulletin strongly recommended that users of the 60-month amortization period for tax purposes carefully consider whether these facilities should be depreciated over a longer period for financial purposes:

... Sound financial accounting procedures do not necessarily coincide with the rules as to what shall be included in the "gross income" or allowed as a deduction therefrom, in arriving at taxable net income. It is well recognized that such rules should not be followed for financial accounting purposes if they do not conform to generally accepted accounting principles. . . .

The board recommended, for the first time, the deferral of differences in income tax resulting from the differing treatment of depreciation for financial and tax purposes:

In those cases in which the amount of depreciation charged in the accounts on that portion of the cost of the facilities for which certificates of necessity have been obtained is materially less than the amount of amortization deducted for income-tax purposes, the amount of income taxes payable annually during the amortization period may be significantly less than it would be on the basis of the income reflected in the financial statements. In such cases, after the close of the amortization period, the income taxes will exceed the amount that would be appropriate on the basis of the income reported in the statements. Accordingly, the committee believes that during the amortization period, where this difference is material, a charge should be made in the income statement to recognize the income tax to be paid in the future on the amount by which amortization for income-tax purposes exceeds the depreciation that would be allowable if certificates of necessity had not been issued. The amount of the charge should be equal to the estimated amount by which the income tax expected to be payable after the amortization period exceeds what would be so expected if amortization had not been claimed for income-tax purposes in the amortization period. The estimated amount should be based on normal and surtax rates in effect during the period covered by the income statement with such changes therein as can be reasonably anticipated at the time the estimate is made. . . .

In accounting for this deferment of income taxes, the committee believes it desirable to treat the charge as being for additional income taxes. The related credit in such cases would properly be made to an account for deferred income taxes. . . .[2]

1953 to 1954

In 1953, U.S. Steel accelerated depreciation, stating in a note to the 1953 financial statement:

[2] *Accounting Research Bulletin No. 43*, chap. 9, section C.

Since 1946, U.S. Steel has followed the policy of reflecting accelerated depreciation on the cost of new facilities in the first few years of their lives when the economic usefulness is greatest. The amounts charged to income for accelerated depreciation have been related to U.S. Steel's rate of operations.

Under the Internal Revenue Code, that portion of the cost of facilities certified by the Defense Production Administration as essential to the defense effort is covered by a Certificate of Necessity and can be written off for tax purposes at the rate of 20 percent per year. The effect of amortization of these facilities is to charge to income a greater portion of their cost in the earlier years of life and, therefore, follows the principle of accelerated depreciation.

U.S. Steel has included in wear and exhaustion in 1953, as a measure of the accelerated depreciation for the year, $105,137,893, representing amortization on its facilities covered by Certificates of Necessity.

In commenting on the effect of accelerated amortization and the tax laws, management pointed out that it had to be regarded as a temporary expedient, since "for many companies the addition of amortization on new facilities to 'so-called' regular depreciation on old facilities may approximate, temporarily, a truer total of wear and exhaustion on all facilities based on current dollar value. But it automatically guarantees something of a *future crisis*." (Emphasis added.)

Management noted in 1954 that the new methods of accelerated depreciation first allowed for tax purposes in 1954 would ease the future crisis, but even these provisions, applicable to new assets only, would fall far short of providing adequate depreciation on the relatively more numerous and older existing facilities.

1956

In its 1956 report, U.S. Steel included a chart (see Exhibit 2) comparing "wear and exhaustion recorded" with "wear and exhaustion needed." To calculate "Total Wear and Exhaustion Needed," as shown in the chart, the following statistical procedure was followed: excluding the amount of nontax-deductible accelerated depreciation from 1947 through 1952 (see Exhibit 3), and including only regular depreciation on emergency facilities, the amount of wear and exhaustion previously recorded for each year included in the chart was subdivided according to the acquisition years of the assets being depreciated. Each yearly subdivision was then adjusted to reflect the change in the *Engineering News-Record*'s index of construction costs from the various earlier acquisition years to any given year included in the chart. The sum of that year's adjusted depreciation amounts gave the "Total Wear and Exhaustion Needed" for that year. The process was repeated for every year in the chart. Notice that each year's deficiency is in dollars of the buying power that prevailed in *that* year.

EXHIBIT 2

U.S. STEEL CORPORATION

Wear and Exhaustion Recorded versus Wear and Exhaustion Needed

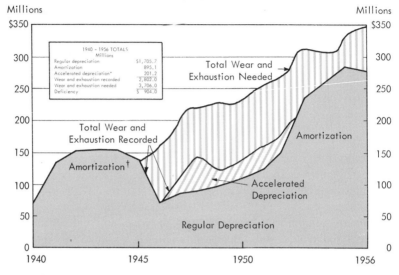

1940 - 1956 TOTALS	
Millions	
Regular depreciation	$1,705.7
Amortization	895.1
Accelerated depreciation*	201.2
Wear and exhaustion recorded	2,802.0
Wear and exhaustion needed	3,706.0
Deficiency	$ 904.0

* Not deductible for tax purposes.

† Additional amortization due to ending of emergency period allocated to years 1941–45.

1957 to 1958

Evidence of the "future crisis" of declining allowable depreciation on emergency facilities first appeared in 1957, and was far more obvious in 1958 (see Exhibit 3). Amortization of emergency facilities, which reached a peak of $147.7 million in 1955, had declined to $57.2 million by 1958.

1959

In 1959, management noted the approaching exhaustion of emergency amortization:

This [depreciation] deficiency has been aggravated by the running out of five-year amortization permitted on varying percentages of the total costs of certain defense and defense supporting facilities covered by Certificates of Necessity. The need for revision of the tax laws as they relate to depreciation . . . continues to be most vital to the maintenance of existing and the addition of new productive capacity.

In the spring of 1959, the representatives of the United Steelworkers of America and the major steel companies met to negotiate a new wage contract to replace the contract expiring in June. The union requested

EXHIBIT 3

U.S. STEEL CORPORATION

Selected Financial Statistics, 1946–67
(millions of dollars)

	Net Income	Depre- ciation	Capital Expen- ditures	Investment Tax Credit Taken	Investment Tax Credit Deferred
1967	$172.5	$354.7	$547.7	$33.4	$26.0
1966	249.2	344.3	440.7	20.8	16.6
1965	275.5	324.5	353.6	13.7	12.4
1964	236.8	335.8	292.6	0.6	12.8
1963	203.5	307.8	244.7	0.6 (est.)	12.0
1962	163.7	265.9	200.6	0.4 (est.)	8.2
				Amortization of Emergency Facilities	
1961	190.2	210.5	326.8	$ 13.7	
1960	304.2	208.4	492.4		
1959	254.5	189.9	366.1	22.2	
1958	301.5	204.9	448.1	57.2	
1957	319.4	276.0	514.9	115.8	
1956	348.1	277.6	311.8	140.2	
1955	348.1	285.2	239.8	147.7	
1954	195.4	261.8	227.4	142.8	
1953	222.1	236.6	361.4	105.1	
1952	143.6	176.9	469.2	46.2	
1951	184.3	162.1	352.4	12.8	
1950	215.5	143.9	179.3	...	
1949	165.9	119.7	179.1	...	
1948	129.6	146.0	275.2	...	
1947	127.1	114.0	206.6	...	
1946	88.6	68.7	201.0	...	

sizable increases in wages and fringe benefits, contending that large steel profits would permit these increases without affecting the prices of finished steel. The steel industry spokesman argued this was not possible; any *sizable* wage increase would have to be passed along in the form of higher prices. There was considerable government pressure for a settlement without the need for a price increase in order to avoid the threat of further inflation.

In May of 1959, the union paid for a series of full-page newspaper advertisements stating its position. A portion of one of these ads, which cites financial data from the United States Steel Corporation's 1952 and 1958 annual reports, is reproduced as Exhibit 4.

Because neither side would compromise its position, a nationwide steel strike resulted, lasting from July until mid-November. The union's advertisement, while failing to arouse sufficient public reaction to prevent the strike, raised some questions about the financial accounting practices of the United States Steel Corporation.

EXHIBIT 4

STEEL WORKERS' SHARE OF
STEEL INDUSTRY'S INCOME HAS
NOT INCREASED SINCE 1952

TRUE, there have been wage increases, but because fewer men are making more steel, the total labor costs have remained the same.

Please examine these LABOR COSTS *

1952 .... 42.1¢ of each sales dollar
1958 .... 42.8¢ of each sales dollar

(notice they are about the same)

Now examine the NET PROFITS

1952 .... $143,678,740
1958 301,558,231

(profits have DOUBLED)

	1952	1958
* Sales (millions)	$3,137.4	$3,472.2
Number of employees	294,263	223,490
Employment costs (millions)	$1,322.1	$1,488.5

SOURCE: *Wall Street Journal*, May 14, 1959. Reproduced by permission.

On December 8, 1959, J. S. Seidman, president of the AICPA, released to the press a statement explaining the issues in the steel strike:

The (steel) industry's contention was that under conventional accounting, depreciation is calculated based on original dollar cost, and that this is inadequate because it fails to give effect to the tremendous change that has taken place in the purchasing power of the dollar, as a result of which it would cost many more dollars today to replace the plant than were originally spent. The industry maintains that realistic profits should be figured by reference to replacement figures. On that basis, the industry's profits are one-half of what the financial statements show.

The labor officials contend that original cost is all that should be recovered, and that anything in excess of that is a profit. Furthermore, they say that the original cost should be spread over the expected period in which the plant will be used. However, the companies have been following the tax laws in the way they write off depreciation, and the tax laws have allowed a higher write-off to be bunched in early years and counterbalanced by a lower write-off in later years. The figures presented by the steel industry cover the earlier years where there is the higher write-off. The labor people say that the depreciation amounts should be reduced by this excess write-off in the early years. Reducing the depreciation would result in an increase in profits.

All of this raises a question as to whether the conventional accounting use of historical dollars is meaningful in an inflationary period.

In commenting on the problem, he expressed a personal opinion that when inflation is significant, managements should issue two financial statements, one in the conventional form based on historical cost and the other adjusted to show the effects of inflation on earnings and financial position. "Basically," he said, "the problem is disclosure." The American Institute's accounting procedures committee had encouraged in 1948 and again in 1953 the use of supplementary financial statements showing the need for retention of a substantial portion of current income (or procurement of funds otherwise) to maintain assets at the same level of productivity. Mr. Seidman felt, in his personal opinion, that the supplementary statements should indicate the effects of inflation on every aspect of financial statements, including bank balances, long-term liabilities, lease commitments, and other items.

Mr. Seidman stated that historical and price-level statements side by side would be useful to indicate what part of the affairs of a business was due to "managing" and what part to government fiscal factors.

The U.S. Steel 1960 annual report contained the following comment related to depreciation:

> . . . Past and prospective dollar debasement is now a continuing—and often overriding—concern of business and government. It intrudes upon, complicates, and warps all business, saving, investing, wage, and tax decisions. It has introduced immeasurable injustice. . . .
>
> Illustrative of the seriousness of these matters are the facts of U.S. Steel. For the postwar years, 1946–1960, U.S. Steel's recorded wear and exhaustion—sometimes called depreciation—aggregated $2,872 million. Of this amount $2,671 million was deductible in determining taxable income. If, each year, depreciation had been sufficient to recover the appropriate buying power—not just the number—of dollars originally expended, the total would have been $4,276 million. The deficiency from this amount needed to stay even was $1,605 million, on which taxes were levied as though it were income. Tax destruction to the flow of dollars that maintains the nation's tools of production in their status quo not only darkens the prospect that new jobs will be created by productive investment, it threatens continuation of existing jobs. It directly handicaps all corporations having depreciable property and especially those corporations heavily invested in long-life facilities. It indirectly handicaps all other enterprises who do business with them as their capabilities as customer or supplier are undermined.
>
> In former times when the tax rate on corporate income was smaller and inflation was not a big factor, these same injustices and impediments to growth were present but not of as great moment. But with the enormous increases in the tax rate until it is now over 50 percent—some *three* times the prewar rates—they are indeed worthy of most serious consideration and correction if we are to have economic growth.

1962 to 1967

In 1962, U.S. Steel obtained some relief in its continuing struggle with the problem of inadequate depreciation. Inflationary pressure on the economy was diminishing; the adoption of Revenue Ruling 62–21 by the Internal Revenue Service set forth new guideline lives for depreciable assets, frequently shorter than the lives previously used; and U.S. Steel added $44 million to the wear and exhaustion amounts previously determined, as a direct result of the new guideline procedures.

In addition, the investment tax credit provided by the Revenue Act of 1962 (later amended and liberalized in the Revenue Act of 1964) provided for U.S. Steel an immediate reduction of $8.2 million in federal income taxes. The investment tax credit was intended to stimulate capital investment; it allowed a credit directly against the company's federal income tax liability of 7 percent of the cost of "qualified" depreciable property. A sliding scale of eligibility for the credit was established on the basis of the life of the property. Assets with a life of eight years or more received the full credit; assets with a life of less than four years were not eligible. U.S. Steel's 1962 annual report stated:

> The guideline procedure and the investment credit against federal income tax are recognitions of the vital depreciation problem that exists. They serve currently to lift total wear and exhaustion to an amount more nearly approaching true depreciation based on current dollars. However, they fall short in dealing with the fundamental facility replacement problem arising from inflation, since total depreciation over the lives of the facilities is still limited to original cost.

The enactment of the investment tax credit raised certain accounting questions regarding the timing for recognition of the benefit in reported income. Two methods evolved for financial statement recognition of the immediate cash benefit from the reduction in the tax liability, based on differing interpretations of the nature of the credit. Proponents of the belief that the credit was a selective reduction in taxes recognized the full amount of the credit in the year of property acquisition—the "flow-through" method; the other group believed the credit to be a reduction in a cost chargeable to future accounting periods, and thus deferred the benefit over the life of the assets being depreciated—the "deferral" method.

The Accounting Principles Board of the AICPA, in March 1964, issued *Opinion No. 4* (superseding its *Opinion No. 2* of December 1962), which, although continuing to find the deferral method preferable, recognized the flow-through method as acceptable. This opinion was in harmony with the Securities and Exchange Commission's *Accounting Series Release No. 96*, issued in January 1963, recognizing both methods.

Following the issuance of APB *Opinion No. 4,* many steel companies adopted the flow-through method of accounting for the investment credit, and also in 1964 recognized the portion of the credit deferred in earlier years. *Barron's* commented, on February 1, 1965:

Some of the corporate reports issued last month call for close analysis . . . steel companies . . . differed widely in the treatment of the investment tax credit. In other instances, investors will have to scrutinize annual reports to learn how management has tailored "profits."

In its 1964 annual report, U.S. Steel continued to defer the investment credit:

. . . The investment tax credit provided for in the Revenue Act of 1962, as amended in 1964, amounted to $12.0 million in 1963 and $13.4 million in 1964. The amount for 1963 was included in wear and exhaustion of facilities in that year and added to the reserve for depreciation; because of amendment of the law, the amount for 1964 was included in a provision for income taxes and established as a deferred investment credit to be amortized over the lives of the property acquired. . . .

Bethlehem Steel Corporation, the second largest steel producer, reported in its annual report for 1964 (see Exhibit 5):

. . . Net income for 1964 reflects a reduction in the provision for federal income taxes equal to the 1964 investment tax credit of approximately $18,300,000

EXHIBIT 5

BETHLEHEM STEEL CORPORATION

Selected Financial Statistics, 1955–67
(millions of dollars)

	Net Income	Depre- ciation	Capital Expen- ditures	Investment Tax Credit Taken	Investment Tax Credit Deferred
1967	$130.4	$214.8	$338.3	$10.1	. . .
1966	170.9	212.0	265.1	20.4	. . .
1965	150.0	196.1	377.6	20.6	. . .
1964	147.9	181.2	385.7	18.3*	$(6.3)*
1963	102.5	163.7	177.3	4.1	4.4
1962	88.7	155.5	144.5	2.2	2.4
1961	122.4	98.1	114.3	. . .	. . .
1960	121.2	94.2	169.9	. . .	. . .
1959	117.2	97.6	86.7	. . .	. . .
1958	137.7	108.7	91.4	. . .	. . .
1957	191.0	110.6	209.0	. . .	. . .
1956	161.4	102.4	211.6	. . .	. . .
1955	180.2	102.6	98.5	. . .	. . .

* A total of $24.6 million was taken in 1964, which is the sum of $18.3 million applicable for 1964 and $6.3 million eliminated as deferrals from prior years.

plus $6,300,000 representing that portion . of the investment tax credit that was applicable to 1962 and 1963 which was deferred in those years.

Another large steel producer, Republic Steel, reported:

. . . The credits for investments in depreciable property . . . for the current year amounting to $5,295,000 and the deferred credits for 1962 and 1963 amounting to $3,837,000 were applied in 1964 as a reduction of the provision for federal taxes on income. . . .

Of the major steel producers, only U.S. Steel and Inland Steel continued to defer the investment tax credit.

1968

In early 1968, economic pressures on steel producers began to increase. The labor contract with the U.S. Steelworkers expired August 1, 1968. There was widespread expectation that a strike would ensue, and steel users stockpiled inventories heavily. The high volume of ordering resulted in capacity operations, requiring the use of less efficient, marginal productive facilities. In addition, foreign imports of steel were growing substantially.

When the labor contract was settled in July without dispute, production fell sharply. Steel users began to reduce their heavy inventories and industry analysts anticipated, in September, that a normal pattern of ordering would not be resumed until January 1969. Further downward pressure on steel production resulted from continued importation of foreign steels at prices as much as $35 a ton lower than domestic producer prices.

The cumulative effect of these pressures was to sharply reduce third-quarter profits for most steel producers located in the United States. Profit declines for the third quarter of 1968 as compared with the third quarter of 1967 were reported in the *Wall Street Journal* as:

U.S. Steel	− 70%
Bethlehem	− 6
Republic	− 31
Jones & Laughlin	− 86
Inland	+ 20
Youngstown Sheet & Tube	− 57
Armco	+ 51

U.S. Steel's third-quarter earnings declined despite an increase in third-quarter sales in 1968. Earnings dropped from the 1967 figure of $36.2 million ($0.67 a share) to $11 million ($0.21 a share) in 1968.

The apparent effect of the decreased third-quarter activity for most manufacturers of steel would have been more severe except for changes made by the majority of the firms in their depreciation policies and in accounting for the investment credit. Exhibit 6 shows the company's earn-

EXHIBIT 6

Operating Earnings for Three Months Ended September 30, 1968
(millions)

	Accelerated Depreciation		Straight-Line Depreciation	
	Earnings	EPS	Earnings	EPS
Bethlehem	...	...	$21.7	$0.49
Republic	$ 8.2	$0.53	11.3	0.72
Jones & Laughlin.	(3.48)*	(0.29)*	0.8	0.05
Inland	9.1**	0.49**	13.7†	0.75†
Youngstown ..... N.A.	N.A.	N.A.	2.5	0.24
U.S. Steel	11.0**	0.21**	33.0	0.61

   ° Loss.
   °° Amortizing investment credit.
   † Does not include nonrecurring gain from property sale of $4.1 million at $0.22
per share.

Operating Earnings for Nine Months Ended September 30, 1968
(millions)

	Accelerated Depreciation		Straight-Line Depreciation	
	Earnings	EPS	Earnings	EPS
Bethlehem	...	...	$115.3	$2.53
Republic	$ 56.1	$3.55	65.0	4.11
Jones & Laughlin	22.5	2.71	26.8	3.25
Inland	50.6*	2.77*	63.7	3.49
Youngstown ... N.A.	N.A.	N.A.	26.8	2.51
U.S. Steel	139.5*	2.58*	205.6	3.80

   ° Amortizing investment credit.
   SOURCE: Computed from *Wall Street Journal* articles of October 1968.

ings for the three- and nine-month periods ended September 30, 1968
under two alternative depreciation methods.

Bethelehem changed from accelerated to straight-line depreciation on
new acquisitions in 1968; equipment acquired in prior periods continued
to be depreciated by accelerated methods. Firms changing from accelerated to straight-line depreciation on all depreciable assets included National Steel, Republic Steel, and Youngstown Sheet & Tube. Inland Steel
changed to straight-line depreciation on all assets and, additionally, flowed
through the investment credit generated by 1968 capital acquisitions. The
deferred investment credit for prior acquisition continued to be amortized
on a straight-line basis.

At the end of the third quarter of 1968, among the major producers,
only U.S. Steel continued to defer the investment credit over the life of
the related assets and to use accelerated depreciation for all assets.

In October 1968, U.S. Steel management stated:

In view of the announced changes by other companies in the industry, U.S. Steel is studying its situation to determine whether it also should change its procedures so as to avoid the possibility of improper conclusions being drawn by attempts to compare operating results that are not comparable.

U.S. Steel said that if it had adopted the depreciation and investment credit accounting methods used by other companies, its earnings would have been significantly higher, increasing earnings to $33 million or $0.61 a share from the third quarter, and $205.6 million or $3.80 a share for the year to date, from $0.21 per share for the third quarter and $2.58 for the year to date previously reported.

Acquisition Challenge

One factor which was considered by many to have a bearing on the accounting change made by the steel companies was the take-over of Jones & Laughlin by Ling-Temco-Vought. Many of the smaller steel producers were considered attractive acquisitions because of their high cash flows, understated assets, low earnings per share and depressed price-earnings ratios.

As an admitted direct response to this potential problem, Armco Steel had changed to straight-line depreciation methods during the first half of 1968. This change had added $0.46 to earnings per share for the first half of the year. By consolidation of European operations, an additional $0.19 per share had been obtained; earnings for the first six months thus ran 25 percent above the comparable period in 1967.

Questions

1. Comment on U.S. Steel's accounting for depreciation between 1946 and 1968.
2. Should U.S. Steel change to straight-line depreciation in 1968?
3. How should U.S. Steel account for the investment tax credit?

Case 14–2. TRANS WORLD AIRLINES, INCORPORATED

Changes in Depreciation Estimates

In early January 1962, the executive committee of the board of directors of Trans World Airlines (TWA) met to discuss certain matters concerning the financial statements to be included in the 1962 annual reports to stockholders. In particular, the committee was trying to determine how best to show for fiscal 1961 financial reporting purposes (*a*) that a large portion of TWA's existing fleet of Lockheed Constellations had become technologically obsolete and probably would be taken out of service before they were fully depreciated, and (*b*) that most of the company's piston fleet of Lockheed Constellations would probably be sold at prices considerably below their previously estimated salvage (residual) values.

The problem facing the TWA executive committee arose primarily because of two factors. First, the adoption of jet aircraft by the company had proceeded at a faster rate than originally anticipated. And, second, there was a worldwide excess of second-hand piston aircraft for sale.

Company Background

TWA was the only United States air carrier providing scheduled service on both a transcontinental and transatlantic route system. It was the third largest domestic carrier, having a route system connecting major East Coast cities with the West Coast as well as extensive routes in the midwest and southwest. As a United States international carrier, TWA ranked second, with a route system that included cities in Western Europe, North Africa, the Middle East and Southeast Asia.

On September 30, 1961, TWA reported current assets of approximately $133 million and current liabilities of about $99 million. Total assets amounted to some $525 million. Exhibit 1 shows comparative balance sheets for the years 1960–61.

During recent years TWA's reported profits had varied greatly. After showing small losses for the three-year period 1956–59, the introduction of jet service on TWA routes in late 1959 turned 1959 and 1960 into profitable years for the company.[1] By mid-1961, however, delays in acquiring additional jets had placed TWA at a serious disadvantage in comparison with its major competitors, and the company was losing substantial amounts of money on its passenger and cargo operations.

During recent years, TWA had also suffered from a lack of continuity of top management. The airline had had six different presidents since the end of World War II. In fact, the company did not have a president from July 1960 until April 1961.

Jet Acquisitions

In 1955, TWA began planning for the acquisition of jet aircraft. In all, some 33 Boeing 707s and 30 Convair 880s costing about $300 million were

---

[1] Commercial jet service by U.S. carrier was introduced internationally by Pan American World Airways in October 1958, and domestically by National Airlines in December 1958. TWA's first domestic jet went into service in March of 1959 while its first international jet service was introduced in November 1959.

EXHIBIT 1

TRANS WORLD AIRLINES, INC.

Comparative Balance Sheet
(in millions)

ASSETS	9/30/61	12/31/60
Current Assets:		
Cash and U.S. government securities	$ 33.5	$ 64.2
Accounts receivable (net)................	55.8	30.8
Inventory of spare parts, etc.	14.3	15.3
Prepayments	29.5	2.7
Total Current Assets	$133.1	$113.0
Noncurrent assets and investments	$ 51.7	$ 21.3
Property and equipment:		
At cost	$554.9	$503.3
Less depreciation	229.3	208.6
Net	$315.6	$294.7
Deferred charges	$ 24.9	$ 21.2
Total Assets	$525.3	$450.2
LIABILITIES AND EQUITY		
Current Liabilities:		
Accounts payable	$ 36.8	$ 35.0
Debt due within 12 months	13.4	12.7
Salaries and wages	11.6	10.6
Taxes	11.3	7.6
Other liabilities	25.7	11.0
Total Current Liabilities	$ 98.8	$ 76.9
Long term debt	$286.5	$223.2
Deferred credits	26.9	24.1
Total Liabilities	$412.2	$324.2
Stockholders' equity:		
Capital paid in	$ 82.3	$ 82.3
Retained earnings	30.8	43.7
Total Stockholders' Equity	$113.1	$126.0
Total Liabilities and Equity	$525.3	$450.2

ordered for delivery between 1959 and 1960. In addition, in 1957, TWA ordered some $90 million worth of Lockheed Constellations and other piston aircraft to meet TWA's aircraft requirements until the delivery of the jets. The acquisition of these piston aircraft was financed through bank loans and a common stock issue.

Originally, TWA's jets were to be delivered to TWA's holding company, the Hughes Tool Company, which in turn would lease the planes to TWA on a short-term basis. However, during 1959, as the jets were delivered to Hughes Tool, Hughes Tool found it increasingly more difficult to meet the payments for the jets. As a result, Hughes Tool released some of the jets it had ordered to other airlines and sought to borrow money to finance the acquisition of the remainder of the ordered jets.

Subsequently, on December 30, 1960, TWA concluded a $164 million loan agreement with nine banks and two insurance companies (an additional $117 million was subsequently borrowed from this same group) for the financing of its jet fleet. As a condition for receiving the loan, representatives of the Hughes Tool Company, owner of nearly 80 percent of the outstanding TWA common stock, signed an agreement to deposit their company's TWA stock in a voting trust controlled by three trustees.[2] Two of the trustees represented the lending institutions. The third trustee represented Hughes Tool.

In February 1961, the voting trust called a special stockholders' meeting and reconstituted the board of directors. The board, in turn, elected a new president. He assumed office in April 1961.

The new management, in an effort to obtain "jet parity" with its major competitors, immediately ordered 26 additional Boeing 707 jets. As a result, TWA's jet fleet was expected to grow from 28 planes in January 1961 to 73 planes by the end of 1962. This substantial growth of the jet fleet, together with the rapid deterioration of the used plane market, raised the question of what to do with the existing piston fleet, which totaled 121 aircraft at the end of 1961.

Depreciation Policy for Piston Planes

Over the years, TWA changed its depreciation to reflect the changing conditions in the airline industry. Typically, because of constant parts replacement and maintenance, the company's airplanes experienced physical lives longer than the lives used for depreciation accounting. TWA's depreciation accounting was based on shorter periods than the physical life because planes were usually replaced long before they were physically exhausted by a more economical plane.

In the early 1950s, most airlines, including TWA, used five-year lives and 5 percent residual values for their planes. However, the Korean war and subsequent events, including the growth of the airline business throughout the world, created a large demand for used piston aircraft. As a result, prices considerably above net book values were frequently realized from the sale of such planes.

In 1956, in an attempt to reduce the high book profits on the sale of used aircraft and in line with Internal Revenue Service objections, the

---

[2] For the events leading up to the creation of the voting trust, see: Charles J. V. Murphy and T. A. Wise, "The Problem of Howard Hughes," *Fortune*, Vol. 59 (January 1959), pp. 79–82; "A Deadline for Howard Hughes?" *Fortune*, Vol. 60 (July 1959), pp. 112–113; T. A. Wise, "The Bankers and the Spook," *Fortune*, Vol. 63 (March 1961), p. 142.

Civil Aeronautics Board (CAB) proposed that the airlines use seven-year lives and 15 percent residual values. TWA adopted the CAB proposals for its aircraft acquired after January 1, 1956.

In 1958, the CAB made its 1956 depreciation accounting proposal mandatory for all planes, whereupon the airlines took the CAB to court and won a judgment in the Supreme Court invalidating this rule on the grounds that the CAB wasn't given the right to set depreciation schedules for financial reporting purposes. At this point, TWA reviewed its depreciation policy and revised downward the residual values used, from 15 to 5 percent for earlier models and 10 percent for later ones. The company continued to use depreciation lives of seven years for its piston aircraft, however.

During 1960, it became apparent to TWA's management that the net book value of many of the company's piston aircraft probably exceeded current market value. However, it appeared to management that these aircraft would remain in service until depreciation charges (at current rates) would eliminate any excess of net book value over market value. Accordingly, management decided that the current depreciation rates in force during 1960 were adequate and, consequently, it was not necessary to mention in the 1960 annual report the possibility of losses on the sale of the aircraft.

Action by the SEC

During early 1961, TWA was planning to offer to its stockholders $100 million of 6.5 percent subordinated income debentures with detachable warrants. The preliminary prospectus in connection with this issue made reference to the market value of the piston planes in the following manner:

If any of these types of aircraft [the piston aircraft] are sold in the immediate future, the Company would expect to record sizable book losses, the amounts of which are not determinable.

This statement did not completely satisfy the SEC, which asked that reference to the possible book losses due to premature disposal be made in the auditor's opinion. (The 1960 year-end statements were still being used at the time.) The auditor's opinion in the final prospectus thus stated:

In our opinion, except that . . . and subject to the possibility of losses, presently indeterminable, arising in the event of disposal of surplus aircraft . . . present fairly . . . in conformity with generally accepted accounting principles.

The Independent Auditors Recommend an Accounting Policy Change

In July, after the issuance of the subordinated debentures, and after discussions with the TWA management, the company's independent auditors suggested a change in TWA's accounting policy. The auditors recommended with respect to aircraft that had become, or were scheduled to become, surplus to the operating requirements of the company, that:

a) The terminal depreciation date of aircraft and related equipment be changed to coincide with the date on which it is anticipated the aircraft will be removed from scheduled service.

b) Residual values be reviewed and established as the lower of present residual value or estimated market value.

Throughout the late summer and fall of 1961, various staff members as well as members of top management discussed ways to implement the above recommendations. The board of directors also discussed this matter and at their December meeting directed the executive committee to determine what, if any, adjustments should be made in the company's depreciation policies concerning surplus or obsolete piston aircraft.

The Situation in Late 1961

During 1961, TWA had recorded book profits on the sale of some of its older types of aircraft, but had shown sizable book losses on the sale of several of the newer Lockheed Constellations bought after 1957 (Exhibit 2).

EXHIBIT 2

TRANS WORLD AIRLINES, INC.

Summary of 1961 Aircraft Sales

A. Aircraft (reverse chronological order):	Book Profit (Loss)	
Number Type	Recorded	Deferred
4—Lockheed L–1049H	$(2,725,521)	
1—Lockheed L–1049G	(234,849)	
1—Lockheed L–749A	65,937	
5—Lockheed L–049	77,806	
20—Martin M–404	228,102	$1,744,563*
1—Douglas DC–4	54,471	
B. Deferred profit from prior years' sales carried into 1961	272,865	
C. Reversal of 1960 profit on two repossessed 1649A's	(844,124)	
Total	$(3,105,313)	$1,744,563

* Profit on conditional sales contracts ·is recorded as payments are received (see items B and C).

By the end of 1961, it became unmistakably clear to top management that the market for used Lockheed Constellations had become saturated, and that prices considerably below present residual values would probably be received by the company when its Lockheed Constellation fleet was

EXHIBIT 3

TRANS WORLD AIRLINES, INC.

Sales Price for Aircraft, 1961–64
(in thousands)

Aircraft	1961 (Actual) Sales		1962–64 (Est.) Sales	
Type*	Isolated	Fleet	Isolated	Fleet
L–1649A	$400	$200	$250	$40
L–1049G	200	100	150	40
L–1049A	175	75	125	40
L–749A	125	40	100	20
L–049	115	20	75	15

° All Lockheed Constellations.

retired. Exhibit 3 shows management's estimates of the anticipated sales price of its Lockheed Constellations during the years 1962–64, inclusive. These estimates of future sales prices for Lockheed Constellations were considerably below the present net book value and the existing residual values set on the aircraft (see Exhibit 4).

Remaining Service Lives

In addition to the effect on the used plane market, the introduction of jets made the TWA's Lockheed L–1649A aircraft almost obsolete. Costing over $2 million each, these planes were delivered to TWA between May 1957 and June 1958, considerably later than the delivery dates of comparable planes of other airlines and just a few months before the delivery of the first jets to commercial airlines. These Lockheed Constellations purchased by TWA had exceedingly long ranges (they were able to fly nonstop from Los Angeles to Paris or New York to Athens, a feat that at the time no jet was able to perform). However, they were best suited for precisely the same type of service as the jets, and public preference for jet service drastically shortened the Lockheed L–1649A's useful life. Consequently, management decided to retire the L–1649A from service as soon as possible.

Other considerations contributed to a decision to retire the obsolete L–1649A's. First, TWA was losing a substantial amount of money. Since the piston flights as a general rule were then unprofitable (whereas most jet flights were making money) and since the L–1649A's were the most uneconomical planes to operate over the short distances now assigned to the piston fleet, there was considerable pressure to take them out of active service at an early date. This pressure was compounded by a second consideration, namely, 1961's lower than expected growth in airplane travel, both for the industry in general and for TWA in particular.

EXHIBIT 4

TRANS WORLD AIRLINES, INC.

Selected Data on Piston Aircraft Fleet Based on Existing Terminal Depreciation Dates
and Residual Values Projected to December 31, 1962

Number	Type*	Average Age (Years)	Terminal Depr. Dates (Fleet)	Net Book Value† (thousands) Fleet	Net Book Value† (thousands) Per Aircraft	Residual Value Per Aircraft
12	L–1649A, cargo	4	5–64 to 6–65	$18,882	$1,573	$ 238,000 (10%) ‡
9	L–1649A, passenger	4	5–64 to 12–64	12,750	1,417	238,000 (10%)
3	L–1649A, charter passenger	4	6–64 and 7–64	3,899	1,300	238,000 (10%)
24	L–1049G	6	3–62 to 9–63	11,700	487	195,400 (10%)
5	L–1049A	9	Fully depr.§	1,193	239	124,200 (10%)
25	L–749A	11	Fully depr.§	3,288	132	89,200 (10%)
12	L–749	14	Fully depr.§	1,030	86	45,000 (5%)
25	L–049	16	Fully depr.§	1,426	57	35,000 (5%)
115 #				$54,168		$14,667,600

* All Lockheed Constellations.
† Includes spare equipment.
‡ Percent of original cost.
§ Certain modification costs being depreciated to Dec. 31, 1962.
\# Does not include five repossessed aircraft (three 1649A, two 1049A) or an FC–82 aircraft used as an engine carrier.

A final consideration was that during 1960, TWA had attempted to counteract the uneconomical passenger carrying use of the L–1649A's by converting 12 of the planes to all-cargo configurations at a total cost of over $3 million. However, the need for these planes didn't develop as expected, largely because regular passenger-carrying jets also had large cargo-carrying capacity.

Retirement Plans

An overall retirement plan for all piston planes had been revised by the end of 1961. The L–049 fleet (refer to Exhibit 4) would be grounded at the end of 1961, largely because they lacked weather radar which would be mandatory after January 1, 1962 by CAB order. A decision had already been reached not to make the necessary modifications to the L–409 fleet because the modifications would not be economically justified. Further retirement plans of regular passenger aircraft would see the

EXHIBIT 5

TRANS WORLD AIRLINES, INC.

Proposed Revision of Aircraft Residuals
and Terminal Depreciation Dates

Schedule A

Number	Type	Residual	Terminal Depr. Date
Aircraft other than L–1649A:			
24:	L–1049G	3%	No change (3–62 to 9–63)
5:	L–1049A	3	No change (fully depr.)
25:	L–749A	3	No change (fully depr.)
12:	L–749	3	No change (fully depr.)
25:	L–049	3	No change (fully depr.)
L–1649A aircraft:			
2:	Reg. pass.	3%	12–31–61
1:	Reg. pass.	3	4–30–62
4:	Reg. pass.	3	9–30–62
2:	Reg. pass.	3	4–30–63
3:	Charter	3	No change (6–64 and 7–64)
4:	Cargo	10*	12–31–61
8:	Cargo	3	No change (5–64 to 4–65)

Schedule B

Aircraft other than L–1649A's:			
Same as Schedule A.			
L–1649A aircraft:			
9:	Reg. pass.	3%	12–31–61
3:	Charter	3	12–31–61
4:	Cargo	10*	12–31–61
8:	Cargo	3	12–31–63

* It was anticipated that these aircraft would be sold in early 1962 at about a 10 percent residual figure.

L–1049A's retired at the end of 1961. The L–1649A passenger aircraft would be taken out of service between the end of 1961 and the middle of 1963, on the average nearly two years before they would become fully depreciated. The L–1049G's would be retired about as they became fully depreciated during 1962 and 1963. Most of the L–749A fleet, already fully depreciated, would be used at least through 1964. Plans for the L–1649A charter aircraft were uncertain. It was anticipated that four of the L–1649A cargo aircraft would be sold early in 1962, while the remaining eight would be used indefinitely.

Alternatives Being Considered

In carrying out the board's October 1961 directive, the executive committee was considering the following four alternatives:

Plan 1. Continue with the present depreciation schedule (see Exhibit 4).

EXHIBIT 6

TRANS WORLD AIRLINES, INC.

Conceptual Scheme of Alternative Ways to Depreciate the Existing Piston Fleet
(end of service, 1962 in all plans)

Plan 1			Plan 2		
Seven-Year Useful Life, 10% Residual (Present Practice)			*Change Terminal Date to 12–31–62, 3% Residual (Normal Method)*		
	Annual Depr.	*Book Value Year-End*		*Annual Depr.*	*Book Value Year-End*
		$1,000			$1,000
1958	$129	871	1958	$129	871
1959	129	742	1959	129	742
1960	129	613	1960	129	613
1961	129	484	1961	291	322
1962	129	355	1962	292	30
1963	129	226	1963	...	...
1964	126	100	1964	...	...

Plan 3			Plan 4		
Change Terminal Date to 12–31–62, 3% Residual (Special Item in 1961)			*Change Terminal Date to 12–31–61, 3% Residual*		
	Annual Depr.	*Book Value Year-End*		*Annual Depr.*	*Book Value Year-End*
		$1,000			$1,000
1958	$129	871	1958	$129	871
1959	129	742	1959	129	742
1960	129	613	1960	129	613
1961	454	159	1961	583	30
1962	129	30	1962	000	30
1963	...	...	1963	...	...
1964	...	...	1964	...	...

Plan 2. Adopt the depreciation terminal dates and residuals shown in Exhibit 5, Schedule A and recompute the depreciation rates, retroactively effective as of January 1, 1961, to provide for depreciation to the residual value at the revised terminal date.

Plan 3. Adopt the same schedule as in Plan 2 and continue with the present depreciation levels to the new terminal dates while charging 1961 income with an additional charge, the sum of which would equal the adjustment of the residual rates plus the normal depreciation charges falling between the revised terminal dates and original terminal dates.

Plan 4. Adopt the depreciation terminal dates and residuals as shown in Exhibit 5, Schedule B and handle the excess as in Plan 3. A conceptual scheme illustrating each of these four plans is shown in Exhibit 6. The actual dollar amounts involved, which management considered to be quite material, particularly in view of an already expected $14 million loss, are shown in Exhibit 7.

EXHIBIT 7

TRANS WORLD AIRLINES, INC.

Total Depreciation Charges, By Plan, By Year
(in thousands)

A. Total Depreciation, By Year, for All Piston Plans

	1961	1962	1963	1964	1965
Plan 1	$20,106	$16,011	$11,509	$ 6,253	$ 551
Plan 2	36,242	18,694	7,659	3,701	436
Plan 3	41,010	12,748	6,620	3,360	380
Plan 4	48,829	9,370	6,162	19	...

*B. Increased (Decreased) Depreciation, By Year,
for Plans 2, 3, and 4*

	1961	1962	1963	1964	1965
Plan 2	$16,136	$ 2,683	$(3,850)	$(2,552)	$(115)
Plan 3	20,904	(3,263)	(4,889)	(2,893)	(171)
Plan 4	28,723	(6,641)	(5,347)	(6,234)	(551)

Because of the magnitude of the adjustment, in addition to deciding which plan to use, the executive committee also had to decide how the adjustment should be charged against income.

The option of making an adjustment by directly charging earned surplus was not available because of a CAB "clean surplus" rule.

Question

1. How should the company report to its stockholders the fact that the original estimates for calculating depreciation charges for the company's Lockheed Constellations were no longer valid in 1962?

CHAPTER 15

PRICE-LEVEL ACCOUNTING

Inflation is a condition of overall rising prices. There is widespread concern throughout the world over the future purchasing power of local currencies. The extent of this interest and the degree of inflation varies from country to country. For example, the purchasing power of the Brazilian cruzeiro declined about 60 percent during 1965, whereas the United States dollar depreciated only 2 percent. This chapter briefly covers some of the more simple technical questions about how inflation and purchasing power are measured by economists and accountants.

MEASURES OF INFLATION

Statisticians and economists measure inflation by selecting a sample of goods and services representative of the economy and recording their price movements, each item being weighted by its relative importance in terms of its total volume of sales related to the sales of all items. Next, a base year is selected and the index number 100 is assigned to represent that year's composite price. The sample's composite price index for subsequent years can then be compiled and compared to the base year to measure changes in the price-level index.

The Consumer Price Index prepared monthly by the Bureau of Labor Statistics of the United States Department of Labor is generally used as an indication of general price-level changes in the United States. The base period for this index is an average of the period 1957, 1958, and 1959. This index is a weighted average of the prices paid by the public for some 398 consumer products in 50 cities. The Consumer Price Index is often used in escalator clauses in wage and lease contracts. It is also recognized by the courts.

A broader measure of the changes in the overall general level of prices is the Implicit Price Deflator for the Gross National Product, which is the total value at current prices of final goods and services produced by a nation before deducting depreciation charges, other similar allowances, and institutional consumption of durable capital goods. This price index, published by the Office of Business Economics, United States Department of Commerce, is used to translate the gross national product from current prices to constant prices. Its base period is 1958.

Another commonly used price index is the Wholesale Price Index compiled by the Bureau of Labor Statistics. It measures price changes in primary producers' markets. Because of its limited coverage, this index is not considered a good measure of inflation.

According to the Consumer Price Index, consumer prices in the first quarter of 1970 were 32.5 percent higher than the base period and 173.8 percent higher than in 1940 (48.4 to 132.5). Similarly, the Implicit Price Deflator Index indicates aggregate prices increased 201.8 percent between 1940 and the first quarter of 1970 (43.9 to 132.5). Clearly, these two measures of price-level changes indicate different rates of inflation between 1940 and 1970. This difference has led to considerable controversy over which index is the more reliable measurement of inflation. The Implicit Price Deflator reflects broader price changes than the Consumer Price Index, since it includes a wider range of goods and services. However, it is apparently not as sensitive as the Consumer Price Index is to short-run price changes.

The principal virtue of the Consumer Price Index is the fact that it is more easily understood by the general public. The principal criticism of it is that it does not adequately take into account changes in product quality. Nevertheless, quality is not ignored, and over the years this index has generally proved to be a reasonably adequate measure of inflation.

Irrespective of how accurately inflation can be measured, there is no question that it has occurred almost continuously in the United States since the beginning of World War II. Also, there is evidence that it will continue for the foreseeable future. Inflation is inherent in the plans of many corporations and governmental agencies and few seem willing to pay the price of stopping it. Also, the public and private debt is now so enormous that should deflation occur, there would most probably be widespread defaulting of debts. Consequently, to support this debt, at least mild inflation will be tolerated. However, most likely, this inflation will lead to further debt expansion and further inflationary pressures.

BUSINESS CONSIDERATIONS

During inflationary periods, businessmen try to minimize their company's purchasing power losses and maximize its purchasing power gains so as to at least maintain the purchasing power equivalent of their stockholders' equity. The ways to do this are well known to businessmen. The problem is to achieve them in practice.

Cash, accounts receivable, and similar monetary assets are all exposed to purchasing power losses in an inflationary economy. For example, a 10,000-cruzeiro check deposited by a Brazilian businessman in the bank on January 1, 1970 will buy fewer goods on December 31, 1970. If the price-level index doubles during this period, the purchasing power of the check will be cut in half. The same is true of accounts and loans receivable held during the same period.

Accounts payable, long-term debt, and similar monetary liabilities are exposed to purchasing power gains. To the extent that these liabilities are extinguished with "cheaper" currency than originally obtained through the incurring of the liability, a company is better off.

Consequently, most businessmen during inflationary times seek to maintain a net monetary liability balance (i.e., monetary liabilities in excess of monetary assets), or at least the minimum net monetary asset balance possible.

To the extent feasible, managers operating in inflationary conditions shift their resources from monetary assets to physical assets, such as inventory, plant, or equipment. They assume that raw materials and finished goods inventories are protected against inflation as long as the prices of raw materials and finished goods keep pace with rate of inflation. Similarly, fixed assets are protected to the extent that their resale or replacement value rises with inflation and their related depreciation expense is recovered through price increases.

ACCOUNTING CONSIDERATIONS

Financial statements are prepared initially in terms of historical costs, and it is assumed that the local currency is a constant unit of measure. However, inasmuch as the amounts shown in the statements result from many transactions occurring at different times, the purchasing power equivalent of these various amounts will not be the same if inflation has taken place during the period when these transactions occurred.

In countries with extreme inflation, it is generally agreed that it is desirable to restate these historical-cost-based statements in terms of current purchasing power equivalents. However, in the United States, the annual rate of inflation has been relatively mild and there is considerable controversy as to the extent to which financial statements ought to be restated to reflect changes in the purchasing power. At present, the practice is not to adjust statements, although a few companies do publish supplemental statements showing the impact of inflation on their businesses.

Restatement Mechanism

Typically, the goal of restatement is to express the financial statements in terms of the purchasing power at the most recent balance sheet date so as to measure the purchasing power gains and losses on holding monetary items. As a practical matter, the process used to restate financial statements in stable amounts having the same purchasing power can be complicated or simple, depending on the particular company involved or the degree of precision sought. In all cases, however, the amounts are restated through the use of an index of changes in the general level of prices. Whether the indexes used for restatement should measure general price-level changes or price changes for specific items or classes of items is debatable. However, the current preference seems to be for using indexes that compare general price-level changes.

Restatement is a statistical procedure independent of other accounting principles and procedures. It starts with the historical cost data and the company's particular accounting policy. Consequently, the restatement process is independent of the accounting principles selected to prepare the statements.

For the purpose of restatement, all items in the financial statements are classified as either being monetary or nonmonetary items. Monetary items are those normally carried in the accounts at current cash values, such as cash, accounts receivable, accounts payable, and long-term debt. The remaining items are classified as nonmonetary. They include inventories, plant and equipment, and capital stock.

Monetary items are worth their face value. Consequently, monetary items do not need to be restated. They are automatically stated in current dollars. The purchasing power of these items does change, however. Consequently, monetary assets held during periods of inflation lose purchasing power, whereas holding monetary liabilities leads to a gain in purchasing power. As noted earlier, one of the principal objectives of restatement is to measure this net gain or loss from holding monetary items.

Nonmonetary items are restated in terms of the currency equivalent of the purchasing power at the time of their acquisition. This is achieved by multiplying the item's historical dollar cost by the current price-level index divided by the price-level index for the period of the original transaction. For example, using the Implicit Price Deflator index to obtain the 1970 current dollar equivalent of the original cost of an asset purchased in 1940, the original cost would be multiplied by 132.5 divided by 43.9, approximately 3.02. Thus, the difference in the amounts shown for nonmonetary assets on the historical-cost-based statements and the restated statements is due entirely to change in the measuring unit. No profit or loss results from this process. The adjustment simply restates the original investment in terms of the current purchasing power situation.

If the nonmonetary accounts and the beginning owners' equity balance are restated in current values and the monetary accounts are unchanged, the two sides of the balance sheet will be out of balance. This difference is the gain or loss from holding monetary items for the accounting period.

Illustration 15–1 presents a simple illustration of this procedure. The Bahia Corporation, a Brazilian company, has been in business one year. Its principal asset is land held for future development. All of the items on the year-end balance sheet have been held for one year, a period during which the local price-level index has doubled. This movement reflects a 50 percent depreciation in the local currency's purchasing power.

ILLUSTRATION 15–1

BAHIA CORPORATION

Balance Sheet
(Cr$ = cruzeiros)

ASSETS	Index = 100	Adjustments	Index = 200
Cash	Cr$10,000		Cr$10,000
Land, at cost	20,000	Cr$20,000 (1)	40,000
Total	Cr$30,000		Cr$50,000
LIABILITIES AND NET WORTH			
Notes payable	Cr$ 5,000		Cr$ 5,000
Capital	25,000	(Cr$25,000) (2)	50,000
Loss from net monetary assets	....	Cr$ 5,000 (3)	(5,000)
Total	Cr$30,000		Cr$50,000

Illustration 15–1 shows that the Bahia Corporation experienced a Cr$5,000 loss on net monetary assets held during its first year of operations. The determination of this loss involved restating in current values the nonmonetary items—land and the beginning owners' equity balance. Step (1) converted the original land cost to its current purchasing power equivalent by multiplying the beginning balance by the change in the price-level index, i.e., 200/100 or 2. Step (2) converted to current cruzeiros the beginning balance of the owners' equity. At this point, the restated assets total is Cr$5,000 less than the restated liabilities and net worth total. Therefore, Step (3) is necessary to bring the two sides of the balance sheet into balance.

If the Bahia Corporation had not been able to offset its monetary asset balance by the notes payable, the company's monetary loss would have been Cr$10,000. This assumes that the beginning owners' equity would have had to be Cr$30,000 to make the two sides of the unadjusted balance sheet balance. Therefore, the restated liabilities balance would have been Cr$60,000 before recognizing the monetary loss of Cr$10,000.

The gains and losses applicable to monetary items can be calculated directly on a monetary item-by-item basis. The Cruzeiro Corporation example included later in this chapter describes this procedure. It also shows how to restate sales, expenses, assets, liabilities, and net worth.

Degree of Restatement

There are three major points of view as to the degree to which financial statements in the United States should be restated in current dollars. These are: no restatement, limited restatement, and complete restatement showing monetary gains and losses.

Those advocating no price-level restatement argue that inflation has been mild in the United States and as such has not resulted in any gross misstatements of income. In addition, they point out: restatement is not considered a generally accepted accounting principle by the Accounting Principles Board or the Securities and Exchange Commission. Price-level adjusted statements would be confusing to the users of financial statements. Price-level adjustments are not acceptable for determining income tax liability. And, there is little demand for price-level adjusted statements. Other arguments include: there is no practical, easy method for making reliable price-level adjustments. The cost principle is easily understood and has proved a useful convention in practice. And, businessmen would not voluntarily adopt price-level accounting that resulted in lower profits, unless they were public utilities seeking to prove that their reported unadjusted cost-based income was overstated for rate-making decisions.

The proponents of limited price-level adjustments support restatement of only the inventory, fixed asset, and depreciation accounts. Generally, these people are sympathetic to the "no-restatement" point of view. However, they feel limited restatement might demonstrate to the taxation authorities the extent to which income taxes confiscate capital in times of inflation. Other advantages claimed for limited restatement are that it will provide management with cost data in current dollars for financial decisions, as well as indicate to stockholders whether or not a company's financial policy is designed to prevent an impairment of capital due to price-level changes. The limited restatement advocates also believe their approach avoids confusing readers of financial statements with the notions of losses and gains on monetary items.

The complete restatement supporters claim that their approach is necessary to avoid having net income measured partly in historical dollars and partly in current dollars, which might result from limited restatement. Also, they believe widespread adoption of their proposal would better increase the chances of some income tax relief. More importantly, however, they argue that matching revenue and expenses in current dollars and showing all balance sheet items in similar dollars would be more useful for measuring performance and judging the effectiveness of financial policies. In addition, the complete restatement proponents claim that the cumulative effect of inflation in the United States over the life of most long-lived assets and liabilities has been far from "mild," and that the notion of gains and losses on monetary items is well understood by most users of financial statements.

Other Issues

Irrespective of whether gains or losses due to inflation are measured on a limited or complete basis, at least four major questions still remain:

1. Should the net price-level gains or losses be charged directly to owners' equity or reported as a separate part of net income?
2. Should the restated figures be presented as the principal statements or only as supplemental statements? On a voluntary or compulsory basis?
3. Should the Consumer Price Index, the Gross National Product (GNP) Implicit Price Deflator or some other set of index numbers be used for restatement purposes?
4. To what extent should the meaning and significance of the price-level restated data and the index used be explained in accompanying foot-notes?

Accounting Research Study No. 6.   *Accounting Research Study No. 6,* by the staff of the Accounting Research Division of the AICPA, con-cluded that the preparation of financial statements showing the effects of price-level changes is feasible and desirable. The study supported the presentation of completely restated statements as a supplement to the statements based on historical cost. The study also expressed a preference for using the GNP Implicit Price Deflator for restatement purposes be-cause of its broad coverage. Nevertheless, the study also recognized that the Consumer Price Index could be used to approximate changes in the general price level.

APB Statement No. 3.   In June 1969, the APB published Statement No. 3, "Financial Statements Restated for General Price Level Changes." It recommended that comprehensive price-level statements be published as a supplement to historical-cost statements. Specific procedures suggested for price-level restatement were:

1. Both price-level statements and historical dollar statements should embody the same accounting principles.
2. An index of the general price level should be used—the GNP Im-plicit Price Deflator was suggested for the United States (except that the Bureau of Labor Statistics' Consumer Price Index might be used as a basis of approximating the GNP Implicit Price Deflator on a monthly basis).
3. General price-level financial statements should be presented in terms of the general purchasing power of the dollar at the latest balance sheet date.

4. Monetary and nonmonetary items should be distinguished for the preparation of price-level financial statements. The statement presentation should emphasize that general price-level gains and losses arise from holding monetary items. Distinguishing monetary and nonmonetary items, the APB believed, would allow (*a*) restatement of nonmonetary items in terms of general purchasing power and (*b*) recognition of general price-level gains and losses on monetary items. Those assets and liabilities that have both monetary and nonmonetary characteristics (debentures held as investment and convertible debt) should be classified as monetary or nonmonetary according to the purpose for which they are held.

5. Nonmonetary items should be restated to dollars of current purchasing power at the end of the period. In the case of inventory, the lower-of-cost-or-market rule should be applied to the restated cost.

6. Monetary assets and liabilities should be stated in dollars of *current* purchasing power. Therefore, for comparative purposes, prior period monetary assets would be updated to dollars of current general purchasing power.

7. The income statement items should be restated to the end-of-period current purchasing power.

8. General price-level gains and losses should be included in current net income, as a separate, clearly identified item.

9. General price-level statements of earlier periods should be updated to dollars of purchasing power at the end of each subsequent period for which they are presented as comparative information. (The APB noted that this "rolling forward" of prior restated results should be carefully described as an updating rather than a restatement of previous information.)

10. Restatement of financial statements of foreign branches or subsidiaries in combined or consolidated financial statements should be based on an index of general price levels in the United States. Foreign branch or subsidiary statements should be stated on an historical basis before restatement for general purchasing power of the U.S. dollar.

11. All general price-level information should be based on complete price-level calculations. As a minimum, the results presented should include sales, net general price-level gains and losses on monetary items, net income, extraordinary items, and common stockholders' equity.

12. The basis of preparation of general price-level information and what it purports to show should be clearly explained in the notes to the general price-level financial statements or other appropriate places. The explanation should include the following points:

a) The general price-level statements (or information) are supplementary to the basic historical-dollar financial statements.

b) All amounts shown in general price-level statements are stated in terms of units of the same general purchasing power by use of an index of changes in the general purchasing power of the dollar.

c) The general price-level gain or loss in the general price-level statements indicates the effects of inflation (or deflation) on the company's net holdings of monetary assets and liabilities. The company gains or loses general purchasing power as a result of holding these assets and liabilities during a period of inflation (deflation).

d) In all other respects, the same generally accepted accounting principles used in the preparation of historical-dollar statements are used in the preparation of general price-level statements (or information).

e) The amounts shown in the general price-level statements do not purport to represent appraised value, replacement cost, or any other measure of the current value of assets or the prices at which transactions would take place currently.

f) The general price-level statements (or information) of prior years presented for comparative purposes have been updated to current dollars. This restatement of prior years' general price-level statements is required to make them comparable with current information. It does not change the prior periods' statements in any way except to update the amounts to dollars of current general purchasing power.

13. Disclosure involving the following items should also be made:

a) The difference between the balance of retained earnings at the end of the preceding year in beginning-of-the-year dollars and at the beginning of the year in end-of-the-year dollars, which arises in the roll-forward process discussed in item 9 above should be explained as follows:

Retained earnings at the beginning of the year:

Restated to general purchasing power at the beginning of the year ... xxx
Amount required to update to general purchasing power at the
    end of the year xxx
Restated to general purchasing power at the end of the year xxx

b) The fact should also be disclosed that when assets are used or sold, federal income taxes are based on cost before restatement for general price-level changes, since inflation is not recognized in the Internal Revenue Code.

AN EXAMPLE: THE CRUZEIRO CORPORATION

The unadjusted statements of the Cruzeiro Corporation, a Brazilian company, are presented in Illustrations 15–2 and 15–3.[1] They will be used to illustrate the technique for adjusting for price-level changes.

ILLUSTRATION 15–2

CRUZEIRO CORPORATION

Comparative Balance Sheets, December 31, 1970 and 1969
(in cruzeiros)

ASSETS	1969	1970	LIABILITIES	1969	1970
Cash	10	20	Accounts payable	60	92
Accounts receivable	100	150			
Inventory	120	185			
Plant and equipment					
(at cost)	260	280	STOCKHOLDERS' EQUITY		
Less accumulated			Common stock	200	200
depreciation	(112)	(138)	Retained earnings	118	205
Total	378	497	Total	378	497

ILLUSTRATION 15–3

CRUZEIRO CORPORATION

1970 Income Statement
(in cruzeiros)

Sales	900
Cost of goods sold	(690)
Gross margin	210
Depreciation	26
Other expenses	97
Net Income	87

The following price index for the period 1960–70 reflects the changes in the year-end Brazilian government's wholesale price index. The index has been restated to show 1970 as the base year (1.0 = base period). These factors will be used to adjust the company's statements to a common purchasing power equivalent.

---

[1] This example is based on material presented in "A Practical Approach to Accounting for the Effects of Price-Level Changes in Brazil" by Thomas Y. S. Summer published in the December 31, 1963 issue of the Arthur Andersen *Chronical*.

December	Factor
1970	1.00
1969	1.45
1968	2.21
1967	2.98
1966	4.04
1965	5.48
1964	5.69
1963	7.16
1962	8.33
1961	10.16
1960	12.52

The price-level factors for the last four months of 1969 and 1970 are:

	1969	1970
September	1.66	1.17
October	1.57	1.13
November	1.50	1.06
December	1.45	1.00

The company's unadjusted balance sheets at the beginning (December 31, 1969) and at the end (December 31, 1970) of the calendar year 1970 are not comparable because the units of measurement in these balance sheets are cruzeiros of different dates and therefore of different purchasing power. Therefore, to make these balance sheets comparable, they will be adjusted to a common unit of measurement, namely, the cruzeiro (Cr$) as of December 31, 1970.

Monetary assets and liabilities at the end of 1970 are already stated in cruzeiros as of the closing balance sheet date. However, the monetary assets and liabilities at the beginning of the year must be translated into year-end cruzeiros so they may be compared with year-end balance sheet figures. The restatement of December 31, 1969 monetary

ILLUSTRATION 15–4

CRUZEIRO CORPORATION

Net Monetary Assets

December 31, 1969 Balances	Before Adjustment	Adjustment Factor	After Adjustment
Cash	Cr$ 10	1.45	Cr$ 14
Receivables	100	1.45	145
Accounts payable	(60)	1.45	(87)
Net Monetary Assets	Cr$ 50		Cr$ 72

assets and liabilities is shown in Illustration 15–4. The adjustment factor of 1.45 is based on the 45 percent increase in the general price level that occurred between December 31, 1969 and December 31, 1970 (i.e., 1.45 = 1.45/1).

The company's inventories are stated at cost in terms of cruzeiros as of date of purchase. To make the beginning and year-end inventory figures comparable, it is necessary to translate them into year-end cruzeiros. Assuming that inventories are valued on the first-in, first-out method and that they represent purchases made during the last months of each year, their restatement to the December 31, 1970 price level is accomplished as shown in Illustration 15–5. The adjustment factors applied are based on increases in the price level from date of purchase to December 31, 1970, as shown by the monthly price-level index.

ILLUSTRATION 15–5

CRUZEIRO CORPORATION

Inventories

	Before Adjustment	Adjustment Factor	After Adjustment
December 31, 1969 Balance			
Purchases:			
October, 1969	Cr$ 30	1.57	Cr$ 47
November, 1969	40	1.50	60
December, 1969	50	1.45	73
Year-end inventory	Cr$120		Cr$180
December 31, 1970 Balance			
Purchases:			
September, 1970	Cr$ 25	1.17	Cr$ 29
October, 1970	45	1.13	51
November, 1970	55	1.06	58
December, 1970	60	1.00	60
Year-end inventory	Cr$185		Cr$198

Typically, the greatest distortion due to inflation is found in the property, plant, and equipment accounts. In order to adjust the property accounts and the related reserves for depreciation to the year-end price level, it is necessary first to analyze the accounts by dates of acquisition. In this example we will assume all acquisitions were made at year-end for cash. The appropriate restatement factors are then applied to the cost and reserve balances as shown in Illustration 15–6. Combining the above price-level adjustments calculations, the adjusted balance sheets are shown in Illustration 15–7.

ILLUSTRATION 15-6

CRUZEIRO CORPORATION

Plant and Equipment

	Before Adjustment		Adjust-ment	After Adjustment	
	Cost	Depr.	Factor	Cost	Depr.
December 31, 1969					
Investments:					
1964	Cr$180	Cr$ 90	5.69	Cr$1,024	Cr$512
1965	50	20	5.48	274	110
1968	20	2	2.21	44	4
1969	10	...	1.45	14	...
Plant and equipment	Cr$260	Cr$112		Cr$1,356	Cr$626
December 31, 1970					
Investments:					
1964	Cr$180	Cr$108	5.69	Cr$1,024	Cr$614
1965	50	25	5.48	274	137
1968	20	4	2.21	44	9
1969	10	1	1.45	14	1
1970	20	...	1.00	20	...
Plant and equipment	Cr$280	Cr$138		Cr$1,376	Cr$761

ILLUSTRATION 15-7

CRUZEIRO CORPORATION

Comparative Balance Sheets, December 31, 1969 and 1970
(in cruzeiros)

	Before Adjustment		After Adjustment	
	1969	1970	1969	1970
Cash	10	20	14	20
Accounts receivable	100	150	145	150
Accounts payable	(60)	(92)	(87)	(92)
Net monetary assets	50	78	72	78
Inventory	120	185	180	198
Plant and equipment (at cost)......	260	280	1,356	1,376
Less accumulated depreciation	(112)	(138)	(626)	(761)
Stockholders' equity	318	405	982	891
Reconciliation of stockholders' equity, beginning of year	...	318	...	982
Net income	...	87	...	(91) *
End of year	...	405	...	891

* Assume for the moment that this is a balancing figure. Derivation and proof are presented in Illustration 15-9.

In addition, the 1970 cost of goods sold must be restated to December 31, 1970 cruzeiros:

	Before Adjustment	Adjustment Factor	After Adjustment
Opening inventory	Cr$ 120	(See Ill. 15-5)	Cr$ 180
Purchases	755	1.225	925
Closing inventory	(185)	(See Ill. 15-5)	(198)
Cost of goods sold ...	Cr$ 690		Cr$ 907

To simplify our calculations, purchases have been adjusted by the average adjustment factor for the year: $(1.45 + 1)/2 = 1.225$.

For the sake of convenience, 1970 sales and other expenses are also adjusted by the average adjustment factor for the year (this implicitly assumes these items were evenly distributed throughout the year):

	Before Adjustment	Adjustment Factor	After Adjustment
Sales	Cr$900	1.225	Cr$1,103
Other expenses	97	1.225	119

In order to adjust the 1970 income statement to year-end 1970 cruzeiros, the 1970 depreciation expense must be stated. Therefore, using the adjusted data determined above, the 1970 depreciation expense is:

	Before Adjustment	After Adjustment
Cost of plant and equipment at Dec. 31, 1970	Cr$280	Cr$1,376
Less Dec. 31, 1970 addition not depreciated	20	20
Total	Cr$260	Cr$1,356
1970 depreciation (at 10% rate).......	Cr$ 26	Cr$ 135

To complete the adjustment of the financial statements to common year-end cruzeiros, it is necessary to calculate the loss for the year on the monetary items and to restate each item in the conventional income statement.

Monetary assets (such as cash, receivables, and deposits) and liabilities (such as bank loans and accounts payable), are stated in fixed cruzeiro amounts. As the price level rises, monetary assets lose purchasing power and liabilities become payable in cruzeiros of decreasing purchasing power. The excess of monetary assets over liabilities represents the "exposure to inflation." The inflation loss may be computed on the basis of the average "exposure to inflation" as shown in Illustration 15–8.

ILLUSTRATION 15–8

CRUZEIRO CORPORATION

Exposure to Inflation

	Balance	
	Beginning of Year	End of Year
Cash	Cr$ 10	Cr$ 20
Receivables	100	150
Accounts payable	(60)	(92)
	Cr$ 50	Cr$ 78
Add: Cash used to acquire property in Dec. 1970	...	20
	Cr$ 50	Cr$ 98

Average exposure, $\dfrac{50 + 98}{2}$ .... Cr$74

Loss on exposure to 45% inflation, 74 × 0.45 .... Cr$33

The income statement before and after the price-level adjustments explained above is summarized in Illustration 15–9. In this example, the results of operations reported in accordance with generally accepted accounting principles indicated a profit, but a loss after price-level adjustments. In addition, the balance sheet financial ratios before price-level adjustments are changed significantly after the price-level adjustments are made.

ILLUSTRATION 15–9

CRUZEIRO CORPORATION

Income Statement

	Before Adjustment	After Adjustment
Sales	Cr$900	Cr$1,103
Cost of goods sold	690	907
Gross margin	Cr$210	Cr$ 196
Depreciation	26	135
Other expenses	97	119
Loss on net monetary assets		33
Net Income (Loss).................	Cr$ 87	Cr$ (91)

SUGGESTED FURTHER READING

AMERICAN INSTITUTE OF CERTIFIED PUBLIC ACCOUNTANTS. *Reporting the Financial Effects of Price Level Changes,* Accounting Research Study No. 6. New York, 1963.

JONES, RALPH. *Effects of Price-Level Changes on Business Income, Capital and Taxes.* Columbus, Ohio: American Accounting Association, 1956.

————. *Price Level Changes and Financial Statements—Case Studies of Four Companies.* Columbus, Ohio: AAA, 1955.

MASON, PERRY E. *Price Level Changes and Financial Statements.* Columbus, Ohio: AAA, 1956.

CASES

Case 15–1. **HOLDEN CORPORATION**
Calculating the Effect of Price Level Changes

The Holden Corporation was a two-year-old merchandising firm. During this period the price-level index changed as follows:

Opening of business	150
First year, average	160
First year, end	175
Second year, average	190
Second year, end	200

The company business was such that all of its revenues and expenses were earned or incurred fairly evenly throughout the year. The only exceptions to this generalization were depreciation and that portion of the merchandise sold represented by the beginning inventory. Inventory was priced on a first-in, first-out basis. Dividends were declared and paid at the end of each year.

EXHIBIT 1

HOLDEN CORPORATION

Comparative Income Statement (Historical Basis)
(in thousands)

	Year 1	Year 2
Sales	$800	$1,000
Operating expenses:		
Cost of goods sold	$470	$ 600
Depreciation	30	40
Other expenses (including income tax)	280	300
Total operating expenses	$780	$ 940
Net Profit from Operations	$ 20	$ 60

383

EXHIBIT 2

HOLDEN CORPORATION

Comparative Statement of Retained Earnings (Historical Basis)
(in thousands)

	Year 1	Year 2
Retained earnings, beginning of year	$..	$15
Net profit from operations	20	60
Total	$20	$75
Dividends to stockholders	5	10
Retained Earnings, End of Year	$15	$65

EXHIBIT 3

HOLDEN CORPORATION

Comparative Balance Sheet (Historical Basis)
(in thousands)

	Opening of Business	End of Year 1	End of Year 2
ASSETS			
Cash, receivables, and other monetary items	$200	$195	$235
Inventories	250	300	200
Plant and equipment	300	400	400
Less: Accumulated depreciation		(30)	(70)
Total Assets	$750	$865	$765
LIABILITIES AND STOCKHOLDERS' EQUITY			
Liabilities:			
Current liabilities	$100	$200	$100
Long-term liabilities	350	350	...
Total Liabilities	$450	$550	$100
Stockholders' Equity:			
Capital stock	$300	$300	$600
Retained earnings	...	15	65
Total Stockholders' Equity	$300	$315	$665
Total Liabilities and Stockholders' Equity	$750	$865	$765

The company's plant and equipment was acquired on the first day of business and at the end of the first year. All of the plant and equipment was depreciated on a straight-line basis over a 10-year life. The land on which the plant was located was held under a long-term lease agreement.

At the beginning of the company's second year, management paid off in cash $50,000 of the company's $350,000 long-term liabilities. The remaining $300,000 was converted to capital stock.

Exhibit 1 presents the company's income statements on an historical basis for each of its first two years of operations. Exhibit 2 shows the unadjusted statement of retained earnings for the same periods. Holden's balance sheets at the opening of business and at the end of each year's operations are presented in Exhibit 3.

At the end of the second year's operations, the management wanted the company's statements restated in "current dollars" to determine whether or not the company had experienced a monetary gain or loss to date. Management also wanted to know how much of this accumulated gain or loss related to the second year of operations.

Question

1. Restate the company's statements for its first two years' operations in current dollars.

Case 15–2. CROSTHWAITE BROTHERS, INCORPORATED

Impact of Price-Level Changes on Management Performance Evaluation

Crosthwaite Brothers, a small West Coast firm with sales of $15 million in 1964, produced industrial pumps, mixers, and specially designed machined castings. The firm had continually expanded since its founding and had only recently begun to experience unsatisfactory profits, although it had always suffered from the wide economic swings characteristic of its industry. Return on stockholders' investment in 1964 was about 12 percent, down from 14.5 percent in 1960 (see Exhibits 1 and 2).

Seattle Division

Crosthwaite Brothers was founded in Seattle, Washington, in 1910 as a producer of a standard line of industrial pumps, custom-designed "special order" pumps, and a small number of industrial mixers, most of which were built to customer specifications. During periods of low sales, the firm had also contracted to cast special items, always to customer specification. In recent years these special castings had become a major part of the Seattle division's (the original Crosthwaite Brothers) sales.

EXHIBIT 1

CROSTHWAITE BROTHERS, INC.

Balance Sheet, December 31, 1964
(in thousands of dollars)

	Seattle	Tacoma	Portland	Total
ASSETS				
Current assets	4,600	1,030	765	6,395
Plant and equipment (net):				
Buildings	140	...	1,100	1,250
Machinery	560	70	700	1,330
Investment in: *				
Tacoma	620	...	...	...
Portland	2,200	...	...	...
Total Assets	8,120	1,100	2,575	8,975
LIABILITIES				
Current liabilities	1,920	480	375	2,775
Long-term debt	400	...	...	400
Due to Seattle *		620	2,200	...
Stockholders' equity	5,800	...	...	5,800
Total Liabilities	8,120	1,100	2,575	8,957

* Interdivisional accounts have been eliminated in the combined balance sheet.

EXHIBIT 2

CROSTHWAITE BROTHERS, INC.

Income Statement for the Year 1964
(in thousands of dollars)

	Seattle	Tacoma	Portland	Total
Sales	8,000	4,000	3,000	15,000
Cost of sales:				
Material	1,700	900	600	3,200
Labor	2,640	1,540	1,070	5,250
Overhead:				
Depreciation:				
Buildings	10		30	40
Machinery	80	70	100	250
Other overhead	1,910	580	970	3,460
Total overhead	2,000	650	1,100	3,750
Total cost of sales	6,340	3,090	2,770	12,200
Gross profit	1,660	910	230	2,800
Selling and general expense	650	300	250	1,200
	1,010	610	(20)	1,600
Home office expense	110	50	40	200
Net income before taxes	900	560	(60)	1,400
Income taxes (50%).............	450	280	(30)	700
Net Income after Taxes	450	280	(30)	700

The original factory, built in 1915, and an addition completed prior to 1940 were still in use; superior maintenance had kept the facilities in a condition favorable to efficient production. New executive offices were planned for 1966. Production equipment had been built or purchased as needed. As Crosthwaite's equipment replacement had been somewhat sporadic over time, the production facilities were of various ages and efficiencies (see Exhibit 3).

EXHIBIT 3

CROSTHWAITE BROTHERS, INC.

Schedule of Plant and Equipment and Depreciation at December 31, 1964
(in thousands of dollars)

	Acquired	Cost	1964 Depreciation	Accumulated Depreciation 12-31-64	Net Book Value
Seattle:					
Buildings	1915	500	...	500	...
	1939	400	10	260	140
		900	10	760	140
Machinery	1930	150	...	150	...
	1942	350	...	350	...
	1954	600	...	600	...
	1962	800	80	240	560
		1,900	80	1,340	560
Tacoma:					
Machinery	1956	700	70	630	70
Portland:					
Buildings	1962	1,200	30	90	1,110
Machinery	1962	1,000	100	300	700
Total		5,700	290	3,120	2,580

NOTE: Straight-line depreciation (without salvage value) has been computed on the basis of estimated lives of 40 years for buildings and 10 years for machinery.

The original Crosthwaite plant had always been quite profitable; the recent increase in the volume of special castings only increased that profitability. Since the costs of assembly operation had been increasing in the past few years, management had gradually moved to counteract this change by shifting emphasis to the casting and machine shops. Control components were increasingly subcontracted.

Tacoma Division

In 1956, a separate division was established in Tacoma, Washington (30 miles from Seattle). The Tacoma plant assembled and marketed a standard line of home sump pumps. Weather conditions in the Pacific Northwest were quite damp; as a result, most new homes with basements were built with pumping systems designed to keep basements dry. The Tacoma plant assembled such a system, consisting of a pump, switch, sensing device, mounting brackets, and a cover.

The Tacoma division purchased pump units from a variety of sources, including the Seattle plant. Fabrication included light stamping and forming. Most of the production activity of the Tacoma plant consisted of the assembly and wiring of the pump units. The division had been profitable from its inception, with return on total assets frequently above 20 percent, although Crosthwaite enjoyed no particular pricing advantage. As volume increased, they had been forced to purchase more and more pump units from outside sources. The higher prices of the outside sources had cut the profit margins somewhat, but management continued to consider the profits satisfactory.

Portland Division

Crosthwaite's latest expansion venture had not proved so successful. Demand for the standard line of Crosthwaite pumps had been moderately increasing. The Tacoma division had been clamoring for more pumps for several years. In addition, the Seattle division had experienced increasing demand for custom castings. To take advantage of this increasing demand, a new plant was begun in Portland, Oregon in 1961. That city was selected for several reasons, chief of which was the opportunity to provide a job-shop casting facility to that city to utilize the pump production facilities that might not immediately consume the plant's capacity.

The plant layout had been made taking into account the best features and the most modern equipment available. The optimum balance between the production shop (for the pump line) and the job shop (for the custom castings) had been the designer's goal.

After two years, operations were still not on a profitable basis. Unit costs continued to be out of line with the Seattle division; the Tacoma plant was reluctant to purchase pumps from Portland, and virtually no special casting orders had been received. In 1964, the plant was operating at about 60 percent of capacity and the plant manager felt that a cut in the labor force might be necessary if more business were not found.

Accounting

In 1961 Crosthwaite moved to a decentralized form of organization. As each plant manager had previously managed his entire operation, including control of current assets and liabilities, the changes brought on were mostly in the accounting area. Beginning in 1962, the divisional accountants prepared separate financial statements that were forwarded to Seattle.

The corporate controller then took these reports and combined them into the corporate financial statements. A comparative analysis was also prepared at this time.

In February 1965, Crosthwaite's president John McGuire was pondering the results of the executive meeting held the previous week. Concerned with the slow increase in profit, Mr. McGuire had proposed an incentive pay plan for the divisional management (including the divisional manager, accountant, and the marketing and production managers). The executive meeting had immediately become embroiled in controversy. The Seattle manager was in favor of the plan, provided he was assured of complete responsibility for the division's operations (as the corporate offices had remained in Seattle, he felt somewhat dominated by Mr. McGuire and the corporate staff).

The other operating managers were not so pleased. The Tacoma manager was skeptical unless a "more fair" method of pricing the pumps he bought from within the company were established. The manager of the Portland division was particularly bitter toward the Seattle division manager: "I can produce pumps better than you've ever done. If I just had your overhead, I'd make you look sick. Unless I get your overhead rates or unless I can produce and sell as I please (prices for the Crosthwaite line and for the special pumps sent to Tacoma were set in Seattle) I'll never show a profit."

After two hours of discussion, the meeting was adjourned. No agreement was made on the incentive pay proposal.

Philips N.V.

Mr. Nash, the corporate controller, had also been troubled by the incentive pay proposal because of some inadequacies in the company's traditional accounting system. He wondered if some of the features of a particular foreign corporation he had read about might prove beneficial. In 1962, Philips N.V., a Netherlands corporation, had to modify its accounting statements somewhat to satisfy the SEC, subsequent to a public offering in the United States. As Philips' accounting concepts were unusual and somewhat controversial to U.S. accountants, their system aroused considerable interest and led to several articles in accounting journals.

In order to get a reaction from his fellow managers, Mr. Nash prepared the following summary which he gave to the president and the other participants in the executive meeting:

Accounting System of Philips N.V.

N. V. Philips Gloeilampersfabrieken is a large Dutch firm similar in product line to the General Electric Corporation; in 1964 sales were about $1.9 billion.

Philips produces and markets a wide variety of products from light bulbs to cyclotrons. In 1965 they announced their first major line of digital computers; at the same time they were a leading firm in European color television technology.

Philips' accounting methods differ from those used in the U.S. in several respects; these methods are based upon the philosophy that no income for a period may be realized until the "purchasing power of the capital at the end of the period is equal to that at the beginning of the period." [1] The major accounting differences are:

a) Provision for depreciation of fixed assets is based upon replacement value.

b) Fully depreciated fixed assets still in use continue to be depreciated on the basis of their replacement value.

c) Inventories and cost of goods sold are based upon replacement value.

d) Gains on sale of stock are included in income.

e) Profit-sharing is shown as a deduction after net income.

The purpose of financial accounting for Philips is also somewhat different than that found in the U.S. For Philips, the primary object of accounting is to provide information for the operating manager. Replacement value theory is the basis of their accounting for management, not just a calculation technique used in the yearly report.

Replacement value is determined on the basis of the trend of the specific price levels for each group of fixed assets, such as buildings, houses, machinery, etc. These groups are revalued regularly on the basis of index numbers maintained separately for each group. When an index has risen significantly to merit revaluation, the asset account is increased as is the contra-revaluation surplus. Accumulated depreciation is also increased proportionately, with revaluation surplus rather than an expense being the contra. Depreciation is based on the remaining life and replacement value.

Inventory, including raw materials through finished goods, is valued on the basis of standard cost. Standard costs are organized by group (all inventory items are grouped—each group using the index value of a representative element). When the index changes materially, the standard costs are revalued on the basis of the group's representative index. A separate revaluation surplus account for inventories is used. Price variances are based upon the latest standard cost.

Generally, Philips carries *intangible assets* at no value. Start-up expenditures are capitalized however, and are depreciated on the basis of volume of production. Until completely written off, these start-up expenditures are revalued in a manner similar to that of inventory.

The decrease in purchasing power of the *net monetary assets* is treated as a period expense and as a reserve. The difference between monetary assets and total liabilities at the close of each period is multiplied by the inflation factor (based on a *cost of living index*) and is credited to a reserve and debited to cost of inflation, an expense account.

---

[1] "An Application of Replacement Value Theory," *Journal of Accountancy*, July 1960, pp. 37–47, by Professor A. Gondeket, chief internal auditor of Philips Industries.

EXHIBIT 4

CROSTHWAITE BROTHERS, INC.

Construction Cost Index and GNP Implicit Price Index, 1915–64

	Construction Cost Index 1964 = 100	GNP Implicit Price Index 1964 = 100
1915	18	31
1916	20	31
1917	25	51
1918	29	51
1919	33	51
1920	41	51
1921	33	51
1922	30	48
1923	33	49
1924	33	48
1925	33	49
1926	33	49
1927	33	48
1928	33	49
1929	33	49
1930	32	47
1931	29	41
1932	26	37
1933	28	36
1934	31	39
1935	30	38
1936	31	40
1937	33	40
1938	33	40
1939	31	40
1940	32	40
1941	35	44
1942	39	50
1943	42	55
1944	41	56
1945	43	57
1946	49	61
1947	60	69
1948	67	72
1949	66	73
1950	69	74
1951	74	80
1952	76	81
1953	78	82
1954	78	83
1955	80	84
1956	85	86
1957	88	90
1958	88	91
1959	90	93
1960	92	95
1961	93	96
1962	95	97
1963	98	98
1964	100	100

Source: Constructed by case writer from various publications of the U.S. Department of Commerce.

Questions

1. What would be the impact of the Philips approach to financial reporting upon Crosthwaite's internal and external financial statements? Would it help the company to resolve some of the difficulties encountered with the introduction of the proposed incentive compensation scheme?
2. Specifically, what is your estimate of the impact on Crosthwaite's 1964 statements of adjusting for price-level changes? (See Exhibit 4.)
3. What is your estimate of Crosthwaite's operating results for 1964? How useful is this figure? For what purposes?

CHAPTER 16

INTANGIBLE ASSETS

Intangible assets are expenditures for special rights, privileges, or competitive advantages which will lead to increased revenues or earnings. They include expenditures for franchises, research and development, patents, corporate organizations, and similar items having no physical existence, but which nevertheless can reasonably be expected to contribute to earnings beyond the current accounting period.

Intangible assets are often thought to be less deserving of being shown as an asset than physical assets because of their nonphysical character. This is incorrect, since accounting regards an asset as being an economic quantum. Whether or not it is represented by a physical item is incidental to the issue of whether or not an expenditure with potential future income benefits should be capitalized. The principal reason for associating asset quanta with specific physical or intangible items is to clarify for communication purposes the kinds of resources in which management has invested the firm's funds.

Accounting Research Bulletin No. 43, Chapter 5, is currently the most authoritative statement dealing with intangible assets. To date, the Accounting Principles Board has not issued a comprehensive opinion on this matter, although the Board has endorsed the conclusions outlined in Chapter 5. In addition, the Accounting Principles Board has commissioned a research study on research and development costs, an important intangible asset.

Accounting for intangible assets raises at least four important problems:

1. Under what conditions is an intangible asset created?
2. What cost items should be capitalized?
3. What amortization policy should be applied to the capitalized cost?
4. How should an intangible asset be written off when it becomes reasonably evident it has lost its value to the company?

Most accountants agree that the answers to these questions should con form to the following basic accounting principles:

1. Intangible assets should be recorded at cost.
2. The cost of intangible assets acquired for other than cash should be measured by the fair value of the asset acquired or by the fair value of the consideration given, whichever is the more definitely determinable.
3. Costs should be matched with revenues whenever possible.
4. Costs should not be deferred to future periods unless there is a reasonable expectation they will be recovered from future revenues resulting from the expenditures.

A number of managements and accountants believe conservatism should govern the accounting for intangibles. Therefore, they would add to the above list the general presumption that intangible asset costs should be written off as incurred or, if capitalized, amortized over a relatively short period of time. Increasingly, however, there is a growing belief that conservatism alone should not justify such actions which might eliminate a valid business asset from the accounts. Rather, the goal of accountancy should be to provide as accurate a record of costs and cost expiration as possible.

Amortization Practices and Theory

For amortization purposes intangible assets can be classified as:

Type A: Those having a limited life either by law, agreement, or their nature (such as patents, copyrights, and research and development).

Type B: Those having no indication of a limited life (such as trade names).

Type A intangibles should be amortized by systematic charges to income over the period during which they create benefits for their owner. Should it become clear while the intangible is being amortized that its actual life will be less than originally estimated, the asset amortization rate should be changed or a lump sum write-off to income be made to reflect the new facts. In this respect, the treatment of intangibles is identical to that for physical assets having limited periods of usefulness.

Type B intangibles can be carried at their full original cost until it becomes evident they have become worthless. At such a time, they become Type A intangibles and subject to amortization or partial lump-sum reduction. Sometimes, because of a desire to be conservative, Type B intangible assets are amortized even though their potential contribution of benefits to future periods remains undiminished.

The costs of intangibles developed in the course of business are usually written off as incurred, principally because it is difficult to determine, as the potential intangible asset is being created, whether or not future benefits will result from its creation. Also, some companies are continuously making expenditures for intangibles, such as research and development, which management considers to be a regular, recurring expense of doing business and, hence, properly charged to income as incurred. In addition, it is sometimes difficult to determine the specific costs related to developing an intangible asset. Under these circumstances, the usual course of action is to expense the costs as incurred on the ground that only those costs that can be specifically identified with an item being capitalized should be recorded as assets.

Payments in Excess of Book Value

A special problem arises when a group of tangible and intangible assets or the stock of a company is purchased at a price greater than the value shown on the books of the seller. The excess purchase price should be allocated to the particular tangible and intangible assets, if practical and justifiable. If the intangibles are Type A, their new cost basis should then be amortized over the remaining productive life.

If an excess of purchase price over the carrying cost of the assets still remains after making a reasonable allocation of acquisition cost to the acquired tangible and intangible assets, it is called goodwill. Before *Opinion No. 16* of the Accounting Principles Board was issued in 1970, the intangible asset goodwill was often retained on the books until it was evident that it had lost its value. Not everyone followed this practice, however. Some companies and some accounting authorities expressed a preference for writing goodwill off against income over time. Henceforth, *Opinion No. 16* requires goodwill created through business acquisitions to be written off during a period not to exceed 40 years. The topic "goodwill" is discussed in greater detail in the chapter related to intercorporate investments and business combinations.

Income Tax Treatment

Intangible property which definitely has a limited life and is used in the business or production of income can be amortized for tax purposes. However, these items cannot be amortized using the declining-balance and sum-of-the-years'-digits methods. Goodwill, trade names, and other intangibles with indefinite useful lives cannot be amortized for tax purposes, although certain organization costs, which are sometimes treated as Type B intangibles for accounting purposes, can be amortized against taxable income over a period of not less than five years.

Research and experimental expenditures may be deducted currently for income tax purposes, irrespective of how they are handled for accounting purposes. Of course, if these costs are expensed on tax returns but capitalized in the accounting records, a deferred tax accounting situation arises. A similar, but somewhat more complex, treatment for tax purposes is available for the exploration and development costs incurred by oil and gas exploration companies.

SPECIFIC INTANGIBLE ASSETS

Research and Development Costs

Research and development costs include those direct and indirect costs related to the creation and development of new processes, techniques, applications, and products with commercial possibilities. These costs can be placed into one of three broad categories: basic research, which deals with research activities with no immediate concern for commercial potential; applied research, which is directed to the discovery of new products or the improvement of existing ones; and development costs, which relate to those activities designed to bring research output to a marketable stage.

Most companies expense their research and development costs as incurred. This follows the treatment generally used for tax purposes. A few companies capitalize and amortize over future periods all or part of such costs. Some authors have suggested that under the appropriate circumstances it may be desirable to provide for research and development costs by a charge against income in advance of the time they are incurred. Very few, if any, companies follow this practice.

A desire to be conservative is usually the reason given for expensing research and development costs as incurred. Others believe that it is not desirable to capitalize such costs, because for any one project they are usually incurred over a long period of time and the probability of ever developing and successfully marketing a commercial product is typically low. In fact, they note, right up to the point when a product is placed on the market, there is considerable uncertainty as to its real commercial value. Thus, they claim, the whole process is too speculative to do otherwise than expense the costs as incurred.

Those supporting capitalization believe that whenever costs can be specifically related to research and development projects it is desirable to defer such costs if there is a reasonable chance that they will be recovered out of future revenues. Such expenditures are similar to investments in "bricks and mortar" and should be accounted for in the same fashion. Under these circumstances, conservatism is not regarded by the capitalization proponents as sufficient justification for tolerating the improper matching of costs and revenues brought about by expensing all research and development costs as incurred. Certainly, it is pointed out, if the product of research and development is purchased from its developer, the purchase cost is typically capitalized and then amortized over subsequent periods, principally because the expenditure is made in the expectation it will lead to future benefits. This practice prompts the capitalization supporters to ask: Why shouldn't the research and development costs of internally generated projects with similar projected benefits be treated in the same way? What is the critical difference in circumstances?

Some companies justify expensing research and development costs on the ground that they spend approximately the same amount on research and development each year. Consequently, they would get the same annual expense irrespective of which method they adopted. This may be true, but expensing does leave management with the ability to regulate annual profits simply by increasing or decreasing their annual expenditures for research and development. Those supporting capitalization claim that this danger is minimized if research and development costs are capitalized. On the other hand, the expense advocates claim that since *Opinion No. 9* requires write-downs of previously capitalized research and development no longer considered to be beneficial to be included in the determination of operating profits, some managements who capitalize research and development may be reluctant to face up to the fact that a lump-sum write-off of their capitalized costs should be made, since this unusual charge will reduce current operating profit. Thus, there may be undesirable potential profit measurement implications associated with either method.

Other propoasls for accounting for research and development include: capitalization of all such costs irrespective of whether or not they are productive, since it can logically be argued that the costs of the unsuccessful projects are part of the costs of the marketable projects. A less acceptable proposal advocated by some writers is that companies with a relatively fixed level of research and development activity on a long-range basis may incur actual expenses in any one year for such costs which are either above or below their long-term average annual expense for this item. In these cases, it may be argued that proper matching of costs and revenues requires that the annual costs be based upon the average annual long-range costs, irrespective of the actual annual expenditures. The difference between costs charged and actual expenditures would be carried in a reserve account. This approach may be justified if one assumes that each dollar of sales consumes past research and development costs and proper matching of costs and revenues requires a provision for replacement of such costs in the future. Others suggest that basic research costs should always be expensed; a portion of applied research capitalized; and development costs always capitalized. In their opinion, accounting should reflect the fact that as one moves from basic research to development activities the likelihood of a marketable product being created increases. Finally, others believe that some of the newer statistical approaches to handling uncertainty in business decisions should be studied by businessmen and their accountants as a possible basis for deciding on a more logical basis how to handle research and development costs in specific situations.

Advertising and Marketing Costs

The general practice is to expense advertising and marketing costs as incurred. To some it seems logical that if research and development costs can be deferred, the same accounting treatment should be given to advertising and marketing costs incurred in the expectation of generating profits in future accounting periods. The standard reply to this proposition is that future benefits from such activities are difficult to determine and most probably are received within a fairly short period of time after the expenditure. Therefore, expensing these costs is appropriate.

This answer is not satisfactory to everyone, however. Dissenters claim that advertising and marketing costs are an important group of intangibles and are clearly related to future deliveries of product. However, because of a slavish adherence to accounting procedures motivated by an arbitrary desire to conform to the tax treatment of such costs, a valid business asset has been suppressed. Therefore, they suggest that greater research attention be given to this subject, with a view to making accounting practices more realistic.

Patents

Patents are granted by the United States Patent Office. They give holders the exclusive rights to control their invention for a period of 17 years. The actual period of control may be extended by obtaining additional patents on improvements to the original item. Patent rights may be sold or granted to others on a royalty basis.

The cost of an internally generated patent usually includes legal fees, patent fees, costs of models and drawings, and related experimental and development costs that can reasonably be identified with the patent. Since the registration of a patent is no guarantee of protection, it is usually necessary to defend the patent in court tests. Accordingly, the costs of successful court tests are generally included in the costs of the patent. When litigation is unsuccessful, the costs of litigation and the other costs of the affected patent should be written off immediately.

In the case of successful litigation, the costs of the patent should be amortized over the useful economic life of the patent. Because of technological or market obsolescence, this period is typically shorter than the patent's legal life. However, if a patent's effective economic life can be extended by an additional patent, it is permissible to write the unamortized balance of the cost of the old patent over the economic life of the new one.

The classification of patent amortization charge depends on the nature of the patent. For instance, patents related to manufacturing activities are charged to manufacturing expenses. Patents used in shipping are charged as selling expenses.

Copyrights

A copyright gives its owner the exclusive right to sell literature, music, and other works of art. The copyright period is 28 years, with the option to renew for another 28 years. The costs of obtaining a copyright are nominal. Therefore, the cost is often written off as incurred. However, the cost of a purchased copyright may be substantial. The common practice is to write such costs off against the income from the first printing or its equivalent.

Franchises

A franchise may be either perpetual, revocable at the option of the grantor, or limited in life. The costs of a franchise includes fees paid to the grantor and legal and other expenditures incurred in obtaining the franchise. When the franchise is perpetual, these costs need not be amortized. If the franchise is for a specific period of time, the franchise costs should be systematically amortized over the franchise period. The costs of revocable franchises, in the absence of a specific time limit on the life of the franchise, are usually accounted for as perpetual franchises, although some accounting authorities believe it is prudent to amortize the costs of such franchises over a relatively short period of time.

Trademarks and Trade Names

Trademarks, trade names, and distinctive symbols, labels, and designs used to differentiate products and brands can be protected from infringement by registering them with the United States Patent Office. Proof of prior and continuous use is required to retain the right to the trade name or marks registered. Protection of trademarks and names that cannot be registered can be sought through common law.

The cost of a trademark includes legal fees associated with successful litigation, registry fees, and all developmental expenditures that can be reasonably associated with the trademark. The cost of a purchased trademark is its purchase price.

As long as they are used continuously, trademarks have an unlimited life. Therefore, they can be treated as a Type B intangible. However, in practice, their costs are often amortized rapidly, since the economic life of a trademark depends on the tastes of consumers.

Leasehold Improvements

Lessees often make alterations or improvements to the property they are leasing. At the end of the lease, such leasehold improvements revert to the lessor. Therefore, the lessee only has the right to use his improvements during the period of this lease. Consequently, leasehold improvements are amortized over the remaining life of the lease or their useful life, whichever is shorter.

Organization Costs

Organization costs include incorporation fees, legal fees, promotion expenditures, and similar costs associated with the initial organization of a company. These costs benefit the corporation during its entire life, which for accounting purposes can be considered to be unlimited. This assumption supports the treatment of organization costs as a permanent asset. Others agree that initial organization costs should be capitalized to avoid starting a business with a deficit, but argue that these costs should be amortized rapidly, since they have no ultimate disposable value. Hence, they should be written off against income before the ultimate income created by the business enterprise is determined. Others justify rapid amortization on the ground of conservatism.

Intangible Development Costs

In the oil and gas industry, all drilling costs, excluding the pipe and equipment used to complete a well, are classified as intangible development costs. Other intangible costs include drill site preparation, roads to the location, grading, logging (electrical well surveys conducted with special downhole instruments), perforating, cementing, and formation stimulation. Such costs are classified as being intangible since they do not give rise to an asset with physical substance or salvage value. There are three different acceptable accounting methods used to handle intangible drilling costs. These are as follows:

1. The costs are charged as an expense during the years incurred.
2. The gross recoverable costs are capitalized and amortized over the productive life of the wells.
3. The gross recoverable costs are capitalized and the related tax reduction is credited to a reserve; both the costs and the reserve are then amortized over the productive life of the related wells.

For tax purposes, most taxpayers deduct their intangible development costs as incurred.

Those companies deducting their intangible development costs as incurred for accounting purposes do so to be conservative or to conform with their treatment of these expenditures for tax purposes, even though this is not necessary to qualify the cost for tax deductibility. Others write these costs off as incurred since they believe that the annual charges approximate the amortization charges that would be recognized if a capitalization policy had been followed in earlier years.

In the opinion of many, capitalization of intangible development costs results in a proper matching of costs and revenues, since these costs are very similar in nature to capital expenditures. A few companies capitalize all of their intangible development costs on the ground that unsuccessful development activities are a necessary part of developing successful wells. The total pooled costs are then written off over the life of the productive wells. However, the more common practice is to capitalize only those intangible development costs associated with wells that appear productive. Intangible development costs for "dry holes" are expensed as exploration costs in the year the well is abandoned.

Capitalizing intangible development costs in the accounting records and expensing them for tax purposes raises the accounting question: What is the appropriate accounting treatment for the tax reduction resulting from expensing intangible development costs as incurred for income tax purposes?

The United States Congress has granted the oil and gas industry a special depletion allowance for tax purposes equivalent to 22 percent of the gross income from oil and gas production. This allowance, calculated separately for each property, is granted in lieu of cost depletion and is limited to an amount not exceeding 50 percent of the net income from the oil and gas production. The allowance for "percentage depletion" can be deducted from taxable income whenever it exceeds cost depletion. Since in most cases it does exceed cost depletion, any intangible costs capitalized for tax purposes (to be recovered by future cost depletion deductions) will not result in any additional tax deductions; whereas if the intangible costs are expensed, they will result in an immediate tax reduction. This explains the industrywide practice of expensing intangible costs for tax purposes.

Unlike the deferred tax situations arising from timing differences which change the pattern of tax payments, the practice of treating intangible development costs differently for tax and book purposes reduces the total amount of tax paid. Therefore, the problem shifts from providing a reserve for the funds obtained now by deferring the payment of taxes to one of matching in the income statement the tax reduction and the expense giving rise to it.

The net effect of the tax reduction, if any, created by currently expensing the intangible development costs for tax purposes is to reduce the company's investment in intangible development costs. Therefore, it is argued, sound accounting requires that the capitalized intangible development costs and their related tax benefit be amortized over the same period. This can be achieved by either (1) establishing a reserve for the related income tax reduction and amortizing it over the same period as the associated intangible asset, or (2) deducting the tax reduction from the related intangible asset and amortizing the net amount. Those who support this position regard as misleading the common practice of capitalizing intangible development costs and writing them off over future periods, but including in current income the related tax deduction as received.

Oil and Gas Exploration Costs

Another special intangible asset problem in the oil and gas industry involves the exploration costs of finding oil and gas. The issue is: Should exploration costs which may reasonably be expected to be recovered out of future production be charged to income as incurred *or* capitalized and amortized over the productive life of the oil and gas properties discovered? Exploration costs are essential in the discovery of oil and gas and include: dry hole costs, expensed or abandoned lease costs, geological and geophysical costs, and other direct and indirect costs related to exploration and development activities. They are incurred prior to the intangible development costs discussed above.

Most oil companies expense their oil and gas exploration costs as incurred. A few companies capitalize anywhere from a small to a substantial proportion of these costs. For tax purposes, any exploration costs capitalized will be recovered through cost depletion deductions. However, since in most cases percentage depletion will apply in lieu of cost depletion, any exploration costs capitalized may not result in any future tax reductions. Consequently, oil and gas companies attempt to expense exploration costs for tax purposes to the extent they are permitted to do so. The Internal Revenue Service has established rather definite, complex rules concerning exploration costs such that a portion of exploration costs must be capitalized. Nevertheless, a significant portion of exploration costs will be expensed for tax purposes to obtain the tax benefit in the year of occurrence. Accordingly, to the extent they are capitalized for reporting to stockholders, the related tax benefit is either included in income as received or netted against the capitalized costs to be amortized over future periods. When recoverable exploration costs are capitalized, the latter treatment of the related tax benefit is preferable.

The speculative nature of gas and oil exploration has been the principal reason for expensing these costs as incurred for book purposes. Other arguments for expensing as incurred include: conservatism; that the charge approximates, in the case of established companies with continuous exploration programs, the amount that would have been written off if a capitalization policy had been followed in previous years; and that capitalization might lead to compulsory capitalization for income tax purposes or the payment of additional state property and income taxes.

The capitalization of oil and gas exploration costs has been justified on the ground that the purpose of exploration is to discover properties which will be productive over a number of years. Therefore, proper matching of costs and revenues requires that the exploration investment be capitalized and amortized over the life of the productive resources discovered.

It is further argued by some that the discovery of productive properties is unlikely without some exploration costs being incurred for unproductive ventures. Therefore, the capitalized cost ought to include exploration costs related to both successful and unsuccessful ventures.

For established companies, it seems reasonable to expect that capitalized costs would not exceed the value of the estimated proven reserves of the company. However, since the practice of capitalizing such costs is fairly new, the limitation for capitalized exploitation costs has not yet been clearly established in practice or in theory.

ROLE OF JUDGMENT

The appropriate accounting for intangible assets is very dependent on the particular circumstances of each situation, perhaps more so than in any other areas of accounting. Seldom does an exhaustive analysis of the facts lead to a clear-cut answer. Therefore, selecting the best approach usually requires the exercise of management judgment.

The public accountant faces the same judgmental situation in deciding what form his opinion statement will take. Sometimes his problem is aggravated, when he is not fully satisfied with management's treatment of the item but is not absolutely convinced that his preferred alternative treatment is the only possible answer. In these situations, the public accountant usually resorts to a "subject to" type of opinion. This warns the reader of the statement that the auditor and management disagree on the handling of the intangible, but the auditor feels management's position has merit. Of course, if the auditor believes management's treatment is inappropriate and management insists on using its approach, the auditor will issue a more drastic form of opinion, or he may even terminate his audit arrangement.

Businesses change over time, and often their past accounting practices become inappropriate for their new conditions. This is particularly true of accounting for intangibles. However, it is seldom clear at what precise point in time a change in accounting policy is justified. Again, responsible management judgment must be exercised. Unfortunately, in most cases changes in accounting for intangibles, such as switching from expensing to capitalizing research and development, are made long after the events justifying a change have occurred. Also, a decline in profitability is often the event that appears to prompt the decision to change accounting methods. Changes under these circumstances inevitably raise questions about the integrity of management's statements and the accounting profession's justification for permitting alternative approaches to accounting for intangibles.

Profit Impact of Shift

It is important to note that when a management changes from expensing to capitalizing the cost of an internally generated tangible, the favorable impact on profit may spread well beyond the year of the change. While there are many possible variations of this impact, depending on the direction and size of the annual expenditures, the following simple example should be sufficient to illustrate the point:

The Viking Chemical Company has a very stable business. The management plans to continue its practice of spending $1 million per year on research and development over the next 10 years. In 1968, the company changed its accounting for research and development from expensing as incurred to capitalization and amortization over five years.

What will be the impact on profits of this decision over the next five years? Illustration 16–1 supplies the answer.

ILLUSTRATION 16–1

VIKING CHEMICAL COMPANY

(in thousands)

	Old Policy: Expense R&D as Incurred	New Policy: Capitalize R&D and Amortize Over 5 Years					
	1967	1968	1969	1970	1971	1972	1973
Profits before taxes and R&D expenses	$4,000	$4,000	$4,000	$4,000	$4,000	$4,000	$4,000
R&D expenses	1,000	200	400	600	800	1,000	1,000
	$3,000	$3,800	$3,600	$3,400	$3,200	$3,000	$3,000
Income taxes (50%).....	1,500	1,900	1,800	1,700	1,600	1,500	1,500
Net profit after taxes and all charges	$1,500	$1,900	$1,800	$1,700	$1,600	$1,500	$1,500
Annual profit improvement ...		400	300	200	100	...	...
Deferred R&D (balance sheet item)... ...		800	1,400	1,800	2,000	2,000	2,000

Inappropriate Practices

It is often difficult to determine whether or not an intangible asset expenditure will be recovered out of future revenues. Typically, this problem of uncertainty is resolved on the basis of conservatism, by expensing the cost as incurred. In the case of many well-established companies run by responsible managers, this treatment is often unnecessarily followed. This can result in an improper matching of costs and revenues and the omission of a valid business asset from the balance sheet. On the other hand, marginal firms often resort to capitalizing intangible asset costs of dubious future value in order to boost earnings. Thus, in practice, the inappropriate treatment is the one most often adopted. Hopefully, the Accounting Principles Board's study and opinion on this subject will lead to an improvement in the accounting for the costs of intangible assets.

SUGGESTED FURTHER READING

McFadden, J. A., Jr., and Tuska, C. D. *Accounting and Tax Aspects of Patents and Research.* Princeton, N.J.: D. Van Nostrand Co., 1960.

National Association of Cost Accountants. "Accounting for Research and Development Costs," NACA *Bulletin 36*, section 3, Research Series 29, pp. 1373–1437.

Paton, William A. *Asset Accounting.* New York: Macmillan Co., 1952.

Sands, J. E. *Wealth, Income and Intangibles.* Toronto: University of Toronto Press, 1963.

CASES

Case 16–1. MULTIPRODUCTS ELECTRONICS CORPORATION

Accounting for Research and Development Expenditure

"I think it's pretty clear that what looks on the surface as though it's a *bookkeeping* decision may be one of our most important management decisions. And that's why we are here today."

Frank Freeman, president of the Multiproducts Electronics Corporation addressed his executive group as they met to consider what had grown into a major corporate issue—namely, the accounting treatment of a special research and development expenditure. The accounting for the costs would make the difference in reporting either continued losses or small profits for the company over the next three years. Because there was no definitive accounting practice to cover the extraordinary costs involved, various members of Multiproducts' management team had been examining the issue to uncover as many of the relevant considerations as possible. The meeting in progress was to try to resolve the question.

Multiproducts Electronics Corporation had been founded in 1957. The company's operations covered the development, manufacture, and sale of electronic equipment for military and civilian use. By 1969, the company employed about 2,200 people. Some 8,000 shareholders owned Multiproducts stock, traded in the over-the-counter market.

In its early years, Multiproducts had rapidly increased its sales and showed increasing earnings per share. This success was due principally to the firm's development of a number of improved electronic components for computers and rocket monitoring systems. As a result, Multiproducts was labeled as a "growth company" and its stock sold at a substantial premium.

About 1962, Multiproducts' sales and profits began to decline, the underlying reason being that the company's line of electronic gear was progressively being made obsolete by a series of rapid changes in computer and rocket technology. Also, Multiproducts' R&D group was unable to come up with any significant improvements in the company's existing products. Consequently, Multiproducts' stock began to sell at a lower price-earnings ratio.

Beginning in 1965, Multiproducts reported losses to its stockholders. However, from the low point in 1966 these losses were reduced somewhat in 1967 and again in 1968, principally because the firm had secured in those years several government cost-plus-fixed-fee contracts related to the manufacture of experimental air-to-air missile guidance systems. But despite the reduced losses, Multiproducts' stock continued to be traded at a substantially lower price than the stock of similar companies.

In 1967, as a result of the reported losses in 1965 and 1966, Multiproducts' management became subject to repeated criticism by a dissident stockholder group. This group accused the management of being "unimaginative" and "incompetent." And as the losses persisted through 1967 and 1968, other stockholders became more and more sympathetic to the dissident group's demands for a "change of management."

In February 1969, encouraged by the trend towards profitable operations, Frank Freeman, Multiproducts' president, promised the company's stockholders that Multiproducts would show a small profit during 1969 and thereafter increased profits. This encouraging news was welcomed by the stockholders. Freeman's promise was reported in all the leading financial journals, and the price of the company's stock improved slightly.

Exhibit 1 shows Multiproducts' financial data for the years 1957–68.

The R&D Program

One month *after* Freeman's promise to the stockholders of future profits, Multiproducts' management committee met and decided to undertake a stepped-up three-year R&D program, which hopefully would revitalize the company. This program grew out of a development by the company's R&D department of a simple pilot model of a computer component, which gave promise of revolutionizing computer memory capacity and allied systems. In this component, management decided, lay the chance for Multiproducts to regain its lost market position.

However, one of Multiproducts' competitors was known to be exploring the same principle of electronics upon which Multiproducts' laboratory model was based. Therefore, in the spring of 1969, Multiproducts decided to accelerate the development of a patentable commercial product by increasing the company's R&D expenses from some $1 million to $1.5 million a year, of which $1 million would be devoted to the new project.

EXHIBIT 1

MULTIPRODUCTS ELECTRONICS CORPORATION

Financial Data, 1957–68

	Gross Sales*	R&D Expense*	Net Profit after Taxes*	Earnings per Share**	Stock Price Yearly Range	
					High	Low
1957	$ 8,000	$ 400	$ 100	$0.10	$ 4	$ 2
1958	21,000	900	600	0.60	42	19
1959	33,000	800	2,000	2.00	119	62
1960	40,100	1,000	2,500	2.50	140	95
1961	42,000	950	2,600	2.60	202	136
1962	42,000	900	2,500	2.50	265	151
1963	40,000	1,000	1,800	1.80	167	111
1964	36,000	1,000	1,200	1.20	121	89
1965	35,500	800	(100)	(0.10)	90	61
1966	33,000	600	(600)	(0.60)	68	37
1967	36,100	1,000	(400)	(0.40)	54	41
1968	36,300	1,000	(10)	(0.01)	72	47

* In thousands.
** One million shares outstanding.

The remaining $500,000 would be used to continue R&D related to other products, most of which the firm was already producing. Previously, Multiproducts had never spent more than $500,000 in total on any single R&D project.

Dr. Peter Hellman, Multiproducts' vice president for research and development, believed that even with the increased R&D expenditures, it would still take nearly three years to develop the laboratory model into a sound commercial product. During the first year, he proposed to conduct some further basic research on the electronic principles incorporated in the model. The actual development of commercial prototypes was scheduled to take place in the second and third years. Dr. Hellman estimated the probability of successfully creating a commercial product at about 7 chances out of 10.

Based on recent studies of the projected demand for computer capacity during the period 1972 to 1977, Multiproducts' vice president for sales, Alan Cross, estimated that the new computer component and its allied systems' sales potential would be about $150 million between 1972 and 1978.

On its past experience with similar technological innovations, management expected that the competitive advantage of the component might be as short as two years, but more likely as long as four years. Thereafter, as similar or better competitive components were developed by either Multiproducts or other companies, it was anticipated that the component would experience declining sales for a period of between two and three years.

Expense or Capitalize?

Shortly after the management committee had decided to go ahead with the new R&D program, Thomas Supple, Multiproducts' controller, circulated among top management a memorandum showing the impact of the extraordinary R&D program on projected earnings for 1969–71 inclusive (see Exhibit 2). According to Supple's projections for these years:

1. Multiproducts would show losses—rather than the small profits anticipated earlier—if the R&D costs were expensed as incurred. The nearly $300,000 spent in 1968 to develop the laboratory model of the component had been charged against 1968 income.
2. On the other hand, if the R&D costs were capitalized and deferred until sales were generated from these expenditures, Multiproducts would report slightly higher profits for 1969–71 than Freeman had originally anticipated, primarily because the firm's expendable R&D costs would be reduced some $500,000 below the initially planned level.

Irrespective of whether the company capitalized or expensed the R&D costs *for book purposes,* the company would report *for tax purposes* losses in 1969 through 1971 inclusive.

Supple's memorandum caused considerable consternation among the management group. As a result, Freeman called a meeting of his management group to discuss the memorandum and the expensing issue. The group consisted of:

1. Frank Freeman, president.
2. Thomas Supple, controller.
3. Dr. Peter Hellman, vice president, research and development.
4. David Smith, vice president, finance.
5. Alan Cross, vice president, sales.
6. Phillip Appleton, vice president, purchasing.
7. James Jackson, vice president, employee and public relations.

After the prefatory remarks quoted at the beginning of the case, Multiproducts' president asked the controller to expand on his memorandum.

FREEMAN: Tom, why don't you discuss your memorandum a bit more extensively? Why do we have to write off, *as they are incurred,* these R&D costs related to the memory storage project?

SUPPLE: Well, first let me explain that *either* deferment or current expensing of R&D costs is an acceptable accounting practice. In fact, both practices are followed within our industry. However, the accounting profession has generally favored current expensing of such costs.

Personally, I believe that we should write off our R&D costs as incurred for several reasons. First, the accounting treatment I propose is conservative. Sec-

EXHIBIT 2

MULTIPRODUCTS ELECTRONICS CORPORATION

MEMORANDUM

To: Frank Freeman
From: Thomas Supple
Re: Revised Pro Forma Income Statements 1969–71

Our decision to increase annual R&D expenses from the original planned level of $1 million to $1.5 million will have a significant impact on our anticipated reported profits for 1969–71.

Therefore, I have revised the earlier profit estimates. The first revision assumes that we charge against income the R&D costs as incurred. The second revision assumes that we defer till 1972 the R&D costs related to the memory storage project.

For tax purposes, we will follow our tax policy of expensing R&D costs currently. As a result, we will not have to pay taxes during 1969–71.

Original (January 1, 1962) and Revised Projections
(in thousands except last column)

	Gross Sales	R&D Expense	Net Profit (Loss) Before	—after Taxes	Earnings per Share
Original:					
1969	$37,500	$1,000	$100	$ 50	$0.05
1970	38,500	1,000	300	150	0.15
1971	38,500	1,000	300	150	0.15
Revised:					
A. Expense R&D as incurred:					
1969	37,500	1,500	. . .	(400)	(0.40)
1970	38,500	1,500	. . .	(200)	(0.20)
1971	38,500	1,500	. . .	(200)	(0.20)
B. Defer R&D:					
1969	37,500	500	600	300 *	0.30
1970	38,500	500	800	400 *	0.40
1971	38,500	500	800	400 *	0.40

° The balance sheet will show the following:

	ASSETS (thousands)			LIABILITIES (thousands)	
1969	Deferred R&D expense	$1,000	Deferred tax liability		$ 300
1970	Deferred R&D expense	2,000	Deferred tax liability		700
1971	Deferred R&D expense	3,000	Deferred tax liability		1,100

Recommendation

I recommend that better accounting practice and consistency with our earlier treatment of R&D costs calls for us to expense these costs currently.

ond, it is highly speculative that we will ever generate future revenues from these R&D costs. Third, if we defer them, we will be overstating our income during the next three years. Fourth, we have always currently expensed our R&D costs, and consistency demands that we treat these anticipated costs in the same fashion.

FREEMAN: Well, Tom, I think this is more than just an accounting question. I am sure there are some additional considerations that we as management will have to evaluate. What thoughts do the rest of you have about Tom's proposed accounting policy to cover the handling of these R&D costs? Peter?

HELLMAN: Speaking for the R&D group, I would reject out of hand Tom's statement that the project is highly speculative. As I've said before, I think our chances for success are 7 out of 10. Those are pretty good odds to me.

One other thing worries me. The morale of the R&D group has been very low in recent years. They feel the losses of the last few years have resulted from *their* failure to come up with a new product. Now, we have a red-hot prospect and everyone is happy. If you write off the costs and we continue to report losses to the stockholders, then the R&D group's morale might fall again during those periods when we have setbacks on the project. And make no mistake about it, this project, like all R&D projects, will have its discouraging moments.

On the other hand, if you capitalize the costs and carry them on the balance sheet as an asset, you will be telling the R&D boys that they have created something of value. Which is true. After all, we wouldn't spend all this money if we didn't think it was of some value to us, would we?

I'm for deferment of these particular costs. In fact, I'm for deferring all our R&D costs which will benefit future accounting periods.

SMITH: I agree with Peter. From our point of view in Finance, there is only one policy to follow—deferment.

If this R&D project is to be completed within three years and turned into a successful commercial venture, we will have to go to the public money markets for capital in 1971, the year before we get into commercial production. And, for the life of me, I don't see how we will get sufficient funds at a reasonable cost if we show losses for the entire period 1965 through 1970.

Now, I can't go along with Tom when he states that deferment would be overstating our income during the next three years. If we defer these costs, what we are really doing is matching our costs with our revenues. These R&D costs are clearly identifiable with the memory storage project. And just as clearly, sensible accounting would say that they be matched with the memory storage revenues. Therefore, since these revenues will not be realized until after 1971, the appropriate R&D costs should be deferred until 1971, and then expensed against the revenues from the project.

To write these R&D costs off as incurred would be misleading. We would understate our income over the next three years. And, because the post-1971 revenues would be relieved of these R&D costs, the post-1971 income would be overstated.

Of course, there would be full disclosure to our stockholders of our accounting policy covering R&D costs. The extraordinary costs related to the memory storage project would be the only ones deferred. They would be clearly labeled as such on the balance sheet with an explanatory footnote. All other R&D costs would be expensed as incurred.

FREEMAN: How does this question look from the sales end, Alan?

CROSS. I go along with both Peter and David. If we are to finance this project we will have to keep our sales volume up over the next few years. And the best way to do this is to continue to get government cost-plus-fixed-fee contracts. However, those people in the Pentagon don't like to let out contracts to unprofitable companies. Therefore, I can't see jeopardizing the whole project just to be "conservative" accounting-wise.

APPLETON: I know one thing—if we are to finance the bulk of this project for at least two years by ourselves, we will have to resort to such measures as drawing down our cash and stretching our accounts payable. And that means our present current ratio of 2.2 to 1 will decrease somewhat, irrespective of whether we expense or defer the R&D costs.

Currently, despite our losses, we have been able to get reasonable trade credit because of our good current ratio. If, however, we have to reduce our current ratio to 1 to 1 or even less, and continue to report losses, I am sure our trade creditors will not be quite so generous. After all, they have seen far too many companies in the electronics business go under in recent years. Admittedly, I don't understand all the fine accounting points, but just from the purchasing angle, I'm for deferment. Our current ratio will decline but at least we will have profits to offset this disadvantage.

FREEMAN: Well, Jim, you are the last one. How do you see this issue from the employee and public relations point of view?

JACKSON: Like Phil, I don't pretend to understand all the fine points of accounting. In contrast, however, to the rest of you I'm not as positive in my position with respect to the issue.

As you all know, over the last few years we have successfully put off the demands of our workers for higher hourly wages. Our principal argument has been that we couldn't afford these increases in view of our losses. Now if we defer the R&D costs, we are going to be showing profits. And under these conditions, I have no doubt that it will be harder to justify denying the employees a pay increase. In addition, I must point out that such wage increases would be an additional *out-of-pocket* expense. They would be an added drain on our resources at the very time we are scratching and scraping to get together enough money to finance the stepped-up R&D program.

As for the stockholders, I am sure they would like to see some profits. And, if we defer the R&D costs, there will be profits.

But, if we expense the R&D cost as Tom suggests, our stockholders are going to be unhappy over the losses. It's going to put you, Frank, in a difficult position, since you promised them profits for 1969.

On balance, I guess I favor deferment. Perhaps we can put the union off a year or two. Frankly, I don't know how we can expense R&D costs for three years and tell the stockholders we are confident of success. The dissident group will say, "Clearly management by its own admission is throwing more money down the rathole."

FREEMAN: Tom?

SUPPLE: If you are all so keen to defer these R&D costs, let me ask you some questions:

1. Why shouldn't we have separate R&D accounts for *all* our projects?
2. What do we do with that $3 million lump deferment if the component project fails?
3. Aren't we just getting ourselves *into* more problems than we're getting *out* of?
4. And finally, over what period do you propose specifically to expense them after we go into production in 1971?

CROSS: On your last question, I believe we should plan to expense these deferred costs equally over the maximum period possible. That is, over the anticipated four years in which we expect to have a competitive advantage with the product, plus the subsequent three years of declining sales. Seven years in all.

In addition, we should also restate the comparative 1968 financial figures in our 1969 annual report. We should take out of the expenses charged against 1968 revenues the $300,000 we have already spent on the memory storage project. These costs should be deferred also. Then, we would show a small profit for 1968, which would be more realistic, since the R&D costs rightly belong on the balance sheet. Both the 1968 and 1969 statements would then be truly comparable.

SUPPLE: My God, Dave, you're trying to bookkeep us to profit!

CROSS: And you, Tom, are trying to bookkeep us to ruin. . . .

Question

1. As the president of Multiproducts, what accounting policy would you recommend should be adopted to account for the R&D costs related to the computer memory storage project? Would you expense or defer all, or some, of these costs? If you elect to defer the R&D costs, what policy would you adopt to cover the eventual expensing of these deferred costs?

Case 16–2. **MILWAUKEE BRAVES, INCORPORATED**

Milwaukee Braves, Inc. was incorporated under the laws of the State of Delaware on November 15, 1962 to operate the Milwaukee Braves baseball team of the National League. This case deals with the Milwaukee Braves' accounting for the costs of the player contracts acquired from a predecessor corporation and the subsequent costs incurred by the company for player development and acquisitions.

Players

The competitive success of a baseball club, which bears a strong relationship to its financial success, depends primarily upon the skill of players under contract to the club. In 1963, the policy of the Braves was to rely primarily upon players who were recruited and developed through the company's own player replacement program in the seven-club farm system it operated. During the period 1958–62, the National League Baseball Club of Milwaukee, Inc. spent about $6.6 million for the cost of scouting and team replacement, including the farm system, bonuses, schools, and tryouts. Occasionally, players' contracts were also acquired in major league trades or purchases. These costs were entirely written off as an expense in the respective years paid.

Forty-three players made up the Braves major league roster as of February 1, 1963. In 1963, Warren Spahn, with 327 major league wins, held the National League record for most games won by a lefthanded pitcher and had two no-hit games. Also, he was a member of the National League All Star team 14 times. Frank Bolling led the league in fielding at his position in 1961 and 1962 and was a member of the National League All Star team in those years. Del Crandell led National League catchers in fielding in 1958, 1959, 1960, and 1962, and had been a member of the All Star squad eight times. Eddie Matthews had hit 399 home runs in his major league career and had played on the All Star team nine times. He ranked eighth on the all-time list of major league home-run hitters. Hank Aaron led the league in total bases in 1956, 1957, 1959, 1960, and 1961, and was on the All Star team eight years. His lifetime major league batting average was .319, which was second highest among all active National League players in 1963.

The Braves controlled approximately 160 additional baseball player contracts. Player contracts were acquired through the services of 15 full-time scouts and 19 part-time scouts who covered the United States, Canada, and Latin America.

Player Acquisition

Young players often required at least three to five years' experience in the minor leagues before acquiring the skills needed to perform in the major leagues. In 1963, the Braves owned and operated two minor league clubs and in addition had working agreements with five other minor league clubs.

Once a player had signed a professional baseball contract with one of the clubs comprising the farm system of the Braves, his contract remained subject to the control of the Braves until such time as it was traded or sold to a club outside the Braves system, or until he was given an outright and unconditional release from his contract, or unless he was selected by another major league club in what was popularly called the baseball draft.

Most major league clubs often were interested in the same young baseball players. As a result of this tremendous competition, the practice developed on the part of many clubs to pay large bonuses to induce free-agent players to sign their first contract.

Capitalization and Amortization of Player Acquisition and Development Costs

On November 16, 1962, the Milwaukee Braves entered into an agreement to purchase all of the outstanding capital stock of the National League Baseball Club of Milwaukee from Perini Corporation. On the closing date for this transaction, November 26, 1962, the National League Baseball Club of Milwaukee was liquidated and its assets and liabilities were transferred to the Milwaukee Braves.

The total cost of the acquisition, including broker's commission, was $6,218,480; the cost was allocated to player contracts ($6,168,480) and league membership ($50,000).

Prior to the acquisition, the predecessor company, the National League Baseball Club of Milwaukee, had expensed all costs in connection with the acquisition and development of players.

Starting with the 1963 season, for financial reporting purposes, the Milwaukee Braves intended to capitalize the total cost of developing players, including the net income or expense from purchase and sale of player contracts. The amounts so capitalized were to be amortized against operating income "over a period equivalent to the actual playing careers of major league players." The cost of player contracts acquired from the predecessor company were to be amortized against operating income "over a period estimated to reflect replacement through future player development expenditures."

For income tax purposes, the company intended to deduct future team replacement expenditures from income as incurred. The cost of player contracts acquired from the predecessor company were to be amortized over a 10-year period, which represented the major league experience of the players of the National League Baseball Club of Milwaukee.

Exhibit 1 is an operating statement for 1962 prepared by the Milwaukee Braves. This statement shows the effect of certain adjustments to be made by the Milwaukee Braves. In the opinion of the company, these adjustments, when applied to the historical statements related to the baseball operations of the National League Club of Milwaukee, fairly presented the results of operation on a pro forma basis for the year ended October 31, 1962.

Questions

1. Do you agree with the decision to capitalize (*a*) the costs of the player contracts acquired from the National League Baseball Club of Milwaukee, and (*b*) future player acquisition and development costs?

EXHIBIT 1

MILWAUKEE BRAVES, INC.

Pro Forma Statement of Income from Baseball Operations
for the Year Ended October 31, 1962

	Historical Statement	Pro Forma Adjustments*	Pro Forma Statement
Operating income	$3,670,417		$3,670,417
Operating expenses:			
Team, park, games, and concessions .	$2,263,706	$(60,032)ᵃ	$2,203,674
Team replacement, including net income or expense from purchase and sale of players	599,433	(599,433)ᵇ	......
Amortization of player costs	......	691,777ᶜ	691,777
Scouting salaries and expense	274,278		274,278
General and administrative	336,718		336,718
	$3,474,135		$3,506,447
Income from baseball operations	$ 196,282		$ 163,970
Interest expense	3,567	150,000ᵈ	153,567
Net income applicable to baseball operations before income taxes	$ 192,715		$ 10,403
Provision for income taxes, applicable to baseball operations† ...	104,000	(100,600)ᵉ	3,400
Net Income Applicable to Baseball Operations	$ 88,715		$ 7,003

* Explanation of pro forma adjustments:
  a) Restatement of rental costs under terms of the new stadium lease.
  b) Reduction in operating expenses for the amount of team replacement expense to be capitalized and amortized over the estimated playing career of major league players.
  c) Amortization of player contracts capitalized upon acquisition of the club and of amounts expended for team replacement subsequent to acquisition.
  d) Annual interest charges estimated at 5 percent on the term note payable to bank.
  e) Adjustments in the provision for income taxes to reflect the foregoing adjustments.
  † On a pro forma basis, amortization of player contracts and future team replacement costs for tax purposes will exceed the amortization recorded in the income statement, and, consequently, there will be no income tax currently payable.

2. Do you approve of the company's policies covering the amortization of the costs referred to in question 1? What accounting techniques do you recommend that the company adopt to achieve its goal of amortizing (a) the acquired player contract costs "over a period estimated to reflect replacement through future player development expenditures," and (b) the future player development and acquisition costs "over a period equivalent to the actual playing careers of major league players"?

3. Comment on the allocation of the purchase price ($6,218,480) between player contracts ($6,168,480) and league membership ($50,000).

Case 16–3. WALT DISNEY PRODUCTIONS

Accounting for Film Inventories

"Our product is practically eternal," declared Roy Disney, president, Walt Disney Productions.[1] The most profitable example of this statement was "Snow White and the Seven Dwarfs," Walt Disney Productions' first feature-length movie. It cost $1.4 million to make. The picture's initial release, in 1937, resulted in a profit of $3.8 million. Its first reissue, in 1944, and its second, in 1951, netted Disney another $3 million. The movie was again reissued in 1958. The master negatives of "Snow White" and all of the other Disney films were kept in a specially built two-story concrete "vault" at the Disney Studios in Burbank, California. This case deals with the company's accounting policies related to the amortization of the costs of these film inventories.

Walt Disney Productions

During fiscal year 1964, Walt Disney Productions earned $7 million profit on a gross income of $87 million. The company's principal sources of income were: theatrical film rentals, television film rentals, and Disneyland Park. In addition, the names, characters, music, and other creative values flowing from the company's theatrical motion pictures, television shows, and Disneyland Park were marketed on records, merchandise, and comic strips by the divisions, subsidiaries, or agents of the company in practically every country in the world.

Over the years, Walt Disney Productions had produced a number of outstanding films for theatrical and television release. The company's film inventory included full-length cartoon features such as "Snow White," "Pinocchio," "Alice in Wonderland," and "The 101 Dalmations"; full-length live features, including "Treasure Island," "Robin Hood," "Old Yellow," and "The Absent-Minded Professor"; full-length "true-life" pictures, such as "Living Desert" and "Nature's Half-Acre"; and about 500 short subjects, consisting mostly of cartoons and travel pictures which were produced before 1954. In addition to the theatrical features, the company's inventory also included films produced for television, such as

---

[1] Exhibit 1 shows the company's inventory balances and results of operations from 1957 to 1964.

EXHIBIT 1

WALT DISNEY PRODUCTIONS

Selected Inventory and Operating Data
(in millions of dollars, except earnings per share)

	1964	1963	1962	1961	1960	1959	1958	1957
Inventories (at lower of cost or market):								
Production in process	10.8	13.6	16.9	15.2	15.1	15.4	20.4	14.5
Completed production, less amortization	12.3	11.1	7.6	8.8	14.0	14.0	5.0	4.4
Story rights and preproduction costs	1.3	0.9	0.8	0.4	0.6	0.5	0.3	0.3
Merchandise, materials, and supplies	1.9	1.7	1.7	1.8	2.7	2.7	2.2	1.4
Less provision for possible excess over estimated realizable amounts	...	...	...	...	...	(1.0)	(0.5)	(0.3)
Total inventories	26.3	27.3	27.0	26.2	32.4	31.6	27.4	20.3
Total theatrical films and television revenues	46.1	49.2	46.8	46.3	23.4	35.3	29.1	24.4
Amortization of theatrical and television production costs	14.5	16.1	15.6	19.2	14.6	19.4	13.7	12.3
Net income after taxes	7.1	6.6	5.3	4.5	(1.3)	3.4	3.9	3.7
Earnings per share	$3.96	$3.81	$3.14	$2.75	$(0.83)	$2.15	$2.51	$2.44

the "Zorro" adventure episodes and the films prepared for the Mickey Mouse Club and "Walt Disney's Wonderful World of Color." Except for a few commercial productions, Walt Disney Productions owned the master negatives of all the films the company had ever produced.

Accounting for Production Costs

The Walt Disney Productions 1964 annual report to stockholders included the following data in the current asset section of the consolidated balance sheet:

Inventories at the lower of cost or market (Note 2):

Productions in process	$10,830,987
Completed productions, less amortization	12,341,914
Story rights and preproduction costs	1,245,824
Merchandise, materials, and supplies	1,905,382
Total inventories	$26,324,107

Note 2 accompanying the financial statements stated:

Note 2—Inventories and Amortization. Costs of completed theatrical and television productions are amortized by charge to the income account in the proportion that the producer's share of income (less distribution, print, and advertising costs) received by the company for each production bears to the estimated total of such income to be received. Such estimates of total income are reviewed periodically and amortization is adjusted accordingly.

For accounting purposes, Walt Disney Productions maintained three major inventory categories for production costs: story right and pre-production costs, productions in process, and completed productions. Most productions began with the acquisition of a story property. Once acquired, the property was assigned an account number and all preproduction costs associated with the story were collected under this account number. These costs included the salary of the writer responsible for preparing the screen version of the story, and any other charges directly related to this activity. Indirect studio overhead was allocated between story accounts on the basis of direct dollar costs, including employee benefits. Should a story be abandoned before going into production, the costs accumulated in the story's account were written off to current income.

Once it was decided to produce a film based upon the story, the story account was closed out and the accumulated costs transferred to a production account. The number assigned to this production account remained with the production throughout its lifetime. Again, all of the costs directly associated with the production were charged to the production, and studio overhead was allocated between productions on the basis of direct dollar costs. Direct cost included such items as the salaries of actors, directors, cameramen, and set designers, as well as the wages of electricians, carpenters, and stagehands. Studio overhead included all those studio costs which could not be directly allocated to a specific production.

The cost of each feature production was charged to income in the proportion the income received [2] during the production's first release bore to the estimated total to be received. This practice was referred to as the "flow-of-income" method. For example, assume a film cost $1 million to produce and management estimated it would earn "net rentals" of $2 million during its first release. In this case, for every dollar of "net rental" from the film included in the income of the current period, 50 cents of production costs would be amortized. "Net rentals" were gross rentals less distribution, print, and advertising costs. These costs were about 40 percent of every gross rental dollar. Only the rental income associated with the production was included in the amortization calculation.

---

[2] Walt Disney Productions recorded domestic film rental income upon actual receipt of remittances. Similarly, the company recorded foreign income at the time of receipt of remittances in United States dollars or at the time of expenditures of foreign currencies abroad for the account of the company. In the case of feature theatrical films released on a national basis, these receipts were typically over a three- to four-year period, with between 70 and 80 percent of the total revenues realized during the first 12 months. About 256 key theaters out of a total 10,000 possible outlets accounted for about 80 percent of these revenues.

The production costs of films produced for television release were written off at the time the film was first shown on television. In those cases where a film previously released for theatrical showing was reissued for use on "Walt Disney's Wonderful World of Color," the costs associated with preparing the film for use on television were charged to income during the period in which the film was first run on television. Examples of theatrical releases later shown on television were "Johnny Tremain" and "The Miracle of the White Stallions."

Thus, the entire production costs of a film were amortized during the film's first release. Unlike several other movie producers, the company did not assign any residual value to its film inventory. These other companies assigned residual values to their theatrical releases based upon the expected revenues from the sale of the rights to the film for subsequent use on television. Walt Disney Productions did not follow this practice, since it was the company's policy not to sell the rights to its old theatrical releases to the television networks. Because of the nature of its product, the company believed it was more profitable to reissue its films for theatrical rather than television distribution. Also, while management intended that every film it produced would be reissuable, they nevertheless recognized that their product was subject to public acceptance, and that no true feeling of reissue possibilities could be estimated at the time a film was first released.

The company's inventories were carried at the "lower of cost or market." For this purpose, "market" was defined as estimated net rentals. For example, assume a film cost $1 million to produce and, based upon the initial public reaction, management estimated the film would generate net rentals to the producer of only $600,000 during its first release. In this case, the inventory value of the film would be written down to $600,000, $400,000 would be charged to income in the current period, and the remaining $600,000 cost would be amortized on the basis of $1 of cost for each $1 of net rental received.

The management of Walt Disney Productions had achieved a high level of competence in estimating film receipts. When a production was completed, key administrative and sales personnel submitted their estimates of the production's revenues. These estimates gave the company an initial feel for the production's income potential. Once the production was released, the company collected detailed statistics on the number of showings, admissions, and cash receipts. These results were then compared to similar statistics for earlier releases. The comparisons, tempered by experienced judgment and adjusted to reflect the actual release schedule, were then used to project the current release's estimated revenues for both financial accounting and cash management purposes. In the case of new releases, these estimates were prepared during the six-week period between the initial release date and the receipt of the first rental income.

Three or four times each year, management reappraised their income estimates. If a production's revenues were likely to fall materially below the prior estimate, the production's inventory value was written down and the loss charged to current income. On the other hand, if it appeared that the production's receipts were going to be materially larger than anticipated, the production's unamortized costs would be written off on the basis of the new income estimate.

1965 Motion Picture Product

It was generally anticipated that fiscal year 1965 would be a banner year for Walt Disney Productions. Based upon early record-shattering box-office receipts, "Mary Poppins" promised to be the most widely acclaimed of all Walt Disney motion pictures. In addition, the company planned to rerelease the classic cartoon feature, "Cinderella." Other 1965 full-length theatrical releases included "Emil and the Detectives," "The Tattooed Police Horse," "Those Calloways," and "The Monkey's Uncle." Scheduled for release in Christmas 1965 was "That Darn Cat." Other features in process included "Jungle Book," "Lt. Robin Crusoe," "Follow Me Boys," "A Son-in-law for Charles McCready," "Bullwhip Criffin," "The Gnomobile," and "The Happiest Millionaire."

Questions

1. Should the company capitalize story right and preproduction costs? Production costs?
2. What amortization policy should the company follow for deferred film costs?
3. Do you agree with the company's policy of reporting its film inventory on a lower-of-cost-or-market basis?

Case 16–4. **R. G. BARRY CORPORATION**
Human Resources Accounting

The R. G. Barry Corporation had sales and earnings for 1969 of $25,310,588 and $700,222 respectively. For the 10 years ending with 1969, Barry's sales grew at a 20 percent compounded annual rate while earnings increased at a 21.5 percent rate.

Barry produced and marketed a broad line of leisure footwear and related products. Its markets were characterized by intense price and style competition, which dictated that management have good internal controls. As part of its controls, Barry introduced in 1967 a "human asset accounting" concept.

The president's letter in the 1967 annual report stated under the subtitle "Organizational Assets":

As managers we are entrusted with the care of three types of assets: physical assets, organizational assets, and customer loyalty assets. Each manager is responsible for effective utilization of these assets to create a profit for the organization while preserving the financial soundness of the business.

If people are treated abusively, short-term profits will be derived at the expense of the company's organizational assets.

Managers now work with accounting data which reflect the condition of physical assets and changes in these assets over a period of time. The assets of human resources and customer loyalty do not appear in dollar terms on the balance sheets. To employ effectively all three types of assets, and realize the objectives of R. G. Barry, equally reliable accounting instruments are required to reflect the condition of organizational assets and customer loyalty and changes in these assets over time.

To fulfill these objectives we are now in the process of developing and installing a Human Resource Accounting system to measure in dollar terms the organizational assets and changes in these assets over time.

In later sections of the 1967 report "people—the human resources of the company" are referred to as that asset "without which all other assets become meaningless in terms of potential and future growth."

The initial development of this human asset accounting system was a joint effort by Barry and the University of Michigan's Institute for Social Research.

Barry's commitment to human asset accounting was further articulated throughout its 1968 annual report:

We set ambitious goals for profitable growth in 1968. We achieved these goals in the principal result areas of the business, namely, (1) to generate a profit on total resources employed, (2) to protect and improve the value of the financial, physical, organizational, and customer loyalty resources of the company, and (3) to manage profits to insure a sound financial position.

The resources of the business are: (1) the financial resources available to the corporation; (2) the technological resources such as buildings, equipment, and production technology; (3) the human resources in terms of the skills and abilities possessed by the people who comprise the organization; (4) the proprietary resources such as corporate name, brand names, copyrights, and patents; (5) the information resources of the business which provide reliable data upon which to make timely decisions.

The 1968 report went on to define the basic objectives of Barry's human resource accounting system as being:

1. To provide Barry managers with specific feedback information on their performance in managing the organizational resources and customer loyalty resources entrusted to their care so that they can make proper adjustments to their pattern of operations to correct adverse trends or further improve the condition of these resources.
2. To provide Barry managers with additional information pertaining to human resources to assist in their decision making.
3. To provide the organization with a more accurate accounting of its return on total resources employed, rather than just the physical resources, and to enable management to analyze how changes in the status of the resources employed affect the achievement of corporate objectives.

Barry clearly noted that the human resource accounting system was a "first pioneering step" and that it lacked refinement. Additionally, Barry stressed that, "The human resource capital accounts are used for internal informational purposes only and are not reflected, of course, in the financial data presented in this report."

The 1969 Barry annual report devoted 2 of its 24 pages to human resource accounting. (See Exhibit 1.) This material was introduced with a disclaimer which cautioned the reader that:

The figures included regarding investments and amortization of human resources are *unaudited* and you are cautioned for purposes of evaluating the performance of this company to refer to the *conventional certified* accounting data further on in this report. [Italics added.]

(Questions follow on page 426.)

EXHIBIT 1

R. G. BARRY CORPORATION AND SUBSIDIARIES

Excerpt from 1969 Annual Report

Balance Sheet

	Financial and Human Resource	Financial Only
ASSETS		
Total current assets	$10,003,628	$10,003,628
Net property, plant, and equipment	1,770,717	1,770,717
Excess of purchase price of subsidiaries over net assets acquired	1,188,704	1,188,704
Net investments in human resources	986,094	......
Other assets	106,783	106,783
Total Assets	$14,055,926	$13,069,832
LIABILITIES AND STOCKHOLDERS' EQUITY		
Total current liabilities	$ 5,715,708	$ 5,715,708
Long-term debt, excluding current installments	1,935,500	1,935,500
Deferred compensation	62,380	62,380
Deferred federal income taxes as a result of appropriation for human resources	493,047	......
Stockholders' Equity:		
Capital stock	879,116	879,116
Additional capital in excess of par value	1,736,253	1,736,253
Retained earnings:		
Financial	2,740,875	2,740,875
Appropriation for human resources	493,047	......
Total Stockholders' Equity	5,849,291	5,356,244
Total Liabilities and Stockholders' Equity .	$14,055,926	$13,069,832

Statement of Income

	Financial and Human Resource	Financial Only
Net sales	$25,310,588	$25,310,588
Cost of sales	16,275,876	16,275,876
Gross profit	$ 9,034,712	$ 9,034,712
Selling, general, and administrative expenses	6,737,313	6,737,313
Operating income	$ 2,297,399	$ 2,297,399
Other deductions, net	953,177	953,177
Income before federal income taxes	$ 1,344,222	$ 1,344,222
Human resource expenses applicable to future periods	173,569	......
Adjusted income before federal income taxes	$ 1,517,791	$ 1,344,222
Federal income taxes	730,785	644,000
Net Income	$ 787,006	$ 700,222

The information presented in this exhibit is provided only to illustrate the information value of human resource accounting for more effective internal management of the business. The figures included regarding investments and amortization of human resources are unaudited and you are cautioned for purposes of evaluating the performance of the company to refer to the conventional certified accounting data further on in this report.

EXHIBIT 1 (*continued*)

Human Resource Accounting

During the past year work continued on the development of Barry's Human Resource Accounting System. The basic purpose of the system is to develop a method of measuring in dollar terms the changes that occur in the human resources of a business that conventional accounting does not currently consider.

Basic Concept

Management can be considered as the process of planning, organizing, leading, and controlling a complex mix of resources to accomplish the objectives of the organization. Those resources, we believe, are: physical resources of the company as represented by buildings and equipment, financial resources, and human resources which consist of the people who comprise the organization and proprietary resources which consist of trademarks, patents, and company name and reputation.

In order to determine more precisely the effectiveness of management's performance it is necessary to have information about the status of investments in the acquisition, maintenance, and utilization of all resources of the company.

Without such information, it is difficult for a company to know whether profit is being generated by converting a resource into cash or conversely whether sub-optimal performance really has been generated by investments in developing the human resources which we expensed under conventional accounting practice.

Definition

Human Resource Accounting is an attempt to identify, quantify, and report investments made in resources of an organization that are not presently accounted for under conventional accounting practice. Basically, it is an information system that tells management what changes over time are occurring to the human resources of the business. It must be considered as an element of a total system of management—not as a separate "device" or "gimmick" to focus attention on human resources.

Objectives

Broadly, the Human Resource Accounting Information System is being designed to provide better answers to these kinds of questions: What is the quality of profit performance? Are sufficient human capabilities being acquired to achieve the objectives of the enterprise? Are they being developed adequately? To what degree are they being properly maintained? Are these capabilities being properly utilized by the organization?

As expressed in our 1968 Annual Report, our specific objectives in development of human resource accounting are . . . [see case for description].

Approach

The approach used has been to account for investments in securing and developing the organization's human resources. Outlay costs for recruiting, acquiring, training, familiarizing, and developing management personnel are accumulated and capitalized. In accordance with the approach conventional accounting employs for classification of an expenditure as an asset, only those outlays which have an expected value beyond the current accounting period deserve consideration as investments. Those outlays which are likely to be consumed within a twelve-month period are properly classified as expense items. The investments in human resources are amortized over the expected useful period of the investment. The basic outlays in connection with acquiring and integrating new management people are amortized over their expected tenure with the company. Investments made for training or development are amortized over a much shorter period of time. The system now covers all management personnel at all locations of the corporation.

Research and development of the system began in late 1966. . . .

EXHIBIT 1 (continued)

Applications

There are many potential applications for human resource accounting. Considering outlays for human resource investments which have a useful life over a number of years would have an impact upon the current year's revenue. Recognizing investments in human resources and their useful lives, losses resulting from improper maintenance of those resources can be shown in dollar terms. Estimating the useful lives of investments also provides a basis for planning for the orderly replacement of human capabilities as they expire, supplementing conventional manpower planning. Finally, recognizing investments in human resources will allow management to calculate dollar return on investment on a more comprehensive resource base for a particular profit center.

Summary

From the standpoint of management, knowledge of the human resource investments, maintenance, and returns is necessary for proper decision making and planning long-range corporate growth. As industry becomes increasingly technical, and management becomes progressively more complex, we believe conventional accounting practice will come to recognize human resource accounting in financial reporting.

At this stage, the Human Resource Accounting System at R. G. Barry is best regarded as a potentially important tool of the overall management system. It is not an end in itself, and needs continuing refinement and development.

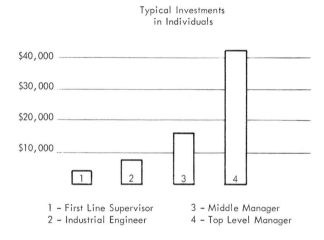

Typical Investments
in Individuals

1 – First Line Supervisor   3 – Middle Manager
2 – Industrial Engineer   4 – Top Level Manager

Questions

1. Comment on the following statement: A favorite cliché for any president's letter in the corporate annual report is, "Our employees are our most important—our most valuable—asset," but when one turns from the president's letter to the remainder of the report, and in particular to the financial statements, there is, typically, never any other indication or acknowledgment of these "vital" human resources beyond that which may be subsumed in *Goodwill* account. Barry has taken bold steps to account for its human

resources . . . . an effort which is, perhaps, not without some very fundamental conceptual problems.

2. Comment on this statement: The essential criterion for determining whether
    an expenditure is an "asset" or an "expense" relates to the notion of future
    service potential. Clearly, if a firm were to retain an upper management
    person under terms of a five-year contract, there would be this notion of
    future service potential and the person could quite properly be regarded as
    an "asset."

3. In order to meaningfully reflect human assets in its financial accounting
    data, how would you suggest that Barry resolve some of the following
    issues?

    a) What is the acquisition cost for each human asset? How much of this
         first cost, once quantified, is allocable to current expense or, vice versa,
         how much of it should be capitalized?

    d) Over what time period should the capitalized portion of the first cost
         be amortized? Should the amortization interval be different for each
         person? Will broad group accounts suffice, e.g., all division managers?

    c) How should continuing investments in people be treated in the ac-
         counts, i.e., expensed or capitalized, and on the basis of what criteria?
         Who should properly make these judgments?

    d) Does the acquisition cost really capture and convey the value of a
         human asset? Although classical accounting theory records assets on
         the books of account at "cost," would it perhaps not be better to use
         some more realistic and current measure of human resource "value"?
         Some alternative methods for valuation might be:

         (1) *Capitalization of Salary:* Using this approach, one would make a
             pro forma projection of a man's salary and discount it to a present
             value at an appropriate discount rate. Aside from the difficulty of
             selecting the "appropriate" discount rate, a definition for "salary"
             will have to be developed. Is "salary" to include stock options,
             executive fringes, pensions, etc., or rather simply just the plain
             cash disbursements across time? In other words, what exactly is
             to be capitalized and at what rate?

         (2) *Replacement Costs:* This method would value human assets at the
             estimated costs to the firm of replacing them with others of "like
             talent and experience." This replacement cost concept would serve
             to adjust the balance sheet value of human resources to current
             price trends in the economy, thereby providing a more realistic
             value during inflationary times. However, it would also be incon-
             sistent with the historical cost approach to valuing assets and
             would thus lead to a balance sheet wherein different assets would
             be denominated in dollars of different years and therefore of dif-
             ferent value. One possible solution to this dilemma would be to
             value all assets at replacement cost.

         (3) *Economic Value:* This approach to valuing the human resources of
             an organization involves discounting to a present value that portion
             of the firm's future earnings which is directly attributable to human

resources. The matter of the appropriate discount rate has, again, to be resolved; but of more importance and difficulty is the problem of properly allocating the future earnings to the several factor inputs of production. People, patents, finance, capital goods, etc., all contribute to a firm's output. Is it practical or even possible to attempt a reasonable partitioning of future earnings among these factor inputs, or would such an exercise degenerate into a totally arbitrary allocative process?

Also to be considered is the very fundamental difference between financial accounting "earnings" and cash flows. The latter can be discounted; the former cannot. Therefore, will the firm be additionally burdened with trying to reconcile pro forma earnings *and* cash flows with the several factor inputs?

Finally, just how reliable and accurate will intermediate to long-term pro forma projections prove to be? Might not dissident stockholders seek legal recourse against those firms who were too optimistic in their projections and who subsequently were forced to write down asset values by virtue of not having been able to produce to the earlier promises?

e) Other problems remain: What attitude will the regulatory agencies adopt toward the inclusion of human resource assets and their concomittant amortization in their determination of allowable investment bases for public utilities? Will government agencies recognize human resource assets as a legitimate balance sheet item in determining proper fees and profits on their contract awards? What are the legal implications of human resource assets? Does a corporation really "own" its human resources?

4. Comment on the following: One view of Barry's Human Resource Accounting system is that it represents an effort to refine and improve its internal management practices and to make its financial accounting system and output data more responsive and relevant to the needs of its users. Another view might be that Barry has embarked on a course which will only add to the lack of objectivity and the problems which already plague generally accepted accounting principles.

CHAPTER 17

INVENTORY PRICING

The selection of a method for pricing inventories represents an important management decision. The procedure selected will have a major impact on the measurement of net income and net working capital.

Inventories include all tangible items held for sale or consumption in the normal course of business for which the company holds title, wherever they might be located. Typically, inventories can be placed in one of four categories: finished goods, goods in process, raw materials, and manufacturing supplies. There are several generally accepted methods for pricing inventories. The significant problems in the area of inventory valuation result from the difficulties involved in allocating costs between periods and products, and the failure of selling prices and costs to move together.

The American Institute of Certified Public Accountants' pronouncement on inventory pricing appears in *Accounting Research Bulletin No. 43*, Chapter 4. This chapter, originally issued in 1947 as *Accounting Research Bulletin No. 29*, sets forth the general principles applicable to the pricing of inventories of mercantile and manufacturing enterprises.

Periodic and Perpetual Inventory Systems

Inventory value is determined by multiplying the quantity of inventory on hand by the price per unit. There are two systems for determining the quantity of inventories: the periodic inventory system and the perpetual inventory system. Irrespective of the system used, it is necessary periodically to inspect physically inventories.

The periodic inventory system involves a periodic determination of beginning inventory, purchases for the period, and ending inventory. These totals are determined by actual count. From these counts the cost of goods sold may be determined by deduction. The basic formula is:

Beginning inventories + purchases − ending inventories =
cost of goods sold

The perpetual inventory system involves the keeping of a running record of all the additions and subtractions to the inventory.

Pricing Bases

Depending on the circumstances, the bases for pricing inventories may be: cost; cost or market, whichever is lower; or selling price. The major objective underlying the selection of a pricing basis in a particular case should be the fairest determination of periodic income.

COST METHODS

Cost is the principal basis for pricing inventories. *Accounting Research Bulletin No. 43*, Chapter 4 states:

The primary basis for accounting for inventories is cost . . . as applied to inventories, cost means in principle the sum of the applicable expenditures and charges directly or indirectly incurred in bringing an article to its existing condition and location.

The inventory prices of manufacturing and merchandising companies reflect the different functions of these two classes of business activity. Manufacturing companies convert raw materials into finished goods. Consequently, their inventory prices reflect the cost of raw materials, direct labor, and factory overhead. Those costs associated with the product are referred to as product costs and are charged against revenues when the products are sold. All other costs, such as general administration and selling costs, are classified as period costs and are charged to the period in which they were incurred. Typically, merchandising businesses do not incur conversion costs. As a result, their inventory prices are the same as the prices the company paid for the products it sells.

Every well-run business maintains some record of its costs. These costs may be collected and recorded on the basis of either individual jobs (a job cost system) or the various production processes (a process cost system). The costs assigned to the various finished and partially finished products may be predetermined standard costs or actual costs. If a standard cost system is used, the common practice is to assign any small difference between actual and standard costs to cost of goods sold. If the variance is relatively large, however, some effort may be made to allocate the variance between the cost of goods sold and ending inventory accounts. In practice, a number of methods are used to allocate overhead costs to inventories. Most cost systems use a standard overhead rate which allocates a fixed amount of overhead per unit to finished or partially finished goods, based upon the amount of, say, direct labor dollars embodied in the inventory. Other common bases for absorbing overhead are machine hours and direct labor hours.

The exclusion of all factory overheads from inventory costs does not constitute an accepted accounting procedure for financial or tax accounting. Some argue that the inclusion of fixed factory overhead in inventory prices (and cost of goods sold) is misleading, since it tends to make a profit a function of production rather than sales. These people advocate "direct costing," a procedure which includes in the inventory price only variable manufacturing costs. The fixed manufacturing costs are treated as period costs and are charged against income during the period in which they are incurred. Irrespective of the method used in financial reports, direct costing can be used for internal accounting purposes.

Often more than one product is produced from the same raw material. In the case of common products and by-products, raw material costs are typically allocated between the products on the basis of relative sales value, although a variety of other methods are permissible as long as the results are not misleading. Often, for example, if the by-products represent a relatively minor portion of the total production, the "by-product cost method" is used. Under this method, the by-product is initially valued at selling price less disposition costs. The total cost of the primary product is then reduced by this net amount. As a result, the profits and losses of the company are recorded on the sale of the primary product.

INVENTORY METHODS

There are a number of generally acceptable methods based on historical costs for determining the price of inventories. The costs selected by these methods for pricing inventories reflect either the flow of goods or the flow of costs. Illustration 17–1 will be used to illustrate briefly a number

ILLUSTRATION 17–1

ABC COMPANY

	Units	Unit Cost	Total
Beginning inventory	2	$10	$20
Purchases:			
1	1	11	11
2	1	10	10
3	1	12	12
4	1	13	13
Cost of goods available for sale			$66
Total quantity available for sale	6		
Total sold during period	4		
Ending inventory	2		

of these cost-based methods (how the actual unit costs were determined will be ignored in these examples).

Specific Identification

The specific identification procedure associates the actual costs to the particular items in inventory. For example, if by inspection the ABC Company determined that its ending inventory consisted of purchases 1 and 3, the ending inventory would be valued at $23. Consequently, the cost of goods for the period would be $43 (total goods available for sale less ending inventory). While this method may directly relate revenues and costs, it is impractical for most businesses. However, it is sometimes used for "big ticket" items, e.g., autos.

Last Invoice Price

The last invoice price method values the ending inventory at the most recent invoice price paid. Under this method, the two units in the ABC Company's ending inventory would be priced at $26 and the cost of goods sold expense would be $40. For those companies with a rapid turnover of inventory and where older inventory items are used first, this method gives inventory prices which are a close approximation of those determined by the specific identification method. This method is not widely used.

Simple Average

The simple average method prices the ending inventory as follows:

$$\frac{\text{Sum of invoice prices per unit}}{\text{Number of invoices}} \times \text{number of units in ending inventory}$$

In the case of the ABC Corporation, this method would lead to an ending inventory value of $22.40 if the beginning inventory value per unit was included as an "invoice price." As a result, the cost of goods sold would be $43.60. The principal weakness of this procedure is that it gives equal weight to the invoice prices of large and small purchases. However, like some of the other methods discussed in this section, because of its simplicity it is used by small businesses.

Weighted Average

The weighted average method assigns to the ending inventory the average cost of the units available for sale during the period. The weighted average cost of the ABC Company's ending inventory is $22 and its cost of goods sold expense for the period is $44:

Cost of goods available for sale $66
Total units available for sale 6
Average cost $11
Ending inventory price (2 units × $11) $22

This method assumes sales are made proportionally from all inventory available. Therefore, the cost of the inventory is influenced by the cost of all of the items available for sale during the period. As a result, if prices are rising, inventory prices may lag behind selling prices based on current purchase costs.

Moving Average

The moving average method computes the average unit price of the inventory after each purchase. The use of a moving average reduces the extent of the possible lag between inventory price and selling prices associated with the weighted average method. Given a perpetual inventory system, the cost of goods sold of the ABC Company is $42.22 and the value of the ending inventory is $23.78 (see Illustration 17–2).

ILLUSTRATION 17–2

	Physical Units			Dollar Costs		
Date	Additions to Stock	Reductions in Stock	Balance	Additions to Stock	Reductions in Stock	Balance
April 1	...	...	2	...	...	$20.00
6	1	...	3	$11	...	31.00
7	...	2	1	...	$20.66	10.34
15	1	...	2	10	...	20.34
16	1	...	3	12	...	32.34
25	...	2	1	...	21.56	10.78
27	1	...	2	13	...	23.78

First-In, First-Out

The first-in, first-out (Fifo) method assumes that the goods remaining in inventory are the most recent purchases: that is, the goods purchased first are sold first. In the case of the ABC Company, the price of the ending inventory using the Fifo procedure is $25 (i.e., the sum of the costs of purchases 3 and 4). As a result, the cost of goods expense is $41. This technique is based upon the flow of goods approach to inventory pricing.

Last-In, First-Out

The last-in, first-out (Lifo) method is based on the flow of costs concept and assumes the most recent purchase costs are related to current revenues. As a result, the ending inventory reflects the oldest costs.

Lifo inventories consist of a series of "cost layers." The initial layer includes the quantities and related prices existing at the time when Lifo was adopted. The ending inventory is the base cost layer plus the older layers of inventory required to equal the quantity of goods at the balance sheet date. In the case of the ABC Company, if Lifo had been adopted before the beginning of the period, the initial cost layer would be two units at $10 (i.e., the beginning inventory). The next layer would have been purchase 1. Under the Lifo method, ABC's ending inventory determined by a *periodic* inventory system is $20 and the resulting cost of goods sold expense is $46. Since unit reductions in inventory equaled purchases, the two units in the ending inventory are valued at the $20 shown for the two units in the beginning inventory. If the ending inventory had been determined by a *perpetual* inventory system, the ending inventory would be $23, because the inventory fell below the Lifo base during the month. The $23 consists of one unit at the initial cost of $10 plus the $13 cost of the earliest purchase after the inventory fell below the base quantity.

A company can adopt the Lifo method for income tax purposes only on the condition that it use this method in its published financial statements.

Lifo versus Fifo

The Lifo and Fifo methods are among the most popular inventory pricing procedures. In practice, each is considered an equally acceptable alternative. However, their impact on working capital and net income can be significantly different. For example, in the ABC situation, the Lifo procedure led to an ending inventory valued at $20, whereas the Fifo method resulted in an ending inventory valued at $25. The cost of goods sold for the period also reflected the different procedures: Lifo led to a cost of goods sold expense of $46 and Fifo resulted in a cost of goods sold expense of $41. The extent of the cost differential in this illustration should not be considered typical. However, it does highlight the relationship between the inventory pricing procedure, the inventory value, and the cost of goods sold expense.

The adoption of Lifo as an acceptable inventory method caused considerable controversy. The advocates of Lifo argued that this procedure stated the cost of goods sold in current dollars. As a consequence, they noted, costs and revenues would be matched in terms of relatively similar dollars, irrespective of the direction of the trend in prices. This result, the advocates of Lifo argued, overcame a major weakness of Fifo, namely, that in periods of rising prices it leads to an "overstatement" of profits, since a portion of these profits have to be used to replace the consumed inventories at higher costs. Similarly, in periods of falling prices, the proponents of Lifo stated, Fifo leads to an "understatement" of profit, since inventories produced or bought during an earlier period of higher prices would be matched with current lower selling prices.

Those who opposed Lifo argued that Lifo leads to an unrealistic balance sheet presentation of inventory. Except in some rare situations, Lifo did not correspond to the actual flow of goods, and Lifo did not necessarily result in an improved matching of costs and revenues. If a Lifo inventory consisting of very old cost layers was depleted, the Lifo opponents argued, the current profits would be misleading, since current revenues would be matched in part against these old unrealistic costs.

While not necessarily agreeing that Lifo is a sound accounting method, a number of people became reconciled to Lifo because it represented a partial recognition of price-level changes for the purpose of determining income. For example, in 1953, the American Accounting Association's Committee on Accounting Concepts and Standards stated:

> . . . LIFO has some usefulness at the present time provided adequate standards of disclosure are utilized. However, strong effort should be applied to experimentation and techniques of price-level adjustment and if techniques eventually are commonly adopted for reflecting in accounting reports the impact of price-level changes, the *artificial* LIFO method should be abandoned entirely in favor of a realistic flow assumption.

Later in 1957, another AAA committee examined the reporting of inventories and the cost of goods sold. Their report said:

> In the majority of companies, the most important category of expense is the cost of goods sold. Ideally, the measurement of this expense should accomplish three related objectives:
> 1. report in current terms the cost of products and services transferred to customers during the period;
> 2. report in current terms the costs present in inventories at the end of the period;
> 3. identify the gains or losses resulting from price changes.

The methods of inventory pricing in common use achieve these objectives in varying degrees. For example, LIFO usually reflects cost of goods sold in relatively current terms, but fails to do the same for inventories, and does not disclose the results of price changes. FIFO and average cost methods are reasonably satisfactory in many cases with respect to the pricing of inventories.

They also reflect the effects of price changes but bury this information in the cost of goods sold figure, thereby failing to distinguish between trading profit or loss and the gains or losses from price movements. Standard cost methods can accomplish the objectives set forth above, but the results of these procedures typically are adjusted to historical outlay cost in published financial reports.

Base Stock

The base or "normal" stock method assumes that a business needs a minimum or basic inventory quantity to carry on normal operations. For example, if the ABC Company needed an inventory of two units to carry on normal operations, the two units could be regarded as the base stock. In a sense, it is argued, this base stock is similar to the company's fixed assets. If the company is to continue operations, the base stock must be preserved. Therefore, the argument continues, if the replacement cost of this minimum inventory rises, the increase in these costs should not be reflected in higher income. To avoid this effect, the base stock is priced at a cost well below current market. In this respect, the base stock method is similar to the Lifo method. Both seek to match current costs with current revenues.

The inventory in excess of the base stock can be valued by Lifo, Fifo or some other method. Should a company cut into its base stock and intend to replace the deficient quantity later, a replacement provision is established equal to the difference between the base price and the current market price of the deficient units. When the units are replaced, they are replaced at the base price and the provision offset by the difference between the base price and the actual cost of the deficient units.

The base stock method is generally accepted for financial accounting purposes. It is not approved for income tax purposes, however. Outside of some companies engaged in processing basic raw materials, this method is not widely used.

COST OR MARKET, WHICHEVER IS LOWER

The primary basis for accounting for inventory is cost. However, *Accounting Research Bulletin No. 43*, Chapter 4 states:

A departure from the cost basis for pricing the inventory *is required* when the utility of the goods is no longer as great as its cost. Where there is evidence that the utility of goods, in their disposal in the ordinary course of business, will be less than cost, whether due to physical deterioration, obsolescence, changes in price levels, or other causes, the difference should be recognized as a loss of the current period. This is generally accomplished by stating such goods at a lower level commonly designated as *market*.

The term "market" means current replacement costs, either by purchase or reproduction. The shift in emphasis from the balance sheet to
the income statement has led to a modification in the application of the
term "market." In the days when the balance sheet was the dominant
statement, the lower of cost or market rule was adopted to report inventories on a "conservative" basis. This approach assumed that lower selling
prices would automatically follow lower replacement costs. However,
with the increased emphasis on net income, businessmen became concerned about the problems caused by the failure of selling prices to follow
replacement cost changes. Accordingly, *Accounting Research Bulletin
No. 43*, Chapter 4 notes:

> The rule of cost or market, whichever is lower, is intended to provide a
> means of measuring the residual usefulness of an inventory expenditure. . . . In
> applying the rule, however, judgment must always be exercised. . . . Replace-
> ment or reproduction prices would not be appropriate as a measure of utility
> when the estimated sales value, reduced by the costs of completion and disposal,
> is lower, in which case the realizable value so determined more appropriately
> measures utility. Furthermore, where the evidence indicates that cost will be
> recovered with an approximately normal profit upon sale in the ordinary course
> of business, no loss should be recognized even though replacement or repro-
> duction costs are lower. . . . It also recognizes that, if a business is expected to
> lose money for a sustained period, the inventory should not be written down
> to offset a loss inherent in the subsequent operations.

The application of the lower of the cost or market (replacement or
reproduction cost) rule is further modified by upper and lower limits:

1. Market should not be greater than net realizable value.
2. Market should not be less than net realizable value less a normal profit
   margin.

The decision process for making the "cost or market" determination is
shown in Illustration 17–3. Illustration 17–4 presents data on four inventory situations with different combinations of original cost, replacement
cost, net realizable value, and the appropriate inventory valuation decision
for each case. Original cost is the price paid to acquire the inventory.
Replacement cost is the price for which the inventory could now be
purchased or reproduced. Net realizable value is the selling price less the
costs of completion and disposal. The normal profile margin associated in
the illustration is 21 percent of the selling price.

In Example A the inventory valuation would be $85 ($140 selling
price −$5 completion −$50 profit margin = $85), or the "lower limit"
of the allowable valuation range. In Example B, the inventory would be
valued at $90 (selling price $95−$5 completion = $90), the "upper limit"
of the allowable inventory valuation.

ILLUSTRATION 17–3

Application of Lower of Cost or Market Rule

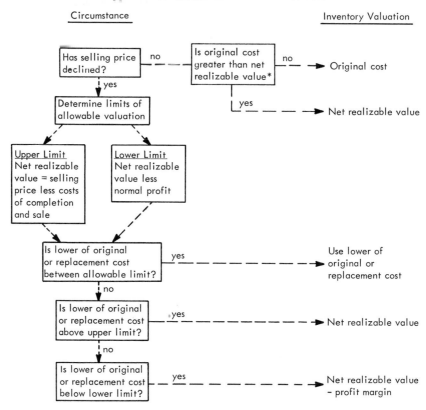

Circumstance   Inventory Valuation

° Net realizable value = selling price — cost of completion and sale.

Loss resulting from inventory write-down may be handled in one of two ways: as a cost of sales, or as a special operating expense item. When the amount of the loss from applying the lower of cost or market rule is substantial, it is good practice to show the charge separately identified from the cost of goods sold.

Some people object to the lower of cost or market basis for pricing inventories. They claim that it is inherently inconsistent. As one dissenter to *Accounting Research Bulletin No. 43* said: "A drop in selling price below cost is no more of a realized loss than a rise above cost is a realized gain under a consistent criterion of realization."

The lower of cost or market rule is acceptable for income tax purposes, except in the case of Lifo inventories. There is no such restriction in the case of financial accounting reports.

ILLUSTRATION 17–4

Lower of Cost or Market Computation

	Examples			
	1	*2*	*3*	*4*
Cost	$2.00 *	$2.00	$2.00	$2.00
Replacement cost	2.10	1.98 *	1.98	1.88
Net realizable value	2.50	2.30	1.90 *	2.40
Net realizable value				
less normal profit	1.98	1.82	1.50	1.90*

    ° Inventory valuation.

To further illustrate the application of the cost or market rule, assume:

	Example A	Example B
Original cost	$100	$100
Replacement cost	80	93
Old selling price	150	150
New selling price	140	95
Cost of completion, sale	5	5

Retail Method

The retail inventory method is used as an approximation of the cost or market method by retailers and others who keep their inventory records on a selling price basis. In order to apply this method, records must be maintained of purchases and returns to manufacturers, showing cost and selling prices; and of customer sales and returns, showing selling prices. The cost of the ending inventory is calculated as follows:

1. Add the purchases during the period at cost to the opening inventory at cost.
2. Add the purchases at retail to the opening inventory at retail.
3. Subtract these two totals. The difference is the so-called cumulative mark-on in dollars. Calculate this amount as a percentage of the total retail price of the goods available for sale during the period.
4. Subtract actual sales from the total retail price of goods available for sale (determined in 2 above) to obtain computed inventory at retail.
5. Multiply the ending inventory at retail by the mark-on percentage (computed in 3 above) and subtract from inventory at retail to determine inventory at cost.

The retail method is widely used in the retail business, since it reduces the clerical work and permits cost to be omitted from price tags.

SELLING PRICE

The third basis for pricing inventories is selling price. According to *Accounting Research Bulletin No. 43*, Chapter 4:

Only in exceptional cases may inventories properly be stated above cost. For example, precious metals having a fixed monetary value with no substantial cost of marketing may be stated at such monetary value; any other exceptions must be justifiable by inability to determine appropriate approximate costs, immediate marketability at quoted market price, and the characteristic of unit interchangeability. When goods are stated above costs this fact should be fully disclosed.

If the selling price basis is used, the cost of disposition should be deducted. The principal arguments for the application of the selling price basis are: first, the inventory is readily marketable at known market prices and, second, production is the critical business activity, rather than selling. In general, the inability to determine cost is the weakest argument for pricing inventories on a selling price basis.

STATEMENT PRESENTATION

Typically, inventories are shown in the current asset section of the balance sheet, immediately after accounts receivable. According to *Accounting Research Bulletin No. 43*, Chapter 4:

The basis of stating inventories must be consistently applied and should be disclosed in the financial statements; whenever a significant change is made therein, there should be disclosed the nature of the change and, if material, the effect on income.

The Securities and Exchange Commission's Regulation S–X requires disclosure of the inventory pricing basis:

The basis of determining the amounts shall be stated. If a basis such as "cost," "market," or "cost or market whichever is lower" is given, there shall also be given, to the extent practicable, a general indication of the method of determining the "cost" or "market": e.g., "average cost," "first-in, first-out," or "last-in, first-out."

A number of people believe that the difference between the stated cost and the current value of inventories kept on a Lifo or base stock method should be disclosed, principally because the inventory values shown on the balance sheet may be only a small fraction of their actual worth. In 1949, a draft of an accounting research bulletin proposing such disclosure was withdrawn. Those who opposed the disclosure stated that it would raise questions among the readers of financial statements as to the validity of the Lifo method; that it was in many cases difficult to objectively determine the current cost of inventory; and that the amount disclosed was unrealizable, unless the inventories were depleted. In contrast, the American Accounting Association Committee on Accounting Concepts and Standards recommended that "when Lifo is used there be reported in the financial statements figures showing the inventory valuation and the operating costs (including tax effects) on a realistic basis." Relatively few companies disclose the effect Lifo has on their balance sheet or income statement, except in the year in which Lifo is adopted.

SUMMARY

The valuation of inventories is critical to the periodic measurement of net working capital and net income. The importance of inventories is further reflected in the prominence this item receives in internal control systems and audit programs. There are many different accepted procedures for valuing inventory, most of which are cost-based. Management should select the inventory pricing method which leads to the fairest determination of periodic income. The discussion of inventories involves considerable controversy: some argue that the number of acceptable inventory procedures should be reduced. Others contend that particular inventory methods are misleading. A number of people believe that the disclosure of inventories is inadequate. Clearly, this is an important area for all those who prepare, audit, or use accounting statements.

SUGGESTED FURTHER READING

ACCOUNTING INTERNATIONAL STUDY GROUP. *Accounting and Auditing Approaches to Inventories in Three Nations: Stock in Trade and Work in Progress in Canada, the United Kingdom and the United States.* London: St. Clements Foot & Cross Ltd., 1968.

AMERICAN INSTITUTE OF PUBLIC ACCOUNTANTS. *Case Studies in the Observation of Inventories.* New York: AICPA, 1959.

BUTLER KEITH J. *Effects of Taxation: Inventory Accounting and Policies.* Cambridge, Mass.: Harvard University, 1949.

HOFFMAN, RAYMOND A. *Inventories: A Guide to their Control, Costing and Effect upon Income and Taxes.* New York: Ronald Press Co., 1962.

MAGEE, JOHN F., and BOODMAN, DAVID M. *Production Planning and Inventory Control.* New York: McGraw-Hill, 1967.

CASES

Case 17–1. **BEALE COMPANY**
Direct and Full Absorption
Costing of Inventory

Early in November 1970, the new president of the Beale Company was eagerly waiting the completion of the profit and loss statement for October. He knew that October sales had exceeded those for September by more than $50,000, and he was anxious to see how much of this increased sales volume was reflected as extra profit. But when the report came in, it showed an overall loss of $5,015 (Exhibit 1) as compared with a September profit of $3,509. The president immediately thought some mistake had been made and called in the controller for an explanation. The controller said the figures were correct, but that in October the company had not produced anywhere near its normal volume and hence the charge for unabsorbed burden had decreased the profit more than the added sales had increased it. He said that if the rate of sales were always the same as the rate of factory production, the kind of distortion that was bothering the president would not appear. However, when the factory operations were out of phase with sales operations, such distortions were almost certain to result so long as the company followed the commonly practiced accounting convention of charging or crediting periodic over- or underabsorbed factory overhead to the current profit and loss account.

The president reacted strongly to the controller's explanations: "I don't care a hoot for your accounting conventions. But I do know this: when our sales go up, with other things reasonably equal, I am going to expect my profit to show an increase. If your reports can't show so simple a thing as that, why do we spend so much money on your department?"

As a matter of fact, the controller had been thinking about much the same problem that disturbed the president, but from a slightly different angle. Accordingly, he seized the opportunity to propose a radically dif-

442

EXHIBIT 1

BEALE COMPANY

Condensed Income Statement, Month of October 1970

Sales	$336,903	
Cost of sales at standard	178,168	
Gross margin above standard costs		$158,735
Less manufacturing variances from standard costs:		
Labor	$ 4,321 *	
Material	3,972	
Overhead:		
Volume †	26,870	
Spending ‡	1,347	
		27,868
Gross profit		$130,867
Selling costs:		
Selling expenses	$ 84,514	
Sales taxes	3,236	
Freight allowed	7,195	
Total selling costs		94,945
Operating profit before administrative costs.		$ 35,922
Administration costs:		
General administrative expenses	$ 20,640	
Research expenses	5,879	
Total administration costs		26,519
Operating profit		$ 9,403
Other income or charges		(14,418)
Loss, Current Month		$(5,015)

* Credit variance.
† Volume variance is the difference between the budgeted cost and the overhead costs charged at the standard overhead cost net unit to the production for the period.
‡ Spending variance is the difference between the actual costs and the budgeted costs.

ferent approach to the problem of overhead: *charge the fixed overhead costs for the month to the current operating statement in a lump sum* just as is commonly done in the case of selling and administrative expenses. Thus there would be no problem of heavy over- or underabsorbed overhead as the volume of operations changed. Cost of goods sold, of course, now would reflect only the nonfixed factory costs, i.e., variable costs, which the controller called "direct costs."

As an illustration, the controller reworked the company's figures for October, with the startling result that the former loss of $5,015 was turned into a profit of $11,028 (Exhibit 2). When this figure was shown to the president, he first exclaimed, "That's more like it." Then he hesitated and started to speculate: "But this means more taxes and more

EXHIBIT 2

BEALE COMPANY

Condensed Income Statement (Proposed Style),
Month of October 1970

Sales	$336,903	
Standard "variable" cost of sales	123,133	
Gross margin above variable costs		$213,770
Selling expenses:		
Selling expenses	$ 84,514	
Sales taxes	3,236	
Freight allowed	7,195	
Total selling expenses		94,945
Merchandising margin		$118,825
Administrative expenses:		
General administrative expenses	$ 20,640	
Research expenses	5,879	
Total		26,519
Additional factory expenses:		
Fixed factory overhead	$ 65,862	
Manufacturing variances from standard costs:		
Labor variance $4,321*		
Material variance 3,972		
Overhead variance (spending).. 1,347	998	66,860
Operating margin		$ 25,446
Other income or charges		(14,418)
Profit, Current Month		$ 11,028

° Credit variance.

demands for wage increases and dividends and what-all. Maybe your idea isn't so good after all."

The controller was in favor of the new plan largely because of its simplified accounting procedures. For one thing, there would be no fixed overhead costs in the standard cost figures for different products but only the three classes of "direct costs":

a) The cost of raw materials.
b) Direct labor.
c) The portion of the outlay for manufacturing expenses which varies directly or closely in proportion to productive activity.

Omission of fixed overhead costs from the individual product costs would mean that the vexing and expensive task of working out an acceptable allocation of overhead to each product would be unnecessary. Inasmuch as many of these prorations had in fact become out of date, the controller was further attracted to his plan by the possibility that the expense of the needed overhauling of the figures might be avoided.

The controller also believed that the proposed system would greatly sharpen the focus of management on the *controllable* portion of costs by spotlighting the variable elements. Standards for the variable costs incurred by the different departments at different levels of output could be worked out by engineering methods. Since the fixed costs pertaining to factory operations tend to fall into quite a different category from that of the variable costs, they should be segregated anyway. By way of analogy, he suggested that, like a retail store, a manufacturing company "purchases" its product for a known "direct cost." Consequently, the chief difference between the two kinds of business is that to make a profit the manufacturing company has to pay the fixed factory costs in addition to the selling salaries, administration costs, storage, etc. Furthermore, the fixed factory costs are like the occupancy costs (rent, maintenance, etc.) of a retail store. On such a basis, the factory's "direct costs," i.e., variable costs, are similar to the retail store's "cost of purchases."

The controller argued that a further advantage of his proposal would be the provision of a more satisfactory basis for making the usual monthly comparison of margin figures in the company's product-by-product "Gross Margin Statement." When recast in the new form (with fixed costs excluded) the figures would be much more meaningful than at present. The new margin figures would be, of course, much higher all down the line, but once the management adjusted its thinking to the new basis, the controller was confident that the value of knowing how much each product was contributing to fixed costs and profit would be greatly appreciated.

One of the sales executives supported the controller's argument on the usefulness of the new margin figures. He pointed out, for example, that if there were two products sold by one of his divisions, products A and B, and if the situation were as described in the following example, product B, in general, would clearly appear to be the more desirable item to sell:

Product	Total Factory Cost per Pound (Std.)	Selling Price	Margin	% of Sales
A	$0.897	$1.55	$0.653	42.1
B	1.015	1.80	0.785	43.6

But if the new margin figures were to work out something as follows, then product A was by all odds the product on which the company's selling effort really should be concentrated:

Product	Variable Factory Cost	Selling Price	New "Margin"	% of Sales
A	$0.413	$1.55	$1.137	73.6
B	0.809	1.80	0.991	55.6

The controller's proposed method of keeping records, the sales executive reasoned, would thus reveal the true opportunities for profit. He cited one company he knew that had so redirected its selling effort that in less than eight months it had shifted from an operating loss to an operating profit and had maintained good profits ever since.

At this point in the discussion the treasurer entered the argument. He observed cynically that if the example cited was typical of the Beale Company, the first thing anyone knew, the sales department in its efforts to get business would be selling at its usual markup over the new standard cost figures (variable costs only). "When that time comes," he snorted, "how are we going to cover the fixed costs? Where do we get our capital replacements? We'll have to pay the piper sooner or later."

Turning to the controller, who had talked of the desired focus of the new system on variable costs, the treasurer gave as his opinion, based on long experience, that it was the lack of control of the long-run costs that really wrecked a company. "You can make mistakes on the direct costs,"

EXHIBIT 3

BEALE COMPANY

Condensed Balance Sheets as Actually Prepared

ASSETS	*Sept. 30, 1970*	*Oct. 31, 1970*
Current Assets:		
Cash	$ 80,560	$ 95,553
Accounts receivable	150,428	178,610
Inventory*	573,630	521,822
Total Current Assets	$ 804,618	$ 795,985
Plant and equipment (net)	2,120,450	2,108,788
Total Assets	$2,925,068	$2,904,773
LIABILITIES AND NET WORTH		
Current liabilities	$ 397,480	$ 382,200
Mortgage payable	560,000	560,000
Total Liabilities	$ 957,480	$ 942,200
Net Worth:		
Capital stock	$1,000,000	$1,000,000
Retained earnings*	967,588	962,573
Total Net Worth	$1,967,588	$1,962,573
Total Liabilities and Net Worth	$2,925,068	$2,904,773

* Had the Beale Company used the direct cost method, its balance sheets would appear as above except for the inventory and retained earnings items. These would appear as shown below:

	Sept. 30	*Oct. 31*
Inventory	$401,541	$365,776
Retained earnings	795,499	806,527

NOTE: In both present and proposed statements, the effect of income taxes is not shown. The Beale Company recorded estimated income tax expense only at the end of the calendar year.

he said, "but because things in this area are constantly changing and because one never makes much of a commitment anyway, the life of the company is really not prejudiced. If necessary, a new management can quickly reverse the trend. But once a company lets the long-run costs get out of control, then the fat really is in the fire. I'm opposed to anything that leads us to take a short-sighted view of cost." To this argument the controller had little to say, except that it was a matter of emphasis, and that he still thought the variable costs the most important.[1]

All of the group discussing the proposal were aware of the effect of the controller's scheme on the inventory item in the balance sheet. The treasurer, and the president too, were worried about this effect, and both wondered if the possible improvement to the operating statement was worth the price of distorting the balance sheet. The controller proposed that a footnote be carried in the balance sheet calling attention to the matter, and perhaps indicating the extent of the distortion. The company's balance sheet as of October 31, 1970 is reproduced in Exhibit 3, together with an indication of how the balance sheet figures would appear had the company used the "direct cost" method. Income statements for September, under both the present and proposed methods are shown in Exhibit 4;

EXHIBIT 4

BEALE COMPANY

Condensed Income Statement, Month of September 1970

	Actually Prepared	Proposed Method
Sales	$283,028	$283,028
Cost of sales at standard	152,604	104,662
Gross margin	$130,424	$178,366
Less: Manufacturing variances:		
Labor	$ 5,426 *	$ 5,426 *
Material	5,081	5,081
Overhead:		
Volume	447 *	....
Spending	2,173	2,173
Fixed factory overhead	....	65,862
Total overhead and variances	$ 1,381	$ 67,960
Profit before expenses	$129,043	$110,676
Selling expenses (total)	$ 85,482	$ 85,482
Administrative expenses (total)	26,026	26,026
Total expenses	$111,508	$111,508
Operating profit	$ 17,535	$(832)
Other income or charges	14,026	14,026
Net Profit or (Loss) Current Month	$ 3,509	$(14,858)

° Credit variance.

[1] Variable costs were 67 percent of total costs during 1970.

nomenclature and arrangement has been changed somewhat in order to facilitate comparison between the present and proposed systems.

When one of the officials asked about the federal income tax implications, the controller pointed out that the tax return was a special report, that it already differed from the company's operating reports in several respects, and that the reports he was suggesting were monthly profit estimates largely for internal use and not annual reports. Furthermore, if the company wished to do so, the annual tax and corporate reports could be computed on the more orthodox basis. "But," he insisted "let's make these monthly reports so that they help us, not handicap us."

Questions

1. What do you recommend?
2. What would be the effects of the controller's proposal on the balance sheet?
3. Approximately how busy (relative to normal volume) was the factory in October?
4. Could the problem in the case ever arise with respect to *annual* statements of profit?

Case 17–2. R. J. REYNOLDS TOBACCO COMPANY

Adoption of Lifo
Inventory Valuation

In 1957, the R. J. Reynolds Tobacco Company adopted the Lifo basis of inventory valuation, with results as indicated by the following quotation from its annual report:

During 1956 and prior years, inventories were valued on the average cost method. Effective for 1957, however, the Company adopted the last-in, first-out (LIFO) method of inventory valuation. By this method, the current costs of replacing materials used are more nearly reflected in determining earnings. In 1957, acquisitions of leaf tobacco were made at prices considerably higher than the average cost of tobacco in inventories at the beginning of the year. The effect of LIFO and related adjustments was to reduce earnings before income taxes by $26,897,049 and net earnings by $12,342,049. The resultant income tax saving for the year amounted to $14,555,000. Inventories at the year end were carried at $28,312,684 less than they would have been under the previous method.

The reaction of investors to this change is indicated by the following quotation from the *Wall Street Journal* for February 3, 1958:

Last week saw a brief wave of selling in the hitherto strong tobacco shares. It apparently grew out of the change by R. J. Reynolds Tobacco Co. to the "last-in-first-out" method of valuing inventories. Although this reduced reported earnings below what they would have been under the old system of accounting, it did not in any way cut Reynolds' real earnings or the company's ability to pay dividends. On the contrary, the change saved the company $14 million, or $1.40 a share, in cash by cutting the Federal income tax that much. Because of increased prices, the tobacco bought by Reynolds in 1957 cost $28 million more than the average cost of its three-year inventory, such as every tobacco company must maintain. Under the LIFO system, that extra cost was charged into the income account, reducing the pre-tax profit by that much. After taxes, it cut profit by $14 million, but it also cut the tax itself, at the 52% rate, by about the same amount. The LIFO system is expected to be put into force by the other tobacco companies. After the brief selling, the Street evidently saw it was unwarranted, because tobacco share prices recovered.

The 1958 annual report of Reynolds contains the following statement:

During the second year of the Company's use of the LIFO method of inventory valuation, first adopted in 1957, acquisitions of both flue-cured and Burley tobaccos were made at prices higher than were paid in the previous year. The resulting LIFO adjustment enabled the Company to effect a further saving in income taxes estimated at $8,500,000. Thus, during the two years under LIFO, the Company has been able to conserve about $23,000,000 that otherwise would have been required for taxes. Inventories at the close of the year were carried at $45,031,770 less than they would have been under the previously used average cost method of inventory valuation.

In its 1959 report, the company reported that inventories at the end of 1959 were carried at $64,399,895 less than they would have been under the average cost method used prior to 1957.

Financial statements of R. J. Reynolds Tobacco Company are given in Exhibit 1. Financial statements of two of its principal competitors are given in Exhibits 2 and 3; these companies continued to use average cost in valuing inventories. These statements have been condensed and rearranged from those presented in the annual reports. Of total operating costs, approximately 50 percent consists of excise taxes paid on finished products, approximately 25 percent is tobacco, and approximately 25 percent is all other manufacturing, selling, and administrative costs.

Inventory Values

Leaf tobacco is the most important element of cost in the manufacture of cigarettes and also the most volatile. Rising tobacco costs normally can be offset by higher prices, particularly since the average inventory method

EXHIBIT 1

R. J. REYNOLDS TOBACCO COMPANY

Financial Statements
(in thousands)

Condensed Position Statements as of December 31

	1959	1958	1957	1956
ASSETS				
Current Assets:				
Cash	$ 27,109	$ 29,646	$ 26,142	$ 23,697
Accounts receivable, customers	44,530	36,990	33,910	30,155
Inventories*	684,507	594,905	586,540	557,247
Total Current Assets	$756,147	$661,542	$646,593	$611,100
Fixed and other assets	97,205	81,791	66,505	48,294
Total Assets	$853,352	$743,333	$713,097	$659,394
EQUITIES				
Current Liabilities:				
Notes and accounts payable	$179,656	$121,196	$106,460	$ 68,131
Federal and state taxes	87,619	75,002	63,744	71,202
Other current	10,470	9,984	9,780	8,231
Total Current Liabilities	$277,744	$206,182	$179,985	$147,564
Funded debt	92,000	98,000	104,000	110,000
Capital stock	136,640	139,260	168,040	169,542
Retained earnings	346,968	299,891	261,073	232,288
Total Equities	$853,352	$743,333	$713,097	$659,394

Statements of Earnings for Years Ended December 31

	1959	1958	1957	1956
Net sales	$1,286,856	$1,146,559	$1,053,326	$957,367
Cost of sales and other expenses	1,082,700	969,712	907,914	815,323
Operating profit	$ 204,156	$ 176,847	$ 145,412	$142,044
Other income and deductions, net ..	−6,386	−4,863	−6,805	−4,942
Income before taxes	$ 197,770	$ 171,984	$ 138,607	$137,102
Taxes on income	107,412	93,658	74,446	75,190
Net earnings	$ 90,358	$ 78,326	$ 64,160	$ 61,913
Dividends†	43,280	39,248	35,375	33,470
Additions to Retained Earnings	$ 47,078	$ 39,078	$ 28,785	$ 28,443
Earnings per Common Share	$4.45	$3.80	$3.08	$2.96

° Inventories at average cost in 1956 and Lifo thereafter.
† Includes preferred dividends of $1,281,000 in 1959, $2,282,000 in 1958, $2,657,000 in 1957, and $2,763,000 in 1956.
Details may not add to totals because of rounding.
SOURCE: Annual reports.

EXHIBIT 2

THE AMERICAN TOBACCO COMPANY

Consolidated Financial Statements
(in thousands)

Condensed Balance Sheets as of December 31

	1959	1958	1957	1956
ASSETS				
Current Assets:				
Cash	$ 17,740	$ 20,696	$ 22,972	$ 23,418
Accounts receivable, customers	51,911	46,943	45,180	44,752
Leaf tobacco, at average cost	586,605	578,305	612,315⎤	
Other inventories, at average			⎥	655,116
cost	70,075	70,000	59,066⎦	
Other current assets	1,697	1,318	950	1,137
Total Current Assets	$728,028	$717,268	$740,483	$724,423
Fixed and other assets	78,498	79,264	74,724	69,981
Total Assets	$806,526	$796,532	$815,207	$794,404
EQUITIES				
Current Liabilities:				
Notes and accounts payable	$ 71,760	$ 81,211	$105,779	$ 93,984
Accrued taxes	53,817	50,655	52,132	51,512
Other current	14,826	11,313	13,227	12,347
Total Current Liabilities	$140,403	$143,179	$171,138	$157,842
Funded debt	150,653	165,402	179,330	193,188
Capital stock	260,561	260,561	260,561	260,561
Retained earnings	254,908	227,390	204,178	182,813
Total Equities	$806,526	$796,532	$815,207	$794,404

Income Statements for Years Ended December 31

	1959	1958	1957	1956
Net sales	$1,161,377	$1,105,176	$1,098,093	$1,091,206
Cost of sales and operating				
expenses	1,019,129	971,132	969,805	971,168
Operating profit	$ 142,248	$ 134,044	$ 128,288	$ 120,039
Other income and deductions, net ..	−6,177	−9,050	−9,683	−8,687
Income before taxes	$ 136,071	$ 124,994	$ 118,605	$ 111,352
Taxes on income	72,823	66,138	61,510	59,663
Net income	$ 63,248	$ 58,856	$ 57,095	$ 51,689
Dividends *	35,730	35,730	35,730	35,730
Additions to Retained Earnings	$ 27,518	$ 23,126	$ 21,365	$ 15,959
Earnings per Common Share	$9.23	$8.55	$8.28	$7.45

* Includes preferred dividends of $3,167,000 each year.
Details may not add to totals because of rounding.
SOURCE: Annual reports.

EXHIBIT 3

LIGGETT & MYERS TOBACCO COMPANY

Consolidated Financial Statements
(in thousands)

Condensed Balance Sheets as of December 31

	1959	1958	1957	1956
ASSETS				
Current Assets:				
Cash and government securities	$ 12,321	$ 4,459	$ 12,263	$ 11,635
Accounts receivable, customers	21,190	23,095	23,090	22,579
Leaf tobacco, at average cost	292,005	306,965	346,472	372,484
Other inventories, at average cost ..	38,388	34,353	34,558	36,587
Other current assets	1,160	1,102	1,030	1,408
Total Current Assets	$365,064	$369,974	$417,412	$444,693
Fixed and other assets	39,327	39,128	39,028	36,978
Total Assets	$404,391	$409,103	$456,440	$481,671
EQUITIES				
Current Liabilities:				
Notes and accounts payable	$ 3,296	$ 7,576	$ 57,119	$ 82,469
Accrued taxes	22,794	23,764	24,992	26,325
Other current liabilities	6,817	5,581	6,930	6,977
Total Current Liabilities	$ 32,907	$ 36,921	$ 89,041	$115,771
Funded debt	84,250	90,000	95,750	101,500
Capital stock	138,066	138,453	138,111	138,111
Retained earnings	149,169	143,729	133,538	126,290
Total Equities	$404,391	$409,103	$456,440	$481,671

Income Statements for Years Ended December 31

	1959	1958	1957	1956
Net sales	$554,936	$556,046	$570,385	$564,966
Cost of sales and operating expenses	488,216	485,935	506.027	503,923
Operating profit	$ 66,720	$ 70,111	$ 64,358	$ 61,043
Other income and deductions, net ..	−1,645	−2,198	−2,463	−2,676
Income before taxes	$ 65,075	$ 67,913	$ 61,895	$ 58,367
Income and franchise taxes	35,036	36,689	33,621	31,916
Net income	$ 30,039	$ 31,223	$ 28,274	$ 26,451
Dividends *	24,015	21,032	21,025	21,023
Additions to Retained Income	$ 6,024	$ 10,191	$ 7,249	$ 5,428
Earnings per Common Share	$7.28	$7.60	$6.85	$6.39

* Includes preferred stock dividends of $1,430,000 in 1959, $1,461,000 in 1958, 1957, and 1956.

Details may not add to totals because of rounding.

SOURCE: Annual reports.

used results in only a gradual increase in tobacco costs charged to any one year's production.

Tobacco has to be aged before it is used in cigarettes, and the quality tends to vary from year to year. Hence, large inventories are needed.

The low point of the year's inventory cycle falls in June or July, when the companies have on hand supplies sufficient for 14 to 18 months' production. Tobacco markets open around the end of July in Georgia, followed by a succession of market openings, moving north, through the following February. Based on estimates made in June, when the inventory is low, the companies purchase according to plan their estimated needs for the succeeding 30 months. The peak of inventory holdings is reached in February.

As the tobacco is purchased at the auctions, the cost for each grade is estimated, adjusting for the loss of weight in drying, stemming, and regrading. The inventory cost for each grade is adjusted to average in new purchases as made. When all purchases for a crop year are completed, costs are reviewed in the light of experience in loss of weight and regrading, and average inventory costs are established for the season for each grade.

It will be seen that the costs of new purchases have an immediate effect on inventory costs of leaf used in manufacture. But it is to be noted that a large factor in that average is the previously established costs of the tobacco in inventory at the start of the buying season, which in turn had been determined by a process of averaging with costs established in former years. Hence, while changing prices of leaf are reflected quickly in costs, the changes in costs are not fully commensurate with the changes in prices paid. In fact, the process of averaging from year to year permits the prices in any one year to influence costs over a long period.

Questions

1. Recast the R. J. Reynolds financial statements for 1957 and 1958 to show how they would have appeared if the company had not shifted to Lifo.

2. As well as you can, compare the performance of the three companies in 1957, 1958, and 1959.

3. Do you agree with R. J. Reynolds' decision to adopt Lifo? Do you think its competitors should also adopt Lifo?

4. Under what conditions do you think the company might consider switching back to the average cost method at a later date?

CHAPTER 18

INTERCORPORATE INVESTMENTS AND BUSINESS COMBINATIONS

Frequently corporations acquire interests in other corporations ranging from a few shares of capital stock to 100 percent ownership. The reasons for these acquisitions vary from temporary short-term investments of excess funds to permanent investments made to control and direct all operations of the company acquired. The corporation in which an interest is acquired usually continues in existence, but in some instances it may be dissolved by merger into the acquiring company.

This wide range of different types of ownership arrangements can be classified into four groups: (1) interests of less than 50 percent, (2) interests of more than 50 percent, (3) interests of 50 percent, and (4) business combinations. The accounting procedures for each of these four situations will be discussed first. Then the topic of business combinations will be covered in considerable detail.

The principal authoritative statements on the accounting for intercorporate investments and business combinations are *Opinion No. 16, Business Combinations*, and *Opinion No. 17, Intangible Assets*. Both of those opinions were published during 1970. Previously, the Accounting Principles Board had sponsored two accounting research studies related to intercorporate investments and business combinations: *A Critical Study of Accounting for Business Combinations* by Arthur Wyatt (ARS No. 5) and *Accounting for Goodwill* by George Catlett and Norman Olson (ARS No. 10).

ACCOUNTING PROCEDURES

Ownership Interests of Less than 50 Percent

The reporting procedures for interest of less than 50 percent depend in part upon the intention of the investor.

Initially, such stock acquisitions are recorded by charging an asset investment account for the cost, which includes the purchase price plus all incidental acquisition costs such as broker's commissions. Dividends received as a distribution of earnings subsequent to acquisition are recognized at the time of receipt. Presentation of these investments on the balance sheet depends upon whether the investment is made for temporary short-term reasons or for the purpose of creating some longer term relationship.

Short-term investments such as readily marketable capital stocks held as temporary investments are presented as current assets. These stocks are valued at the lower of original cost or market value. (The APB in mid–1971 proposed these investments be carried at their current market value and changes in this value reflected in current income.)

Marketable securities held for longer term investment of funds are usually valued at original cost on the balance sheet. They are valued at the lower of original cost or current market value only if the decline in value is thought by the holder of the securities to be "permanent" (i.e., the market value will not at least equal the original cost within the next few years).

With few exceptions, the appreciation of securities (i.e., the increase in market value) is not recognized until the securities are sold. This difference between the selling price and the original cost is termed "gain on sale of securities" in the income statement, under "other income" or "extraordinary income."

Long-term investments of capital stock held to maintain a continuing business relationship are usually included among noncurrent assets at original cost. Write-downs to values less than cost are made only to recognize significant and apparently permanent declines in value.

If market quotations are available, full and fair disclosure requires that the market value of investments be disclosed either in footnotes or parenthetically in the balance sheet. Investments in affiliates should be reported separately from other investments.

It is usual for both short- and long-term investments in securities shown as investments on the balance sheet to present, parenthetically, the market value of the investment, as:

Investment in securities, at cost (market value, $1,417,000) $1,273,000

Ownership Interests of More than 50 Percent

The acquisition of more than one half of the voting capital stock of a corporation creates a parent and subsidiary relationship. The company owning the controlling interest is the parent (or holding) company, and the controlled corporation is the subsidiary company.

The parent corporation records the acquisition by charging the cost of the stock purchased to an investment account. Cost is the cash price paid or the fair market value of the property exchanged. Subsequent to acquisition, the relationship with the subsidiary may be recorded by the parent using either (1) the cost method, or (2) the equity method.

The *cost method* maintains the separate legal distinction between corporate entities. This method gives no recognition to the subsidiary company's earnings or losses in the parent's records. As a result, the investment accounting showing the acquisition cost usually remains unchanged throughout the period of ownership. Dividends from the subsidiary are credited to income at time of receipt. In effect, the cost method is the same as the method previously described for handling long-term ownership of corporate interests of less than 50 percent.

After the initial acquisition cost has been entered in the parent's investment account, the *equity method* subsequently adds or subtracts from this amount the parent's proportional share of the changes in the subsidiary's retained earnings. The investment account increases as the parent's share of the subsidiary's reported earnings is credited to an income account. Dividends received from the subsidiary reduce the investment account. As a result of these entries, the investment account reflects initial cost plus or minus the parent's share of the change in the subsidiary's net worth subsequent to acquisition.

Illustration 18–1 summarizes the accounting entries in the parent's books applying the cost method and the equity method.

Under the equity method, it may be appropriate for the parent to charge against the income from the subsidiary a portion of the difference between the cost of the parent's investment in the subsidiary and the net worth of the subsidiary represented by the parent's investment. If a parent purchased a subsidiary company with net worth of $1.5 million for $2 million, the $500,000 differential might be amortized against that portion of the subsidiary's income recognized in the parent's accounts over a reasonable period. However, the parent should not recognize appreciation in the subsidiary's net worth, except that provided by earnings.

Accounting Principles Board *Opinion No. 10* indicated that all investments in domestic subsidiaries not consolidated should be reported on the equity basis,[1] principally because it conforms to the objectives of consoli-

---

[1] In late 1970, the APB was considering extension of the requirement for the equity method to ownership interest of more than 20 percent.

ILLUSTRATION 18-1

Cost and Equity Methods of Accounting for Subsidiaries

Transaction	Cost Method	Equity Method

(1) Parent acquires 80% of a company's stock for $200,000	(1) Investment in Subsidiary 200,000
	    Cash 200,000
		(1) Investment in Subsidiary 200,000
		    Cash 200,000

(2) Subsidiary reports $40,000 earnings	(2) No entry	(2) Investment in Subsidiary ...... 32,000 Income 32,000

(3) Subsidiary pays $20,000 in dividends	(3) Cash 16,000
	    Dividend Income 16,000
		(3) Cash 16,000
		    Investment in Subsidiary .. 16,000

(4) Subsidiary reports $20,000 loss	(4) No entry	(4) Income from Subsidiary ...... 16,000 Investment in Subsidiary .. 16,000

dated statements: to present the results of operations and financial condition essentially as if the group were a single economic unit. Also, the equity method eliminates the possibility available under the cost method of manipulating consolidated earnings through the control of dividends received by the parent. The only exceptions to the requirement of the consolidation or equity method are cases where the parent's control is likely to be temporary; where the control of the subsidiary does not rest with the majority owners (such as bankruptcy); or where the existence of a large minority interest makes it more useful to present separate financial statements for the two companies.

In the case of unconsolidated foreign subsidiaries, *ARB No. 43*, Chapter 12, and *ARB No. 51* both recommend that the cost method be used to report these investments where there is any question as to whether an increase in a foreign subsidiary's equity will accrue to the credit of the parent company. Caution in reporting foreign earnings is required because in many cases foreign assets stand in some degree of jeopardy as to their ultimate realization by U.S. owners due to actual or possible political instability, exchange controls, or expropriation by local authorities.

When the investment in unconsolidated subsidiaries is material relative to the consolidated entity's financial position or income, the cost of the investment in the unconsolidated subsidiaries and the equity of the consolidated group in the assets, liabilities, and operating results of the unconsolidated subsidiaries, individually or collectively, should be disclosed in the footnotes. Alternatively, these data may be shown in separate statements. In addition, dividends received by the consolidated group from unconsolidated subsidiaries accounted for by the equity method may be disclosed parenthetically or by footnote.

Ownership Interest of 50 Percent

When a company owns exactly one half of another corporation's capital it is usually treated in the owner's accounts in the same way as an ownership interest of less than 50 percent, principally because the owner lacks effective control. However, other possible alternatives for accounting for 50 percent owned companies include: use of the equity method; full consolidation; or use of hybrid techniques which recognize one half of the subsidiary's assets, liabilities, and net income in the owner's accounts.

Some accountants argue that if the owner of a 50 percent interest in a company has effective operating control, then full consolidation should be permitted. Others object to this proposal because (1) the Securities and Exchange Commission does not allow such a consolidation, and (2) if two companies both owning a 50 percent interest in the same subsidiary company fully consolidated it, the same assets and liabilities of the jointly owned company would be included in the two sets of consolidated financial statements, even though each owned only 50 percent of the subsidiary.

Split consolidation, whereby each of the owners of a joint venture company would include only 50 percent of the subsidiary's assets, liabilities, revenues, and costs in its consolidated statements, is an approach that some believe overcomes the double accounting criticism of full consolidation by both owners. However, in practice split consolidation is seldom considered appropriate, since each owner of capital stock has an undivided interest in the assets, liabilities, revenues, and costs of the joint-venture company. For example, the 50 percent owner does not in any sense own half of each asset on the balance sheet. His claim is equivalent to 50 percent of the company's net worth.

Supporters of the equity method for handling investments in 50 percent owned companies claim the cost approach is unnecessarily conservative and does not reflect in the parent's statements the benefits attributable to ownership due to changes in the net assets and income of the 50 percent owned company. The equity method overcomes these objections. Therefore, it is claimed, it represents a better presentation of the facts.

Business Combinations: Two Approaches

A business combination occurs when two or more businesses are joined together as one entity to continue the same business activities each had carried on previously. Business combinations include all those changes in corporate ownership which are termed mergers, purchases, consolidations, poolings, amalgamations, and acquisitions. The financial accounting issue raised in recording and reporting business combinations centers upon the valuation of the assets which are brought together in a business unit. The two methods used to record business combinations are: (1) the purchase method, and (2) the pooling of interest method.

Purchase Method. Under the purchase method of recording a business combination, the assets of the acquired entity are recorded at their fair market value on the books of the acquirer. This alternative treats the acquisition as if the dominant business had bought the net assets of another business and established a new cost basis for these acquired assets. All acquisitions of other companies except those involving an exchange of common stock which meets all of the restrictive conditions for a pooling of interest set forth in *Opinion No. 16* must be recorded by the purchase method. (Those that meet these specific conditions for a pooling of interest *must* be accounted for by the pooling of interest method, as indicated later.)

Purchase Method Illustration. The accounting for purchases can be illustrated by a relatively simple example of a business combination.

Company A acquired Company B intending to continue the operations of both companies as a single unit. Company B's financial position at the date of acquisition was as follows:

	Book Value	Fair Market Value
Net current assets	$100,000	$100,000
Fixed assets	400,000	700,000
Total	$500,000	$800,000
Capital stock	$300,000	
Retained earnings	200,000	
Total	$500,000	

Company A paid $900,000 cash for Company B. The accounting entry in Company A's records is:

Net Current Assets	100,000	
Fixed Assets	700,000	
Goodwill	100,000	
Cash		900,000

This transaction is clearly a purchase of Company B by Company A. The previous owners of Company B received cash and retained no ownership in the new business unit. Consequently, subsequent operations will be charged with depreciation based on fixed asset costs of $700,000, which is the fair market value of the assets acquired. The excess of the purchase price over the assets acquired is called goodwill. It is first recorded as an asset and subsequently charged to operations over a period of years not to exceed 40, as specified in *Opinion No. 17*. It is important to note that income from the acquired company will be included in Company A's accounts only from the date of acquisition, and Company B's retained earnings at acquisition are not carried over to Company A.

Pooling of Interest Method. Under the pooling of interest method, all assets of the newly combined group are valued at the same amounts at which they were previously carried in the accounts of the individual predecessor businesses. Underlying this alternative is the presumption that no new business entity had been created. Instead, it is assumed that ownership groups have merely contributed assets (or pooled resources) to carry on operations in an organization which is substantially a continuation of the preceding entities. Therefore, there is no reason to change asset values from those carried by the predecessor businesses.

Pooling of Interest Illustration. Using the example presented earlier, assume that Company A issued its own capital stock with a par value of $200,000 and a fair market value of $900,000 in payment for Company B, instead of paying $900,000 cash. In this transaction, the choice of the pooling of interest method can be strongly supported. The new entity is owned jointly by all stockholders of the previously separate corporations. The total assets and liabilities and retained earnings are undiminished and unchanged by the combinations. The stockholders of two corporations have merely pooled assets and liabilities and retained pro rata ownership in the new entity.

The combination would be entered on Company A's records as follows:

Net Current Assets	100,000	
Fixed Assets	400,000	
Capital Stock		200,000
Capital Surplus		100,000
Retained Earnings		200,000

It should be noted that subsequent operations of the combined companies will be charged with depreciation based upon the original $400,000 book value of Company B's fixed assets. Also, no goodwill is recognized and no related problems of subsequent amortization or write-off are encountered. Further, the retained earnings of Company B are carried over into the combination, and the paid-in capital accounts are adjusted to reflect any differences between the par value of Company B stock and the par value of stock issued by Company A.

Company A's statement of results of operations for the accounting period in which Company B was acquired will include the combined results of operations of the constituent interests for the entire annual accounting period in which the combination was effected.

DEVELOPMENT OF THE BUSINESS COMBINATION PROBLEM

For a number of years prior to World War II, the legal form of the business combination dominated the accounting for these transactions. Consequently, most business combinations were treated as purchases of one company by another and were recorded by the purchase method. In a few cases, the combination of companies of comparable size was recorded for accounting purposes as if a new corporation was formed. Typically, businessmen believed that the creation of goodwill from mergers was a real deterrent to business mergers. It could not be used to reduce taxable income; it represented a potential charge against income; and most bankers regarded it as an asset of dubious value for credit extension purposes.

Following World War II, accountants and businessmen began to distinguish between combinations that resulted in a continuance of the former ownership interests and those that did not carry over the old ownership interests to the combined companies. Clearly, cash purchases of another company should be accounted for by the purchase method. However, acquisitions for stock did involve a continuation of ownership interests, and in such cases the accounting treatment of the combination was either the pooling of interest or the purchase method. The latter method proved very popular, since no goodwill was recorded.

To clarify when pooling of interest was appropriate, *ARB No. 40* was published in 1950. It set forth criteria for the application of the pooling of interest method; namely, continuation of the previous ownership interests in the same proportions in the new entity; the combination of companies of comparable size; similar or complementary business activities; and continuation of the management of both parties.

During the early fifties, the frequency and level of business mergers began to rise, encouraged in large part by pooling of interest accounting. The most attractive features of this method were: instant earnings created by taking up the acquired companies' earnings from the beginning of the accounting period; an automatic improvement of earnings per share by acquiring companies with a lower price-earnings ratio than that of the acquiring company; an upward-sweeping annual sales and profit trend over time, since there was no restriction on comparing this year's pooled results with last year's results as previously reported in last year's statements before poolings took place; the inclusion of poolings that occurred after the close of the accounting period but before the release of the annual results to the stockholders in the results reported for the closed period. This allowed companies to make up through acquisitions any deficiencies in their earnings per share after operations had been completed for the year.

Subsequently, in 1957, *ARB No. 47* was released. It redefined the criteria for pooling to bring them more in line with current pooling applications, which typically ignored the comparable size and similar business tests of *ARB No. 40*. The new criteria were: the combination results in a distribution of capital stock which is in proportion to prior ownership and no substantial change in ownership is expected to occur shortly after the combination; there is a continuity of all of the constituent businesses in the combined business; there is a continuity of the constituent management or power to control management; the relative size of individual businesses joined are significant in comparison to the combined group. ("Significant" was defined as at least 5 percent of the combined company.) The bulletin still permitted stock acquisitions to be treated as either poolings or purchases. In addition, it did not significantly diminish any of the attractiveness of the pooling method.

The trend toward growth by acquisition increased in the early 1960s. In practice, the size test was ignored, and some acquisitions that represented less than one half of 1 percent of the size of the acquiring company were pooled. In addition, many managements seemed to choose between the purchase or pooling accounting method for stock acquisitions solely for their impact on earnings data. Often, purchases for stock and cash were treated as part pooling, part purchase.

The growth and spread of the conglomerate companies, with the attendant rocketing stock prices, was encouraged by the liberal interpretation of pooling criteria. Fearful of its consequences, in 1965 the APB published *Opinion No. 6*, in part to get some realism back into pooling accounting by having accountants use better judgment in their approval of the use of the pooling method. The opinion reaffirmed *ARB No. 48* and said the criteria specified in *ARB No. 47* were "illustrative guides and not necessary literal requirements." The distinction between a pooling and purchase was "to be found in the attendant circumstances." In addition, the Board improved the disclosure requirements for pooling transactions.

The bursting of the conglomerate bubble and the increasing criticism of the liberal pooling practices that arose during the late 1960s made it imperative that the criteria for the pooling method be tightened quickly. Some proposed the elimination of the method entirely. Others wanted to limit its application to combinations effected by common stock of companies of comparable size. Many wanted to eliminate management's choice of pooling or purchase accounting in stock acquisition situations. In addition, while there was relatively less controversy over the purchase method, a number of proposals were made involving a compulsory write-off of goodwill.

OPINION NO. 16, BUSINESS COMBINATIONS

In August 1970, the APB issued *Opinion No. 16, Business Combinations* to clarify criteria for using the purchase and pooling methods to account for business combinations. It concluded that both methods were acceptable in accounting for business combinations, but not as alternatives under the same conditions. A business combination meeting specified conditions *required* the pooling of interest method. All other combinations were *required* to use the purchase method. Furthermore, a single method must be applied. Therefore such transactions as a part purchase, part pooling were no longer acceptable.

Conditions Requiring Pooling Treatment

Pooling of interest was defined in *Opinion No. 16* as the presentation as a single interest of two or more common stockholder interests that were previously independent and the combined rights and risks represented by those interests. The use of this method showed that the combining stockholder groups neither withdrew nor invested assets, but simply exchanged voting common stock in a ratio that determined their respective interests in the combined corporation.

The pooling of interest method could only be used if the transaction met all of the conditions specified in the opinion. In fact, if all of these conditions were met, the pooling of interest method had to be used. These basic conditions fall under three categories:

1. With Respect to the Combining Companies

a) Each of the combining companies is autonomous and has not been a subsidiary or a division of another company within two years before the plan of combination is initiated.

b) Each of the combining companies is independent of the other companies. (Independence existed if neither of the combining companies held as intercorporate investments more than 10 percent in total of the outstanding voting common stock of the other combining company).

2. With Respect to the Manner of Combining of Interests

a) The combination is effected in a single transaction or is completed in accordance with a specific plan within one year after the plan is initiated.

b) A corporation offers and issues only common stock with rights identical to those of the majority of its outstanding voting common stock in exchange for substantially all of the voting common stock interest of another company at the date the plan of combination is consummated.

c) None of the combining companies changes the equity interests of the voting common stock in contemplation of effecting the combination, either within two years before the plan of combination is initiated or between the dates the combination is initiated and consummated; changes in contemplation of effecting the combination may include distributions to stockholders and additional issuances, exchanges, and retirement of securities.

d) Each of the combining companies reacquires shares of voting common stock only for purposes other than business combinations, and no company reacquires more than a normal number of shares between the dates the plan of combination is initiated and consummated.

e) The ratio of the interest of an individual common stockholder to those of other common stockholders in a combining company remains the same as a result of the exchange of stock to effect the combination.

f) The voting rights to which the common stock ownership interests in the resulting combined corporation are entitled are exercisable by the stockholder; the stockholders are neither deprived nor restricted in exercising those rights for a period of years.

g) The combination is resolved at the date the plan is consummated, and no provision of the plan relating to the issue of securities or other considerations is pending.

3. With Respect to the Absence of Planned Transactions

a) The combined corporation does not agree directly or indirectly to retire or reacquire all or part of the common stock issued to effect the combination.

b) The combined corporation does not enter into other financial arrangements for the benefit of the former stockholders of a combining company, such as a guaranty of loans secured by stock issued in the combination which in effect negates the exchange of equity securities.

c) The combined corporation does not intend or plan to dispose of a significant part of the assets of the combining companies within two years after the combination, other than disposals in the ordinary course of business of the formerly separate companies and to eliminate duplicated facilities of excess capacity.

Originally the Board had proposed to include a size test in *Opinion No. 16*. The first proposal was to limit poolings to acquisitions of companies that were at least 25 percent of the size of the combined company based on the distribution of relative voting rights in the new entity. Later, this test was reduced to 10 percent after considerable opposition by businessmen to the original proposal. Eventually, the Board failed to get approval of this more limited size test among its members and, as a result, *Opinion No. 16* did not include a size test.

The 90 Percent Test

The primary source of technical problems in applying these criteria is the definition of "substantially all of the voting common stock" which must be exchanged (see 2*b* above).

The text of *Opinion No. 16* states that substantially all of the voting common stock means "90 percent or more." That is, at the date the combination is consummated, one of the combining companies (issuing corporation) issues voting common stock in exchange for at least 90 percent of the outstanding voting common stock of the other company (combining company).

For the purposes of computing the 90 percent figure, shares of the combining company are excluded if they were (1) acquired before and held by the issuing corporation and its subsidiaries at the date the plan of combination is initiated, regardless of the form of consideration; (2) acquired by the issuing corporation and its subsidiaries after the date the plan of combination is initiated other than by issuing its own voting common stock; or (3) outstanding after the date the combination is consummated.

An investment in the stock of the issuing corporation by a combining company may prevent a combination from meeting the 90 percent criterion, even though the investment of the combining company may not be more than 10 percent of the outstanding stock of the issuing corporation. To determine whether or not an investment by the company being acquired in the stock of the issuing corporation precludes use of the pooling method, this stock investment must be expressed as an equivalent number of shares of the combining company, because the 90 percent of shares exchanged criterion is expressed in terms of shares of stock of the combining company. The procedure for this translation is shown in Illustration 18–2.

ILLUSTRATION 18–2

Reduction of Shares Exchanged Due to Intercorporate Investment

Assume:

1. Company A (issuing company) agrees on March 31, 1970 to issue one share of A stock for each four shares of Company B.
2. Company B on March 31 has 100,000 shares of its own stock outstanding, and holds 2,000 shares of A as an investment.*
3. By March 31, 1971, Company A has issued 24,000 shares of its stock for 96,000 shares of B.

The required computation:

Shares of B exchanged for A	96,000
Shares of A held by B restated on basis of rate of exchange (2,000 sh. of A @ 4:1)	8,000
Defined number of shares exchanged	88,000
Number of shares exchanged required for pooling	90,000

* The effect of the computation would be the same if B had purchased all or part of the 2,000 shares for cash after the combination plan had been initiated.

A combination of more than two companies is evaluated essentially as a combination of two companies. The percentage of voting common stock is measured separately for each combining company.

Accounting Mechanics

The pooling of interest method requires that the recorded assets and liabilities of the separate companies be combined at their historical cost basis. However, since the separate companies may have recorded assets and liabilities under differing methods of accounting, it is permisisble to adjust the amounts to the same basis of accounting if the change would otherwise have been appropriate for the separate company. Such a change in accounting method to make the accounts conform should be applied retroactively and financial statements for prior periods should be restated.

The stockholders' equities are also combined as part of the pooling of interests, including the capital stock, capital in excess of par value, and retained earnings or deficits. If the value of the outstanding shares of stock exceeds the capital stock of the separate combining companies, the excess is deducted first from contributed capital, then from retained earnings.

If treasury stock is used to effect a combination, this treasury stock should first be treated as retired, and the stock issued in the combination then treated as if it were previously unissued shares.

The treatment of stock of the combining companies held by another company depends on whether the holder is the issuing company or another combining company. If the investment of a combining company is in the common stock of the issuing company, it is, in effect, returned to the resulting combined corporation and should be treated as treasury stock. In contrast, an investment in the common stock of another combining company (not the issuing company) is an investment in stock that is exchanged in the combination for the common stock issued. This stock is in effect eliminated in the combination, and would be treated as retired stock.

Reporting Requirements

A corporation that uses the pooling of interests method of accounting for a combination should report results of operations for the period in which the combination occurs as though the companies had been combined as of the beginning of the period. Results of operations for that period thus comprise those of the separate companies combined from the beginning of the period to the date the combination is consummated, and those of the combined operations from that date to the end of the period. The effects of intercompany transactions on current assets, liabilities, revenues, and cost of sales for the periods presented, and on retained earnings at the beginning of the periods presented, should be eliminated to the extent possible. The nature of and effects on earnings per share of nonrecurring intercompany transactions involving long-term assets and liabilities (such as fixed assets purchased before the combining date), need not be eliminated, but should be disclosed.

The combined corporation should disclose in notes to its financial statements the revenue, extraordinary items, and net income of each of the separate companies from the beginning of the period to the date of combination. In addition, balance sheet and financial information presented for prior years should be restated on a combined basis to furnish comparative information. Such data should clearly indicate the nature of the information.

Expenses incurred in effecting a business combination accounted for as a pooling of interests should be deducted in determining the net income of the combined corporation for the period in which the expenses are incurred. Such expenses include such items as registration fees and costs of furnishing information to stockholders.

Disclosure of Poolings

A combined corporation is required to disclose in its financial statements that a combination which is accounted for by the pooling of interests method has occurred during the period. The basis of the current presentation and restatements of prior periods may be disclosed in the financial statements by captions or by reference to the notes.

Notes to the financial statements of a combined corporation should disclose the following for the period in which a business combination occurs:

1. Name and brief description of the companies combined, except a corporation whose name is carried forward.
2. Description and number of shares of stock issued.
3. Details of the results of operations of the previously separate companies for the period before the combination was consummated that are included in the current combined income. The details should include revenue, extraordinary items, net income, other changes in stockholders' equity, and the amount of and manner of accounting for intercompany transactions.
4. Descriptions of the nature of any adjustments of net assets of the combining companies in order to adopt the same accounting practices and the effects of these changes on net income reported previously by the separate companies and now presented in comparative financial statements.
5. Details of an increase or decrease in retained earnings from changing the fiscal year of a combining company. The details should include at least revenue, expenses, extraordinary items, net income, and other changes in stockholders' equity for the period excluded from the reported results of operations.
6. Reconciliations of amounts of revenue and earnings previously reported by the corporation that issues the stock to effect the combination with the combined amounts currently presented in financial statements and summaries. A new corporation formed to effect a combination may instead disclose the earnings of separate companies which comprise combined earnings for the prior periods.

Business combinations consummated before the financial statements are issued, but which are either incomplete as of the date of the financial statements or initiated after that date, cannot be included in the statements of the prior period. However, the notes to the financial statements should disclose details of the effects of such combinations. The details should include revenue, net income, earnings per share, and the effects of anticipated changes in accounting methods as if the combination had been consummated at the date of the financial statements.

Conditions Requiring Purchase Accounting

The principal accounting issues to be decided in mergers required to be accounted for by the purchase method are:

1. Which company is the acquirer?
2. How much did the acquirer pay for the purchase?
3. What adjustments are required to the book values of the individual assets acquired and liabilities assumed so that these values on the acquirer's book reflect their net realizable value or fair market value?
4. How should any differences between the purchase price and those adjusted book values be handled in the accounts of the acquired?

Opinions No. 16 and *17*, which were issued concurrently, discuss these issues.

Acquirer Characteristics. A corporation which distributes cash or other assets or incurs liabilities to obtain the assets or stock of another corporation is clearly the acquirer. In most cases involving exchanges of stock, the Board concluded that presumptive evidence of the acquiring corporation in combinations effected by an exchange of stock is obtained by identifying the former common stockholder interests which either retain or receive the larger portion of the voting rights in the combined corporation, unless other evidence clearly indicates that another corporation is the acquirer.

Purchase Price Determination. The responsibility for determining the purchase price rests with the acquiring company. The general principles governing this determination are:

1. Assets acquired by exchanging cash or other assets are recorded at cost, which is the amount of cash disbursed or the fair value of the assets distributed.
2. Assest acquired by assuming liabilities are recorded at cost, which is the present value of the amounts to be paid.
3. Assets acquired by issuing stock are recorded at the fair value of the stock or the fair value of the consideration given up for the stock.

The difficulty of determining the "fair value" of noncash assets or stock given up by the acquirer has led to the rule that their "cost may be determined either by the fair value of the consideration given or by the fair value of the property acquired, whichever is more clearly evident."

Book Value Adjustments. The acquiring company is responsible for making any required adjustment to the book values of assets acquired and liabilities assumed as a result of the purchase. *Opinion No. 16* presented some guidelines for this assignment of the purchase price. They are:

1. Marketable securities should be recorded at their current net realizable values.

2. The amounts shown for receivables should be the present values of amounts to be received determined at appropriate current interest rates, less allowances for uncollectibility and collection costs, if necessary.

3. Inventories:

   a) Finished goods and merchandise should be recorded at their selling prices less the sum of (1) cost of disposal and (2) a reasonable profit allowance for the selling effort of the acquiring corporation.

   b) Work in process must be valued at the estimated selling prices of finished goods less the sum of (1) costs to complete, (2) costs of disposal, and (3) a reasonable profit allowance for the completing and selling effort of the acquiring corporation based on profit for similar finished goods.

   c) Raw materials have to be restated to their current replacement costs.

4. Plant and equipment: (a) to be used, stated at current replacement costs for similar capacity unless the expected future use of the assets indicated a lower value to the acquirer; (b) to be sold or held for later sale rather than used, adjusted to its current net realizable value; and (c) to be used temporarily, presented at its current net realizable value recognizing future depreciation for the expected period of use.

5. Intangible assets which can be identified and named, including contracts, patents, franchises, customer and supplier lists, and favorable leases, should be recorded at their appraised values.[2]

6. Other assets, including land, natural resources, and nonmarketable securities, must be presented at their appraised values.

7. The amounts shown for accounts and notes payable, long-term debt, and other claims payable should be the present values of amounts to be paid determined at appropriate current interest rates.

8. Similarly, the amounts recorded for liabilities and accruals—for example, accruals for pension cost, warranties, vacation pay, deferred compensation—must be present values of amounts to be paid determined at appropriate current interest rates.

9. Other liabilities and commitments, including unfavorable leases, contracts, and commitments, and plant closing expense incident to the acquisition, should be recorded at the present value of amounts to be paid determined at appropriate current interest rates.

Additional rules are: an acquiring corporation should record periodically as a part of income the accrual of interest on assets and liabilities

---

[2] Fair values should be ascribed to specific assets; identifiable assets should not be included in goodwill.

recorded at acquisition date at the discounted values of amounts to be received or paid (see Illustration 18–3). An acquiring corporation should not record as a separate asset the goodwill previously recorded by an acquired company and should not record deferred income taxes recorded by an acquired company before its acquisition. An acquiring corporation should reduce the acquired goodwill retroactively for the realized tax benefits of loss carry-forwards of an acquired company not previously recorded by the acquiring corporation.

GOODWILL

Goodwill purchased as a part of an acquisition must be amortized, according to *Opinion No. 17*. (Previously, the common practice was not to amortize goodwill.) The goodwill amortization can be based on anticipated loss in value if a logical basis can be determined. Otherwise, it must be amortized over a period not to exceed 40 years on a straight-line basis.

ILLUSTRATION 18–3

Implementation of APB Opinion No. 16
Purchase Accounting Using Discounted Values

	Book Value	Basis of Valuation	Value for Purchase Accounting
Current Assets:			
Cash	$ 10,000	Actual	$ 10,000
Accounts receivable (net)	90,000	Discounted @ 8%, 1 year* .	83,340
Fixed assets	400,000	Reproduction cost	700,000
	$500,000		$793,340
Accounts payable	$ 10,000	Actual	$ 10,000
Long-term debt	90,000	5 years @ 8%	61,290
	$100,000		$ 71,290
Net Value of Purchases	$400,000		$722,050

Net Charge against Income:
In Year 1: Income (accounts receivable, 90,000 — 83,340) ..$6,660
Expense (long-term debt †) 4,860
Net Credit to Income $1,800

* Assume, for the purposes of the example, that accounts receivable are due one year from this date (90,000 @ 0.926).

† Present value of debt @ 8%, payable in 4 years (90,000 @ 0.735)................$66,150
Present value of debt @ 8%, payable in 5 years (90,000 @ 0.681)................ 61,290
Change in present value of debt...$ 4,860

The Nature of Goodwill

It is difficult to give a precise definition of the nature of goodwill, since every business situation gives rise to a different mutation. However, in most situations it can be considered, in the technical sense, as simply being the cost paid for a business in excess of the fair market value of its net tangible and intangible assets for the expectation of earnings in excess of a normal return on these assets. It is only through such a transaction that goodwill can be recognized on the books of a company.

Originally, the concept of goodwill was more narrow. It was considered to represent the value of customer loyalty, habitual return, or some other such advantageous relations between a proprietor and his customers. Another early concept stressed the importance to the determination of goodwill of the exclusive location of a business, or one in close proximity to suppliers and customers. Other early writings related goodwill to the personal qualities of the proprietor.

During the late 19th century, as the business system became more complex, so did the notion of goodwill. Now, businesses tended to be more diversified and less personal; their success was due to such intangibles as trademarks, advertising, managerial skills, technological advantage, and financial resources. Under these conditions, goodwill was considered to be the excess of value of a going business over starting one from nothing. The starting costs were considered to include the costs of fixed assets, organization and initial start-up.

During the early 20th century, business valuation approaches began to place increasing weight on profit potential. This led to the belief that goodwill somehow reflected all of the variables which led to a business having an above-average earnings capacity for its industry. In this sense, goodwill is an integral part of a business and cannot be regarded as an asset which is salable independent of the business. Consequently, today goodwill is considered to be a residual item.

Technically, goodwill is what is left after the sum of the fair market values of the individual assets acquired is deducted from the total price paid for the business in excess of any liabilities acquired. It is not directly relatable to the costs of doing business which may have led to its creation. Also, its exact measurement will probably always be imperfect because of the problems associated with valuing individually the tangible and intangible assets which together give rise to the excess earnings capacity.

"Negative Goodwill"

Sometimes companies are purchased for a price less than their net book value. In these so-called bargain purchase cases, a "negative goodwill" or an "excess of book value of assets acquired over cost" item is created. If, after adjusting the book value of the assets acquired and liabilities assumed, the sum of the market or appraisal values of the assets acquired less liabilities still exceeds the purchase cost, the values assignable to non-current assets acquired (except marketable securities) should be reduced proportionately. Under *Opinion No. 16*, negative goodwill is prohibited unless such long-term assets are reduced to zero value. If such negative goodwill is then recorded, it must be amortized systematically as a credit to income over the period estimated to be benefited, so long as the period is not in excess of 40 years. In addition, the method and period of amortization must be disclosed in the financial statements.[3]

Goodwill Tax Consideration

Under Section 162 of the Internal Revenue Code of 1954, the cost of self-developed intangibles and goodwill is deductible in the year paid or incurred, even though it may have a useful life extending beyond the taxable year. Such items are considered to be an ordinary and necessary expense of doing business. In contrast, the cost of a purchased intangible cannot be amortized or depreciated for tax purposes, unless it can be demonstrated that it has a limited life which can be estimated with reasonable accuracy. Under this provision, the purchase price of intangibles such as copyrights, patents, and other contracts of limited duration may be deducted from taxable income. However, purchased goodwill is expressly denied this treatment. The tax cost assumes that the life of goodwill can not be estimated reasonably. Consequently, the asset goodwill must, for tax purposes, be carried as an asset until the business giving rise to this item is sold. At that time the tax basis of the business sold will be the market price paid originally for the business, which included goodwill.

DIFFERENT CONCEPTS

Pooling of Interests

Pooling of interests method supporters believe a merger effected through an exchange of stock is in substance a combination of stockholder

---

[3] Before *Opinions 16* and *17*, to the extent that negative goodwill was attributable to certain depreciable assets it was allocated to them. This resulted in a corresponding downward adjustment of the assets' related depreciation. Any negative goodwill was either combined with any positive goodwill already on the balance sheet or carried on the right-hand side of the balance sheet and amortized over some appropriate period. The netting approach was defended on the basis of conservatism. However, since there was no logical relationship between the negative and positive goodwill items created in separate transactions, the preferred method became that of crediting the excess to income in future periods on a reasonable and systematic basis.

groups and as such does not involve the corporate entities. Therefore, no new basis of accountability is required In their opinion, the pooling of interests method has:

Validity. The combination of two or more stockholder groups in a pooling is effected without change in the net assets, liabilities, and capital of the combining companies. Aggregate income is unchanged, as the resources are unchanged. The stockholders exchange risks and benefits by combining, but do not alter the essential characteristics of the corporate entities.

Consistency. The pooling theory was developed within the boundaries of the historical cost convention and is compatible with it. Accounting as a pooling of interests for business combinations arranged through the issuance of common shares is based on existing accounting concepts and is not an occasion for revising historical cost data. Both constituents usually have elements of appreciation and of goodwill which are recognized and offset, at least to some extent, in setting a share exchange ratio. The bargaining which takes place in setting an exchange ratio usually reflects the relative earning capacities (measured by historical cost accounts) of the constituents and frequently gives recognition to the relative market values of the two stocks, which in turn reflect this earning capacity, goodwill, or other values. Accounting recognition is given this bargaining by means of the new number of shares outstanding distributed in accordance with the bargained ratio, which has a direct effect on earnings per share after the combination.

Usefulness. The economic substance of a combination is best reflected by reporting operations up to the date of the exchange of shares based on the same historical cost information used to develop the separate operating results of each constituent; and informative comparison with periods prior to the business combination is facilitated by maintaining historical costs as the basis of reporting combined operations subsequent to the combination.

Those opposed to the pooling of interest method doubt that it is based upon a sound concept. In their view, it is primarily an accounting subterfuge for recording an acquisition of a company without recognizing the current fair values of the assets and goodwill underlying the transaction. They view the difficulty in defining the criteria for the application of the pooling method, particularly as to whether relative size is a substantive factor, as a major obstacle to its acceptance. In their opinion, the absence of any effective criteria resulted in the use of this method to account for numerous business combinations which are clearly in substance the acquisition of one company by another. Whether or not *Opinion No. 16* will overcome these objections to the use of the pooling method has yet to be determined.

The most serious defect attributed to the pooling of interests method by its opponents is that it does not accurately reflect the economic substance of the business combination transaction. They claim that it ignores the economic bargaining which resulted in the combination terms by accounting only for the amounts previously shown in accounts of the combining companies. This bargaining usually involves fair market value consideration, not past costs. In addition, opponents of the pooling method claim that the subsequent issuance of stock by one of the parties on the occurrence of particular, predicted events, is unilateral and tends to point to the reality that one of the parties is in fact being acquired.

Purchase Method

Those favoring the purchase method of accounting for business combinations believe, as a practical matter, that one company acquires another in almost every combination involving stock. They base their opinion on the following assumptions:

Acquisitions.   Generally one company in the combination is clearly the dominant and continuing entity, and one or more companies cease to control their own assets.

Bargained Transaction.   Combination is a significant economic event resulting from bargaining between independent parties. The agreed terms recognize primarily the bargained values and only secondarily the constituent's costs. The bargain rests on the assessment of the current status and future prospects of each of the units as a contributor to the combined corporation.

Reporting Economic Substance.   The acquisition is recorded at its economic value, irrespective of whether by stock, cash, or a combination of these. The purchase method recognizes all the assets and liabilities of the acquired company, not merely those previously shown on the financial statements of the acquired company.

Opposition to applying the purchase method to business combinations effected primarily by issuing stock is sometimes based on the difficulties in measuring the fair market value of the stock issued in the acquisition. The reliability of the measure is diminished as neither the fair value of the consideration given nor the fair value of the property acquired is clearly evident. Measuring fair values of assets acquired is complicated by the presence of intangible assets or other assets which do not have discernible market price.

The fair value of stock issued is not always objectively determinable. A market price may not be available for a newly issued security or for securities of a closely held corporation. Even an available quoted market price may not always be a reliable indicator of the fair value of consideration received, because the number of shares issued is relatively large, the market for the security is thin, the stock price is volatile, or other uncertainties influence the quoted price.

Those who oppose applying the purchase method to some or most business combinations effected by stock also challenge the theoretical merits of the method. They contend that the goodwill acquired is stated only by coincidence at the fair value which would be determined by direct valuation. The weakness is attributed, not to measurement difficulties (direct valuation of goodwill is assumed), but to the underlying basis for an exchange of shares of stock. Bargaining in that type of transaction is normally based on the market prices of the equity securities. Market prices of the securities exchanged are more likely to be influenced by anticipated earnings capacities of the companies than by evaluations of individual assets.

A related argument is that the purchase method is improper accounting for a business combination in which a relatively large number of shares of stock is issued because it records the goodwill and fair values of only the acquired company. Those who support this view prefer that assets and liabilities of both companies be combined at existing recorded amounts; but if one side is to be stated at fair values, they believe that both sides should be recorded at fair values.

Criticism of the purchase method is directed not only to the theoretical and practical problems of measuring goodwill in combinations effected primarily by stock but also to accounting for goodwill after the combination. Intangible assets acquired, including goodwill, often have indeterminate useful lives, and alternative methods of accounting are followed. Retaining the cost as an asset is criticized because it may overstate net income before the loss of value is recognized and understate income in the period of write-offs. Present accounting for goodwill is cited as an example of lack of uniformity, because selecting among alternative write-off periods is discretionary.

RESEARCH EFFORTS OF THE APB

As indicated earlier, over the years the accounting for business combinations deteriorated to the point where it was one of the most controversial unresolved problem areas in financial accounting in the late 1960s. Most of the controversy centered on two issues: the criteria for a pooling of interests and the treatment of goodwill. Two APB research studies examined these problems.

ARS No. 10

In 1968, Catlett and Olson concluded that business combinations in which a continuing entity survives are in essence purchase transactions and that the pooling of interests method is not appropriate in such combinations. Furthermore, they concluded that in those "relatively rare" combinations where no constituent company clearly emerges as the continuing entity, a new business has in effect been created. In these cases, the accounting should be similar to that for new companies: the assets and rights should be recorded at fair market value and no goodwill recognized. Based on these conclusions, they recommended that the pooling of interests method be discontinued as an acceptable accounting practice.

ARS No. 10 argued that by treating most combinations that then qualified as pooling of interests as purchases, financial statements would be more useful to investors. First, the fair market value of separable assets and property rights would be disclosed. Second, assigning fair market, rather than book, values to acquired assets would result in more realistic depreciation charges. Third, the amount paid for goodwill would be fully disclosed. The goodwill would be charged directly against the retained earnings of the acquiring corporation as an advance payment by the current stockholders for excess future earnings.

ARS No. 5

Earlier, in 1963, Wyatt had reached similar conclusions. He recommended that the pooling of interests concept be dropped and replaced by a "fair-value pooling" concept. He argued that the fair-value pooling treatment should only be applied to those business combinations in which (a) the constituent combinations approximate each other in size; (b) it is difficult to determine which constituent acquired the other; and (c) the facts of the transaction clearly indicate that the combined entity is a new enterprise. All other combinations should be treated as purchases.

The fair-value pooling method records the assets of the new enterprise created through a combination at their fair market value. Normally, because it is essentially a new enterprise, the combined entity would not begin operations with any retained earnings. However, if required for legal or regulatory purpose, the combined entity may record as retained earnings that amount of the constituent companies' retained earnings which is legally available for dividends.

Criticisms

A number of accountants and businessmen disagreed with the conclusions of Wyatt, Catlett, and Olson. They argued that pooling of interests and purchase accounting were appropriate methods for accounting for business combinations and that many combinations were in effect poolings of interests. The challenge, they believed, was to identify the proper circumstances when each approach is appropriate.

Some accountants argue that combinations effected by cash are in substance different from those effected by stock, and a different method of accounting should be applied to each. Acquisitions for cash, they argue, should be treated as purchases, since one company gains control over the assets of another. An exchange of shares means that both groups of stockholders continue their ownership interest and a genuine pooling of interests takes place, a fact which the accounting should reflect. While agreeing with this basic position, those who consider continuity of ownership interest as the key criteria for pooling believe purchase accounting is appropriate for combinations if either a material minority interest in a subsidiary company exists after acquisition of the subsidiary or if a material amount of preferred stock, either voting or nonvoting, has been used for the acquisition.

Others question the practicality of the fair-value pooling concept proposed by Wyatt for combinations which in essence create "a new enterprise." In their opinion, the tests for determining whether or not a new enterprise has in fact been created are not clear and, hence, not operational.

SUGGESTED FURTHER READING

CATLETT, GEORGE R., and OLSON, NORMAN O. *Accounting for Goodwill.* New York: AICPA, Accounting Research Study No. 10, 1968.

HARVEY, JOHN L., and NEWGARDEN, ALBERT. *Management Guides to Mergers and Acquisitions.* New York: John Wiley & Sons, 1969.

MACE, MYLES L., and MONTGOMERY, GEORGE O. *Planning for Growth Through Acquisition.* Boston: Division of Research, Graduate School of Business Administration, Harvard University, 1962.

WYATT, ARTHUR R. *A Critical Study of Accounting for Business Combinations.* New York: AICPA, Accounting Research Study No. 5, 1963.

CASES

Case 18–1. **SOUTHERN PAPER COMPANY**
Business Acquisition
Accounting

In 1970, the Southern Paper Company sales of paper and paper products in the United States exceeded $800 million. Its highly integrated timber, pulp, paper, and related operations included plants and mills throughout the United States and in several foreign countries. During the 1950s and 1960s Southern had acquired stock in a number of companies in a program of rapid growth and expansion. The majority of these acquisitions had been treated as purchases, but several were recorded as poolings of interest.

In December 1970, Southern acquired all of the business and properties of the American Sisalkraft Corporation, a worldwide producer of reinforced paper products, by exchanging 291,236 shares of Southern's regular common stock for all of the 485,392 outstanding common shares of American Sisalkraft. This exchange rate of 0.6 share of Southern for each share of American Sisalkraft had been determined by negotiation between the managements of the two companies. The values of the properties owned, past earnings records, prospective earnings, financial conditions of the two companies, and market values of the outstanding shares of common stock were among the relevant factors considered.

The merger agreement provided that the business previously conducted by American Sisalkraft as a separate corporation would be treated as a division of Southern. No material changes in the management of the new division were anticipated.

Sales of American Sisalkraft had ranged from $11.6 million in 1965 to $14.9 million in 1969. Net earnings per share declined from $1.48 in 1965 to $1.11 in 1967 and rose to a high of $1.70 for 1969. Sales for the first two months of 1970 were about 3.1 percent greater than the first two months of 1969, but net income was almost 25 percent lower because American Sisalkraft had not been able to increase selling prices to cover increased manufacturing costs. During the period 1965 through 1969, American Sisalkraft paid dividends equal to about 60 percent of net income.

The highest and lowest prices for Southern's common stock on the New York Stock Exchange on December 13, 1970 were 36½ and 35½. Over-the-counter quotations on the same date for American Sisalkraft's stock were 18 bid and 22 asked. These quotations for American shares were approximately double those during the first half of 1969. Southern's common prices had ranged from the low 20s to a high of 60 during the six years preceding this acquisition. The shares issued to American by Southern represented about 2 percent of the total Southern common stock outstanding.

Condensed balance sheets for Southern and its consolidated subsidiaries and for American Sisalkraft are presented in Exhibit 1.

EXHIBIT 1

SOUTHERN PAPER COMPANY AND CONSOLIDATED
SUBSIDIARIES AND AMERICAN SISALKRAFT
CORPORATION

Balance Sheets
(in thousands)

	Southern Apr. 2, 1970	American Sisalkraft Feb. 27, 1970
ASSETS		
Current assets	$161,175	$3,646
Investments	61,340	815
Other assets	18,815	10
Property, plant, and equipment (net)	246,592	3,139
Deferred charges	6,570	86
Total Assets	$494,492	$7,696
LIABILITIES		
Current liabilities	$ 47,148	$1,230
Long-term debt	91,552	
	$138,700	$1,230
Stockholders' Equity:		
Preferred stock	$ 9,727	....
Common stock:		
Southern ($5 par value)	51,742	....
Sisalkraft ($5 par value)		$2,427
Capital surplus	104,090	131
Retained earnings	190,233	3,908
Total Stockholders' Equity	$355,792	$6,466
Total Liabilities	$494,492	$7,696

SOURCE: Prepared by case writer from prospectus dated July 18, 1970.

Questions

1. How would the acquisition of American Sisalkraft Corporation be recorded by Southern if the acquisition were to be treated as a pooling of interests?

2. *a*) How would the acquisition of American Sisalkraft be recorded by Southern if the acquisition were to be treated as a purchase and Southern common was valued at:
   (1) $40 per share?
   (2) $20 per share?
   b) How should any difference between cost and book value of assets be handled subsequent to purchase?

3. Which method of recording the acquisition do you believe Southern must adopt? Why?

4. Disregarding any current or past opinions of the Accounting Principles Board, which method of recording the acquisition do you believe Southern *should* adopt? Why?

Case 18–2. FOSTER-MARTIN, INCORPORATED

Analysis of Criteria for Pooling of Interest Accounting

Foster-Martin, Inc., a manufacturer of television sets, intends to acquire all the outstanding stock of Comet Tube Company, a manufacturer of television tubes. It is expected that Foster-Martin will issue 175,000 shares of its capital stock in a nontaxable exchange for the net assets of Comet, which will then be liquidated. The data in Exhibit 1 are taken from the financial statements of the companies at the close of the most recent fiscal year.

Foster-Martin has 457,500 shares of capital stock outstanding, of which 398,792 shares are owned directly or beneficially by Tom Foster and 118,400 are owned directly or beneficially by Lowell Martin. The remainder of the stock is widely held and is from time to time on the over-the-counter market.

Comet Tube Company was organized in 1955 by Messrs. Thomas and Hinchey, who own 75 and 25 percent of the company, respectively. The company has proved very profitable, net income after taxes having varied

EXHIBIT 1

FOSTER-MARTIN, INC.

Current assets................................	$2,100,000
Property, plant, and equipment (net).........,.,	2,399,000
Other assets ....,,.	331,700
Current liabilities	852,700
Long-term debt ,............................	1,875,000
Capital stock	457,500
Retained earnings	1,645,500
Sales and other revenues	6,582,500
Net income before taxes	687,500
Net income after taxes	394,750
Recent market price	31

COMET TUBE COMPANY

Current assets	$1,317,000
Current liabilities	750,000
Working capital	567,000
Fixed assets, net	574,000
Capital stock	175,000
Retained earnings	966,000
Sales	2,665,000
Other revenues	135,000
Net profit before taxes	775,000
Federal income tax	410,000

from 9 to 14 percent of sales in the past few years. Comet's product line will complement lines now manufactured by Foster-Martin, and the marketability of the Foster-Martin shares makes the transaction attractive to Thomas and Hinchey. Thomas and Hinchey have agreed not to dispose of any shares acquired in the transaction for a period of 12 months after its consummation.

All of the ownership interest in the original business will be represented in the surviving business. Mr. Thomas, who is now president of Comet, will continue as general manager of these operations and will also be placed on the Foster-Martin board of directors. Hinchey is now production manager of Comet and will continue in that capacity. Foster-Martin intends to sign employment contracts with both men.

Questions

1. Does the case outlined above qualify as a pooling of interests? List the factors to be considered in determining whether a particular transaction is a pooling of interests or a purchase, and apply each of these factors to this case.

2. State whether your conclusion in 1 above would be changed by each of the following changes in facts, and why (changes should be considered individually and not cumulatively):

a) Comet Tube Company is not liquidated after the acquisition, but, because of certain local tax advantages, is operated as a subsidiary.

b) Thomas and Hinchey have indicated their intention to sell, shortly after the consummation of the transaction, 50,000 of the shares they acquire thereby and agree to hold the remainder for a period of 12 months.

c) The 175,000 shares issued to Thomas and Hinchey are a special Class B common stock that differs from the common stock already outstanding only with respect to voting rights, which are one 10th that of the other common shares.

d) Only 100,000 shares are issued to Thomas and Hinchey and the remainder of the consideration for the transaction is paid in cash.

3. Assume that Foster-Martin, Inc. publishes an annual report containing comparative financial statements and a 10-year financial summary. If the transaction qualifies as a pooling of interests, what changes if any should be made in the prior year financial statements and the 10-year summary in the next annual report?

4. Assume that Foster-Martin acquired the capital stock of Comet Tube and continues to operate it as a subsidiary. How should the transactions be recorded on the books of Foster-Martin?

5. How should Foster-Martin account for the Comet acquisition if the company were acquired for $5.5 million cash?

Case 18–3. LAWRENCE PAPER COMPANY
Accounting for Joint Ventures

In 1964, Facts Inc. and Lehman Paper Corporation jointly formed the Lawrence Paper Company to build and operate a $31 million mill to produce high quality machine-coated paper.

Under the terms of a long-term purchase contract described in a footnote to the December 31, 1964 balance sheet of Facts Inc., and in the text of the annual report of Lehman Paper for 1964, Facts and Lehman were each obligated to buy one half of the output of the Lawrence Paper Company.

In addition to an initial investment by Facts and Lehman in all of the common stock and some subordinated notes of Lawrence, the new company obtained financing by means of first mortgage bonds issued to four institutional investors. The latter source represented about 60 percent of the initial financing of the mill. The mortgage lenders viewed Facts' and Lehman's long-term purchase contracts with Lawrence as a form of security for the bonds.

The Lawrence Paper Company began operations in June 1966, and its output reached 75,600 tons in 1969 and 86,100 tons in 1970, the latter amounting to over 100 percent of the rated capacity of the mill. A $29 million expansion program announced in 1970 and scheduled for completion by 1973 was expected to raise the annual capacity of the mill from 78,000 tons to 233,000 tons.

Facts Incorporated

Facts Inc. published *Facts*, several other popular weekly magazines, and a number of trade journals. Combined annual periodical circulation was over 12 million in 1970. Early in 1968, Facts entered the book publishing business. Facts had a subsidiary which operated paper and board mills and timberlands in Oklahoma and a paperboard converter facility in South Carolina. Facts also owned several radio and television stations.

Net profit, earnings per share, and common stock prices of Facts Inc. for the years 1963–70, as reported in *Moody's*, are given in Exhibit 1. Selected balance sheet data for Facts are presented in Exhibit 2.

EXHIBIT 1

FACTS INC.

Earnings and Stock Price Record

	Net Income (Millions)	Earnings per Share	Common Stock Prices High	Low
1963	$13.9	$7.10	$ 80½	$54
1964	12.0	6.15	70½	51¾
1965	8.7	4.47	69	52
1966	9.0	4.60	75	63¼
1967	9.3	4.75	86	55½
1968	8.7	4.27	106½	78
1969	10.2	4.76	89¾	56
1970	14.2	6.55	91¾	63¾

In reporting the Lawrence joint venture to its stockholders, Facts Inc. listed the following item immediately beneath the "current assets" on its balance sheet for December 31, 1964:

Investments, at cost:
   Rock Real Estate and Lawrence Paper Company (Note E)... 13,051,181

Note E read as follows:

The Company and Lehman Paper Corporation each own 50% of the capital stock of Lawrence Paper Company (a corporation formed in January 1964, which is constructing a groundwood pulp and paper mill at Lawrence, Texas, at an estimated cost (including working capital) of approximately $31,000,000. Initially, the mill will contain one paper machine designed to produce approxi-

EXHIBIT 2

FACTS INC.

Selected Balance Sheet Data
(in millions)

	1964	1967	1970
Current assets	$101	$ 98	$129
Net buildings, equipment, and land	45	59	85
Timber and timberland (net)............	28	26	25
Other assets	34	48	54
Total Assets	$208	$231	$293
Current liabilities	$ 29	$ 31	$ 39
Long-term debt	45	45	65
Other liabilities	46	59	71
Stockholders' equity	88	96	118
Total Liabilities and Equity	$208	$231	$293

mately 78,000 tons of machine coated printing paper annually. Lehman will manage the mill and supply its requirements of bleached chemical pulp. In addition to their stock ownership, the Company and Lehman have made, and have agreed to make in the future, certain loans to Lawrence which will be evidenced by subordinated notes. At December 31, 1964, the total investment of the Company and Lehman in the stock and notes of Lawrence amounted to $5,000,000 and $3,500,000 respectively, and, based on present estimates, the additional cash required from the Company and Lehman for this purpose during 1965 will be approximately $2,600,000 and $1,300,000, respectively. Lawrence has arranged for additional financing from four institutional investors in the maximum amount of $18,600,000 first mortgage bonds. In the event that (1) funds required for certain purposes by Lawrence should exceed a specified amount, or (2) the corporation's "quick assets" (as defined) should be reduced below a specified amount, or (3) the mill should not be completed, or certain other conditions should not have been met, by stipulated dates, or (4) the corporation should determine not to complete such a mill, the Company and Lehman are obligated on a 50–50 basis to purchase additional subordinated notes or to purchase the then outstanding first mortgage bonds of Lawrence and, under certain of the above-mentioned circumstances, to pay a termination fee to the purchasers of such bonds, as the case may be. The Company is obligated under a long-term contract to purchase paper produced during 50% of the total available operating time of the paper machine or machines at the mill of Lawrence as well as to pay certain shutdown costs. Lehman is similarly obligated. The payments by the Company and Lehman under such paper contracts are to be (1) amounts sufficient to enable Lawrence to recoup all costs, charges and expenses (other than Federal and state income taxes) properly includable in the determination of its net income and not attributable to periods of disability resulting from any act of God, fire, strike or certain other causes, and (2) a fixed annual amount of $500,000 each as long as the mill contains only one paper machine.

From 1965 to 1970, Facts reported the investment in Lawrence separately from the Rock Real Estate investment, showing it always immediately following the current assets. The amount reported December 31, 1965 was $9.1 million, and from 1966 through 1970, $7,209,000.

The financial statements for 1965, 1966, and 1967 included a footnote containing information similar to the last part of the 1964 Note E. In addition, in 1966 and 1967, the amount of the Lawrence first mortgage bonds outstanding as of the end of the year was included in the footnote. The amount was $17,011,000 at December 31, 1966 and $16,301,000 at December 31, 1970. It was noted that Facts and Lehman were obligated to purchase these bonds if the four conditions described in the 1964 Note E were not met.

For the years 1968 through 1970, Facts' balance sheet continued to disclose the Lawrence investment as a separate item, reported at the cost of $7,209,000, but without any explanatory footnote. *Moody's* reported that the amount of Lawrence first mortgage bonds outstanding as of December 31, 1968 was $14,881,000.

Between 1966 and 1970, each of Facts' annual reports included brief, one-paragraph comments on the Lawrence joint venture. These comments indicated that the joint venture represented a hedge by Facts against anticipated shortages of the special paper used by *Facts;* the mill supplied one fifth of *Facts'* paper requirements, used the most modern equipment available, and was operating at capacity.

Lehman Paper Corporation

Lehman Paper Corporation ranked as one of the world's largest paper companies. As of December 31, 1970, the plants of this company and its subsidiaries (excluding Lawrence Paper Company) had an approximate annual capacity of 1,876,000 tons of paper.

Earnings per share and common stock price data for Lehman Paper for the years 1963–70 as reported in *Moody's* are given in Exhibit 3. Exhibit 4 contains selected balance sheet data for Lehman Paper Corporation.

Lehman Paper reported its investment in Lawrence under the balance sheet caption "other assets," appearing after the property accounts. In 1964 it was reported without an explanatory footnote as follows:

Investment in Lawrence Paper Company (at cost)..... $3,500,000

In the president's covering letter for Lehman's 1964 annual report to stockholders, a brief reference was made to the plans for the new mill being built in conjunction with Facts Inc., noting that it would be completed some time in 1966. The following additional comments were included in the text of this same annual report in a section titled "Sales and Marketing":

EXHIBIT 3

LEHMAN PAPER CORPORATION

Earnings per Share and Stock Price Data, 1963–70

	Earnings per Share	*Common Stock Price*	
		High	*Low*
1963	$3.53	69⅞	50⅛
1964	2.63	58½	40⅛
1965	2.32	58¾	42½
1966	2.76	60⅜	50¼
1967	2.81	54½	39¾
1968	2.33 *	67	51¼
1969	2.47	59⅞	37½
1970	2.50	60⅝	45

* After 10 percent stock dividend.

EXHIBIT 4

LEHMAN PAPER CORPORATION

Selected Balance Sheet Data
(in millions)

	1964	*1967*	*1970*
Current assets	$180	$201	$224
Net property	320	345	298
Other assets	37	29	20
Total Assets	$537	$575	$642
Current liabilities	$ 44	$ 57	$ 77
Long-term debt	110	90	78
Deferred income taxes	0	19	39
Other liabilities	5	5	13
Stockholders' equity	378	404	435
Total Liabilities and Equity	$537	$575	$642

. . . In anticipation of the high-quality output of the new mill under construction at Lawrence, Texas, we are developing new markets for the company's coated printing papers in the Midwest, South, and East. The Lawrence mill is owned jointly with Facts Inc., which will share its production with Lehman. . . .

In a later section of the 1964 report, titled "Financial Review," the following description of the Lawrence Paper Company was presented:

Lawrence common stock is owned 50% by Lehman and 50% by Facts Inc. During the year Lehman purchased 20,000 shares of common stock of this company at a cost of $2 million and made long-term advances of $1.5 million; Facts Inc., also purchased 20,000 shares of common stock for $2 million and made long-term advances of $3 million. These advances will be secured by subordinated notes.

It is contemplated that Lehman Paper will similarly advance an additional $1.3 million and Facts Inc. an additional $2.6 million during 1965, and that Lawrence will sell approximately $18.6 million of 25-year, 5% first mortgage and collateral bonds to four institutional investors.

In 1965, the explanation of the Lawrence financing was moved from the text of Lehman's annual report to a footnote to the financial statements. The amount reported to stockholders in 1965 as the investment in Lawrence was $4.8 million. This was again shown under "other assets." The footnote read as follows:

Investments. The investment in Lawrence Paper Company represents 20,000 shares of common stock (50% of the common stock outstanding) at a cost of $2,000,000 and long-term advances of $2,800,000. Lawrence is constructing a paper mill in Texas which will commence operation early in 1966. Lehman Paper Corporation will manage the mill and has contracts to purchase a portion of the output and to furnish certain amounts of pulp.

Lehman Paper Corporation has also made temporary advances of $1,500,000 to Lawrence which will be repaid from the proceeds of the sale of bonds upon completion of the mill.

In 1966, the company's investment was reported at $4,605,000 and the footnote was similar to the 1965 footnote, except that it indicated the mill had begun operation in May 1966. The company's president, in his letter to stockholders, indicated that the mill was operating on a 24-hour, seven-day week schedule.

In 1967, the balance sheet item and footnote were about the same as in 1966. That year, the president's letter included the following comments:

In the growing field of double-coated magazine papers, the new mill owned jointly with Facts Inc. at Lawrence, Texas, remained in a startup status during much of 1967, the first full year of operations, as technological problems were smoothed out. Production and efficiency steadily improved, and by the end of the year Lawrence paper contributed to the rise in corporate sales volume, although the mill's high startup costs offset any benefits to 1967 earnings.

In 1968, Lehman again reported on its balance sheet the investment in Lawrence at a cost of $4,605,000. This year, however, the following additional information was included in the footnote on investments:

. . . The corporation's equity in profits on Lawrence for the year ended December 31, 1968, was $373,546; Lawrence paid no dividends during the year. The corporation's equity in the capital of Lawrence at December 31, 1968 was $2,508,839.

The president's letter in 1968 did not include a comment on Lawrence Paper Company. The text of the annual report made a brief reference to the fact that 1,300 acres of cottonwood were planted for the Lawrence mill.

In 1969, Lehman reported an amount in the "other assets" section on its balance sheet in a renamed account titled "Investment in Affiliated Companies at Cost." The 1969 balance sheet, showing comparative figures for December 31, 1969 and December 31, 1968 for this account, reported $6,288,000 and $4,605,000 respectively. An explanatory footnote read as follows:

Investments in Affiliated Companies. The corporation's equity in the net assets of 50% owned affiliated companies at December 31, 1969, was $820,000 in excess of the cost of its investments. The corporation's equity in the net income of these companies during 1969 amounted to $311,000. These companies paid no dividends during the year.

The text of the annual report in 1969 included the following comment:

Printing papers sales were also above the previous year as we expanded distribution through paper merchants in the Midwest and East, and new offset grades were marketed from the printing papers mill at Lawrence, Texas.

The 1970 balance sheet showed $7,131,000 as the amount in the account Investments in Affiliated Companies at Cost, with the following related footnote:

Investment in Affiliated Companies. The Corporation holds 50% equity in three operating companies, two of which were in a start-up stage at December 31, 1970. The Corporation's equity in the fully operating company at that date was $1,032,000 in excess of the cost of its investment; and its equity in its net income during 1970 amounted to $207,000. The Corporation's equity in the two companies in a start-up stage at that date was $403,000 less than the cost of its investment; and its share of preoperating expenses during 1970 amounted to $397,000.

These companies paid no dividends during the year.

The president's covering letter to the 1970 report included the following two paragraphs:

In addition to the Framingham program we are making good progress in construction of the new kraft pulp and paper mill at Lawrence. This major project, authorized last year, the largest of its kind we have undertaken, will place the company in a much better position to serve its eastern markets with bleached specialty grades. The new mill, wholly-owned by Lehman, will also furnish the expanding pulp requirements of the Lawrence mill, jointly owned by Lehman and Facts Inc. Shortly after the first of the year, the two companies announced the installation of a new Number 2 paper machine in the printing papers mill for the manufacture of coated magazine and other printing paper grades. It is expected that the new machine will be in operation in early 1973.

When these projects are completed, Lawrence will be transformed into one of the major pulp and paper complexes in the country.

Later in the text of the same annual report, in the "Financial Review" section, the following comments were noted:

Capital for the $29-million expansion of the Lawrence Paper Company, jointly owned by Lehman and Facts Inc., is being provided largely through funds borrowed from three institutional lenders who participated in the original financing of the venture. The lending institutions are providing $25 million of the required capital and $4 million is being provided from funds generated internally by Lawrence Paper Company.

Financing of the expansion has not necessitated any additional capital investment by Lehman.

Questions

1. How should Lehman and Facts account for their investment in the Lawrence Paper Company? Why?
2. How adequate are the methods they now use?
3. How should Lehman and Facts account for their long-term purchase contracts with Lawrence?

PART VI
Long-Term Commitments

CHAPTER 19

ACCOUNTING FOR LEASES

The use of leases by businessmen to finance asset acquisitions has grown substantially in recent years. This chapter discusses the accounting by lessees and lessors for long-term personal and property leases. Lease agreements involving natural resources are not covered, principally because of their complex and varied nature.

In September 1964, the Accounting Principles Board issued *Opinion No. 5, Reporting of Leases in Financial Statements of Lessees.* This opinion dealt primarily with the question: Are assets and liabilities created on the lessee's books by entering a noncancellable agreement to lease property on a rental basis? The Board concluded that unless the lease agreement was in substance an installment purchase of property, no assets or related liabilities need be shown on the lessee's balance sheet. The Board further stated that financial statements should disclose sufficient information regarding material noncancellable leases ". . . to enable the reader to assess the effect of lease commitments upon the financial position and results of operations, both present and prospective, of the lessee." *Opinion No. 5* also indicated that leases which were substantially installment purchases of property should be treated as purchases. Finally, the Board recommended that gains and losses on sale and leaseback agreements be amortized over the life of the lease as an adjustment to the rental cost.

Subsequently, in May 1966, the Accounting Principles Board issued *Opinion No. 7, Accounting for Leases in Financial Statements of Lessors.* This opinion dealt principally with the allocation by lessors of revenue and expenses to the periods covered by the lease. The Board recognized there were two generally accepted methods of accounting for leases by lessors: the so-called financing and operating methods (described below). The Board believed that the financing method should be used to account for those leases which pass many of the risks or rewards of ownership, such as maintenance, to the lessee. The Board also recommended that the operating method be used in those instances where the lessor retains the risks and rewards of ownership, such as in the case of automotive equipment leases where the lessor maintains the leased property. In addition, the Board suggested that it was preferable to initially defer the costs of writing leases and then allocate them to expenses over the life of the lease. In those cases where a manufacturer uses leases as part of his marketing activities, the Board recommended that if certain conditions were met, the manufacturer should recognize his normal manufacturing profit when the lease agreement was signed and defer the lease income over the life of the lease, using the financing method. In other cases, the Board recommended that both the manufacturing and lease incomes be deferred and recognized over the lease's life, using the operating method. Finally, *Opinion No.* 7 recommended that significant leasing activities should be disclosed in the lessor's balance sheet in a manner which best describes the nature of his investment in leased assets.

LEASING PRACTICES

A lease agreement conveys the right to use property in return for a series of specified future rental payments over a definite period.

There are a great many different leasing agreements in practice. A typical lease contract contains provisions covering the following areas:

a) The duration of the lease, which can run from a few hours to the expected economic life of the asset.

b) The options open, if any, to renew the lease or purchase the property at the end of the lease's term. In many cases these renewal or purchase options can be exercised for a nominal consideration.

c) The duties of the lessee to service the leased property. The service duties may range from none to complete maintenance.

d) The restrictions, if any, on the lessee's business activities, such as paying dividends or entering new bank loans.

e) The penalties for early termination of the lease. Often, the cost of termination is the lessor's unrecovered costs plus a penalty payment.

f) The consequences of default. Usually, the lease agreement requires the lessee to pay immediately all future payments in the event of default. However, in practice this provision may be difficult to enforce.

g) The obligation of the lessor to provide the lessee with "quiet enjoyment" of the leased property.

There are a number of advantages and disadvantages to leasing assets. One of the major advantages claimed by leasing companies is that current accounting practices do not list lease obligations among a company's liabilities, whereas loan obligations must be recorded. Consequently, by financing asset acquisitions with leases, rather than borrowing, a company can report a better debt-equity ratio. Some of the other advantages cited by leasing companies include: shifting the risks of ownership, such as technological obsolescence, onto the lessor; freeing of capital to finance working capital needs; possible tax advantages in certain cases that makes leasing cheaper on an after-tax basis than owning; 100 percent financing; and additional cost recovery for those companies operating under certain government contracts which allow recovery of rent, but not interest costs.

Offsetting these possible advantages of leasing is the disadvantage of its cost. Depending on the company's credit standing, lease costs before income tax considerations can range from one half of 1 percent to 8 percent higher than would be paid for comparable debt financing, if available.

LESSEE'S STATEMENTS

Nearly all of the companies leasing property or equipment do not list the related property rights and rental obligations in their balance sheets. *Opinion No. 5* of the Accounting Principles Board approved this practice, principally because leases were similar to executory contracts. According to *Opinion No. 5:*

It seems clear that leases covering merely the right to use property in exchange for future rental payments do not create an equity in the property and are thus nothing more than executory contracts requiring continuing performance on the part of both the lessor and the lessee for the full period covered by the leases. The question of whether assets and liabilities should be recorded in connection with leases of this type is, therefore, part of the larger issue of whether the rights and obligations that exist under executory contracts in general (e.g., purchase commitments and employment contracts) give rise to assets and liabilities which should be recorded.

The rights and obligations related to unperformed portions of executory contracts are not recognized as assets and liabilities in financial statements under generally accepted accounting principles as presently understood. Generally accepted accounting principles require the disclosure of the rights and obligations under executory contracts in separate schedules or notes to the financial statements if the omission of this information would tend to make the financial statements misleading. The rights and obligations under leases which convey merely the right to use property, without an equity in the property accruing to the lessee, fall into the category of pertinent information which should be disclosed in schedules or notes rather than by recording assets and liabilities in the financial statements.

In addition to the Board's conclusions, others have objected to showing leases in balance sheets for some of the following reasons: the rental obligation does not represent a liability to repay borrowed funds; it is simply a commitment for future rent expenses. Also, the legal rights of the lessor are different from those of lenders in bankruptcy. Others argue that the right to use leased property is not the same as ownership, and hence the lease right is not an asset. According to this point of view, assets are rights acquired irrevocably, whereas a lease provides for services yet to be rendered and which may not be performed. Another argument against recording lease rights and obligations is that if some companies were forced to capitalize leases, they would default under their present loan indentures. Thus, a change in accounting would precipitate action on the part of creditors and investors to the detriment of the reporting company, despite the fact that the basic financial condition of the company had not changed.

Those who support the recording of lease rights and obligations claim that leasing is a form of financing which has many similarities to conventional debt financing, rather than executory contracts. Typically, the proponents of lease capitalization claim that the lessor essentially completes his part of the agreement when he delivers the leased property. Consequently, the lease agreement is different from the typical executory contract, since no significant future service is to be performed by the lessor. In addition, those supporting capitalization claim that the lessee is committed to making a series of fixed cash payments which reduce his ability to meet a similar obligation to other creditors. Accounting, they point out, is interested in presenting a useful report of the company's financial condition. Given this purpose, it is indefensible, the argument runs, to omit a significant asset and liability simply because its inclusion in the balance sheet would hurt the company.

If lease obligations were recorded in the body of the financial statements, an asset account, Right to Use Leased Property, and a liability account, Rental Obligations under Leases, would be shown. Measuring these accounts presents some difficulties, however. One of the many different suggested solutions is to make the initial entry in both the asset and liability accounts equal to the present value of the future rental payments during the first period of the lease, discounted by the interest rate used in establishing the rental charges.

Subsequently, as the leased property right is "consumed" and the rental payments made, the two balance sheet accounts must be amortized. One of the many different suggested procedures is that the asset account, Right to Use Leased Property, be amortized in the same manner as owned property is depreciated. This treatment recognizes the fact that depreciation schedules reflect the characteristics of the property, not the means used to finance its acquisition.

Next, it is proposed that the liability account, Rental Obligations under Leases, be reduced by the principal repayment amount implicit in the rental payment. The remaining portion of the rental payment would be charged to the income statement as an interest expense. Typically, rental payments are level. Therefore, in the case of long-term leases, the liability account would be extinguished slowly at first, since the bulk of the rental payment would be interest on the unpaid balance of the obligation. Toward the end of the lease, the opposite would occur, because the unpaid balance and related interest charges would be smaller.

It is important to note that under this suggested capitalization and amortization method, the total expenses charged to the income statement would be the same as under the conventional method, which simply charges the rent payment as an expense whenever it falls due. The timing of the expenses during the life of the lease would be different under the two approaches, however.

As a transition measure, some advocates of capitalization suggest that lease asset and liability accounts might be presented "short" in the balance sheet, i.e., the accounts and related amounts might be listed on the balance sheet but the amounts not included in the totals for the assets and liabilities money columns. This method of presentation is accepted by the Securities and Exchange Commission, which does not accept statements capitalizing lease rights and obligations.

Accounting Entries

In order to illustrate the accounting entries by a lessee, assume that the lessee signs a 10-year lease payable in annual amounts of $1,000. The implicit interest rate of the lease financing is 6 percent.

Under normal accounting for leases, the lessee's books simply record the rental payment for the lease as an expense at the time of payment:

Equipment Rental 1,000
    Cash   1,000

If the lease obligation was capitalized, as some suggest, the following entries would be made at the time the lease was signed by the lessee to recognize an asset and a related liability:

Right to Use Leased Property 7,360
    Rental Obligation under Leases   7,360
    To recognize the present value of future lease obligations, in this
    case $1,000 a year for 10 years at 6%.[1]

The first rental payment would be recorded as follows:

Rental Obligation under Leases 558
Interest Expense (6% of $7,360) 442
    Cash   1,000

---

[1] The present value of a stream of payments or receipts is the amount that would have had to be invested today to generate that cash flow at a given rate of interest. For example, if $7,360 were invested today at 6 percent it would return $1,000 per year for 10 years to the investor. At the end of that time the investment would be recouped and the return would be 6 percent. Thus, the present value of $1,000 per year for 10 years discounted at 10 percent is $7,360. Present value tables that can be used to make this calculation are included at the end of this book.

Next year, the interest expense would be less, since the balance of the rental obligation had been reduced by $560 during the first year. The second-year entries are:

Rental Obligation under Leases	592	
Interest Expense (6% of $7,360 — $558)	408	
Cash		1,000

In subsequent years, more of the $1,000 lease payment will go to reducing the balance of the Rental Obligation under Leases as the annual interest on the declining balance of this account gets smaller. At the end of the lease period, the rental obligation liability account will be reduced to zero by the last lease payment.

An additional entry each year would be made to recognize the depreciation of equipment.

Depreciation Expense (10% of $7,360)	736	
Allowance for Depreciation of Leased Equipment		736

The Allowance for Depreciation of Leased Equipment account is shown on the balance sheet as a contra account to Right to Use Leased Property.

Over the life of the lease, the depreciation and interest expenses will be equal to the total lease payment.

Disclosure

The current standards of lease disclosure in footnotes were established by *Opinion No. 5*, which stated:

The Board believes that financial statements should disclose sufficient information regarding material, non-cancellable leases which are not recorded as assets and liabilities . . . to enable the reader to assess the effect of lease commitments upon the financial position and results of operations, both present and prospective, of the lessee. Consequently, the financial statements or the accompanying notes should disclose the minimum annual rentals under such leases and the period over which the outlays will be made.

In many cases, additional disclosure will be required. The Board believes that rentals for the current year on leases covered by this Opinion should be disclosed if they differ significantly from the minimum rentals under the leases. Type or types of property leased, obligations assumed or guarantees made, and significant provisions of lease agreements (such as restrictions on dividends, debt, or further leasing or unusual options) are examples of other types of information which should also usually be disclosed.

The specific details to be disclosed and the method of disclosure will vary from one situation to another depending upon the circumstances. In many cases, a simple statement will suffice. In more complicated situations, more detailed disclosure will be appropriate. For example, it may be useful to provide a schedule of rentals by years or by three- or five-year periods if annual rentals will fluctuate significantly; or it may be desirable to provide a brief description of the basis for calculating the rental if the amount of rent is dependent upon some factor other than the lapse of time; or it may be necessary to indicate the effect of lease renewals in order to avoid misleading implications.

Most people agree that financial statements should disclose information regarding material noncancellable leases. Some proponents of noncapitalization of leases argue that adequate footnote disclosure is preferable to capitalization, since it permits the reader to adjust the statements to meet his particular analytical needs. The common reply to this argument by capitalization advocates is that footnote disclosure should supplement financial statements, not supplant them.

Installment Purchases of Property

Opinion No. 5 of the Accounting Principles Board noted that some leases were in substance installment purchases of property and should be accounted for as property purchases. In these cases the Board recommended:

The property and the obligation should be stated in the balance sheet at an appropriate discounted amount of future payments under the lease agreement. A note or schedule may be required to disclose significant provisions of the transaction. The method of amortizing the amount of the asset to income should be appropriate to the nature and use of the asset and should be chosen without reference to the period over which the related obligation is discharged.

To help management and accountants distinguish between conventional leases and leases which result in the lessee acquiring equity in the property, the Accounting Principles Board suggested the following criteria:

The presence, in a non-cancellable lease or in a lease cancellable only upon the occurrence of some remote contingency, of either of the two following conditions will usually establish that a lease should be considered to be in substance a purchase:

(*a*) The initial term is materially less than the useful life of the property, and the lessee has the option to renew the lease for the remaining useful life of the property at substantially less than the fair rental value; or

(*b*) The lessee has the right, during or at the expiration of the lease, to acquire the property at a price which at the inception of the lease appears to be substantially less than the probable fair value of the property at the time or times of permitted acquisition by the lessee.

In these cases, the fact that the rental payments usually run well ahead of any reasonable measure of the expiration of the service value of the property, coupled with the options which permit either a bargain purchase by the lessee or the renewal of the lease during the anticipated useful life at bargain rentals, constitutes convincing evidence that an equity in the property is being built up as rental payments are made and that the transaction is essentially equivalent to a purchase.

Other circumstances which the Board believed might indicate a lease should be accounted for as a purchase were:

The determination that lease payments result in the creation of an equity in the property obviously requires a careful evaluation of the facts and probabilities surrounding a given case. Unless it is clear that no material equity in the property will result from the lease, the existence, in connection with a non-cancellable lease or a lease cancellable only upon the occurrence of some remote contingency, of one or more circumstances such as those shown below tend to indicate that the lease arrangement is in substance a purchase and should be accounted for as such.

(a) The property was acquired by the lessor to meet the special needs of the lessee and will probably be usable only for that purpose and only by the lessee.

(b) The term of the lease corresponds substantially to the estimated useful life of the property, and the lessee is obligated to pay costs such as taxes, insurance, and maintenance, which are usually considered incidental to ownership.

(c) The lessee has guaranteed the obligations of the lessor with respect to the property leased.

(d) The lessee has treated the lease as a purchase for tax purposes.

The Accounting Principles Board also suggested that leases between lessees and lessors who are related in business should often be accounted for as purchases, even though the lessee is not building up direct equity in the leased property. According to *Opinion No. 5:*

In cases in which the lessee and the lessor are related, leases should often be treated as purchases even though they do not meet the criteria set forth [earlier in the opinion], i.e., even though no direct equity is being built up by the lessee. In these cases, a lease should be recorded as a purchase if a primary purpose of ownership of the property by the lessor is to lease it to the lessee and (1) the lease payments are pledged to secure the debts of the lessor or (2) the lessee is able, directly or indirectly, to control or influence significantly the actions of the lessor with respect to the lease. The following illustrate situations in which these conditions are frequently present:

(a) The lessor is an unconsolidated subsidiary of the lessee, or the lessee and the lessor are subsidiaries of the same parent and either is unconsolidated.

(b) The lessee and the lessor have common officers, directors, or shareholders to a significant degree.

(c) The lessor has been created, directly or indirectly, by the lessee and is substantially dependent on the lessee for its operations.

(d) The lessee (or its parent) has the right, through options, or otherwise, to acquire control of the lessor.

In 1966, the APB published *Opinion No. 10* which required that a subsidiary whose principal business is leasing property or facilities to its parent or an affiliate should be consolidated into the parent company statements.

Sale and Lease-Back

The sale and lease-back is a financing device whereby the owner of property sells it and simultaneously leases it back from the buyer. The lease portion of the transaction presents no accounting problem. The lease is treated like any other lease. An accounting problem arises when there is a gain or loss on the sale of the asset, however. In the past, some companies reported the gain or loss in the current income statement. Others deferred the gain or loss and wrote it off over the lease-back period.

The Accounting Principles Board believes that the sale and the concurrent lease cannot be accounted for as separate transactions. Accordingly, the Board recommended that any material gains and losses arising from sale and lease-back transactions, together with the related tax effect, should be deferred and amortized over the life of the lease as an adjustment to the rental cost. Deferred gains are recorded as liabilities and deferred losses as assets. In those cases where the lease was accounted for as a purchase, the Board recommended the adjustment should be to depreciation.

LESSOR'S STATEMENTS

The accounting for leases on the lessor's statements raises several problems: the allocation of the rental revenues and costs to the appropriate accounting periods; the allocation of lease acquisition, operating, and closing costs in a manner which is systematic, fair, and consistent with the revenue recognition method; the appropriate description and classification of leased assets in the balance sheet. *Opinion No. 7, Accounting for Leases in Financial Statements of Lessors* of the Accounting Principles Board, dealt with these problems.

There are two basic methods used by lessors to record lease expenses and revenues: the operating and financing methods.

Operating Method

The operating method (sometimes called the rental method) recognizes revenue as each rental receipt is received. Costs related to the leased asset, such as depreciation and service costs, are expensed as incurred.

Illustration 19–1 illustrates the operating method with different depreciation schedules. The illustration assumes that equipment costing $10,000 is leased for a five-year period with 60 noncancellable monthly payments of $225 each. At the end of five years, the lessee has the option of renewing for one year at a time for a nominal annual rental of $100. In the illustration it is assumed that five renewal payments are received and at

ILLUSTRATION 19–1

Operating Method

Year	Lease Payments Received (a)	Sum-of-the-Years'-Digits		Straight-Line Depreciation	
		Deprec. Expense (b)	Gross Profit or (Loss) (c)=(a)—(b)	Deprec. Expense (d)	Gross Profit or (Loss) (e)=(a)—(d)
1	$ 2,700	$ 3,167	$ (467)	$ 1,900	$ 800
2	2,700	2,533	167	1,900	800
3	2,700	1,900	800	1,900	800
4	2,700	1,267	1,433	1,900	800
5	2,700	633	2,067	1,900	800
6	100	100	0	100	0
7	100	100	0	100	0
8	100	100	0	100	0
9	100	100	0	100	0
10	100	100	0	100	0
Totals ...	$14,000	$10,000	$4,000	$10,000	$4,000

the end of 10 years the equipment is abandoned by the lessor. The total revenue for the 10 years is thus $14,000, and the lessor's total gross profit is $4,000. Assuming 95 percent of the equipment cost is amortized during the initial term of the lease, the problem is: How much of the $4,000 gross profit should be recognized each year?

The Accounting Principles Board recommended that the operating method be used in those cases where the lessor substantially retains the risks or rewards of ownership in connection with his leased assets. According to *Opinion No. 7*:

... there are companies (e.g., the owner-operator of an office building, the lessor of automotive equipment on short-term leases—daily, weekly or monthly) which retain the usual risks or rewards of ownership in connection with their leasing activity. They may also assume responsibilities for maintaining the leased property or furnishing certain related services which will give rise to costs to be incurred in the future. Rental revenues are designed to cover the costs of these services, depreciation and obsolescence, and to provide an adequate profit for assuming the risks involved. In these cases the operating method is appropriate for measuring periodic net income from leasing activities. The operating method is also appropriate if the leasing activity is an integral part of manufacturing, marketing or other operations of a business which generate revenues and costs which must be considered along with revenues and costs from the leasing activities in arriving at appropriate methods for measuring the overall periodic net income (examples are leases of retail outlets with lease provisions deliberately made favorable to induce lessee to handle lessor's product and leases which generate significant servicing revenues and costs). The operating method likewise is appropriate for leasing activities for an otherwise strictly financing institution if such activities are characterized as set forth in this paragraph.

Financing Method

The financing method (sometimes called financial method) regards the lease as being similar to a sale on credit. The excess of aggregate rentals over the cost of the leased asset (reduced by estimated residual values) is considered to be the lessor's compensation for financing the property acquisition. This income is then spread over the period of the lease so that the amount of income recognized each period bears the same relationship to the unpaid balance of the loan. The receivable shown as an asset is reduced by the difference between the gross rental receipt and the amount allocated to income.

ILLUSTRATION 19–2

Financing Method

Year	Months in Year*	Gross Profit
1	60 through 49	$1,251
2	48 through 37	975
3	36 through 25	700
4	24 through 13	425
5	12 through 1	149
6	....	100
7	....	100
8	....	100
9	....	100
10	....	100
Total	....	$4,000

* The sum of 60 months' digits is 1,830. During the first year the sum of the 49th through the 60th months is 654/1830, so 35.7 percent of the income is recognized during the first year.

Illustration 19–2 illustrates the application of the financing method to the same example presented earlier (see Illustration 19–1). In Illustration 19–2, the deferred gross income is recognized over the initial lease period on the sum-of-the-month'-digits basis.[2] This technique approximates com-

---

[2] Rather than actually working out what the unpaid principal amounts to each month, which would require splitting each lease payment into an interest portion and a principal repayment portion, the total amount of gross profit is simply spread over the life of the lease on a declining scale. The method is called "sum-of-the-months'-digits," or sometimes, the "rule of 78." Some banks use it for their consumer installment loans; a 12-month loan has 78 months' digits, and during the first month the bank recognizes 12/78 of the total interest charge. This is a reasonable approximation to the result obtained by using a more scientific method based on compound interest, even though it does tend to recognize income slightly earlier than a true compound interest-based method.

pound interest calculations. The income over the renewal periods is equal to the option period payments of $100 per year.

The Accounting Principles Board believes that the financing method is generally appropriate where the lessor does not retain the risks or rewards of ownership. According to *Opinion No. 7:*

The financing method is generally appropriate for measuring periodic net income from leasing activities of entities engaged in, perhaps among other things, lending money at interest—e.g., lease-finance companies, banks, insurance companies or pension funds. Lease agreements of institutions of this kind typically are designed to pass all or most of the usual ownership risks or rewards to the lessee, and to assure the lessor of, and generally limit him to, a full recovery of his investment plus a reasonable return on the use of the funds invested, subject only to the credit risks generally associated with secured loans. Usually, the financing method is similar to the method of accounting for revenue already in use for other lending activities of the institutions. The financing method is also appropriate for a leasing activity of an entity which is not identified as a financial institution, such as a manufacturer, if the lease agreements have the characteristics described earlier in this paragraph.

Accounting Entries

Using the same example as Illustration 19–1, which assumes that a company purchases an asset for $10,000 and then leases it, the operating method recognizes the income as the cash from the $2,700 annual lease rental charge is received. The leased asset owned by the lessor is depreciated in this case on a straight-line basis of $1,900 per year. The gross profit is the difference between these amounts.

Cash	2,700	
Rental Income		2,700
Depreciation Expense	1,900	
Allowance for Depreciation		1,900

Based on the gross profit schedule in Illustration 19–2 and the aggregate lease payments and asset cost in Illustration 19–1, the financing method recognized at the time the lease is signed the following asset and liability accounts:

Lease Payments Receivable	14,000	
Deferred Profit on Leasing		4,000
Cost of Leased Asset		10,000

The profit is recognized as each $2,700 payment is received:

Cash	2,700	
Lease Payments Receivable		2,700
Deferred Profit on Leasing	1,251	
Current Profit on Leasing		1,251

The amount of the last entry is the first-year, sum-of-the-months'-digits figure shown in Illustration 19–2.

Therefore, at the end of the first year, the receivable from leasing would be $11,300 and the remaining deferred profit $2,749 ($4,000 − 1,251). At the end of the second year, the lease receivable would be $8,600 ($11,300 − 2,700) and the deferred profit account $1,774 ($2,749 − 975).

Balance Sheet Presentation and Disclosure

Leased assets fit neither of the conventional balance sheet categories of "loans receivable" or "property employed in operations." Accordingly, the Accounting Principles Board recommends that significant amounts invested by lessors in leased assets should be shown separately in the balance sheet. Also, these assets should be presented "in a manner which best describes the nature of the investment." *Opinion No.* 7 states:

The classification and description of the investment should be appropriate in the circumstances and should depend upon whether the financing or operating method of accounting is used.

When the financing method is used, the aggregate rentals called for in the lease should be classified with or near receivables and a description used along the lines of "receivables under contracts for equipment rentals" or "contracts receivable for equipment rentals." When a company is predominantly engaged in leasing activities for which the financing method is appropriate, information should be disclosed regarding future maturities of the rentals receivable. Unearned finance charges of interest (as defined in Paragraph 5) included in the aggregate rentals should be shown as a deduction therefrom. Estimated residual value should be classified separately with or near property, plant and equipment unless the residual value represents an amount expected to be collected from the lessee (e.g., when a favorable purchase option exists), in which case it should be classified with or near notes and accounts receivable. Thus, the investment is represented by the net rentals receivable plus the residual value. Receivables under financing leases are subject to the same considerations as to current or noncurrent classification, where such segregation is appropriate in the balance sheet, as are assets resulting from other activities.

When the operating method is used, the investment should be classified with or near property, plant and equipment and a description used along the lines of "investment in leased property," "property held for or under lease," or "property (equipment, buildings, machines, etc.) leased to others"; accumulated allowances for depreciation and obsolescence should be known as a deduction from the investment.

In addition to the appropriate balance sheet presentation, the Accounting Principles Board believes that the footnotes to the financial statements should disclose at least the accounting methods used, as well as sufficient information to enable the reader to assess the significance of leasing activities to the company.

Initial Direct Cost

Leasing companies incur costs, such as commissions and legal fees, which can be directly associated with consummating particular leases. For a number of years, it was a common practice to recognize an immediate recovery of these costs out of expected gross income at the time the lease agreement was signed. Rather than accelerate the recognition of income, the Accounting Principles Board expressed a preference for deferring negotiation and closing costs and amortizing them over the life of the lease. *Opinion No. 7* said:

When initial direct cost of negotiating and closing leases are reasonably expected to be recovered from revenues, these costs should preferably be deferred and allocated to future periods in which the related revenues are reported. In this context, "initial direct" costs are those costs which are directly associated with consummating the lease (e.g., commissions, legal fees, costs of investigating the lessee's financial status and of preparing and processing documents). The method of allocation to future periods should be consistent with that used to recognize revenue under the financing or operating methods. However, substantially the same net income would be reported under the financing method by expensing initial costs as incurred and recognizing as revenue in the same period, in addition to the normal revenue, a portion of the unearned revenue equal to the initial costs; this method is also acceptable. When initial direct costs of a lessor are reasonably constant in relation to revenues, no practical objection can be raised to a practice of consistently expensing these costs as incurred and recognizing revenue without compensating for initial costs.

Leasing by Manufacturers

As part of their regular marketing program, a number of manufacturers are willing to lease, rather than sell, their products to customers. In these cases, the manufacturer receives his normal manufacturing profit margin as well as a return for lease financing, if provided. Depending on the circumstances, the manufacturing profit on leased assets should be recognized at either the time the lease agreement is signed or over the lease period. *Opinion No. 7* states:

When manufacturers use leases to assist in marketing products or services, the Board believes that the guidelines described [earlier] indicate whether the financing or operating method is appropriate. Manufacturing revenues (amounts which would have been obtained in a regular sale or the discounted amount of future rentals whichever is lower), costs and profit should be determined at the time of entering into the lease and reported in the income statement of the lessor on the same basis as outright sales of similar manufactured property, provided all of these conditions are met: (*a*) credit risks are reasonably predictable, (*b*) the lessor does not retain sizable risks of ownership of the nature described [earlier] and (*c*) there are no important uncertainties surrounding the amount of costs yet to be incurred or revenues yet to be earned under the lease. If any of these conditions is not met, manufacturing profit should be recognized, using the operating method, only as realized in the form of rental revenue over the term of the lease. If manufacturing revenue is determined at the time of entering into the lease, the conditions described above having been met, the financing method should be used and the amount of the manufacturing revenue becomes the "cost of the leased property." When it is feasible to determine normal selling prices, then revenues, costs and trading profits of dealers and other middlemen should be recognized in the same manner and under the same conditions described above for manufacturers.

Accounting Entries

A manufacturer using leasing as a marketing aid might have the following breakdown for the "sale" of one unit on a 10-year lease contract:

Cost	$ 9,000
Manufacturing profit	1,000
Deferred leasing profit	2,000
Selling price	$12,000

If the conditions listed above were met, the $1,000 profit from manufacturing would be recognized immediately, and the profit from leasing the equipment would be recognized under the financing method.

Under the *financing* method (using the sum of the year's digits), the entries would be:

1. Immediate (to recognize manufacturing profit):

Accounts Receivable	12,000	
Sales		10,000
Deferred Profit on Leasing		2,000
Cost of Goods Sold	9,000	
Inventory		9,000

2. As payment is received (to recognize leasing revenue):

Cash	1,200	
Accounts Receivable		1,200
Deferred Profit on Leasing	360	
Leasing Profit		360

If there were substantial risk in the lease, recognition under the *operating method* would be required. Accounting entries (in this case under a straight-line method) would be made as each payment is received:

Cash	1,200	
Rental Income		200
Sales		1,000
Depreciation Expense	900	
Allowance for Depreciation		900

The Continuing Controversy

Accounting for leases by lessors is a fairly settled issue. The controversy over the proper accounting for leases by lessees continues, however. For example, the Accounting Principles Board, commenting in *Opinion No. 7* upon the consistency of *Opinion No. 5* and *No. 7*, said:

The Board takes notice of a question that has been raised as to whether certain conclusions herein are inconsistent with conclusions in *Opinion No. 5, Reporting of Leases in Financial Statements of Lessee*—specifically, the question is whether leases accounted for on the financing method by lessors should be capitalized by lessees. As indicated in Paragraphs 2 and 7, the Board considers the principal accounting problem of lessors to be the allocation of revenue and expense to accounting periods covered by the lease in a manner that meets the objective of fairly stating the lessors' net income; the Board believes that this objective can be met by application of the financing method when the circumstances are as described in this Opinion. As to the lessee, however, capitalization of leases, other than those which are in substance installment purchases of property, may not be necessary in order to state net income fairly since the amount of the lease rentals may represent a proper charge to income. There continues to be a question as to whether assets and the related obligations should be reflected in the balance sheet for leases other than those that are in substance installment purchases. The Board will continue to give consideration to this question.

In mid–1971 the APB was considering proposals that lessees capitalize leases when either the expected residual value of the leased asset at the end of the lease term was nominal or the lease term approximated the asset's life. Another proposal would require capitalization of financing-type leases.

SUGGESTED FURTHER READING

MEYERS, JOHN H. *Reporting of Leases in Financial Statements.* American Institute of Certified Public Accountants Research Study No. 4, 1962.
VANCIL, RICHARD F. *Leasing of Industrial Equipment.* New York: McGraw-Hill, 1963.

CASES

Case 19–1. **DRAXSON INDUSTRIES**
Accounting for Sale and Lease-Backs and Lessee's Lease Commitments

In May 1970, the officers of Draxson Industries were considering the presentation of the company's lease transactions in the 1970 financial statements.

Draxson Industries was incorporated in Pennsylvania in 1947 as the successor to a family-owned business formed two decades earlier. The company sold supplies and equipment to the commercial dry-cleaning and laundry industries.

The Company

In 1969, sales and net income reached all-time highs of $16.4 million and $343,000, respectively. Stockholders' equity at the close of that year totaled $2.6 million.

Operations of the company had always been profitable. In the 10-year period from 1960 to 1969, net income had ranged from 9 to 22.8 percent of shareholders' equity at the beginning of the year. Book value per share of stock had climbed from $2.68 to $10.54 during the same period. A 10-year summary of selected operating and financial information is shown in Exhibit 1.

From its earliest years, Draxson Industries sought to build a reputation for offering its customers a full line of high-quality equipment and operating supplies. The dry-cleaning and laundry industries in the nationwide market looked to Draxson leadership in the development of new equipment, accessories, and specialized consumable supplies.

The company acted primarily as a national distributor for a number of relatively small manufacturers and as exclusive representative for others

EXHIBIT 1

DRAXSON INDUSTRIES

Ten-Year Summary

(figures in thousands of dollars except percentages and per share figures)

	1969	1968	1967	1966	1965	1964	1963	1962	1961	1960
Operations:										
Net sales	16,418	15,222	13,056	11,659	10,516	10,099	9,340	7,711	6,246	5,379
Income before federal income tax	750	539	507	286	246	375	402	308	183	188
Percentage of sales	4.3%	3.5%	3.9%	2.5%	2.3%	3.7%	4.3%	4.0%	3.0%	3.5%
Net income to shareholders	343*	259	240	134	118	178	183	145	90	77
Percentage of sales	2.1%	1.7%	1.9%	1.1%	1.1%	1.8%	1.9%	1.9%	1.4%	1.4%
Per share †	$1.39	$1.16	$1.09	$0.60	$0.53	$0.80	$0.82	$0.65	$0.41	$0.34
Dividends paid in cash	94	14	7	2	2	15	...	15	15	15
Financial position:										
Current assets	4,633	4,423	3,490	2,915	2,742	2,634	2,345	1,978	1,566	1,278
Current liabilities	1,988	2,289	1,415	1,282	1,201	1,164	1,156	995	865	647
Working capital	2,645	2,134	2,075	1,633	1,541	1,470	1,189	983	701	631
Current ratio	2.3	1.9	2.5	2.3	2.3	2.3	2.0	2.0	1.8	1.9
Long-term debt	371	424	472	262	390	428	315	441	186	178
Shareholders' equity	2,605	2,036	1,852	1,552	1,420	1,305	1,127	801	672	397
Percentage of net income to shareholders' equity at beginning of year	16.8%	14.0%	15.5%	9.6%	9.0%	15.8%	22.8%	21.6%	15.0%	14.3%
Book value per share †	$10.54	$9.16	$8.33	$6.99	$6.39	$5.87	$5.07	$3.61	$3.02	$2.68

* Does not include income tax refund of 23¢ per share.

† Based on 247,000 shares outstanding at December 31, 1969 and 222,000 shares outstanding in 1968 and prior years.

in limited geographic areas. About 90 percent of the products sold by Draxson were manufactured by others. The balance, consisting of replacement parts for standard laundry and dry-cleaning equipment such as belts, padded rollers, and chemically treated press covers, were manufactured in the company's Philadelphia plant.

In 1958, following the death of the company's president and principal stockholder, the management of the company changed. The new management embarked upon an aggressive expansion program. Existing branches were strengthened by adding sales personnel and increasing inventories. The company's geographic sales coverage became nationwide as branches were established in new cities.

Funds for Draxson's expansion program had been obtained from several sources. The largest part of increased working capital requirements was internally generated. Minimum dividends were paid to stockholders during the expansion period. In 1959, capital stock sold to several members of the new management team provided about $100,000. The balance was obtained by borrowing on long-term notes, which were refinanced late in 1967. In 1969, the company's working capital position was improved by the sale of 25,000 additional shares of capital stock to the general public. At the close of 1969, Draxson's stock was held by about 600 stockholders.

Draxson's Lease Activities

Since 1947, the company had signed a number of lease agreements involving real estate. In 1969, a sale and lease-back arrangement was used to acquire a building to house the New York branch. Also in 1969, management was considering the leasing of automobiles needed in company operations.

Real Estate Leases.   Since 1947, Draxson had leased all of the physical facilities used in operations. In 1947, when the home office and plant space requirements exceeded its Philadelphia building, the company sold its plant and moved into leased property.

Branch operations had always been conducted in leased facilities. In most cases, new branches were established in very low-rent districts under three- to five-year leases. After sufficient sales volume was obtained, the branches were moved to larger and better buildings. At the close of 1969, all of Draxson's operations except the New York branch were housed in fairly new, modern buildings. A schedule of the company's real estate leases is shown in Exhibit 2.

Draxson's management had subscribed to a principle of leasing real estate to conserve working capital for inventory and accounts receivable expansion. Early in 1969, the company's treasurer said,

EXHIBIT 2

DRAXSON INDUSTRIES

Real Estate Leases at May 28, 1970

	Philadelphia	New York	Chicago	Cleveland	Atlanta	Kansas City	Dallas	Los Angeles	Seattle
Date of lease	5-1-68	11-1-60	2-1-66	5-1-67	10-1-69	9-1-67	7-1-69	4-1-68	8-1-67
Length of lease	20 yrs.*	10 yrs.	10 yrs.	10 yrs.	5 yrs.	5 yrs.	10 yrs.#	10 yrs.	5 yrs.
Probable life of property (from date of lease)	50 yrs.	30 yrs.	30 yrs.	50 yrs.	30 yrs.	20 yrs.	50 yrs.	50 yrs.	20 yrs.
Option to buy at a nominal price?	no	no	no	no	no	no	no	no	no
Cancellation provisions	none	none	none	none	none	none	none	none	none
Amount of annual rental	$45,400*	†	$18,000	$13,900	$9,600	$3,600	$12,600	$13,500	$5,800
Other payments by lessee?									
Taxes	yes	no‡	no	no‡	no‡	no	no‡	yes	no
Insurance	yes	no‡	no	no	no	no	no	yes	no
Maintenance	yes	yes	yes	yes	yes	yes	yes	yes	yes
Heat	yes	yes	no	yes	yes	yes	yes	yes	yes
Light	yes	yes	yes	yes	yes	yes	yes	yes	yes

* Plus three five-year renewal options with annual rentals of $24,100, $22,900, and $22,900 respectively.

† $39,700 for first five years and $40,700 for second five years.

‡ Payments required by lessee equal to increases over the initial base year of the lease.

Plus two five-year renewal options.

We have always leased, but I would be inclined to say that leasing is not an industry practice. Many of our competitors, I know, own their own buildings, but this may well be one of the reasons that they have failed to expand from more than one or two locations.

All our leases are negotiated at the best possible price to the company. We do not know exactly what percentage of net income the lessor receives on his investment, but we assume it to be in the 6 to 10 percent range. As our annual report for 1969 indicates, we earned 16.8 percent on our shareholders' money, using it for trading purposes.

No attempt has been made to compare the cost of leasing either with long-term debt or equity capital. These are studies that probably should have been made, but I doubt that they would have seriously altered the company's leasing program. Any method of obtaining equity or long-term capital immediately requires some extra strings on management. This is a factor that we are reluctant to assume, especially when any resultant savings is hit by high income tax rates and earnings at present are satisfactory.

Planned Sale and Lease-Back. For a number of years, Draxson had been planning to move its New York City branch to better facilities in a more desirable location. The lease on the New York premises was to terminate November 1, 1969.

After exhausting all efforts to find suitable existing space, arrangements were completed early in 1970 to obtain required facilities through a sale and lease-back transaction. Unimproved land was purchased at a cost of $300,000. A contract had been signed with a New York contractor for the construction of a one-story building on the site. Interim financing had been obtained from the company's Philadelphia bank. The building scheduled for completion early in September 1970 was to cost $500,000, including all financing and related costs. The completed building, together with the land, was to be sold to the Old Quaker Life Insurance Company of Philadelphia for $750,000 and immediately leased by Draxson for a period of 25 years at a monthly lease rental of $4,500. The lease provided that Draxson would pay all costs of maintaining the property as well as periodic amounts equal to the property taxes and insurance costs. At the expiration of the lease, Draxson was to have the option of purchasing the property for $250,000. It was estimated that the steel and masonry building would have a physical life of 40 years.

Automobile Leasing. In May 1970, management of Draxson Industries was considering the adoption of a policy of providing automobiles for certain key sales personnel in all branches. Currently, company-owned automobiles were used only by executives at Philadelphia. Under the contemplated plans, a fleet of about 20 automobiles would be leased from a national firm of automotive equipment lessors. The plan, if adopted, would probably be effected later in 1970 when 1971 model autos became available.

Approximate costs were available, although the lessor had not submitted his detailed proposals. Under a typical lease arrangement, the lessor would provide new autos at the estimated fleet cost price of about $3,500 for periods of two years. In addition to a monthly payment of $100 per unit, the lessee would pay an annual charge for insurance, taxes, and licensing, depending upon the location of the auto's use. The lessee would, of course, pay all costs of operation and normal maintenance.

Questions

1. What recognition, if any, should be given in Draxson Industries' 1970 financial statements to:
    a) Real estate leases?
    b) Automobile leases?
2. How should the sale and lease-back of the New York branch property be reflected in 1970 financial statements?
3. Draft the appropriate footnotes to the 1970 financial statements regarding lease transactions.
4. List alternative methods of presenting leases in the financial statements. Describe how the amounts shown in the financial statements for each of these methods might be calculated.

Case 19–2. LEASCO DATA PROCESSING EQUIPMENT CORPORATION

Accounting for Sales by Lessors

Leasco Data Processing Equipment Corporation, founded in 1961, was a computer-based service organization engaged in several business activities: (1) leasing computers and related data processing equipment to users; (2) furnishing computer information services, including the design, analysis, and operaton of computer-based systems for problem solving, operations research, and information storage and retrieval; and (3) warehousing, servicing, and delivery of domestic and imported automobiles. During the six months ended March 31, 1968, approximately 69 percent of Leasco's net income came from leasing activities, 26 percent from information services, and 5 percent from automotive operations. Its domestic business was conducted through wholly owned subsidiaries, and its foreign leasing activities through Leasco Europa, 76 percent of whose stock was owned by Leasco's wholly owned subsidiary, Leasco World Trade. Exhibits 1 and 2 contain financial statements for the firm.

Computer Leasing

In 1968, Leasco wrote two types of leases for computer equipment: full payout leases and operating leases. Prior to May 1967, Leasco had written exclusively full payout leases. The full payout lease obligated the lessee to a sum of rental payments that was sufficient to return to the lessor the invoice cost of the equipment plus interest charges and other related expenses. On March 31, 1968, amounts receivable under full payout leases, included estimated additional amounts to be realized at the end of the leases, totaled approximately $56.6 million; the corresponding unrecovered cost of the equipment subject to such leases was about $45 million. At the end of the lease term, lessees could normally renew the lease at a negotiated rental rate which was not lower than one 12th of the original rate. Some full payout leases contained purchase options at the end of the lease term. The purchase price was customarily set at the fair market value of the equipment, or in some cases, at the residual salvage value, which typically was estimated to be 10 percent of the equipment's original cost. If the equipment was not purchased or its lease extended, then it was to be returned to Leasco.

In May 1967, Leasco commenced writing operating leases in addition to full payout leases. Operating leases were leases in which the cost of the equipment and related expenses would not be recovered over the initial term of the lease. By March 31, 1968, operating leases were in effect for equipment having an original cost of $56.4 million, with an accumulated depreciation allowance of $2.2 million. The monthly rate of rentals due under the operating leases totaled approximately $920,000. Leasco's policy was to write operating leases for only IBM System 360 computers. Conversely, almost all IBM System 360 equipment owned by Leasco was leased under operating leases. Cancellation of an operating lease required 180 days prior notice and payment of a penalty, usually about 50 percent of the unpaid rentals to the end of the lease term. While the operating leases involved greater risk to Leasco than full payout leases, Leasco's management felt such leases were justified by their increased profit potential. Leasco's operating leases were written for a three-and-a-half- to five-year initial commitment, as compared to the one- to three-year operating leases customarily written by computer manufacturers and other leasing companies.

For the fiscal year ended September 30, 1967, approximately 46 percent of the cost of equipment under new leases was for equipment manufac-

EXHIBIT 1

LEASCO DATA PROCESSING EQUIPMENT

Statement of Consolidated Income

	Year Ended September 30					(Unaudited) Six Months Ended March 31	
	1963	1964	1965	1966	1967	1967	1968
Income:							
Income from information services	$3,729,242	$5,162,369	$6,957,181	$ 7,652,107	$ 8,456,429	$ 4,327,110	$ 4,592,741
Earned income on lease contracts*	274,756	496,284	869,965	1,995,023	4,394,164	1,916,054	3,086,703
Computer rental income†	...	...	...	...	853,690	...	4,068,827
Income from automotive services	411,692	477,112	560,512	703,783	696,827	363,628	635,096
	$4,415,690	$6,135,765	$8,387,658	$10,350,913	$14,401,110	$ 6,606,792	$12,383,367
Expenses:							
Cost of sales—information services	$3,584,150	$4,870,306	$6,734,198	$ 7,293,406	$ 7,846,424	$ 4,023,803	$ 4,233,717
Operating expenses—automotive services	245,100	273,482	342,533	387,147	322,642	161,694	218,549
Interest	122,326	175,602	291,725	616,778	1,657,717	696,431	2,427,467
Depreciation, computer rental equipment	...	...	...	...	377,756	...	1,845,427
Selling, general, and administrative	190,154	372,932	508,077	1,115,952	2,374,660	1,014,886	1,734,296
	$4,141,730	$5,692,322	$7,876,533	$ 9,413,283	$12,579,199	$ 5,896,814	$10,509,456

Income before provision for federal income taxes	$ 273,960	$ 443,443	$ 511,125	$ 937,630	$ 1,821,911	$ 709,978	$ 1,973,911
Provision for federal income taxes							
Current	$ 81,100	$ 129,900	$ 77,254	$ 110,062	$ 75,000	$ 91,573	.....
Deferred	10,200	17,000	81,760	120,100	358,000	88,700	473,000
	$ 91,300	$ 146,900	$ 159,014	$ 230,162	$ 433,000	$ 180,273	$ 473,000
Net income	$ 182,660	$ 296,543	$ 352,111	$ 707,468	$ 1,388,911	$ 529,705	$ 1,500,911
Dividend requirements on preferred stock	15,000	15,000	15,000	15,000	15,000	7,500	7,500
Net income applicable to common stock	$ 167,660	$ 281,543	$ 337,111	$ 692,468	$ 1,373,911	$ 522,205	$ 1,493,411
Average number of shares of common stock outstanding	959,526	959,540	1,001,032	1,383,950	1,728,138	1,590,830	2,109,540
Per share:							
Net income as above	$0.17	$0.29	$0.34	$0.50	$0.80	$0.33	$0.71
Pro forma net income per share including issuance of additional shares upon exercise of certain outstanding options and certain warrants resulting in dilution and conversion of Series A convertible preferred stock					$0.73	$0.30	$0.64
No cash dividends have been paid on the Company's common stock.							
Amounts of investment credit utilized in the determination of the provision for federal income taxes and its effect on the provision are as follows:							
Amounts of investment credit utilized, total	$ 29,163	$ 30,673	$ 44,486	$ 132,833	$ 430,756	$ 96,657	$ 472,380
Per share	$0.03	$0.03	$0.04	$0.10	$0.25	$0.06	$0.22

* Full payout leases.
† Operating leases.

EXHIBIT 2

LFASCO DATA PROCESSING EQUIPMENT

Consolidated Balance Sheet
(in thousands)

	September 30, 1966		September 30, 1967	March 31, 1968 (Unaudited)
ASSETS				
Cash		$ 1,889	$16,307	$ 15,684
Marketable securities, at cost		36	46	3,869
Notes and accounts receivable		943	943	1,535
Lease receivables:				
Aggregate future rentals	$19,606		$42,101	$51,718
Estimated additional amounts at end of lease	1,355		4,061	4,800
	$20,961		$46,162	$56,518
Unearned income to be included in future gross earnings	4,464		9,717	11,565
Net lease receivables		16,497	36,445	44,953
Computer rental equipment, at cost, less accumulated depreciation of 0, $378,000, and $2,223,000, respectively		0	16,583	54,172
Inventories, lower of cost or market		290	249	59
Equipment, fixtures, and improvements		383	1,161	1,190
Other assets		888	1,505	2,307
Deferred debt expense and discount		74	969	949
Total Assets		$21,000	$74,208	$124,718
LIABILITIES AND EQUITY				
Notes payable		$10,989	$19,353	$ 71,668
Accounts payable		3,308	11,076	4,482
Accrued expenses		535	1,195	2,710
Customers' deposits on leases		59	111	115
Federal income taxes, deferred		287	593	1,061
Subordinated note, 6%		500	500	500
Convertible debentures, 6.5%		0	226	0
Senior subordinated debentures, 5.75%		0	25,000	25,000
Total liabilities		$15,678	$58,054	$105,536
Minority interests		0	0	736
Preferred stock	$ 250		$ 250	$ 250
Common stock	198		262	267
Paid-in capital	3,252		12,646	13,441
Retained earnings	1,622		2,996	4,488
Total Equity		5,322	16,154	18,446
Total Liabilities and Equity..		$21,000	$74,208	$124,718

tured by International Business Machines Corporation and 12 percent for equipment manufactured by National Cash Register Corporation. No other manufacturer accounted for as much as 10 percent of the new equipment leased. During the six months ended March 31, 1968, approximately 65 percent of the cost of equipment under new leases was for IBM computer equipment.

Exhibit 3 presents data related to Leasco's leasing operations during 1963–68.

EXHIBIT 3

LEASCO DATA PROCESSING EQUIPMENT

| Period | Ending | Leases Written during Period | | On Full Payout Leases, at End of Period | |
		Aggregate Face Amount	Cost of Leased Equipment Purchased	Receivables	Unearned Rental Income
Six months,	Mar. 31, 1968 ...	$49,521,815	$53,377,846	$51,717,960	$11,565,008
Six months,	Mar. 31, 1967 ...	20,659,954	16,364,978	31,945,091	7,230,786
Year,	Sept. 30, 1967 ...	57,125,661	54,101,124	42,101,192	9,716,651
Year,	Sept. 30, 1966 ...	23,046,546	17,960,113	19,605,719	4,463,542
Year,	Sept. 30, 1965 ...	7,158,000	5,664,279	7,845,664	1,594,706
Year,	Sept. 30, 1964 ...	3,982,177	3,051,837	4,358,497	997,817
Year,	Sept. 30, 1963 ...	2,158,934	1,695,280	2,538,127	564,623

Source: Leasco Prospectus, August 12, 1968.

Approximately 7,100 leases for computers or related equipment were in force at March 31, 1968 with approximately 5,500 lessees. Seven lessees accounted for approximately 17 percent of the total amount receivable from these leases. The maximum total rental obligation for a single lessee was about $3.5 million.

Leasco conducted a credit investigation of all prospective lessees, and financial statements were usually required except where such information was publicly available. More than 80 percent of amounts due under current leases were from concerns having AAA–1 ratings by a major credit rating organization. Prior to January 1, 1968, Leasco had a credit insurance policy which insured the payment of rentals to Leasco under its equipment leases. The policy was terminated on January 1, 1968 as a result of litigation between Leasco and the insurance company over claims arising from nonpayment of lease contracts which the insurance company had refused to cover.

Leasco's leases generally provided that in the event the lessee should default in the payment of a lease installment, Leasco could either declare the entire balance on the lease due and immediately payable, repossess the leased equipment without recourse to legal proceedings, or retain all prior payments under the lease and cause the sale of the leased equipment in order to recover the balance due.

All lessees were responsible for maintaining the leased equipment, and were required to contract with the manufacturer for regular maintenance service for the original lease and all renewal periods.

By January 1968, Leasco had extended its leasing operations to Europe, operating through Leasco Europa. Leasco, through Leasco World Trade, owned about 76 percent of the common stock of Leasco Europa; the balance was owned by a group of European banks and Bankers Trust, International.

The initial equity capitalization of Leasco Europa was $3 million, of which Leasco's share was about $2.27 million. Leasco did not intend to utilize its domestic lines of credit in pursuing the European business. The European banking co-owners had agreed to lend to Leasco Europa's operating subsidiaries approximately $25 million for computer purchases. Such loans would be secured by leases and by the underlying equipment. In addition, Leasco World Trade was arranging for the sale of $20 million of 5 percent convertible debentures in June 1968. The payment of principal and interest would be guaranteed by Leasco and the debentures were convertible into Leasco common stock. The debentures would not be offered for sale or registered in the United States.

Financing

To expand its leasing activities, Leasco relied heavily on borrowed capital from banks. The loans available to Leasco were dependent upon the company's "borrowing base." The borrowing base consisted of either 85 percent of the total lease payments to be made or the depreciated cost of the rental equipment, whichever was less, for all unencumbered leased equipment. A critical measure for the banks, according to a Leasco executive, was a leasing company's ability to generate a positive cash flow from the net of rentals less operating cash expenditures, interest payments, and the amortization of debt. Leasco had always been able to show such a positive cash flow.

Leasco also obtained financing by assigning leases without recourse to financial institutions, who advanced a portion of the present value of the noncancellable receivable. On September 30, 1967, Leasco had assigned as collateral rental equipment having a depreciated cost of $6,627,500 for a loan of $3,885,000 and on March 31, 1968 equipment valued at $26,025,000 for a loan of $14,551,000.

The following summarizes the anticipated future payments of notes payable in connection with financing agreements existing in 1968:

Fiscal Year	Amount
1969	$17,002,000
1970	17,554,000
1971	13,328,000
1972	8,823,000
1973 and after	4,376,000
	$61,083,000
Revolving credit	10,000,000
Total	$71,083,000

Exhibit 4 contains a statement of the sources and uses of funds for the 18-month period from September 30, 1966 to March 31, 1968.

EXHIBIT 4

LEASCO DATA PROCESSING EQUIPMENT

Sources and Uses of Funds Statement
for Sept. 30, 1966 to Mar. 31, 1968
(in thousands)

Sources:	
Profits	$ 2,867
Depreciation	2,223
Increase in notes payable	60,679
Increase in accounts payable and accruals	3,352
Senior subordinated debentures	25,000
Sale of common stock	10,189
Deferred federal income taxes	774
Other	856
Total sources	$105,940
Uses:	
Increase in cash	$ 13,795
Increase in marketable securities	3,833
Increase in leases receivable	29,048
Increase in computer equipment (operating lease)	56,395
Other	2,869
Total uses	$105,940

Computed from the Sept. 30, 1966 and Mar. 31, 1968 Leasco balance sheet and income statement, respectively.

Common Stock

The common stock of Leasco Data Processing Equipment Corporation had performed over the years as a glamour issue for stockholders. The common stock had gone from a 1965 low of $7⅛ on the over-the-counter market to a high of $73⅛ on the American Stock Exchange for the first quarter of 1968, and had risen as high as $114¾ through August 12, 1968. The common stock had consistently maintained a price-earnings ratio of

70 to 90 times the prior year's earnings. Brokers and analysts had justified Leasco's high P/E ratio with comments such as earnings growth, industry potential, market opportunities, quality of the leases, and management capability. Leasco's P/E ratio was not at all unique to the computer leasing industry, where P/E ratios generally ranged from 50 to over 100.

On March 31, 1968, there were approximately 2,134,000 shares of common stock outstanding. However, stock options and warrants potentially could have increased the common stock by an additional 767,640 shares. The option price ranged from $2.50 to $53.50. The price range of the warrants was $2.50 to $41.25.

In accordance with indenture provisions from the financing agreement, Leasco could not declare a dividend on its common stock if as a result the outstanding indebtedness (excluding subordinated debt) were to exceed 350 percent of the consolidated net worth.

Accounting Policies

Leasco's accounting policies for tax and shareholder reporting of leasing income were similar to industry practices for both full payout and operating leases. For full payout leases, total lease income was the excess of gross rentals plus the estimated salvage or residual value of the equipment at the end of the lease over the cost of the equipment and related marketing expenses. Total lease income was taken into earned income monthly over the term of the lease by the sum-of-the-years'-digits method. The estimated residual value of the equipment was based on a purchase option of up to 10 percent of the equipment's original cost or on a salvage value of about 5 percent. The historical residual value averaged about 6 percent.

On Leasco's balance sheet, full payout leases were represented by leases receivable (the total amount of lease payments to be received) and were shown net of the income to be realized in future periods. The following is a summary of anticipated collections of the full payout leases represented by leases receivable in the balance sheet on March 31, 1968:

Fiscal Year	Amount to Be Collected
1969	$14,112,000
1970	12,476,000
1971	10,243,000
1972	8,497,000
1973 and later	11,190,000
Total leases receivable	$56,518,000

As an example of the accounting for a full payout noncancellable lease, assume a computer costing $1 million was leased for a period of six and a half years, with the lessee having the option to purchase the equipment at the end of the lease period for $100,000. The annual rental was $204,800 and the cost to the lessor of securing the lease was $37,600. Also, assume the lessor borrowed $800,000 for the purchase of the computer. The lessor's accounting entry to record the above transaction would be as follows:

	Debit	*Credit*
(Asset) Lease Receivable (6½ × 204,800)..........	1,331,200	
(Asset) Residual Value	100,000	
(Contra to Lease Receivable) Unearned Income ...		393,600
(Liability) Notes Payable		800,000
(Asset) Cash		237,600

The unearned income from the lease contract would be credited to Earned Income over the life of the lease, using the sum-of-the-years'-digits method. Thus the earned income in any one period would be in proportion to the lessor's outstanding lease receivable.

For operating leases, where the cost of the equipment would not be recovered during the initial term of the lease, net income was the total lease payments received during the reporting period, minus depreciation, interest, selling expenses, etc. The cost of the leased equipment, net of the depreciation allowance, for an operating lease was shown as an asset on the balance sheet. For shareholder reporting, Leasco depreciated the cost of the equipment under operating leases on a straight-line method over 8 or 10 years.

As a result of accelerated depreciation for tax reports and the investment credit, Leasco actually paid very low income taxes. Leasco's heavy computer purchases generated a substantial amount of investment tax credits. The tax law allowed the investment credit to be deducted from income taxes up to a maximum of 50 percent of the tax otherwise payable in any one year. Unused portions of the investment credit could be carried back three years or carried forward seven years. It can be seen from Exhibit 1 that in 1967 and 1968 Leasco was deducting close to the maximum allowable.

Future Outlook

The successful performance of Leasco's common shares was attributable in large part to the company's ability to double or triple its base of leased equipment in each of the past five years. The continuation of such results could become increasingly difficult over time for two reasons: the sheer size of the future investment base and the life cycle of third-generation equipment. With an initial annual investment of only about

$1.7 million, rapid percentage growth was feasible. For 1967, however, investments in new equipment were $51.1 million and for the first six months of 1968 had reached $53.4 million.

"Any slowdown in computer purchases," a Leasco executive pointed out, "might mean that Leasco would show an annual growth of 40 to 50 percent instead of 200 percent, and that is not really too bad. Besides, it is not at all clear just how much Leasco's common share price depends on earnings performance. Some informed analysts claim that the stock price represents almost wholly a speculation on the residual value of the equipment we own. For example, the IBM 1401 Series still has a value of around 30 to 40 percent of its initial cost, almost 10 years after purchase and 6 years after introduction of the third-generation equipment. In our accounting, we have only allowed for a 10 percent residual value."

The life cycle of computer equipment posed another problem. The principal obsolescence of computer equipment resulted from technological innovation rather than physical wear. The fact that a family of equipment started to become obsolescent at a specific point in time (when a new computer generation was announced) rather than after an elapsed period of time made the continued purchase of third-generation machines (e.g., IBM System 360) an increasingly hazardous undertaking over time. Thus, Leasco was faced with the need to invest increasingly large amounts in third-generation equipment each year with prospects of smaller returns from each round. However, the decrease in equipment value resulting from the introduction of fourth-generation equipment could not be exactly forecast. As the executive quoted above pointed out, the IBM 1401 Series had an economic life of almost 10 years even though its generation life was only 5 years.

The cutoff date for purchases of third-generation computer equipment was a critical decision for the company. Because of debt repayment terms, it would be about four years after the cessation of computer purchases before the company could avail itself of any significant portion of its cash inflow for reinvestment or return to the shareholders.

Questions

1. How should Leasco have accounted for its full payout and operating leases? (Industry experts generally agreed that the advent of fourth-generation computers would be "evolutionary rather than revolutionary." In addition, they were also in general agreement that the computer leasing market was becoming a "lessee's market.")

2. How significant was the choice of accounting for leases to Leasco's success?

CHAPTER 20

PENSION COSTS

A pension plan is an arrangement whereby a company provides for retired employees' benefits which can be determined in advance. Since World War II, the accounting for private pension plans has become a major accounting issue, principally because of the rapid growth in the number, scope, and size of these plans. The major accounting controversy revolves around the timing of the cost of these plans to income. Other related issues involve accounting for changes in the actuarial assumptions, appreciation of the pension fund assets, and revisions to the plan.

By 1980, it is estimated, 42 million employees will be covered by private pension plans with total reserves of $225 billion. A number of factors have contributed to the growth of pension plans. The passage of the Social Security Act in 1935 created considerable public interest in pensions. During World War II, pension benefits were exempt from wage stabilization controls. From 1949 onwards, following a federal court ruling, pensions were wages and hence bargainable issues; organized labor has vigorously presented demands for expanded private pension coverage. At the same time, employers have increasingly used pension plans as part of their personnel policy to attract, motivate, and hold better qualified workers and executives. This trend was motivated in large part by the tax inducements offered to employers by the federal government to encourage the creation of "qualified" pension plans.

PENSION PLANS

A full understanding of the accounting for pension costs requires an appreciation of the variety of actuarial valuation techniques and funding instruments, agencies, and methods involved in determining the financial provisions for pension benefits. Therefore, the discussion of the accounting for pension costs is preceded by a brief description of pension plans. This description is a summary of the material included in Ernest Hicks' *Accounting for the Cost of Pension Plans,* Accounting Research Study No. 8.

Valuation

Actuarial valuation is the process of determining the amounts needed to finance a pension plan. This process relies on three principal concepts. First, the valuation is for a closed group of employees. Second, the ultimate cost of the plan is primarily the present value, as of the valuation date, of the expected future benefit payments. Third, the valuation is merely an approximation, since the assumptions underlying the calculations (actuarial assumptions) involve considerable uncertainty. The valuation of a pension plan is sometimes separated, after it is determined, into two portions: past service costs (also called "prior service costs") and normal costs (sometimes called "current service costs"). Past service costs are those pension costs assigned under the valuation method used to those years prior to the inception of the plan. Normal costs are those pension benefits based on service after the inception of the plan. In making the actuarial valuation, however, the past service and normal costs are not considered separately.

Assumptions

When estimating the cost of pension plans, actuaries must make a number of difficult assumptions regarding uncertain future events. For example, estimates are made of the expected rate of return on the pension fund, the fund's administrative expenses, and the amounts and timing of future benefits. The future benefit estimates, in turn, may involve estimates of future employee compensation levels, cost-of-living indices, mortality rates (both before and after retirement), retirement ages, employee turnover, vesting privileges, and social security benefits.

Clearly, it is most unlikely that the actuarial assumptions will be realized in practice. Therefore, it is necessary to review and change the actuarial assumptions from time to time. If the original assumptions turn out to have been conservative in terms of actual events, the pension fund may become overfunded and an actuarial gain results. If the assumptions turn out to have been optimistic, there will be an actuarial loss.

The net adjustment for actuarial gains and losses is handled by actuaries in one of two ways when revising valuations and contribution patterns. The so-called immediate method applies the net actuarial gain to reduce the next employer contribution. This method is typically not used for net losses. The spread method spreads the net gain or loss over the present and expected future contributions. Some actuaries use the immediate method for handling net gains and the spread method for losses.

Funding Instruments and Agencies

Typically, employers make some financial provision for the current and future benefits payable under pension plans, irrespective of whether or not the plan stipulates funding. There are a variety of funding instruments, the most popular being contracts with life insurance companies (insured plans) and trust agreements (trust fund plans).

Insured plans cover a variety of arrangements. For example, individual policies providing death and retirement benefits may be issued to a trustee for each employee. A similar arrangement is a group annuity contract issued to the employer. Both of these arrangements specify the premiums and benefits.

Other popular insured funding arrangements are deposit administration contracts and immediate participation guarantee contracts. Essentially, both of these plans require the employer to open an account with an insurance company and make regular contributions to this account. The insurance company in turn adds interest to the account at an agreed rate. When the employee retires, the insurance company issues an annuity providing the stipulated benefits and the annuity premium is withdrawn from the employer's account.

Trust fund plans require the employer's contributions to be made to a trustee who invests the funds and pays retirement benefits according to the terms of the trust agreement. Trustees may be an individual, a bank, or a group of individuals. The terms of trust agreements may give the trustee full power to select investments or he may be subject to the general direction of the employer.

Funding Methods

Once an employer adopts a pension plan he has wide choice of funding alternatives. Some of the more common methods are:

1. Pay-as-you-go method.
2. Terminal funding method.
3. Unit credit method.
4. Entry age normal method.
5. Individual level premium method.
6. Aggregate method.
7. Attaining age normal method.

Each of these methods produces varying periodic contribution patterns.

Illustration 20–1 illustrates the different financial cost—in contrast to accounting—patterns of some common funding methods. The assumptions underlying Illustration 20–1 are:

The calculations are based on a hypothetical employee group. At the inception of the plan, none of the employees has retired. As employees retire and are replaced, the group approaches maturity—a condition in which the age distri-

ILLUSTRATION 20-1

Comparison of Results under Various Methods of Funding Pension Cost

	Pay-as-You-Go ‡	Terminal Funding‡	Unit Credit Method Past Service Cost Funded: Over 20 years	Unit Credit Method Past Service Cost Funded: As to Interest Only	Entry Age Normal Method Past Service Cost Funded: Over 20 years	Entry Age Normal Method Past Service Cost Funded: As to Interest Only	Individual Level Premium Method	Aggregate Method	Attained Age Normal Method Past Service Cost Funded: Over 20 years	Attained Age Normal Method Past Service Cost Funded: As to Interest Only
Past service cost	...	...	$ 431,924	$431,924	$ 661,315	$661,315	...$	...$	$ 431,924	$ 431,924
Initial normal cost	...	...	26,371	26,371	27,101	27,101	...$	...$	50,858	50,858
Ultimate normal cost	...	...	33,563	33,563	27,101	27,101	...$	...$	27,101	27,101
Contribution—beginning of year:										
1	...	...	53,402	36,906	68,488	43,230	$ 126,488	$ 95,591	77,889	61,393
2	$ 840	$ 10,151	54,398	37,902	68,488	43,230	112,337	89,867	75,903	59,407
3	2,100	15,226	55,267	38,771	68,488	43,230	101,472	84,635	74,106	57,610
4	3,543	18,456	56,058	39,562	68,488	43,230	92,778	79,995	72,479	55,983
5	5,326	23,070	56,731	40,234	68,488	43,230	85,061	75,728	70,999	54,503
10	17,270	39,041	58,821	42,324	68,488	43,230	57,235	59,233	65,277	48,781
15	30,006	42,295	59,933	43,437	68,488	43,230	42,032	43,331	61,484	44,988
20	40,582	44,134	60,863	44,367	68,488	43,230	34,060	37,730	58,947	42,451
21	42,356	44,409	34,008	44,543	27,101	43,230	33,002	36,858	31,521	42,056
25	48,158	45,316	34,694	45,229	27,101	43,230	29,971	34,015	30,233	40,768

30	54,443	55,829	34,934	45,463	27,101	43,230	27,900	31,568	29,125	39,660
35	62,999	63,442	33,480	44,014	27,101	43,230	27,101	29,949	28,391	38,926
40	65,559	50,369	33,077	43,612	27,101	43,230	27,101	28,930	27,929	38,464
50	64,249	49,227	33,388	43,923	27,101	43,230	27,101	27,867	27,448	37,983
Limit	63,000	50,753	33,563	44,098	27,101	43,230	27,101	27,101	27,101	37,636
Fund balance—end of year:										
1	...	54,737	37,823	70,200		44,311	129,651	97,981	79,836	62,928
2	9,543	111,002	76,762	141,293		88,869	247,228	191,683	158,772	124,532
3	23,236	168,273	116,269	212,873		133,249	355,265	281,125	236,547	184,543
4	39,103	226,307	156,094	284,763		177,260	455,613	366,515	313,120	242,907
5	58,267	284,655	195,777	356,622		220,543	548,731	447,840	388,263	299,385
10	178,161	569,997	380,564	707,342		417,303	918,561	794,067	737,424	547,991
15	288,002	831,283	528,079	1,035,096		570,864	1,160,317	1,090,139	1,039,107	735,903
20	364,714	1,070,060	638,136	1,343,743		682,428	1,315,863	1,251,691	1,302,039	870,115
21	375,937	1,088,255	656,331	1,361,700		700,385	1,339,177	1,277,347	1,323,484	891,560
25	410,140	1,151,400	719,556	1,422,100		760,785	1,410,822	1,362,729	1,395,201	963,277
30	454,999	1,213,230	781,305	1,476,931		815,616	1,475,905	1,438,799	1,459,655	1,027,731
35	528,172	1,235,435	803,511	1,495,910		834,594	1,495,910	1,471,378	1,484,796	1,052,872
40	536,121	1,225,500	793,576	1,487,884		826,569	1,487,884	1,472,026	1,480,699	1,048,775
50	501,002	1,202,048	770,124	1,467,601		806,286	1,467,601	1,460,955	1,464,588	1,032,664
Limit	502,104	1,206,924	775,000	1,471,873		810,558	1,471,873	1,471,873	1,471,873	1,039,949

† Pay-as-you-go and terminal funding are not considered to be "actuarial cost methods"; the results under these procedures are included in the table for comparative purposes.

§ Past service cost and normal cost are not determined separately under either the individual level premium method or the aggregate method. The annual contributions under these methods include amortization (not separately identified) of past service cost.

SOURCE: Ernest R. Hicks, *Accounting for the Cost of Pension Plans*, Accounting Research Study No. 8 (New York: AICPA, 1965). Adapted from a table appearing in "Fundamentals of Pension Funding," by Charles L. Trowbridge, *Transactions of the Society of Actuaries*, Vol. IV, 1952, p. 36.

bution, including the ages of employees who have retired, approximates a distribution which is expected to be duplicated year after year. If this condition
were reached or approximated, the annual contribution (payment) under any
particular funding method would remain the same or approximately so. This
theoretical result is represented in [Illustration 20–1] by the entries under
"Contribution," captioned "Limit." (The assumption of an initially immature
group of employees is applicable to pension plans recently adopted and to plans
of employers whose operations are growing. In both instances, the proportion
of pensioners to active employees is low in relation to the proportion represented by the theoretical condition of maturity.) Other assumptions are an
interest rate of 2.5 percent and a retirement benefit of $420 annually. The past
service cost, when developed under a particular funding method, has been
amortized in the illustration over a period of 20 years. Changes in the conditions and assumptions specified would, of course, vary the amounts appearing
in the illustration, but the trend indicated would remain.[1]

An employer may pay pension benefits on a pay-as-you-go basis, i.e.,
the employer pays benefits when they become due. Strictly speaking,
this is not a funding method, since no pension fund is established. Thus,
the pension contributions depend solely on the amount of the current
retirement benefits paid.

In terminal funding, the employer makes provision for the payment
of benefits at the time the employee retires, i.e., no payments to funds are
made during the employee's active service. This terminal funding method
may involve a single-premium annuity or an equivalent contribution to a
trust. The terminal funding method is often used in situations where union
contracts require pensions only for those employees retiring during a
certain period.

The unit credit method funds future service benefits as they accrue.
The normal annual cost under this method is the present value of the units
of future benefit credited to employees for service during the year. The
total annual contribution ordinarily comprises two parts: (1) the normal
cost and (2) an amount for past service cost, which may include the
interest on the unfunded past service cost as well as an amount to reduce
the unfunded past service cost balance.

In contrast to the unit credit method, which looks only at services performed, the entry age normal method apportions to past, present, and
future periods the estimated cost of an employee's projected benefits,
without regard to the timing of the service giving rise to the benefits. This
method assumes that (1) every employee entered the plan at the earliest
possible time, and (2) contributions have been made from the time of
entry into the plan to the actuarial valuation date. In theory, the normal
costs under this plan are level amounts. The sum of these payments plus

---

[1] Ernest R. Hicks, *Accounting for the Cost of Pension Plans*, Accounting Research
Study No. 8 (New York: American Institute of Certified Public Accountants, 1965).

accumulated interest should provide fully for the employee's pension at retirement. The entry age normal method can be applied on an aggregate or individual basis.

The individual level premium method requires the payment of a level annual amount over the period from the employee's actual entry into the plan until his retirement. This method is commonly used where the funding instrument is individual insurance or annuity plans.

When the level premium method is applied on a collective basis, it is called the aggregate method. The aggregate method implicitly amortizes past service costs over the average remaining service life of the participants, whereas the individual level premium method amortized the implicit past service costs over the expected remaining life of the participants. This difference in handling past service costs (which are not separately identified) accounts for the different contribution patterns between the individual and aggregate methods in Illustration 20–1.

The attained age normal method is similar to the aggregate method, except the past service cost is specifically determined at the beginning of the plan as it is under the unit credit method. As in the unit cost and entry age methods, the past service cost may be amortized through a variety of contribution patterns.

Income Tax Considerations in Plan Selection

Most pension plans are designed so that the employer contributions are deductible for tax purposes during the year contributed. To qualify for this status, pension plans must meet certain requirements specified by the Internal Revenue Code and the Internal Revenue Service.

There are several other tax aspects which should be noted. First, the tax treatment of pension costs follows cash, rather than accrual, accounting. Second, the earnings of qualified trust plans are tax free. Third, there is no tax requirement that past service costs be funded. Fourth, employer contributions to the fund are not taxable income to employees until distributed as retirement benefits.

Summary

The variety of pension agreements, funding arrangements, and the different relevance of the income tax consideration to individual companies results in a wide variety of pension obligations among businesses. This leads to numerous accounting variations for pension costs.

ACCOUNTING CONSIDERATIONS

Most proposed accounting proposals related to pension costs, in contrast to funding patterns, fall into one of four basic variations:

a) Pay-as-you-go.
b) Annual recognition of future liability for benefits to retired employees only.
c) Annual recognition of the normal cost plus an amount equal to the interest on any unfunded past service cost.
d) Annual recognition of the normal cost plus an amount amortizing past service costs over a period which in practice may range anywhere from 10 to 40 years, plus interest on unfunded prior service cost.

Opinion No. 8 of the Accounting Principles Board supports methods (*c*) and (*d*). Before *Opinion No. 8* was issued in 1967, all of these methods were found in practice.

The accounting controversy over pension costs revolves around these fundamental questions: Should accounting for pension costs be on an accrual basis? What actuarial method should this accrual basis follow? What disclosure standards should be applied to pension plans and costs? Other related questions include: How should one account for changes in pension plans? What is the proper accounting treatment of actuarial gains and losses? What is the correct way to account for unrealized appreciation (or depreciation) of pension funds? How should one account for possible pension costs related to employees who may become eligible for coverage at a later date?

Cash versus Accrual

Whether or not generally accepted accounting principles should require the accrual method to be used for relating pension costs to fiscal periods is basic to the pension cost controversy. The alternative is to follow a cash flow accounting method.

The following accounting entries illustrate the difference between the cash and one of the accrual methods for a new pension plan with a first-year normal cost of $100,000 (including interest on the amortized past service cost). The past service cost is $300,000,

a) At the time the plan is established:

Cash Method

No entry

Accrual Method

No entry

b) After the first year the actuarially determined payment to the fund is $100,000:

Cash Method

No entry

Accrual Method

```
Pension Expense ....................................... 100,000
    Pension Payment Liability ........................            100,000
```

c) The company makes a payment of $50,000 to the pension fund:

Cash Method

```
Pension Expense ....................................... 50,000
    Cash ...........................................            50,000
```

Accrual Method

```
Pension Payment Liability ........................... 50,000
    Cash ...........................................            50,000
```

It is important to note that under both methods, no entry in the company's books is made to record the past service cost at the time the plan is established, or at any other time in the future. Also, under the cash method, the pension expense is equal to the cash actually paid into the pension fund by the company.

Those who argue that the cash amount paid is the appropriate pension expense stress the uncertainties and diversity of practices involved in making actuarial valuations. Under these conditions, the argument runs, the actual contribution to the fund is the only reliable measure of the periodic cost of pension plans. Others point to the fact that some employers believe they will never have to pay the entire amount of an actuarially calculated pension accrual, because the pension fund is being continuously replenished by new contributions which are adequate to cover current payments from the fund. Therefore, it is not necessary to fully fund the pension fund. If these costs will never have to be paid into the fund, it is argued, the accrued amounts are not true costs. Furthermore, in these cases, if the accrued costs were significantly larger than the amounts funded, large deferred pension liabilities would be shown on the balance sheet. These liabilities might be misinterpreted and union pressure might develop to make additional contributions to the pension fund, thereby placing an unwarranted and unnecessary financial burden on the company.

Those who support accounting for pension costs on an accrual basis consider that credits for future pension benefits are part of an employee's current compensation. This employment cost, they maintain should be accounted for when incurred, irrespective of how the plan is funded. The funding of a pension plan, they state, is a financial management decision completely unrelated to accounting considerations.

OPINION NO. 8

Opinion No. 8, Accounting for the Cost of Pension Plans supports the accrual approach to pension accounting. The pension cost may be determined by an actuarial cost method which is rational, systematic, and consistent with the accrual approach to accounting. Both the accounting method and the actuarial cost method should be consistently applied from year to year. *Opinion No. 8* places limits on the maximum and minimum annual provision for pension costs.

An Overview

The basic accounting for pension plans recommended in the opinion is relatively straightforward: the provision for pension cost should be based on an actuarial cost method that gives effect, in a consistent manner, to employee group data, pension benefits, pension fund earnings, investment gains or losses, and other assumptions regarding future events. The actuarial cost method selected should result in a systematic and rational allocation of the total cost of pensions among the employees' years of active service. If the actuarial cost method selected includes past service cost as an integral part of normal cost, the provision for pension cost should be the pension cost adjusted for the effect on pension fund earnings of differences between amounts accrued and amounts funded. If the actuarial cost method deals with past service cost separately from normal cost, the provision for pension cost should include normal cost, an amount for past service cost, and an adjustment for the effect on pension fund earnings of differences between amounts accrued and amounts funded.

Pension Costs: Maximum and Minimum Limits

In developing APB *Opinion No. 8*, the Board agreed unanimously concerning the need (1) to eliminate fluctuations in annual pension costs that can result from cash based methods, and (2) to prescribe the accrual basis for accounting for pension costs. Pension costs are an important cost of doing business. Except in rare cases, when a company commits itself to pay pensions to its employees upon their retirement, the cost of those pensions may be expected to continue as long as the company has employees. Furthermore, year-by-year pension cost should not be greatly out of line with the size or compensation of the employee group. (For example, it does not appear reasonable for a company with a stable or growing employee group to have pension costs of $50,000 one year, $100,000 the next, and $10,000 the next. This could happen, for instance, if the company followed the policy of only charging as its periodic pension expense an amount equal to its annual cash contribution to the pension fund.

The Board encountered considerable disagreement as to the appropriate definition of pension costs. One view was that pension cost should "take into account all estimated prospective benefit payments under a plan with respect to the *existing employee group.*" The principal opposing view was that "pension cost is related to the pension benefits to be paid to the *continuing employee group as a whole.*" Under either view, annual pension cost would include normal cost. The essential difference between the two views is in their accounting for past service costs.

The Board agreed, as had the predecessor Committee on Accounting Procedure, that past service costs relate to periods subsequent to the adoption or amendment of a plan and should not be charged against retained earnings as something applicable to the past, since the benefits are available for future periods.

Some members of the Board believed past service cost should be specifically recognized in annual provisions over a period of years, although there were some differences in views concerning the appropriate period to use. Other members believed it unnecessary to make specific provisions for past service cost if all benefit payments could be met on a continuing basis by annual provisions representing normal cost plus an amount equivalent to the interest on unfunded prior service cost.[2]

There is merit to both positions. Although the Board stated a preference for past service cost being amortized, it concluded, due to differing opinions as to the real long-run costs of pensions, that it should not at this time rule out either approach as an acceptable measure of pension costs. Accordingly, in order to substantially narrow the difference in account-

---

[2] In many places, the opinion refers to "amounts equivalent to interest" or "interest equivalents." As used in the opinion and in the actuarial profession, "interest" is a simple way of referring to the earnings, assumed or actual, of a pension fund. The need to take interest equivalents into account in computing the pension cost provision arises when the actual pension fund differs from a theoretical fund and when the amounts funded differ from the amounts which have been recorded for accounting purposes.

Under the present-worth basis used for pension cost accounting, it is assumed that amounts equivalent to prior service cost and normal cost will be contributed to a fund and that the fund will produce earnings (interest) at an assumed rate. If contributions for these amounts are not made, they will not be available to produce earnings, and it becomes necessary to make an additional provision equivalent to what the earnings would have been if the contributions had been made. This assumption is extended to past service cost even though it is known at the outset that the amounts will not be funded until sometime in the future, or not at all.

For this reason, the opinion calls for the pension cost provision to include an amount equivalent to interest on unfunded prior service cost. Such interest may be included as a separate component of the provision or it may be included in the amortization of the past service cost. Whenever past service cost is being amortized and the prior year pension cost provisions have not been funded, an amount equivalent to interest on the unfunded provisions should be added to the provision for the year in addition to any amount included in the amortization. Conversely, when the amounts funded exceed the prior year pension cost provisions, a reduction of the provision for the year is needed to reflect the interest equivalents on the excess amounts funded.

ing for the cost of pension plans, the Board expressed its opinion in terms of a minimum method based on the normal cost plus interest concept, and a maximum method based upon the amortization of past service cost concept. One result of this conclusion is that any period may be selected for the amortization of past service cost, as long as the total annual provision falls between the minimum and maximum. As the opinion is written, it allows a company to fit its accounting for the cost of its pension plan to the facts and circumstances in its particular case.

The essential difference betwen the minimum and maximum methods is the extent to which past service cost is included in the pension cost provision. Under the defined minimum, only interest on unfunded prior service cost (plus any indicated provision for vested benefits) is included. Under the defined maximum, 10 percent of the past service cost is included.[3] Normal cost is the same under both.

It is important to note that the 10 percent limitation applies separately to past service cost at the adoption of a plan and to changes in prior service cost that result from amendments of the plan. For example, disregarding interest equivalents, if a company adopts a pension plan with past service cost of $100,000, the maximum accounting provision would be normal cost plus $10,000 (10 percent of $100,000) of past service cost. If the company later amends the plan to increase benefits, and the cost of the increased benefits related to service prior to the amendment is an additional $50,000, the maximum would be normal cost plus $15,000 (10 percent of the total $150,000) until such time as the original past service cost has been fully amortized; after that time the maximum becomes normal cost plus $5,000 (10 percent of the $50,000 increase). This can be significant when there is a series of increases in benefits over a period of time.

As previously indicated, whenever the funding differs from the cost provision, the cost provision must be increased or decreased by interest equivalents on the difference between the amount provided and the amount funded. An illustration may be helpful. When a company adopts a pension plan, it may fund immediately all of the past service cost in order to gain the advantage of the tax-free income from the investment of the funds by the pension trust. Because the pension cost provision with respect to the past service cost is limited to 10 percent, there will be a deferral on the balance sheet for the other 90 percent. Again taking past service cost of $100,000, $10,000 would be included in the pension cost provision for the year and the other $90,000 would appear as a deferred charge on the asset side of the balance sheet. In this situation, the accrual

---

[3] The maximum cost is the sum of the normal cost, 10 percent of past service cost, 10 percent of increases or decreases in prior service cost arising from plan amendment, and interest equivalents on the difference between provisions necessary for the plan and amounts funded.

for the following year would be reduced by the earnings of the $90,000. If the assumed interest rate was 4 percent, the cost provision for the succeeding year would be reduced by $3,600. Because of these reductions, the amortization period will be somewhat longer than 10 years.

Conversely, if the company decides to make the maximum pension cost provisions but does not immediately make contributions to the fund or makes contributions in smaller amounts than provided, there will be an accrued pension liability for the unfunded amount on the balance sheet. The pension cost provision for subsequent years should include an amount equivalent to interest on whatever amount is shown as an accrual on the balance sheet.

In two frequently used actuarial cost methods, the "individual level premium" and "aggregate" methods, past service cost is not measured separately. That is, it is included in normal cost. Because there is no separately computed amount for past service cost, the defined minimum and maximum are the same under these methods.

On the other hand, in many other frequently used actuarial cost methods, such as the unit-credit (accrued benefit), entry age normal, and attained age normal methods, past service cost is measured separately. It is only when methods such as these are used that there is a difference between the defined minimum and maximum. However, if the past service cost has been fully amortized, there is no difference between the defined minimum and maximum.

Opinion No. 8 assumes that the defined minimum, the defined maximum, and the provision for the year will all be computed using the actuarial cost method selected by the reporting corporation. For example, if the pension cost provision is based on the unit credit method, the defined maximum should also be based on that method and not on the entry age normal method, which usually would give a greater maximum amount.

The opinion also contemplates that in all cases, the provision for pension cost will be based on an acceptable actuarial cost method, with all variable factors consistently applied. Furthermore, the treatment of actuarial gains and losses, the actuarial assumptions, and the like should conform with the recommendations of the opinion, and should be applied consistently from year to year (see below).

As to past service cost, except for a special vested-interest provision,[4] the opinion assumes the company will select the interest-only or some amortization plan (not exceeding the 10 percent limitation) and apply whatever it selects consistently. If this is done, pension cost provisions will not fluctuate greatly from year to year, unless caused by such factors as

---

[4] Vested benefits are due to employees whether or not they remain employees. For our purposes we can ignore this provision.

major changes in the size, composition, or compensation of the employee group. If the vested-benefit provision is required, it could cause some variations from year to year. However, the effect is not likely to be material.

Income Taxes

In many cases, the maximum annual pension cost defined in the opinion is the same as the maximum allowed for federal income tax purposes. Generally speaking, the Internal Revenue Service will allow an annual deduction for the normal cost of a qualified plan plus not more than 10 percent of the past service cost. This is also the general maximum limitation included in the opinion. Differences between the maximum tax deduction and the maximum pension cost provision can arise, however, as a result of unrealized appreciation or depreciation, or as a result of the application of the actuarial cost method. Probably the outstanding example of the latter is where the unit credit actuarial cost method is used for tax purposes. When this method is used, actuarial gains usually reduce the pension cost deduction in the year they occur or in the following year. In these cases, it may be necessary to make accounting adjustments to effect a spreading or averaging in the gains.

Major Objective

The major objective of *Opinion No. 8* was the elimination of inappropriate fluctuations in the annual charge for pension costs. To a large degree, the use of the accrual method accomplishes this goal. However, the opinion also dealt with potential fluctuations in the annual pension expense due to (1) actuarial gains and losses, (2) the funding of pension plans, and (3) legal safeguards typically written into the plans. In addition, it provided guidelines on such aspects as a change in method and disclosure.

Actuarial Gains and Losses.   Before *Opinion No. 8*, some companies made substantial reductions in their annual cash funding provision for pension cost when investment gains were realized by the pension fund, the estimated future earnings rate of the fund was increased, or accumulated appreciation in pension fund investments was recognized in the actuarial valuation. All of these events are "actuarial gains." The Board concluded that actuarial gains—and, in like manner, actuarial losses—"should be given effect in the provision for pension cost in a consistent manner that reflects the long-range nature of pension cost." The recommended way to accomplish this was to "spread" or "average" actuarial gains and losses over a period of years.

Funding.   Some companies based their provision for pension cost on the amount funded, that is, the amount paid to the pension fund. The amounts funded frequently varied widely from year to year because of working capital availability, tax considerations, and other factors. The opinion makes it clear that under accounting, amounts funded are not determinants of pension costs.

Accrual accounting is based on the assignment of costs among years on the basis of the economic benefits derived from the incurrence of the cost. Funding arrangements may not, and often do not, follow the pattern of economic benefits. As previously indicated, funding is a matter of financial management. It may be discretionary and as such is not a matter of accounting principles.

Legal Safeguards. Somewhat related to funding is the influence of legal safeguards that limit the company's liability for the payment of pensions to the amount in the pension fund. As a matter of business prudence, most companies include a clause in their pension plans to the effect that the company may, at its discretion, discontinue the plan or discontinue contributions. In those cases, the employees have no rights to any benefits beyond those that can be paid from the assets in the pension fund. Relying on these clauses, some companies took the position that they had no liability for pensions and therefore did not need to record pension cost beyond the amounts contributed to the pension fund. The Board concluded that clauses such as these could not, as a practical matter, be brought into play by a business that expected to continue to operate in today's economy. In short, these clauses should have little effect on the incurrence of pension cost. Except in rare instances, therefore, they should be ignored in determining the amount of pension cost to be provided.

Change in Method. In the case of a change from one acceptable method to another (such as in the actuarial cost method employed, and in the treatment of past or prior service costs or of actuarial gains and losses) the Accounting Principles Board believed that prior cost should be left unchanged; the effect of the change should be applied prospectively (i.e., to future periods). Similarly, if change is made to an acceptable method, any unamortized prior service cost (computed under the actuarial cost method to be used for accounting purposes in the future) may be treated as an amendment of the plan on the date of change, rather than on the date of adoption or amendment of the plan.

Deferred Taxes. If pension costs are recognized for tax purposes in a period other than the one in which it is recognized for financial reporting, consideration should be given to allocation of income taxes among accounting periods.

Disclosure. *Opinion No. 8* required the following disclosure:

1. A statement that such plans exist, identifying or describing the employee groups covered.
2. A statement of the company's accounting and funding policies.

3. The provision for pension cost for the period.
4. The excess, if any, of the actuarially computed value of vested benefits over the total of the pension fund and any balance sheet pension accruals, less any pension prepayments or deferred charges.
5. The nature and effect of significant matters affecting comparability for all periods presented, such as changes in accounting methods (actuarial cost method, amortization of past and prior service cost, treatment of actuarial gains and losses, etc.), changes in circumstances (actuarial assumptions, etc.), or adoption or amendment of the plan.

An example of appropriate disclosure was presented in *Opinion No. 8:*

The company and its subsidiaries have several pension plans covering substantially all of their employees, including certain employees in foreign countries. The total pension expense for the year was $———, which includes, as to certain of the plans, amortization of prior service cost over periods ranging from 25 to 40 years. The company's policy is to fund pension cost accrued. The actuarially computed value of vested benefits for all plans as of December 31, 19—, exceeded the total of the pension fund and balance sheet accruals less pension prepayments and deferred charges by approximately $———. A change during the year in the actuarial cost method used in computing pension cost had the effect of reducing net income for the year by approximately $———.

After *Opinion No. 8*

Opinion No. 8 was adopted in November 1966. The first year in which its effects began to emerge was in 1967; the number of companies reporting pension plans included in the 600-company sample in *Accounting Trends and Techniques, 1968* increased from 462 to 576. The diversity in the treatment of pension costs is shown in Illustration 20–2 on the treatment of past service cost.

ILLUSTRATION 20–2

Accounting for Pension Plans, 1967

	Number Reporting
Past service amortized over:	
More than 10 years, but less than 40	241
40 years or more	44
10 years or less	31
Number of years not stated	59
Only interest on past service benefits being charged	55
No disclosure whether there is charge for past service benefits	66
Other (including plans for which past service charges are fully amortized)	68
Report refers to pension plan, but does not disclose treatment of costs	12
Total presentations	576

Opinion No. 8 succeeded in eliminating wide fluctuation in the annual pension costs of companies. However, there are many accounting commentators who would like to see the differences in current practice still further reduced. The complexity of the area and the great diversity of company practices will make this difficult to achieve.

SUGGESTED FURTHER READING

HICKS, ERNEST R. *Accounting for the Cost of Pension Plans*, Accounting Research Study No. 8. New York: American Institute of Certified Public Accountants, 1965.

GRIFFIN, FRANK L., and TROWBRIDGE, CHARLES L. *Status of Funding Under Private Pension Plans*. Homewood, Ill.: Richard D. Irwin, 1969.

CASES

Case 20–1. ALLEN MANUFACTURING COMPANY

Accounting for a New Pension Plan

The Allen Manufacturing Company planned in the near future to discontinue its present informal pension arrangements for hourly rated employees, and to adopt a formal plan of retirement benefits under which the actuarially determined costs of past and current services would be funded through a qualified pension trust. Company management considered a formal plan necessary to maintain good employee relations (there was no union) and to obtain the advantages of a funded pension plan.

Previously, the company had been charging to income the cost of the monthly allowances paid retired employees. Retired employees had received $235,000 in the past year. The present value of the past service cost of these 435 retired employees was actuarially estimated at $1,934,000. The management planned to fund this cost immediately upon adoption of the formal plan; in addition, past service cost of $4,614,000 was estimated for the 3,500 present employees. Current service cost for the present employees was estimated at $220,000 annually.

The financial data for the company was:

Total assets	$47,098,000
Total liabilities	5,480,000
Capital stock	14,120,000
Retained earnings	27,498,000
Sales	57,199,000
Net income	2,009,000

The company management was considering the accounting to be followed in adoption of the pension plan:

542

1. The present value of the past service costs for the 435 retired employees, net of tax effect, would be charged to retained earnings, since it was related to prior period wages paid.
2. Past service costs related to current employees would be charged against income over a 25-year period, which was the estimated service life of these employees.
3. Current service costs would be charged to income as paid.

The immediate funding of the past service costs of retired employees would be charged off on the federal income tax return over a 10-year period.

Questions

1. Is the proposed accounting acceptable? What are the available alternative methods?
2. What information should be included on the balance sheet of Allen Manufacturing Company?
3. Compute the tax effect of the proposed pension plan, assuming a 4 percent interest rate.
4. Eight years after the adoption of the pension plan, the company has its actuary make a new study of the assumptions on which the estimated pension costs were based. The study indicates that, due to higher than anticipated interest rates on investments and favorable mortality experience, the amount of money in the fund at the end of the eighth year exceeds the amount originally expected to be on hand at the end of the ninth year. Since the company's earnings for the year are poor and its cash position is low, it has been decided that no payments to the pension trust fund will be made. What would be the impact of this policy change on the company's financial statements?

Case 20–2. DYNAMIC INDUSTRIES, INCORPORATED
Acounting for Pension Plan Revisions

Dynamic Industries, Inc. was one of the nation's largest producers of basic materials for industry and had pursued a dynamic policy of vertical forward integration which had moved it up near the top in *Fortune's* 500 companies. Its original pension plan was created in 1925. During the ensuing years, this plan was modified and the corporation's annual pension costs increased. In 1958, the corporation and its union signed a revised pension plan which materially increased the corporation's annual pension costs. The corporation estimated that the settlement package, including the new pension terms, would increase annual employment costs significantly.

Over the years, the company's income had moved closely with the cyclical swings in the nation's economy. During the last 10 years, the company had experienced several bitter struggles with unions over wage issues. In addition, the company's pricing policy was constantly under government scrutiny, since increases in the prices of the company's products were considered to have an inflationary effect on the nation's economy.

The 1925 Pension Plan

From its inception in 1925, the corporation's voluntary pension plan provided noncontributory pensions. These retirement benefits were based upon 1 percent of the retiring employee's average earnings during the last 10 years of his service, multiplied by the number of years of service. In 1935, due to the corporation's unprofitable position, all pensions were reduced according to a sliding scale. In 1936, a further change in the plan provided for the deduction of public pensions (i.e., social security) from the pension payable by the corporation.

Since the amounts available for pension payments from the pension fund were relatively small, the corporation's annual contributions to the fund were about equal to the fund's current benefit payments. Thus the annual pension expense shown in the corporation's income statements was equivalent to accounting for pension costs on a pay-as-you-go basis.

The 1945 Revision

In 1945, the corporation adopted a revised pension plan providing retirement benefits through joint contributions of the employee and the company. Under the contributory part of this plan, employees having at least 25 years of continuous service could elect to participate in the scheme and contribute 3 percent of their compensation to the scheme. The corporation agreed to contribute such additional amounts as were sufficient, according to the determination of an actuary, to cover present and prospective pension benefits and expenses. The contributions of the corporation were restricted to a ceiling of 5 percent of that portion of the earnings of the eligible employees above the maximum earnings taxable for federal old age security benefits. All contributions were held by a trustee.

In addition, the plan included a noncontributory part which continued the eligibility of employees for pensions with respect to service prior to January 1, 1945. Commencing in 1945, the noncontributory part of the plan provided for payments by the corporation, to a trustee, of the present value (as determined by an actuary) of the expected future payments of pensions granted to employees retiring under the noncontributory part of the plan. No provision for the payment of pensions granted prior to 1945 was made as part of the noncontributory plan. Therefore these payments were still treated as a current expense.

The new pension plan almost doubled the corporation's pension costs. About half of the total was paid each year to the plan's trustees for future benefits. Under the contributory part of the pension plan, employees and the company paid annually about $0.5 million and $1 million, respectively.

The 1958 Revision

The 1958 revisions to the corporation's pension plan added to the noncontributory part the features of minimum pensions and extended pension benefits to employees with less than 25 years service but at least 15 years of continuous service. These benefits applied to employees retiring on or after January 1, 1958.

This noncontributory portion of the plan was also amended to restore pensions of retired employees to the level provided prior to the pension benefit reduction made in 1935. The 1936 change deducting public pensions from the pension determined under the 1925 formula was, however, continued. These amendments related to employees with 25 years or more of continuous service who were retired before January 1, 1958.

Estimated Cost of the 1958 Revision

Based upon certain conservative actuarial assumptions, the corporation's management estimated that the past service cost of the 1958 pension plan was almost $450 million and the estimated 1958 charge for future service costs was $38.5 million.

On June 16, 1958, a special meeting of the corporation's stockholders was held to consider and take action upon the 1958 revisions to the pension plan. Exhibit 1 contains excerpts from the proxy statement issued to stockholders prior to the meeting. Exhibits 2 and 3 are the balance sheet of the corporation at December 31, 1957 and the income statement for 1957.

EXHIBIT 1

DYNAMIC INDUSTRIES, INC.

Proxy Statement

Estimates of the Cost of the Proposed Insurance and Pension Benefits

It is estimated that the annual cost to the Corporation of providing the insurance benefits now contemplated will approximate $12.5 million at full operations. In determining the cost of pensions various factors have an important bearing, such as the age at which employees retire, the methods of financing

EXHIBIT 1 (*continued*)

used, and the interest rate assumed for invested funds. Actuarial estimates of the cost of the proposed pension benefits have been prepared by independent actuaries, using a method which recognizes the cost of the pension of an employee during the period of his active employment. In the financing of pensions, the principle of accruing the cost of an employee's pension prior to the time he retires is deemed proper by insurance companies, by the Pension Trust Division of the United States Treasury Department, and by actuarial societies in this country and abroad.

Under the method used, the cost of pensions is divided into two parts, one for *future* service and the other for past service. For *future* service the annual cost is expressed as a level percentage of payroll, such percentage to be computed so as to remain constant. For past service the total cost is expressed as a lump sum amount at the start of the plan. Under the United States Treasury Department tax regulations for funding pensions, the minimum requirement is that the annual *future* service cost must be met in full plus at least an amount equal to the interest on the past service cost, at the rate assumed in actuarial estimates. Also under the Treasury Department regulations the maximum amount that may be used as a deductible item for tax purposes in any year is the full annual cost of *future* service, plus 10% of the total past service cost at the start of the plan. The minimum method of financing does not cover the entire cost of the pensions, but only provides that the total unfunded cost at any time shall not be greater than it was when the plan started. On this minimum basis of funding, and on the basis of the pension provisions previously described, cost estimates are set forth below.

A. *Estimated Cost of Proposed New Noncontributory Pension Benefits for Present Employees*

> Future Service: On the basis of present payroll, the estimated cost for 1958 on an annual basis is.......................... $38.5 million
>
> Past Service: The lump sum cost for present employees in excess of that under present noncontributory pension provisions is estimated to be $450 million. The annual amount needed to meet the interest requirement is.................. 11.5 million
>
> Total .... $50.0 million

B. *Estimated Cost of Proposed Noncontributory Pension Benefits for Employees Retired Prior to January 1, 1958*

The lump sum cost of the proposed noncontributory pension benefits for employees retired prior to January 1, 1958, is estimated to be $49 million in excess of that under present noncontributory pension provisions. On the basis outlined above for paying the amount needed to meet the interest requirement for minimum finding of the lump sum cost of past service for employees who retired since January 1, 1945, and continuing the past practice of making direct payments to pensioners, rather than advance payments into a trust fund for employees who retired prior to January 1, 1945, the estimated cost for 1958 on an annual basis is $3 million, an increase of $1 million over the present estimated annual cost.

EXHIBIT 1 (continued)

C. Estimated Cost of Contributory Pensions

Contributory pensions became operative in 1945, and no credit was allowed for service prior to that date. Therefore there is no past service cost involved for contributory pensions.

Using the same actuarial method of determining cost described above, the annual future service cost for 1958 is estimated to be $3 million, a reduction of $0.5 million from the present estimated annual cost.

The following table shows a summary of the estimates of the costs of the respective elements of the proposed pension and insurance provisions on the minimum basis of funding stated compared with the costs of the present provisions, all of which costs are before the effect of income taxes:

	Total Lump Sum Cost of Past Service				Estimated Annual Cost Cost 1958		
		Under Proposed Plan					
	Under Present Plan	Total Cost	Less Funds Now Trusteed	Un-funded Cost	Present Plan	Proposed Plan	Income
(Costs Shown in Millions)							
Noncontributory pensions:							
Present employees	$ 58	$505	$55	$450	$2.0	$50.0	$48.0
Retired employees	57	104	32	72	2.0 *	3.0	1.0
Total	$115	$609	$87	$522	$4.0	$53.0	$49.0
Contributory pensions					3.5	3.0	−0.5
Total for pensions					$7.5	$56.0	$48.5
Insurance benefits					1.0	12.5	11.5
Total for pensions and insurance					$8.5	$68.5	$60.0

* Represents estimated cost for 1958 of unfunded pensions and is applicable to employees who retired prior to January 1, 1945.

Since the noncontributory pensions are based on the earnings during the ten years prior to retirement, the amount of pensions to be provided for employees who retire in the future will be related to wage and salary levels of the future. Accordingly, the annual cost estimates are subject to revision upward if the total payroll cost should increase or revision downward if the total payroll cost should decrease.

The estimate also assumes the present level of public pensions. If the Federal Social Security Act is amended so as to increase retirement benefits, the direct cost to the Corporation for pensions under the proposed plan would be reduced, but the present cost of social security taxes would be increased to support the increased public pensions. No estimate is attempted with respect to the amount of any change in costs by reason thereof.

There are many factors relating to financing the cost of pensions, particularly noncontributory pensions, which make desirable, from time to time, changes in the method of making financial provision for these costs and in the amounts set aside in any year. The Board of Directors of the Corporation proposes to use its discretion from time to time with respect to such financing.

EXHIBIT 2

DYNAMIC INDUSTRIES, INC.

Balance Sheet at December 31, 1957
(in thousands)

ASSETS

Current Assets:

Cash		$ 191,542
Marketable securities, at cost............................		324,600
Accounts receivable, less estimated bad debts..............		154,784
Inventories at lower of cost or market....................		335,438
Total Current Assets		$1,006,364

Long-Term Assets:

Property, plant, and equipment.........................	$2,475,281	
Less accumulated depreciation..........................	1,231,355	1,231,335

Other Assets:

Costs applicable to future periods.......................		63,912
Investments		24,222
Total Assets		$2,338,424

LIABILITIES AND STOCKHOLDERS' EQUITY

Current Liabilities:

Accounts payable		$ 200,171
Accrued taxes		183,914
Dividends payable		6,833
Long-term debt due within one year....................		5,340
Total Current Liabilities.............................		$ 396,258
Long-term debt		59,870

Stockholders' Equity:

Preferred stock, 6% cumulative par value $100		
(3,252,000 shares)	$ 325,200	
Common stock (78,200,000 shares), stated capital		
$10 per share..	762,000	
Income reinvested in the business.......................	775,096	1,882,296
Total Liabilities and Equity........................		$2,338,424

Management Issues

Prior to the time the 1958 plan went into effect, there were a number of accounting policy issues raised during management's discussions of the plan. For example, one executive wanted to know how to account for the past service costs. He suggested that this entire amount be written off against retained earnings. Another executive suggested that the potential cost of the plan might not be as much as stated in the proxy plan, since the pension fund would probably appreciate in value more rapidly than the actuarial assumptions assumed. If this occurred, the executive stated, the company should be able to cut back in any one year its cash payment to the fund and the company's related pension cost, since the fund would be more than adequate to meet pension payments. Other executives were concerned with how to handle actuarial gains or losses should the plan or its actuarial assumptions be revised at some future date. Another issue

EXHIBIT 3

DYNAMIC INDUSTRIES, INC.

Statement of Income for the Year Ended December 31, 1957
(in thousands)

Sales	$2,076,617
Costs:	
Employment costs:	
Wages and salaries	$ 818,421
Pensions, social security taxes, insurance and other employee benefits	35,523
	$ 853,944
Products and services bought	798,309
Depreciation of facilities	108,309
Interest	1,997
State, local, and miscellaneous taxes	51,220
Estimated federal taxes on income	113,000
	$1,927,142
Net Income	$ 149,475

Statement of Retained Earnings
(in thousands)

Retained earnings at January 1, 1957		$652,953
Net income for the year ended December 31, 1957		149,475
		$802,428
Less dividends declared:		
Preferred stock	$19,512	
Common stock	7,820	27,332
Retained Earnings at December 31, 1957		$775,096

raised during these discussions was the extent of the footnote disclosure which should accompany the pension cost in the financial statements.

Questions

1. During 1958, it was anticipated that the corporation's cost of pensions, social security, taxes, insurance, and other employee benefits under the 1958 revised plan would be (in millions):

	1957 (Actual)	1958 (Estimated)	1959 (Estimated)
Noncontributory part of pension plan:			
Funding of current service	$ 4.0	$ 49.0	$ 52.0
Funding of portion of past service costs ($45 million initially, $32 million per year thereafter)	...	45.0	32.0
Contributory part of pension plan	3.5	3.0	3.5
Total pension cost	$ 7.5	$ 97.0	$ 87.5
Social security taxes	16.0	17.5	19.0
Insurance costs	1.0	12.5	14.0
Payments to welfare and funds for other employee benefits	11.0	15.0	17.0
Total	$35.5	$142.0	$137.5

How do you think Dynamic Industries should account for its pension plan revision: in 1958? In subsequent years? First, assume the company follows its projected 1958 and 1959 funding plans. Next, assume the company funds only the projected 1958 and 1959 current service costs. Finally, assume the company funds the 1958 projected amounts, but does not make any contributions to the fund in 1959. (Assume *Opinion No. 8* does not apply in this question.)

2. Given the facts and the various assumptions in Question 1, if *Opinion No. 8* had been in effect in 1958 (rather than for periods after 1967), how would the company have accounted for its pension plan in 1958? In 1959? What factors might have influenced its decision?

CHAPTER 21

LONG-TERM DEBT

Long-term debt includes all creditor claims upon a company that are not payable within 12 months or the normal operating cycle, whichever is longer. These obligations include mortgage notes, bonds, installment payment contracts, and long-term notes.

This chapter deals only with those forms of long-term debt issued under formal agreements. Within this broad category, bonds payable in one form or another is the predominant type of debt and the subject of the major accounting controversy in this area. Consequently, the bulk of this chapter concentrates on accounting for bonds payable. The accounting for other forms of long-term debt is similar.

CHARACTERISTICS OF LONG-TERM DEBT

Long-term debt issued by corporations to raise funds from credit sources represents a promise (1) to repay the sum of money at a specified future date, and (2) to compensate the lender for the use of his money through periodic interest payments. The basic conditions of the debt are printed on the face of the bond certificate. The full details of the contract between the company and the bondholders are contained in the bond indenture, which is held by a representative of the bondholder, who is known as the trustee under the indenture. In bankruptcy, the claims of the bondholders rank ahead of those of stockholders.

Long-term debt may come in a variety of forms. It may be secured or unsecured; if unsecured, it is termed a debenture. Secured debt often takes its name from the character of the collateral pledged. For example, bonds secured by marketable securities are known as collateral trust bonds. Mortgage bonds or notes are secured by all or some of the fixed assets of the borrower. Securities backed by chattel mortgages may be called equipment trust certificates. Within the various categories of long-term debt some debt instruments, such as subordinated debentures, may rank lower than others in their claims upon the company's assets in bankruptcy.

There are many variations in the method and timing of the repayment of the principal amount of long-term debt. The basic bond is repayable in a lump sum at a specific future date. The sinking-fund bond is a modification of this form. Its indenture requires the borrower to make periodic cash payments into a sinking fund. This cash, plus the accumulated interest on it, is used to retire the bonds at maturity. A more common type of sinking fund bond indenture calls for payments to a trustee, who uses the funds accumulated for making periodic bond retirements. This practice increases the probability that the lender will be repaid.

Serial bonds are another type of bond with provisions designed to reduce the risk to the bondholders. These bonds are repayable in a series over the life of the issue instead of a single maturity date.

Callable bonds give the borrower the option, after a certain period of time, to redeem all or some of the debt prior to maturity for the payment of a specified call premium beyond the principal amount. The call provision gives the borrower greater flexibility in the design of his capital structure, in that as interest rates change he can replace old bonds with less expensive new ones.

Long-term debt indentures contain a number of provisions. Some provisions may restrict the dividend payments of the borrower. These restrictions often limit the use of additional short- or long-term debt, or require that the borrower stay within certain debt-to-equity and working capital ratio limits. Other provisions may include the right to convert the bonds to other securities, such as stock.

Typically, the borrower's obligation to pay interest is fixed. It is not conditional upon company earnings, except for income and participating bonds. The payment of interest on income bonds is conditional upon the earning of income: if the income is not sufficient to pay interest, no payments need be made. The interest obligation may or may not be cumulative (i.e., interest not paid in one year becomes a lien against future earnings). These bonds usually result from corporate reorganizations, where it is necessary to give old security holders a less desirable form of security so that new senior securities can be sold. Participating bonds entitle the holder to share in earnings with the stockholders in a pro rata or limited way, in addition to the bondholder's usual fixed interest.

Bond Prices

The price of a bond is determined by the relationship between its nominal rate (the fixed interest payment specified in the terms of the indenture) and the prevailing market interest rate for the bonds of similar investment quality. For example, if the Viking Chemical Company issued $1 million worth of 5 percent bonds repayable in 10 years and the current market interest rate for comparable bonds was 6 percent, the company would receive $926,000 from the buyers of the bonds. Assuming interest is paid annually, this sum represents the present value of 10 annual payments of $50,000 plus a payment of $1 million 10 years hence, all discounted at 6 percent. If the bondholder held the Viking bonds to maturity, the return on his investment of $926,000 would be 6 percent. The computation would be made as shown in Illustration 21–1.

ILLUSTRATION 21–1

	Cash Flow	Times	Equals
Years	Item	P.V. Factor (6%) *	Present Value
1–10	Annual interest payments, $50,000............. 7.360		$368,000
10	Repayment of principal, $1,000,000............ 0.558		558,000
			$926,000

* See Tables A and B in Appendix.

The market price of a bond can vary during its life as the level of interest rates shift or the quality of the company's credit changes. For example, assume that after five years pass, the market rate for bonds similar to the Viking Chemical Company's bonds falls to 4 percent. Since the Viking bond pays a 5 percent nominal rate, its market price will rise to $1,044,600. Anyone buying the bonds in the market for this price would get a yield of 4 percent on his investment if he held the bonds to maturity. Assuming annual interest payments, the present value calculations are shown in Illustration 21–2.

ILLUSTRATION 21–2

	Cash Inflow	Times	Equals
Years	Item	P.V. Factor (4%)	Present Value
1–5	Annual interest payments, $50,000............. 4.452		$ 222,600
5	Principal repayment, $1,000,000................ 0.822		822,000
			$1,044,600

Generally, interest payments are made semiannually, but for the sake of simplicity it will be sufficient for our purposes to assume annual payments. For semiannual payments, the present value results can be closely approximated by halving the annual interest payment and doubling the number of periods over which the payments are received.

Bond tables are available for determining bond prices and yield rates. The tables are based on present value calculations. They consider five elements of a bond: nominal rate, number of periods to maturity, maturity value, market price, and yield rate. Illustration 21–3 reproduces an excerpt from a typical bond table.

ILLUSTRATION 21–3

Bond Value Table

Purchase Price of a $100 Bond at 5% Nominal Rate,
Payable Semiannually

Yield	Maturity (Years)			
	4	4.5	5	5.5
4.8%	$100.67	$100.80	$100.88	$100.96
4.9	100.33	100.40	100.44	100.48
5.0	100.00	100.00	100.00	100.00
5.1	99.64	99.60	99.56	99.53
5.2	99.29	99.21	99.13	99.05

When bonds are bought between interest dates, the purchase price includes the accrued interest.

Registration

Bonds may be registered in one of three ways in the books of the issuer. Some are registered with respect to both principal and interest; that is, the name of the owner is recorded in the issuer's records and checks for interest and principal payments are sent directly to him by the issuer. This protects the bondholder from losses or theft of his certificates, since the transfer of ownership benefits can only be effectively made by changing the owner's name in the issuer's books. Other bonds are registered as to principal only. This protects the bondholder from loss or theft of principal. Interest is received by detaching on the appropriate interest dates interest coupons attached to the certificate and presenting them to a bank for deposit or collection. Occasionally, bonds are not registered as to either interest or principal and are freely transferable.

Financial Consideration

The long-term fund requirements of corporations are usually satisfied through the issuance of a combination of stocks and bonds and the retention of earnings. Compared to stocks, bonds have some attractive features. The interest payments are deductible as a business expense in determining taxable income, whereas dividends are not. The ownership interest is not diluted when bonds are issued. The earnings on the funds obtained through a bond issue may be greater than the related interest charge, with the result that the earnings per share of the stockholders increase since no additional equity shares are issued. This effect is called "leverage."

The major disadvantage of bonds is the fixed requirement to repay principal and to pay interest periodically. If a corporation fails to meet these obligations, the bondholders may assume control of the company or force it into bankruptcy.

ACCOUNTING PRACTICES

The principal controversy concerning accounting for bonds revolves around the handling of unamortized discount, issue costs, and redemption premiums on bonds refunded. These matters are discussed in *Accounting Research Bulletin No. 43*, Chapter 15, and *Opinions No. 6* and *No. 14*.

Issuance of Bonds

When bonds are issued, they are recorded at their face value in the long-term liability account. Any difference between the proceeds of the sale and the face value of the bond is put into the liability account Bond Premium or the asset account Bond Discount. The premium or discount balance is then written off to the Bond Interest account over the life of the issue.

The accounting entry to record an issue of one thousand $1,000 bonds at their face value is:

```
Cash .............................................. 1,000,000
    Bonds Payable ...................................        1,000,000
```

If these bonds had been issued at a premium of $100,000, the entry would have been:

```
Cash .............................................. 1,100,000
    Bonds Payable ...................................        1,000,000
    Bond Premium ...................................          100,000
```

The accounting entry for a $100,000 discount is:

```
Cash ..............................................   900,000
Bond Discount ....................................    100,000
    Bonds Payable ...................................        1,000,000
```

Bond premium is generally shown on the liability side of the balance sheet as a deferred credit, between the long-term debt and capital sections. Bond discount is most often presented in the noncurrent asset section of the balance sheet, as a deferred cost. Both accounts are regarded as being future adjustments to the interest expense. Bond premium is viewed as an "interest advance" from bondholders and is treated as a reduction of future interest charges. Bond discount is considered to be a "prepayment of interest" by the issuer. It is added to interest charges in future period. When both discounts and premiums on bonds payable are present, it is permissible to show them on a net basis.

An alternative method which conforms to the desire of some to measure liabilities in terms of cash received is to show bond discounts and premiums on the balance sheet as valuation accounts related to bonds payable. A bond premium is added to bonds payable at par and a discount is subtracted from the par value. Thus, the initial carrying value equals the cash consideration received, rather than the face value typically reported. (As indicated later, this approach also results in a carrying value which is equivalent to the carrying value shown in the bondholder's accounts.) The main objectiion to this method is that the face value is the amount for which the corporation is liable throughout the life of the bond, not the current cash equivalent of the bond.

The costs associated with issuing bonds include underwriting fees, taxes, printing, and engraving. When bond discounts and premiums are treated as valuation accounts, the issuing costs are often accounted for as a deferred cost and amortized over the life of the issue. Frequently, when bond discounts and premiums are shown as deferred items, the issuing costs are treated as deductions from the proceeds of the issue. This has the effect of including them as part of the bond discount or premium.

When there is more than one bond issue, each issue should be listed separately on the balance sheet. Fair disclosure requires that the interest rate, maturity date, collateral data, and the number of authorized and issued bonds be shown for each issue. Any convertibility and subordination of long-term debt should also be indicated. In addition, violations of any of the indenture stipulations should be disclosed.

Amortization of Bond Premium and Discount

There are two acceptable methods for amortizing bond premium and discount items, both of which, as indicated earlier, are considered to be adjustments to future interest expense. The straight-line method takes this discount or premium into the interest expense account over the life of the bond in equal amounts. This procedure results in an equal interest charge each period. The compound-interest method reduces the discount or premium by the amount needed to make the nominal interest expense equal to the effective rate of interest.

Illustration 21–4 presents an example of the straight-line amortization method. It assumes a five-year $1 million bond issue with a nominal rate of 5 percent sold at a discount to yield approximately 6 percent paid annually.

Illustration 21–5 demonstrates the compound-interest method, using the same example presented in Illustration 21–4.

ILLUSTRATION 21–4

Discount Amortization, Straight-Line Method

($1 million 5-year bonds, nominal rate 5% payable annually,
sold at $957,600 to yield approximately 6%)

Interest Payment Periods	A Cash Interest Payment	B Bond Discount Amortization ($42,400/5)	C Effective Interest Expense (A + B)	D Unamortized Bond Discount Balance (D — B)	E Bond Carrying Value * ($1 Million —D)
0	...	...	...	$42,400	$ 957,600
1	$50,000	$ 8,480	$58,480	33,920	966,080
2	50,000	8,480	58,480	25,440	974,560
3	50,000	8,480	58,480	16,960	983,040
4	50,000	8,480	58,480	8,480	991,520
5	50,000	8,480	58,480	...	1,000,000

* Carrying value on the balance sheet if bond discount is treated as a valuation account rather than an asset.

Using the amounts in Illustration 21–4 for each interest period, the accounting entries for recording periodic interest payment and adjustment to the bond discount account are:

```
Bond Interest Expense...................................  58,480
    Cash  ..............................................          50,000
    Bond Discount  ....................................           8,480
```

The entries for amortizing bond premium are similar, except the amortization charge is debited to the bond premium account.

ILLUSTRATION 21–5

Discount Amortization, Compound-Interest Method

($1 million 5-year bonds, nominal rate 5% payable annually,
sold at $957,600 to yield approximately 6%)

Interest Payment Periods	A Cash Interest Payment	B Effective Interest Expense (6% of E)	C Bond Discount Amortization (B — A)	D Unamortized Bond Discount Balance (D — C)	E Bond Carrying Value *—(P.V. of Future Interest + Principal Payments Discounted at 6%)
0 ...	...	...	...	$42,400	$ 957,600
1 ...	$50,000	$57,456	$ 7,456	34,944	965,250
2 ...	50,000	57,915	7,915	27,029	973,650
3 ...	50,000	58,419	8,419	18,610	981,650
4 ...	50,000	58,899	8,899	9,711 †	990,150
5 ...	50,000	59,711	9,711 †	...	1,000,000

* Carrying value on the balance sheet if the bond discount is treated as a valuation account rather than as an asset.

† Slightly more than 6 percent. This small discrepancy is due to rounding in the present value tables. On the final payment, the bond discount account is closed. Whatever balance remains is charged to interest expense.

Even though the compound-interest method gives a more accurate measure of income, bond issuers frequently use the straight-line method because of its simplicity. Also, it is sufficiently accurate in most cases and is easy for stockholders to understand.

A number of years ago, some companies wrote bond discount directly off to retained earnings at the date of issuance. In their opinion, it was a desirable general policy to account conservatively for such intangible assets. Today, this practice and the similar one of crediting bond premiums directly to retained earnings at issuance are not permissible, since they lead to an improper matching of costs and revenues.

Retirement before Maturity

Bonds may be redeemed before maturity through the exercise of their call provisions or by purchase in the open market. Bonds retired by call are usually called at a periodic interest date, after paying and recognizing in the accounts the interest due for the period. Any related bond discount or bond premium is adjusted to reflect the new status of the issue.

To illustrate the accounting entries, assume that $100,000 par value of bonds with a related discount of $3,000 are retired after paying a call premium of $2,000. The entries to record the call and retirement are:

Bonds Payable	100,000	
Loss on Bond Retirement	5,000	
Cash		102,000
Bond Discount		3,000

The accounting entries to record the call and retirement of a similar issue, except that it had originally been sold at a premium of $3,000, are:

Bonds Payable	100,000	
Bond Premium	3,000	
Cash		102,000
Gain on Bond Retirement		1,000

Material losses or gains on bond retirements are treated as extraordinary items in the income statement.

Refunding

When interest rates decline, corporations often take advantage of the call provisions of their bonds outstanding to float a new, cheaper issue to obtain funds which are then used to call and retire the outstanding more expensive issue.

From the finance point of view, savings result from refunding when the present value of the new issue discounted by the current interest rate over the unexpired portion of the outstanding issue is greater than the call price of the outstanding bonds. Refundings involve out-of-pocket payment beyond the call price for such items as engraving, printing, underwriting, and legal services. Since similar outlays probably would be made for a new issue at the maturity date of the old issue, to pay off the existing bondholders, some corporate treasurers do not consider these costs in their analysis. Other treasurers include an opportunity cost equivalent to the return the company is forgoing on these funds by paying them out now rather than at some future date.

Refunding creates a significant accounting problem, namely: What is the proper accounting treatment for any (a) unamortized bond discount and issue costs and (b) call premium related to the old issue? For example, assume a $5 million 10-year 5 percent bond issue sold at a $300,000 discount is redeemed after 5 years at a call price of 104. The issue costs connected with these bonds was $100,000. To finance the redemption of the old issue, a new 15-year 3 percent bond issue is sold. The management must now decide how to account for the following charges related to the old bond issue:

Unamortized discount and issue costs	$200,000
Call premium (50,000 shares × $4)........	200,000
Total	$400,000

There are three acceptable methods for handling these costs:

1. Write the $400,000 off directly to income as a nonrecurring extraordinary charge.
2. Amortize the $400,000 over the remaining five-year life of the original issue.
3. Amortize the $400,000 over the 15-year life of the new issue.

ARB No. 43, Chapter 15, supported the first two methods but rejected the third. Later, in *Opinion No. 6*, the Accounting Principles Board approved the third approach under appropriate circumstances. The direct write-off to income approach is the only method for handling these costs permitted for tax purposes.

The direct write-off to income method considers the $400,000 to be the cost of the privilege of terminating a disadvantageous borrowing contract. As such, some have argued that the accounting for it should reflect the accepted practice of recognizing an expense no later than the time when the transaction creating it is completed. Also, to capitalize the $400,000, some argue, is equivalent to capitalizing the unrecovered book value of assets replaced by new assets, which is generally rejected as an appropriate accounting practice.

Amortizing the $400,000 over the remaining life of the original issue assumes that this amount is the cost of making a more attractive arrangement which will accrue to the company over the unexpired term of the old issue. This point of view regards bond discount created at the time the bonds were issued as part of the cost to a corporation for the right to subsequently call bonds for retirement before maturity. Furthermore, the cost of borrowing over the entire period of the original issue is influenced by the terms of the original agreement, and if any cost of anticipating maturity is incurred, it is only because it is attractive to do so. Therefore, if this advantage over the remaining life of the old issue exceeds the unamortized bond discount balance, such discount should be regarded as an element of the cost of borrowed money and properly spread over the unexpired term. The Committee on Accounting Procedure preferred this alternative, although some critics objected to the fact that no bonds would be shown on the books of the issuer to which this cost could be related.

The amortization of the $400,000 over the life of the new issue reflects the belief that the expense of retiring the old issue is part of the cost of the new issue. The Committee on Accounting Procedure considered this justification to be untenable. Nevertheless, a number of corporations adopted this alternative because it related the cost to bonds on the books of the company as well as presenting what they considered to be a better measure of their long-run interest cost. In view of its widespread acceptance and the practical reasons supporting its use, the Accounting Principles Board in *Opinion No. 6* specifically approved this approach where "the refunding takes place because of currently lower interest rates or anticipation of higher interest rates in the future."

Conversion

In order to make bonds more attractive to buyers, some issues give the bondholder the right under certain conditions to convert his bonds into stock. The conversion terms can vary: the conversion ratio may specify a certain number of shares of stock to be issued for each bond, or it may simply indicate that stock of an equivalent par value to the bond's value may be issued. Sometimes the conversion right can be exercised only after a specific period of time.

Whether or not the bondholder exercises his right to convert depends on a number of factors. For example, a $1,000 bond with a nominal interest rate and yield of 6 percent, convertible into 10 shares of stock, will sell as a bond as long as the market value of the stock is less than $100 per share. However, should the market price of the stock rise to $150 per share, the bond's price will reflect the fact that it is equivalent to 10 shares of stock. Under these conditions bondholders would probably not consider converting their bonds into stock until the annual dividends paid on 10 shares of stock are greater than the $60 annual interest payments received, or until the bonds reach maturity or conversion is forced by the borrower.

When bonds are converted, the first step is to correct the current balances by recording any accrued interest, and by adjusting, if necessary, the unamortized bond discount or premium accounts. The next step is to record the conversion. This can be done in one of two ways.

The first method records the conversion on a market value basis. The newly issued security is recorded at either its market value or the market value of the bonds, whichever is more readily determinable; the appropriate bonds payable account is reduced by the par value of the bonds converted; and any difference between par value of the bonds and the market value assigned to the new securities is reported as a gain or loss on conversion. This method assumes that the conversion terminates the bond transaction and begins a new one for the stock. Therefore, the relevant value associated with this transaction is the amount that would be received today if the bonds were sold, or if the stock was sold rather than exchanged. If the market values of the bonds and equity differ, the market value of the bonds is the preferred measure of the new equity created.

The alternative approach assumes that the original issue price of the bonds represented in large part a sum paid for the future delivery of stock. Therefore, when conversion occurs, the book value of the bonds should be transferred to the newly issued stock.

To illustrate, the Ronald Company offers bondholders 20 shares of $5 par value stock in exchange for each $1,000 6 percent bond they hold. The market value of the stock is $60 per share and of the bonds $1,200 per bond. All accrued interest has been paid and the balance of the unamortized premium account is equivalent to $20 per bond. Holders of 600 bonds exercise their conversion right. The accounting entries are:

Market Value Method (Based on bonds' market value of $720,000)

Bonds Payable (600 bonds @ $1,000).....................	600,000	
Bond Premium (600 × $20)...........................	12,000	
Loss on Bond Conversion	108,000	
Common Stock (12,000 shares × $5 par value)........		60,000
Premium on Common Stock [600 × 1,200] − 60,000 ..		660,000

Book Value Method (Based on bonds' book value of $612,000)

Bonds Payable (600 bonds @ $1,000).....................	600,000	
Bond Premium (600 × $20)...........................	12,000	
Common Stock (12,000 shares × $5 par value)		60,000
Premium on Common Stock (612,000 − 60,000)		552,000

The conversion of bonds into other bonds in the same company which are substantially the same, or into stock in accordance with the bond indenture, is considered by the Internal Revenue Service as a nontaxable transaction to the bondholder. All exchanges of bonds for other securities or property are taxable.

Debt Issued with Stock Warrants

The interest rate of bonds issued with warrants is typically lower than the rate for similar quality bonds without warrants. Therefore, the issuer is able to get a higher price for his bonds by adding stock warrant features than he would otherwise. This difference in the proceeds is in substance a payment by the bondholder for a future "call" on the stock of the issuer. The proceeds minus this amount can be considered as the imputed cost of the straight bond portion of the security.

In March 1969, the Accounting Principles Board issued *Opinion No. 14, Accounting for Convertible Debt and Debt Issued with Stock Purchase Warrants.* In the case of convertible debt and debt issued with stock warrants where the debt must be converted to obtain the advantage of the warrants, the Board recommended that no portion of the proceeds from the issuance be accounted for as attributable to the conversion feature. The Board noted that the inseparability of the debt and conversion feature was the primary difficulty, rather than the practical problems of valuing the conversion feature.

If the debt were issued with detachable stock warrants, the Board stated that the portion of the proceeds allocable to the warrants should be accounted for as a credit to paid-in capital. Since the face value of the debt obligation remains unchanged, the offsetting credit is to the discount or premium on debt accounts, depending upon the relationship between the proceeds of the issue and the face amount of the obligation. This has the effect of recording the discount that would have been recorded if the issue had been sold as straight debt.

Warrants are often traded, and their fair market value can usually be determined by their market price at the issue date. This value is the basis for allocating the proceeds of the issue between the debt obligation and warrants. If no market exists for the warrants, the relative market values for the debt with and without warrants must be estimated.

Debt Issued with Conversion Privileges

Beginning December 31, 1966, *Opinion No. 10* of the Accounting Principles Board recommended that the conversion features of debt obligations be accounted for in a similar fashion to debt with detachable warrants, principally because the full extent of the actual discount on the bond portion of the convertible bonds is not recorded at the time of issuance. Since only the difference between the proceeds and the face value is charged as bond discount, the real interest cost of the debt obligation portion of the security is understated compared to similar straight debt, since the proceeds include the value of the future conversion privilege. However, there were a number of practical problems related to estimating the value of the conversion right. Therefore, the Board in *Opinion No. 12* rescinded its recommendation until the question could be studied further. Also, the Board felt that the classification of convertible debt as a residual security for computing primary or fully diluted earnings per share would offset some of the distortion in income measurement resulting from the understatement of bond discount.

ACCOUNTING PRACTICES: THE BUYER

Purchase of Bonds

Bonds may be bought at their face value or at a price which represents either a premium or discount from the face value. The accounting entries in the bondholder's books to record the purchase of bonds are:

```
Investment in Bonds ...........................................  xxx
    Cash  ....................................................        xxx
```

The amount recorded by the purchaser as the asset Investment in Bonds is always the bondholder's cost.

Interest Payments Received

When bonds are bought at their face value, the bondholder records his periodic interest payments by a simple debit to Cash and credit to Interest Income. If the purchase involved a premium or discount and the bondholder intends to hold his bonds as a long-term investment, the accounting is more complex.

The carrying value of a bond bought at a discount gradually rises to par at maturity. Rather than wait until the maturity date to recognize all of this gain over cost, it is customary to record in the bondholder's accounts the increase as it accrues as part of his interest income. Thus, the interest income includes the interest payment received plus the change in the carrying value of the bond. The accounting entries are:

```
Cash  .........................................................  xxx
Investment in Bonds ...........................................  xxx
    Bond Interest Income  .....................................        xxx
```

This treatment assumes that the discount is analogous to a prepayment of interest by the issuer. It also assumes that the bond will be held to maturity.

The carrying value of a bond purchased at a premium slowly declines to par at maturity. The accounting treatment for recognizing this change in carrying value is the reverse of the bond discount situation. However, the carrying value at any point in time should not be greater than the redemption value at the issuer's next optional redemption date. The accounting entries are:

```
Cash  .........................................................  xxx
    Investment in Bonds  .......................................        xxx
    Interest Income  ...........................................        xxx
```

The change in the carrying value is the difference between the present value of future interest payments and the redemption payment at maturity at the current interest payment date and the date of the prior interest payment. The discount rate used to compute these present values is the yield to maturity rate implicit in the purchase price. If the bondholder's balance sheet date does not match the interest payment date, the accrued interest to date is the difference between the carrying values at the two dates bounding the current accounting period.

ILLUSTRATION 21–6

Calculation of Carrying Value Charge at End of Year 1

Years	Item	Times P.V. Factor (6%)	Equals Present Value
1–9	Annual interest payments, $50,000	6.802	$340,100
9	Principal repayment, $1,000,000	0.592	592,000
	Present value on first payment date		$932,100
	Present value at purchase date		926,000
	Change in Bond Investment		$ 6,100

To illustrate the calculation of change in carrying value, assume that $1 million of 10-year bonds paying 5 percent annually is bought for $926,000 to yield 6% to maturity. Illustration 21–6 reflects the carrying value *after* one year. At the end of this year, the first annual interest payment of $50,000 is received.

The accounting entries to record interest income are:

```
Cash  ......................................................  50,000
Investment in Bonds  .......................................  6,100
    Interest Income  .......................................         56,100
```

A similar entry at the end of each period will result in a level effective *rate* of interest income being recognized on the carrying value of the bond (i.e., $56,100/$932,000=6\%$, approximately). As the bond approaches maturity, the related interest income will slowly increase to reflect the increasing carrying value.

Alternatively, for convenience, investors often adjust the carrying value of their investment in bonds by an amount equal to the bond discount (or premium) divided by the number of interest periods to maturity. This amount is added or deducted, depending on whether it relates to discount or premium, from the periodic interest payment received to determine interest income. This approach leads to the recognition of a level interest income item over the life of the bonds. However, since the carrying value is slowly increasing as maturity approaches, the effective rate of interest obtained by relating interest income to carrying value declines.

Changes in carrying value are not recognized when the issuer's financial condition makes the collection of par at maturity doubtful. Also, bonds held for short-term investments are carried at cost and are not typically adjusted for changes in carrying value. Such short-term investments are usually reported on the basis of lower of cost or market, but unless a decline in market price is significant and appears to be permanent the carrying value is seldom reduced to market. In all cases, the current market value should be disclosed parenthetically on the balance sheet.

The income tax regulations related to bonds are complicated. However, in most cases, for income tax purposes the investor reports as interest income the interest payments actually received. Upon disposal of the bonds, any difference between the amount received and the purchase price is reported as a taxable gain or loss. In general, the bond's original purchaser will be taxed at ordinary rates on these gains up to the amount of the original discount at the issue date. Other purchasers will pay capital gains rates on gains above their original purchase price. No gains or losses can be recognized before disposal.

SUGGESTED FURTHER READING

GRAHAM, BENJAMIN; DODD, DAVID L.; and COTTLE, SIDNEY. *Security Analyses.* 4th ed. New York: McGraw-Hill, 1962.

CASES

Case 21–1. **PACE CORPORATION**
Accounting For Bonds

On June 30, 1961, Pace Corporation issued 4 percent first mortgage 10-year bonds having a maturity value of $3 million. The bonds were issued at a price to yield 5 percent.

The Pace bonds were dated June 30, 1961 and required semiannual interest payments. They were redeemable after June 30, 1966 and before June 30, 1968 at 104; thereafter until maturity they were redeemable at 102. They were also convertible into Pace $10 par value common stock according to the following schedule:

Before June 30, 1966: 60 shares of common stock for each
$1,000 bond.
July 1, 1966 to June 30, 1969: 50 shares of common stock for
each $1,000 bond.
After June 30, 1969: 40 shares of common stock for each
$1,000 bond.

The following transactions occurred in connection with Pace's bonds.

July 1, 1967. Bonds having a maturity value of $500,000 were converted into common stock.

December 30, 1968. Bonds having a maturity value of $500,000 were reacquired by Pace Corporation by purchase on the market at 99¼ and accrued interest. The reacquired bonds were cancelled immediately.

June 30, 1969. Pace Corporation called the remaining bonds for redemption. In order to obtain the cash necessary for the redemption and for business expansion, a $4 million issue of 20-year 3 percent sinking fund debenture bonds were issued at a price to yield 3 percent. The new bonds were dated June 30, 1969 and also called for semiannual interest payments.

Questions

1. Determine the amount of the proceeds from the June 30, 1961 bond issue. Illustrate the December 31, 1961 balance sheet disclosure(s) related to this indebtedness. (Use tables at the end of Question 4.)
2. Determine the amount of "interest expense" to be deducted in arriving at the net income for the year ending December 31, 1962.
3. Describe the balance sheet and income statement effects of the July 1, 1967, conversion, including dollar amounts involved.
4. Describe the balance sheet and income statement effects of the June 30, 1969, redemption, including dollar amounts involved.

Present Value of $1

Periods	1.5%	2%	2.5%	3%	4%	5%
10	0.862	0.820	0.781	0.744	0.676	0.614
20	0.742	0.673	0.610	0.554	0.456	0.377
40	0.551	0.453	0.372	0.307	0.208	0.142

Present Value of $1 per Period

Periods	1.5%	2%	2.5%	3%	4%	5%
10	9.222	8.983	8.752	8.530	8.111	7.722
20	17.169	16.351	15.589	14.877	13.590	12.462
40	29.916	27.355	25.103	23.115	19.793	17.159

Case 21–2. **UNITED CORPORATION**

Accounting for
Unamortized Bond Discount

The financial statements of United Corporation prepared for the fiscal year ending December 31, 1970, disclosed as a long-term liability outstanding 10-year 5 percent debenture bonds in the amount of $10 million. These bonds were scheduled to mature in another five years, on January 2, 1975. The bond indenture provided that subsequent to January 1, 1971, the bonds were callable at 102. Interest payments were required semiannually on July 1 and January 1.

The bonds were originally issued at a price which yielded 6 percent. Accordingly, "unamortized bond discount" in the amount of $371,875 was reported as a deferred charge among the assets in the December 31, 1970 balance sheet.

At a meeting of the company officers, Benton Bishop, treasurer, proposed that the outstanding bonds be refunded by means of a new issue of 5 percent 10-year debenture bonds also having a maturity value of $10 million and requiring semiannual interest payments. Bishop explained that he had good reason to believe that the new bonds could be issued to yield 4 percent. He also explained that he was convinced interest rates would not decline further during at least the next three or four years. Bishop made the following estimates of the out-of-pocket costs that the company would incur in connection with recalling outstanding bonds and issuing new securities:

Internal administrative costs of calling the old issue ...	$ 15,000
Company's cost of preparing and issuing new bonds ...	85,000
Total costs	$100,000

Similar costs would normally be incurred upon regular maturity or refinancing.

One of the vice presidents, Chatfield Sharkey, suggested that paying the premium call price and an extra $100,000 in expenses to substitute new 5 percent bonds due in 10 years for old 5 percent bonds due in 5 years was ridiculous and wasteful.

SHARKEY: Furthermore, wouldn't that wipe out this $371,825 asset shown on our balance sheet? I have noticed that this asset has been getting smaller every year. I understand that it exists only because of the outstanding bonds and that it will disappear completely when the bonds are retired. Your recommendation would cost the company nearly $700,000—this $371,825 asset, the $200,000 call premium, and $100,000 for fees and red tape. That seems like an awful lot just to get a five-year extension on our long-term debt!

BISHOP: Let me say two things about the $371,825 asset. First of all, our auditors tell me that we can continue to carry the asset in our balance sheet, just as we have been, even if we refund the old bonds. We would simply continue to amortize it over the remaining five-year life of the old bonds, even though they are no longer outstanding. I admit this seems a little strange and I am not thoroughly familiar with the reasoning underlying the procedure, but they assured me that it was in accordance with generally accepted accounting principles. Frankly, I have been more concerned about the advantages of refunding now while conditions seem to be favorable. I haven't really looked into the way in which the accounting would have to be handled.

I do want to point out, however, that the loss of that asset would not be very serious. It is not like losing cash or inventory or having $370,000 worth of plant burn down. We have to make the same cash interest payments and retire the bonds when they mature, whether we have the asset or not.

At this point, Martin Schwarz, vice president for public relations, interrupted.

SCHWARZ: I don't understand that. Do you mean to say that year after year we have been telling our stockholders and creditors that we have an asset worth $700,000, or $500,000 or now $370,000, although having that asset doesn't do us one bit of good? Some of these people compute the rate of return we are able to earn year by year. If that asset doesn't help us earn more, we should have written it off a long time ago.

Bishop: Well, we couldn't just get rid of it. It is a type of prepaid interest. When we first issued our bonds, the purchasers didn't pay us face value because our interest rate wasn't high enough. Instead, they paid us less than face value and the difference was additional interest which, in effect, we paid in advance.

Sharkey: If we have already paid in advance some of the interest on our outstanding bonds, that would be wasted if we now call the bonds and pay a 2 percent premium. Surely there must be a cheaper way to get a five-year extension on our $10 million debt. In fact, what's the hurry? We have five years to worry about the debt. Maybe we won't even need an extension by the time our bonds mature.

Schwarz: This reference to the interest we have paid in advance reminds me of a question I have been wondering about for some time. Ever since we first issued our 5 percent debentures, we have shown as a liability only the $10 million which would have to be paid when the bonds mature—initially this was looking 10 years into the future. At no time have we shown as a liability the $250,000 cash interest payments which the bond indenture requires to be made every January 1 and July 1. At the outset those totaled $5 million—half as much as the $10 million due at maturity. Indeed, it seems to me that the interest payments are a much more important liability than the face value. After all, if we make our interest payments regularly, probably we can issue new bonds any time we need money to retire old ones. On the other hand, we can't keep borrowing every six months just to make interest payments. Yet, we have never reported to our stockholders the amount of our liability for interest payments. I realize, of course, that the interest payments actually show up in our income statement, but that doesn't seem to me to take care of our liability for future interest payments.

Questions

1. What is the nature of the $371,875 "unamortized bond discount"? What attributes cause "unamortized bond discount" to be classified among the assets? How was the amount $371,875 determined? Do you consider any alternative method of measurement to be acceptable or preferable? What effect would refunding have on this account? (Use tables at the end of question 4, if necessary.)

2. Is the amount of the liability on the December 31, 1970 balance sheet correctly reported at $10 million? Or, as Martin Schwarz suggested, should it be shown at $12.5 million in order to include interest payments? Or, should the liability be shown at some other amount? What are the attributes of "liabilities" and the methods of measuring them which support your answers to these questions?

3. Based solely on the information provided in this case, what is your recommendation with respect to the proposed refunding? Be prepared to support

your recommendation with a computation of any dollar advantage or disadvantage.

1. Without prejudice to your answers to the foregoing questions, assume that it is decided to undertake the refunding operation on January 2, 1971. What effects, if any, would refunding have on the December 31, 1971 balance sheet and the statement of income and statement of retained earnings for the year ending December 31, 1971? At what dollar amounts should the related accounts appear in those statements?

Present Value of $1

Periods	2%	2.5%	3%	4%	5%	6%
5	0.9057	0.8838	0.8626	0.8219	0.7835	0.7473
10	0.8203	0.7812	0.7441	0.6756	0.6139	0.5584
20	0.6730	0.6103	0.5537	0.4564	0.3769	0.3118

Present Value of $1 per Period

Periods	2%	2.5%	3%	4%	5%	6%
5	4.7135	4.6458	4.5797	4.4518	4.3295	4.2124
10	8.9826	8.7521	8.5302	8.1109	7.7217	7.3601
20	16.3514	15.5892	14.8775	13.5903	12.4622	11.4699

PART VII

Stockholders' Equity

CHAPTER **22**

EQUITY CAPITAL TRANSACTIONS

The owners' equity or net worth section of the balance sheet shows the accumulated investment of the owners of the corporation, the stockholders. The stockholders' investment may be made "directly" through purchase of common or preferred stock, or "indirectly" through the corporations' retention of earnings which might have been paid out to stockholders. The net worth represents the "book" or residual value of the corporation; this residual is the assets less the liabilities.

In its balance sheet, the corporation discloses the sources and nature of equity capital, including the types of stock authorized and outstanding and any statutory or contractual limitations. To use this data effectively, the reader of the report must understand the accounting, legal, and financial distinctions between the various accounts comprising the equity section.

OWNERS' EQUITY

The stockholders' investment in the corporation is represented by either common or preferred stock. More than one type of each kind of stock may be issued. If there is more than one class of stockholder, the equity interests of each class should be disclosed fully in either the financial statements or the accompanying footnotes. Accounting treats both classes of stock in a similar fashion.

Owners of preferred stock have certain privileges ahead of the common stockholders, such as a preference in dividends or liquidation. Preferred stock dividends are usually fixed in amount and can be noncumulative or cumulative; usually no dividend can be paid on the common stock until preferred dividends previously earned but not declared are paid. Preferred shares may be classified as participating. That is, the owners

573

can participate in dividend distribution with the common shareholders once a specified level of dividends has been paid to the common shareholders. In liquidation, after the claims of creditors have been settled, preferred stockholders have a preferred fixed claim on assets relative to the common stockholders. Typically, preferred stock does not carry voting rights. Most preferred stock is redeemable under certain conditions, at the corporation's option, at a specified price schedule which usually includes a special premium. Sometimes preferred stockholders are granted the privilege of converting their stock into shares of common stock. The conversion ratio and conditions vary from issue to issue, but the intent of the company is usually the same: to make the preferred stock more attractive to potential purchasers.

Common stock represents the residual ownership interest in a company after recognizing the preferred stockholders' preferred position. Common stockholders elect directors, share in the profits of the business after preferred dividends are paid, and in liquidation share in the residual assets of the company after the claims of all creditors and preferred stockholders have been settled. Sometimes, common stockholders have the option to purchase any new common shares issued by their company in proportion to their holdings. This is called a "preemptive" right.

The common stockholders' investment in a company is typically shown in three parts:

1. Capital stock.
2. Capital in excess of par value (sometimes called "capital surplus").[1]
3. Retained earnings (sometimes called "earned surplus").

The capital stock account shows the par or stated value of the common shares issued. It is customary to disclose the number of shares authorized by the board of directors for the company, the number issued, and the number owned by the company as treasury stock, if any. The par value of a share bears no relationship to actual value. It is simply the amount engraved on the face of the stock certificate. This practice satisfies a legal requirement and indicates the limit of the stockholders' liability for the debts of the company. To limit legal liability and lessen certain stock transfer taxes, the par value is usually arbitrarily set as low as possible. Some states permit companies to issue no-par stock. In these cases, the no-par stock is assigned an arbitrary value and recorded on the books at this stated value, which is usually very low.

Typically, shares are issued at a price in excess of their par or stated value. In these cases, the excess amount is shown in the capital surplus

---

[1] The use of the term "surplus" is discouraged because of the misleading inferences readers of financial statements may draw from its use. However, in this chapter for the sake of convenience we will use "capital surplus" rather than the preferred, but longer caption "capital in excess of par value."

account. In addition, the value of any capital received by the company which did not involve issuing shares, such as donated assets, is included in this account. Other transactions which are described later that could affect the capital surplus account include: treasury stock transactions, stock dividends, and stock splits. The adjustments to the capital surplus account associated with accounting for "poolings of interest" has been discussed previously.

The accounting entries for a new stock issue are fairly straightforward. For example, assume the Lawson Corporation issued at a price of $25 per share 10,000 new common shares with a par value of $5 per share. The underwriting costs were $15,000. Consequently, the net proceeds to the company from the issue were $235,000. The accounting entries are:

```
Cash ................................................... 235,000
        Capital Stock .........................................    50,000
        Capital Surplus .......................................   185,000
```

None of these transactions, including the underwriting costs, affect net income. It is the preferred practice to show the increase in the capital accounts net of the costs associated with the stock issue.

Retained earnings represents the accumulated earnings of the company less dividends. It also includes the cumulative effect of any special credits and charges, such as prior period income adjustments, not included in the income computation. If there is no capital surplus available, the retained earnings account may properly be charged with those items normally absorbed by the capital surplus account. Also, under some circumstances, such as the declaration of a stock dividend, a portion of the retained earnings account may be transferred to the capital account. It is not considered good practice to add to retained earnings the net worth increments created by reappraisal of assets or the purchase of other companies at less than their book value. These increments should be clearly segregated from retained earnings and their source indicated by an appropriate account title.

Treasury Stock

Treasury stock is a company's own stock which has been issued and subsequently reacquired by the company but not yet retired formally. Treasury stock is shown as a deduction at cost from capital, rather than as an asset since legally a company can only reacquire its own stock with unrestricted capital. Treasury stock does not have voting privileges and does not enter into the computation of earnings per share.

When treasury stock is retired, the capital account is reduced by its par or stated value. The number of shares authorized remains unchanged, but the number of shares issued is reduced by the stock retired. Any difference between the retired treasury stock's cost and the amount charged to the capital account is deducted from the capital surplus account applicable to the retired class of shares. If the capital surplus account is inadequate to absorb the full excess of cost over par value, any remaining excess is charged to retained earnings.

When treasury stock is resold, the capital surplus account is adjusted to reflect any difference between the stock's cost and selling price. As far as accounting is concerned, such transactions do not give rise to corporate profits or losses.

Dividends

Dividends are pro rata distribution to stockholders of retained earnings. They can be in the form of cash, stock, or property. Generally, corporations can only declare dividends out of earnings, although some state laws and corporate agreements permit the declaration of dividends from sources other than earnings.

The declaration of dividends in cash or property by the board of directors legally binds the company to pay the dividends, unless the decision is rescinded by the stockholders receiving the dividends. Therefore, at the time dividends in cash or property are declared, retained earnings is charged with the amount of the dividend and a current liability account, Dividends Payable, is established. When the dividends are distributed, this account is reduced accordingly. Typically, when property is distributed as dividends, the retained earnings account is reduced by the book value of the property. However, some people argue that in those cases where the fair market value of the property distributed is different from its book value, the difference should be credited or charged to either income or retained earnings, depending on the circumstances.

Sometimes the directors of a company may segregate in a separate account in the owners' equity section of the balance sheet a portion of the retained earnings account and label it as being a restricted or appropriated reserve. This practice indicates that the reserved amount is not legally available for distribution to stockholders as dividends until the restrictions are removed. When the conditions leading to the segregation of retained earnings no longer exist, the reserve should be eliminated and credited to retained earnings directly. Irrespective of whether or not a special reserve is created, any restrictions of retained earnings as to dividend distributions should be fully disclosed in footnotes or parenthetical notation.

Ordinarily, dividends are not paid on treasury stock.

Stock Dividends and Splits

Stock dividends and splits are treated differently for accounting purposes, although they are generally regarded as being essentially the same from the financial point of view, since they both leave the shareholders' proportional share of equity unchanged.

Accounting Research Bulletin No. 43 distinguishes between stock dividends and stock splits as follows. A stock dividend "is prompted mainly by a desire to give the recipient shareholder some ostensibly separate evidence of a part of their respective interests in accumulated corporate earnings without distribution of cash or other property which the board of directors deems necessary or desirable to retain in the business." In contrast, a stock split-up "is prompted mainly by a desire to increase the number of outstanding shares for the purpose of effecting a reduction in their unit market price and, thereby, of obtaining wider distribution and improved marketability of the shares."

Accounting practice and the Internal Revenue Service do not regard a stock dividend or split as income to the recipient. The rationale for this position was cited in *Eisner* v. *Macomber* (252 U.S. 189), wherein it was held that stock dividends are not income under the Sixteenth Amendment. The court ruled:

A stock dividend really takes nothing from the property of the corporation and adds nothing to the interests of the stockholders. Its property is not diminished and their interests are not increased . . . the proportional interest of each shareholder remains the same. The only change is in the evidence which represents that interest, the new shares and the original shares together representing the same proportional interests that the original shares represented before the issue of the new ones.

Since a shareholder's interest in the corporation remains unchanged by a stock dividend or split-up except as to the number of share units constituting such interest, the cost of the shares previously held should be allocated equitably to the total shares held after receipt of the stock dividend or split-up. When any shares are later disposed of, a gain or loss should be determined on the basis of the adjusted cost per share.

Nevertheless, accounting practice does treat a stock dividend on the books of the issuing company as if it were income to the recipient, principally because many recipients appear to regard it as such. *ARB No. 43* states:

A stock dividend does not, in fact, give rise to any change whatsoever in either the corporation's assets or its respective shareholders' proportionate interests therein. However, it cannot fail to be recognized that, merely as a consequence of the expressed purpose of the transaction and its characterization as a *dividend* in related notices to shareholders and the public at large, many recipients of stock dividends look upon them as distributions of corporate earnings and usually in an amount equivalent to the fair value of the additional shares received. Furthermore, it is to be presumed that such views of recipients are materially strengthened in those instances, which are by far the most numerous, where the issuances are so small in comparison with the shares previously outstanding that they do not have any apparent effect upon the share market price and, consequently, the market value of the shares previously held remains substantially unchanged.

The Committee on Accounting Procedure believed that where these circumstances existed, the company should "in the public interest" account for the transaction by transferring from retained earnings to the permanent equity capital accounts (i.e., the capital stock and capital surplus accounts) an amount equal to the "fair value" of the additional shares issued. For example, to account for the issuance of 10,000 shares with a par value of $5 and fair value of $25 as a stock dividend, the following entries would be required.

Retained Earnings	250,000	
Capital Stock		50,000
Capital Surplus		200,000

Unless this approach was used, the CAP believed "the amount of earnings which the shareholder may believe to have been distributed to him will be left, except to the extent otherwise dictated by legal requirements, in earned surplus subject to possible further similar stock issuances or cash distributions." [2]

Where the number of additional shares issued as a stock dividend was so great that it had, or may reasonably be expected to have, the effect of materially reducing the market value per share, the CAP believed that the dividend income implications and possible other constructions stockholders attributed to stock dividends were not likely to occur. Under these circumstances, the nature of the transaction clearly indicates it is a stock split. Consequently, the CAP considered there was no need to capitalize retained earnings, other than to the extent required by law. For example, assume a company split its stock two for one, issued 100,000 new shares, and reduced its par value per common share from $5 to $2.50. Under these circumstances, no accounting entries would be required. The capital stock account would remain unchanged. However, compared to the situation before the split, the footnotes to the capital section of the balance sheet would now show twice as many authorized and outstanding shares and a par value per share of half the original value. Now, assume the company did not reduce its par value per share. In order to reflect the fact that the par value of the stock issued had increased by $500,000, the following entries would be required:

Retained Earnings	500,000	
Capital Stock		500,000

[2] The accounting for stock dividends recommended by the CAP will in most cases result in capitalization of retained earnings in an amount in excess of that called for by the laws of the state of incorporation. Such laws usually require capitalization of the par value of the shares issued. However, these legal requirements are minimum requirements and do not prevent the capitalization of a larger amount.

In addition, when the circumstances indicated that a stock split had occurred, the CAP believed that the use of the word "dividend" should be avoided in related corporate resolutions, notices, and announcements. In those cases where because of legal requirements this could not be done, the CAP recommended that the transaction be described as a "split-up effected in the form of a dividend."

The problem of resolving at what point a stock dividend becomes so big as to constitute a stock split was resolved by *ARB No. 43* as follows:

Obviously the point at which the relative size of the additional shares issued becomes large enough to materially influence the unit market price of the stock will vary with individual companies and under differing market conditions and, hence, no single percentage can be laid down as a standard for determining when capitalization of earned surplus in excess of legal requirements is called for and when it is not. However, on the basis of a review of market action in the case of shares of a number of companies having relatively recent stock distributions, it would appear that there would be few instances involving the issuance of additional shares of less than, say 20% or 25% of the number previously outstanding where the effect would not be such as to call for the procedure [described for accounting for stock dividends].

Bulletin No. 43 does not indicate the appropriate date for determining the fair market value of stock dividends. Typically, the declaration date is used, although in practice the ex-dividend and payment dates have also been used.

Stock Option and Purchase Plans

In order to compensate managers and to increase their interest in their company's activities, companies sometimes issue to managers nontransferable rights entitling them to buy a stated number of shares of stock at a specific price during some limited time period. The terms of such stock options granted should be clearly disclosed in the balance sheet, so that stockholders and prospective purchasers of stock are aware of the potential dilution of their equity.

If the fair market value of a stock option is more than the option price at the time the option is granted, any gain the recipient realizes at the time the option is exercised may be taxed as ordinary income. Consequently, the option price is usually close to the market price at the time the right is granted.

The hope of those granting stock options is that through the efforts of those receiving them the price of the company's stock will rise above the option price. If this expectation is realized, the stock option recipient regards the increase in value of his stock purchase right as additional compensation.

For a number of years, there was considerable accounting controversy as to how to measure such compensation and over what period to expense it. For example:

On January 1, 1965, John Lester, the president of a publicly owned company, is granted the right to purchase 10,000 shares of the company $5 par value stock at a price of $10 per share. The earliest time he can exercise this right is December 1, 1965. His right expires on December 31, 1968. The market price of this stock on January 1, 1965 was $12 per share. By December 31, 1965 the price had reached $20 per share. On January 25, 1968, John Lester exercised his right and was issued 10,000 shares at $10 per share. The current market price was $35 per share.

To ignore the compensation element of these events would lead to an overstatement of the company's income and an understatement of John Lester's cost of services. The problem is how to measure the compensation. Is it the difference between the grant price and the market price at the grant date? The difference between the grant price and the market price at the time the option is exercised? Or, the difference between the grant price and the price of the stock when the grantee sells it?

The conclusion of *ARB No. 43* concerning the measurement of the stock option compensation was that no compensation is involved if the option price is near to or above the market price at the time the option was granted. *ARB No. 43* argues:

When compensation is paid in a form other than cash the *amount* of compensation is ordinarily determined by the fair value of the property which was agreed to be given in exchange for the services to be rendered. The time at which such fair value is to be determined may be subject to some difference of opinion, but it appears that the date on which an option is granted to a specific individual would be the appropriate point at which to evaluate the cost to the employer, since it was the value at that date which the employer may be presumed to have had in mind. In most of the cases under discussion, moreover, the only important contingency involved is the continuance of the grantee in the employment of the corporation, a matter very largely within the control of the grantee and usually the main objective of the grantor. Under such circumstances it may be assumed that if the stock option were granted as a part of an employment contract, both parties had in mind a valuation of the option at the date of the contract; and accordingly, value at that date should be used as the amount to be accounted for as compensation. If the option were granted as a form of supplementary compensation otherwise than as an integral part of an employment contract, the grantor is nevertheless governed in determining the option price and the number of shares by conditions then existing. It follows that it is the value of the option at that time, rather than the grantee's ultimate gain or loss on the transaction, which for accounting purposes constitutes whatever compensation the grantor intends to pay. The committee therefore concludes that in most cases, including situations where the right to exercise is conditional upon continued employment, valuation should be made of the option as of the date of grant.

ARB No. 43 indicated that these conclusions were applicable to employee stock purchase plans also.

If compensation is involved in a stock option plan, the amount of the compensation should be charged to income in some reasonable manner consistent with the facts of the situation in the period during which the services of the employee covered by the plan are rendered. Sometimes the stock option plan states that the employee can exercise the option only if he agrees to stay with the company for a specified period of time. In this case, it is reasonable to charge the compensation to income during this specified period. The offset to the income charge should be a credit to the Accumulated Credit under Stock Option Plan account, which is shown in the owners' equity section of the balance sheet. When the stock option is exercised, the credit item is eliminated.

Using the John Lester example, the accounting entries would be:

a) When the option was granted:

```
Additional Compensation ............................    20,000
     Accumulated Credit under Stock Option Plan* .....            20,000
```

* 10,000 shares times the difference between the option price and the market price at the grant date.

b) When the option was exercised:

```
Cash ................................................  100,000
Accumulated Credit under Stock Option Plan ...........   20,000
     Common Stock, $5 par value ......................            50,000
     Capital Surplus .................................            70,000
     Issuance of 10,000 shares at $10 per share
     pursuant to stock option plan.
```

There is disagreement in the disposition of a balance in the Accumulated Credit under Stock Option Plan account if the stock option is not exercised before the expiration date. Some consider the elimination should be a correction of prior year's net income. Others favor treating it as an addition to owners' equity, much like donated capital.

Convertible Securities

A number of companies have issued bonds and other debt obligations which have future implications for the stockholders' equity accounts because they are either convertible into stock or carry detachable warrants to purchase stock. Chapter 21 indicated the appropriate accounting for these conversion privileges and warrants.

SUGGESTED FURTHER READING

RAPPAPORT, LOUIS H. *SEC Accounting Practice and Procedure.* New York: Ronald Press Co., 1966.

CASES

Case 22–1. KEMP FOODS CORPORATION
Accounting for Changes in Net Worth Accounts

"Here's the entire mess," said Ed McCowan, as papers of vario⟩   ⌐es and colors fluttered from the large manila envelope and spread over the desk of Dan Conner, CPA. "I bought 40 shares of Kemp Foods common last year in May. Since then I've received proxy statements, notices of stock splits, stock certificates, quarterly financial statements, and a few dividend checks. When this thick annual report came in yesterday's mail, I called you. I knew what to do with those little dividend checks, but to tell the truth I don't know what the rest of this means. I thought the annual report would explain things, but I don't see any relationship between my 40 shares and the big numbers and big words in the report."

"It appears that you saved everything, Ed," said Dan Conner. "Let's see if we can list things as they happened from the beginning." He made these notes on a desk pad as he selected papers from the assortment before him:

```
May 5, 1964, bought 40 common at 38 plus commission ........ $1,539.60
July 20, 1964, received cash dividends, 40 at 25¢ ..............   10.00
Oct. 20, 1964, received cash dividends, 40 at 25¢ ..............   10.00
Oct. 25, 1964, received 2 shares, common stock dividend.
Jan. 20, 1965, received cash dividends, 42 at 25¢ ..............   10.50
Mar. 15, 1965, received 21 shares, 3 for 2 stock split.
Apr. 20, 1965, received cash dividends, 63 at 20¢ ..............   12.60
```

"Now, let's look at the quotations in today's *Wall Street Journal* and see how you've made out over the past year. Here it is on the Pacific Coast

Exchange. The closing price yesterday was 28½. Now we'll look at the April 30, 1965 annual report together and see what it tells us."

This case concerns corporate financial reporting for changes in stockholders' equity and its meaning to the investor.

The Company

Kemp Foods Corporation was established in Illinois in 1927 to acquire and operate three small vegetable canning plants. Operations were expanded to include canning of fruits and frozen fruit processing. The growth of these newer activities in the late 1940s was responsible for transfer of company headquarters to California. In 1965, the company had 15 canning and processing plants throughout the Midwest and on the West Coast.

Kemp's operations had always been profitable. Earnings per share of common reached an historic high of $2.27 in the fiscal year ended April 30, 1965. Net income for the year was $1.3 million on sales of almost $59 million. Stockholders' equity at April 30, 1965 exceeded $13 million. The company's comparative balance sheets at the close of the two most recent years are shown in Exhibit 1. An analysis of common stock, paid-in surplus, and retained earnings is shown in Exhibit 2.

Most of the funds needed to finance the company's growth had been provided internally. Modest cash dividends had been paid quarterly without interruption since 1946, when the common stock was split three for one. In 1952, after a public offering of preferred and common stock, a policy of supplementing the regular cash dividends with stock dividends to common stockholders was adopted. Five percent stock dividends were declared in each year thereafter except for 1955 and 1956, when stock dividends were 20 percent and 10 percent respectively. The 4 percent preferred stock was gradually being retired as it became available in the market at an attractive price. Some funds had been obtained by the use of long-term debt and future expansion was to be financed more extensively in this way.

The price of Kemp Foods' common stock had risen steadily since the early 1950s. For example, the price had ranged from a low of 12¾ to a high of 18⅜ in the year 1959 and reached an all time high of 43½ in 1964.

Questions

1. Evaluate Ed McCowan's investment at June 10, 1965.
2. Examine the stockholders' equity section of Kemp Foods' balance sheet to:
   a) Determine how each item was originally created.
   b) Explain changes during the year ended April 30, 1965.
3. Contrast Kemps methods of reporting preferred treasury stock and common treasury stock.

EXHIBIT 1

KEMP FOODS CORPORATION

Comparative Balance Sheets, April 30, 1965 and 1964

ASSETS	1965	1964
Current Assets:		
Cash	$ 996,020	$ 1,124,588
Receivables (net)	5,076,894	5,084,087
Inventories, at the lower of cost		
(Fifo basis) or market	10,440,509	8,708,578
Total Current Assets	$16,513,423	$14,917,253
Prepaid expenses	133,434	230,002
Plant and Equipment:		
Land	$ 290,349	$ 346,319
Buildings and leasehold improvements	4,200,760	4,719,515
Machinery and equipment	3,916,508	4,275,927
Automotive equipment	601,393	586,030
Construction in progress	2,033,324	...
	$11,042,334	$ 9,927,791
Less: Accumulated depreciation and amortization	5,038,251	4,532,968
Net Plant and Equipment	$ 6,004,083	$ 5,394,823
Total Assets	$22,650,940	$20,542,078

LIABILITIES		
Current Liabilities:		
Bank loans	$ 2,192,500	$ 1,350,000
Current maturities of long-term debt	170,790	163,478
Accounts payable and accrued liabilities	2,187,440	1,770,026
Income taxes	1,014,527	936,889
Dividends payable	126,811	102,554
Total Current Liabilities	$ 5,692,068	$ 4,322,947
Long-term debt, noncurrent portion	3,660,223	3,831,013
Deferred income taxes and other expenses	273,850	174,225
	$ 9,626,141	$ 8,328,185
Stockholders' Equity:		
Cumulative 4% preferred stock, par value $100; authorized 15,000 shares, issued 8,995 shares less 198 shares in treasury	$ 879,700	
Common stock, par value $5; authorized 1,000,000 shares, issued 590,552 shares, (4,482 shares in treasury, see below)	2,952,760	
Paid-in surplus (Exhibit 2)	2,853,702	
Retained earnings (Exhibit 2):		
Reserve for plant expansion	1,466,676	
Unappropriated *	4,997,457	
	$13,150,295	
Less: Treasury stock, common (4,482 shares at cost)	125,496	
Total Stockholders' Equity	$13,024,799	12,213,893
Total Liabilities	$22,650,940	$20,542,078

* Under terms of the long-term debt agreement $2,330,808 of retained earnings at April 30, 1965 is restricted against payment of cash dividends on or purchase of common stock.

EXHIBIT 2

KEMP FOODS CORPORATION

Common Stock, Paid-In Surplus, and Retained Earnings
For the Year Ended April 30, 1965

| | Common Stock | | Paid-In | Retained Earnings | |
	Shares	Par Value	Surplus	Reserve for Plant Exp.	Unappro-priated
Balance at May 1, 1964	375,130	$1,875,650	$3,197,277	$3,500,000	$2,742,831
Add:					
Net income for the year..	...	...	...	...	1,376,871
Gain on sale of 600 shares common treasury stock	...	...	17,716	...	...
Discount on 245 shares of preferred stock purchased	...	...	4,003	...	...
Reduction in reserve for plant expansion	...	...	...	(2,003,324)	2,033,324
Total	375,130	$1,875,650	$3,218,996	$1,466,676	$6,153,026
Add or (deduct):					
Transfer to common stock in connection with 3 for 2 stock split	196,690	983,450	(983,450)	...	...
Cash dividends					
Preferred ($4 per share)	...	...	...	...	(35,386)
Common ($0.95 per share)	...	...	...	...	(408,367)
5% stock dividend, recorded at fair market value of $38 per share..	18,732	93,660	618,156	...	(711,816)
Balance at April 30, 1965 ..	590,552	$2,952,760	$2,853,702	$1,466,676	$4,997,457

4. What is the effect of Kemp's acquisition of treasury stock upon investor McCowan's holdings?

5. Suggest improvements Kemp might make in reporting stockholders' equity information on its balance sheet.

6. How does the issuance of stock options to the management change the company's net worth accounts at (*a*) date of issuance, (*b*) date the options are first exercisable, and (*c*) date exercised? Assume options to buy 2,000 shares are first exercisable in 1965. (These were issued originally at a price equal to the then current market price of 20.) What would be the accounting entry for these options if they were exercised during 1965, when the market price of Kemp stock was 26? Not exercised? How did the company originally account for the granting of these options?

Case 22–2. **GENERAL HOST CORPORATION**

Accounting for Warrants

During the first quarter of 1969, General Host acquired a majority interest in Armour and Company. The March 1969 interim report to the stockholders announced that the acquisition would make General Host "one of the largest [companies] in the country with consolidated annual sales approximating $2.2 billion." General Host's 1968 sales equaled $202 million (including $43 million sales of L'il General, which merged with General Host in July 1968). The October 1969 interim report announced an agreement to sell substantially all of its investment in Armour and Company to the Greyhound Corporation for $50 million less than the $261 million recorded on the books of General Host as the value of the company's investment in Armour.

General Host

General Host Corporation was incorporated as General Baking Company in 1911. The present name was adopted in 1967. Three of the company's divisions manufactured and sold complete lines of baked goods. The fourth division, "Li'l General," operated convenience stores and small self-service grocery stores. Two wholly owned subsidiaries, Yellowstone Park Company and Everglades Park Company Inc., operated inns, lodges, restaurants, gasoline service stations, and recreational facilities.

Armour

In 1969, Armour and Company was the second largest meat packer in the United States and among the leaders in the fields of household soaps, fatty chemicals, hydraulic turbines, governors and valves, ship propellers, electronic force measurement equipment, and desalination systems.

Acquisition of Armour

By the end of 1968, General Host owned approximately 16.5 percent of the outstanding shares of Armour common stock; 750,000 shares had been purchased from Gulf and Western Industries, Inc. between August and October. An additional 252,500 shares had been purchased in the open market. The $60,535,000 investment in this stock was carried on the balance sheet at cost.

On January 20, 1969, the General Host shareholders approved an exchange offer to the holders of common stock of Armour through which General Host would exchange $60 principal amount of its 7 percent subordinated debentures due February 1, 1994, and warrants expiring January 31, 1979 to purchase two and a half of its shares of common stock at $40 per share, for each share of Armour common stock offered. At the expiration of the exchange offer on February 14, 1969, the company had received approximately 2,700,000 shares of the common stock of Armour and Company, giving it an aggregate of 3,700,000 shares, representing approximately 57 percent of Armour's outstanding common stock. In payment for the 2,700,000 shares received under the exchange offer, the company issued approximately $159 million of its 7 percent subordinated debentures and 6,750,000 of its warrants.

The 57 percent in Armour was recorded in the March 1969 interim report of Armour as follows:

> Investment in Armour at cost, plus equity
> in undistributed earnings $261,000,000

The October 1969 interim report explained that the $261 million carrying value of Armour:

> ... comprises $59 million of cash purchases, while the balance was acquired in exchange for approximately $159 million principal amount of 7% subordinated debentures and 6.6 million ten-year warrants to purchase General Host common stock at $40 per share. For accounting purposes, the 7% debentures were assumed to have had an estimated fair market value of approximately $124 million at the time of their issuance in February, 1969, and, similarly, the warrants were assigned a value of approximately $74 million, based on their approximate market value at the time of issuance. Additional expenses relating to the issuance of debentures and warrants amounted to approximately $4 million.

If the expenses were paid in cash the bookkeeping entry would be:

Investment in Armour	261,000,000	
Unamortized Bond Discount	35,000,000	
Cash		63,000,000
7% Subordinated Debentures Due 2-1-94		159,000,000
Capital in Excess of Par (Assigned Value of Warrants)		74,000,000

Competing Tender Offer

On January 28, 1969, the Greyhound Corporation, through a subsidiary, offered to purchase up to 41 percent of Armour's common stock for cash at a price of $65 per share. On January 30, 1969, this offer was increased to $70 per share. Greyhound obtained 2,096,000 shares (about 33 percent of the outstanding stock of Armour) and blocked a takeover by General Host.

Resale

On October 27, 1969, General Host signed an agreement for the sale of its investment in Armour to Greyhound for a package valued at $211 million, including $77 million in cash, $36 million in a five-year interest-bearing note, and the remainder in Greyhound warrants and convertible preferreds. The agreement was subject to the approval of the stockholders of both companies as well as the Interstate Commerce Commission. General Host commented on the agreement:

Your management's decision to sell the company's investment in Armour was motivated primarily by the tight money market which would have made it difficult to finance the acquisition of the remaining minority interest in Armour. The alternative to selling the Armour stock was to risk tieing up a major portion of the company's capital for a considerable period of time in an investment where the carrying cost substantially exceeds the cash dividends therefrom. On the other hand, selling to Greyhound will put the company in the position of having substantial liquid assets to use in acquisitions at a time when good solid companies are selling at a low earnings multiple and, therefore, at attractive prices. Your management continues to actively study opportunities for acquisitions which will enhance its earnings and strengthen its position in the convenience and leisure time fields.

Accounting for the Sale

General Host stated that the $50 million loss on the sale of its Armour stock would be recorded as an extraordinary loss for financial reporting purposes when the transaction is consummated.

On February 15, 1970, *Forbes* magazine, in an article on General Host titled "It's All Done With Arithmetic," asked the question, "How can a $50 million loss be a profit?" The article answered this question in part as follows:

It all depends on how you choose to keep your books.

Will the miracles of certified public accounting never cease? Listen how Harris J. Ashton, president of General Host Corporation, can prove that although his company will lose $50 million on the sale of its 57% holdings in Armour & Company to Greyhound, it will come out $23 million ahead.

Anyone who can do simple arithmetic should understand his reasoning. . . .

Since the warrants cost General Host nothing (except for possible future dilution) the full $74 million was profit—or at least credit to capital surplus.

On the books, this $74 million "profit" more than offsets the $50 million "loss" to be incurred in the sale. . . .

Follow? No? Well, never mind, because all that has really happened is that large amounts of paper have been shuffled back and forth. . . . Ashton . . . claims that all of this shuffling has been a good thing for General Host. He says: In a period of tight money I'd rather have the $211 million than the Armour stocks. The truth is, of course, that General Host won't really have $211 million. Nearly $100 million of the deal is in Greyhound warrants and convertible preferred, which are not easily traded in today's turbulent market.

In February, 1970, the warrants General Host valued at $11 each in the Armour tender were selling for about $3 each and General Host stock was trading at about $12 per share. The $1,000 debentures issued for the Armour stock by General Host were selling in the open market at about $460.

Question

1. What is your appraisal of General Host's accounting for its investment in the Armour stock obtained through the 1969 exchange offer?

PART VIII

Special Accounting Problems

CHAPTER 23

MEASURING OVERSEAS ACTIVITIES

The manager of an international company must deal with financial statements from different foreign subsidiaries which are stated in terms of more than one local currency. This is a major difference between managing domestic and foreign operations. Typically, the parent company manager overcomes this difficulty by translating the foreign subsidiary statements into the domestic currency of the parent company. If the exchange rate between the domestic and foreign currency has changed since the last balance sheet date, translation gains and losses will be generated by this procedure. In addition, if a foreign or domestic company has debts or receivables which are payable in another currency and the local exchange rate changes, an exchange gain or loss related to this item must be recognized on the local company's statements irrespective of whether or not they are translated into another currency.

Accounting Research Bulletin No. 43, Chapter 12, and APB *Opinion No. 6* govern the determination and disposition of these gains and losses for public reporting purposes. The Accounting Principles Board is currently making a study of accounting for foreign operations. An earlier study in 1960 by the National Association of Accountants indicated that a number of the practices described in Chapter 12 of *ARB No. 43* were outmoded in relationship to current practices.

EXCHANGE RATES

The exchange rate is the amount of one currency which must be exchanged for one unit of another. For example $1 (Australian) is equivalent to $1.125 (U.S.). Conversely, one would have to pay $0.899 (Australian) to purchase $1 (U.S.), which is the reciprocal U.S. dollar price for Australian dollars. Since each country has its own currency, there are a multiplicity of exchange rates. The rates for the major countries involved in international trade are published daily in most of the leading newspapers.

At any moment, more than one exchange rate may exist between two currencies. Most countries have an official or "par" rate, but exchange dealers may quote prices different from this rate, depending on their stocks of the currency and the general level of the supply and demand for it. In addition, the rates dealers quote may be influenced by the length of time before which they must deliver the currency. For example, the "spot" or immediate delivery rate is usually different from the forward rate for delivery in, say, 90 days. Sometimes, countries use different rates for financing different types of goods and services. Also, in some cases, a black market rate might exist alongside the official government rate.

The supply and demand for foreign currencies is influenced by international movements involving goods, services, and investments as well as speculative activities in foreign currencies. For example, when United States residents export goods or services overseas they receive payment in U.S. dollars. To obtain these U.S. dollars, the foreign importers must exchange some foreign currency. Thus, the U.S. exports increase the supply of foreign currency and the demand for U.S. dollars in the foreign exchange market. The reverse situation exists when U.S. residents import goods or services from overseas.

In a free market, the exchange rate will tend to stabilize at the point where the supply and demand for a currency are in balance. This balance can be influenced by a variety of factors. Since a country's exports and imports often reflect its internal cost-price structure, changes in the domestic purchasing power of different currencies may influence their relative exchange rates. The exchange rate in free markets is also influenced by the fact that not all imports and exports are bought on price alone. For example, consumer preferences for certain imports and inelastic demand situations can complicate the adjustment mechanism. Also, if any discrepancies between foreign exchange markets exist, arbitrage activities by foreign currency traders will soon eliminate the discrepancies.

Since World War II, government planners have increasingly recognized that freely fluctuating exchange rates can cause distortions in a country's balance of payments and internal economy. Consequently, most of the world's major trading nations have adopted fixed exchange rate policies and declared a par value of their currency expressed in terms of gold or U.S. dollars. In addition, the 107 nations who are members of the International Monetary Fund have agreed to keep their exchange rate fluctuations within 1 percent of parity. A member country can still change its exchange rate, but such changes are supposed to be infrequent.

Governments use a number of devices that increase the supply or decrease the demand for their currency to keep their exchange rates close to par. These include: selling or adding to foreign exchange reserves, establishing foreign exchange controls, imposing import controls, subsidizing exports, and reducing foreign aid programs.

Restrictions upon the free exchange of currencies can lead to a currency being overvalued. In these cases, it becomes desirable to shift funds from the overvalued currency to the more normally valued currencies. In order to halt this flight from the overvalued ("soft") currency to the normally valued ("hard") currencies, the soft currency can be declared inconvertible by its government. Thus, the currency can not be freely exchanged for other currencies. Countries can make their currencies wholly inconvertible for all people, or for residents but not foreigners; for some but not all other currencies; and for certain types of transactions only.

Devaluation

At times, governments with serious adverse balance of payments problems are unable to maintain their currency's par value. The classical solution to this problem is to devaluate the currency. It is hoped that this step will improve the balance of trade by making it more expensive for citizens to import goods and less expensive for foreigners to buy exports. Successful devaluation requires an increase in exports and, since local prices of imported goods will rise, an antiinflationary domestic fiscal policy must be instituted. However, since trade is only one part of the total international payments system, currency speculation, foreign investments, and military aid may also affect the payments balance.

Devaluation can be continuous or one-time. For example, the Brazilian cruzeiro has declined in value at a fairly steady rate since World War II. In contrast, the British pound was devalued in 1949 and 1967.

Since World War II, devaluations have been common. In fact, only a few of the world's 120 currencies (those of the United States, Cuba, Ethiopia, Haiti, Honduras, Liberia, and El Salvador) have not been formally devalued since 1946. Since 1949, Chile has devalued nearly 50 times and Brazil over 30 times. The Russian ruble has been devalued three times in that period, principally to reduce domestic purchasing power. In its 179-year history, the United States has only devalued the dollar in terms of gold once, in 1934.

Multiple exchange rates are an intermediate form of devaluation, since they devalue the currency for specific kinds of transactions. Under this arrangement, all foreign exchange receipts from exports are sold to the exchange administration and all foreign exchange required for payment is bought from the administration. Multiple rates are then used for both the buying and selling of exchange. A high selling rate discourages imports and a high buying rate encourages exporters. By having different buying and selling rates for different types of transactions, the government is able to encourage or discourage certain kinds of imports and exports. Today, the use of multiple exchange rates is limited mainly to Latin America and underdeveloped countries.

Upward revaluing of a currency's par value has been fairly rare since World War II. However, it has occurred. For example, in 1961, West Germany and the Netherlands revalued their currencies upward by 5 percent. Subsequently, in 1969, West Germany again revalued its currency upward.

EXCHANGE GAINS AND LOSSES

Some companies hold foreign currency and accounts or notes receivable which are payable in a foreign currency. Fluctuations in the exchange rates of these currencies create exchange gains or losses on these items for the company holding them. For example, if a Brazilian company bought 10 tractors from a U.S. company for $50,000 (U.S.), and between the time the company received the invoice and the payment of the $50,000 (U.S.) the Brazilian cruzeiro was devalued from 1,200 to 1,800 cruzeiros ($Cr.) to the dollar, the Brazilian company would have experienced an exchange loss of Cr$30 million. Originally, the payment of the invoice would have required Cr$60 million. After the devaluation, repayment requires Cr$90 million, a difference of Cr$30 million. Conversely, if the Brazilian company was owed $50,000 (U.S.), the devaluation would have created a potential exchange gain of Cr$30 million. For example, if the Brazilian company had sold the tractors to the U.S. company and the exchange rate changed before the account receivable was paid, the Brazilian company would receive an exchange gain on its account receivable asset.

Exchange gains and losses are recognized on the books of the company whose assets or liabilities give rise to the gains or losses. Realized gains or losses on foreign exchange items are credited or charged against operations. Typically, however, unrealized losses are charged to operations. In contrast, unrealized gains are carried to a suspense account, except to the extent that they offset previous provisions for unrealized losses, in which case they may be credited to the account previously charged.

TRANSLATION OF STATEMENTS

Managers and stockholders of U.S. companies with overseas subsidiaries generally measure the success of these overseas operations in terms of the changes in the U.S. dollar equivalent of their net worth. In order to do this, the statements of the foreign subsidiary must be converted from the local currency to its U.S. dollar equivalent. No actual cash changes hands in this process. It is simply a work sheet adjustment. For example, to convert statements in Australian dollars to U.S. dollars, each item on the Australian statement is multiplied by 1.125, since $1 (Australian) equals $1.125 (U.S.). If there has been a change in the exchange rate, as explained later, some items on the balance sheet and statement of retained earnings will be multiplied by the old rate and some by the new. Thus, when each item is converted to dollars the statements will be out of balance. The balancing item is the translation gain or loss.

Once each of the items on the right-hand side of the following equation have been converted from local currency to U.S. dollars, the translation gain or loss can be computed as follows:

$$\text{Translation gains or losses} = \text{Assets} - (\text{liabilities} + \text{beginning net worth} + \text{profit} - \text{dividends})$$

If the answer is a negative amount, then a loss has occurred. It must be deducted from the owners' equity portion of the right-hand side of the balance sheet to bring the right and left sides into balance. That will occur if after translation:

$$\text{Assets} < (\text{liabilities} + \text{beginning net worth} + \text{profit} - \text{dividends})$$

Conversely, if the assets are greater than the right-hand side of the equation, a translation gain will occur.

There are a variety of ways to translate each of the items in the equation from local currency to U.S. dollars. Each is discussed below.

Stable Exchange Rate

There are few problems involved in translation when the exchange rate between the base currency and the overseas currency has been stable over a long period of time. To convert the amounts shown on the foreign currency statements to their base currency equivalents, the exchange rate is applied directly to the amounts shown on the local currency statements. Since the same rate will most likely be applied to each item in the statements, the equality of the right and left sides of the balance sheet is maintained, as is the relationship between current financial statements and those for prior periods.

Fluctuating Exchange Rate

When there has been a change in the exchange rate, the task of converting statements from one currency to another becomes more difficult.

These difficulties arise because not all of the items on the financial state-ments are affected by the devaluation or appreciation in the exchange rate in the same manner. For example, in the case of a devaluation, the equiva-lent dollar values of the foreign currency cash balances will decline. The cash will now buy fewer dollars. However, the dollar equivalent value of the foreign inventory might remain unchanged, because management may be able to raise its selling prices sufficiently to offset the devaluation effect. This is usually possible if the devaluation is the result of locally inflated price levels.

Recognizing that different items are affected differently by exchange rate changes, the accountant has grouped assets into categories which re-flect their responsiveness to exchange changes. The first category is finan-cial or monetary assets. These assets which are cash or "near-cash." Cash, accounts receivable, and investments in securities fall into this category. The second category is physical or nonmonetary assets, which includes inventories and fixed assets. On the liabilities side, all of the items can be considered to be financial in nature.

The exchange rate used to translate statements is either the current or the historical rate. The current rate is the exchange rate prevailing on the date of the statement. The historical rate is the rate of exchange existing on the date the transaction took place. For example, in the case of fixed assets, the historical rate would be the rate prevailing at the time the com-pany acquired the assets.

The selection of the appropriate current rate presents problems in those cases where multiple rates exist or the currency is not freely convertible. In most other cases involving free convertibility of reasonably stable cur-rencies, the par rate is used. Small fluctuations from it are ignored. For example, in the case of a British subsidiary, its statements may be converted at the parity rate of $2.40 = £1, even though the current exchange rate may be $2.39 = £1. When multiple rates are encountered, the rate for remitting dividends to U.S. shareholders is often used, since the ultimate objective of doing business overseas is to return profits in the form of dividends to the U.S. investors.

Financial Method

The most common method for translating statements is the financial method. It translates monetary assets and liabilities at the current rate (i.e., rate at the balance sheet date) and physical assets at the historical rate (i.e., rate at the time the transactions occurred). The rationale under-lying this approach is discussed below. From the point of view of the U.S. investor, the dollar equivalent of the foreign currency (cash) and claims to receive a fixed number of local currency units (accounts receivable) depreciates in terms of U.S. dollars immediately when devaluation occurs.

Consequently, the current rate of exchange gives the best translation for such financial assets expressed in foreign currency.

Similarly, the dollar equivalent of local currency liabilities is also affected by a change in the exchange rate. The effect is the reverse of the financial asset situation, however. Following devaluation, debts payable in local currency can be satisfied with local currency which is the equivalent of fewer dollars. Again, because the dollar equivalent of these financial items is immediately affected by changes in the exchange rate, the current rate is used to translate liabilities.

The risks of being exposed to devaluation losses can be minimized if the local manager keeps his net financial assets (financial assets minus liabilities) in as big a net negative position as possible. This is because unfavorable movements in exchange rates reduce the dollar value of local financial assets. Conversely, these same changes reduce the dollar equivalent needed to extinguish local debts. Of course, the opposite is true in those cases where appreciation in the exchange rate is anticipated.

The dollar equivalent of the local currency values assigned to physical assets, such as inventory and plant, are often regarded as being unaffected by exchange rate changes. Therefore, they are translated at the relevant historical rate (i.e., the rate prevailing at the time the particular asset was acquired). Underlying this practice is the assumption that devaluation is usually the consequence of inflation within the foreign country and that the local selling prices of the inventory and the other goods or services which will eventually be produced from using the fixed assets will increase sufficiently to offset the devaluation.

In the case of inventory, the normal cost or market rule is applied. That is, if the dollar equivalent of local currency selling margin equivalent after devaluation can not be realized through raising local prices, the inventory value is reduced. This situation could arise in cases where price controls exist or local competitors do not respond to the devaluation with higher prices because they are measuring their profit in local currency, rather than dollars or some other relatively more stable currency. Under these circumstances, the practice is to determine the dollar cost of the inventory at the rates prevailing at the time the inventory was recorded on the books of the company. The market cost is the local currency selling price less the costs of disposition translated at the current rate on the balance sheet date. For example:

	Local Currency	Rate	U.S. Dollars
Inventory cost at acquisition date rate ...	200,000	0.60	120,000
Market value at current rate	250,000	0.30	75,000

In this case, the inventory would be stated in the translated balance sheet at $75,000 and a loss of $45,000 charged to income.

Local managers can protect themselves against the risk of translation losses by converting financial assets into physical assets, since physical assets are translated at their appropriate historical rate except when this assumption that local prices can be increased to recover devaluation losses is not realistic. No translation gain or loss occurs when there is a change in the exchange rate. On the other hand, if they anticipate an appreciation in the exchange rate, they can gain from this event by shifting funds from physical assets into financial assets.

Local currency profits of the foreign subsidiary accrue as local sales are recognized and the related costs are incurred. Local currency revenues are recorded in current funds and hence are usually translated at the prevailing exchange rate at the time they are recorded in the company's books. Typically, the average rate for the month in which they are recognized is used to translate revenues.

The local currency costs used to determine local profits can be of two kinds: those using current funds, such as wages and expenses; and those using funds incurred in previous periods, such as depreciation which relates to fixed assets acquired in prior periods. Those involving current funds, such as salary and utilities expenses, are translated at the average rate for the month during which the expenses were incurred. Depreciation, cost of goods sold, and other expense items related to fund expenditures made in prior periods are translated at the historical rate at the time they were recorded during the prior period.

The difference between the translated local revenue and local costs is the dollar equivalent of the local profit.

Profits create financial assets. Therefore, in a year when exchange rates are declining while profits are being earned, the local manager should take whatever steps he can, consistent with sound business practices, to minimize the increase in financial assets created by profits.

Net worth includes capital stock and retained earnings. Capital items are translated at their historical rate to maintain consistency with the parent company's records. Retained earnings include an accumulation of the amounts added in each of the prior years. Each of these amounts (annual profit less dividends) is translated at the rate originally used at the time of its addition to retained earnings. The current period's addition to the translated retained account is the dollar profit equivalent obtained from the translated income statement less any dividends translated at the rate prevailing at the time declared.

As indicated earlier, no gain or loss on translation has occurred if after translation the sum of the assets equals the liabilities plus net worth accounts. If the translated assets are greater than the translated right-hand side of the balance sheet, a translation gain has occurred. This gain is the amount needed to make the sum of the liabilities and net worth equal to the total assets. On the other hand, if the right-hand side is greater than assets, the amount needed to bring it into balance with the assets is the translation loss.

The translation gain or loss balancing figure represents the dollar change in the U.S. investor's dollar equity in the foreign company due to exchange rate changes. Irrespective of whether they are realized or not in terms of actual currency transfers, translation losses are charged to income in the parent's statements.

Material translation gains by parent companies have been rare in recent years. The preferred practice is to show the unrealized portion of the gain as a reserve above the stockholders' equity section of the balance sheet, although, since this amount arises from appreciation of the net financial assets, it might well be regarded as part of owner's equity and treated in much the same fashion as a revaluation reserve arising from the upward valuation of fixed assets in a domestic situation. To the extent that the parent company actually realizes a translation gain, it can be included in income.

Other Methods

There are other procedures for translating statements from one currency to another. For reference purposes we will refer to them as the:

1. Current asset method.
2. Modified financial method.
3. Net asset method.

The differences between these methods and the financial method is shown in Illustration 23–1.

ILLUSTRATION 23–1

Differences between Translation Methods

		Method and Rates		
	Financial	Current Asset	Modified Financial	Net Asset
Inventory	Historical	Current	Current	Current
Long-term debt	Current	Historical	Current	Current
Fixed assets	Historical	Historical	Historical	Current

Current Asset Method

The current asset method differs from the financial method in that it translates all current assets and liabilities at the current rate, irrespective of whether or not the current asset is a financial or a physical asset. All non-current assets or liabilities are translated at their appropriate historical rate.

In this latter respect it also differs from the financial method, which translates long-term liabilities at the current, rather than historical, rate.

The current asset method was originally advocated by *Accounting Research Bulletin No. 43*. With respect to inventories, the bulletin said:

> Inventory should follow the standard rule of cost or market whichever is lower in dollars. When accounts are to be stated in which the question of foreign exchange enters and the inventory is not translated at the rate of exchange prevailing on the date of the balance sheet, as is usually done with current assets, the burden of proof is on those who wish to follow some other procedure.

More recent studies indicate that the prevalence of the practice of translating inventories at the current rate is declining.

With respect to long-term liabilities, *ARB No. 43* said:

> Long-term liabilities and capital stock stated in foreign currency should not be translated at the closing rate, but at the rates of exchange prevailing when they were originally incurred or issued. This is a general rule, but an exception may exist in respect to long-term debt incurred or capital stock issued in connection with the acquisition of fixed assets, permanent investments, or long-term receivables a short time before a substantial and presumably permanent change in the exchange rate. In such instances it may be appropriate to state the long-term debt or the capital stock at the new rate and proper to deal with the exchange differences as an adjustment of the cost of the assets acquired.

Modified Financial Method

In October 1965, *Opinion No. 6* of the Accounting Principles Board modified *ARB No. 43*'s position with respect to long-term financial items by stating that translation of long-term receivables and long-term payables at current exchange rates is appropriate in many circumstances. This amendment gave authoritative support to a common translating practice which might be called the modified financial method. This translation procedure is the same as the financial method except that it translates inventory at the current rather than historical rate. In this respect, it is similar to the current asset method. It is similar to the financial method in its treatment of current and noncurrent financial items, however.

Net Asset Method

The net asset method translates all of the items on the balance sheet, except capital stock and retained earnings, at the current rate. This practice assumes that a company's entire net worth is exposed to exchange rate changes. Capital and retained earnings are translated at their appropriate historical rate to maintain consistency with the parent company's dollar investment account related to the subsidiary. This is not a very common method. However, when applied to price-level-adjusted local statements, it opens up the intriguing analytical possibility of separating losses and gains due to local price-level shifts from gains and losses due to exchange rate movements.

An Illustration

The effect of the various translation methods is shown in Illustration 23–2. The 1968 exchange rate was 4 local units to $1 (U.S.) and the rate in 1969 was 8 local units to $1 (U.S.). The inventory was purchased equally in 1968 and 1969, and has a local market value of 32 units, so a "cost or market" adjustment may be necessary.

ILLUSTRATION 23–2

Effect of Methods of Currency Translation

	(local currency) 1969 Financial Statement	Methods (U.S. dollars)			
		Financial	Current Asset	Modified Financial	Net Asset
ASSETS					
Cash	40	5	5	5	5
Inventory	24	4	3	3	3
Plant:					
Purchased 1969	96	24	24	24	12
Purchased 1968	200	25	25	25	25
Total	360	58	57	57	45
LIABILITIES					
Current liabilities	88	11	11	11	11
Long-term liabilities	72	9	18	9	9
Stock	80	20	20	20	20
Earned surplus:					
1968	40	10	10	10	10
1969	80	10	10	10	10
Total	360	60	69	60	60
Translation (loss)		(2)	(12)	(3)	(15)
		58	57	57	45
Computation of inventory purchased:					
1968	12	3.0	1.5	1.5	1.5
1969	12	1.5	1.5	1.5	1.5
	24	4.5	3.0	3.0	3.0
Market value	32	4.0	4.0	4.0	4.0

SEPARATING PRICE-LEVEL AND TRANSLATION GAINS AND LOSSES

Inflation and currency depreciation can differ with respect to timing and magnitude. Using the translation methods discussed previously, this fact can create distortions in the translated net worth of subsidiaries in economically unstable countries.

Many countries have experienced mild, steady inflation since World War II. In most of these cases, if devaluation occurred it did so in one sharp reduction in the currency's value. Certainly, this sharp movement did not parallel the gradual loss of purchasing power within the country of its currency. In fact, even though Germany and the Netherlands revalued their currencies upward in 1961, their internal price levels were rising.

The currency of other countries, such as Brazil and Argentina, has devalued on an almost continuous basis subject to the supply and demand for their currency in the foreign exchange market. Even in these situations, the currency devaluation has not paralleled the internal inflation.

In situations where significant inflation exists, it may be useful to separate the impact of both shifts in the local price level and exchange rate on translated profits. This can be done as follows: first, adjust the local statements for changes in the local price levels in order to determine whether a purchasing power "gain" or "loss" has occurred. After this adjustment, all of the items on the local statements will be in local units of current purchasing power. Next, translate the price-level-adjusted local statements into dollars using the net asset method, i.e., translate all of the local statement items at the current rate except capital stock and surplus, which are translated at the historical rate. This step gives a translation gain and loss figure in cost results from the fact that changes in the local prices and exchange rates differ in magnitude and timing.

MEASUREMENT AND MOTIVATION

Local managers in economically unstable countries are often held responsible for translated profits after translation gains and losses. This measure of performance puts pressure upon them to take, with the cooperation of the parent company, whatever steps are possible to reduce their exposure to exchange gains and losses. In inflationary economies, many of these same steps also protect against inflation eroding the U.S. stockholders' investment.

The interest a manager shows in taking particular steps to reduce his exposure to devaluation may be biased somewhat by the translation method used. For example, the financial method biases a manager toward shifting funds from cash to inventories because inventories are translated at the historical rate, and hence, are not exposed to devaluation. On the other hand, cash is translated at the current rate, which means it is exposed to devaluation losses. The current asset method translates both cash and inventories at the current rate. So, the local manager is biased by this method toward being indifferent between holding cash or inventories. They both are exposed to devaluation losses. Of course, to the extent the local manager believes local prices for his products will rise after devaluation, he will be biased toward preferring to hold inventory rather than cash. He can recapture some of his devaluation loss through these higher prices.

There are other possible measures of management performance. Some companies, for example, use the profit shown on the local currency statements. This can be a misleading indication of management's performance, since the rising local profit margins may be inadequate to offset local currency devaluation of the U.S. stockholders' dollar equity in the subsidiary. If the local manager has no responsibility for the financial aspects of his business, he may be measured in terms of translated profits before translation gains and losses.

Regardless of how the local manager is measured and the degree of control he has over his company's financial activities, someone in the organization must be responsible for seeing that the company's exposure to devaluation is minimized. This requires active, continuous planning and an aggressive approach to financial management.

SUGGESTED FURTHER READING

Hepworth, Samuel R. *Reporting Foreign Operations*. Ann Arbor: University of Michigan, Bureau of Business Research, 1956.

National Association of Accountants. *Management Accounting Problems in Foreign Operations*, Research Report No. 36. New York, 1960.

Wasserman, Max J.; Hultman, Charles W.; and Zaoldos, Laszlo. *International Finance*. New York: Simmons-Boardman Publishing Co., 1963.

CASES

Case 23–1. HEMISPHERE TRADING COMPANY

Translation of Foreign Currency Statements

On January 1, 1970, the Hemisphere Trading Company, with head-quarters offices in New York, established the Overseas Company. This new wholly owned subsidiary located in a foreign country was to carry on its merchandising activities entirely within that country. Hemisphere's investment of $60,000 (exchanged for the foreign country's currency, pintos, at the rate of 5 pintos for $1) was paid into the Overseas Company for all of its authorized capital stock.

Immediately, on January 1, Overseas borrowed 400,000 pintos from a local bank on a five-year note with a 20 percent interest rate. Fixed assets were purchased at a cost of 600,000 pintos, merchandise was acquired from local suppliers, and operations began on the same date.

Overseas' operations were spread evenly through the year. Interest on the long-term note was paid on the last day of each month. Overseas paid no dividends in 1970.

The following information about the price-level index in the foreign country and the official rate of exchange was available.

	Price-Level Index	Exchange Rate, Pintos to U.S. $
Jan. 1, 1970	100	5.0 to 1
July 1, 1970	125	5.5 to 1
Dec. 31, 1970	150	6.0 to 1

Changes in price levels and exchange rates occurred at a constant rate throughout 1970 and were expected to continue in 1971 and thereafter.

At the close of the 1970 year, the Overseas Company submitted the income statement and balance sheet shown in Exhibits 1 and 2 to Hemisphere Trading Company.

EXHIBIT 1

OVERSEAS COMPANY

Income Statement for the Year Ended December 31, 1970
(in thousands)

	Pintos	Rate	U.S. Dollars
Sales	1,000		
Cost of sales:			
Purchases	800		
Less inventory	200		
Cost of sales	600		
Gross profit	400		
Expenses:			
Depreciation	60		
Interest	80		
Other expenses	120		
Total	260		
Net income before taxes	140		
Income taxes	70		
Net Income after Taxes	70		

EXHIBIT 2

OVERSEAS COMPANY

Balance Sheet, December 31, 1970
(in thousands)

	Pintos	Rate	U.S. Dollars
ASSETS			
Cash	80		
Accounts receivable	300		
Inventories	200		
Fixed assets	600		
Accumulated depreciation	(60)		
Total Assets	1,120		
LIABILITIES			
Accounts payable	280		
Taxes payable	70		
Notes payable	400		
Capital stock	300		
Retained earnings	70		
Total Liabilities	1,120		

Questions

1 Using space provided in Exhibits 1 and 2, translate Overseas' statements into U.S. dollars. (Do not make any price-level adjustments prior to translation.)

2. After you have completed question 1, consider the effect that the following transactions would have upon translation:
    a) Overseas borrowed funds from its U.S. parent.
    b) Overseas borrowed locally, but its U.S. parent guaranteed the loan.
    c) Dividends were declared by Overseas on December 31, 1970 but were not remittable to its parent until June 30, 1971 because of exchange control restrictions.
    d) Purchases of equipment and merchandise for dollars were made from the parent, rather than purchasing locally.

3. Should price level be taken into account before translating into dollars? For what purposes would this be useful?

Case 23–2. **KIBON, S.A.**

Influence of Price-Level Shifts and Exchange Fluctuations on Management's Decisions

In 1941, Kibon, S.A. was established in Sao Paulo, Brazil, to manufacture and distribute dried egg products, ice cream, and confectionery products. Early in 1960, General Foods (GFC) acquired 75 percent of the outstanding Kibon stock. This case deals with the problem of translating Kibon's financial statements from cruzeiros into U.S. dollars. To help the reader understand the managerial implications of this problem, a brief survey of Kibon's operations is included.

Financial Results

Between the fiscal years (FY) ending March 31, 1962 and March 31, 1964, Kibon's annual sales rose from Cr$2.9 [1] billion to Cr$9.8 billion, and profits before taxes increased from Cr$288 million to Cr$1.7 billion. When translated into dollars at the average dollar exchange rate prevailing during this period, between the fiscal years 1962 and 1964, net sales rose slightly,

---

[1] Cr$ = cruzeiro.

from \$9.2 million to \$9.7 million, and profit before taxes increased from \$845,000 to \$1,723,000. Exhibit 1 presents comparative income statements for the fiscal years 1962 through 1964, inclusive. Exhibit 2 presents comparative balance sheets for the fiscal years 1963 and 1964. Both Exhibits 1 and 2 show the financial results in cruzeiros and dollars.

EXHIBIT 1

KIBON, S.A.

Income Statements, FY 1962 to FY 1964

	(thousands of U.S. \$)			(millions of Cr\$)		
	1962	1963	1964	1962	1963	1964
Net sales	9,177	9,495	9,763	2,910	5,379	9,767
Cost of goods sold	4,908	4,703	4,450	1,544	2,632	4,427
Gross margin	4,269	4,792	5,313	1,366	2,747	5,340
Marketing expense	2,600	2,399	2,430	813	1,300	2,342
General and administrative expense	375	320	321	116	178	311
Operating profit	1,294	2,073	2,562	437	1,269	2,687
Other (income) and expenses	363	509	623	121	297	738
Technical service fees and intercompany interest	86	210	216	27	117	242
Net Profit before Taxes	845	1,354	1,723	289	855	1,707

EXHIBIT 2

KIBON, S.A.

Comparative Balance Sheets as of March 31, 1963 and 1964
(in thousands)

	1963		1964	
	U.S. \$	Cr\$	U.S. \$	Cr\$
ASSETS				
Total current assets	4,095	2,457,514	3,149	4,093,490
Other assets	285	171,777	320	417,519
Net plant and equipment	3,190	995,791	2,704	1,354,980
Goodwill	31	9,565	101	59,818
Total Assets	7,601	3,634,647	6,274	5,925,807
EQUITIES				
Total current liabilities	2,994	1,810,959	1,610	2,093,769
Advances from GFC	1,000	596,688	823	1,070,551
Capital stock *	2,444	255,769	2,789	475,620
Retained earnings	1,163	971,231	1,052	2,285,867
Total Equities	7,601	3,634,647	7,274	5,925,807

* In 1963 and 1964, stock dividends were declared and an appropriate amount was transferred from retained earnings to the capital stock account.

Referring to the fiscal year 1964 profits, Mr. S. M. Jarvis, financial vice president for Kibon commented:

Profits are elusive in Brazil. You may be making book profits but you may not be making a "cash profit." Much of the profit we report has to be put back into the business to meet the increased costs of acquiring and holding adequate inventories.

Twenty-five percent of Kibon's stock was held by the public and was regularly traded. The Kibon stock was generally regarded as a "blue chip," although it had never paid a cash dividend. On several occasions during recent years, the stock had been split either two or four for one (called a "stock dividend" in Brazil).

Company Facilities

Kibon had three manufacturing facilities in Brazil. In the Rio area, and to a lesser degree in the Sao Paulo area, the company depended upon street vendors operating company-owned pushcarts for the distribution of its ice cream products. Kibon employed a large number of people in all of its operations. It was Kibon's policy to follow the cost-of-living index increases by making periodical adjustments to employees' wages. As a result, management believed that Kibon enjoyed excellent employee relations.

Marketing Prices

Mr. Jarvis believed that the rate of inflation had considerable effect on marketing practices. He commented:

Every time we increase our prices, we obviously lose customers. Special promotions help offset the negative impact of price increases, but we cannot expect them to have long-term results. Advertising funds would normally be better spent in establishing a solid consumer franchise. Nevertheless, with the pressure of inflation, we find it necessary to resort to planned promotions designed to help us reach our volume estimates in the face of consumer resistance.

We have been forced to raise our prices on popsicles from 10 cruzeiros to 60 cruzeiros within two years. Most of the people buying these popsicles are children; their income has not gone up six times during this period. Perhaps I am even exaggerating if I say that their income has gone up two times. As you see, every price rise cuts us off from a segment of the market that can no longer afford these particular impulse items. Our problem is to undertake price rises only as the need arises and to do this in a series of small steps so as to minimize the impact on the consumer. If you are able to make a small jump, say from 50 cruzeiros to 60 cruzeiros, you need to have some sort of promotion to offset the shock.

Product Line Development

Speaking of the company's product line development, one executive said:

The lines in which we are able to do effective development work are typically lines where we have the equipment needed to produce products. Most of our development work is limited by capital. We have to work within our existing equipment limits.

Legal, Financial, and Economic Problems

In 1964, much of Kibon top management's time was devoted to two legal matters: registration of the GFC investment in Brazil, and litigation involving pension payments to the Brazilian government on behalf of the company's ice cream pushcart vendors.

In 1960, when GFC bought a majority interest in Kibon from its former owners, the payment was not registered in Brazil. Subsequently, in September 1962, the Brazilian government passed a profits remittance law that limited annual remittances of profits abroad to 10 percent of a company's investment in foreign currency that was registered in Brazil. In addition, the repatriation of capital was limited to 10 percent per year of this registered investment. Since GFC's investment was not registered, GFC was unable to receive dollar dividends from Kibon. Immediately after the passage of this law, GFC began negotiating with the Brazilian government to register its Kibon investment. As of 1965, the investment had not been registered.

The lawsuit brought by the Brazilian Government Pension Institute maintained that the ice cream pushcart operators were employees of Kibon and, hence, should be covered by the government's pension plan. If Kibon lost this case, it was potentially liable to pay the government a substantial sum in past benefit costs (payable in cruzeiros and adjusted to reflect changes in purchasing power since the debt was incurred). The company had not created a reserve for contingencies to cover any losses that might arise from the Government Pension Institute litigation, because to do so involved certain risks. For instance, the company's books were continually examined by government officials who might conclude, if they saw the provision for this loss, that Kibon was admitting defeat. Mr. Jarvis estimated Kibon's chance of winning the case at "50–50."

Obtaining Funds

Another area of critical importance to Kibon top management was cash flow management. As Kibon no longer received funds from GFC (the parent corporation was reluctant to do so until its investment was registered in Brazil) and because of the general economic and political uncertainties, Kibon had to rely on funds generated internally or raised from local banks. During the fiscal year 1964, Kibon borrowed and repaid about Cr$664 million from local banks. The interest rate on these loans ranged from 2 to 3 percent a month (a few months' loan was regarded as a "long-term" loan in Brazil).

However, other loan arrangements were causing problems. In 1961, GFC made a *direct* unsecured dollar loan to Kibon of $360,000. By September 1962, when the new Profit Remittance Law was passed, Kibon had repaid $134,000 of this loan. But the new law blocked further repayments. Therefore, as of 1962, Kibon owed GFC $226,000 and interest payable on this loan had accumulated on Kibon's books and would continue to do so until Kibon could get the loan exchange registered under the Profit Remittance Law. (It was considered advisable to place this interest on Kibon's books so as to show proof of the foreign liability.) Kibon had to pay withholding taxes on the booked but not remitted interest because unbooked interest was not deductible under Brazilian tax law. Also Kibon incurred "exchange losses" [2] on this liability.

In 1960, GFC and the Banco do Brasil entered into a "swap loan" agreement whereby Kibon received a Cr$285 million loan carrying nominal interest rates from the Sao Paulo office of the Banco do Brasil; the New York office of Banco do Brasil received a $3 million interest-free loan from GFC in exchange. This five-year loan agreement was still outstanding. Mr. Jarvis was anxious to repay this loan, as he believed there was some risk that the Brazilian government might change its policy toward repayments. Also, for negotiating the loan GFC charged Kibon 1 percent interest on $3 million payable in dollars, which, of course, was accumulating on Kibon's books as a liability and causing further exchange losses.

Taxation Problems

Taxation decisions also consumed a lot of Kibon top management time. These decisions included: Should Kibon prepay next year's taxes and get a deduction from this year's taxable income, or should Kibon delay payment of taxes until after the close of the year so as to pay its tax bill with "cheaper" cruzeiros? Should Kibon reappraise its assets to reflect current replacement costs and pay a tax of 10 percent on the increase in asset values, so as to raise its capital base and reduce its exposure to excess

---

[2] Since Kibon's books were kept in cruzeiros and the loan was repayable in dollars, whenever the cruzeiro was devaluated the amount of cruzeiros needed to repay the loan increased. This increase represented an "exchange loss" to Kibon and was treated as a cruzeiro expense of the current period. This accounting entry was made only in the Kibon books.

profits taxes which were based on the relationship of profit to capital? Or would it be more economical to pay the 30 percent tax on "effective capital," i.e., paid-up capital plus undistributed profits?

The Cost-Price-Profit Spiral

Another area of concern to management was the maintenance of satisfactory gross profit margins in the face of rapidly rising costs. Management believed that it was necessary to raise prices whenever costs went up in order to be in a position to have the cash necessary to replace the inventories and therefore stay in business. These problems of gross margins and inventories were closely tied to the overall problem of purchasing. According to management, commodity buying was a hectic operation in Brazil. Anticipated price rises always resulted in a temporary shortage as well as temporary overstocking on the part of both customers and suppliers. Management believed that it was difficult to predict just what customers would do and just what suppliers would have available. This problem was further compounded by the uncertainty of crop conditions in Brazil, especially in cotton, peanuts, and sugar.

Long-Run Financial Planning

While short-run cash management taxed management's capacities to the utmost, long-run financial planning was a "nightmare." Kibon's financial policy, designed to "preserve General Foods' dollar equity in Kibon," was based on three assumptions: continued cruzeiro inflation; continued devaluation of the cruzeiro in terms of U.S. dollars; and an unwillingness on General Foods' part to invest more dollars in Brazil, at least until the Brazilian government registered General Foods' investment in Kibon.

Mr. Jarvis outlined Kibon's financial policy as follows:

1. Have Kibon repay as soon as possible its dollar loans, swap loans, and interest commitments.
2. As soon as Kibon could afford to pay dividends, amortize GFC's dollar investment in Kibon through dollar dividends to GFC.
3. If dividends were not possible, preserve or improve GFC's dollar equity investment in Kibon.
4. Hedge GFC's losses in Kibon by finding ways to use Kibon to benefit GFC domestic earnings indirectly.

In order to implement this financial policy: first, Kibon sought to have available sufficient working capital to maintain and, if possible, reasonably expand the business while at the same time having enough cash available to repay GFC dollar loans, swap loans, and interest.

Second, Kibon management sought to reduce the exposure to "translation losses" on GFC's books incurred through the devaluation of the cruzeiro. Therefore, management attempted to generate through operations sufficient earnings after taxes to offset these translation losses, as well as provide cash flows to finance productive capital investments which in turn would yield higher profits as a further hedge against the devaluation of the cruzeiro.

Third, to further limit this erosion, Kibon attempted to reduce working capital to a minimum and, at the same time, increase long-term assets and liabilities.

Kibon management believed that the company could minimize its current tax payments by expensing for tax purposes as many items as possible. This practice, of course, reduced profits after taxes, but it further increased translation losses by increasing cash in future years. Thus, Kibon management did not consider it advantageous to reduce taxes unless the tax benefit offset the accompanying translations losses.

As long as inflation continued and tax rates were high, Kibon management did not anticipate the accumulation of large cash reserves. Therefore, it attempted to keep avenues of local credit open, especially to finance the more profitable portions of its business. To do this, however, Kibon had to leave cash balances in its bank accounts to assure future financing in sufficiently large amounts.

Kibon's financial policy provided for limited acquisition of fixed assets in the near future because the company had first to repay loans and interest to GFC, and not because of any absence of profitable investment opportunities. Productive assets, executives believed, which created additional sales in turn created additional receivables and cash. These current asset items in turn created translation losses. Hence, when evaluating capital investment projects, management measured the return from those investments in terms of the additional profits earned after taxes, less the related translation losses. On the other hand, long-term fixed assets, such as building and land, offered no expense advantages, but their net book value did offer a dollar translation advantage.

The Kibon financial policy also encouraged the acquisition of inventories and raw and packing materials. These purchases made no change in the company's total working capital position and hence had no effect on translation losses or gains. While the company incurred inventory carrying expenses, it also had significant opportunities for "paper" inventory profits.

Investment of cash in commercial paper was considered advantageous by management, but only if the interest received offset the devaluation rate. (Current interest rates were 2.5 to 3 percent per month.) This alternative, however, was less productive than investing in inventory, because the net return from interest was very small. Lending excess cruzeiros to third parties offered possibilities only when substantial dollar interest on the loan could be paid in the United States. Banking regulations, however, limited Kibon's efforts in this area.

Internal Financial Analysis

All of Kibon's internal financial analyses were made in dollars, rather than cruzeiros. According to Mr. Jarvis:

In evaluating our business our utmost concern is its health in stable currency; namely, dollars. This is the way most successful independent Brazilian businessmen look at their businesses also. Sometimes when a business looks very good in cruzeiros but poor in dollars, it is a sign that business is rapidly heading toward bankruptcy.

GFC's Translation Policy

In order to convert foreign subsidiaries' financial statements into dollar terms for consolidation purposes, the book value of the assets and liabilities of the foreign subsidiaries were translated by General Foods from the local currencies into dollars at the rates of exchange prevailing at the year end. Land, building, and equipment and related depreciation, however, were included in the corporation's consolidated financial statement at the rates of exchange prevailing on the date the assets were acquired. Income and expense accounts, except depreciation, were translated at the average exchange rates prevailing during the fiscal year. The depreciation expenses and reserves were translated at the exchange rates related to the assets giving rise to the depreciation (Exhibit 3 shows rates for 1960–64).

The income statement for fiscal year 1964 of the corporation and its international division included an exchange loss of about $800,000, due to the devaluation of the Brazilian cruzeiro.

No adjustment was made by General Foods in the accounts of any of its subsidiaries to reflect changes in the local price levels prior to or after

EXHIBIT 3

KIBON, S.A.

Exchange Rates, Cost of Living Index, and Wholesale Price Index

	1960	1961	1962	1963	1964
Cruzeiros per U.S. dollar	205.14	218.50	475.00	620.00	1,850
Cost of living index (1958 = 100):					
All items	185	256	390	882	1,399
Food	208	280	442	993	1,617
Wholesale price index (1958 = 100).	181	250	383	853	1,354

SOURCE: *United Nations Statistical Yearbook,* 1963; and *United Nations Monthly Bulletin of Statistics,* March 1964.

translating the local currencies into dollars. Exhibit 3 also shows changes in the cost of living and wholesale price indices of Brazil during the period 1960–64.

Nearly all of the corporation's and the international division's accounting problems concerning exchange rates, exchange losses, and inflation involved the Brazilian subsidiary, Kibon, S.A. According to a GFC executive:

It's a neat question always which exchange rate to apply in the case of Brazil. The year-end rate can be most misleading, since the exchange rate is very volatile. For instance, the rate during the early part of 1964 jumped almost overnight from 1,300 to 2,000 cruzeiros to the dollar. In addition, there are at least three exchange rates: a free market rate to buy cruzeiros, a free market rate to sell cruzeiros, and the official rate. We usually take an average of the two rates we think are the most realistic at the time.

For accounting purposes, our Brazilian subsidiary does not revalue its assets in cruzeiros to reflect the changes in the general price levels since the assets were acquired. Since long-term credit is not available in Brazil, there is no problem about adjusting long-term liabilities for changes in price levels. According to our Brazilian management, to account for the impact of price levels would mean an increase of about 30 people in the accounting department. You see, they don't have very advanced accounting machines and many of their records must by law be entered by hand in bound ledgers. Also, they maintain that by translating their financial reports into dollars they approximate the impact of inflation. The devaluation of the currency reflects the rate of price inflation, they claim. . . .

Typically when assets are written up for tax purposes, depreciation charges remain unchanged for financial reporting purposes. . . . If a Brazilian company reappraised its assets for book purposes, but not for tax purposes, this might well result in pressure from the tax authorities upon the company to enter a tax return based on the reappraised values. Of course, this wouldn't prevent us from making the adjustments to reflect price levels at Rye if we wanted to do it. . . .

Questions

1. What is the difference between an "exchange" gain or loss and a "translation" gain or loss? Should Kibon include both translation and exchange gains and losses in its financial reports to its Brazilian stockholders? How would you report these items?

2. Assume General Foods wants to present to its stockholders consolidated financial statements including Kibon's balance sheet and income statement, what policy would you recommend that General Foods adopt with respect to translating Kibon's cruzeiro financial statements into U.S. dollars? Why? (In particular, indicate how you would handle the following items: cash, inventories, accounts receivable, fixed assets bought in the United States with U.S. dollars and exported to Brazil, fixed assets bought with local cur-

rency, depreciation, accounts payable, long-term debt, common stock, retained earnings, and bond interest.)

3. Do you believe the Kibon management is correct in maintaining that "by translating their financial reports into dollars they approximate the impact of inflation"?

4. Should General Foods apply the same policy you recommend for external reporting to the translation of Kibon's statements for internal management control policies? Currently, Mr. Jarvis is held responsible for achieving a "dollar profit before taxes, but after translation and exchange gains or losses." Therefore, the method used to measure exchange and translation gains or losses could have a significant influence on the measurement of his performance.

Case 23–3. ESQUIRE HOTELS CORPORATION

Measurement for U.S. Stockholder Reporting Purposes of the Annual Profitability of Investments in Overseas Operations

The footnotes to the 1969 financial statements of the Esquire Hotels Corporation annual report to stockholders included the following note regarding the company's consolidation policy:

The consolidated statements include all subsidiaries with the exception that the wholly-owned subsidiary, Esquire Hotels International, Inc., included in consolidation, adopted the policy, beginning January 1, 1969, of excluding from its consolidation the operation of certain foreign subsidiaries and divisions (formerly included in consolidation), due either to unstable political situations or to currency restrictions or both. The operation now excluded are those in Berlin, West Germany; Barcelona, Spain; Port-Au-Prince, Haiti; Istanbul, Turkey; and, Beirut, Lebanon. These operations are now carried as investments and income therefrom will be included in consolidation when received.

Investments in and advances to nonconsolidated foreign subsidiaries and divisions of $2,720,794 at December 31, 1969 exceeded the Company's equity in the net assets of such subsidiaries and divisions by approximately $1,340,000. In the opinion of management, there has been no permanent impairment in the value of the investments in foreign companies and divisions, and consequently, no provision has been made for possible losses.

Consolidated earned surplus at December 31, 1969 included $8,488,129, representing the combined undisturbed net earnings of consolidated subsidiaries.

EXHIBIT 1

ESQUIRE HOTELS CORPORATION

Esquire Hotels International, Inc. and Subsidiaries Consolidated Comparative
Statement of Profit and Loss for the Year 1968 (Audited) and 1969 (Unaudited)

	1968 All Units	1969 Consolidated Units	1969 All Units
Net operating profit:			
Acapulco Esquire	...	$ 18,543	$ 18,543
Puerto Rico Esquire	$ 643,703	855,618	855,618
Mexico City Esquire	48,696	255,711	255,711
Panama Esquire	145,907	188,466	118,466
Toronto Esquire	165,184	844,185	844,185
Istanbul Esquire	297,612	...	278,252
Berlin Esquire	(35,530)	...	31,745
Barcelona Esquire	122,435	...	143,156
Port-Au-Prince Esquire	(737,559)	...	(796,004)
Beirut Esquire	*	...	111,542
Total net operating profit	$ 650,448	$2,092,523	$1,861,214
Headquarters office expenses	675,678	482,159	482,159
Total net operating profit after headquarters expenses	$ (25,230)	$1,610,364	$1,379,055
Additions to or (deductions from) income	33,729	(355,931)	(350,888)
Total net profit before foreign income taxes	$ 8,499	$1,254,433	$1,028,167
Foreign income taxes	320,012	423,856	535,169
Total net profit or (loss)	$(311,513)	$ 830,577	492,998
Plus: Beirut Esquire net profits, 1968, received in 1969	...	144,606	...
	$(311,513)	$ 975,183	$ 492,988

* Opened 1969.

Exhibit 1 shows a breakdown of 1968 and 1969 income of Esquire
Hotels International by countries. It also indicates which of the subsidiaries was included in the consolidated statement of income presented to
stockholders. The information contained in Exhibit 1 was not available to
stockholders—it was used solely for internal management purposes.

Question

1. In your opinion, what were the profits for Esquire International in 1968
   and 1969?

CHAPTER 24

DISCLOSURE BY DIVERSIFIED COMPANIES

In recent years, a number of companies have diversified into more than one industry, principally through acquisitions and mergers. This change in the business environment led to a new demand from investors that the stockholder reports of all diversified companies disclose supplemental financial information related to the principal segments of their business. Previously, it had not been considered essential for fair disclosure that this data be published.

The principal issues raised by this new business development were:

1. Are there any circumstances under which the issuers of financial data should report the results of operations on some basis other than total company figures?
2. If so, what, and how should they be reported?

In September 1967, the Accounting Principles Board issued a statement, "Disclosure of Supplemental Financial Information by Diversified Companies." The board believed that there were:

. . . few practical problems involved in determining sales or revenues for segments of a diversified company. However, determining of profitability by segments in a form suitable for reporting to investors raises many complex problems.

Pending further study of these problems, the board's recommendation was that diversified companies:

. . . review their own circumstances carefully and objectively with a view toward disclosing voluntarily supplemental financial information as to industry segments of the business.

In the future, after evaluating the results of the studies of the Financial Executives Institute (FEI) and others, the board indicated that it planned to issue a definitive pronouncement on the subject.

In the meantime, in 1969, the Securities and Exchange Commission instituted a requirement that companies registering securities disclose the related contribution their major product lines and services make to sales and earnings (see below).

Diversification Trend

The diversification movement of the 1960s was characterized by the joining together of companies operating in unrelated or only slightly related industries. This type of expansion was in contrast to earlier corporate growth patterns which involved companies either integrating vertically to become distributors and suppliers of their products or horizontally to enter related businesses.

The principal corporate reasons for this diversification were:

1. To minimize economic instability resulting from cyclical market factors or overreliance on a single product line.
2. To acquire new products, technological know-how, and management skills more cheaply and with less risk through acquisition than by means of internal development.
3. To expand into nonrelated businesses so as to avoid the antitrust laws restricting horizontal and vertical growth.
4. To take advantage through mergers of the opportunity to boost earnings and sales through the "pooling-of-interest" treatment of acquisitions.

Investment Analysis

Concurrent with the diversification trend was a significant increase in the emphasis in the stock market on financial analysis and the role of the financial analyst. Increasingly, these analysts and astute, analytically inclined stockholders were frustrated in their evaluation of diversified companies because of their inability to relate the total revenues and operating results of these companies to their various segments.

The industry identification of the segments was essential in order to appraise properly for investment purposes the past performance and future risk and prospects of this type of company. For example, analysts noted, the fact that a company was losing money in one segment could be obscured from investors. These losses would be combined with the profits produced by other segments in the total company profit figure released to the public. Also, the relative importance of the diverse segments of the business changed over time. Without knowledge of the parts of the business, investors could not appraise how these changes affected the stability or risk associated with the total enterprise.

Management Reaction

Management was responsive to these requests and increasingly more and more annual reports contained data related to the parts of a business. Specific examples of disclosure noted by the APB in its 1967 statement were:

a) Revenues by industry activity or type of customer.

b) Revenues and profits by separable industry segment.

c) Separate financial statements of segments of the business which operate autonomously and employ distinctly different types of capital structure, such as insurance or bank subsidiaries of merchandising or manufacturing companies.

d) Revenues by type of industry activity and type of customer, together with a general indication of the profitability of each category.

e) Information that the operations of a segment of the enterprise are resulting in a loss, with or without disclosure of the amount of such loss.

The positive reaction of most companies to the Board's statement indicated that management supported the basic concept of full and fair disclosure. However, many of them, in letters to the Board, expressed a strong conviction that this should be on a voluntary basis and appropriate to the companies' interests. Forced disclosure of profits and revenues by business segments, they argued, might be:

1. Harmful, since it could be used against the companys' interests by customers, competitors, labor unions, and governmental agencies.

2. Misleading, if it led to uniform rules for reporting the results of operations by segments that did not permit the reports to reflect the unique characteristics of a company.

3. Misinterpreted, due to the public's general lack of appreciation of the limitations of the somewhat arbitrary basis for most cost allocations.

Financial Executives Institute Study

In proposing its new rules, the SEC considered an extensive study of accounting practices for diversified companies conducted by Professor Mautz under the sponsorship of the FEI.[1] This study involved an analysis

---

[1] R. Mautz, *Financial Reporting by Diversified Companies* (New York: Financial Executives Research Foundation, 1967).

of detailed questionnaires completed by some 218 financial analysts and investment advisors and 412 companies.

The study's findings were released in December 1967. Its conclusions stressed the necessity for the management of diversified companies, working within recommended guidelines, to make the determination of the information and group breakdowns which would be meaningful to investors. "Management, because of its familiarity with company structure," states the study, "is in the most informed position to separate the company into realistic components for reporting purposes. To require reporting on some rigid basis might fractionalize a company into unnatural parts which would not fairly reflect the results of its operations."

The report concluded that companies which operate almost completely within a single broadly defined industry, or which are highly integrated, should not be required to break themselves into smaller segments for reporting to stockholders. Companies which, to a material degree, have operations in more than one broadly defined industry should disclose meaningful information concerning their major segments.

The study suggested that any activity in a particular segment accounting for 15 percent of a company's gross revenue should be considered "material" and, hence, disclosable. In Professor Mautz's opinion, no present system of industry or product classification was suitable for the identification of industry groups for financial reporting practices. So, he concluded, it was essential to allow management discretion in defining the broad industry groupings used for reporting purposes.

Professor Mautz also recommended that disclosures be permitted in parts of the annual report other than the formal statements. Whether in narrative or tabular form, the disclosures related to business segments should be grouped and carry a clear indication of the limitations of their usefulness. The type of disclosure he recommended should include:

1. Identification and description of the components subject to separate reporting.
2. Disclosure of any significant changes from previous reports in the composition of the reporting components.
3. Disclosure of sales or gross revenues for each reporting component and the relative contribution in percentage terms that the unit makes to the parent's overall income.
4. Disclosure of the method for allocating common costs or pricing intracompany transfers of goods and services if it significantly affects the reported results.

Investors Survey

The Mautz study surveyed financial analysts, investment advisors, and corporate officers. The results of this survey indicated that the more important investment objective was a maximum return in the long run from a combination of dividends and capital appreciation. The most important company characteristics in achieving this goal were considered to be growth potential, managerial ability, and profits, in that order. The most useful measures of profitability were stated to be return on common stock equity, return on total assets, and net income as a percentage of sales. The preferred indicators of managerial ability were growth of the company, the return on common stock equity, and the personal reputation of key personnel. The growth potential of a company was best indicated, the analysts said, by the growth of its major markets, rate of growth in earnings per share, and research and development expenditures.

In the case of diversified companies, the analysts agreed that it was necessary to appraise the major segments of the business on an industry by industry basis before they could be considered in combination. They felt it was not possible to do this adequately from data currently supplied in annual reports, although a large number of them tried to do it by estimation.

The information concerning business components considered most useful by analysts was: net income and operating income, sales or gross revenues, and total or net assets devoted to the operations of the component, in that order. Most analysts apparently did not feel it was necessary for the independent auditor's opinion to cover this data. However, a large number of them did express a desire for a standard approach to defining reporting components on some product basis, such as the Standard Industrial Classification.

The minimum point at which it becomes necessary to report separately for a component was considered by most of the analysts to be when the component accounts for between 10 and 14 percent of whatever base was eventually selected. Some of the bases suggested were: sales, net income, assets employed, net income before allocation of common costs, and total expenses. Most respondents also indicated the maximum number of components reported upon should be 11 or less, in most cases.

Corporate Survey

After examining the results of the survey of corporations, Mautz was struck by the lack of unanimity or even proposed unanimity on any important point covered by the survey. He believed that this diversity of opinion was due principally to the great variety in business structure and practice.

While he was not able to come up with a precise figure, it was clear to Mautz that companies covered by the survey collected data for management purposes on the basis of organizational units. However, this was done in a variety of ways for a variety of management control purposes.

The sample companies split almost equally between those with a close relationship between organizational units and product lines and those with little relationship between units and product lines. More than half of the survey companies indicated they prepared fairly complete income statements by organizational units, whereas the remainder stated they prepared partial income statements of one sort or another for organizational units. Typically, the amount of information collected by product lines was significantly less than that available for organizational units. Yet, 34 percent of the respondents believed that the most appropriate basis for reporting data was by product lines; 31 percent supported an organizational unit basis for reporting; and 14 percent proposed legal corporate entities.

An analysis of the survey results shows that a large number of corporations could not directly associate their assets with either organizational units or product lines. About 40 percent stated that they could identify less than 50 percent of their total assets with business segments. Slightly more than 40 percent indicated that they could associate 80 percent or more of their assets with either organizational units or product lines.

Nearly half of the surveyed corporations expressed a preference for reporting the results of operations on a less than total company basis in the text of the annual report. Using the footnotes to the financial statements as the most appropriate method was proposed by 26 percent of the respondents. The other respondents indicated a variety of different methods.

Common Costs

A difficult problem in trying to determine the profits of business segments is how to handle common or joint costs. Common costs are those costs that are jointly shared by more than one business segment. For example, the headquarters accounting staff may keep the accounts for each of the company's components. The costs of this department are common to all of the company's operations. Typically, there is no clearly discernible way to associate these costs with the particular parts of a business. They must be allocated on some reasonable but nevertheless arbitrary basis if they are to be assigned to other parts of the business.

The FEI study showed that a great variety of allocation bases are used in practice to assign common costs to organizational units or product lines. Excluding common production costs, the study also indicated that common costs exceeded 10 percent of sales for 38 percent of the companies that reported internally by organizational unit. In the case of companies reporting internally on a product line basis, 57 percent of the respondents had common noninventoriable (nonproduction) costs in excess of 10 percent of sales.

While most companies allocated all of their noninventoriable common costs to business segments, the study revealed that not all companies allocated all of their common costs to components of their business, principally because they considered that some costs could not be charged to segments on any reasonable basis.

Irrespective of the degree to which common costs were allocated, a substantial variety of cost allocation bases are used. Some companies spread common costs on the basis of segment sales or profit before common noninventoriable cost allocations. Others use component asset or investment as the basis. Some allocate noninventoriable common costs on the basis of specific segment expense items, whereas others do it through negotiations with the managers of the operation affected by the allocations. Another approach was to use a basis combining several of these methods. In addition, many companies use more than one method for allocating costs among the components of their company.

Defined Profit

One way to minimize the subjective element introduced into segment reporting through the allocating of joint costs is to report the profitability of segments before joint cost allocations. This so-called defined profit approach divides costs into two categories: those directly attributable to a single unit and those not directly relatable to a single unit. The defined profit of the reporting segment is the difference between the unit's revenue and costs directly attributable to the reporting unit or product.

Defined profit is the contribution a unit makes to covering the company's total common costs. If the total defined profit of all of the segments is greater than the total common costs, the company will be profitable. The relationship between segment defined profit and company profit varies from industry to industry, depending on the mix of common and direct costs. For example, common costs such as advertising represent a higher proportion of total costs for companies dealing with consumer products than they do for manufacturers of industrial goods, such as machine tool companies. Consequently, the defined profit as a percentage of sales for these two business categories will differ.

A number of questions have been raised concerning the usefulness of defined profits: Will readers understand the limitations of this figure? For example, will they recognize that the relationship between assets employed and defined profit is in many cases meaningless? Will readers try to make their own joint cost allocations, based on an inadequate appreciation of the situation? What are the dangers for management in publishing this figure? For example, the defined profit for a segment will be higher than its profits after joint cost allocations. Will customers use this defined profit as an argument for reduced prices? Will labor unions use it, rather than the total company profit, as a basis for justifying wage increases?

Despite the fact that these and other similar questions have yet to be answered, nearly all of the investors covered by the Mautz study said they would find defined profit for segments useful in those cases where the allocation of joint costs destroyed the usefulness of the segment net income figure. Management was somewhat less enthusiastic about disclosing defined profits. They preferred a net income after cost allocation, since they thought it was less liable to be misinterpreted. About a third of the companies surveyed indicated they thought defined profit might be useful, however.

Transfer Prices

Transfer prices are those prices charged for goods and services transferred between units in the same company. The transfer price is revenue to the selling unit and a cost to the buying unit. These prices are not subjected to the pressures of arm's-length bargaining that exist in the marketplace, and hence lack the objectivity usually associated with sales to those outside the company. The costs and revenues created by these internal transfers are eliminated in the preparation of consolidated statements, since the transfers are offsetting and do not involve parties outside of the corporate entity. However, in the case of segment reports, these transfers would not be eliminated. Thus, the sales and costs of the individual segments may total more than those reported for the entire company on a consolidated basis.

According to the Mautz study, transfer prices represent somewhat less of a problem than joint costs. For example, only 24 percent of those companies surveyed reporting for internal purposes on an organizational basis estimated that their internal sales were equivalent to 10 percent or more of total sales. Of the companies with product line based internal reports, 37 percent used products internally which amounted to more than 10 percent of total production costs.

A variety of transfer pricing practices exist in practice, often in the same company. Transfer prices range from the equivalent of market prices to direct costs. Some companies base their prices on established pricing formulas. Others leave the establishment of the price of internally transferred products or services to negotiations between the units involved.

A number of factors influence the setting of transfer prices. In some situations, the prices of goods moved into states that levy taxes on inventories are deliberately set at a low value in order to minimize taxes. Some companies use their transfer price system as a management control device. The pricing approach used will vary with the different motivational objectives top management hopes to achieve through its control system. Transfer prices between foreign and domestic operations are sometimes used as a device to repatriate cash from foreign operations, rather than through cash dividends which may be restricted by exchange controls.

Reporting Bases

There are a number of different possible ways a diversified company could be divided for reporting purposes. These include:

1. Legal entities.
2. Organizational units.
3. Type of customer.
4. Geographical distribution of activities.
5. Product categories.
6. Industry groupings.

In many cases, there will be a close relationship between some of these bases. For instance, a legal entity may be identical to an organizational unit or to a product line. The rest of this section examines the appropriateness of these segments for reporting to public investors. The issue raised is: Can one basis be applied effectively and fairly to all companies?

The *legal entities* through which a company operates often bear little relationship to the operating structure of the company. Some companies maintain separate corporate entities to hold property, to meet state legal requirements, to protect company names, or to lease property to other entities within the corporate structure. In such cases, corporate operations are often conducted without regard for these legal subdivisions. Also, unless required by law, financial statements are seldom prepared for these operationally insignificant entities. Many argue that to ask corporations to prepare statements for such entities would be an unreasonable requirement.

Since most companies maintain fairly detailed records by *organizational divisions*, it has been suggested this segment might be an appropriate basis for reporting purposes. Certainly, for most companies, organizational data is readily available and could be put in a form suitable for publication at little additional cost. However, there are considerations that may make this kind of data irrelevant for security investment decisions. For example, the organization of most diversified companies is constantly in a state of flux as new companies are added. This makes year-to-year comparisons difficult. Sometimes the activities of divisions are closely related to each other, as they are in vertically integrated companies. In these cases, it may be misleading to split their common activity into parts based on divisions. Other arguments against using divisional bases for reporting are: the divisional organization may reflect historical patterns of doing business, rather than the current realities. In some companies, the availability of talented executives may determine how the divisional units are structured. Then, there is always the question concerning the ability of uninformed investors to use data prepared for managers who have considerable knowledge about the industries involved, reasons for the divisional structure, and the limitations of the data.

The risk of diversified companies depends in large measure on the *type of customer* they serve. One important breakdown of a business for investment appraisal purposes is between government and civilian business. Another is between ultimate consumers; middlemen, such as wholesalers and jobbers; and those who add value to purchased items, such as manufacturers. Dealings with each of these customers typically have different risk and profit characteristics. For example, the margins on government business are often less than on civilian business. Also, generally, the risk of a sudden cutback in the level of government is considered to be higher than for nongovernment sales. In addition, the things a company must do to be successful vary somewhat by the kinds of customers it serves.

Companies seem to be able to generate reports of revenues by type of customer fairly readily. However, very few companies keep records of profitability by customer, and to require them to do so might impose a burden upon them.

Investors are often interested in the *geographical distribution* of a company's business, since this is a variable that may affect the risk and profit characteristics of a company. The economic fortunes of regions change, and the extent to which a company has facilities and markets in these regions will affect its future prospects. Most companies split their financial records between foreign and domestic operations. Thus, these figures can be made available to investors with little additional effort. However, few companies keep records by regions within the United States or the foreign countries in which they operate. Consequently, to give regional data to investors may require recasting the accounting systems of a great number of companies. Some argue that the cost of this change may not be worth the value of the data to investors.

Product lines seem to be the most often-suggested basis for segment reporting. Clearly, it is of interest to investors to know how much each of the broadly defined product categories of a company contributes to its success. For example, it makes a considerable difference to investors if the success of a diversified company with computer, typewriter, business machine, and office furniture products is due mainly to its computer or office furniture products, principally because a higher price-earnings multiplier may be applied to the earnings of computer-oriented companies than to those of office furniture companies.

There is little agreement on what constitutes a product line. Also, there are many practical problems to establishing an all-inclusive, well-defined list of product categories which could be uniformly used by all corporations. Some companies, particularly diversified companies, view their product lines very broadly. Others see their product lines in narrow terms. One company selling canned foods may simply view itself as being in the food business. Another company in the same business may regard its product lines as being canned fish, canned meats, and canned soups. It may go even further and break these categories down by different trademarks or container size.

The product lines of some companies tend to blend together. For example, it may be difficult for a company that makes soaps, detergents, window cleaners, waxes, and polish to draw a clear distinction between the cleaning compounds and polishing products, particularly as some products both clean and wax.

Two other problems are encountered in trying to define a set of product lines as a common basis for component reporting. First, some products are used in other products. For instance, one diversified company makes circuit boards which it and its customers use in computers, communications equipment, television sets, and satellites. In this case, it is not clear to what product category the circuit boards belong. Second, product innovation is widespread and frequent in our economy. This creates a problem in that any set of established product categories may well become obsolete in a relatively short period of time.

Reporting segments of a business by *industry groupings* is similar in approach to product line reporting, except the categories are broader. It also has many of the same problems: there is no common agreement as to what constitutes an industry; industries tend not to be discrete, and they are constantly changing as new products and markets are created and old ones disappear. The APB's interim recommendation nevertheless did suggest disclosure of information by "industry segments of the business."

The Standard Industrial Classification and the Standard Enterprise Classification prepared by the Technical Committee on Industrial Classification, a committee of representatives of government agencies concerned with the collection and use of industrial statistics, have been suggested as possible uniform bases for product line reporting. The Mautz study does not recommend these systems for business segment identification because the business segments comprising the complex structures of diversified companies typically could fall into one or more categories of these classification systems.

NAA Study

In April 1968, the National Association of Accountants released an extensive study of external reporting for segments of a business by Morton Backer and Walter McFarland.[2] This report considered two major

---

[2] *External Reporting for Segments of a Business* (New York: NAA, 1968).

questions: What are the definitions of business segments that are significant to suppliers of capital? What kinds of segment financial data would best serve the purposes of investors?

The study's conclusions, which were similar to those of the Mautz study, were:

1. Investors and creditors have an important need for operating results of major segments of diversified companies.
2. Disclosure of sales and contributions to consolidated profits is needed when segments are affected differently by economic conditions, have different profit rates, or make a material contribution to company sales or profits.
3. No standard classification of business segments can yield meaningful results when applied to companies with diverse organizational patterns.
4. A uniform segment classification is not needed, since analysts do not regard intercompany comparisons of segments results to be significant in their work.
5. In each case, management can best define the most meaningful definition of business segments.
6. Contribution is the most meaningful measure of segment profitability where there are material amounts of joint revenues and cost.
7. No serious opposition to disclosing segment sales exists among executives.
8. Strong opposition exists among executives to disclosing segment contributions to profits.
9. Companies reporting segment earnings stated that the practice led to better understanding of their companies without any objectionable reaction of consequence.
10. Investor confidence in segment reports will be improved if these reports are covered by the auditor's opinion.

Securities and Exchange Commission

Until 1965, the Securities and Exchange Commission refrained from requiring corporations to disclose in reports to stockholders financial data related to their principal business segments. The Commission was reluctant to take action until full consideration had been given to:

1. The value of such data compared to its cost.
2. The usefulness of the data, given the problems associated with allocating costs and revenues between business segments.
3. The difficulties of establishing rules and penalties.
4. The existing trend toward fuller disclosure by corporations of product line data.

In addition, the SEC was already being furnished with some of this data. Form S–1 required a descriptive disclosure, insofar as practical, of the relative importance of each class of products or services which contributed 15 percent or more to the gross volume of business done.

The step-up in merger activity during the post 1965 years; the more insistent investor demands for fuller financial disclosure by the laggard corporations; and a greater interest in corporate disclosure by Congress led the Commission to take a stronger stand. During 1966, the Commission's chairman clearly indicated that unless all of the conglomerate corporations did not voluntarily improve their disclosure practices, the SEC would be forced to set disclosure requirements.

Subsequently, in 1969, the SEC amended its previous registration requirements related to the disclosure of product lines and services. Now, companies registering securities were to disclose the revenues and net income for those products or services that during the previous two fiscal years contributed at least 10 percent to total sales and operating revenue, or to income before taxes and extraordinary items had been deducted. For each product or service falling into this category, the company must disclose the approximate amount or percentage that each contributed to revenue and net income during each of the previous five years. If this is not practical, the company should disclose whatever figures they can that most clearly indicate how much of a profit or loss resulted from a particular product line.

Originally, in the notice preceding its pronouncement, the Securities and Exchange Commission had proposed that to the extent practicable companies registering securities report the approximate amount of assets employed in each segment of the business. Further, the proposed requirement would have required disclosure of revenues and net income arising from foreign sources and from government or any single, large customer accounting for 10 percent of total company sales, revenue, or net income.

Different Views

No one basis appears to be universally practicable for segment reporting. However, elements of all the possibilities discussed (with perhaps the exception of legal entities) can be appropriate in some cases. Also, the disadvantages of the Technical Committee's industrial and enterprise classification codes should not rule out the possibility of developing a similar system for component disclosure, although the task may be a long, difficult, and frustrating one. In the meantime, it has been suggested that the best solution is a flexible one which leaves it up to each corporation to use the basis most appropriate to its specific case.

Those who doubt management's ability to be objective in such matters are dissatisfied with this latter approach. To make it operational, they suggest that at least concrete minimum reporting requirements using some uniform system applicable to all corporations should be defined. In addition, others believe that the authority for determining the number of reporting units and the kind of data disclosed should rest with the independent auditor rather than management. Also, any departure from the minimum guidelines would have to be justified by management and the company's independent auditors. However, even those who take this position agree that the bases for disclosure should be broadly defined. Also, they concede that the base selected should most probably be related to markets, products, or industry, which, when broadly defined, are all very similar in meaning.

There are others who, while agreeing that investors probably need segment data, are concerned that component reporting will only increase the misuse of accounting statements by investors, unions, and government agencies. In addition, they argue, to pile the vagaries of component reporting on top of the existing uncertainties of financial reporting will only make the corporate reporting system more chaotic and less useful.

Component reporting is already an established corporate reporting requirement. The ultimate form it will take has not been determined. Even when some detailed concrete guidelines have been developed, the investor will have to be wary of how he uses such data. It can be very misleading unless the user has a firm grasp of the definition of the reporting base, the nature of joint cost allocation, the method used to price intercompany transfers, and the appropriateness of these three items to the company and its industry.

SUGGESTED FURTHER READING

ACCOUNTING PRINCIPLES BOARD. *Disclosure of Supplemental Financial Information by Diversified Companies.* New York: American Institute of Certified Public Accountants, 1967.

BACKER, MORTON, and McFARLAND, WALTER. *External Reporting for Segments of a Business.* New York: National Association of Accountants, 1968.

BAUMES, CARL G. *Allocating Corporate Expenses,* Studies in Business Policy No. 108; A Research Report from the Conference Board. New York: National Industrial Conference Board, 1963.

MAUTZ, R. K. *Financial Reporting by Diversified Companies.* New York: Financial Executives Research Foundation, 1967.

RAPPAPORT, ALFRED; FIRMIN, PETER A.; and ZEFF, STEPHEN A. (eds.). *Public Reporting by Conglomerates, The Issues, The Problems, and Some Possible Solutions.* Englewood Cliffs, N.J.: Prentice-Hall, 1968.

SOLOMONS, DAVE. *Divisional Performance: Measurement and Control.* New York: Financial Executives Research Foundation, 1965.

U. S. Congress, Subcommittee on Antitrust and Monopoly of the Committee on the Judiciary. *Hearings on Economic Concentration.* Washington, D.C.:

U.S. Government Printing Office:

Part 1.   "Overall and Conglomerate Aspects," 1964.
Part 2.   "Mergers and Other Factors Affecting Industry Concentrations," 1965.
Part 3.   "Concentration, Invention, and Innovation," 1965.
Part 4.   "Concentration and Efficiency," 1965.
Part 5.   "Concentration and Divisional Reporting," 1966.

CASES

Case 24–1. **QUAKER OATS COMPANY**

Business Segment Disclosure

The 1970 annual report of the Quaker Oats Company took special note of the death of John Stuart, who had been president of the company from 1922 to 1942, chairman of the board from 1942 to 1956, and a director from 1956 to 1964. The annual report stated:

When he joined Quaker in 1900, the company had one business—oatmeal. Under Mr. Stuart's leadership, the product base was broadened, and the Aunt Jemima, Ken-L-Rations, and Puss'n Boots brands were acquired. He was also responsible for Quaker's entry into the chemicals business and many international markets. . . . He had a special appreciation of the value of brand reputations, as illustrated by his comment . . . to Chairman Donald B. Lourie: "If this business were to be split up, I would take the brands, trademarks, and goodwill and you could have all the bricks and mortar—and I would fare better than you."

The 1970 Quaker Oats Company annual report presented as part of the text preceding the financial statements, a "Consolidated Sales Growth" chart (Exhibit 1).

The text of the annual report described each of the operating divisions: New Business: Fisher Price Toys (acquired September 1969); U.S. Grocery products: Cereals, Mixes and Frozen Foods, Corn Products, Burry, Pet Foods; Canadian Grocery Products; International Grocery Products; and Chemicals. The report also contained a description of many operating divisions (see Exhibits 2, 3, and 4).

Questions

1. Do the product line presentations give you a clear picture of the company's operations?
2. What additional information do you think should be included?

EXHIBIT 1

QUAKER OATS COMPANY

Consolidated Sales Growth
(adjusted to exclude divested businesses)

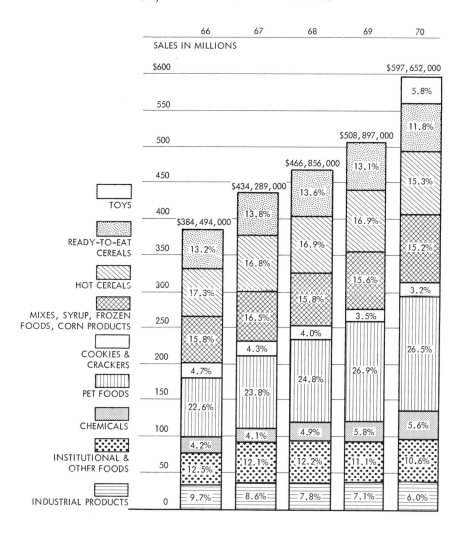

EXHIBIT 2

QUAKER OATS COMPANY

Financial Summary

financial summary

year ended June 30	1970	1969	% INCREASE (DECREASE)
	thousands of dollars		
Net sales	**$597,652**	$553,879	7.9
Income before income taxes	**53,966**	49,198	9.7
Income taxes	**25,823**	23,492	9.9
Income before extraordinary charges	**28,143**	25,706	9.5
Extraordinary charges	—	1,092	—
Net income	**28,143**	24,614	14.3
Preferred dividends	**490**	495	(1.0)
Common dividends	**11,737**	10,704	9.7
Earnings reinvested during the year	**15,916**	13,415	18.6
	per common share		
Income before income taxes	**$4.27**	$3.94	8.4
Income taxes	**2.06**	1.90	8.4
Income before extraordinary charges	**2.21**	2.04	8.3
Extraordinary charges	—	.09	—
Net income	**2.21**	1.95	13.3
Dividends declared	**.94**	.87	8.0
	thousands of dollars		
Net current assets (working capital)	**$ 89,901**	$ 80,241	12.0
Property, plant and equipment	**179,732**	141,399	27.1
Other assets	**31,205**	6,853	355.3
Long-term debt and preferred stock	**76,110**	26,719	184.9
Deferred income taxes	**16,931**	14,258	18.7
Common shareholders' equity	**207,797**	187,516	10.8

EXHIBIT 3

QUAKER OATS COMPANY

Financial Summary

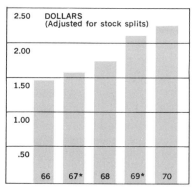

earnings per share

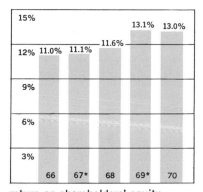

return on shareholders' equity

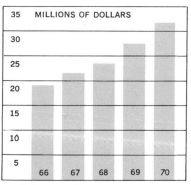

capital expenditures

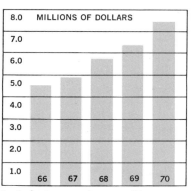

technical research expenditures

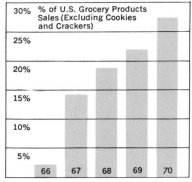

sales growth through new products
introduced since Fiscal 1966

* Excludes extraordinary items

EXHIBIT 4

QUAKER OATS COMPANY

New Business

Among the most significant developments of the year was the acquisition of Fisher-Price Toys in September, 1969. Fisher-Price is the leader in preschool toys, and one of the nation's major toy companies. The acquisition of this fine company in a growing and profitable industry significantly expands our business in the young family market.

Several Fisher-Price characteristics are illustrative of the type of company that is being sought in our acquisition program: high quality products, outstanding consumer reputation, solid base for growth, good management, and a logical relationship to our existing businesses.

We are pleased to report that Fisher-Price performance since our association has been excellent. Sales and profits increased substantially, continuing a long-term growth pattern. The rate of Fisher-Price sales increases compared to the year earlier was more than double that for the toy industry as a whole.

New products made substantial contributions to the good results. The Play Family Farm and Play Family House, introduced to the trade in March, 1968 and March, 1969, respectively, were of particular significance, and demand for them continues strong. Two new products introduced in March, 1970—the Play Family Action Garage and the Play Family Fun Jet—are receiving excellent trade acceptance. There are more than 70 items in the Fisher-Price line, 12 of them new in 1970.

In order to continue this flow of successful new products Fisher-Price's traditionally strong emphasis on research and development is being increased. The company's record of R & D innovation, in combination with its reputation for quality, is a very positive indication of future potential.

Since the acquisition in September, major additions have been made to Fisher-Price's facilities. Operations were begun in a Medina, New York, plant complex consisting of 42 acres and approximately 400,000 square feet of manufacturing and warehouse space. A 57,000-square-foot warehouse was built in Holland, New York. These moves have put us in a position to handle an increasing volume of business more efficiently.

U.S. Grocery Products

Cereals. Quaker cereal sales in the U.S. showed an overall increase of 8%. We believe that the increased public emphasis on nutrition is highly appropriate. In that context, the traditional value of oatmeal, which is still available at less than 2¢ a serving, is a distinct Company strength.

New high shares of market were achieved in hot cereals through the success of new varieties of Instant Quaker Oatmeal. Instant Oatmeal with Maple & Brown Sugar was added nationally during the year and Instant Oatmeal with Dates & Brown Sugar was introduced into 30% of the country. These flavored convenience hot cereals have not only increased our sales; through their high taste appeal and convenience they have brought the benefits of a nourishing oatmeal breakfast to many additional children.

Quaker ready-to-eat cereals also reached a new high market share at year-end, benefiting from two new product introductions and continued good sales of Cap'n Crunch's Crunch Berries, which were introduced in Fiscal 1969. Cap'n Crunch's Peanut Butter Cereal was introduced nationally late in Fiscal 1970. King Vitaman, which has unique taste appeal and 100% of daily vitamin requirements, was introduced into two-thirds of the country in June, with complete national distribution planned by fall.

On August 4, 1970, in response to the widely publicized and unjustified criticism of the nutritional worth of many ready-to-eat cereals, Dr. Robert O. Nesheim, Vice President—Research and Development, appeared before the U.S. Senate Subcommittee on the Consumer. Dr. Nesheim explained in detail the positive nutritional values

EXHIBIT 4 (*continued*)

of our ready-to-eat cereals, our emphasis on nutrition education, and the quality of our marketing efforts.

The original publicity had resulted from testimony by a civil engineer who has crusaded for elimination of hunger, an objective which we share. All of the professional nutritionists who subsequently made statements to the Subcommittee, including Dr. Nesheim and five senior university professors, cited the fact that cereals are nutritionally good foods. Continued increased public consumption of cereals is both appropriate in terms of good nutrition, and anticipated in terms of our business development.

During the year we also had some significant disappointments in three new products that failed to meet our expectations in the market place, and as a result have been discontinued. These were a nutritious oat flake cereal, a high-protein, vitamin-rich children's instant breakfast product, and our entries in the specialty snacks area. The food business is highly competitive, and when new products do not succeed in test markets there is naturally a negative effect on overall profits.

Mixes and Frozen Foods. Good sales gains were registered by the frozen foods, mixes, and syrup sold under the Aunt Jemima brand. Of particular importance was the continued sales growth of frozen waffles, where our products lead the market; the successful introduction of Aunt Jemima Complete Pancake Mix; and the encouraging test market results on Aunt Jemima Frozen French Toast.

In June, plans were announced for a major addition to our frozen foods capacity—a new plant which will be built this year in Jackson, Tennessee. The investment in this plant is indicative of the expectations we have for specialty frozen foods.

Corn Products. Considerable effort in research and marketing is being made to expand our basic corn meal and grits business through new products. Quaker Instant Grits, which like Instant Oatmeal require only the addition of hot water to be ready to eat, were very successfully marketed in three major areas of the Southeast. Instant Grits are being introduced throughout the country currently.

Burry. The overall results of the Burry Division were once again disappointing, although portions of the business performed well. Accordingly, at year-end we decided to discontinue Burry's high-cost store-door delivery system in the Eastern part of the country. Instead, we will sell through specialized distributors, which we have used in some other areas. While we cannot expect the same quality of distribution or level of sales for the Burry line in grocery outlets, we will have eliminated a major cost load that has handicapped the Division's performance. There will be some expense associated with this change, but the growing and profitable Girl Scout and Institutional segments of this Division should benefit from the action taken.

Case 24–2. INTERNATIONAL TELEPHONE AND TELEGRAPH

Business Segment Reporting

During the 1960s, in the attempt to maintain sales and profits, many United States based companies were expanding overseas. In contrast, International Telephone and Telegraph (IT&T), during this 10-year period sought to develop operating strength within the United States, rather than abroad. For example, in 1959, IT&T's operations were substantially outside the United States. By 1969, 61 percent of the company's sales and 55 percent of its profits of $234 million were generated by its United States and Canadian operations.

The company's 1969 annual report contained two presentations related to the major product groups of the company. The "Principal Product Groups" data were summarized on page 5 of the report (Exhibit 1), and a "General Grouping of Net Assets" exhibit was included as part of the financial statements (Exhibit 2).

Although no complete listing of companies included in the consolidation was presented, some specific companies were pictured or described in the text of the annual report. These included the following: ITT Avis, ITT Continental Baking, ITT Sheraton, ITT Levitt & Sons, ITT Jennings of California, ITT Howard Sams, ITT Hamilton Management Corporation, ITT Rayonier, ITT Pennsylvania Glass Sand Corporation, ITT Southern Wood Preserving Company, ITT Standard Telephone & Cables (Great Britain), ITT Alcoa, and ITT Bobbs Merrill.

In addition, each product group was described individually in the annual report, as shown in Exhibits 3 and 4.

Questions

1. Do the product line presentations give you a clear picture of the companies' operations?
2. What additional information do you think should be included?

EXHIBIT 1

INTERNATIONAL TELEPHONE AND TELEGRAPH

Principal Product Groups

Dollar amounts in millions

	Sales and Revenues				Net Income			
	1969		1968		1969		1968*	
Manufacturing—								
Telecommunications Equipment	$1,017	19%	$ 846	18%	$ 49	21%	$ 47	23%
Industrial and Consumer Products	1,533	28	1,290	27	66	28	44	21
Natural Resources	270	5	225	5	26	11	22	11
Defense and Space Programs	289	5	274	6	2	1	1	1
	3,109	57	2,635	56	143	61	114	56
Consumer and Business Services—								
Food Processing and Services	1,086	20	985	21	24	10	25	12
Consumer Services	791	14	683	14	23	10	20	10
Business and Financial Services	259	5	220	5	14	6	16	8
	2,136	39	1,888	40	61	26	61	30
Utility Operations	230	4	201	4	30	13	29	14
Total	$5,475	100%	$4,724	100%	$234	100%	$204	100%

*Before extraordinary items

EXHIBIT 2

INTERNATIONAL TELEPHONE AND TELEGRAPH

General Grouping of Net Assets as of December 31, 1969
(thousands of dollars)

	Consolidated	Manufacturing	Consumer and Business Services	Telecommunication Utilities
ASSETS				
Current Assets	$2,313,558	$1,628,453	$ 607,708	$ 77,397
Investments, Deferred Receivables and Other Assets .	667,551	254,518	351,201	61,832
Plant, Property and Equipment	3,498,244	1,786,677	1,044,175	667,392
Accumulated Depreciation	(1,286,766)	(766,025)	(384,881)	(135,860)
	5,192,587	2,903,623	1,618,203	670,761
LIABILITIES				
Current Liabilities	1,540,747	942,031	400,156	193,560
Reserves and Deferred Liabilities . . .	341,987	249,045	55,370	37,572
Long-Term Debt	1,145,383	528,518	400,733	216,132
Minority Equity in Subsidiaries Consolidated . .	83,161	47,585	15,046	20,550
	3,111,278	1,767,179	871,305	472,794
NET ASSETS	$2,081,309	$1,136,444	$ 746,898	$197,967
NET ASSETS EMPLOYED				
United States and Canada	$1,427,061	$ 675,622	$ 677,171	$ 74,268
Foreign	654,248	460,822	69,727	123,699
	$2,081,309	$1,136,444	$ 746,898	$197,967

EXHIBIT 3

INTERNATIONAL TELEPHONE AND TELEGRAPH

Social/Environmental Relations

1970 begins not only a new decade but a new era. Suddenly, new problems and ideas are matters of public concern: Environmental pollution. Ecology. Social Ambience. Public accountability. Involvement. Business is confronted with a demand that it show not only profits for shareholders but also contributions to the general welfare.

Historically, ITT has maintained throughout the System active social-environmental relations.

In 1968, ITT Chairman and President Harold S. Geneen served as honorary chairman of the first Plans for Progress conference—to promote equal employment opportunity in business and upgrade the skills of minorities. During that year, ITT loaned one of its executives to Washington to serve as administrative director of Plans for Progress, which is supported by 400 corporations.

Also, during 1968 and 1969, Mr. Geneen served on the first Executive Board of the National Alliance of Businessmen (NAB) and was chairman of NAB's Region II—New York and New Jersey (containing one-fifth of the nation's industry). During this period, NAB trained and employed more than 125,000 hard-core unemployed workers, and ITT alone hired four times as many as it had originally pledged—or a total of over 1,000 workers. Since 1963, Company workers from all minority groups increased from 2½% to 21%.

Representative recent ITT activities in the public interest include:

Pollution Control. All three companies in ITT's Natural Resources Group—Rayonier, Pennsylvania Glass Sand and Southern Wood Preserving—conduct continuous research into methods of combating air and water pollution.

Narcotics Education. ITT sponsors, in cooperation with the Institute for the Advancement of Criminal Justice, a unique program of drug education aimed at community leaders and the public. Through an ITT grant to the Institute, 20 seminars are being held in 1970 to alert communities to the drug problem, its growth patterns, individual symptoms, facilities for treatment and methods of curbing drug abuse.

Minority Entrepreneurship. ITT announced early in 1970 that it is sponsoring a Minority Enterprise Small Business Investment Corporation (MESBIC) in cooperation with the Commerce Department's Office of Minority Business Enterprise. ITT's MESBIC will provide venture capital for qualified minority businessmen who might otherwise be unable to obtain these funds from conventional sources.

In a depressed area of Boston, ITT Continental Baking Co. set up a baked goods store, trained workers to run it and turned it over to a community group which keeps the profits.

Job Training. ITT's Semi-conductor Division in West Palm Beach, working with Florida's Community Action Migrant Program (CAMP), established a unique project for field workers to become skilled assembly line workers.

Under the guidance of ITT's Industrial Relations Department, several operating divisions wrote specialized production-line manuals to train people from disadvantaged backgrounds. The manuals incorporated special methods where language was an obstacle.

Levitt and Sons operates training centers in Burlington, N.J., and Bowie, Md., for training unemployed to become carpentry mechanics.

ITT Gilfillan trains school dropouts to become sheet metal assemblers.

Public Recreation. ITT Rayonier offers the public free use of almost all of its 350,000 acres of land in Washington state for hunting and recreation, and also provides camping areas with cooking facilities. Over 50,000 people used these lands in a recent one-year period.

A bakery in St. Louis was given by ITT Continental to a local church. Community members in the depressed area surrounding the bakery converted it into a community center.

EXHIBIT 3 (continued)

The Future. A basic principle of our economic system has been that in the long run private enterprise will best allocate most goods and resources and serve the public interest. The achievements of this system have been immense, particularly in technology and economics. The new era challenges business to achieve social objectives directly and quickly. Business cannot solve all social problems, but it can contribute its special skills, methods, and resources to the search for solutions. ITT will bear its full share of responsibility as a business leader in social as in technological and economic fields, and will give even broader meaning to its objective of serving people and nations everywhere.

EXHIBIT 4

INTERNATIONAL TELEPHONE AND TELEGRAPH

Defense-Space

In 1969, ITT made significant contributions to defense of the Western World and exploration of space through both its manufacturing and service activities.

ITT Arctic Services, Inc. was established to assume U.S. Air Force contracts formerly held in the far North by ITT's Federal Electric Corporation. It operates, maintains, and supports nearly 100 communication sites that make up the White Alice Communication System in Alaska; it also mans the Distant Early Warning (DEW) System's radar and communication stations, and the giant Ballistic Missile Early Warning System (BMEWS) sites in Greenland and Alaska.

ITT Gilfillan, Inc., designer and manufacturer of advanced radar systems and navigational aids, received contracts from Government agencies for development of solid state, phased array radar—an advanced concept in the radar field and Gilfillan produced and delivered to the U.S. Navy 12 precision approach radar systems enabling aircraft to land in adverse weather.

Our Avionics Division contributed to the improvement of air traffic control with its new radar display BRITE, which enables control towers to view radar position of aircraft in daylight environment. This equipment is being installed in major airports by the Federal Aviation Administartion (FAA). Also, advanced air-to-ground and ground-to-air voice transmission for traffic control information is now being supplied to the FAA.

We continued to work with NASA's Nimbus weather satellite program. The Nimbus IV, scheduled for launch in 1970, will contain not only a night infrared camera and a day camera for weather mapping but also the new Filter Wedge Spectrometer, designed and built by our Aerospace/Optical Division, adding a new dimension to weather forecasting by measuring water vapor content of the earth's atmosphere.

ITT Space Communications, Inc. received contracts for large commercial satellite communication earth stations from the governments of Spain, Greece, and Colombia, and from RCA Global Communications Inc. to provide an antenna system for the Guam earth station, as well as for the complete earth station to be operative in 1970. Also, our major German company, Standard Elektrik Lorenz, received a contract to provide 12 satellite communication earth stations for NATO countries.

Natural Resources

ITT's Natural Resources Group is dedicated to use of the physical environment in the most enlightened possible way.

One example is that of ITT Rayonier Incorporated, one of three companies that make up the Natural Resources Group. Rayonier, whose basic business is converting trees into useful products, concentrates on raising the productivity of lands by growing timber as a renewable crop and by creating and applying new technology to harvesting and processing.

No less concerned with intelligent use of natural resources are the Group's other two companies—Pennsylvania Glass Sand Corporation and Southern Wood Preserv-

EXHIBIT 4 (continued)

ing Company. All three firms conduct continuous research into methods of controlling pollution of air and water.

Rayonier is a major producer of cellulose acetate, a highly-purified form of wood pulp used as a basic material in many high-volume products such as rayon, acetate, tire cord, cellophane, films, sponges, plastics. It also turns out other types of wood pulps, lumber, and a new generation of wood-derived materials known as silvichemicals. Its fastest growing segment is in cellulose for cellulosic fibers, one of the 15 major growth industries in the United States.

Pennsylvania Glass Sand is a producer of high-purity silica and special clay products that go into the glass, chemical, metallurgical, ceramic and building industries. Its basic raw materials come directly from nature—silica and attapulgite clay. PGS's extensive facility expansion is spurred by growing world-wide demands, including the need for special drilling muds in petroleum-producing areas such as Kuwait, Venezuela, and the North Sea, and by new oil fields being developed along the Alaskan North Slope where clay products are a constituent of Arctic-type drilling fluids. Also, major development is going on in suspension fertilizer technology and in new products for the paint and metallurgical industries.

Southern Wood Preserving Company protects one of man's oldest resources, wood, from the ravages of decay, insects, and other wood-destroying organisms. The firm also stresses proper procurement, handling, and seasoning before the wood is brought to the treating cylinders. SWP's first process, in 1908, was creosoting pine blocks to be used for street paving. Today the firm produces a full line of treated forest products.

PART IX

Financial Accounting Policy: Review Cases

REVIEW CASES

Review Case 1. **THE BOSTON PATRIOTS**
Setting Corporate Financial Reporting Policy for a New Company

The American Football League was organized in August 1959. Initially, it granted franchises to teams in eight cities, including Boston. The football season commencing September 1960 was to be the league's first season and the schedule called for each team to play each of the other seven teams once at home and once away. A postseason championship game between the winners of the Eastern and Western divisions of the league was also planned.

Organization of the Boston Patriots

The Boston club's franchise had been granted to William Sullivan, Jr., in November 1959. The club was incorporated in Massachusetts in March 1960 and was authorized to issue 100,000 shares of Class A common stock and 150,000 shares of common stock. Both classes of stock had a $1 par value and were identical in every respect except that only the Class A stock carried voting rights. Mr. Sullivan and nine other prominent New England businessmen each purchased 10,000 shares of the Class A stock for $2.50 per share.

In August 1960, the Patriots offered 120,000 shares of nonvoting common stock to the public at $5 per share. The Patriots hoped that this public stock offering would stimulate interest in the Patriots' football team and would also broaden their financial base. The underwriters of the stock anticipated that the entire issue would be sold immediately and that the remaining 30,000 shares of authorized common stock would not be offered for public sale. The underwriting discounts and commissions for the public issue were $0.50 per share.

The Patriots paid the American Football League $25,000 for the Boston franchise. Any proposed transfer of the franchise had to be approved by an 80 percent vote of the league members In addition to the original payment, the league received an annual membership charge of $1,000 from each team and 3 percent of the gross gate receipts from each preseason and regular season league game. The league also received 15 percent of the gross receipts from the postseason championship game. In addition, if the league required additional funds to meet its expenses, each team could be assessed equally.

The Patriots signed Edward McKeever as general manager under a one-year contract for a $20,000 annual salary. Mr. McKeever had been the head coach at Notre Dame, Cornell, and the University of San Francisco, and more recently had been engaged in public relations work.

Anticipated Operating Expenses for the Boston Patriots

The prospectus offering this nonvoting stock to the public included a "Statement of Assets and Unrecovered Promotional Costs" and a "Statement of Cash Receipts and Disbursements" from the date of incorporation through June 30, 1960. These statements are reproduced in Exhibit 1 and Column (1) of Exhibit 2.

In addition to these expense figures, certain additional expense information was available. Columns (2) and (3) of Exhibit 2 summarize this information.

Players' Travel Advances, Salary Advances, and Bonuses

The Patriots started preseason training with a squad of 100 players which was to be gradually reduced to the League maximum of 33 players by the start of the regular 1960 season. In order to induce players to sign up with the Patriots, $27,975 was paid in bonuses to players that showed up for practice. Three of these players received a total of $18,400 and a two-year contract with an option to renew their contracts for additional periods at a salary of not less than 90 percent of the original salary contract amount. All other players were signed to one-year contracts with options to renew at not less than 100 percent of the original contract amount. The contracts of the top three bonus players contained nonrelease clauses binding on the club. The other 97 players could be released (dismissed) by the team manager, thus relieving the club from the responsibility of honoring the salary contracts.

EXHIBIT 1

THE BOSTON PATRIOTS

Balance Sheet, June 30, 1960

ASSETS AND UNRECOVERED PROMOTIONAL COSTS

Current Assets:

Cash	$ 97,546.78	
Stock subscriptions receivable, due June 1, 1960	55,000.00	
Salary advances	10,507.77	
Deposits receivable	425.00	
Total Current Assets		$163,479.55

Other Assets and Unrecovered Promotional Costs:

Leasehold improvements, at cost, office and stadium		$ 4,589.00	
Furniture and fixtures, at cost		4,054.90	
League franchise fee		25,000.00	
Unrecovered promotional costs:			
General administrative expenses	$63,405.05		
Bonuses paid to players	27,975.00		
Other expenses	25,234.86	116,614.91	
Prepaid expenses		3,692.77	
Total Other Assets and Unrecovered Promotional Costs			153,951.58
Total Assets and Unrecovered Promotional Costs ..			$317,431.13

LIABILITIES AND CAPITAL STOCK

Current Liabilities:

Accounts payable	$ 1,000.00	
Accrued liabilities	576.14	
Other current liabilities	1,959.99	
Total Current Liabilities		$ 3,536.13
Deferred income, advance sale of tickets		63,895.00
Total Liabilities		$ 67,431.13

Capital Stock:

Nonvoting common stock ($1 par value) 150,000 shares
authorized, no shares outstanding.

Class A common stock ($1 par value) 100,000 shares
authorized:

Shares issued for cash (78,000)	$195,000	
Shares subscribed to and to be issued June 1, 1960 (22,000)	55,000	
Total Capital Stock		250,000.00
Total Liabilities and Capital Stock		$317,431.13

In addition to the bonus payments, salary and travel advances of $10,508 were made to 28 of the original 100 players. These advances were to be deducted from future salary payments and were not considered as bonuses. However, by August 1960, 9 of these 28 players had already been released and it was doubtful that their advances amounting to $4,318 would be recovered.

Salaries and Wages

Mr. McKeever received a one-year contract for $20,000 and Lou Saban, head coach of the Patriots, signed a three-year contract for an aggregate payment of $50,000. If, for any reason, Mr. Saban was relieved of this position before his three-year contract expired, he was still to receive the $50,000 contract amount. Mr. Sullivan received $25,000 for

EXHIBIT 2

THE BOSTON PATRIOTS

Statement of Receipts and Disbursements and Anticipated
Operating Expenses for the Boston Patriots

	(1) Statement of Cash Receipts and Disbursements to June 30, 1960	(2) Expenses Anticipated for First Season (to Dec. 31, 1960)	(3) Recurring Annual Expenses Anticipated after 1960
Receipts:			
Sale of 78,000 shares of Class A floating stock	$195,000.00	...	...
Advance sale of tickets	63,895.00	...	...
Total receipts	$258,895.00	...	...
Disbursements:			
Airline deposit	$ 425.00	$ 425	...
League franchise fee	25,000.00	25,000	...
Office construction payments	2,850.00	4,600	...
Stadium construction payments	1,739.00	200,000	...
Furniture and fixtures	4,055.00	4,055	...
Bonuses to players	27,975.00	27,975	... *
Salary advance to players	10,508.00	10,508	$ 11,000
Annual league membership fee	1,000.00	1,000	1,000
Salaries of directors and officers, to Mr. Sullivan	15,000.00	25,000	20,000
Other salaries and wages, office and coaching	31,208.60	88,500	88,500
Office rent	3,276.00	7,776	9,000
Telephone and telegraph	3,304.66	7,600	7,600
Hotel, travel, functions and scouting expense	12,277.80	22,300	22,300
Professional services, legal and accounting	3,750.00	6,750	7,000
Advertising and promotional expenses	9,795.17	13,000	13,000
Office supplies and expense	5,798.70	6,300	5,300
Insurance performance bond	2,000.00	2,000	...
Payroll tax expense	686.70	12,000	12,000
Players' uniforms	698.59	13,900	7,400
Total disbursements to June 30, 1960	$161,348.22		
Cash balance as of June 30, 1960	$ 97,546.78		

EXHIBIT 2 (continued)

	(1) Statement of Cash Receipts and Disbursements to June 30, 1960	(2) Expenses Anticipated for First Season (to Dec. 31, 1960)	(3) Recurring Annual Expenses Anticipated after 1960
Anticipated disbursements:			
Mr. McKeever's annual salary.....	...	$ 20,000	$ 20,000
Mr. Saban's annual salary..........	...	16,667	16,667
Players' salaries	...	289,080	297,000
Automobile expense	...	751	751
Trust account under B.U. indemnity agreement	...	50,000	... *
Liability insurance	...	22,000	... *
Surgical and hospitalization insurance	...	25,000	25,000
Annual stadium maintenance expense	...	25,000	25,000
Training equipment	...	8,300	3,800
Food and lodging at training camp.	...	32,800	32,800
Travel expenses while team is on the road	...	57,500	57,500
Total anticipated annual disbursements	...	$1,250,787	$682,618

° Uncertain or variable over a period of time (see text).

services rendered through the end of 1960 and had accepted a salary of $20,000 for the 1961 season. Mr. McKeever commented that $15,000 of Mr. Sullivan's 1960 salary was remuneration for expenses he incurred in obtaining the League franchise, $5,000 was payment for the time he spent in organizing the team, obtaining its financial backing, and scouting for prospective football players, and the remaining $5,000 was his salary as president for 1960.

Administrative and office salaries, in addition to those of Mr. McKeever and Mr. Sullivan were expected to total $46,500 annually, and coaching salaries over and above Mr. Saban's were anticipated at $42,000 annually.

No salaries were paid to any of the players during preseason training, but the contracted salary amounts were to be paid to each of the retained 33 players during the regular season. The players' salaries ranged from $7,000 to $15,000 with an average salary of $8,760. The salary contract provided that each player was to receive 1/14 of 75 percent of his contracted salary at the end of each game and the final 25 percent at the completion of the season.

Office Expense

The Patriots signed a three-year lease for office space for $750 a month and made certain improvements and changes to the building. Leasehold improvements were expected to cost a total of $4,600 and $2,850 of this amount had been paid to the contractor prior to June 30, 1960. The physical life of the improvements was estimated at 15 years.

Office equipment costing $4,055 was purchased for use by the office staff. The estimated life of all the equipment was five years with an estimated scrap value of approximately 10 percent of original cost.

Advertising and Promotion Expense

The cost of scouting for new players including entertainment of prospective players, dining with college coaches, and complimentary travel passes to Boston amounted to $22,200 for the 1960 season and was not expected to change materially in succeeding years.

The cost of promotional devices amounted to $9,795 by June 30, 1960. Mr. Moore, director of public relations, stated that this amount represented 75 percent of the annual amount he had budgeted for this purpose. He further commented that approximatetly $4,800 of this budgeted figure was the anticipated cost of 35,000 programs to be sold at the season games. Mr. Moore's annual salary of $7,500 was included in the figure for administrative and office salaries.

Cost of Professional Services and Insurance

The corporation agreed to indemnify Boston University against certain liabilities which may be assessed against it as a result of the use of its field by the Patriots, but not in excess of $150,000. The Patriots agreed to deposit $50,000 cash in a trust account which was used as security for this indemnity agreement. Mr. Sullivan stated that he was unable to estimate the possible liability under this agreement and no policy could be obtained to insure against this liability. Only the maximum limit was certain.

The corporation posted a surety company performance bond for $100,000 with the league to guarantee that the Patriots would field a team and play each scheduled game during the season. This performance bond cost the Patriots $2,000.

Liability insurance was purchased by the Patriots at a total cost of $22,000. This amount provided for a three-year contract that required annual payments of $10,000, $7,000, and $5,000, respectively, during the first three years. The coverage provided under this contract was deemed sufficient to cover any liability incurred by the Patriots. The contract provided for equal coverage during each of the three years.

The corporation's CPA believed that some amount should be set up as organization expense and amortized over a period of time of not less than 60 months as set forth in Section 248 of the Internal Revenue Code. It was his feeling that the entire SEC registration expense of $21,000, and some portion of the accounting and legal fees, should be capitalized since these were costs associated with establishing the company, not costs of current operation. However, the Patriots' management felt that since these were out-of-pocket costs, they should be charged off against current operations.

Stadium Expense

The Patriots contracted to use Boston University's football field for all home games on a rent-free basis. However, they agreed to make certain improvements to the field and bear one half of the cost of such improvements themselves, as well as to maintain the field in good playing condition. They agreed to bring the seating capacity up to 25,000; install adequate lighting facilities for night games; build and equip press, radio, and television broadcasting boxes; and make certain other improvements to the field. The anticipated total cost of such expenditures was $400,000.

The lease contract with B.U. provided that the Patriots could use the field for the 1960 and 1961 seasons, with an additional two-year renewal option available at that time, with no further improvements required under such contract. Mr. McKeever pointed out that a group of private individuals was considering the construction of a $25 million sports stadium with a retractable metal dome; an attached hotel, swimming pool, and nightclub; adequate parking facilities; and a capacity well over 50,000. He estimated that if this group decided to build such a stadium, it would be completed by June 1962. In view of the limited capacity, inadequate parking facilities, and other temporary arrangements of their present home field, the Patriots' management welcomed the construction plans for such a stadium and offered to lease it, when and if built, for $100,000 per year.

Training Camp Expenses

The cost of the football training camp for the 1960 season was estimated at $55,000 annually by Mr. Saban. This included the cost of food, lodging, uniforms, and training equipment at the camp.

The University of Massachusetts at Amherst permitted the Patriots to use the university's field for training purposes in exchange for certain training equipment purchased by the Patriots. The equipment cost $8,300 in 1960, but it was anticipated that only $3,800 would be needed during each of the two succeeding years, since some of the previous season's equipment could be reused during the following years.

Players' uniforms and equipment cost $13,900 for the 1960 season. Many of the training uniforms would be worn out at the end of the 1960 season and the 1960 game uniforms would probably be used as practice uniforms in 1961. The cost of replacing the game uniforms and damaged equipment and purchasing odd-sized uniforms was estimated at $7,400 for each year succeeding 1960.

Anticipated Income for the Boston Patriots

Television Rights.   In June 1960, the league entered into a contract with the American Broadcasting Company covering the sale of television rights to all 1960–64 regular season and championship games. The amount to be paid to the league by ABC depended upon the percentage of sponsorship of broadcasts of the games, varying from $965,000 at 50 percent to $2,120,000 at 100 percent. The Patriots had been informed that to date, 100 percent of the broadcasts for 1960 had been sponsored and that at least 50 percent of the broadcasts anticipated for the succeeding four years had also been sponsored. Each league team received one eighth of the total television contract payments, payable in equal installments in October, November, December, and January. Under the contract, ABC had to pay 10, 5, 10, and 5 percent over the sponsorship amounts called for the preceding year during the period 1961–64.

Radio Rights.   The Patriots arranged to have all of their games during the first three seasons broadcast over WEEI for fees of $9,000, $10,000, and $11,000 in the years, 1960, 1961, and 1962, respectively.

Concession Rights.   An independent concessionaire agreed to take over the concession operation for the Patriots at their home games. All concession income belonged solely to the home team. The contract specified that the Patriots were to receive 25 percent of the gross sales for granting exclusive concession rights to the concessionaire. Based on his experience, the concessionaire stated that he anticipated typical concession sales for an attendance of 12,000 would be from $2,200 to $2,800. The closer the attendance at the game approached capacity, the less would be the anticipated dollar purchase per person, he said.

The concessionaire also contracted to sell football programs at the games for a 20 percent commission. The programs sold for 50 cents each. and the concessionaire anticipated that 25 to 35 percent of the people at each game would purchase programs.

Gate Receipts.   The gate receipts were based upon the attendance at both home and away games. Under the constitution and bylaws of the league, which bound all teams, the home team guaranteed the visiting team $20,000 or 40 percent of the net gate receipts, whichever was greater. In August 1960, approximately 1,820 season tickets to the 1960 home games had been sold at $35 each. Tickets to the home games had an average price of $5 each. In August 1960, the corporation said it was impossible to make any estimate of the income from ticket sales.

Boston University Field had a capacity of 25,000 seats, comprised of 5,000 end-zone seats at $4 each, 1,500 box seats at $6 each, and 18,500 reserved grandstand seats at $5 each.

The Patriots were the sixth professional football team to be established in Boston. All of these teams failed financially, primarily due to a lack of public support.

Questions

1. What accounting policies would you recommend that Mr. McKeever establish for the preparation of financial statements of a publicly owned professional football team?

2. Would you support the argument of the CPA or the Patriots' management concerning organization expense? If you would support neither of these arguments, what would be your recommendation relative to the organization expense?

3. Prepare financial statements for the 1960 season, assuming that total current liabilities as of December 31, 1960 were $11,000. Calculate the balance in the cash account on December 31, 1960, based on information in the case and on the income assumptions you made.

4. Should the same financial statements be used both in assessing the Patriots as an investment opportunity and in reporting to the Patriots' shareholders at the end of the season?

5. Should the Patriots choose a fiscal year ending on a date other than December 31?

Review Case 2. TEXAS LAND AND ROYALTY COMPANY
Evaluation of a Corporate Financial Reporting Policy

On June 1, 1971, Peter Small, a faculty member of an eastern business school, interviewed Phillip Lord, financial vice president of Texas Land and Royalty Company. During their interview, they discussed Texas Land and Royalty's policies regarding the recognition of income from the company's various activities.

Texas Land and Royalty Company

The Texas Land and Royalty Company was founded in 1888 to develop certain Texas real estate holdings. Over the years, this land and royalty company became involved, through a series of wholly owned subsidiary companies, in a number of activities related to agriculture, real estate, and oil (see Exhibit 1).

EXHIBIT 1

TEXAS LAND AND ROYALTY COMPANY

Corporate Relationships

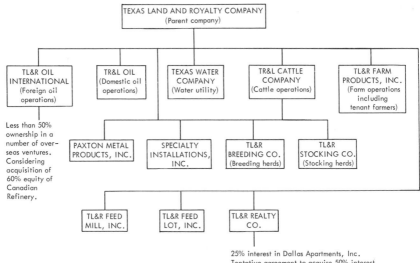

25% interest in Dallas Apartments, Inc.
Tentative agreement to acquire 50% interest
in New Orleans Industrial Park.

Initially, the company bred calves and range-fattened steers. Later, around 1903, the company created a water utility subsidiary to build an extensive irrigation system on the company's property. Subsequently, cotton was raised on this irrigated land by both the company and tenant farmers, who turned over part of their harvest to the company as rent. Both the company and the tenant farmers purchased their water from the company-owned water utility.

In 1938, oil was discovered on the Texas Land and Royalty properties. During World War II, the company leased its oil lands to a number of major oil companies who proceeded to develop the leases. In return, Texas Land and Royalty received a royalty on every barrel of oil extracted from its land. During the war and early postwar years, the company built up large cash reserves from these oil royalties. During 1969, oil royalties accounted for some 10 percent of the company's revenues.

Beginning in 1950, the company began to expand its operations. First, the company built a feed mill and acquired some feed lots in northeast Texas. The output of the feed mill was sold to the feed lots and used to fatten the company's beef cattle just prior to sale. In addition, the company contracted to fatten in its feed lots the cattle of other cattle companies.

Next, in 1958 Texas Land and Royalty acquired two manufacturing companies. The first company, Paxton Metal Products, sold small component parts to the capital goods industry. The second company, Specialty Installations Inc., custom-built and installed large machinery installations, such as complete automobile body production lines. Both these companies were wholly owned subsidiaries. In 1970 they accounted for about 18 percent of the company's assets and 8 percent of its profits.

In 1969, Texas Land and Royalty expanded its oil activities by entering into several agreements with major oil companies to explore and develop oil concessions in Canada and South America. Recently, one of these ventures had discovered oil in commercial quantities in northern Canada. In all of these joint ventures, Texas Land and Royalty held less than a 50 percent interest. In June 1971, the company was considering the acquisition of a 60 percent interest in a proposed Canadian refining company to refine the newly discovered Canadian crude oil.

During 1969, Texas Land and Royalty became involved in the residential real estate business. The company purchased a 25 percent equity interest in a newly formed real estate development company, Dallas Apartments, Inc. (the remaining 75 percent of the equity was owned by two national real estate development companies). After making this investment, Texas Land and Royalty entered into a sale and option agreement with Dallas Apartments to sell to the development company certain parcels of land owned by Texas Land and Royalty in the Dallas area. The first parcel was transferred during 1970. In return, Texas Land and Royalty received a note for $4 million, collectible during a period extending to a maximum of 10 years. These collections were contingent on Dallas Apartments selling the developed property to others.

More recently, Texas Land and Royalty Company had entered into a tentative agreement with another national development company to acquire land and build a $50 million industrial park in New Orleans, Louisiana.

Financial information related to Texas Land and Royalty Company is shown in Exhibits 2 and 3. Exhibit 2 presents comparative balance sheet data for the years 1969 and 1970. Exhibit 3 presents profit and loss information during this same period.

Recognition of Income

The following are excerpts from Peter Small's interview with Phillip Lord:

LORD: As I understand it, you are interested in the policies Texas Land and Royalty follows with respect to the recognition of income from its various operations.

SMALL: Well, why don't you tell me about your company's consolidation policy? This policy, I believe, is relevant to all the topics I plan to discuss.

LORD: Our policy is simple. We consolidate the operations of all compa-

EXHIBIT 2

TEXAS LAND AND ROYALTY COMPANY

Consolidated Balance Sheet, December 31, 1969 and 1970
(in thousands)

ASSETS	1970	1969
Current Assets:		
Cash	$ 2,402	$ 2,316
Marketable securities (Note 1)	14,100	12,600
Accounts receivable	11,000	10,012
Inventories (Note 2)	18,269	17,889
Other current assets	2,275	1,783
Total Current Assets	$48,046	$44,600
Investment and loans to associated companies	4,000	3,200
Property, Plant, and Equipment (Note 3):		
Land	$ 8,233	$ 8,483
Buildings	24,005	23,912
Machinery and equipment	21,293	20,665
Leaseholds	5,143	4,922
Land Improvement	9,201	8,436
	$67,875	$66,418
Less: Accumulated depreciation, depletion, and amortization	20,005	18,967
Net Property, Plant, and Equipment	$47,870	$47,451
Total Assets	$99,916	$95,251

LIABILITIES		
Current Liabilities:		
Federal and state income taxes	$ 4,601	$ 4,991
Accounts payable	3,500	3,406
Accrued property taxes	1,401	1,296
Other current liabilities	2,264	3,090
Total Current Liabilities	$11,766	$12,783
Long-term debt	2,600	6,600
Deferred profit (Note 4)	3,750	...
Capital stock (Note 5)	20,000	20,000
Retained earnings	61,800	55,868
Total Liabilities	$99,916	$95,251

The accompanying Notes to Financial Statements are an integral part of these statements (see Exhibit 3).

nies in which we have at least a 50 percent equity interest. . . . Incidentally, we report our investments in nonconsolidated subsidiaries on a cost basis.

SMALL: I have another general question: What do you think the stockholders of Texas Land and Royalty are primarily interested in? Current earnings or long-term capital appreciation?

LORD: Because we are the kind of company we are, asset values ought to be the most important consideration of our investors. Certainly our company policy is to develop future earning power. And, in an important respect, our assets represent the current value of these future earnings. Of course, this value is only significant when you produce the earnings. Nevertheless, the assets we hold currently determine to a large extent the future prospects for appreciation of our stockholders' investment.

EXHIBIT 3

TEXAS LAND AND ROYALTY COMPANY

Consolidated Income Statement, Years Ended December 31, 1969 and 1970
(in thousands)

	1970	1969
Revenues:		
Sales, royalties, and rent	$93,968	$92,111
Interest and other revenues	1,846	1,202
Total revenue	$95,814	$93,313
Expenses:		
Costs and operating expenses	$71,426	$70,001
Oil and mineral exploration	4,204	3,906
Selling, administrative, and general	7,016	6,847
Federal and state taxes	4,236	4,001
Total expenses	$86,882	$84,755
Net income	$ 8,932	$ 8,558
Less: Dividends	3,000	3,000
Amount Transferred to Retained Earnings	$ 5,932	$ 5,558

The accompanying Notes to Financial Statements are an integral part of these statements:

Note 1: Marketable securities are stated at cost, adjusted for amortization of premium or discount. On December 31, the market value of these securities amounted to $15,120,000 in 1970 and $11,3000,000 in 1969.

Note 2: Inventories as of December 31 were as follows:

	1970	1969
Manufacturing:		
Raw material and work-in-process	$ 3,211	$ 3,004
Finished goods	4,122	4,006
Cattle:		
Market herd	5,267	5,331
Breeding herd	3,621	3,100
Farm produce	1,233	1,640
Other inventories	815	808
Total	$18,269	$17,889

Note 3: All property, plant, and equipment is stated at cost. No discovery value has been assigned to the oil reserves related to the company's holdings in Texas. The cost of improvements to real property and of machinery and other equipment is being charged to operations in equal annual installments over their respective useful lives. For financial statement purposes, intangible drilling costs are capitalized and charged to operations on a unit-of-production basis. In determination of taxable income, these costs are deducted in the year incurred.

Note 4: In 1969, the Company purchased an interest in the Dallas Apartments, Inc. At the same time, the Company entered into a sale and option agreement with that Company relating to some of Texas Land and Royalty's land in Dallas. During 1970, certain parcels of land were transferred under this agreement. In payment the Company received a note for $4,000,000 collectible during a period extending to a maximum of 10 years. The profit from this sale was deferred and is being taken into income, subject to applicable taxes, as collections are received.

Note 5: Under the Company's incentive stock option plan, options at prices no less than 95 percent of market value at date of grant are held by 10 key employees and officers. These options amount to less than 2 percent of the outstanding stock held by the Company's 6,052 shareholders.

We feel that by all odds the most significant factor determining the value of the company is the earnings that it produces. The assets derive their value essentially from their earning power. The assets otherwise are of value only as a matter of ultimate liquidation. Therefore, we feel, as management, our primary function is to generate further earning capacity from the assets which we now have.

The foregoing is not to say that it might not be desirable to give share owners a more accurate or better informed opinion concerning the value of the assets of the company as related to current market. There is serious distortion in our balance sheet when viewed in terms of present worth. I think it can very well be argued that share owners deserve to have further information concerning present worth of the assets of the company. This, however, should not be construed as meaning that the management considers this to be a significant factor in determining the market value of the stock.

SMALL: If you don't mind, I'd like now to talk about specific aspects of your operations. Why don't we begin with the manufacturing operations?

LORD: Fine. That's a fairly straightforward situation. We treat Paxton Metal products as a regular manufacturing company. We are essentially producing to orders, and we recognize income as of the date we invoice the customer. Most of the orders are small and the production cycle is short. Few items are produced for inventory.

SMALL: Does Paxton Metals ever get involved in situations involving progress payments?

LORD: Occasionally Paxton gets into progress payment situations. They usually involve government contracts. However, because these progress payments contracts are so rare and involve small amounts of money, typically we expense the costs of these projects as incurred and treat the progress payments as income when received.

SMALL: You said "few items are produced for inventory." Does this mean some items are produced for inventory?

LORD: Yes. One of Paxton's biggest customers is the appliance industry. Each year Paxton supplies component parts to the appliance manufacturers. We build up large inventories of these items during our slow production months because we know we have *almost* assured sales. This practice smooths out our production cycle and helps us to avoid laying off our workers.

SMALL: When do you recognize the income from these sales to the appliance manufacturers?

LORD: When we ship and invoice the items. This is consistent with Paxton's general policy with respect to income recognition.

SMALL: I see, but what about Specialty Installations, Inc.?

LORD: That's a completely different kind of operation. Specialty Installations makes and installs a few large custom machine installations each year. These contracts typically involve progress payments, large sums of money, and take many, many months to complete.

In this case we pick up the profits as we accumulate the costs on each job. We take into revenue the percentage of the contract's total selling price to the contract's total expected costs times the accumulated costs. We follow this policy to avoid great distortions in income from year to year.

SMALL: Are there ever sales between Paxton Metals and Specialty Installations?

LORD: Sometimes, but these profits are washed out in consolidation.

SMALL: Could we now turn to your real estate operations?

LORD: Surely.

SMALL: As I understand it, most of the land Texas Land and Royalty Company owns was acquired before 1890. Also, this land is carried on the books at its original cost. Is this correct?

LORD: Yes. Our land is shown on the balance sheet at some $8 million.

SMALL: Do you think the stockholders would be more interested in knowing the appreciation in the value of this land, year by year, rather than just its historical cost?

Also, wouldn't the balance sheet be a more meaningful document if the land was shown at, say, its current market value and in current-value dollars? After all, the consumer price index has risen from, say, 100 in 1890 to something over 350 today.

Similarly, don't you think the annual increase or decrease in the value of the land should be recorded as some form of income?

LORD: Now you're putting me on the hot seat. Frankly, I have no idea of the value of our land, before or after federal taxes. There are parts of our holdings we could sell for $2,000 or more an acre. Whereas, there are other parcels we couldn't give away.

Also, there is another complication. We use our land primarily for cattle and farming operations. Now, if we began selling our land off in the fashion of a dealer in real estate, we would have to pay ordinary income taxes on the gain. We intend to remain in the farming and cattle business, so we are locked into holding our land. Under these conditions I am not sure it makes sense to talk about "market values...."

In many respects, the balance sheet is one of the world's most misleading documents. Therefore, it is important for people to understand what its limitations are. Certainly, it doesn't show economic values. Yet, if we tried to portray current market values or price-level-adjusted values, I think we might well destroy the continuity of the balance sheet, which I believe is important.

I will readily agree that assets are seldom, if ever, worth in market terms the values shown on the balance sheet. But would these figures be any more meaningful if I inserted your estimate of the market value for the historic cost? Perhaps we could have a professional geologist estimate each year the value of our oil reserves. Yet, from experience, I know that professional geologists change their minds about the characteristics of a field and amount of recoverable oil.

I suspect I would be willing to accept discounted future market values if there was some systematic way of arriving at these values. To date, I can't convince myself that a systematic procedure has been proposed.

What I try to do is produce an honest income statement which gives a reasonable picture of earnings based on conservative accounting practices. . . .

SMALL: Recently, you sold some land to Dallas Apartments, Inc. How do you propose to handle the profit on that sale?

LORD: First of all, let me say that this was a nonrecurring sale of property no longer economically employed in our business. Therefore, it qualified for capital gains treatment.

Now, as to how we propose to recognize the profits. Basically, after applicable taxes are deducted, we will defer the $3,750,000 profit on this sale and take it into income as collections are made. Also, we will recognize the income from this investment in Dallas Apartments as it is received as dividends. This will avoid distorting our income statement.

Incidentally, we have loaned Dallas Apartments some $2 million. We will recognize the interest on this loan as it accrues, because it will be interest income from a nonconsolidated associated company.

SMALL: Talking about investments, I notice you have some marketable securities listed as current assets. Why do you report these at original cost rather than current market value?

LORD: As you probably noticed, we do give the market values of these securities in the footnotes to our financial statements. However, to answer your question, we are not holding these securities for speculation. We are not a mutual fund. These securities are like our cash balances; they are simply liquid resources that we need to hold in order to efficiently operate our cattle and our farming business.

SMALL: You mentioned the farm operations—what policies do you follow here for the recognition of income?

LORD: In practice, this presents few problems. For instance, our policy is to recognize profit at the time the cotton crop is baled. We have a known market for the crop at that time.

Most of our farm income is derived from our share-rental agreements. That is, when our tenants pick their cotton crop, we get credit for one bale out of every four they press. The bales are not physically separated, they all go to market together. In fact, the cotton of the tenant farmers and the company is all sold through the same outlets. At year-end, about seven eighths of the crop is harvested. For practical reasons, we don't try to accrue the income on the unharvested crop.

SMALL: Is cotton the only crop you raise?

LORD: No. Currently we are developing some citrus groves on one of our properties. We are deferring the costs of these groves until they bear commercial quantities of fruit. This should take about three years.

Also, we grow some barley, which we sell to the feed mill. This profit is washed out in consolidation.

SMALL: What is the policy with respect to your cattle operations?

LORD: Our cattle operations are decentralized. We have three breeding ranches, four stocker ranches, and a feed lot.

SMALL: What is the difference between these three types of operations?

LORD: At the breeding ranch, we breed and raise calves. The breeding herd can be regarded as a fixed asset. The calves are then moved to the stocker ranches and fed on range grass until the cattle obtain a weight of about 600 pounds. This takes about 15 months. Then the cattle are transferred to the feed lot. After about 120 days in the feed lot on a concentrated high protein diet, the cattle reach weights of 1,000 pounds or more and are ready for slaughter.

Each of these operations is managed as a separate unit with a profit and loss responsibility. A breeding ranch manager may sell to one of our stocker ranches or to buyers outside the company, depending on prices. The same company policy applies to the stocker ranches. In line with this policy, we transfer cattle from one inventory to another, say, stocker inventory to the feed lot inventory, at market price.

SMALL: I gather a known current market price exists for cattle at each stage of their development from breeding ranch to feed lot.

LORD: Yes. From the overall company point of view, our policy with respect to cattle is to recognize profits at the time of sale to persons outside the company. Thus, when a stocking manager moves his cattle to our feed lot, the profit we credit to the stocker is for internal management purposes only. This profit is eliminated in consolidation. However, should a stocking manager sell to an outsider, that profit is recognized for external reporting purposes.

SMALL: Why do you use the "outside sale" criterion as the basis for recognizing income from cattle operations?

LORD: I think it is prudent. Also, our various herds are so large—about 200,000 cattle in all—that it would be a tremendous problem to come up with a reliable income figure based on the herd's appreciation and depreciation in value based on changes in market prices.

Incidentally, you may be interested in our inventory pricing policies. Except for our breeding herd and company-produced farm products, inventories are stated at the lower of cost or market. The breeding herd is carried at cost less accumulated depreciation. The company-produced farm products are stated at their market value at the time of harvest or market at year-end, whichever is lower.

All inventories are costed on a first-in, first-out and specific identification basis.

SMALL: That's interesting. You said earlier you had a feed mill operation. . . .

LORD: Yes. This is truly an integrated operation. The feed lot uses the barley grown on our own land irrigated by our own water utility. Let me take you through the whole operation.

When the water utility sells water to the company, the utility recognizes the profit. It is required to do this for utility regulation purposes. We in turn recognize the full utility price as part of the cost of producing barley. Insofar as the profit of the utility is included in our barley costs, the profits from intracompany transfers of water are not eliminated. There is always a slight time lag, however, since the costs of the barley not harvested at the end of the year are deferred, not expensed. These amounts are not material. Therefore, we don't worry.

Now, the barley is transferred to the feed mill at market price. This profit gets washed out in consolidation. However, we do recognize and report as part of our annual profit the feed mill's profit from the sale of feed to our feed lots. We do this for two reasons. First, we regard our feed mill and feed yard as two distinct profit centers. Second, the feed cost is an important ingredient in the formula for determining what is owed to us by those outside the company for whom we fatten cattle.

Let me explain. We sell feed to those outsiders who place cattle in our feed lots under two types of arrangements. First, we might sell grain by the ton. Second, we might sell an increase of so many pounds weight on the animals.

Under both of these arrangements, we are prepared to finance the outsider's purchase of both cattle and grain. As security we hold the title to his cattle when they are placed in the lot. We also agree to handle the sale of the fattened cattle.

In return, we charge the outsider the cost of the feed plus an interest charge on our capital invested in his animals and feed. These interests costs are accrued.

For parent company financial reporting purposes, the milling profit is recognized when the feed is sold to the feed lot, irrespective of whether or not the feed is given to company- or outsider-owned cattle. The cost of feed is then incorporated in the deferred costs related to the cattle operation. These deferrals are expensed when the cattle are sold.

All of these sales of feed to the lots are made at market price.

SMALL: Can we now turn to your oil operations?

LORD: We have two types of oil operations: domestic and foreign. Domestically, our oil revenues are the royalties we receive from our leased oil lands. The lessees pay us a royalty based on the number of barrels of oil they extract. We recognize the income at the time the oil is extracted.

Now, internationally, because we own less than 50 percent of the companies involved, we will not consolidate these operations. Rather, we will recognize the income from these operations when dividends are *received* in the United States. In fact, even if we owned over 50 percent in these companies, I think I would still follow this policy.

SMALL: Why?

LORD: Primarily because of the risks involved. The political climate of the countries touched by our Latin American ventures is very unstable. In particular, the threat of nationalization is always present in the international oil business. Also, there are numerous currency exchange restrictions which make it difficult to repatriate all of your current earnings.

SMALL: Is this true of Canada? It is a fairly stable country, isn't it?

LORD: Perhaps you have a point there. Maybe because of the relatively stable political picture, I should recognize the refinery income as earned and set up a reserve to take care of possible future exchange losses. Obviously, I'll have to think more about this issue.

SMALL: If you go ahead with the New Orleans industrial park venture, how will you account for its income?

LORD: If we go into this deal, we will have a 50 percent equity. Like most real estate ventures, this will be heavily leveraged. I think we plan to use about 90 percent debt and 10 percent equity. This presents a problem because, say we picked up all the assets and liabilities on our balance sheet and showed a 50 percent minority interest, Texas Land and Royalty's whole balance sheet would be radically altered, especially with regard to our debit-equity ratio. The numbers are so big, I am in a quandary just what to do. . . .

Question

1.   Evaluate the corporate reporting policy of Texas Land and Royalty Company. Do you believe the company's financial statements "fairly" report the financial condition of the company and its results of operations?

Review Case 3. **CONTROL DATA CORPORATION**

Changing a Corporate
Financial Reporting
Policy

Mr. William C. Norris, president of Control Data Corporation, included the following comments as part of the midyear report to the stockholders dated January 28, 1965.

The sales, rentals, and service income of Control Data Corporation and its subsidiaries amounted to $75,527,059 for the first six months ended December 31, 1964, as compared with $51,175,818 in the same period last year.

Net earnings for the six months ended December 31, 1964 were $3,256,136 compared with $2,504,446 for the same period in 1963. Per-share earnings on the common stock were $0.45 and $0.36 in the two periods, respectively.

The current outlook continues to be encouraging, with growing customer interest in the new 6000 line as well as the complete 3000 line of computers.

It is important always to bear in mind that Control Data both leases and sells outright its computer products. As I advised at the last stockholders' meeting, outright sales have the effect of producing income currently; however, income is realized in future periods when equipment is rented. Because of variations in the relative amounts of outright sales and rentals, earnings vary from quarter to quarter and year to year. It is expected that the business of Control Data will continue to increase at a substantial rate. There is no assurance, however, that the past relatively consistent rate of earnings growth can be maintained, due to the fluctuations referred to above. During the past few months we have noted a proportional increase in the number of rentals of our very large computer systems. Whether or not this is a temporary trend and will reverse itself in the near future is of course not known.

The "proportional increase in the number of rentals" accelerated following the release of the midyear report. As a result, the top financial officers of the company questioned the appropriateness of two particular accounting policies:

1. Accelerated depreciation of leased equipment (modified double-declining-balance basis).
2. Write-off to expense of all research, development, and marketing expenditures in the year incurred.

Introduction to the Company

Control Data Corporation was organized in July 1957 by William C. Norris, previously vice president and general manager of Sperry Rand's Univac Division, together with a group of engineers who had worked with him at Sperry Rand. Before that, Mr. Norris and some of these Sperry associates had helped start Engineering Research Associates, Inc., an early pioneer in electronic computers which was acquired by Remington Rand in 1952 and became part of the Univac Division of Sperry Rand by merger in 1955.

Control Data Corporation and its subsidiaries developed, designed, manufactured, and marketed advanced, fully transistorized, high-speed digital computing systems and related component and peripheral equipment, including input-output devices for use with computers.

Control Data emphasized applied research and development in both the development of programs (software) to apply computers to the solution of problems and the development of the equipment (hardware) itself.

The product lines of the company were either sold or leased to its customers, and data processing and other technical services were provided by data centers as well as through other divisions and subsidiaries. Approximately 50 percent of the company's business was transacted with the United States government and its prime contractors. The three major functional market areas served by the company were:

Industrial and business	25%
Space and defense	45%
Science and education	30%

From its incorporation on July 8, 1957, the company had experienced rapid growth through the development of new products and market areas and through the acquisition of more than 20 companies.

Exhibits 1 and 2 contain summary consolidated balance sheets and consolidated statements of earnings for the seven years from 1958 to 1964.

The Industry

Only a dozen years old, the electronic data processing industry had in service about 20,000 general-purpose computers worth about $7 billion at original sales value, of which $1.75 billion was estimated to have been installed in 1963. These figures do not include special computers for military and space applications, which probably added another $1 billion in 1963.

Projections for the future were subject to particular uncertainties: prices and obsolescence rates could be affected by design improvements;

EXHIBIT 1

CONTROL DATA CORPORATION

Summary Consolidated Balance Sheets for Years Ending June 30
(in millions)

	1958	1959	1960	1961	1962	1963	1964
Current assets	$1	$2	$6	$14	$27	$47	$ 99
Net property, plant, and equipment	..	..	2	5	13	21	32
Investments and other assets	..	..	..	...	...	2	2
	$1	$2	$8	$19	$40	$70	$133
Current liabilities	$.	$.	$4	$ 9	$17	$21	$ 36
Long-term debt	..	..	..	...	...	20	37
Stockholders' equity	..	2	4	10	23	29	60
	$1	$2	$8	$19	$40	$70	$133

Columns do not necessarily add due to rounding.
SOURCE: Prepared by the casewriter from annual reports of Control Data.

EXHIBIT 2

CONTROL DATA CORPORATION

Summary Consolidated Statement of Earnings for Years Ended June 30
(in millions)

	1958	1959	1960	1961	1962	1963	1964
Net sales	$1	$5	$9	$18	$32	$45	$ 96
Rentals and service income	..	..	..	2	9	18	26
Total revenues	$1	$5	$9	$20	$41	$63	$ 122
All expenses	1	5	8	18	37	55	107
Profit before income tax	..	..	$1	$ 2	$ 4	$ 8	$ 15
Income tax	..	..	..	1	2	5	9
Profit after tax	..	..	$1	$ 1	$ 2	$ 3	$ 6
Earnings per share*	$(0.04)	$0.07	$0.12	$0.16	$0.26	$0.50	$0.88

* Adjusted for stock splits.
SOURCE: Prepared by the casewriter from annual reports.

the ratio of sales to rentals could shift; revenues from new equipment could be limited by the growing availability of serviceable used equipment. Nevertheless, the most conservative estimates indicated that the average annual compound growth between 1964 and 1970 would be 20 percent.

Many well-known companies shared a part of the electronic data processing industry. The market shares, based on the selling value of installed equipment, were estimated by one firm of security analysts in a report made available to the investing public in January 1965:

International Business Machines 72.0%
Sperry Rand 8.7
Control Data 4.5
Radio Corp. of America ,,, ,,,,.............. 2.9
Honeywell 2.5
Burroughs 2.4
National Cash Register 2.2
General Electric 2.1
All others 2.7
                                            ───────
                                             100.0%

Of the above-named firms, Control Data was the only company producing just computers and peripheral equipment. IBM, for example, produced typewriters, dictating equipment, etc., in addition to computers. Thus it was not possible to say for certain how profitable the computer segment was for each of the companies in the industry, based on public documents. However, it was widely speculated that IBM and Control Data were the only companies "making a profit" on their computer business.

Growth of Control Data

As noted in Exhibits 1 and 2, the company had expanded rapidly since its inception in 1957. Although all of the expansion had been in computers, peripheral equipment, and software, the growth cannot be described as uniform. That is, new models of computers were added to "first-generation" computers, "second-generation" computers were delivered, marketing strategy was altered, prices were changed, and new peripheral products were developed.

Leasing Trends

Traditionally the company's orders for equipment were in the form of sales rather than leases. The first lease revenue appeared in the 1960 financial statements. The percentage of rentals and service income relative to total revenue was as follows:

1958 .... 0%[1]
1959 0
1960 2
1961 9
1962 22
1963 29
1964 21
1965 .... N.A.

[1] These figures were calculated from the company's annual reports. N.A. indicates not available in the midyear report.

The above figures reflected the impact on the financial statements of the switch on the part of customers from buying to leasing computers. The trend toward leasing was even more pronounced than is indicated above, and can be measured by the percentage of sales orders which represents sales value of lease orders:

1961	25%
1962	30
1963	40
1964	40
1965	N.A.

Thus in 1964, 40 percent of the equivalent sales value of orders signed during the year was for leased equipment. Note from the preceding table that only 21 percent of the total revenue for the year was from rental and service income. The difference in the percentages reflected the fact that one year's rental was equal to about one fourth of the total sales price. Thus, during the first year of a lease, only one fourth of the equivalent sales price was received as revenue.

Pricing Policy

As noted earlier, the company accepted orders for sale and rental of its products. Exhibit 3 presents the price of the average installation of key models, based on information in an analyst's report.

EXHIBIT 3

Equipment Prices before and after July 1, 1964
(in thousands)

Model	Average Price		Rental per Month	
	Before	After	Before	After
3200	$ 700	$ 500	$ 15	$ 12
3600	2,400	2,300	60	41
6600	7,900	6,900	197	116

In the report of the seventh annual stockholders' meeting in September 1964, the president commented that,

Today the rate of gross profit on our computer systems is greater than any time in the history of Control Data . . . even though we are also at the same time offering more computing per dollar to our customers through reduced selling prices. These reductions in selling prices have come about for a number of reasons, the principal one being the reduction in manufacturing costs, particularly in the cost of components.

EXHIBIT 4

CONTROL DATA CORPORATION

Summary Statement of Sources and Uses of Funds
For the Two Years Ended June 30, 1964
(in thousands)

Sources of Funds:
Long-term debt:
Convertible subordinated

debentures, 3.75%, due February 1, 1989	$35,000	
Equipment purchase contract	2,210	
Other mortgages and debt (net increase)	63	$37,273
Common stock, new issues		29,163
Net earnings	$ 8,748	
Add charges not representing current outlays of funds:		
depreciation, amortization, etc.	22,269	31,017
Total Sources of Funds		$97,453

Uses of Funds:

Investment in property, plant, equipment, and		
other deferred charges		$42,455
Reduction in 6% cumulative preferred stock		350
Treasury stock held by consolidated subsidiary		1,332
Increase in working capital (see below)		53,316
Total Uses of Funds		$97,453

Summary Statement of Changes in Working Capital
For the Two Years Ended June 30, 1964
(in thousands)

Investment in current assets:		
Cash		$ 2,760
Receivables:		
Trade accounts	$12,858	
Unbilled costs and earnings	19,566	
Other	555	32,979
Inventories:		
Work in process	$24,204	
Raw materials and purchased parts	11,703	35,907
Prepaid expenses and deposits		772
Net investment in current assets		$72,418
Less: Increase in current liabilities:		
Notes payable to banks (decrease)		$(7,299)
Current maturities of long-term debt		1,320
Accounts payable		4,894
Customer advances		6,242
Accrued taxes		11,261
Other accrued liabilities		2,684
		$19,102
Increase in Working Capital		$53,316

SOURCE: Prepared by the casewriter from annual reports.

Financing

Exhibit 4 presents a summary statement of the sources and uses of funds for the two-year period from June 30, 1962 to June 30, 1964.

Based on an analysis of annual reports for 1962 and 1964, certain investments increased substantially during the two-year period (percentages are of the dollar amounts of investment at June 30, 1962):

Property, plant, and equipment 330%
Trade accounts receivable 220
Unbilled costs and earnings on contracts in process 270
Work-in-process inventory 250
Raw materials and purchased parts 530

The sources of funds for these investments were, about equally, long-term debt, common stock, and net earnings plus charges not representing current outlays of funds—depreciation, amortization, etc.

The latest public financing was the 3.75 percent convertible subordinated debentures, due February 1, 1989, issued at 102 in February 1964 and convertible at $86.67. This issue raised $35 million to pay outstanding bank loans and to redeem the company's outstanding 6 percent preferred stock. Prior to this undertaking, the company called for redemption all of the 4.25 percent convertible subordinated debentures issued in September 1962. Before the redemption date, substantially all of these debentures were converted into common stock at $43 per share. Exhibit 5 contains a list of public financing for 1962–64.

EXHIBIT 5

CONTROL DATA CORPORATION

Public Financing, 1962–64
(in thousands)

Year Ended June 30		Approximate Amount*
1962	Common stock	$12,000
1963	Common stock	$ 3,000
	Equipment purchase contract	4,500
	Convertible subordinated debentures, 4.25%	15,000
		$22,500
1964	Common stock	$23,000
	Convertible subordinated debentures, 3.75%	35,000
		$58,000

* Approximate amounts do not necessarily represent cash received. In each of the three years, some of the common stock issued was for acquisition of other companies. Also, the $15 million 4.25 percent convertible subordinated debentures issued in fiscal 1963 were called for redemption in fiscal 1964, and substantially all of them were converted into common stock.

SOURCE: Prepared by the casewriter from annual reports.

Future Growth

At the seventh annual stockholders' meeting of the company, Mr. Norris told the stockholders:

> ... Simply stated, in my opinion the outlook is very good for substantial continued growth in sales and earnings for Control Data.
>
> As a matter of policy, we never have publicly announced numbers on what we are planning for in the way of future sales and earnings, and this policy is still the right one for us. There are a number of reasons why we believe this is the proper policy . . . [because] it is extremely difficult for us to accurately forecast sales and earnings. The primary reason for this difficulty is the fact that our average unit sale is large in value. A number of "uncertainty" factors result from this. I will mention a few of the most important.
>
> First, an error in forecasts for even a small number of sales will cause a large dollar error. Second, inability to forecast whether "sale" or "rental" will similarly mean a large dollar error. Third, because of the large commitment involved for the buyer, many approvals are necessary. . . . Thus it is hard to "pin down" probable order dates. Fourth, the entire computer industry changes so fast that competitive actions or slight delays in new product deliveries can throw forecasts off in either direction, up or down.
>
> We do not wish to mislead anyone by making public forecasts which could be significantly in error. So when I say that the outlook is very good for substantial continued growth in sales and earnings, I am speaking more in the long-term sense—in other words, averaging out the peaks and valleys; the highs and the lows.[1]

The growth of the company's revenues and profits over the last six years is depicted graphically in Exhibit 6. During fiscal 1964, the increase in revenues and earnings was 100 percent over the respective amounts for fiscal 1963.

The market range of the company's common stock from 1960 to 1965 appears in Exhibit 7.

Depreciation Policy for Leased Computers

The company consistently followed the practice of depreciating *leased* computing systems over a four-year period on an accelerated basis: a modified double-declining-balance method. For example, assuming a cost of $1 million to be depreciated over four years, the charges for depreciation would be as shown in Exhibit 8.

The company used the same basis (double-declining-balance) on its tax returns as it did for financial reporting purposes.

---

[1] From the report of the seventh annual stockholders' meeting of Control Data Corporation.

EXHIBIT 6

Earnings
Per Common
Share After
Preferred
Stock
Dividends

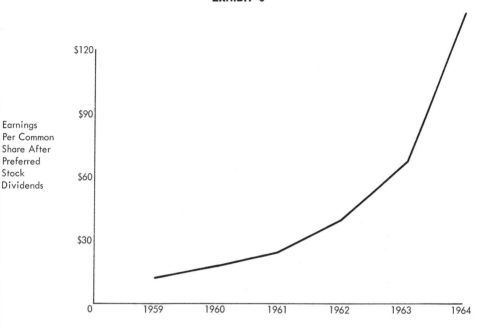

Net Sales,
Rentals
and Service
Income
(Dollars in
Millions)

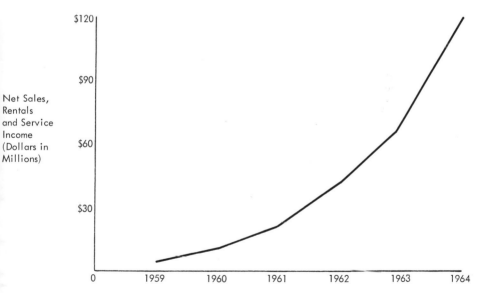

SOURCE: Prepared by the casewriter from annual reports.

EXHIBIT 7

CONTROL DATA CORPORATION

Market Range of Common Stock

Calendar Year	High	Low
1900	$15.45	$ 6.11
1961	29.33	13.95
1962	34.67	13.00
1963	75.58	19.67
1964	74.58	45.25
1965 (early January).............	$56.00	

NOTE: Adjustments in the above prices have been made for the three for one stock split in September 1961 and the three for two stock split in September 1964. Prices are based on over-the-counter markets prior to March 6, 1963 and on the New York Stock Exchange thereafter.

EXHIBIT 8

(in thousands)

Year	Factor	×	Cost of System	Depreciation Charge	Assumed Rental Revenue
1......4/8			$1,000	$ 500	$ 500
2......2/8			$1,000	250	500
3......1/8			$1,000	125	500
4......1/8			$1,000	125	500
				$1,000	$2,000

The total dollar amount of depreciation and amortization is compared to several items in Exhibit 9. The figures were taken from annual and mid-year reports (N.A. indicates figures not available at midyear).

Research and Development Activities

In the annual report to stockholders for the year ended June 30, 1963, the programming activities of the company were described:

Control Data is placing ever-increasing emphasis on the development of programs (software) to apply computers to the solution of problems. We are now developing and "manufacturing" software in Control Data in much the same manner as we do hardware.

In the initial phase, software is planned along with hardware as part of the total product plan. The next phase is the software development phase. Following this, we have a rather extensive quality assurance phase, during which the software is subjected to thorough evaluation and testing before it is released to the field.

EXHIBIT 9

(in millions)

	1962	1963	1964	First Half 1965
Net sales, rentals, and service income	$41.0	$66.1	$131.1	$75.5
Net earnings	1.5	2.7	6.0	3.3
Depreciation and amortization for year*	5.2	9.0	13.8	8.6
Machinery and equipment at cost	17.2	33.7	16.3	N.A.
Leased computing systems at cost	....†	....†	32.6	N.A.
Accumulated depreciation and amortization	6.8	15.2	24.1	N.A.

° Includes depreciation of computers (leased to customers), buildings, and machinery; amortization of patents; etc.
† Included in machinery and equipment.

The total research and development carried out by the Company during the year, including contract and Company-sponsored projects, amounted to approximately $13 million as compared to $8.5 million in the previous fiscal year (1962). The Company-sponsored portion of this program was approximately $5 million (and $2.6 million in fiscal 1962). Included in these amounts was substantial effort for research and development of programs for computers (software).

In 1964, the total research and development carried out by the company amounted to $20 million, of which the company-sponsored portion amounted to $12 million.

The president, Mr. Norris, noted in the 1964 annual report that

Research and development work continues on faster, more advanced computers, so that Control Data will be in a position to offer its customers the services that computers afford at a steadily decreasing cost. Increasing effort is being put into the development of computer peripheral equipment such as mass memories, printers, card readers, automatic tape handlers, data collection devices, and communications equipment.

The dollar amount of research and development expenses since 1962 is summarized in Exhibit 10, based on data which appeared in the annual and interim reports.

Marketing Activities

Marketing at Control Data included analysis of customer needs, systems analysis, selling, demonstration, customer support, programming assistance, etc. These activities occurred at headquarters in Minneapolis, in regional offices, district offices, and in the field.

Expenditures on marketing were not disclosed separately and were included in selling, administrative, and general expenses in the interim and annual financial statements (see Exhibit 11).

EXHIBIT 10

(in millions)

	Year Ended June 30			Six Mos. Ended Dec. 31
	1962	1963	1964	1964
Sales rentals and service income	$41.0	$66.1	$131.1	$75.5
Net earnings	1.5	2.7	6.0	3.3
Research and development expenses	2.6	5.6	12.3	7.1
R&D as percentage of sales	6.3%	8.5%	9.4%	9.4%

EXHIBIT 11

(in millions)

	Year Ended June 30			Six Mos. Ended Dec. 31
	1962	1963	1964	1964
Sales, rentals, and service income	$41.0	$66.1	$131.1	$75.5
Selling, administrative, and general expenses	$ 5.9	$ 9.5	$ 23.1	$14.9
As percentage of sales	14%	14%	18%	20%

Accounting Policy for R&D and Marketing

From its inception in 1957, the company expensed all costs of research, development, selling, etc., as they were incurred. This conservative policy was considered appropriate during the company's early stages of development and before the switch in a substantial number of computer orders from outright sales to leases. The present policy was being reconsidered in recognition of the fact that a significant and growing portion of Control Data's development, programming, and marketing expenses were spent in obtaining orders for leases, the income from which was spread over several years.

About the same time that the company was considering these changes in accounting policies, the Accounting Principles Board of the American Institute of Certified Public Accountants was studying the problems of accounting for leases in the financial statements of lessors. In December 1965, Control Data received the exposure draft of *Accounting for Leases in Financial Statements of Lessors.*

Question

1. What accounting policy do you believe Control Data should adopt for (a) the depreciation of leased equipment, and (b) research, development, and marketing expenditures? Describe and support your recommendations.

(*Additional Information:* During the third quarter of the company's fiscal year 1965 (January 1, 1965 to March 31, 1965) it became clear to management that 1965 net income would be significantly lower than 1964 net income if they continued to use 1964 accounting policies during 1965. 1965 sales were expected to be about $20 million more than 1964 sales. Also, approximately 55 percent of the *orders booked* by the company during 1965 were expected to be lease orders, compared to about 40 percent during 1964.)

Appendix: Present Value Tables

TABLE A: Present Value of $1

Table A shows the present value of one dollar received n years hence at i annual rate of return on the original investment. For example, to find the amount that would have to be invested today (the "present value") to receive one dollar 10 years hence if the annual rate of return earned was 10 percent, follow these steps:

First, go across the top of the table to the 10 percent column. Next, go down this column until the 10 years line is reached. The factor 0.386 is found at this location in the table. This factor indicates that an investment of approximately 38 cents today at 10 percent annual interest will grow to $1 in 10 years.

Years Hence	1%	2%	4%	6%	8%	10%	12%	14%	15%	16%	18%	20%	22%	24%	25%	26%	28%	30%	35%	40%	45%	50%
1	0.990	0.980	0.962	0.943	0.926	0.909	0.893	0.877	0.870	0.862	0.847	0.833	0.820	0.806	0.800	0.794	0.781	0.769	0.741	0.714	0.690	0.667
2	0.980	0.961	0.925	0.890	0.857	0.826	0.797	0.769	0.756	0.743	0.718	0.694	0.672	0.650	0.640	0.630	0.610	0.592	0.549	0.510	0.476	0.444
3	0.971	0.942	0.889	0.840	0.794	0.751	0.712	0.675	0.658	0.641	0.609	0.579	0.551	0.524	0.512	0.500	0.477	0.455	0.406	0.364	0.328	0.296
4	0.951	0.924	0.855	0.792	0.735	0.683	0.636	0.592	0.572	0.552	0.516	0.482	0.451	0.423	0.410	0.397	0.373	0.350	0.301	0.260	0.226	0.193
5	0.951	0.906	0.822	0.747	0.681	0.621	0.567	0.519	0.497	0.476	0.437	0.402	0.370	0.341	0.328	0.315	0.291	0.269	0.223	0.186	0.156	0.132
6	0.942	0.888	0.790	0.705	0.630	0.564	0.507	0.456	0.432	0.410	0.370	0.335	0.303	0.275	0.262	0.250	0.227	0.207	0.165	0.133	0.108	0.088
7	0.933	0.871	0.760	0.665	0.583	0.513	0.452	0.400	0.376	0.354	0.314	0.279	0.249	0.222	0.210	0.198	0.178	0.159	0.122	0.095	0.074	0.059
8	0.923	0.853	0.731	0.627	0.540	0.467	0.404	0.351	0.327	0.305	0.266	0.233	0.204	0.179	0.168	0.157	0.139	0.123	0.091	0.068	0.051	0.039
9	0.914	0.837	0.703	0.592	0.500	0.424	0.361	0.308	0.284	0.263	0.225	0.194	0.167	0.144	0.134	0.125	0.108	0.094	0.067	0.048	0.035	0.026
10	0.905	0.820	0.676	0.558	0.463	0.386	0.322	0.270	0.247	0.227	0.191	0.162	0.137	0.116	0.107	0.099	0.085	0.073	0.050	0.035	0.024	0.017
11	0.896	0.804	0.650	0.527	0.429	0.350	0.287	0.237	0.215	0.195	0.162	0.135	0.112	0.094	0.086	0.079	0.066	0.056	0.037	0.025	0.017	0.012
12	0.887	0.788	0.625	0.497	0.397	0.319	0.257	0.208	0.187	0.168	0.137	0.112	0.092	0.076	0.069	0.062	0.052	0.043	0.027	0.018	0.012	0.008
13	0.879	0.773	0.601	0.469	0.368	0.290	0.229	0.182	0.163	0.145	0.116	0.093	0.075	0.061	0.055	0.050	0.040	0.033	0.020	0.013	0.008	0.005
14	0.870	0.758	0.577	0.442	0.340	0.263	0.205	0.160	0.141	0.125	0.099	0.078	0.062	0.049	0.044	0.039	0.032	0.025	0.015	0.009	0.006	0.003
15	0.861	0.743	0.555	0.417	0.315	0.239	0.183	0.140	0.123	0.108	0.084	0.065	0.051	0.040	0.035	0.031	0.025	0.020	0.011	0.006	0.004	0.002
16	0.853	0.728	0.534	0.394	0.292	0.218	0.163	0.123	0.107	0.093	0.071	0.054	0.042	0.032	0.028	0.025	0.019	0.015	0.008	0.005	0.003	0.002
17	0.844	0.714	0.513	0.371	0.270	0.198	0.146	0.108	0.093	0.080	0.060	0.045	0.034	0.026	0.023	0.020	0.015	0.012	0.006	0.003	0.002	0.001
18	0.836	0.700	0.494	0.350	0.250	0.180	0.130	0.095	0.081	0.069	0.051	0.038	0.028	0.021	0.018	0.016	0.012	0.009	0.005	0.002	0.001	0.001
19	0.828	0.686	0.475	0.331	0.232	0.164	0.116	0.083	0.070	0.060	0.043	0.031	0.023	0.017	0.014	0.012	0.009	0.007	0.003	0.002	0.001	
20	0.820	0.673	0.456	0.312	0.215	0.149	0.104	0.073	0.061	0.051	0.037	0.026	0.019	0.014	0.012	0.010	0.007	0.005	0.002	0.001	0.001	
21	0.811	0.660	0.439	0.294	0.199	0.135	0.093	0.064	0.053	0.044	0.031	0.022	0.015	0.011	0.009	0.008	0.006	0.004	0.002	0.001	0.001	
22	0.803	0.647	0.422	0.278	0.184	0.123	0.083	0.056	0.046	0.038	0.026	0.018	0.013	0.009	0.007	0.006	0.004	0.003	0.001	0.001	0.001	
23	0.795	0.634	0.406	0.262	0.170	0.112	0.074	0.049	0.040	0.033	0.022	0.015	0.010	0.007	0.006	0.005	0.003	0.002	0.001			
24	0.788	0.622	0.390	0.247	0.158	0.102	0.066	0.043	0.035	0.024	0.019	0.013	0.008	0.006	0.005	0.004	0.003	0.002	0.001			
25	0.780	0.610	0.375	0.233	0.146	0.092	0.059	0.038	0.030	0.024	0.016	0.010	0.007	0.005	0.004	0.003	0.002	0.001	0.001			
26	0.772	0.598	0.361	0.220	0.135	0.084	0.053	0.033	0.026	0.021	0.014	0.009	0.006	0.004	0.003	0.002	0.002	0.001				
27	0.764	0.586	0.347	0.207	0.125	0.076	0.047	0.029	0.023	0.018	0.011	0.007	0.005	0.003	0.002	0.002	0.001	0.001				
28	0.757	0.574	0.333	0.196	0.116	0.069	0.042	0.026	0.020	0.016	0.010	0.006	0.004	0.002	0.002	0.002	0.001	0.001				
29	0.749	0.563	0.321	0.185	0.107	0.063	0.037	0.022	0.017	0.014	0.008	0.005	0.003	0.002	0.002	0.001	0.001	0.001				
30	0.742	0.552	0.308	0.174	0.099	0.057	0.033	0.020	0.015	0.012	0.007	0.004	0.003	0.002	0.001	0.001	0.001					
40	0.672	0.453	0.208	0.097	0.046	0.022	0.011	0.005	0.004	0.003	0.001	0.001										
50	0.608	0.372	0.141	0.054	0.021	0.009	0.003	0.001	0.001	0.001												

TABLE B: Present Value of $1 Received Annually for N Years Table B shows the present value of $1 received annually for each of the next *n* years if *i* annual rate of return is earned on the remaining balance of the original investment throughout this period. For example, to find the amount needed to be invested today to receive one dollar for each of the next 20 years if 10 percent can be earned on the investment, follow these steps: First, go across the top of the Table in the 10 percent column.

Next, go down the column to the 20 years line. The factor 8.514 is shown at this spot. This factor tells us that a 10 percent investment of $8.51 today will return to the investor $1 for each of the next 20 years. At the end of that time the investor will have recovered all of his original investment plus a return of 10 percent. Therefore, the present value of $1 per year for 20 years discounted at 10 percent is $8.51.

Years (N)	1%	2%	4%	6%	8%	10%	12%	14%	15%	16%	18%	20%	22%	24%	25%	26%	28%	30%	35%	40%	45%	50%
1	0.990	0.980	0.962	0.943	0.926	0.909	0.893	0.877	0.870	0.862	0.847	0.833	0.820	0.806	0.800	0.794	0.781	0.769	0.741	0.714	0.690	0.667
2	1.970	1.942	1.886	1.833	1.783	1.736	1.690	1.647	1.626	1.605	1.566	1.528	1.492	1.457	1.440	1.424	1.392	1.361	1.289	1.224	1.165	1.111
3	2.941	2.884	2.775	2.673	2.577	2.487	2.402	2.322	2.283	2.246	2.174	2.106	2.042	1.981	1.952	1.923	1.868	1.816	1.696	1.589	1.493	1.407
4	3.902	3.808	3.630	3.465	3.312	3.170	3.037	2.914	2.855	2.798	2.690	2.589	2.494	2.404	2.362	2.320	2.241	2.166	1.997	1.849	1.720	1.605
5	4.853	4.713	4.452	4.212	3.993	3.791	3.605	3.433	3.352	3.274	3.127	2.991	2.864	2.745	2.689	2.635	2.532	2.436	2.220	2.035	1.876	1.737
6	5.795	5.601	5.242	4.917	4.623	4.355	4.111	3.889	3.784	3.685	3.498	3.326	3.167	3.020	2.951	2.885	2.759	2.643	2.385	2.168	1.983	1.824
7	6.728	6.472	6.002	5.582	5.206	4.868	4.564	4.288	4.160	4.039	3.812	3.605	3.416	3.242	3.161	3.083	2.937	2.802	2.508	2.263	2.057	1.883
8	7.652	7.325	6.733	6.210	5.747	5.335	4.968	4.639	4.487	4.344	4.078	3.837	3.619	3.421	3.329	3.241	3.076	2.925	2.598	2.331	2.108	1.922
9	8.566	8.162	7.435	6.802	6.247	5.759	5.328	4.946	4.772	4.607	4.303	4.031	3.786	3.566	3.463	3.366	3.184	3.019	2.665	2.379	2.144	1.948
10	9.471	8.983	8.111	7.360	6.710	6.145	5.650	5.216	5.019	4.833	4.494	4.192	3.923	3.682	3.571	3.465	3.269	3.092	2.715	2.414	2.168	1.965
11	10.368	9.787	8.760	7.887	7.139	6.495	5.937	5.453	5.234	5.029	4.656	4.327	4.035	3.776	3.656	3.544	3.335	3.147	2.752	2.438	2.185	1.977
12	11.255	10.575	9.385	8.384	7.536	6.814	6.194	5.660	5.421	5.197	4.793	4.439	4.127	3.851	3.725	3.606	3.387	3.190	2.779	2.456	2.196	1.985
13	12.134	11.343	9.986	8.853	7.904	7.103	6.424	5.842	5.583	5.342	4.910	4.533	4.203	3.912	3.780	3.656	3.427	3.223	2.799	2.468	2.204	1.990
14	13.004	12.106	10.563	9.295	8.244	7.367	6.628	6.002	5.724	5.468	5.008	4.611	4.265	3.962	3.824	3.695	3.459	3.249	2.814	2.477	2.210	1.993
15	13.865	12.849	11.118	9.712	8.559	7.606	6.811	6.142	5.847	5.575	5.092	4.675	4.315	4.001	3.859	3.726	3.483	3.268	2.825	2.484	2.214	1.995
16	14.718	13.578	11.652	10.106	8.851	7.824	6.974	6.265	5.954	5.669	5.162	4.730	4.357	4.033	3.887	3.751	3.503	3.283	2.834	2.489	2.216	1.997
17	15.562	14.292	12.166	10.477	9.122	8.022	7.120	6.373	6.047	5.749	5.222	4.775	4.391	4.059	3.910	3.771	3.518	3.295	2.840	2.492	2.218	1.998
18	16.398	14.992	12.659	10.828	9.372	8.201	7.250	6.467	6.128	5.818	5.273	4.812	4.419	4.080	3.928	3.786	3.529	3.304	2.844	2.494	2.219	1.999
19	17.226	15.678	13.134	11.158	9.604	8.365	7.366	6.550	6.198	5.877	5.316	4.844	4.442	4.097	3.942	3.799	3.539	3.311	2.848	2.496	2.220	1.999
20	18.046	16.351	13.590	11.470	9.818	8.514	7.469	6.623	6.259	5.929	5.353	4.870	4.460	4.110	3.954	3.808	3.546	3.316	2.850	2.497	2.221	1.999
21	18.857	17.011	14.029	11.764	10.017	8.649	7.562	6.687	6.312	5.973	5.384	4.891	4.476	4.121	3.963	3.816	3.551	3.320	2.852	2.498	2.221	2.000
22	19.660	17.658	14.451	12.042	10.201	8.772	7.645	6.743	6.359	6.011	5.410	4.909	4.488	4.130	3.970	3.822	3.556	3.323	2.853	2.498	2.222	2.000
23	20.456	18.292	14.857	12.303	10.371	8.883	7.718	6.792	6.399	6.044	5.432	4.925	4.499	4.137	3.976	3.827	3.559	3.325	2.854	2.499	2.222	2.000
24	21.243	18.914	15.247	12.550	10.529	8.985	7.784	6.835	6.434	6.073	5.451	4.937	4.507	4.143	3.981	3.831	3.562	3.327	2.855	2.499	2.222	2.000
25	22.023	19.523	15.622	12.783	10.675	9.077	7.843	6.873	6.464	6.097	5.467	4.948	4.514	4.147	3.985	3.834	3.564	3.329	2.856	2.499	2.222	2.000
26	22.795	20.121	15.983	13.003	10.810	9.161	7.896	6.906	6.491	6.118	5.480	4.956	4.520	4.151	3.988	3.837	3.566	3.330	2.856	2.500	2.222	2.000
27	23.560	20.707	16.330	13.211	10.935	9.237	7.943	6.935	6.514	6.136	5.492	4.964	4.524	4.154	3.990	3.839	3.567	3.331	2.856	2.500	2.222	2.000
28	24.316	21.281	16.663	13.406	11.051	9.307	7.984	6.961	6.534	6.152	5.502	4.970	4.528	4.157	3.992	3.840	3.568	3.331	2.857	2.500	2.222	2.000
29	25.066	21.844	16.984	13.591	11.158	9.370	8.022	6.983	6.551	6.166	5.510	4.975	4.531	4.159	3.994	3.841	3.569	3.332	2.857	2.500	2.222	2.000
30	25.808	22.396	17.292	13.765	11.258	9.427	8.055	7.003	6.566	6.177	5.517	4.979	4.534	4.160	3.995	3.842	3.569	3.332	2.857	2.500	2.222	2.000
40	32.835	27.355	19.793	15.046	11.925	9.779	8.244	7.105	6.642	6.234	5.548	4.997	4.544	4.166	3.999	3.846	3.571	3.333	2.857	2.500	2.222	2.000
50	39.196	31.424	21.482	15.762	12.234	9.915	8.304	7.133	6.661	6.246	5.554	4.999	4.545	4.167	4.000	3.846	3.571	3.333	2.857	2.500	2.222	2.000

Indexes

INDEX OF CASES

SUBJECT INDEX

This book has been set in 10 point and 9 point Janson, leaded 2 points. Part titles and chapter numbers are in 18 point and 12 point Helvetica. Part numbers and chapter titles are in 18 point and 16 point Helvetica Medium. The size of the type page is 27 by 45½ picas.